Inflation Theory in Economics

In recent years inflation has again grown to become a worldwide phenomena. Contrary to the direction of research in which money has no role, here the major theme that runs throughout the book is that in order to do monetary economics well in general equilibrium, it helps to have a good money demand underlying the theory. A proper underlying money demand sets up arguably the best foundation from which to make extensions of monetary economics from the basic model. At the same time that money demand is modelled, this also "endogenizes" the velocity of money.

Solving this problem, in a way that is a natural, direct, and "micro-founded" extension of the standard monetary theory, is one key major contribution of the collection. The other key contribution is the extension of the neoclassical monetary models, using this solution, to reinvigorate classic issues of monetary economics and extend them into the stochastic dynamic general equilibrium dimension.

Through his new monograph Professor Gillman brings together a collection of recently published articles in inflation theory, reasserting the importance of money within the neoclassical model of monetary economics. Topics include money demand and velocity, inflation and its effects on endogenous growth, and monetary business cycles. It will therefore be of interest to postgraduate students and researchers of inflation, monetary economies, welfare, growth, and business cycles.

Max Gillman is currently Professor of Economics at Cardiff Business School, Cardiff.

Routledge International Studies in Money and Banking

1 Private Banking in Europe
Lynn Bicker

2 Bank Deregulation and Monetary Order
George Selgin

3 Money in Islam
A study in Islamic political economy
Masudul Alam Choudhury

4 The Future of European Financial Centres
Kirsten Bindemann

5 Payment Systems in Global Perspective
Maxwell J. Fry, Isaak Kilato, Sandra Roger, Krzysztof Senderowicz, David Sheppard, Francisco Solis and John Trundle

6 What is Money?
John Smithin

7 Finance
A characteristics approach
Edited by David Blake

8 Organisational Change and Retail Finance
An ethnographic perspective
Richard Harper, Dave Randall and Mark Rouncefield

9 The History of the Bundesbank
Lessons for the European Central Bank
Jakob de Haan

10 The Euro
A challenge and opportunity for financial markets
Published on behalf of *Société Universitaire Européenne de Recherches Financières (SUERF)*
Edited by Michael Artis, Axel Weber and Elizabeth Hennessy

11 Central Banking in Eastern Europe
Edited by Nigel Healey and Barry Harrison

12 Money, Credit and Prices Stability
Paul Dalziel

13 Monetary Policy, Capital Flows and Exchange Rates
Essays in memory of Maxwell Fry
Edited by William Allen and David Dickinson

14 Adapting to Financial Globalisation
Published on behalf of *Société Universitaire Européenne de Recherches Financières (SUERF)*
Edited by Morten Balling, Eduard H. Hochreiter and Elizabeth Hennessy

15 Monetary Macroeconomics
A new approach
Alvaro Cencini

16 Monetary Stability in Europe
Stefan Collignon

17 Technology and Finance
Challenges for financial markets, business strategies and policy makers
Published on behalf of *Société Universitaire Européenne de Recherches Financières (SUERF)*
Edited by Morten Balling, Frank Lierman, and Andrew Mullineux

18 Monetary Unions
Theory, history, public choice
Edited by Forrest H. Capie and Geoffrey E. Wood

19 HRM and Occupational Health and Safety
Carol Boyd

20 Central Banking Systems Compared
The ECB, The pre-Euro Bundesbank and the Federal Reserve System
Emmanuel Apel

21 A History of Monetary Unions
John Chown

22 Dollarization
Lessons from Europe and the Americas
Edited by Louis-Philippe Rochon and Mario Seccareccia

23 Islamic Economics and Finance: A Glossary, 2nd Edition
Muhammad Akram Khan

24 Financial Market Risk
Measurement and analysis
Cornelis A. Los

25 Financial Geography
A banker's view
Risto Laulajainen

26 Money Doctors
The experience of international financial advising 1850–2000
Edited by Marc Flandreau

27 Exchange Rate Dynamics
A new open economy macroeconomics perspective
Edited by Jean-Oliver Hairault and Thepthida Sopraseuth

28 Fixing Financial Crises in the 21st Century
Edited by Andrew G. Haldane

29 Monetary Policy and Unemployment
The U.S., Euro-area and Japan
Edited by Willi Semmler

30 Exchange Rates, Capital Flows and Policy
Edited by Peter Sinclair, Rebecca Driver and Christoph Thoenissen

31 Great Architects of International Finance
The Bretton Woods era
Anthony M. Endres

32 The Means to Prosperity
Fiscal policy reconsidered
Edited by Per Gunnar Berglund and Matias Vernengo

33 Competition and Profitability in European Financial Services
Strategic, systemic and policy issues
Edited by Morten Balling, Frank Lierman and Andy Mullineux

34 Tax Systems and Tax Reforms in South and East Asia
Edited by Luigi Bernardi, Angela Fraschini and Parthasarathi Shome

35 **Institutional Change in the Payments System and Monetary Policy**
Edited by Stefan W. Schmitz and Geoffrey E. Wood

36 **The Lender of Last Resort**
Edited by F.H. Capie and G.E. Wood

37 **The Structure of Financial Regulation**
Edited by David G. Mayes and Geoffrey E. Wood

38 **Monetary Policy in Central Europe**
Miroslav Beblavý

39 **Money and Payments in Theory and Practice**
Sergio Rossi

40 **Open Market Operations and Financial Markets**
Edited by David G. Mayes and Jan Toporowski

41 **Banking in Central and Eastern Europe 1980–2006:**
A comprehensive analysis of banking sector transformation in the former Soviet Union, Czechoslovakia, East Germany, Yugoslavia, Belarus, Bulgaria, Croatia, the Czech Republic, Hungary, Kazakhstan, Poland, Romania, the Russian Federation, Serbia and Montenegro, Slovakia, Ukraine and Uzbekistan
Stephan Barisitz

42 **Debt, Risk and Liquidity in Futures Markets**
Edited by Barry A. Goss

43 **The Future of Payment Systems**
Edited by Stephen Millard, Andrew G. Haldane and Victoria Saporta

44 **Credit and Collateral**
Vania Sena

45 **Tax Systems and Tax Reforms in Latin America**
Edited by Luigi Bernardi, Alberto Barreix, Anna Marenzi and Paola Profeta

46 **The Dynamics of Organizational Collapse**
The case of Barings Bank
Helga Drummond

47 **International Financial Co-operation**
Political economics of compliance with the 1988 Basel Accord
Bryce Quillin

48 **Bank Performance**
A theoretical and empirical framework for the analysis of profitability, competition and efficiency
Jacob Bikker and Jaap W.B. Bos

49 **Monetary Growth Theory**
Money, interest, prices, capital, knowledge and economic structure over time and space
Wei-Bin Zhang

50 **Money, Uncertainty and Time**
Giuseppe Fontana

51 **Central Banking, Asset Prices and Financial Fragility**
Éric Tymoigne

52 **Financial Markets and the Macroeconomy**
Willi Semmler, Peter Flaschel, Carl Chiarella and Reiner Franke

53 **Inflation Theory in Economics**
Welfare, velocity, growth and business cycles
Max Gillman

Inflation Theory in Economics

Welfare, velocity, growth and business cycles

Max Gillman

With co-authors

Routledge
Taylor & Francis Group
LONDON AND NEW YORK

First published 2009
by Routledge
2 Park Square, Milton Park, Abingdon, Oxon, OX14 4RN

Simultaneously published in the USA and Canada
by Routledge
270 Madison Avenue, New York, NY 10016

Routledge is an imprint of the Taylor & Francis Group, an informa business

Typeset in Times New Roman by
RefineCatch Limited, Bungay, Suffolk

British Library Cataloguing in Publication Data
A catalogue record for this book is available from the British Library

Library of Congress Cataloging-in-Publication Data
Gillman, Max.
Inflation theory in economics : welfare, velocity, growth and business cycles / by Max Gillman.
p. cm.
Includes bibliographical references and index.
1. Inflation (Finance) 2. Monetary policy. I. Title.
HG229.G55 2009
332.4′101–dc22

2008041582

ISBN10: 0–415–47768–9 (hbk)
ISBN10: 0–203–88018–8 (ebk)

ISBN13: 978–0–415–47768–0 (hbk)
ISBN13: 978–0–203–88018–0 (ebk)

Contents

Figures

Tables

Contributors

Szilárd Benk is Economist, Magyar Nemzeti Bank.

Dario Cziráky is Senior Quantitative Analyst, Barclays Capital, London.

Max Gillman is Professor of Economics at Cardiff Business School, Cardiff, Wales.

Mark N. Harris is Associate Professor at Monash University, Clayton Victoria, Australia.

Michal Kejak is Associate Professor at the Center for Economic Research and Graduate Education Economics Institute (CERGE-EI), Prague, Czech Republic.

László Mátyás is Professor at Central European University, Budapest, Hungary.

Anton Nakov is Economist, Research Division, Bank of Spain, Barcelona, Spain.

Glen Otto is Associate Professor, School of Economics, University of New South Wales, Sydney, Australia.

Pierre L. Siklos is Professor, Department of Economics, Wilfrid Laurier University, Waterloo, Ontario, Canada and Department of Economics, University of California, San Diego, California, USA.

J. Lew Silver is Associate Professor, Department of Economics, Finance and Legal Studies, University of Alabama, Tuscaloosa, Alabama, USA.

Oleg Yerokhin is Lecturer, University of Wollongong, Australia.

Preface

The chapters here are the result of enjoyable collaboration with my co-authors. I dedicate the book to Anita Gillman. And I am grateful to the editors at Routledge, in particular Terry Clague, Thomas Sutton and Robert Langham.

1 Overview

"The inflation tax is an issue of the first importance."
(R. E. Lucas, Jr., 1996, Nobel Lecture, p. 675)

Bob Lucas describes in his Nobel Address (Lucas 1996) the temporary positive relation between inflation and employment that can exist in a Phillips curve relation, as in his Nobel cited paper that modeled a Phillips curve in general equilibrium (Lucas 1972). But Lucas also emphasizes in his Nobel address the permanent long run effects of inflation, and in particular the distortions caused by the inflation tax. This collection focuses on the inflation tax distortions.

Inflation has fluctuated greatly over the last century. For the US, Figure 1.1 shows the large swings during the Depression, WWII, and the 1970s and 1980s "Great Inflation". Here the absolute value of the inflation rate (left axis) and its volatility (right axis) are given from 1919 to 2007, and they are seen to move together. Despite the advent of inflation targeting, recent inflation has surged again; inflation has risen more than four-fold from an annual rate of 1.1% in June 2002 to 5.0% in June 2008.[1]

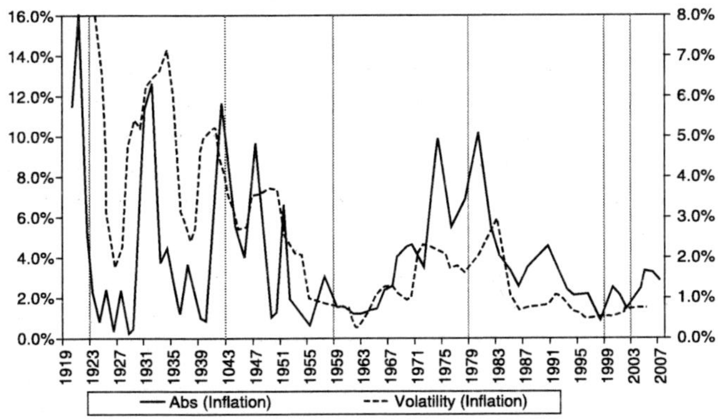

Figure 1.1 Absolute value of US inflation and its volatility, 1919–2007.

Recurrent inflation means that the distortions of the inflation tax unremittingly continue to affect the economy. This book brings together chapters that build a progression in inflation tax theory, with the aim of enabling better analysis of the many distortions that inflation causes. The chapters start with a simple way to add credit into a general equilibrium stationary model, so that any good can be bought with cash or credit. They end with a fully micro-founded bank production technology that produces the credit as in the financial intermediation approach to banking. On the way, the chapters develop extensions which transform a primitive approach towards including credit into a more advanced approach, while building the neoclassical monetary model. And they go from an initial deterministic economy with no growth to a setting of stochastic shocks with endogenous growth, a new frontier.

A theme running through the papers is that monetary economics in general equilibrium is helped by having a good money demand function underlying the theory.[2] A proper endogenous money demand sets up arguably the best foundation from which to make extensions of monetary economics from the basic model. At the same time that money demand is better modelled, this also "endogenizes" the velocity of money in a viable way.

Endogenizing velocity has been a challenge in the literature. For example, Lucas lets velocity be exogenous in Lucas (1988a) and Alvarez, Lucas, and Weber (2001), while setting it at one in his original cash-in-advance economy. Lucas and Stokey (1983) endogenize velocity using a credit good in the utility function. This makes velocity a function of utility parameters, and leaves no role for the cost of credit versus the cost of cash. And Hodrick, Kocherlakota, and Lucas (1991) find this cash-credit good model was not able to fit the velocity data well. Lucas (2000) also endogenizes velocity using the most standard models of money-in-the-utility function and shopping time, although again the velocity depends closely on utility parameters and hard-to-interpret transaction cost specifications. Typically these parameters are set so as to yield a constant interest elasticity of money demand, as in the partial equilibrium Baumol (1952) money demand model.

In contrast, this collection solves the velocity problem by the way in which the cost of exchange credit enters the economy. This gives a natural, direct, and microfounded way to solve the problem. At the same time, it opens up a way to extend the standard monetary economy in the direction of greater realism. By bringing in banking to produce the credit, the financial sector becomes the direct determinate of the shape of the money demand function, because the credit is a perfect substitute for the fiat money in exchange.

With velocity built upon solid banking foundations, calibrating money demand is no longer a task of assigning utility parameters, or general transactions function parameters in order to get some constant interest elasticity. Nor is money demand an exogonous function assumed at the end of a model in order to residually determine money supply from an ad hoc Taylor rule.

Rather it is an integral part of the model that largely determines the nature of the monetary results. And money demand ends up being well-defined across the whole range of inflation rates, including at the Friedman (1969) optimum. The result is arguably a greater realism of money demand functions per se, and a further development of the inflation tax analysis, as Lucas (1996) encourages in his Nobel lecture.

The book's collection gives a new perspective on some classic issues and leads to new results which range from welfare theory, including the welfare cost of inflation, and first and second-best money and credit optimums (Part I), to money demand and velocity investigations (Part II), to growth (Part III), and business cycle theory (Part IV).

Part I (Chapters 2–6) shows how to develop the basic cash-in-advance model so as to include exchange credit, endogenize velocity in a rudimentary way, and to show how this compares to traditional partial equilibrium theories, in terms of the cost of inflation. The optimality of money and credit is then examined within such models, as well as within a model that uses the more advanced single-consumption approach to including credit that forms the basis for the money demand, growth and business cycle applications.

Indeed, starting from the Chapter 2 article, a type of standard microfoundation is built in the collection here. This microfoundation is based in the traditional sense that an industry produces a product with profit maximization and an industry production function that is consistence with industry-level empirical evidence. While taking only small steps in Chapter 2, by Chapter 19 a fully microfounded banking production function is used to supply the credit. And note that all of the eleven chapters with a single good approach with credit, these being Chapters 6–9, 11–15, and 17–18, have the same type of credit production function as in Chapter 19, even though in these other chapters the explicit link to the banking microfoundations is not made, as it is in Chapter 19.

The result is to endogenize velocity so that any degree of money is used depending on the relative cost of money versus credit, and so that the use of the cash constraint cannot easily be viewed as being exogenously imposed. In fact, over the course of the chapters, it emerges that the cash constraint embodies the credit production technology, and is in fact the "exchange technology", rather than the "cash constraint" per se.

Part II (Chapters 7–10) develops and tests the money demand and velocity functions; empirical estimations are done for both developed and transition countries studies. Parts III and IV show useful applications of this theory: as a means of seeing how inflation as a tax can lower growth, be inter-related with financial development, and can explain monetary business cycles. The collection goes to the ever-shifting frontier in its topics of welfare cost, money demand, velocity, inflation effects on endogenous growth, and monetary business cycles.

1.1 Inflation and welfare

Lucas (1980) suggested in a footnote that velocity could be endogenized by having a *credit technology* for buying goods with credit alongside the ability to buy goods with money (cash). Prescott (1987) developed such a technology with both cash and credit use across a store continuum. He specified exogenously a marginal store that divided the continuum between stores using cash and those using credit. On the chalk board, Bob Lucas demonstrated how to endogenize the choice of this Prescott marginal store in a static model, whereby the choice to use cash versus credit at a particular store depended upon the time cost of using credit at each store (motivated by Karni, 1974), as compared to the foregone interest cost of using money.

Making the choice of the marginal store endogenous within a dynamic Lucas (1980) type model led to the first article in this collection, Chapter 2 "The Welfare Costs of Inflation in a Cash-in-Advance Model with Costly Credit". Here an extra first-order condition is added to the standard cash-only Lucas (1980) economy, this being the choice of the marginal store of the Prescott continuum. During the revisions of the Chapter 2 article, Bob King helpfully pointed out that this additional condition made the model a generalization of Baumol's (1952) original transactions cost model, in which the costs of alternative means of exchange (carrying cash or using banking) are minimized optimally.

Baumol's (1952) model implies the well-known square root money demand function, with a constant interest elasticity of money demand equal to –0.5, the number for example that Lucas (2000) uses to specify his shopping time model. However, the money demand function results by rearranging the first-order condition that sets the marginal cost of money equal to the marginal cost of banking. Chapter 2 focuses on this aspect: the equating the marginal cost of different means of exchange. The chapter derives the interest elasticity of money demand to emphasize that the credit option makes the money demand much more interest elastic. Consequently, as follows from Ramsey (1927) logic, when taxing a much more elastic good (money), the welfare cost of the inflation tax is higher than in models omitting such a Prescott exchange credit channel. And by including this exchange credit, which requires the use of time within a technology of credit production, the velocity of money is endogenized in a way suggested by Lucas (1980).

The Chapter 2 article lays the foundation of the remaining papers in the collection. It provides a feasible way to model exchange credit, but in an abstract way, in that its credit production technology is an arbitrary linear one at each store. Although this still gives a type of upward sloping marginal cost function for credit use the store continuum set-up does not make it easy to integrate credit use within the mainstream neoclassical growth and business cycle theory; in contrast Lucas's (1980) economy starts with a similar continuum of goods but he creates a composite aggregate consumption basket that allows for easy integration of the cash-in-advance approach within the neoclassical model. However, this endogenous store continuum approach with credit is useful and does continue to be used, as in Ireland (1994b), Marquis and Reffett (1994), Erosa and Ventura (2002), and Khan, King, and Wolman (2003).

One immediate consequence of the Chapter 2 velocity solution is that it addresses a criticism of the basic Lucas (1980) model, this being that the cash constraint is exogenously imposed. This criticism is rather unfair, and inaccurate, in that Lucas (1980) goes to some length to prove that the original cash-only constraint is endogenously found to be binding, and not assumed exogenously. Yet this criticism is still invoked, especially in "deep foundation" literature that claims to provide a non-standard "microfoundations" for the existence of Lucas's cash-in-advance constraint, as based in search within decentralized markets; see also Townsend (1978). Meeting this criticism head-on, Chapter 2 marks a way forward with velocity endogenous, with cash and credit being perfect substitutes, with costs determining the consumer choice of the mix of exchange means, and with near zero or 100% cash use being possible outcomes of the consumer choice based on relative cost.

Chapter 3, "A Comparison of Partial and General Equilibrium Estimates of the Welfare Cost of Inflation", looks more in depth at what is behind the welfare cost estimate of the Chapter 2 model, and compares this measure to measures based on the traditional partial equilibrium money demand literature. It asks whether partial equilibrium estimates are consistent with, or somehow superseded by, the newer general equilibrium measures such as that put forth in Lucas's (1993a) Chicago working paper (published later as Lucas 2000). The main puzzle tackled in Chapter 3 is that partial equilibrium based estimates tend to be below general equilibrium based estimates. To resolve this, the paper sets out how partial equilibrium estimates are simply the area of the lost consumer surplus under the money demand function due to an inflation tax, as first described by Martin Bailey (1956). In contrast the general equilibrium estimates are equal to the real income necessary to compensate the representative agent for having to face some positive inflation tax instead of a zero tax at the first-best optimum. Are these estimates one and the same? The paper shows that within the Chapter 2 economy the general equilibrium compensating income is almost exactly equal to the lost consumer surplus under the money demand function of the same Chapter 2 economy. And further, the implication is that the composition of the lost surplus depends on what is built into the economy.

In the Chapter 2 economy, the welfare cost estimate includes both the resource cost of producing the exchange credit, in order to avoid the inflation tax; plus it includes the distortion of the ensuing goods to leisure substitution that is caused by the inflation tax. By comparison, Lucas (2000) excludes the leisure channel and focuses on just the resource cost that results from avoiding the use of money (within a shopping time economy). So the welfare cost of inflation, which is the area under the money demand within the general equilibrium model, may represent just the resource cost of avoidance or also other distortions; if these are built into the economy. Lucas (2000) makes a similar point to that of Chapter 3 in that Lucas shows how to compute the general equilibrium estimate directly as a function of the model's own money demand. The implication is that the money demand function of partial equilibrium approaches fully underlies the general equilibrium estimate of the compensating income, as long as the money demand used in the comparison is exactly that function that is derived from the general equilibrium economy, rather than some separately estimated money demand function.

The Chapter 3 paper is also interesting because the literature has suggested different answers to the question of how partial and general equilibrium estimates compare. For example, Dotsey and Ireland (1996) calibrate an estimate of the welfare cost of inflation from a general equilibrium shopping time economy and compare this to an econometrically estimated partial equilibrium estimate of the cost of inflation. They find the general equilibrium estimate is higher than the partial equilibrium estimate. This comparison suggests that estimated money demand functions may not capture what we think money demand actually should be according to our particular general equilibrium economy. But this is different from suggesting that the area under the money demand function is not the same as the compensating income of general equilibrium approaches. The answer of Chapter 3 is that these approaches are in fact the same as long as the experiment is done in an internally consistent fashion: using either the money demand integration or the value-function-based compensating income *from the same economy*.

Part I "Inflation and Welfare" includes three more articles on welfare that investigate the optimal inflation tax under a variety of assumptions. Chapter 4, "The Optimality of a Zero Inflation Rate: Australia", addresses the inconsistency between the accepted Friedman (1969) optimal rate of inflation being equal to deflation at the real rate of interest, and the typical policy prescription worldwide that the best inflation rate is either zero or a somewhat higher rate (as in the 2% now used in many central banks). Chapter 4 gives a simple rationale for a zero inflation as being optimal as based on there being costly price adjustment, using an extension of the Chapter 2 economy. Here, the result depends on the level of the calibrated velocity and the cost of adjusting prices; it is possible that the optimal inflation rate can also be above zero in some cases.

Recent efforts using Neo-Keynesian models have also established a zero inflation rate as optimal, although these results are within models with no inflationary tax finance. Instead they use only relative price distortions from inflation to derive the result, whereby this distortion dominates output stabilization reasons to push the inflation rate above zero (and so decrease the monopoly distortion so that output is induced towards its higher competitive equilibrium level).[3] Chapter 4 in contrast points out a simple way of using the cash-in-advance economy to resolve theory with practical policy making, but leaves open a more elegant, and possibly fundamental, way to resolve this puzzle.

Chapter 5, "On the Optimality of Restricting Credit: Inflation-avoidance and Productivity", examines second best exchange credit policy given that the agent has to face a positive inflation tax. The chapter again extends the Chapter 2 economy, now to include a credit tax. It shows the effect of the tax on the interest elasticity of money demand and on the welfare cost of inflation. It also sets up decentralized credit production problem, whereby it results that the market price of credit in equilibrium is the nominal interest rate. The results on the optimal level of the credit tax clarify the role of exchange credit in the cash-in-advance economy: it provides a way to avoid the inflation tax. And because real resources (time used to produce the credit) are used up avoiding the inflation tax, it is optimal not to allow such evasion of the inflation tax. The paper assumes further that there could be other (unspecified) benefits of the exchange credit, other than being able to avoid the inflation tax, such as some joint use as intertemporal credit. Then the optimal credit tax can be some positive amount of credit use.

The last article of Part I is Chapter 6, "Ramsey-Friedman Optimality with Banking Time". Here the optimality of the inflation tax is examined in a second-best framework in which revenues have to be raised somehow in order to finance government spending. In this literature the Ramsey optimal nominal interest rate has been shown to be zero under certain conditions for example on the utility function, when money enters the utility function; so with these conditions the inflation rate optimum is deflation at the rate of the real interest rate as in Friedman (1969). The problem is that such utility restrictions are very hard to interpret in a simple economic fashion, thus suggesting that the issue is not fully clarified under this approach. Further, several papers have focused on how the Ramsey optimum allows the inflation rate not only to be above the Friedman optimum but even to be positive in different frameworks (Braun 1994b, Lucas 2000).

In contrast, Chapter 6 uses the credit production approach to argue that the Ramsey optimal rate of inflation is exactly zero under very simple conditions: in particular that the production function for the credit takes on a Cobb-Douglas form. In other words, the only requirement necessary in order to show a Ramsey nominal interest rate of zero is that the normalized labor factor used in credit production has a diminishing marginal product. To show this, the economy is now a single consumption good economy as in the typical real business cycle, or neoclassical growth model, instead of a continuum of goods sold at different stores as in Chapter 2.

The production function for the credit takes a form consistent with the "financial intermediation approach" of the banking industry literature, in which deposits are an additional input. In Chapter 6, consumption enters the production function instead of deposits; but since consumption equals deposits in an equilibrium decentralized version of the model, this is a self-production version of the model that is equivalent to the banking industry function that is seen in Chapter 19.

The contribution of the chapter is to show that with a production approach, using "banking time" instead of a general "shopping time" transaction cost, the assumptions required to re-establish the Friedman optimum in the second-best setting are very simple, and easily met. This makes much stronger the robustness of the Friedman optimum as also being Ramsey optimal, as compared to existing literature.

1.2 Money demand and velocity

The next part of the book consists of four chapters on the theory and evidence for money demand and its velocity. Chapter 7, "The Demand for Bank Reserves and Other Monetary Aggregates", sets out a theoretical model of the monetary aggregates of the monetary base, M1 and M2, and shows how to explain the trends in the velocity of these aggregates relative to US empirical evidence.

Explaining velocity trends has been a challenge. Approaches have varied. Friedman (1960) suggested that velocity trends down in the long run by one percent (page 91). Others have suggested that velocity trends upwards because of increasing technological innovation in the banking sector. Chapter 7 takes an approach that allows for either of these outcomes, but only under certain conditions.

Chapter 7 presents models that use a production approach to credit in an economy with a single consumption good, as in Chapter 6. By using this approach, they provide a way to model velocity that is consistent with the microfoundations found in the financial intermediation literature. And more importantly, they show that a shift up in the productivity of credit production can help explain the velocity shifts that occurred after the financial deregulation of the 1980s, which continued into the 1990s.

Here, the only way there can be a secular increase in velocity is if the productivity in the goods sector rises at a faster rate than in the credit production (financial intermediation) sector; and conversely, a continued secular decrease in velocity only results if productivity in the credit production sector rises at a faster rate than in the goods production sector. More generally, what is more likely is that there are periods when the credit productivity is higher because of special productivity shifting events, like financial deregulation; and there can be periods when credit productivity is lower because of productivity set-backs in the financial intermediation sector. One such set-back was the US savings and loan banking crisis of late 1980s and early 1990s. And now there is the 2008–9 international credit contraction.

In this way, Chapter 7 provides a way to explain the "missing money" of the early 1980s, when it appeared that the money demand shifted downwards and that money demand was instable (Friedman and Kuttner, 1992). Instead, the approach of Chapter 7 is that the substitute for money, which is exchange credit, was left out of the money demand functions. In particular, the price of the money substitute, which includes the productivity factor in credit production, went down; and within the money demand function that includes the price of the substitute, there was substitution away from money and towards credit. Money demand was not instable. It simply requires modeling the substitutes to money within the money demand function in order to explain money demand during periods when the prices of such substitutes are undergoing large changes.

Chapter 8, "Money Velocity with Costly Credit", continues this theme of building the price of the substitute to money, this being exchange credit, into the money demand function and then taking this to the US data. Many authors, as far back as Friedman and Schwartz (1982), have put dummy variables into money demand functions to capture the shift in the money demand due to financial deregulation. Chapter 8 instead uses a time series to capture the price of the substitute to money, this being exchange credit. Adding this time series for credit is rare in the literature, although the real wage has been included in money demand estimation (Dowd 1990). Chapter 8 does this by presenting a version of the model that is presented in Chapter 7, and arguing that the productivity of the credit production sector can be captured by the marginal product of labor in that sector, since this should reflect any productivity increases. In this way, it includes a time series of the real wage in the finance sector within the money demand function and finds it to be significant. At the same time the model tries to capture the permanent income hypothesis of money demand that Friedman and Schwartz (1963b) put forth, by including an income ratio that reflects the contribution of this effect.

The approaches to money demand and its velocity of Chapters 7 and 8 is extended in Chapter 9, "Money Demand in General Equilibrium Endogenous Growth: Estimating the Role of a Variable Interest Elasticity". Here both the US and Australian money demand is estimated, using time series for the cost of credit via the real wage in the finance sectors; and a focus is put on the type of interest elasticity contained in this model. Chapter 9 shows that the interest elasticity of money demand rises as the nominal interest rate rises, and also as the cost of credit goes down. Therefore, instead of the interest elasticity falling in the 1980s, as the nominal interest rate fell down, the interest elasticity remained high, and this is attributed to another facet of the finance deregulation and its declining cost of exchange credit. And without the credit cost being included, the results give the standard lack of cointegration often found in the literature for the period.

Such a money demand function, with a rising interest elasticity as the nominal interest rate rises, is a result of the modeling approach that specifies a constant returns to scale production of the exchange credit. It results in a Cagan (1956) type function, which also has the interest elasticity rising with the nominal interest rate, and this feature becomes an important part of the explanation of the relation between inflation and growth in Part III of the collection.

Chapter 10 faces the problem in money demand estimation that a time series for the finance sector productivity may not be available, as is common for example for transition countries. This chapter examines the money demand in Croatia, and is forced to depart from a straightforward money demand approach. There is a focus on whether the Fisher equation of interest rates can be assumed to hold, as is implicit in standard money demand estimations. The expectation that such a relation does not hold is born out and so both the nominal interest rate and the inflation rate are brought into the model. This results in a reasonable money demand function, in a country where again the literature suggests that a stable money demand function may not exist.

Therefore Part II, the "Money Demand and Velocity," takes on the notion that money demand is instable and shows instead how to make the models more inclusive in a reasonable way that captures the likely sources of instability. Investigating thoroughly the money demand is useful since this is another dimension that general equilibrium monetary models can succeed or fail to explain. And with a money demand that is consistent with evidence, it may just happen that the model is better able to explain related phenomena. This in part is what the next Part III demonstrates.

1.3 Inflation and growth

In Part III, "Inflation and Growth," the credit production approach is applied to study the effect of inflation on output growth, when the growth rate is determined by human capital accumulation. Here inflation is a tax, and such taxes affect the return to capital. Chapter 11, "Inflation and Balanced-Path Growth with Alternative Payment Mechanisms", puts forth how the return on human capital is reduced by inflation. And it emphasizes that the return is reduced at a decreasing rate as the inflation rate is increased. This gives rise to a nonlinear profile of inflation versus the output growth rate. And Chapter 11 shows how the rising interest elasticity of money demand underlies the ability of the model to capture the nonlinear effect, which is also what empirical evidence has found.

Chapter 11 emphasizes how the Baumol tradeoff between money and credit costs in making exchanges is captured in this general equilibrium with a single consumption good. It shows that in fact the Baumol condition is not a special condition unique to monetary theory. Rather, by taking an industry approach to the production of credit with a constant returns to scale function, it shows that the Baumol condition is nothing more than the price-theoretic, or microeconomic, equalizing of the marginal cost of the credit output to the ratio of the marginal factor cost to the marginal factor product. This is a condition found in the theory of the firm for any output. In this case the output is the exchange credit.

The money demand of the model follows directly from the Baumol condition equilibrium condition, and the technology coefficients of the credit production function are only parameters of the money demand function that need to be specified that are not completely standard. Chapter 11 shows that the rising interest elasticity, and the nonlinear negative inflation-growth effect is robust to variation in the credit production parameters. And the result is that inflation induces greater leisure use, since inflation taxes exchange and induces substitution to the non-exchange good of leisure, and as a result the utilization of human capital in productive activity goes down. The growth rate follows downwards the lower return on human capital.

Besides the effect of inflation on growth, Chapter 11 also focuses on a secondary effect of inflation. A reallocation of factor inputs results in order to better use resources in the face of the inflation tax. In particular a higher cost of labor, from more leisure use, and a lower capital return, again from more leisure use, results in substitution from labor to capital in production. This creates a generalized Tobin (1965) effect whereby the increase in inflation results in a greater capital to effective-labor ratio. Chapter 11 thereby provides a strong statement on how to view the Tobin effect in general equilibrium: going beyond the exogenous growth Solow framework that Tobin employed, now it is true that capital use relatively rises because of inflation, but at the same time the output growth rate falls, an effect not part of Tobin's analysis. Further, through the better utilization of factor inputs, this Tobin type effect still leaves the growth rate falling because of inflation, but the growth rate falls by less as resources are better used.

Chapter 11 confronts the controversy on how inflation may cause a negative growth effect by showing within a very standard model how this occurs. Its only extension really is to add the exchange credit production structure, and as a result the growth rate falls in a nonlinear fashion. In addition, the chapter brings to light how the Tobin effect operates in general equilibrium.

Chapter 12, "Contrasting Models of the Effect of Inflation on Growth", focuses on the controversy about how a negative growth effect can result in standard neoclassical monetary models. It shows a ready ability to produce an empirically plausible decrease in the output growth rate from a variety of general equilibrium models. The qualification here is that these decreases are plausible in terms of a particular point estimate: such as a 10% increase in inflation causing a certain decrease in the growth rate.

Chapter 12 shows how the models produce different inflation rate changes over the whole range of the inflation rate levels. Linear inflation-growth profiles result in certain cases that are not consistent with the evidence of nonlinearity. Further, the models are distinguished by there secondary effects in terms of the Tobin effect. Some of the models produce reverse Tobin effects that are not consistent with evidence that continues to support the existence of a Tobin effect empirically. Thus the chapter brings into play the importance of both the money demand that underlies the general equilibrium model, in terms of its role in producing the nonlinearity, and the nature of a particular model's Tobin effect, in being able to explain the set of closely related inflation-growth evidence.

Chapter 13, "A Revised Tobin Effect from Inflation: Relative Input Price and Capital Ratio Realignments, USA and UK, 1959–1999", turns to empirical evidence that bears upon the set of related inflation-growth related events. As the statement of the Tobin effect in general equilibrium is new with these chapters, ample room is left to study their implications empirically. Chapter 13 specifically studies for the US and UK how the capital to effective labor ratio is affected by the inflation rate. It presents evidence of cointegration of the factor input ratio and inflation, and Granger causality evidence of inflation causing this ratio to rise, as is consistent with the general equilibrium effect of the Chapter 12 model. This is the first evidence of the Tobin effect that focuses exactly on the factor input ratio, and hopefully more such evidence will be investigated.

Chapter 14, "Inflation and Growth: Explaining a Negative Effect", focuses on details of the empirical evidence that demonstrates a negative and nonlinear inflation-growth effect. The controversy addressed here is that while the literature finds a strong and nonlinear negative inflation effect for most levels of the inflation rate, it also reports a positive and insignificant effect of inflation on growth for the lowest range of inflation, for example up to 1% for developed country samples. Chapter 14 investigates how endogeneity between inflation and growth at low levels of the inflation rate may give rise to a spurious result. By taking account for such endogeneity, Chapter 14 reports that the negative and nonlinear inflation-growth effect is found throughout the whole range of inflation for both developed and less developed panel data samples.

Chapter 15, "Granger Causality of the Inflation–Growth Mirror in Accession Countries", investigates the empirical relation between inflation and growth in time series evidence, and for Eastern European transition countries. There is a striking negative correlation between inflation and growth in Hungary and Poland, giving rise to the mirror of the chapter title. Here a vector autoregression (VAR) is estimated for each of these countries, between, the money stock, the price level and the output level.

Structural breaks are found and these are interpreted as breaks in velocity, since this is equal to the ratio of real money to output that is within the VAR. And the interpretation of these breaks is made using the model of Chapter 12. Chapter 15 argues that changes in the banking legislation lead to deregulatory type shifts in banking productivity that result in shifts in velocity as in Chapter 7. These shifts include the similar bank sector liberalization and restructuring laws in both countries, and in addition views their similar adoption of inflation rate targeting in this vein.

Chapter 15 provides the surprising perspective of how standard monetary growth theory can be applied to seemingly non-standard economies, rather than taking recourse to a start-from-scratch approach in modeling such economies. In particular, Chapter 15 shows how the developed country long term negative inflation-growth effect is not restricted just to developed countries, and instead may apply to all economies. Data limitations make such applications more difficult. But for example, the transition countries now acceding to the European Union already have many years of post-communist data from which to make a study.

1.4 Monetary business cycles

Part IV, "Monetary Business Cycles," includes the business cycle effects of inflation. It starts with a Keynesian perspective of the setting of the aggregate price level over the business cycle. Here the price is set according to marginal cost, which is the basis of the Neo-Keynesian models now popular today (with a monopoly mark-up to price being the cause of "inflation"). Chapter 16, "On Keynes's *Treatise*: Aggregate Price Theory Modern Analysis?" shows how Keynes replaced Fisher's quantity theory with a more Marshallian determination of the aggregate price level.

The chapter argues that Keynes's *Treatise* theory can be used directly to construct the well-known Keynesian "cross" analysis, from which IS-LM analysis is often thought to derive, and from which results a theory of the business cycle. The chapter points out that Keynes's business cycle theory and his non-Fisher price theory uses an assumption that is clearly inconsistent with what economic theory generally accepts to be valid. In particular, Marshallian profit is defined as per unit investment minus savings. Without this assumption, the cross analysis cannot be derived and instead the resulting world is that of neoclassical economics with its aggregate supply and demand coming from a standard model, which is presented.

Chapter 17, "Credit Shocks in the Financial Deregulatory Era: Not the Usual Suspects", provides a framework for examining the effect of inflation in a standard neo-classical business cycle setting. Here, as in the other chapters in Part IV, the usual money supply and goods productivity shocks are supplemented by an additional shock. This added shock is to the productivity of the credit production sector, consistent with the velocity explanation for example in Chapter 7. Chapter 17 uses the model to construct shocks from US data. It then analyses the shocks in terms of their plausibility relative to the US financial deregulation. It finds a set of positive credit shocks consistent with the financial deregulation period, and a negative shock consistent with the credit crisis during the savings and loan crash.

The details of how the model of Chapter 17 compares to more standard monetary business cycle models is the topic of the next chapter. Chapter 18, "A Comparison of Exchange Economies within a Monetary Business Cycle", shows how the additional features of the credit production and credit productivity shock allows the model to have some performance advantages relative to the cash-only cash-in-advance economy, and the shopping time economy.

Combining the endogenous growth framework of Chapter 12 with the monetary business cycle setting of Chapter 18, the next chapter brings together all of these elements. Chapter 19, "Money Velocity in an Endogenous Growth Business Cycle with Credit Shocks", shows how velocity's correlation and volatility over the business cycle is well captured. And it shows how the credit shock contributes more to volatility during the deregulatory subperiod, as might be expected. This chapter also makes the link explicit to the microfoundations literature in financial intermediation, to show how the credit production model used throughout Parts II, III and IV, is based on the banking industry production function. This linkage is useful in that it provides a novel way to calibrate the credit production technology parameters as based on industry evidence.

Chapter 19 marks an advance in using the endogenous growth framework in the business cycle setting. And it provides a more comprehensive way to include both long term inflation tax effects from long-lasting money supply shocks with shorter term business cycle effects from the more temporary goods productivity shocks. And as in Chapters 17 and 18, the shocks are constructed using the equilibrium solutions of the economy's variables, as functions of the shocks and the state variable, and data series for a set of these variables. This framework for the construction of the shocks within dynamic stochastic general equilibrium models holds much promise for future work.

Notes

1 There was deflation in the 1930s that appears in Figure 1.1 in absolute value as being positive; and note that here the volatility of inflation (π_t) is calculated as the standard deviation of the inflation rate (defined using the Consumer Price Index) over a 7 year window, where $k = 3$, and

$$volatility(\pi_t) = SD\,(\pi_{t-k}, \pi_{t-k+1}, \ldots \pi_t, \ldots, \pi_{t+k}).$$

2 And thereby avoiding the problems that Bewley (1983) raises, of infinite money demand in log utility money-in-the-utility function specifications; see McCandless (2008) for a discussion, pp. 241–242.

3 See also Gaspar, Smets, and Vestin (2007).

Part I

Inflation and welfare

2 The welfare costs of inflation in a cash-in-advance model with costly credit*

Max Gillman†

Summary

The chapter presents a modification of the Lucas–Stokey (1983) cash-in-advance economy in which the representative consumer decides, based on relative prices, which goods to buy with cash and which with costly credit An explicit Baumol (1952) condition emerges that guides this consumer choice. Deriving and estimating a closed-form welfare cost function in an example economy, the paper shows that the welfare cost of inflation depends on the margins of substitution. The consumer avoids inflation through costly credit and faces higher welfare costs of inflation than in standard cash-in-advance economies.

2.1 Introduction

The cash-in-advance economies of Lucas (1980, 1984) and Lucas and Stokey (1983, 1987) serve monetary theory well by explicitly modeling the exchange function of cash. However, some criticism centers on the requirement that the consumer use cash: the exogenously imposed Clower (1967) constraint.[1] Relatedly, the exogenous determination of goods as cash-purchased or credit-purchased according to preference specification arbitrarily impedes consumer choice; the consumer lacks the flexibility to use cash or credit in the purchase of any particular good.[2] This paper redresses these issues, within a cash-in-advance economy, by specifying an exchange function through which the consumer decides whether to use cash or costly credit to purchase a good.

Making credit costly in time creates the flexibility in exchange and facilitates empirical applications like the welfare costs of inflation. The theory of the welfare costs of inflation [Bailey (1956)] describes how consumers spend real resources in alternative means of exchange to avoid the inflation tax. Yet estimates of the welfare cost of inflation, such as in Cooley and Hansen (1989), follow from the Lucas (1980) cash-only economy that lacks any alternative means of exchange to cash. Such estimates capture only the inefficiency of inflation-induced substitution from goods to leisure rather than any real resource cost. Estimates such as in Cooley and Hansen (1991) follow from the Lucas–Stokey (1983) economy that has a costless alternative means of exchange to cash. These estimates capture only the inflation-induced inefficiency of substitution towards leisure and credit goods, and again exclude any Bailey-type real resource cost of avoiding inflation.

In this chapter, the consumer chooses between a foregone-interest cost of cash and a time cost of credit when purchasing any one good. Avoiding the inflation tax means switching from flat that uses no resources to exchange credit that uses up societal resources. Inflation acts through cash as a public tax with real proceeds returned in a lump sum fashion, while it acts through credit as a private societal tax with real proceeds destroyed.[3]

Having the ability to switch to costly credit during a stable inflation, the consumer faces higher welfare costs in comparison to standard cash-in-advance economies. This may seem counter-intuitive. However, it results because of the unrealistic assumption in standard cash-in-advance economies that exchange credit is either absent or costless, while here the consumer dissipates real resources when avoiding inflation.

Driving the result of comparatively higher welfare costs, the consumer substitutes away from cash until the marginal costs of avoiding inflation, through credit use, equal the marginal inflation rate tax on cash use. This balances the marginal costs of the means of exchange through a tax avoidance margin analogous to Baumol's (1952) exchange margin. The Baumol-type function of balancing exchange costs extends the Lucas–Stokey (1983) economy, and distinguishes it from Townsend (1989) and Den Haan (1990), both of which also endogenize the cash—credit mix but lack an explicit Baumol-type condition. D. Romer (1986, 1987) also generalizes the Baumol condition, but does not employ the cash-in-advance framework.

The Baumol condition emerges from the exchange technology that specifies the use of Beckerian time [Becker (1965)] for exchange credit. In Den Haan (1990), the exchange technology also induces tradeoffs between the means of exchange. His novel model differs from that presented here by requiring time for cash exchange as well as for credit-type exchange, and by making the cash-in-advance structure apply only in the special case where the consumer uses only cash. The related exchange technologies make the tradeoffs in Den Haan similar to this paper, while the explicit Baumol margin here makes the study of the cash–credit tradeoff simpler.

This chapter indicates that the margins of substitution significantly affect the welfare costs of inflation. Computing a closed-form welfare cost function for an example economy, the paper finds a higher welfare cost of inflation and a more negative interest elasticity of money demand in the costly credit economy than in the cash-only and the costless credit economies. The higher welfare cost and more negative interest elasticity align with Bailey's (1956) logic. Lastly, the chapter estimates the consumer's welfare cost of inflation, compares it with the literature, and finds support for the analysis.

2.2 The deterministic costly credit economy

2.2.1 Exchange structure

The consumer as banker 'self-produces' exchange credit in an implicit banking sector that requires labor.[4] Proportional to the size of the purchase per store and varying continuously by store, the consumer allocates time for exchange credit across a store continuum. Analogous to the color spectrum of Lucas (1980), each store on the continuum sells a different necessity produced with the same technology. The continuum here is similar to Prescott's (1987) continuum in its infinite number of stores and in its division into two segments of purchases, by cash or by exchange credit, but differs in that the consumer chooses the point of division on the continuum rather than taking it as given.

Assume the index $s \in [0, 1]$ marks a store's place along the continuum of stores. Let $\tau(s, t)$ be the proportional time per good that the consumer employs when buying a good with credit at store s. Assume $\tau(s, t) \geq 0$ and $\partial\tau / \partial s < 0$. Since $\tau(s, t)$ is decreasing in s, at low s stores the consumer requires more time for credit use and at high s stores less time for credit use. Since $\tau(s, t)$ is strictly monotonic, there exists a store, say $\bar{s}(t) \in [0, 1]$, which divides the continuum between cash and credit use.

The consumer chooses $\bar{s}$ in deciding where to use credit and where to use cash, buying goods with cash from stores with high time costs of credit, indexed from 0 to $\bar{s}$, and buying goods with credit from stores with low time costs of credit, indexed from $\bar{s}$ to 1. Let $c(s, t)$ be the amount of good purchased at store s at time t; then the consumer makes the good a cash good for $0 \leq s < \bar{s}$ and a credit good for $\bar{s} \leq s \leq 1$. That the exchange technology induces the consumer to choose low s goods as cash goods and high s goods as credit goods makes them analogous to the Lucas–Stokey (1983) cash good c_1 and credit good c_2. Alternatively, the choice of $\bar{s}$ can be thought of as determining the color composition of each of a single cash good and a single credit good.

Assume perfect competition and identical production technology in the market of each store's good. Then the consumer pays the same positive price at time t, denoted as $P(t)$, for any good across all of the stores. This price holds whether using cash or credit. The consumer either uses cash held in advance of trading or uses credit and pays off the debt at the beginning of the next period. Either way, the storekeeper finds the receipts from the period's trading available to him for further trading only at the beginning of the next period.

2.2.2 Cash constraint

To buy goods with cash across the low s stores, the consumer receives a lump sum transfer of cash, $H(t)$, at the end of each period t. Given an initial cash stock of $M(0)$, the cash stock at the beginning of period $t + 1$ is

$$M(t + 1) = M(t) + H(t). \tag{1}$$

The consumer cash expenditures are constrained by the cash stock:

$$P(t) \int_{0}^{\bar{s}} c(s, t)\, \mathrm{d}s \leq M(t). \tag{2}$$

2.2.3 Credit time constraint

When buying goods with credit across the high s stores, the amount of time spent at each store equals $\tau(s, t)\, c(s, t)$. With a given time endowment of one, the total time spent buying goods with credit falls between zero and one:

$$0 \leq \int_{\bar{s}(t)}^{1} \tau(s, t)\, c(s, t)\, \mathrm{d}s \leq 1. \tag{3}$$

2.2.4 Production

The consumer as producer uses the same production function for all goods, assumed linear in the labor input. Labor input equals the time endowment, 1, minus leisure time, $x(t)$, and minus total time in exchange credit activity, as given in eq. (3). Total goods production equals $w(t)$ multiplied by the labor input.

$$\int_{0}^{1} c(s, t)\, \mathrm{d}s = w(t) \left[1 - x(t) - \int_{\bar{s}(t)}^{1} \tau(s, t)\, c(s, t)\, \mathrm{d}s\right]. \tag{4}$$

In a decentralized economy with profit-maximizing firms, $w(t)$ would be equal to the positive real wage.

2.2.5 Wealth constraint

The consumer's end-of-period receipts equal the nominal wages from labor, $P(t)\, w(t)\, [1 - x(t) - \int_{\bar{s}}^{1} \tau(s, t)\, c(s, t)\, \mathrm{d}s]$, plus the lump sum cash transfers, $H(t)$, and the nominal goods endowment, $P(t)\, a(t)$. End-of-period expenditures equal the cash set aside for next period's cash purchases, $M(t + 1)$, and the payment of debt from exchange credit, $P(t) \int_{\bar{s}}^{1} c(s, t)\, \mathrm{d}s$. Defining $i(t)$ as the nominal (discrete time) interest rate, with $q^t \equiv 1/[1 + i(1)]\, [1 + i(2)]\, \ldots\, [1 + i(t)]$, the consumer discounts the stream of nominal income minus expenditures to get net wealth:

$$\sum_{t=0}^{x} q^t \left(P(t)\, w(t) \left[1 - x(t) - \int_{\bar{s}}^{1} \tau(s, t)\, c(s, t)\, \mathrm{d}s \right] \right.$$

$$\left. + H(t) + P(t)\, a(t) - M(t+1) - P(t) \int_{\bar{s}}^{1} c(s, t)\, \mathrm{d}s \right) = 0. \tag{5}$$

2.2.6 *Preferences*

The consumer's utility at time t, $U(t)$, with $a \geq 0$, is defined as

$$U(t) \equiv \int_{0}^{1} [\ln c(s, t) + a \ln x(t)]\, \mathrm{d}s. \tag{6}$$

2.2.7 *Equilibrium*

The representative consumer defines the equilibrium as the quantity and price sequence $\{c(s, t), x(t), \bar{s}(t), M(t), P(t)\}$, for $t = 0, \ldots, \infty$, which maximizes utility in eq. (6), subject to the cash constraint in eq. (2), discounted by time preference over the infinite horizon, and subject to the wealth constraint in eq. (5). The equilibrium sequence also satisfies nonnegativity constraints on $c(s, t)$ and $x(t)$, the credit time constraint of eq. (3), and the cash market clearing condition of eq. (1). To keep the economy monetary with defined prices, assume henceforth that $s \neq 0$, so that $\bar{s} \in (0, 1]$. This excludes the case of a pure credit economy, which can occur only during extreme hyperinflation with no cash use and which apparently has never been experienced.[5] For a study of a nonbinding cash-in-advance constraint, see Svensson (1985).

2.2.8 *The consumer maximization problem*

Discounting utility by $\beta \in (0, 1)$, the consumer's Lagrangian is

$$\max_{\substack{\{c(s,t),\, x(t),\, \bar{s}(t),\, M(t)\} \\ t = 0, \ldots \infty,}} \quad \mathcal{L} = \sum_{t=0}^{x} \beta^t \left(\int_{0}^{1} [\ln c(s, t) + a \ln x(t)]\, \mathrm{d}s \right.$$

$$\left. + \lambda(t) \left[M(t) - P(t) \int_{0}^{\bar{s}} c(s, t)\, \mathrm{d}s \right] \right)$$

$$+ \mu \left\{ \sum_{t=0}^{\infty} q^t \left(P(t)\, w(t) \left[1 - x(t) - \int_{\bar{s}}^{1} \tau(s, t)\, c(s, t)\, \mathrm{d}s \right] \right. \right.$$

$$\left. \left. - M(t+1) - P(t) \int_{\bar{s}}^{1} c(s, t)\, \mathrm{d}s + H(t) + P(t)\, a(t) \right) \right\}, \tag{7}$$

with first-order conditions

$$\beta^t \lambda(t) - \mu q^{t-1} = 0, \tag{8}$$

$$\beta^t \frac{1}{c(s, t)} - \beta^t \lambda(t) P(t) = 0 \quad \text{for} \quad 0 < s < \bar{s}, \tag{9}$$

$$\beta^t \frac{1}{c(s, t)} - \mu q^t P(t)[w(t) \tau(s, t) + 1] = 0 \quad \text{for} \quad \bar{s} \leq s \leq 1, \tag{10}$$

$$\beta^t \int_0^1 \frac{\alpha}{x(t)} \mathrm{d}s - \mu q^t P(t) w(t) = 0, \tag{11}$$

$$-\beta^t \lambda(t) P(t) c(\bar{s}, t) + \mu q^t P(t)[w(t)\tau(\bar{s}, t)c(\bar{s}, t) + c(\bar{s}, t)] = 0. \tag{12}$$

2.3 Discussion of first-order conditions

The relative price of cash to wealth, from eq. (8) and with π the inflation rate, equals $\lambda(t)/\mu = (1 + i)/(1 + \pi)^t$ and shows the relative discounting of the value of money due to inflation. Substituting on the basis of eq. (8), write eq. (9) as

$$\beta^t \frac{1}{c(s, t)} = \mu q^t p(t)[1 + i(t)], \quad 0 < s < \bar{s}. \tag{13}$$

This states that the discounted marginal utility of cash goods equals the product of the discounted marginal utility of nominal wealth and the shadow price of the cash good. The shadow price of the cash good consists of a real goods cost of 1 and a real exchange cost of $i(t)$. Eq. (10) shows that the marginal utility of credit goods equals a similar product $\mu q^t P(t)[1 + w(t) \tau(s, t)]$, $\bar{s} \leq s \leq 1$. The shadow price of the credit good consists of a real goods price of 1 and a real exchange cost of $w(t)\ \tau(s, t)$. Similarly, in eq. (11), the real shadow price of leisure equals $w(t)$.

Combining the first-order condition for money, in eq. (8), with the first-order condition with respect to the marginal store $\bar{s}$ at which to use exchange credit, in eq. (12), shows the Baumol-type condition that balances marginal exchange costs:

$$i(t) = w(t)\ \tau(\bar{s}, t). \tag{14}$$

The consumer sets the time cost of cash equal to the time cost of credit at the marginal store $\bar{s}$ (see Figure 2.1). In Baumol (1952), this equating of the marginal costs of exchange appears by algebraically rearranging the first-order condition to show that the interest rate equals the marginal (and average) costs of a dollar from the bank.[6] This condition also relates to the legal

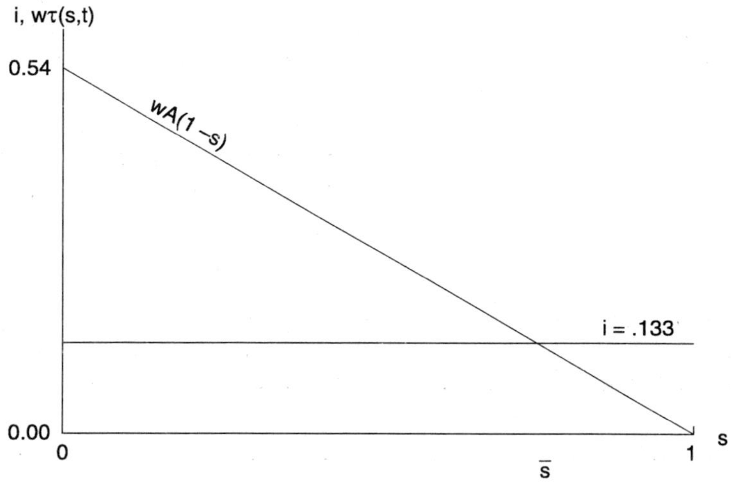

Figure 2.1 Determination of the marginal credit store. Balancing exchange costs through a Baumol-type condition. Example: $w\tau(s,\ t) = Aw(1 - s)$, $Aw = 0.54$, $t = 0.133$.

restrictions description of equilibrium, such as in Eichenbaum and Wallace (1985), in which equilibrium among different types of money occurs at the point of equality among the marginal transactions costs for each of the different types of money. Equating marginal costs here provides the solution of $\bar{s}$ from eq. (14), $\bar{s} = \tau^{-1}(i(t)/w(t))$, shows how the consumer's decision depends on relative prices, and provides the additional margin that extends the standard cash-in-advance economies.

2.4 Substitution rates in the cash-in-advance economies

The consumer's marginal rate of substitution between cash and credit goods, from eqs. (13) and (10), equals $(1 + i(t))/(1 + w\tau(s, t))$, with $\bar{s} \leq s \leq 1$. In cash-only economies like Lucas (1980), $1 + i(t)$ gives the only relevant shadow price for goods consumption. In Lucas and Stokey (1983), the rate between cash goods and credit goods equals $(1 + i(t))/1$. To see how this paper's economy includes the deterministic cash-only and costless credit cases, first note the cash-only case. If $\tau(s, t) = \infty$ for all s, so that $w\tau(s, t) > i(t)$ for all s, then the Baumol-type eq. (14) becomes nonbinding, $\bar{s} = 1$, and prohibitive credit costs reduce the economy to the cash-only case; $1 + i(t)$ would be the only shadow price of consumption goods.

Secondly, again relax the assumption of strict monotonicity for $\tau(s, t)$ to monotonicity, so that $\tau' \leq 0$ instead of $\tau' < 0$. Exogenously divide the goods into cash and costless credit goods by setting $\tau(s, t) = \infty$ for $s < \bar{s}$ and $\tau(s, t) = 0$ for $s \geq \bar{s}$, and by assuming that $\bar{s} \equiv \tau^{-1}i(t)/w(t))$; the consumer takes $\bar{s}$ as given instead of as a choice variable. The marginal rate of substitution between cash and credit goods collapses to $(1 + i(t))/1$ as in Lucas and Stokey (1983). This gives a cash good with a goods' cost of 1 and an exchange cost of $i(t)$, and a credit good with a goods' cost of 1 and an exchange cost of 0. Through a dichotomized relative price specification instead of their preference specification, these assumptions create the same marginal rates of substitution as in the Lucas–Stokey economy.

A more general case exists in the model here: the color spectrum division between cash and credit changes in response to changes in the relative costs of exchange. The resulting marginal rate of substitution of $(1 + i(t))/(1 + w(t)\tau(s, t))$ is generally lower than $(1 + i(t))/1$, since credit is costly here instead of costless as in Lucas and Stokey (1983). A rate of $(1 + i(t))/1$ still holds in the economy here for the least credit-costly store ($s = 1$) if those costs equal 0 [if $\tau(1, t) = 0$]. Otherwise the rate lies below $(1 + i(t))/1$, falls as s goes from 1 to $\bar{s}$, and equals 1 at the marginal store $\bar{s}$, where the shadow exchange costs of cash and credit are equal [$i = w\tau(\bar{s}, t)$].

The rate of substitution also equals 1 at the optimum, both here and in Lucas and Stokey (1983). However, the Lucas–Stokey consumer at the optimum faces zero exchange costs both for cash and for credit and so uses both. The consumer at the optimum here faces zero exchange costs for cash, but positive costs for credit, and so uses only cash. The latter result naturally follows in economies where, independent of preferences, costly credit serves only an exchange function.[7]

Altogether, the consumer finds an added first-order condition and a generally lower marginal rate of substitution between cash and credit goods as compared to Lucas and Stokey (1983). These differences show the sense in which the economy is an extension of the costless credit economy, now including costly credit use alongside cash use and additionally having the consumer decide on the composition of the cash and credit goods. Without preferences tying down cash usage, the consumer can substitute between cash and costly credit to buy any good: doing so alters the welfare costs of inflation.

2.5 The welfare costs of stable inflation

Through derivation of a closed-form welfare cost function, this section compares the costs of inflation among the costly credit, cash-only, and costless credit economies. The log-utility example economy yields a relatively simple closed-form function for the welfare costs of inflation and facilitates comparison to Cooley and Hansen (1989, 1991) who also use log-utility. For the technology of exchange credit, assume a linear function: $\tau(s, t) = A(1 - s)$, for all t, with $A > 0$. The consumer as storekeeper can be thought of as providing credit 'paper work' time for a variable fee, dependent on the store index, so that the time cost of credit is replaced by an explicit cost $A(1 - s)$.[8]

Define the welfare cost of inflation as the real goods endowment, $a(t)$, needed to make the consumer indifferent between the optimum with zero goods endowment and a nonoptimal inflation rate combined with the real goods endowment. Assume the inflation rate, the real goods endowment, and the marginal product of labor constant over time. Appendix A presents the implied closed-form stationary equilibrium. Using the equilibrium solution, the welfare cost function follows by first forming indirect utility.

Define V as indirect utility.

$$V \equiv U[c^*(i, a, \cdot), x^*(i, a, \cdot)], \tag{15}$$

where U equals the log-utility of eq. (6) and $c^*(i, a, \cdot)$ and $x^*(i, a, \cdot)$ equal the equilibrium goods and leisure consumption from eqs. (26)–(28) of appendix A. Note that $i = 0$ is the Friedman (1969) optimum of deflation at the rate of time preference, which equates the competitive equilibrium to the Pareto optimum.[9] Then the welfare cost of inflation is the $a = f(i, \cdot)$ that solves

$$V(i, a, \cdot) - V(0, 0, \cdot) = 0. \tag{16}$$

Presenting welfare costs as a percent of full income, where full income equals the time endowment 1 multiplied by the marginal product of labor w, percentage welfare costs equal

$$\frac{a}{w} = \frac{f(i)}{w} = e^{X} \cdot (1 + i)^{Y} \cdot Z - 1, \tag{17}$$

$$X = \frac{-i}{(1 + a)\,Aw}, \quad Y = \left(\frac{1}{1 + a}\right)\left(1 + \frac{1}{Aw}\right),$$

$$Z = 1 - \frac{i\left(1 - \dfrac{i}{Aw}\right)}{(1 + i)\,(1 + \alpha)}. \tag{18}$$

This assumes that $i < Aw$ so that the economy remains monetary with $\bar{s} = [1 - i/(Aw)] > 0$.

As the interest rate rises from 0, percentage welfare costs rise monotonically from 0, cash use falls, and the economy approaches all credit. Increases in a and Aw cause percentage welfare costs to decrease. Increasing Aw to infinity, and making $\bar{s} = 1 - i/(Aw) = 1$, collapses the cost function in (17) and (18) to the function for the cash-only economy, with an 'N' subscript:

$$\frac{a_N}{w} = \frac{f_N(i, \cdot)}{w} = (1 + i)^{\tilde{Y}}\,\tilde{Z} - 1, \tag{19}$$

$$\widetilde{Y} = \frac{1}{1+a}, \widetilde{Z} = 1 - \frac{i}{(1+i)(1+a)}. \tag{20}$$

The X-term of eqs. (17) and (18), which contains the shadow exchange cost of cash goods relative to that of credit goods, drops out in this cost function as do the other components with Aw. Without these credit costs and the flexibility between cash and credit, the welfare costs of inflation in the cash-only economy are less than welfare costs in the costly credit economy: $f_N \leq f$. Except in the optimum when welfare costs are the same in both economies, the consumer is better off without the option to spend resources avoiding the inflation tax.

The consumer faces the same welfare costs in the cash-only economy of eqs. (19) and (20) as found in Cooley and Hansen (1989) in the special case of certainty, zero capital, and linear production technology. Cash-in-advance economies with costless credit, as in Lucas and Stokey (1983) and Cooley and Hansen (1991), face a different cost function than in either the costly credit or the cash-only economy above. To derive the welfare cost of inflation for the costless credit economy, as before set up the indirect utility eq. (16) from which to form the cost function; then set $\bar{s}$ equal to some arbitrary number, say $\hat{s}$; and make credit costs equal 0, $Aw = 0$. This yields the welfare cost function, similar to the cash-only case, for the economy with a predetermined division between cash and costless credit:

$$\frac{a}{w} = \frac{f(i, \hat{s})}{w} = (1+i)^{\hat{Y}} \cdot \hat{Z} \cdot - 1, \tag{21}$$

$$\hat{Y} = \frac{\hat{s}}{1+a}, \hat{Z} = 1 - \frac{i\hat{s}}{(1+i)(1+a)}. \tag{22}$$

For $a \geq 1$ and $i > 0$, the welfare cost of inflation in this costless credit economy is less than the cost in the cash-only economy and the difference increases as $\hat{s}$ decreases; $\partial f / \partial \hat{s} \geq 0$, for $a \geq 1$, and so $f(i, \hat{s}, \cdot) \leq f_N(i, \cdot)$. The estimate for a in the paper is $a = 2.27$ (see Appendix 2.B), and a similar estimate in Den Haan (1990) is 2.571. With $a \geq 1$ satisfied, this means that the consumer faces a simple hierarchy of welfare costs across the costless credit, no-credit, and costly credit economies: $f(i, \hat{s}, \cdot) \leq f_N(i, \cdot) \leq f(i, \cdot)$.

2.6 Comparison of the interest elasticities of money demand

The interest elasticity of money demand is highest in absolute value in the costly credit economy, given that $a \geq 1$, $Aw \leq 1$, just as the welfare cost of inflation is highest in the costly credit economy for $a \geq 1$. The smallest elasticity in absolute value is found in the cash-only economy, whereas the smallest welfare cost of inflation occurs in the costless credit economy. From eqs. (29) and (30) of Appendix 2A, the costly credit elasticity, denoted by σ, equals

$$\sigma = -\frac{1-\bar{s}}{\bar{s}} - \frac{i}{1+i} + \frac{i[\bar{s}-(1-\bar{s})(1+i)]}{(1+i)^2\left[1+a-\bar{s}\left(\frac{i}{1+i}\right)\right]}. \tag{23}$$

The three terms of eq. (23) compare to the X, Y, and Z terms of the welfare cost function in eqs. (17) and (18). The first term captures the substitution between cash and credit in the face of inflation. At a 10% inflation rate, and with parameter values as given in Appendix 2B, this term accounts for the main part of the elasticity.

Setting $\bar{s}$ equal to 1, in the equilibrium solution given in Appendix 2.A, yields the interest elasticity for the cash-only economy, denoted by σ_N:

$$\sigma_N = -\frac{i}{1+i} + \frac{i}{(1+i)^2\left(1+a-\frac{i}{1+i}\right)}. \tag{24}$$

Compared to eq. (23), eq. (24) lacks the negative first term and has a more positive last term (a larger return of inflation proceeds). This makes the cash-only elasticity less negative than the costless credit elasticity: $|\sigma_N| \leq |\sigma|$. The main difference is the missing first term that reflects the flexibility between means of exchange.

Setting $\bar{s} = \hat{s}$ and $Aw = 0$, in the equilibrium solution given in appendix A, yields the elasticity for the costless credit economy:

$$\sigma_{\hat{s}} = -\frac{i}{1+i} + \frac{i\hat{s}}{(1+i)^2\left(1+a-\frac{i\hat{s}}{1+i}\right)}. \tag{25}$$

This elasticity is generally less than the elasticity in the costly credit economy; with $a \geq 1$ and $Aw \leq 1$, nonbinding constraints according to the parameter specifications of $a = 2.27$ and $Aw = 0.54$ in Appendix 2.B, $|\sigma_{\hat{s}}| \leq |\sigma|$. Similar to the cash-only elasticity in eq. (24), the costless credit elasticity in eq. (25) also lacks the first term in eq. (23), and so reflects an inflexibility between means of exchange. In comparing the costless credit to the cash-only economy, $\partial|\sigma_{\hat{s}}|/\partial\hat{s} \leq 0$ implies that $|\sigma_{\hat{s}}| \geq |\sigma_N|$; that is, the elasticity in the costly credit economy is higher in absolute value than in the cash-only economy. Intuitively, money demand is more interest-elastic in the costless credit economy than in the cash-only economy because the taxed good, cash, comprises a smaller percent of expenditures in the costless credit economy.

By Bailey's (1956) logic, for the costly credit and the cash-only economies, the ranking of the interest elasticities confirms the ranking of the welfare costs functions. The comparative rankings for the costless credit economy are different because the Bailey logic does not apply. The costless credit economy allows avoidance of the inflation tax without using real resources; it lacks the Bailey link between the interest elasticity, real resource use, and the welfare cost of inflation; and it provides the consumer a more negative higher elasticity than in the cash-only economy, but the lowest welfare costs of inflation.

2.7 Estimates of welfare costs and elasticities

Estimating the welfare costs of inflation allows a comparison to other estimates and further tests the paper's analysis. Details of the data specifications are in Appendix 2.B. Comparison to existing estimates in the literature requires distinguishing between welfare costs as a percent of full income, as in eqs. (17)–(22), and as a percent of current income, as is common. The full income measure captures the substitution effects of inflation, while the current income measure adds an income effect of less work because of inflation. Computing current income from either side of the resource constraint in eq. (4) (with $a = 0$), panel A of Table 2.1 presents the estimates using both full and current income bases. The table shows that the 'sign' of the effect of a on welfare costs, but not of the cost of credit Aw, depends on the income basis.

Using averaged annual U.S. data for the years 1948–1988, the measure of the welfare cost of a 10% inflation rate equals 2.19% of current income for the costly credit economy [eqs. (17) and (18)]. The comparable estimates for the cash-only and costless credit economies equal 0.582% and, assuming

Table 2.1 Sensitivity of welfare cost and velocity estimates to parameter changes

A. Welfare costs

	Welfare costs as percent of full income [from (17)–(18)] *(A)*	*Current income [from (4)]* *(B)*	*Welfare costs as percent of current income* *(A) · w/(B)*
$a = 2.27$, $Aw = 0.54$	0.617	$w \cdot (0.2818)$	2.190
$Aw = 0.594$	0.576	$w \cdot (0.2816)$	2.046
$Aw = 1.08$	0.391	$w \cdot (0.2532)$	1.543
$Aw = 0.54$, $a = 2.27$	0.617	$w \cdot (0.2818)$	2.190
$a = 2.497$	0.579	$w \cdot (0.2630)$	2.202
$a = 4.54$	0.373	$w \cdot (0.1644)$	2.268

B. Velocity: Approximation using $1/\bar{s} = 1/(1 - i/Aw)$ *with* $i = 0.133$ *(10% inflation)*

$Aw =$	0.133	0.162	0.20	0.35	0.50	0.54	0.65	0.80
$1/\bar{s} =$	a	5.66	2.99	1.63	1.36	1.33	1.25	1.20

$\hat{s} = 0.5$, 0.098% [eqs. (19)–(22)]. This assumes that the real rate of interest equals 3% [$i = (1.10)(1.03) - 1 = 0.133$], and that $Aw = 0.54$ and $a = 2.27$. The interest elasticity in the costly credit, cash-only, and costless credit economies, in eqs. (23)–(25), equal –0.429, –0.085, and –0.101, respectively.

For a perspective on the economy's realism, the economy's income velocity of money can also be computed. Defining income equal to consumption, and approximating the consumption as $c(s)$, for $0 < s < \bar{s}$ [instead of $\int_0^1 c(s)\,ds$], gives an income velocity of money equal to $1/\bar{s}$. A 10% inflation sets this velocity equal to 1.33 (compared to 1 for the cash-only economy). As shown in panel B of Table 2.1], to get a reasonable estimate of U.S. velocity at a 10% inflation, say equal to 5.66,[10] would require a lower estimate of the cost of credit: $Aw = 0.162$ instead of the actual $Aw = 0.54$. $Aw = 0.162$ would yield an interest elasticity of –4.73 instead of –0.429, and a welfare cost of 5.79% instead of 2.19%.

Still, the welfare cost estimates compare to the literature as expected. Cooley and Hansen's (1989) estimate of the welfare cost of a 10% inflation is 0.521% of current income for quarterly data. Since their economy allows only cash use, 0.521% compares to the cash-only economy of this paper and its estimate of 0.582%. The closeness of the estimates (within 12%) and the small magnitude of 0.521%, compared to the 2.19% estimate for the costly credit economy, does not contradict this paper's finding that allowing only cash yields 'low' estimates of the welfare cost of inflation.

Cooley and Hansen's (1991) estimate of the welfare costs of a 10% inflation is less than their (1989) estimate (0.357% compared to 0.521%). As in this paper, Wright (1991) attributes the difference to the ability of the consumer to costlessly avoid the inflation tax through the credit goods in the Cooley–Hansen (1991) economy. These estimates support this paper's finding that the welfare costs of inflation in the costless credit economy are less than those in the cash-only economy.

Den Haan's (1990) estimate of the costs of going to a 5% inflation rate from 0% is comparatively high at 4.68%. While not directly comparable to the 2.19% estimate in the economy here, the principal difference is that the Den Haan exchange technology requires time use for all means of exchange; this would in itself give rise to expectations of a higher estimate than found here where only credit uses up time.

This paper's 2.19% estimate is significantly higher than the partial equilibrium estimates in the 0.3% range, such as in McCallum (1990) and Fischer (1981). The income decrease that occurs when inflation increases in the general equilibrium economy here, as opposed to holding income constant for the partial equilibrium estimates, explains a small part of the difference. The larger part of the difference seems to be that the partial equilibrium estimates assume 'small' interest (or semi-interest) elasticities. The economy here suggests assuming elasticities from the upper half of the estimated ranges, such as in Lucas (1988a).

2.8 Qualifications

The cash-in-advance economy in this paper facilitates analyses that require flexibility between means of exchange, such as the examination of the income velocity of money, the specification of a stable money demand function, and the determination of a rule of money supply growth. Adding a feature of realism, the costly credit extension also leaves open the merging of the transactions and asset functions of money through the introduction of intertemporal credit. For the equity premium puzzle [Mehra and Prescott (1985)], the model adds one feature, that the marginal rate of substitution in consumption over time depends on the change in the relative price of exchange. Instead of depending on just the interest rate as in Bohn (1991), the marginal rate of substitution depends on changes in the interest-rate/real-wage-rate and the productivity in finance. In itself, this feature of the credit friction may make for better adjustment of prices to shocks, less movement in consumption, and even more difficult the generation of the change in consumption demanded by the Mehra and Prescott 'friction'.

However, within a cash-in-advance economy that depends on the real-wage/interest-rate, it seems possible to envision incorporating both human and physical capital with adjustment costs, adding intertemporal credit, and moving towards resolution of the equity premium puzzle. If the real wage rises because of rising labor productivity in a cycle, and its income effect combines with the income effect of rising real returns to physical capital in a cycle, then the income effect of more consumption may dominate the substitution effect of less consumption as the result of a cyclically rising interest rate. This may produce the needed covariance of consumption and the risk-free rate. Adjustment between human and physical capital would still require flexibility within the consumption-investment process, and perhaps even more flexibility within the cash-credit process, even while leaving room for an Eichenbaum and Christiano (1992) friction.

Appendix 2.A: stationary equilibrium solution

$$c^*(s) = \frac{w + a}{(1 + i)\left[1 + a - \left(\frac{i}{1 + i}\right)\left(1 - \frac{i}{Aw}\right)\right]} \quad \text{for} \quad 0 < s < \bar{s}, \tag{26}$$

$$c^*(s) = \frac{w + a}{[1 + Aw(1 - s)]\left[1 + a - \left(\frac{i}{1 + i}\right)\left(1 - \frac{i}{Aw}\right)\right]} \quad \text{for} \quad \bar{s} \leq s \leq 1, \tag{27}$$

$$x^* = \frac{a(w + a)}{w\left[1 + a - \left(\frac{i}{1 + i}\right)\left(1 - \frac{i}{Aw}\right)\right]}, \tag{28}$$

$$\frac{M^*(t)}{P(t)} = \frac{\left(1 - \frac{i}{Aw}\right)(w + a)}{(1 + i)\left[1 + a - \left(\frac{i}{1 + i}\right)\left(1 - \frac{i}{Aw}\right)\right]}, \tag{29}$$

$$\bar{s}^* = 1 - \frac{i}{Aw}, \tag{30}$$

$$\lambda^*(t)\, P(t) = \frac{(1 + i)\left[1 + a - \left(\frac{i}{1 + i}\right)\left(1 - \frac{i}{Aw}\right)\right]}{w + a}. \tag{31}$$

Appendix 2.B: parameter specification and data description

A, w, and a are the parameters requiring specification for the welfare cost and elasticity estimations. In these estimates, of eqs. (18), (20), (22), and (23), A and w appear everywhere as the product Aw and so are here computed as this product. Annual averages are computed from U.S. annual data for the 1948–1988 period.

The average time costs per good over the continuum of stores which offer exchange credit is

$$\int_{\bar{s}(t)}^{1} \tau(s, t)\, \mathrm{d}s = \int_{\bar{s}}^{1} A(1 - s)\, \mathrm{d}s = \frac{A}{2}.$$

These costs equal labor hours, L, per output, Y, in the credit sector, or L/Y, so that $A/2 = L/Y$. Multiply both sides of the latter equation by the real wage, w, to estimate Aw: $Aw/2 = wL/Y$. Aw equals twice the share of labor in output in the credit sector (abstracting from the model's feature of no capital).

The Finance, Real Estate, and Insurance (FIR) sector is chosen to measure the model's credit sector, picking a broader rather than narrower sector on the assumption that technological innovation would affect average costs equally across the entire sector. The broader sector also provides longer time series data on which to draw a stationary estimate. A gauge of the significance of labor in this sector is that annual hours worked by all employees in FIR, as a percent of total hours worked by all employees in all U.S. sectors, has risen steadily from 3% in 1948 to 6% in 1988.[11]

The labor share in output in FIR is measured by the ratio of the product of the annual wages and the number of full-time equivalent employees in FIR to the value of annual GNP in FIR; this yields an average of 0.27 for 1948–1988[12] and makes $Aw = 0.54$. Measurement errors in FIR make the Aw estimate uncertain, though the stability of the average may decrease this risk and is evidenced by the range of (0.22, 0.33) for the 1948–1988 period.

Derive a from eq. (26), which sets out the solution for equilibrium leisure in the log-utility economy. Assuming that $a = 0$ (zero goods endowment),

$$a = \left(\frac{x}{1-x}\right)\left(1 - \frac{i\bar{s}}{1+i}\right).$$

This implies that a is the share of leisure in hours worked at the economy's optimum ($i = 0$). Then $1/(1 + a)$ and $a/(1 + a)$ are the share of work and leisure in total allocated time. Excluding 1/3 of time for sleep, measure the share of working time in total time to derive a. Divide annual hours worked, by all full- and part-time workers in the U.S., by the annual number of full- and part-time workers in the U.S. Then take the annual average, over 1948–1988, to get $a = 2.27$.[13] Heuristically, $1/(1 + a)$ would be between about 1/4 for a 40-hour work week, or 40/168 of awake time, and about 1/3 for a 60-hour work week, or 60/168 of awake time; its measure of $1/(1 + 2.27)$ falls in between. Also $a = 2.27$ is close to a similar measure (equal to 2.571) in Den Haan (1990).

Notes

* Gillman, Max, (1993), 'The Welfare Costs of Inflation in a Cash-in-Advance Model with Costly Credit', *Journal of Monetary Economics*, 31(1) 97–116. Reprinted: Gillman, Max, 1994, 'The Welfare Costs of Inflation in a Cash in Advance Model with Costly Credit', chapter 10 in *The Theory of Inflation*, ed. Michael Parkin, The International Library of Critical Writings in Economics, An Elgar Reference Collection, volume 41, edited by Mark Blaug, Edward Elgar, Aldershot, England, pp. 348–366.

† I wish to thank especially Robert E. Lucas, Gary S. Becker, and Yair Mundlak as advisors for my dissertation, from which this paper originated. I am also grateful to Glenn Boyle, Dorian Owen, the University of Otago Department of Economics Seminar Series, and the University of Auckland Department of Economics Seminar Series.

1 For example, Plosser (1984) comments on the limits of the exogenous Clower constraint.

2 Coleman (1989) cites this lack of flexibility as the possible failure to get reasonable estimates concerning the term structure of interest rates; Hodrick, Kocherlakota, and Lucas (1991) find a lack of success in tracking velocity with a Lucas–Stokey (1987) economy. Relatedly, Lucas (1988a) describes a velocity more dependent on relative prices than Lucas and Stokey (1983), and King (1988) emphasizes the need for a more variable velocity. Manuelli and Sargent (1988) cite the inflexibility as an issue in applying the cash-in-advance economy to business cycle study. King and Plosser (1986) recommend an endogenization of the cash–credit mix.

3 I owe the societal tax point to the referee.

4 Lucas (1980, p. 144) suggests: 'With the introduction of some real cost associated with dealing in a credit market (say the time involved for one's credit worthiness to be established), one can imagine a model in which currency demand is governed by a mechanism such as that studied above coexisting with a credit mechanism. . . .' While lacking such a mechanism, McCallum (1983) introduces similar time as 'shopping time'. Hicks (1935) states: '. . . my suggestion can be expressed by saying

that we ought to regard every individual in the community as being, on a small scale, a bank. Monetary theory becomes a sort of generalization of banking theory.' Baltensperger (1980) emphasizes the potential from modeling real banking costs in developing the theory of the banking firm.

5 More generally, uniqueness and existence of the general equilibrium follows if utility, defined $U[c(s, t), x(t)]$: $(0, 1]\ X N_{+}^{2} \rightarrow R_{+}$, is monotonic, pairwise continuous, and twice differentiable in goods and leisure, if for all $s \in (0, 1]$, $\lim_{c(s,t) \rightarrow \infty} U_{c(s,t)} = 0$, $\lim_{c(s,t) \rightarrow 0} U_{c(s,t)} = \infty$, $\lim_{x(t) \rightarrow \infty} U_{x(t)} = 0$, $\lim_{x(t) \rightarrow 0} U_{x(t)} = \infty$, and if $U_{cc} < 0$, $U_{xx} < 0$, and $U_{cc} U_{xx} - U_{cx}^{2} \geq 0$, for the satisfaction of second-order conditions, and $U_{cx} > 0$ for uniqueness. Uniqueness also requires continuity of various functions, for the implicit function theorem and a simple fixed point theorem. Proof of the existence of the general equilibrium follows with modification from Lucas and Stokey (1987).

6 In Baumol's notation, $i = b[(T/C)/(C/2)]$.

7 Pointed out to me by Gary S. Becker.

8 Martin J. Bailey suggested to me the analogy of paper work time.

9 The Friedman (1969) optimum is verified by evaluating the derivative of indirect utility with respect to i at $i = 0$.

10 The GNP velocity of M1 in the U.S. averaged 5.66 for the high inflation years of 1973–1981 when the annual percentage increase in the Consumer Price Index for all items averaged 9.24%; tables B-1, 62, 67 [Council of Economic Advisors (1991)].

11 Table 6.11. *The National Income and Product Accounts, 1929–1982*, and *Survey of Current Business*, July 1989 [U.S. Department of Commerce, Bureau of Economic Analysis].

12 Tables 6.3, 6.7, 6.8, ibid, and July 1985–1988.

13 Tables 6.6, 6.11, ibid.

3 A comparison of partial and general equilibrium estimates of the welfare cost of inflation*

Max Gillman†

Summary

Reserve banks worldwide have been moving towards zero inflation policies. Confusion clouds the welfare cost of maintaining such inflation policies despite the best attempts at clarification. Monetary theory research has shifted from partial to general equilibrium economies. This shift has left the partial equilibrium estimates of the welfare cost of inflation below most of the general equilibrium estimates. Put on a comparable basis, partial equilibrium estimates compare more closely with the general equilibrium estimates. Furthermore, evidence suggests that integration under the money demand function appears applicable in general equilibrium economies. Finally, the estimates depend on the elasticities of money demand and the underlying structural parameters.

3.1 Introduction

Estimates of the welfare cost of inflation serve vital functions in research and policy. They help in comparing model economies and in evaluating the policy of sustained inflation. Partial equilibrium estimates confuse these tasks and fall well below newer general equilibrium estimates. Calculations here suggest that lower mean partial equilibrium estimates result because of incomplete accounting of costs, different bases for the calculations, and assumed interest elasticities at the low end of the range. General equilibrium estimates also display a larger variance, which evidence suggests results from a greater diversity in the underlying money demand functions. As Friedman (1956), Bailey (1956), and Eckstein and Leiderman (1992) suggest, trustworthy welfare cost estimates require trustworthy money demand functions.

Inflation imposes a broad array of costs (Dowd, 1992). Baumol's (1952) and Bailey's (1956) "shoe-leather" costs represent resources used in avoiding a sustained inflation tax through alternative exchange technologies. Bailey's (1992) review suggests that these costs provide a lower bound on the total costs of inflation. In partial equilibrium, the utility-based formula measures the real value of the surplus under the money demand curve that the inflation tax eliminates. Lucas (1993a, p. 1) states that in general equilibrium, "The thought experiment underlying the formulas is exactly the same as that used in Bailey's (1956) original study"—that is, a determination of the real cost of compensating a consumer for losing utility as a result of being taxed at some rate of inflation.

Cost estimates of inflation tax avoidance give Cagan (1956), Bailey (1956), and Eckstein and Leiderman (1992) a basis on which to evaluate seignorage policy. These estimates provide Fischer (1981) and Lucas (1981) with a platform to debate the scope of monetary theory and supply Cooley and Hansen (1989, 1991, 1992) with a means to study a Friedman and Schwartz (1963b) type shock on business cycles and tax policy. Gromme (1993) and Black et al. (1993) use such cost estimates to analyze endogenous growth. And as Carlstrom and Gavin (1993) and Braun (1994a) discuss, the cost of zero inflation demands attention as reserve banks move towards such policies (see Dotsey, 1991; Leigh-Pemberton, 1992; Fuhrer and Moore, 1992).

The problem in using the estimates as a standard for analysis is that they differ so much across the literature. A shift from partial to general equilibrium analysis has fragmented the estimates and made comparing them difficult. Consider, for example, estimates of the welfare cost as a percent of GNP resulting from a 10 percent inflation. Partial equilibrium estimates range from 0.22 percent, (Eckstein and Leiderman, 1992) to 0.45 percent (Lucas, 1981). The general equilibrium estimates come in as low as 0.11 percent (Cooley and Hansen, 1989) and as high as 7.15 percent (Marquis and Reffett, 1994).

Seen on a comparable basis, the partial equilibrium estimates in section 3.2 depend largely on the assumed interest elasticities of money demand. Further, the methods of partial equilibrium in section 3.3 give good cost approximations for some example general equilibrium economies. Variations among the general equilibrium estimates in section 3.4 are partly due to elasticity differences in the underlying money demand functions.

3.2 Partial equilibrium differences

Different bases have led researchers to establish low "priors" for the magnitude of the estimates. The problem of selecting the basis at which welfare costs equal zero, goes back to Friedman's (1953) "Inflationary Gap" article. Friedman describes a 10 percent inflation rate as "a stable price level plus a tax of 10 percent per year on the average amount of cash balances." But does a stable price level already impose a positive or a zero level of taxation? As in Friedman (1969), Bailey (1956) states that the inflation "tax" is zero at a nominal interest rate of zero. This means that the stable price level imposes a positive tax and that the tax makes positive the welfare cost of a stable price level. However, as Tower (1971) emphasizes, Bailey calculates welfare costs as being equal to zero at a stable price level. He then calculates the welfare costs of a zero to 10 percent inflation rate increase as a triangle of lost consumer surplus instead of as a triangle plus the box below it (see Figure 3.1).

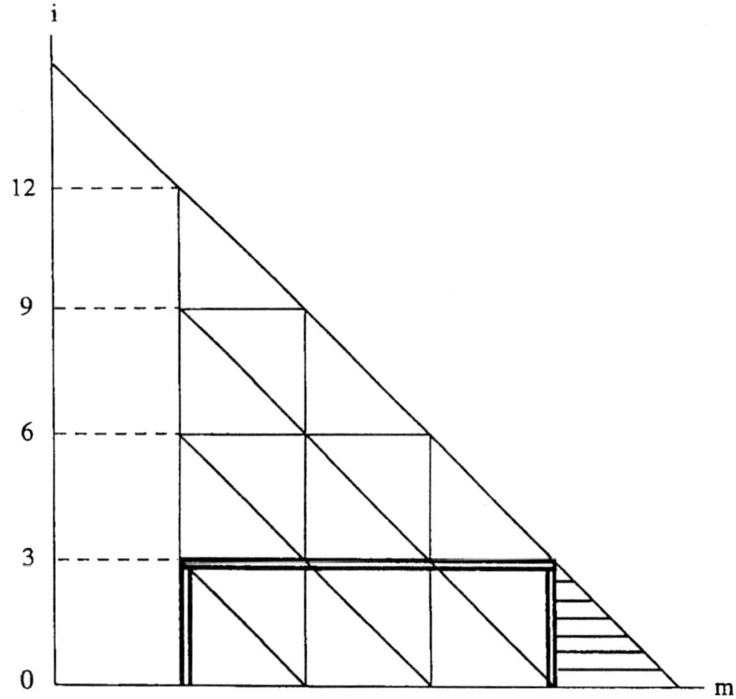

Figure 3.1 The Tower box (double-lined) and Frenkel-Triangle (cross-lined).

Setting the zero-cost basis at the zero inflation rate instead of at the optimal inflation rate would be unimportant if the resulting difference in estimates were negligible. Yet the difference can exceed 50 percent depending on the money demand specification. For a linear money demand, the Tower box in Figure 3.1 represents an amount that is similar to what Bailey mathematically omits. With a 3 percent real interest rate and a zero to 9 percent increase in the inflation rate, this box geometrically equals 6/15 or 41 percent of the lost surplus.

For 1980 M1 data, an approximation of a Cagan money demand function, and a constant semi-interest elasticity of –5, Lucas estimates the welfare loss at 0.45 percent of GNP. To keep the estimate comparable with Bailey's measure, Lucas uses the same cost basis of a zero inflation rate. For correctness, Lucas references Frenkel's (1976) Cagan-based measure that uses the zero nominal interest rate as the zero-cost basis. Thus, the 0.45 percent estimate omits the Tower-type box. For 1989 M1 data, the Cagan money demand function, and a semi-interest elasticity of –5, the Tower-like box is 0.228/0.577 or 39.5 percent of the more inclusive Frenkel measure.

For the central partial equilibrium money demand functions, Table 3.1 shows that omitting the Tower-type box decreases estimates by 38 percent to

Table 3.1 Comparison of partial equilibrium estimates as a percent of income; 1989 U.S. M1 = 783.7, GNP = 5234, $i = 0.0811$; $i = \pi + \rho$; $\rho \equiv .03$

A. Constant semi-interest elasticity: Cagan: $m = ce^{-a\pi}y$; Frenkel: $m = ce^{-a(\pi+\rho)}y$.[a]

Semi-elasticity a	*constant c*	*π: 0 to 10% Welfare cost: Cagan function (1)*	*constant c*	*π: 0 to 10% Welfare cost: Frenkel function (2)*	*"Tower Box" (3)*	*Box as % of (2)*	*π: −.3 to 10% Welfare cost: Frenkel function (4)*	*"Frenkel Triangle" [(4)–(2)] as % of (4)*
1	0.1576	0.00074	0.1624	0.00119	0.00045	37.9	0.00126	5.6
3	0.1745	0.00215	0.1910	0.00351	0.00136	38.7	0.00371	5.6
5	0.1933	0.00349	0.2246	0.00577	0.00228	39.5	0.00609	5.6
7	0.2141	0.00477	0.2642	0.00800	0.00323	40.4	0.00844	5.5
9	0.2372	0.00600	0.3107	0.01022	0.00422	41.3	0.01078	5.4
10	0.2496	0.00660	0.3369	0.01133	0.00473	41.8	0.01194	5.4

B. Constant interest elasticity: $m = ci^{-\eta}y$.[b]

Elasticity η	*constant c*	*0 to 10% Welfare cost: (1)*	*"Tower Box" (2)*	*Box as % of (1)*	*−.3 to 10% Welfare cost (3)*	*"Frenkel Triangle" [(3)–(1)] as % of (3)*
0.10	0.1165	0.00151	0.00068	44.7	0.00206	37
0.20	0.0906	0.00306	0.00139	45.6	0.00443	45
0.30	0.0705	0.00465	0.00216	46.3	0.00724	56
0.40	0.0548	0.00629	0.00297	47.2	0.01074	71
0.50	0.0426	0.00799	0.00383	48.0	0.01537	92
0.60	0.0332	0.00976	0.00478	49.0	0.02200	125
0.70	0.0258	0.01162	0.00528	49.8	0.03264	181
0.80	0.0201	0.01357	0.00687	50.7	0.05338	293

(Continued Overleaf)

Table 3.1 Continued.

C. Constant semi-interest elasticities α and interest elasticities η						
Welfare costs α: (1)	*α*	*Interst rate: i*	*conversion α . i = η*	*Welfare costs η: η*	*(2)*	*Comparison of welfare costs [(2)–(1)]*
0.00119	1	0.0811	0.0811	0.0811	0.00122	0.00004
0.00351	3	0.0811	0.2433	0.2433	0.00374	0.00023
0.00577	5	0.0811	0.4055	0.4055	0.00638	0.00061
0.00800	7	0.0811	0.5677	0.5677	0.00918	0.00118
0.01022	9	0.0811	0.7299	0.7299	0.01219	0.00197
0.01133	10	0.0811	0.8110	0.8110	0.01379	0.00246

[a] The formula for column (1) is $w/y \equiv (c/a)[1 - e^{-a(.10)}(1 + a[.10])]$; for column (2) $w/y \equiv (c/a)e^{-a(.03)}[1 + a(.03) - e^{-a(.10)}[1 + a(.13)]]$; for column (3) $c(.03)[e^{-a(.03)} - e^{-a(.13)}]$; for column (4) $(c/a)e^{-a(.0811)}[e^{a(.03)} - (1 + a(.03))]$.

[b] The formula for column (1) is $w/y \equiv c(\eta/[1 - \eta])[.13^{1-\eta} - .03^{1-\eta}]$; for column (2) $c(.03)[.03^{-\eta} - .13^{-\eta}]$; for column (3) $w/y \equiv c(\eta/[1 - \eta])[.13^{1-\eta}]$.

51 percent. For the Cagan function, Table 3.1. A reports the underestimation at 38 to 41 percent. For a constant interest elasticity, Table 3.1.B reports the underestimation at 45 to 51 percent.

The range of the assumed increase in the inflation rate also affects the estimates. Measuring the cost of the 10 percent inflation rate as compared to the *optimum* rather than to a zero inflation rate is a common practice in the general equilibrium estimates. This practice corresponds to adding another "triangle" to the zero-to-10 percent cost estimate. The cross-lined triangle in Figure 3.1 shows this triangle, which Frenkel describes as the welfare loss due to the "non-payment of interest on money." For the constant semi-elasticity function, Table 3.1.A shows that this Frenkel triangle adds approximately 5.6 percent to the cost estimate. For the constant elasticity function, Table 3.1.B shows that the triangle adds from 37 percent to 93 percent to the estimate. The increase is less for the constant semi-interest elastic function than for the constant interest elastic function because of the hyperbolic shape of the constant elasticity function.

Table 3.1.C shows that the constant semi-elasticity and the constant elasticity estimates can be similar even though they be have differently across the range of interest rates. Excluding the Frenkel triangle, the last column of Table 3.1.C shows that an elasticity conversion with the market interest rate makes the cost estimates nearly equivalent. This explains how estimates from the Cagan function can be low relative to the constant elasticity function. The difference results mainly from the different magnitudes of the Frenkel triangle.

In addition to the contribution of the Tower-box and the Frenkel-triangle, Table 3.1 also shows that the assumed interest elasticity largely determines the magnitude of the estimate. The well-known 0.3 percent estimate fits into the low end of the range in Table 3.1.B. Assuming a –0.25 constant interest elasticity, a monetary base aggregate, and the Friedman (1969) basis, Fischer (1981) calculates a 0.3 percent cost for a 10 percent inflation rate instead of for a zero inflation rate. (The correct estimate with Fischer's assumptions and methodology is 0.17 percent rather than 0.3 percent).[1] Assuming a –0.20 constant interest elasticity, an M1 aggregate, and the Friedman basis, McCallum (1989) approximately reproduces the Fischer convention with a 0.28 percent estimate. In Table 3.1B, the 0.28 percent number rises slightly to 0.31 percent as a result of using 1989 data instead of McCallum's 1987 data. Table 3.1.B shows that taking the measure from the optimum to 10 percent instead of from zero to 10 percent, increases the estimate of 0.31 percent by 45 percent to 0.44 percent. More significantly, however, an increase in the –0.2 constant interest elasticity up to a mid-range of –0.5 more than triples the welfare cost estimate to 1.54 percent.

Table 3.1 illustrates the factors that have helped make the partial equilibrium estimates low in comparison to the general equilibrium estimates. Omitting the Tower box or the. Frenkel triangle or choosing a low interest elasticity knocks down the partial equilibrium estimate. In contrast, the

1.54 percent estimate uses a mid-range constant elasticity, sheds the low "priors," and yields a partial equilibrium estimate more squarely within the general equilibrium range.

3.3 Partial versus general equilibrium

The longevity of the partial equilibrium estimates depends on whether integrating under the money demand function can yield an accurate estimate in general equilibrium economies. For example, Dotsey and Ireland (1994) report that their partial equilibrium-style estimate yields "only a fraction" of the actual general equilibrium cost (reported in Table 3.2). However, evidence here suggests an integrity of such methods. The broader question instead becomes one of plausibility: what factors determine the cost estimate?

Table 3.2 General equilibrium estimates

	Inflation experiment	*Money stock*	*Interest elasticity, or semi-elasticity*	*Welfare cost estimate**
Money in the utility function				
Eckstein and Leiderman (1992)	0 to 10%	n.a.	0.24	0.85–1.93%
Lucas (Section 2, 1993a)	optimum to 10%	M1	7	1.64%
Cash-in-Advance				
Cooley and Hansen (1989)	optimum to 10%	base	n.a.	0.11%
	optimum to 10%	M1	n.a.	0.39%
Cooley and Hansen (1991)	optimum to 10%	M1	n.a.	0.36%
Gillman (1993)	−2.9 to 10%	M1	0.43	2.19%
Ireland (1994b)	optimum to 10%	n.a.	n.a.	0.62%
McCallum and Goodfriend exchange				
Den Haan (1990)	0 to 5%	n.a.	n.a.	4.60%
Black, Macklem, and Poloz (1993)	0 to 10%	M1	0.31	3.04–3.14%
Lucas (Section 3, 1993a)	optimum to 10%	M1	0.5	1.50%
(Section 5, 1993a)	optimum to 10%	M1	0.13	1.00%
Braun (1994a)	optimum to 4%	base	0.55	0.95%
Dotsey and Ireland (1994)	0 to 10%	base	2.73	0.92%
		M1	*5.95*	1.73%
Growth Theory context				
Gromme (1993)	optimum to 8.5%	n.a.	n.a.	0.03%
Black, Macklem, and Poloz (1993)	0 to 10%	M1	0.31	4.82–5.06%
Marquis and Reffett (1994)	optimum to 10%	M1	*0.04*	7.15%
Dotsey and Ireland (1994)	0 to 10%	base	2.73	0.20%
	0 to 10%	M1	*5.95*	0.92%

Take, for example, Gillman's (1993) general equilibrium estimate of 2.19 percent. This estimates the cost of a 10 percent, non-optimal inflation rate from the general equilibrium closed form cost function. The interest rate equals 0.133: the 0.10 inflation rate plus the assumed time preference of 0.03 plus a factor of 0.003 that accounts for the discrete time framework. To derive a partial equilibrium-style estimate in the same economy, consider again the Harberger-type formula of Table 3.1 for welfare costs w as a percent of income y. (The cost of a zero to 0.133 interest rate increase can be measured either by the Harberger (1974) measure

$$\int_{.00}^{.13} i \frac{\partial m}{\partial i} di$$

or the Hotelling (1938) measure

$$\int_{m\,[.00]}^{m\,[.13]} i \cdot dm,$$

where i denotes the interest rate and m denotes real money demand.) Let η denote the (positively defined) interest elasticity of money demand and write the cost function as

$$w/y = \int_{0}^{.133} \eta m \, di.$$

Consider substituting in from Gillman an approximation of the given interest elasticity (his equation [23]). In particular, dropping the negligible last term gives the elasticity as

$$\eta = [(i/Aw)/(1 - [i/Aw])] + i/(1 + i),$$

where $Aw = 0.54$ denotes the calibrated cost of exchange credit. Writing the money demand (Gillman's equation [29]) as $m = (1 - i/Aw)c_1$ with c_1 denoting the cash good, the cost formula becomes

$$w/c_1 = \int_{0}^{133} \{(i/.54) + (i/[1 + i])(1 - [i/.54])\} \, di.$$

Finally, multiplying through by c_1/y, calibrated from his equations (4) and (26) as (0.2774/0.2828), gives the partial equilibrium style estimate of $w/y = 2.28$ percent. This compares closely in magnitude to the exact 2.19 percent estimate.

Note that integrating the money demand function does not necessarily imply holding constant the marginal utility of income. It remains unclear how to hold this fixed in general equilibrium, as one might attempt in order to simulate Marshall's partial equilibrium description. For example, Gillman's (1994a) cash good c_1 exactly equals the inverse of the real marginal utility of a dollar. Holding this marginal utility constant means fixing the consumption of the cash good. Yet the basic experiment is to test the consumer's response to inflation. For one approach, however, consider again the interest elasticity in Gillman (1993). It breaks down into the interest elasticity of approximately the inverse of the money velocity in the first term, $(i/Aw)(1 - i/[Aw])$, plus the interest elasticity of the cash good in the other two terms. Dropping the last two terms, holding the marginal utility of a dollar constant in some sense, and recalculating the partial equilibrium style estimate gives a 29 percent lower estimate of $w/y = 1.61$ percent.

Lucas (1993a) provides another example of how integration under the general equilibrium money demand function yields an estimate that compares well with the general equilibrium estimate. As Table 3.2 indicates, he provides four estimates from three different general equilibrium economies. From the money-in-the-utility function, Sidrauski (1967b)-type economy, Lucas (section 2) first calculates a Taylor-type approximation of $w/y \approx (0.89)i^2$, or 1.57 percent for $i = 0.133$. With a 0.5 elasticity of substitution between money and goods, Lucas derives a second more exact cost estimate for this economy of $w/y = (0.45)i^{0.5}$, or 1.64 percent for $i = 0.133$. Compare these estimates to the Harberger-type triangle by integrating the money demand function. Lucas provides this as $m = i^{-1/(1+\xi)}\,[\delta/(1+\delta)]^{-1/(1+\xi)}y$. Making the assumption that $\xi = 1$, for an elasticity of substitution of 0.5, Lucas calibrates that $\delta = 0.998$. This gives

$$w/y = \int_0^{i_0} \eta m \, di = (0.45)i^{0.5}, \text{ or } 1.64 \text{ percent.}$$

It equals Lucas's exact estimate. The result strikingly indicates an applicability of the partial equilibrium methods.

Equivalently, assume as in Table 3.1.B that $m = ci^{-0.5}y$. Solve for c as $c = i^{0.5}/\upsilon_0$, where υ_0 is the given period velocity. This gives an alternative formula for the partial equilibrium integration:

$$w/y = \int_0^{i_0} \eta m \, di = (\eta/([1-\eta])(i/\upsilon_0).$$

In Lucas's Sidrauski-style economy (Sidrauski, 1967b), the interest elasticity is constant at -0.5 and velocity equals $[(.998/.001)i]^{0.5}$. Making the substitutions yields the same formula of $w/y = (0.45)i^{0.5}$ and the same estimate of 1.64 percent. With this alternative partial equilibrium-type approach, just three numbers determine the estimate: the interest elasticity, the interest rate, and the velocity.

For practical purposes, Lucas's other two economies and the corresponding estimates show the limits of using partial equilibrium methods. In section 3, Lucas specifies a McCallum and Goodfriend-type (McCallum and Goodfriend, 1987) exchange economy and approximates the general equilibrium welfare costs by $w/y \approx (0.41)i^{0.5}$. The cost estimate equals 1.50 percent for $i = 0.133$. This compares closely to the section 2 estimates of 1.57 percent and 1.64 percent. But an integration approach faces hurdles here. The underlying money demand function, as derived from Lucas's equations (3.8, 3.10, 3.11, 3.13), equals $m = (.2866)i^{-0.5}y^{0.5}$ and includes a 0.5 income elasticity. As a result, one must include a value for income in order to calculate by the Harberger triangle method.

Second, consider Lucas's final estimate from an extended McCallum and Goodfriend (1987) economy in section 5. This results from a complex general equilibrium closed form function of the interest rate. While the analysis here does not present this formula, one can approximate the cost estimate of about 1.00 percent for an interest rate of 0.133 from Lucas's table 3.1. The underlying money demand function, which can be computed from the equilibrium solution, has a unitary income elasticity. But the money demand function remains quite complex. Computing the Harberger triangle may be no easier than computing the general equilibrium closed form cost function.

Partial equilibrium methods can offer simple, accurate formulas for the general equilibrium economy. Yet they offer no guarantee of a less complicated approximation than do the general equilibrium methods. Offering an alternative to the partial equilibrium methods, Lucas's (1993a) paper emphasizes that general equilibrium approximations can give simple formulas for the estimates. These formulas depend on the interest rate and on the underlying structural parameters: from preferences in Sidrauski-type economies or from the exchange technology in McCallum and Goodfriend-type economies.

The general equilibrium approximation advantageously reveals the layer beneath the partial equilibrium elasticities. For example, the Taylor approximation of the inflation cost in Gillman's (1987) cash-in-advance economy depends on the calibrated cost of exchange credit, $Aw = .54$, and on the log-utility preference for leisure, $a = 2.27$:

$$w/y \approx [(1/[1 + a])(1 + [1/Aw] - [1/(1 + a)])][i^2/2]/.2818.$$

For $i = 0.133$, this estimate equals 2.44 percent as compared to the exact estimate of 2.19 percent. Besides a simpler formula than the closed form function for the exact estimate, the approximation reveals the likely comparative statics of the structural parameters, just as Bailey (1956) and Lucas (1981) put the focus on the effects of the behavioral parameters. This clarifies testable hypotheses—for example that the cost estimate will trend upwards because the cost of exchange credit trends downwards.

3.4 General equilibrium differences

Differences in calibrated structural parameters and their effects on the economies cause differences amongst the general equilibrium estimates given in Table 3.2. Figure 3.2 (from Gillman, 1994b) shows a way to view the effect of the specification of the exchange parameters in terms of the implied interest and income elasticities of money demand. It shows the combination of real money M/P and real credit Cr/P along an isoquant that represents a given amount of exchange. The level of exchange is produced by the function $e(M/P, Cr/P)$ and equals the level of real output y in equilibrium: $e(M/P, Cr/P) = y$. With a unitary income velocity of money, the parameter specifications would require the function e to be homogeneous of degree one in M/P.

The curvature of the isoquant in Figure 3.2 depends inversely on the elasticity of substitution between money and credit. In Gillman (1993), the interest elasticity exactly equals the elasticity of substitution between cash and credit plus a factor for changes in the marginal utility of income (see Gillman, 1994a). With a high interest elasticity, the curvature is slight, the decrease in utility from tax distortions is large, and the welfare cost of inflation is high.

For example, the Cooley and Hansen (1989) estimate of 0.39 percent (quarterly data) results when the consumer can avoid inflation only with substitution from goods to leisure. With no exchange credit, the money demand is relatively inelastic. Reproducing the leisure-only channel, Gillman (1993) estimates a comparable cost at 0.58 percent. Adding a cash-to-costly-

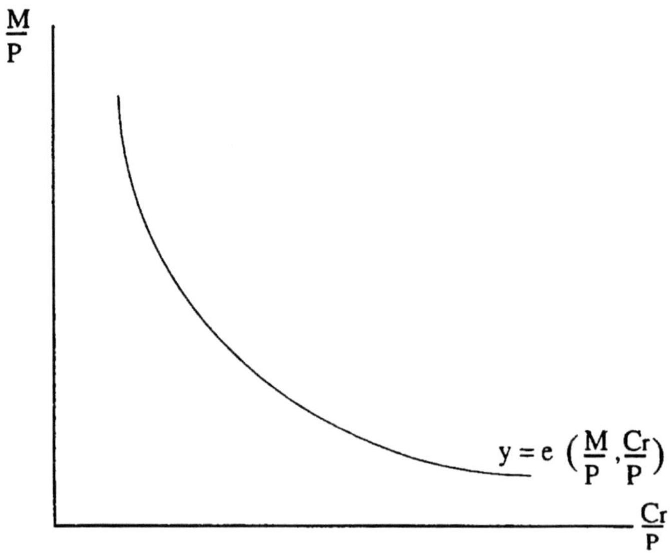

Figure 3.2 An isoquant for exchange.

credit channel and maintaining an approximate unitary income elasticity, Gillman's estimate rises from 0.58 percent to 2.19 percent as the interest elasticity rises from 0.11 to 0.43.

Black et al. (1993) offer similar evidence. Including a cash-to-costly-credit channel and a unitary income elasticity, they find a cost estimate of 3.04 percent and an interest elasticity of 0.31 for a 10 percent inflation rate. Including endogenous economic growth in the analysis, they report a higher estimate of the welfare cost of inflation than for a comparable economy found in Gromme that lacks the cash-to-costly-credit channel. The Bailey-type interest elasticity link also helps explain the magnitude of the estimates reported by Lucas (1993a), Braun (1994a), Dotsey and Ireland (1994), and Eckstein and Leiderman (1992).

3.5 Conclusion

The nature of the welfare cost of inflation supplies evidence for monetary theory. This helps us "to work 'toward isolating numerical constants of monetary behavior" (see Lucas, 1988a, p. 137; Friedman, 1956). The chapter finds reasons why the 0.3 percent standard of partial equilibrium estimates is low and supplies evidence on why the method of integrating under the money demand function remains valid. The wide variance of the general equilibrium estimates apparently results from various specifications of the exchange technology and the related structural parameters. Neither partial nor general equilibrium contradicts a central concept of Bailey (1956)—that is, the higher the interest elasticity of money demand within a given economy, the more the substitution to costly exchange alternatives and the higher the welfare cost of inflation. Assuming a comparable basis, a mid-range interest elasticity, and a 10 percent non-optimal inflation rate, a conservative estimate range is 0.85 percent to 3 percent for the different economies reported here. In terms of U.S. GNP for 1994, a cost of 0.85 percent translates into a loss of $58 billion.

Research could identify further the linkage between the structural parameters, the elasticity features of money demand, and the welfare cost estimates. Focusing on exchange credit markets' technology and distortions and on the ability to avoid the inflation tax also may refine cost estimates (see Gillman, 1994a; Lucas, 1993a; Ireland, 1995). Different optimum quantities of money also affect the cost estimates. For example, the optimum occurs at a zero inflation rate in Gillman (1996b) when accounting for menu costs and at a positive inflation rate in Braun (1994b) when incorporating a Ramsey tax framework. Dynamically, an advancing technology of credit production implies increasingly less expensive credit alternatives, more substitutes to cash, and a more interest elastic cash demand. This suggests that the base welfare cost of a given inflation rate will trend upwards and that sustained inflation will become an increasingly less attractive policy.

Notes

* Gillman, Max, (1995), 'A Comparison of Partial and General Equilibrium Estimates of the Welfare Cost of Inflation', *Contemporary Economic Policy*, 13(4), October, 60–71.

† The author thanks Bob Lucas for suggesting the topic; Sue Cathro for research assistance; and Bennett McCallum, Glenn Boyle, Dorian Owen, Milton Kafoglis, Dick Muth, and Martin Bailey for comments.

1. Fisher (1981) assumes that the monetary base is 150, GNP = 2600, $i = .12$, the real rate of interest .02, and $m = i^{-.25}yc$. Then

$$c = (150/2600)(.12)^{.25}$$

$$= .03396;\ w/y \equiv \int_{.02}^{.12} (.25)i^{-.25}(.03396)\ di$$

$$= (.03396/3)\ (.12^{.75} - .02^{.75}) = .001706.$$

4 The optimality of a zero inflation rate: Australia*

Max Gillman†

Summary

This chapter juxtaposes the policy trend towards a zero inflation rate against the theoretical standard of optimal deflation at the real interest rate. It extends an example monetary economy to include a simple form of nominal adjustment costs and calibrates the model with recent evidence on Australian money demand. There is a critical value that the calibrated parameter for menu costs must exceed in order for a zero inflation rate to be optimal. An inflation rate of − 2 per cent to 0 per cent is found to be optimal. The quantitative results, of whether inflation-adjustment costs imply a zero inflation rate policy for Australia, are tempered by the abstraction of the model and its sensitivity to parameters. Qualitatively, the chapter shows the effects of changes in the adjustment cost function and in the structural parameters.

4.1 Introduction: menu costs and suboptimality of the Friedman deflation

A near-zero inflation rate increasingly has become a focus of policy and research (Leigh-Pemberton 1992; Ireland 1993; Dowd 1994; Stemp 1996). Estimates of the welfare cost of inflation have been calibrated to show the gains from achieving a zero inflation rate (Carlstrom and Gavin 1993; Lucas 2000; Braun 1994a). Yet the accepted first-best optimum of monetary theory remains Friedman's (1969) deflation at the rate of time preference (deflation at the real rate of interest).[1]

Howitt (1987) suggests that 'menu costs' may make deflation unattractive. The menu cost literature has been strong on theoretical results but criticised for its dearth of empirical support. Levy et al. (1997) help fill this gap by providing new evidence that shows this cost to be significant for a set of supermarkets. Another management/accounting type of literature discusses how inflation requires reevaluation of cash flows, inventory values, and capital replacement in such a way that can distort optimal investment strategies (for example, as in Beaurepaire, Higgins and Mercovich 1974).[2] A zero inflation rate eliminates these adjustment costs that waste resources.

Alternatively, frictions and second-best considerations can alter the optimum. Taub (1989) allows informational externalities to drive the optimum above the Friedman rate. Gillman (1996a) introduces a positive externality from costly-credit use to get a similar result. In a Ramsey optimal tax framework, with inflation as one such tax, Braun (1994b) finds a positive inflation rate to be optimal. However, in a similar Ramsey framework, but with positive costs of using a cash alternative, Lucas (2000) finds a nearly trivial departure from the Friedman deflation.

This chapter explores the route of menu costs in that they seem to be pervasive empirically, accepted intuitively, and a direct way to consider more fully the costs of government taxation through inflation. And they can imply an optimum with an exactly zero rate of inflation. Bringing these costs into a monetary general equilibrium, the paper starts from the first-best Friedman optimum and introduces an inflation-induced, menu-type, adjustment cost that reduces profits. The profit reduction is related to the non-monetary, profit maximisation, economies of Barro (1972), Mankiw (1985), and Parkin (1986), or more recently Fluet and Phaneuf (1997). Using a representative agent approach, the paper is able to show how a zero inflation rate can be optimal. This depends critically on the adjustment cost function. Here the paper assumes alternative forms including one similar to Mussa (1977) and Fender (1990). It extends such previous work by calibrating an adjustment cost parameter (based on Levy et al. 1997) and by using this to quantify the optimal rate of inflation.

4.1.1 A baseline case: quantitative and qualitative results

Another advantage of monetary optimisation is that it shows, through the margins of substitution and an explicit welfare cost function, how the Friedman deflation is gradually made more suboptimal as the level of the inflation-adjustment cost increases. The explicit welfare cost function also allows a sensitivity analysis with respect to the model's structural parameters, the adjustment cost parameter, and the inflation-adjustment cost function. This gives qualitative results on what conditions make a zero inflation rate optimal because of inflation-adjustment costs.

The results are suggestive of policy directives, but remain preliminary. The paper's choice of model structure, parameter calibrations, and other assumptions gives a baseline case for whether menu costs cause a zero inflation rate to be optimal. To comfortably allow a policy recommendation, the results would need to be enhanced through expanded efforts to measure the inflation-adjustment costs and through refinements of the general equilibrium model and its calibration.

The abstraction of the model of the paper does not allow, for example, for an Ireland (1996)-type framing of the rules versus discretion debate, or for analysis of how to target a zero inflation rate (see, for example, Svensson 1997). Rather it gives a qualified representative agent formulation of the possibility in Australia of a zero inflation rate optimum as a result of menu-type costs due to inflation. The analysis can be extended to include capital, more general utility specifications, Ramsey-type taxation, relative price variability, and shocks to money supply, goods technology, and finance sector technology. It can be applied to other countries.

4.1.2 Costly credit and a zero inflation optimum

The paper uses an economy in the class with costly-credit technologies that avoid a bias in the results. A standard cash-in-advance economy has a relatively interest-inelastic money demand and its corollary of a less variable velocity, as in for example Cooley and Hansen (1995).[3] This causes an exaggerated effect of the inflation-adjustment cost factor, gives a lower critical value for the cost of adjustment, and makes it easier to accept the hypothesis that the optimum occurs at a zero inflation rate. The agent in the standard model finds a zero inflation rate optimal at a lower level of the adjustment cost factor.

This paper uses my 1993 economy as extended with inflation-adjustment costs. This model is within a group with costly exchange means that help make velocity realistically variable.[4] Here, velocity endogenously depends on the shadow cost of money versus the shadow cost of the exchange credit alternative. Gillman and Otto (1997) show that this explanation leads to a cointegrated Australian demand for money with error correction. And this velocity feature eliminates the bias towards finding a zero inflation rate as optimal, which is demonstrated by examining a special case of the economy that represents the standard model.

4.2 Economy with costly inflation adjustment: reducing the real wage

Expressing profit as revenue minus costs, $R - C$, and letting the inflation-adjustment cost raise total costs by the factor $D(\pi)$, profit is given by $R - [1 + D(\pi)]C$.[5] With P the price of the good c, with linear production that depends only on labour n, and with w the constant marginal product of labour, the production function is $c = wn$. The revenues R are given by Pc and, with W the nominal wage, the costs are given by the nominal wages Wn. Profit maximisation in competitive markets implies that the adjustment cost $D(\pi)$ functions as a tax (with proceeds destroyed) that reduces the real wage w to $w/[1 + D(\pi)]$. The resource constraint becomes:

$$c = wn/[1 + D(\pi)] \tag{1}$$

Within the monetary economy, it enables an analysis of inflation rate optimality.

4.2.1 Choosing cash or credit to purchase goods at stores

Goods differ across a store continuum that is indexed by s which takes on values from 0 to 1. Each store s sells a different colour of the same good $c(s)$ and the agent likes the different colours.[6] The agent uses either cash or credit at each store. The price of the good that is bought with cash at any store equals only the goods price P, since the production technology is the same for all goods. There remains the cost of using cash as the exchange medium, which is the interest foregone by carrying around cash. This is a cost borne implicitly by the agent when combining both exchange and goods in order to yield consumption of the goods. This exchange cost equals the product Pi, where i is the nominal interest rate. The total *shadow* cost of consuming the cash good is $P(1 + i)$, comprising the goods production cost plus the exchange cost.

The production cost of a good bought with credit is the same P at any store. This is also the case in Lucas and Stokey (1983) in which the cash good and credit good each enter as a separate argument in the utility function. There the shadow cost of using credit is zero because credit requires no production resources. Here, the shadow cost of exchange for a credit good is positive. The credit cost, just like the exchange cost of using cash, is not part of the goods market price because the exchange activity is being done by the agent rather than by the store selling the goods.

4.2.2 The technology for credit production and the cash constraint

The agent acts in part like a bank (as Hicks, 1935, suggests) by inputing time into a given credit service technology for each store s, in order to then buy a good on credit at store s. Let $\tau(s)$ denote the average time required per good that is bought on credit at store s. The exchange cost of the good is the value of the time used in credit activity at the store: $Pw\tau(s)$. Just as $P(1 + i)$ is the shadow cost of goods bought with cash, $P[1 + w\tau(s)]$ is the shadow cost of goods bought on credit. Optimally, the agent provides credit services at stores where $w\tau(s) < i$. The agent uses cash at stores where $i \leq w\tau(s)$. In the example economy, $\tau(s)$ is specified to be linear in the store index: $\tau(s) = A(1 - s)$ where A is a positive constant. For example, at the store $s = 1$ the credit cost is lowest (zero) and the agent provides/uses credit there if $i > 0$. the highest cost store at which the agent uses credit services is the one indexed just above the marginal store $\bar{s}$. The marginal store $\bar{s}$ is determined by the equilibrium condition that results from optimisation with respect to $\bar{s}$. This condition weighs the exchange cost of cash against exchange cost of credit use at the marginal store (it is given by $i = w\tau(\bar{s})$).[7]

Given that cash is used at stores indexed from 0 to $\bar{s}$ where credit costs are relatively high, that $M(t)$ denotes the pre-transfer level of cash at time period t, and that $P(t)$ denotes the price of a good at any s store at time t, the cash constraint that gives rise to money demand is:

$$M(t) \geq P(t) \int_{0}^{\bar{s}} c(s, t)ds \quad (2)$$

The composite cash good can be thought of as $\int_0^{\bar{s}} c(s, t)ds$. Next period's money supply $M(t + 1)$ equals this period's money supply $M(t)$ plus an end-of-period lump sum government transfer of cash denoted by $H(t)$:

$$M(t + 1) = M(t) + H(t) \quad (3)$$

In order to get a closed-form solution, the paper assumes a constant rate of inflation π, defined by $\pi \equiv H(t)/M(t)$, so that $M(t + 1) = (1 + \pi)M(t)$.

4.2.3 Income constraint and equilibrium

At the end of the period the agent sets aside cash for trading next period, $M(t + 1)$, and pays off credit debt, $P(t) \int_{\bar{s}}^{1} c(s, t)ds$, while receiving a cash transfer $H(t)$, an asset endowment, $P(t)a(t)$, and wages. Nominal wages equal the wage rate as decreased by the inflation-adjustment factor and multiplied by the time spent working: $\{P(t)w(t)/[1 + D(\pi)]\}$ $[1 - x(t) - \int_{\bar{s}}^{1} A(1 - s)c(s, t)ds]$, where 1 is the Beckerian (1965) time endowment, $x(t)$ is leisure, and the sum $\int_{\bar{s}}^{1} A(1 - s)c(s, t)ds$ is the total Karni (1974)-type time used up in credit activity. During each period, the agent purchases, consumes, and produces goods, as well as producing credit services and incurring the inflation-adjustment cost.

Consider initially specifying the adjustment cost $D(\pi)$ so that it is symmetrically proportional to the level of inflation or deflation: with the parameter $d \geq 0$, let $D(\pi) = d|\pi|$. Discounting over the infinite horizon, by a market discount factor $q \geq 0$, makes the wealth constraint:

$$\sum_{t=0}^{\infty} \{[P(t)w(t)/(1 + d|\pi|)][1 - x(t)$$

$$- \int_{\bar{s}}^{1} A(1 - s)c(s, t)ds] + H(t) + P(t)a(t)$$

$$- M(t + 1) - P(t) \int_{\bar{s}}^{1} c(s, t)ds\} \geq 0 \quad (4)$$

Setting $a(t) = 0$ and substituting in from equations (2) and (3), the time period t net revenue of equation (4) can be rewritten as the social resource constraint $\int_0^1 c(s)ds = [w(t)/(1 + d|\pi|)][1 - x(t) - \int_{\bar{s}}^{1} A(1 - s)c(s, t)ds]$, corresponding to equation (1).

Let preferences at time period t be given by the log-utility function: $u(t) \equiv \int_0^1 \{\ln[c(s, t)] + a \ln[x(t)]\}$, where $a \geq 0$. The representative agent maximises the time-preference discounted utility subject to the cash constraint (2), and subject to the interest-discounted wealth constraint (4). Combining the market clearing equation (3) with the first-order conditions yields the equilibrium $c^*(s, t)$, $0 < s \leq \bar{s}$; $c^*(s, t)$, $\bar{s} < s \leq 1$;$x^*(t)$; $[M(t)/P(t)]^*$; $\bar{s}^*$; and the marginal utility of real income $[\lambda(t)P(t)]^*$, where $\lambda(t)$ is the multiplier of the cash constraint. The deterministic Fisher (1907) equation of interest rates follows by introducing a bond market as in Lucas and Stokey (1983). Although suppressed here, the paper uses the resulting equilibrium condition in the form of $1/q \equiv (1 + i) = (1 + \pi)(1 + \rho)$, where ρ is the rate of time preference. The equilibrium is as in Gillman (1993) except that the marginal product of labour is everywhere reduced by the inflation-adjustment cost factor.

4.3 The effect of menu costs on the equilibrium

Consider first the cash-only economy without the implicit banking sector or the inflation-adjustment cost. This is the special case of $\bar{s} \equiv 1$. The marginal rate of substitution between goods and leisure shows how the inflation-adjustment cost creates pressure towards a zero optimal inflation rate. Denoted $MRS_{c1,\ x}$, this rate equals $(1 + \pi)(1 + \rho)/w$, as in Lucas and Stokey (1983) with leisure added. At $\pi = -\rho/(1 + \rho)$, the rate equals the marginal rate of transformation between goods and time, $1/w$ (from the goods production function), and the first-best Friedman optimum results. With the inflation-adjustment cost, the rate between a cash good and leisure is proportionately affected:

$$MRS_{c1,\,x} = [(1 + \pi)(1 + \rho)(1 + d|\pi|)]/w$$

For inflation rates above zero, the adjustment cost increases the inefficient substitution away from cash goods and towards leisure. For inflation rates below zero, there are opposing effects. As the inflation rate falls below zero, the adjustment cost becomes higher and pressures the agent away from cash. But also, the foregone interest cost of cash becomes lower and pressures the agent towards more cash. With a sufficiently high magnitude of d, the adjustment cost effect dominates and pushes the optimum towards a zero inflation rate.

4.3.1 Relatively less substitution from credit to leisure

With the availability of credit, and with $\bar{s} < 1$, the effect of the inflation-adjustment cost is partly diffused; the adjustment cost affects the shadow cost of cash goods proportionately but affects the shadow cost of the credit goods less than proportionately. Denoted $MRS_{c2,\ x}$, the rate of substitution between a credit good at store s and leisure is:

$$MRS_{c2,\,x} = [(1 + d|\,\pi|) + Aw(1 - s)]/w$$

In the first term, the ratio of the goods cost of the credit good relative to the real wage cost of leisure ($1/w$) is factored by ($1 + d|\pi|$). However, in the second term, the shadow exchange cost of credit and the shadow price of leisure both are factors of the real wage. The inflation-adjustment distortion cancels out and leaves this term as $A(1 - s)$. Because of the first term, increasing or decreasing the inflation rate from a zero level induces substitution from credit goods towards leisure, and a zero inflation rate eliminates this marginal effect. Without this effect in the second term, the overall impact of the inflation-adjustment cost is less than proportional to its level.

In the Lucas and Stokey (1983) economy, the rate between a credit good and leisure is just $1/w$ as there is no cost of credit; the inflation-adjustment cost would affect the credit good in the same proportionate way as it would the cash good. In contrast, with credit use determined by its cost, an increase in the inflation-adjustment cost d induces less overall substitution from goods to leisure since the distortion is not as strong for each credit good as it is for each cash good. Further weakening the overall distortion of a given d, the agent also can substitute from using cash to using credit for the purchase of goods at any s store. This is seen in the other 'external' margin that decides the cash–credit ratio amongst the store continuum.

4.3.2 *Additional 'external' margin of the costly credit economy*

An added external margin as compared to Lucas and Stokey (1983), the agent solves also for $\bar{s}$ from the condition $i = w\tau(\bar{s})$. The solution is $\bar{s}^* = 1 - \{[\rho + \pi(1 + \rho)](1 + d|\pi|)\}/Aw$, where $i = \rho + \pi(1 + \rho)$. As the inflation rate increases above zero, the adjustment cost reinforces the direct effect of the inflation rate increase in causing a decrease in $\bar{s}^*$ and the use of cash at fewer stores. Reducing the inflation rate to a negative level from zero, the adjustment cost offsets the lower foregone interest cost and induces substitution towards credit use at more stores. Thus there are two qualitative features. First, at both internal and external margins the adjustment cost clashes with the low foregone interest cost of cash when the inflation rate is negative. Second, by making the costly credit option available to the agent, the effect of a given level of d is less since it affects the overall purchase of goods less than proportionately if some credit is used. With credit being used, it takes a higher level of d in order to imply the optimality of a zero inflation rate.

4.4 The cost of inflation with the adjustment cost

To sort out the exact effect of stationary inflation and its adjustment cost on utility, a function is derived that gives the Bailey (1956)-type welfare cost of inflation for different levels of the adjustment cost.[8] This welfare cost is defined as the amount of real assets, denoted here by a, that the agent must be compensated with in order to be indifferent to a rate of inflation above the optimal rate. With welfare costs defined as being equal to zero at the Friedman rate of deflation, the function can take on negative values as the inflation rate rises from the negative rate of time preference up towards the optimum. Where the welfare cost function is lowest, at a zero or negative value, the corresponding level of inflation is the optimal inflation rate.[9]

Let $v(\bullet)$ represent the level of utility at the economy's equilibrium, so that v is the indirect utility function. Consider setting indirect utility, with a zero level of real asset endowment and with a Friedman deflation at the rate of $-\rho/(1+\rho)$, equal to indirect utility, with some positive level of real asset endowment a and with some level of inflation π above $-\rho/(1+\rho)$. This gives $v[0, -\rho/(1+\rho)] = v(a, \pi)$. Solving for a and dividing by full income $w{\cdot}1$, the cost function for any given level of inflation is $a/w = f(\pi, \alpha, Aw, \rho, d)$.[10] The leisure preference parameter α is set as in Gillman (1993) at 2.27. Calibrations are then required for Aw, ρ and d.

4.4.1 Calibrating Aw and ρ with Australian data

To calibrate the cost of credit parameter Aw, consider that the income velocity of money in the economy approximately equals $1/\bar{s}$. With $\bar{s}^* = 1 - i/(Aw)$ when adjustment costs are zero, Aw can be computed for a given velocity and an interest rate. First consider to which monetary aggregate the model economy corresponds. Money in the model economy is that which does not earn interest while being used in exchange. This suggests using currency plus non-interest bearing demand deposits, which Gillman and Otto (1997) call non-interest bearing money (NIBM). (This abstracts from the costs of the non-interest bearing demand deposits since the model includes no other costs for money but the foregone interest costs.) The average annual velocity of Australian NIBM over the 1975–96 quarterly period is 11.16 in the Gillman and Otto database. (This is the standard RBA database from 1984 onwards; it uses exponential interpolation for the non-interest bearing deposits from 1976–84.) The average 90-day government bond interest rate is 0.1142 over the same period. From the approximation to velocity given by $1/\bar{s}$ when adjustment costs are zero, this gives an average value of $Aw = 0.1254$. As a test of these parameter specifications, the interest elasticity of money demand can be calibrated with $Aw = 0.1254$ in the model economy and compared to the actual estimated elasticity in Gillman and Otto. From an approximation of equation (23) in Gillman (1993), the model gives an elasticity of –1.89.[11] This compares to the estimated time series elasticity of –1.06 in Gillman and Otto.

An alternative calibration gives a higher value of Aw, by equating the –1.06 elasticity estimate to the model's approximation of the interest elasticity (given in endnote 11). Given an interest rate of 0.1142, this gives a value of $Aw = 0.2335$. A lower value of Aw makes it harder to find optimal a zero inflation rate for any given adjustment cost parameter. This makes $Aw = 0.1254$ more conservative than $Aw = 0.2335$ relative to the experiments of the paper. Another approach is to start with a more conventional, lower, estimate of the interest elasticity, say, –0.5 (as is implied by the Baumol, 1952, model). Calibrating Aw again from the elasticity approximation given in Gillman (1993) implies that $Aw = 0.4015$.

A different alternative is to calculate Aw directly. Gillman (1993) interprets Aw in terms of the share of labour hours in the Finance sector. This again gives a value of Aw that is higher than 0.2335. Another option is to separate out A and w. The real wage in Australia can be measured but there is a problem in measuring A. This parameter is interpreted in Gillman as being proportional to the labour hours per unit of output in the Finance sector. The Australian Bureau of Statistics measure the Finance output by extrapolating from hours worked. The ratio of hours to output, or the inverse of productivity, is therefore based on only the hours series. Lowe (1995) concludes this measure contains significant error and so it is not used in this paper.

The rate of time preference is calibrated as the average real interest rate over the same 1975–96 period. The CPI Australian average inflation rate is equal to 0.0731 over the period. The real rate in a discrete model framework, with discretely observed data, is $(i - \pi)/(1 + \pi)$. With $i = 0.1142$, this gives a real rate of 0.0395.

4.4.2 Calibrating the d factor

Calibrating the d factor of the function $D(\pi) = d|\pi|$ requires two sources of data, for the total menu cost $D(\pi)$, and for the inflation rate that corresponds to that cost. The total menu cost is taken from evidence reported by Levy et al. (1997) for four major US grocery store chains over the 1991–92 period. They find a 0.7 per cent reduction in revenue. To be able to use this as a measure of the model's per cent increase in cost, $D(\pi)$, it is necessary to state the model in terms of a reduction in revenue (instead of an increase in cost) as a result of menu costs, and then show how this corresponds to $D(\pi)$. Let revenue be given as $Pc[1 - \hat{D}(\pi)]$ and costs as wn. Then profit maximisation under perfect competition implies that the real wage equals $(\partial c/\partial n)[1 - \hat{D}(\pi)]$. Equating this alternative to the real wage embodied in equation (1) yields that $1/[1 + D(\pi)] = 1 - \hat{D}(\pi)$. With $\hat{D}(\pi) \equiv 0.007$ in our use of the evidence in Levy et al., we solve for $D(\pi)$ and find that it also equals 0.007.

Second, the relevant inflation rate must be inserted into $D(\pi) = d|\pi| = 0.007$ in order to solve for d. The adjustment cost function should use the inflation rate that corresponds to the time period during which Levy et al. report 0.007. This period is 1991–92 and the average annnual US CPI inflation rate over 1991–92 is 0.0354. Then $0.007 = d|0.0354|$; and $d = 0.1977$ is the calibrated level for d. Notice that this level of inflation is close to the Australian rate in recent years, which averaged 0.0253 over 1990–96. Also making the data comparable to Australia, the technology of grocery store chains presumably is not very different in Australia from the United States since both countries are 'first-world'. There appear to be few if any alternative sources of data from which d can at present be calibrated.

4.4.3 Results for the linear inflation-adjustment cost technology

Substituting $Aw = 0.1254$ and $\rho = 0.0395$ into the welfare cost function $f(\pi)$, a critical level of d can be found. In particular, a zero inflation rate is optimal for values of d that exceed 0.3341. It is found that an interest rate of 0.0395 (a zero inflation rate) becomes optimal once d rises above the critical level of $d^* = 0.3341$. Table 4.1 shows, at $d = 0.1977$ the optimal rate of inflation turns out to be a deflation of 1.70 per cent, more than halfway towards a zero rate from the Friedman deflation of 0.0395 (the calibration for π). This result is sensitive to the value of Aw, π and d. As Aw goes up, the critical d^* goes down. At a value of $Aw = 0.2271$, the critical level of d^* just falls down to the level equal to the calibrated level of $d = 0.1977$, and makes a zero inflation rate optimal. Therefore, at the higher, alternative, calibrated value of $Aw = 0.2335$, which exceeds 0.2271, a zero rate of inflation is optimal. A decrease in r also causes the critical d^* to go down.

4.5 Alternative adjustment cost functions

More generally, the adjustment cost function can be specified as $D(\pi) = d|\pi|^{\beta}$, where β is equal to one for the linear case, less than one for concave cases, and greater than one for convex cases. Research into the form of this cost function appears to be scarce and so the linear case is used as a baseline example. Theory suggests both concave and convex specifications. Fender (1990) derives a concave function, with the cost depending on the inflation rate raised to the (2/3) power ($\beta = 0.67$). Derived from a partial equilibrium with menu costs from changing prices, Fender suggests that menu costs will at first

Table 4.1 Optimal inflation rate under alternative adjustment cost functions ($\rho = 0.0395$)

Adjustment cost function	*Actual d calibrated*	*d* critical Aw = 0.1254*	*Optimal interest rate Aw = 0.1254*	*Optimal inflation rate Aw = 0.1254*	*Minimum Aw at which $\pi = 0$ is optimal at calibrated d*	*Optimal inflation rate Aw = 0.2335*
$d\|\pi\|^{0.67}$	0.0657	0.0694	0.0175	–0.0220	0.1333	0.0000
$d\|\pi\|^{0.78}$	0.0948	0.1087	0.0201	–0.0194	0.1458	0.0000
$d\ln(1 + \|\pi\|)$	0.2012	0.3341	0.0225	–0.0170	0.2226	0.0000
$d\|\pi\|$	0.1977	0.3341	0.0225	–0.0170	0.2271	0.0000
$d\pi^2$	5.59	∞	0.0235	–0.0160	**	–0.0111

Note: ** Raising Aw to 0.467 for this cost function gives an optimal inflation rate of –0.0071.

be high as inflation starts up from a zero level. Then the adjustment cost will rise at a decreasing rate with the level of the inflation rate. Mussa (1977) considers a similar case in which he derives the same (2/3) power. He additionally considers relative price changes, or 'relative demand pressures'. Here some prices need to be, say, raised while the inflation rate is already raising the general price level, and this decreases the menu cost of the inflation adjustment. For this case, Mussa derives convexity in the adjustment cost function for low levels of the inflation rate, and concavity for higher levels of the inflation rate. Empirically, it is only possible to report a β on the basis of calibrations made from an unpublished thesis by Beaurepaire et al. (1974); this gives a power coefficient of 0.78 (see Gillman 1996b), which is not very different from Fender's and Mussa's 0.67.

4.5.1 Sensitivity to concavity versus convexity

To show how both concave and convex specifications affect the results, Table 4.1 presents four more specifications, of $\beta = 0.67$, 0.78 and 2.0, and a natural log case (which is concave but close to linear at near-zero levels of the inflation rate). For $Aw = 0.1254$, all of the alternatives, as with the linear case, imply an optimal deflation rate near the 2 per cent level. This deflation is greatest for the most concave case of $\beta = 0.67$, and least for the convex quadratic case of $\beta = 2.0$. However while the most concave case implies the optimum furthest away from the zero inflation level, it also implies the greatest sensitivity of the optimal deflation rate to the Aw calibration level. For $\beta = 0.67$, Aw need rise less than 10 per cent to imply an optimum of a zero inflation rate. For the convex case of $\beta = 2.0$, a near-infinite rise in Aw would still leave a slight deflation as the optimum. With $Aw = 0.2335$ in the concave and linear cases, a zero inflation rate is optimal; the convex case implies an optimal deflation of 1.1 per cent. In general, the more convex is the specification, the more sensitive is the level of the optimal inflation rate to the calibration of d. For $\beta = 0.67$, a 10 per cent increase in d pushes the optimum to a zero inflation; for $\beta = 2.0$, a 10 per cent increase in d slightly changes the optimal deflation rate.

4.5.2 Skewness and the model without costly credit

Another type of sensitivity analysis would be to skew the $D(\pi)$ functions towards a higher relative cost from either inflation or deflation. Mussa (1977) reasons that wage decreases are more problematic than price increases (which can decrease customer goodwill), and that wage changes are passed through to price changes. He interprets this as a higher inflation-adjustment cost for negative rates of inflation than for positive rates of inflation. Such skewness means for our analysis that the optimal inflation rate would be further pushed up towards zero.

Lastly, suppose that cash is the only means of exchange ($\bar{s} \equiv 1$). Given

$Aw = 0.1254$, the zero rate of inflation would be optimal in all specifications of the inflation-adjustment cost function except for the quadratic specification. For $\beta = 2.0$, the optimal inflation rate would be -0.002, only slightly different from zero. These results are biased towards finding a zero inflation rate in that the model without credit over-emphasises the role of the adjustment cost factor. With costly credit included, the model in a sense automatically indexes the payment to inflation when the purchase is made by credit. Or more exactly, using credit foregoes the interest cost of cash and the adjustment to a different inflation rate.

4.6 Conclusions and qualifications

The chapter finds some cases in which a zero inflation rate is optimal for Australia. For a lower-valued calibration of Aw, a deflation of around 2 per cent is found to be optimal across the alternative specifications of the inflation-adjustment cost function. For the alternative higher-valued Aw, a zero inflation rate is found to be optimal for the linear and concave adjustment cost specifications; a 1.1. per cent deflation is found for the convex specification. These results are more sensitive to the calibration for the menu cost parameter the more concave is the inflation-adjustment cost function.

The study gives estimates of the optimal inflation rate that are designed to be at the low end. An extension could look beyond just the cost of changing prices. There are likely to be tax-like effects of inflation adjustment on the firm's capital and labour demand, and goods supply, as well as on the consumer's capital and labour supply and goods demand, that would increase the inflation-adjustment cost above that of the menu cost interpretation. Much of these added costs conceivably come from uncertainty of the inflation rate, and are an increasing function of the absolute value of the mean inflation rate (as in Lourenco and Gruen 1995). Incorporating such costs would give a higher cost parameter that would push the optimal inflation rate farther towards zero. Further research on the empirical magnitude of menu costs or other inflation-adjustment costs, as well as refinement of the model, would be useful.

The comparative static results can be applied to a given country over time and across countries. For example, a decrease in the real rate of time preference implies a decrease in the critical value that the calibrated adjustment cost parameter d must exceed in order for a zero inflation rate to be optimal. Slightly extending the model conceptually so that the rate of time preference is set equal to the real marginal product of capital, we can think of what has happened to the real interest rate in Australia over time. The not-fully anticipated, early 1990s, inflation deceleration apparently contributed to an increase in the ex post real interest rate until the low inflation rate became more fully expected. By the mid-1990s, it is plausible that a low rate was expected and that a lower inflation risk premium was built into real interest rates. Ceteris paribus, a decrease in the real interest rate makes the optimality in Australia of a zero inflation rate more likely. And with the inflation rates of the United States, European Union and Japan now hovering near 1 per cent, this comparative static result adds weight to the argument for keeping the Australian dollar internationally competitive by maintaining a near-zero inflation rate.

Or consider illustratively the transition European and Asian economies that still are experiencing high and variable inflation rates that can make the real rates high (Gillman, 1998, computes these rates for eleven transition countries). Second, because of newly evolving financial sectors, and with a limited dispersion of information technologies, the menu costs would seem to be relatively high in such economies. The less advanced financial sectors also imply a higher cost of the credit services, which in the model corresponds to a higher Aw. In sum, there are opposing effects. A higher ρ makes a zero inflation rate less likely to be optimal, while a higher d and a higher Aw make the zero rate more likely to be optimal.

Over the secular trend in any given country, the real interest rate tends to be stable, while the cost of credit services, Aw, seems likely to trend down. The menu cost parameter d might seem likely to fall because of technological advance in information technology. However a scale effect on d from a growth in the number of products for sale could make d rise. It is even more difficult to discern a trend for a broader definition of d that includes other costs of inflation in distorting the production/consumption process.

The model's assumption of a zero marginal cost of producing money is a pillar of monetary theory, and is assumed in this model as in most. In qualification, if a government, or a private bank, uses resources to generate the credit necessary to instill confidence for using their debt as a means of exchange, then the marginal cost of money could be positive. Should the marginal cost of all sovereign debt including currency be driven to the competitive real interest rate, then the first-best optimal inflation rate would be zero. In such as optimum, seigniorage would be a competitive return for a stable fiat supply. And menu costs from non-zero inflation would be merely a symptom of departures from the optimum. Assuming zero marginal costs, this paper clarifies how an adjustment friction empirically can make zero the optimal inflation rate in Australia. This result should be strengthened by a theoretical marginal cost of money that is above zero and no greater than the market cost of capital.

Notes

* Gillman, Max, (1998), 'The Optimality of a Zero Inflation Rate: Australia', *The Australian Economic Review*, 31(3), 211–223.

† I gratefully acknowledge the discussion at the Australian 24th Conference of Economists, and at seminars at the University of Melbourne, the University of New South Wales, the Australian National University, Monash University, and

the Center for Economic Research and Graduate Education – Economics Institute of Prague. I especially thank Lance Fisher, Simon Grant and Adrian Pagan for insightful comments and references.

1 Irving Fisher wrote pervasively of 'price stability' with respect to the aggregate price level and not relative prices (for example, Fisher 1920), and helped develop the price index literature (see Persky 1998). He advocated a zero inflation rate policy and was criticised for this (Schumpeter 1952).

2 Harberger (1998) analyses in a growth context 'real cost reduction' as is 'on the mind of most business executives'. He reasons that 'people must perceive real costs in order to reduce them', and that 'inflation is the most obvious, probably the most pervasive, and almost *certainly the most noxious of such policies*' that 'impede the accurate perception of real costs' (italics in original).

3 Gillman, Siklos and Silver (1997), Collins and Anderson (1998), and Gillman and Otto (1997) find a larger-than-standard estimated interest elasticity of money when including cash alternatives. Ireland (1994a) uses the costly credit feature to simulate the u-shaped US historical velocity path.

4 Examples are the McCallum and Goodfriend (1987) and Lucas (2000) 'shopping time' economies that do not specify credit explicitly, and the Bansal and Coleman (1996) 'transaction cost' economy that explicitly includes credit. Related is the Lacker and Schreft (1996) economy in which the use of explicit credit is decided before optimisation on the basis of distance.

5 Balvers and Ran (1997) include within their profit function a related adjustment cost due to the time change in the price, yielding price stickiness. Mussa (1977) and Fender (1990) derive from a monetary setting of costly price changes an adjustment cost function that depends explicitly on the inflation rate. See Christiano, Eichenbaum and Evans (1997) for a comparison of a mark-up sticky-price model and a monetary model with a (costless) financial intermediary.

6 Lucas (1980) uses such a continuum of similar goods that can be aggregated together. Gillman, Siklos and Silver (1997) and Gillman and Otto (1997) use a one-good version of a costly credit model that is similar to the one here.

7 Note that the banking sector is implicit in how the time supplied for producing the credit enters into the optimisation problem. Alternatively, and with identical equilibrium conditions, the banking sector can be made explicit by specifying a separate bank profit maximisation problem and transferring bank profits to the agent's income. To simplify the model's structure, this explicit version is not presented (for a related explicit bank model, see Aiyagari, Braun & Eckstein (1998)).

8 See for example Lucas (2000), Braun (1994a) and Gillman (1995) for such welfare cost measures.

9 Lucas (2000) and Gillman (1996a) similarly allow for negative values of the welfare cost function of inflation at the optimum.

10 Writing the welfare cost function in terms of the nominal interest rate for presentation purposes:

$$a/w =$$
$$\{[Z(\{1 + d|\pi|\}/\{1 + d[0.0395]/[1.0395]\})$$
$$\text{exponent}(1/\{1 + \alpha\})] - 1\}\ \{1/(1 + d|\pi|]\}$$

where:

$$Z \equiv \{1 - [(i\{1 - [i(1 + d|\pi|)/Aw]/[(1 + i)$$
$$(1 + \alpha])]\} \cdot \{([1 + i]\ \text{exponent}[1/(1 + \alpha)])/$$
$$(e\ \text{exponent}[([i - \ln(1 + i)][1 + d|\pi|])/$$
$$(Aw[1 + \alpha])])\}$$

11 The formula used for the interest elasticity is $-\{[(1 - \bar{s})/\bar{s}] + i/(1 + i)\}$, which approximates equation (23) given in Gillman (1993) by omitting the last negligible term that is due to changes in the marginal utility of income.

5 On the optimality of restricting credit: inflation-avoidance and productivity*

Max Gillman†

Summary

The chapter presents a model in which the consumer uses up resources in order to avoid the inflation tax through the use of exchange credit. In an example economy without capital, the credit tax is optimal when the resource loss from credit use dominates the productivity effect and the inefficiency of substitution towards leisure as a result of the credit tax. The chapter also examines second-best inflation policy in this context, given a credit tax. It then extends the economy to an endogenous growth setting and shows how restricting inflation avoidance can increase productivity.

5.1 Introduction

Roubini and Sala-i-Martin (1995) suggest that credit restrictions can be good for decreasing the avoidance of inflation tax but bad for accumulating capital. In their model, the government controls the given level of financial intermediation, which negatively affects the consumer's utility value of money and positively affects the accumulation rate of the capital stock. An increase in intermediation decreases the demand for money and the inflation tax proceeds. It can be optimal to repress intermediation despite a decrease in the growth rate.

Alternative approaches focus on inflation tax avoidance by modelling intermediation endogenously through an exchange technology. In Schreft (1992) and Gillman (1993), the consumer chooses how many resources to devote to producing exchange (trade) credit, and thereby to avoid the inflation tax. For tax avoidance alone, Schreft (1992) and Gillman (1987) find it socially optimal to eliminate the waste of resources in tax avoidance by prohibiting such avoidance activity. A restriction on avoidance may work at first, but over time taxpayers will tend to avoid such restrictions, as the existence of "non-bank" banks may illustrate. Using an explicit exchange technology and a particular example of a credit restriction, Lucas (1993a) lets the consumer avoid reserve requirements in a way that uses up even more resources in total inflation tax avoidance. The government restricts the first exchange alternative and the agent produces a second unrestricted exchange alternative, using a costlier technology than for the first. The restriction thereby induces less efficient inflation tax avoidance activity, which can cause an even larger waste of resources in the total avoidance activity. Such literature further develops the issue of inflation avoidance, but leaves unanswered the broader Roubini and Sala-i-Martin (1995) question about the tradeoff between the costs and benefits of credit use in a second-best world with the inflation rate given.[1] In particular, what if endogenous financial intermediation also furthers intertemporal accumulation?

This chapter addresses the issue from a base model of intermediation that is endogenously produced in order to avoid the inflation tax. This further develops inflation analysis as part of the standard tax analysis of first- and second-best optima (Lipsey and Lancaster, 1956). First, in exploring inflation tax avoidance in the base model, the paper separates bank and consumer problems to show that the equilibrium relative price of the credit services is equal to the nominal interest rate net of the credit tax (see Aiyagari et al., 1998). In the context of the margins of substitution, the elasticities and the inflation cost calibration, this explains why a second-best optimum can be a credit tax that is only as big as the nominal interest rate. Intuitively, the consumer as banker sets the marginal cost of credit service production (the marginal avoidance cost) equal to the credit service price. Making a tax on credit use as high as the marginal cost of production pushes the net supply price of credit services to zero, induces only money use, and deters all inflation tax avoidance except the substitution of leisure for goods. If the latter effect is of small importance relative to the gain in resources from no credit use, then this is second-best optimal.

To include real benefits of the use of credit, the chapter initially introduces an economy-wide increase in the marginal product of labour from the average level of exchange credit use. With a tradeoff comparable to Roubini and Sala-i-Martin (1995), the paper finds a range in which restricting the credit is optimal only when the inflation rate becomes moderately high and inflation avoidance activity begins using up more resources than are generated by the higher marginal product of labour. This extends the application of the theory of the second-best optimum to money and credit markets, including a first-best optimum that extends Friedman (1969). The example also shows how second-best credit tax and inflation tax policies depend on the nature of the economy, in terms of "developed" or "developing".

The paper also discusses related results from the base model as extended to a Lucas (1988b) endogenous growth model (see also Ireland, 1994b, and Marquis and Reffett, 1995). A credit tax has only a level effect rather than a growth effect when there is no leisure use, and this effect is interpreted as increasing the efficiency of human capital. Positive leisure use implies a lower return on human capital and a lower growth rate; when inflation increases leisure, credit restrictions can increase the growth rate only by decreasing the leisure use. In Roubini and Sala-i-Martin (1995), in which there is no leisure, the growth rate changes because financial intermediation is assumed to increase the rate of change of the capital stock. With a different approach, Hartley (1998) shows how financial intermediation can affect the stock of capital rather than its growth rate, using information asymmetry and a credit constraint. Kiyotaki (1998) also uses a credit constraint, whereby the physical capital stock equals the collateral value of the intertemporal credit that is made available. Given a Kiyotaki-type effect, if exchange credit use leads to a higher collateral value being put on the intertemporal credit, then the capital stock ends up being higher. With this literature as a motivation for making a somewhat weaker assumption than Roubini and Sala-i-Martin, the paper lastly considers restricting financial intermediation when it is assumed to affect the average level of the capital stock in the growth model.

5.2 The economy with an explicit financial intermediation sector

Consider an economy with an explicit bank sector that produces credit services only for exchange transactions; and let there be a tax on exchanges made with credit. Exchange occurs across a (0, 1] continuum of stores as indexed by s.[2] The stores each sell a consumption basket or good that differs by colour (as in Lucas, 1980). Let the good at store s and at time t be denoted by $c(s, t)$. This continuum can be thought of as existing across a geographical region in which the average consumer values the different cultural dimensions of each region. Utility depends equally on each colour of good, and induces "rainbow" consumption. The only other difference on the continuum is that the cost of exchange through private banking services gradually increases as the distance increases from the store, indexed by $s = 1$. With the lowest cost at $s = 1$, this can be thought of as an international financial centre; an index near zero can be thought of as isolated banks with a relatively high production cost for exchange services.

Let $P(t)$ denote the price of any good at any store at time t. In equilibrium, the good's price must be the same across all stores because it reflects only the production cost of the good, and each good is produced by the same linear, labour-only technology, with w the given, constant marginal product of labour. The shadow price, in contrast, will differ across stores, as this includes both the goods price of $P(t)$ and a shadow cost of exchange. Exchange induces a shadow cost because it is "self-produced" by the average agent who acts either as a consumer carrying around money or as a bank that produces the credit services. The shadow exchange cost is the same for all goods purchased by money and is just the interest forgone from carrying around money, $P(t)i(t)$, where $i(t)$ is the nominal interest rate. Since the production of credit services varies across the continuum, the shadow cost of credit varies with the store index. In particular, let the time per good that is used to produce credit services at store s be denoted by $\tau(s)$, and let this production time be given as a linear, decreasing function of the store index

s: $\tau(s) = A(1 - s)$, with $A \in R_{++}$. From the equilibrium conditions, the shadow cost of exchange by credit at store s equals the value of the production time, or $wP(t)A(1 - s)$.

If the financial intermediation activity is restricted in any way, then this can be thought of as raising the implicit price of purchasing a good with credit. Let this restriction be represented by an explicit tax that adds $T_e(t) \geq 0$ to the explicit goods price $P(t)$, making the price of credit goods $P(t) + T_e(t)$, where the tax proceeds are returned lump-sum to the consumer through a transfer, denoted $G(t)$. Defining $t_e \equiv T_e(t)/P(t)$, so that t_e is constant for all time periods, the price of a good bought with credit at store s becomes $P(t)(1 + t_e)$, while the total shadow price s is $P(t)[1 + t_e + wA(1 - s)]$, in the equilibrium marginal rates of substitution.

5.2.1 The agent as a money user

On the basis of the shadow costs of the exchange of money versus credit, which are affected by the credit tax, the representative agent chooses the point in the continuum at which to switch between credit and money. Call this marginal store $\bar{s}(t)$, now another choice variable along with goods, leisure (also in the utility function below) and the money stock. The consumer uses credit where its shadow cost is below the nominal interest rate, and this occurs for the relatively less expensive stores indexed from $\bar{s}(t)$ to 1. More formally, the money goods are $c(s, t)$, $s \in (0, \bar{s}(t)]$, and the credit goods are $c(s, t)$, $s \in (\bar{s}(t), 1]$.[3] The aggregate, or composite, money and credit goods are $\int_0^{\bar{s}(t)} c(s, t)\, ds$ and $\int_{\bar{s}(t)}^{1} c(s, t)\, ds$. Letting $M(t)$ denote the money stock at time t, the agent's demand for credit through the choice of $\bar{s}(t)$ gives rise to the model's particular form of the "Clower" or "cash" constraint.

$$M(t) \geq P(t) \int_0^{\bar{s}(t)} c(s, t)\, \mathrm{d}s, \tag{1}$$

and the supply of money enters the economy through lump-sum transfers of $V(t)$:

$$M(t + 1) = M(t) + V(t). \tag{2}$$

Assuming a constant inflation rate in order to derive a closed-form solution, define $V(t) \equiv \pi M(t)$, with $\pi \in R$, so that $M(t + 1) = M(t)(1 + \pi)$.

5.2.2 The agent as banker

The agent as banker in effect has "plants", "branches" or we could just say locations across the continuum, each with a differentiated cost and profit. Let the profit per unit of consumption at each location be denoted as $\Pi(s, t)$ with total profit at location s equal to $\Pi(s, t)c(s, t)$. Let the bank sell the credit service at any store for $P_F(s, t)$. In the competitive equilibrium below (equation (5)), $P_F(s, t) = P_F(t)$, for all s; the fee is the same across all stores. Costs at each location s are the marginal product w as factored by the labour hours used in the credit production, specified linearly as $A(1 - s)$. Per unit profit at each location is given by

$$\Pi(s, t) = P_F(t) - wP(t)A(1 - s). \tag{3}$$

The total profit across the continuum at locations at which the consumer uses credit is given by $\int_{\bar{s}(t)}^{1} \Pi(s, t)c(s, t)\,ds$; total revenues of the bank from all of its locations are $P_F(t) \int_{\bar{s}(t}^{1} c(s, t)ds$; and total costs are $wP(t) \int_{\bar{s}(t)}^{1} A(1 - s)c(s, t)ds$. With technology linear for each store, there is a greater time required per good at the locations that are added on the margin when the range of the use of credit spreads on the continuum. This gives the bank's aggregate operations an increasing marginal cost of expanding the range of credit use through a lower $\bar{s}(t)$. Given $P_F(t)$ and $c(s, t)$, the bank's profit problem is to find the marginal location for production of credit services:

$$\max_{\bar{s}} \int_{\bar{s}}^{1} \Pi(s, t)c(s, t)\,ds = P_F(t) \int_{\bar{s}}^{1} c(s, t)\,ds - wP(t) \int_{\bar{s}}^{1} A(1 - s)x(s, t)\,ds. \tag{4}$$

The first-order condition states that the relative price of finance equals the value of the time required at the marginal store $\bar{s}(t)$ at which the bank offers credit; this can be thought of as the marginal (time) cost of the credit service:

$$P_F(t)/P(t) = Aw(1 - \bar{s}(t)). \tag{5}$$

This implies that bank profits are zero at the marginal location $\bar{s}(t)$, which is used to substitute in for $\Pi(\bar{s}, t)$ in the consumer's first-order condition with respect to $\bar{s}(t)$. At every other store s, bank profits in equilibrium are $\Pi(s, t) = P_F(t) - wP(t)A(1 - s)$, which is used to substitute in for $\Pi(s, t) - P_F(t)$ in the consumer's first-order condition with respect to the credit good, $c(s, t)$, $\bar{s}(t) < s \leq 1$, in order to determine that the shadow cost of a credit good is $P(t)[1 + t_e + wA(1 - s)]$.

5.2.3 The agent as consumer

The consumer receives the profit from the banking activity as part of income. The other earned income is derived from working for wages, supplying labour for goods production and for banking. This equals the marginal product of labour w factored by the total time endowment of 1 less leisure, denoted

$x(t)$, or $w[1 - x(t)]$. The consumer also receives the lump-sum money supply transfer $V(t)$, and the lump-sum transfer of the credit tax revenues $G(t)$, where in equilibrium

$$G(t) = t_e P(t) \int_{\bar{s}(t)}^{1} c(s, t)\mathrm{d}s. \tag{6}$$

Also assume there is an exogenous real asset endowment of $a \in R_+$. The expenditures on goods using credit equals $P(t)(1 + t_e) \int_{\bar{s}(t)}^{1} c(s, t)\, \mathrm{d}s$, and the purchases paid for with money equals $P(t) \int_0^{\bar{s}(t)} c(s, t)\, \mathrm{d}s$. The consumer also pays $P_F(t) \int_{\bar{s}(t)}^{1} c(s, t)\mathrm{d}s$ for the credit services. The net income equals the change in money holdings between periods, $M(t + 1) - M(t)$. With a market discount rate of $q \equiv 1/(1 + i)$, the discounted stream of nominal asset value is

$$\sum_0^t q^t[M(t+1) - M(t) - \int_{\bar{s}(t)}^{1} \Pi(s, t)c(s, t)\, \mathrm{d}s$$
$$- wP(t)(1 - x(t)) - V(t) - P(t)a$$
$$- G(t) + P(t) \int_0^1 c(s, t)\mathrm{d}s + (P_F(t) + t_e P(t)) \int_{\bar{s}(t)}^{1} c(s, t)\, \mathrm{d}s] = 0. \tag{7}$$

The utility function, with $a \geq 0$, is the log example: $U(t) \equiv \int_0^1 (\ln]c(s, t)] + a \ln[x(t)])\, \mathrm{d}s$. Given the preference discount factor β, the consumer maximizes the discounted utility with respect to $c(s, t)$, $0 < s \leq \bar{s}$; $c(s, t)$, $\bar{s} < s \leq 1$; $x(t)$; $M(t + 1)$; $\bar{s}(t)$, subject to (1), and (7), with $\lambda(t)$ and μ as the multipliers. The full solution, given in Appendix 5.A, requires the consumer first-order conditions, the market-clearing conditions (2) and (3), the bank's first-order condition (5) and the government constraint (6), with the restriction that $t_e \leq i < Aw$ so that $\bar{s} \in (0, 1]$. Also, in lieu of an explicit bond market, to save on notation, we will assume the Fisher equation of $q = \beta/(1 + \pi)$.

Given that the bank profit is zero at the marginal store $\bar{s}(t)$, the first-order condition with respect to $\bar{s}(t)$ plus other first-order conditions imply that the relative price of the credit service in equilibrium equals the nominal interest rate net of the credit tax:

$$P_F(t) \,/\, P(t) = i - t_e. \tag{8}$$

5.3 Levelling the inflation distortion through credit taxes

Along the "external" $\bar{s}(t)$ margin, the bank and consumer problems imply that $Aw(1 - \bar{s}(t)) = P_F(t)/P(t) = i - t_e$. The solution is $\bar{s}(t) = \bar{s} = 1 - (P_F(t) / P(t))/Aw$. The credit tax pushes down the net supply price of credit so that the credit supply and its use fall to zero while $\bar{s}$ goes to one. This does not indicate the second-best optimum, but this and other parts of the equilibrium indicate the effect of the credit tax in a way suggestive of the optimum.

5.3.1 The margins of substitution

The credit tax also raises the consumer's shadow price of using credit. From equations (A1–A5) of Appendix 5A, the marginal rate of substitution between any money good and a credit good at store s equals the ratio of the relative shadow prices, or $(1 + i) / [1 + t_e + Aw(1 - s)]$. Raising t_e to i makes the cost of credit greater than the interest rate at all stores in the (0, 1] s-index continuum, and so fully offsets the inflation distortion towards using credit. With $i = t_e$ and only money usage, the shadow price of goods consumption equals $(1 + i)$ for all goods, and the shadow cost of goods relative to leisure equals $(1 + i)/w$. This ratio is higher than when some credit is used at a lower exchange cost than i; the credit tax induces substitution towards leisure. Because the first-best ($i = 0$) optimum has a comparable ratio of $1/w$, this substitution goes in the wrong direction in terms of efficiency, and leaves unclear what is the second-best optimum.

5.3.2 The elasticities

The relative impact of the different effects of the credit tax, on money-versus-credit use and on goods-versus-leisure use, can be seen to some extent within the interest elasticity of money demand, denoted $\eta_i^{M/P}$:

$$\eta_i^{M/P} = -\left[\frac{i}{Aw} \Big/ \left(1 - \frac{i - t_e}{Aw}\right)\right] - \frac{i}{1 + i} - \frac{i[(2 + i)(i - t_e) - Aw]/[Aw(1 + i)^2]}{\left(1 + a - \frac{i}{1 + i}\left[1 - \frac{(i - t_e)}{Aw}\right] - \frac{t_e}{Aw}\ln\left[\frac{1 + i}{1 + t_e}\right]\right)}. \tag{9}$$

The credit tax primarily affects the first term, which equals $-(1 - \bar{s})/\bar{s}$ and shows the extra-marginal effect of substitution of credit for money in the purchase of any good. This tends to dominate the second term, $i/(1 + i)$, which is the effect of the substitution of money/goods for leisure (see Gillman, 1993) and is unaffected by the credit tax. The third term is the interest elasticity of the marginal utility of income. This includes the effects of the change in tax revenues from inflation and from the credit tax, and of the change in income as a result of a change in leisure, and has a negligible magnitude for moderate inflation rates.

This suggests that the main effect of the credit tax, rather than an increase in the substitution of leisure for goods, is a decrease in the substitution of credit for money in the purchase of any good. Through this substitution in the first term, the credit tax decreases the magnitude of the interest elasticity. A corollary view comes through computation of the elasticity of substitution between the money and credit inputs (to exchange). Defining money as $\int_0^{\bar{s}(t)} c(s,\ t)\ \mathrm{d}s$, credit as $\int_{\bar{s}(t)}^1 c(s,\ t)\ \mathrm{d}s$ and the relative price of money to credit as i/Aw, the elasticity of substitution between money and credit, denoted σ, is

$$\sigma \equiv \left[\partial\left(\frac{\int_{\bar{s}(t)}^{1} c(s)\ \mathrm{d}s}{\int_{0}^{1} c(s,\ t)\ \mathrm{d}s}\right) \Big/ \partial\left(\frac{i}{Aw}\right)\right]\left[\frac{i}{Aw} \Big/ \frac{\int_{\bar{s}(t)}^{1} c(s)\ \mathrm{d}s}{\int_{0}^{1} c(s,\ t)\ \mathrm{d}s}\right]$$

$$= \left[\frac{i}{Aw}\Big/\left(1 - \frac{i - t_e}{Aw}\right)\right] + \frac{i}{1 + i}. \qquad (10)$$

The first two terms of the interest elasticity, denoted $\hat{\eta}$, equal the negative of the elasticity of substitution between money and credit: $-\hat{\eta} = \sigma$. And $\partial\sigma/\partial t_e < 0$ (for $t_e \leq i < Aw$, so that $\bar{s} \in (0,1]$). The credit tax unambiguously decreases the elasticity of substitution between money and credit, and the interest elasticity of money demand, with marginal utility held constant. By Bailey (1956) type logic, which positively links the magnitude of the money demand elasticity to the magnitude of welfare cost estimate, this increased inelasticity from the credit tax lowers the welfare cost of a given inflation.[4] And equation (9) suggests that Bailey's result, in which he ignores changes in the marginal utility of income, can be more precisely stated as a positive link between the magnitude of the elasticity of substitution between money and credit and the welfare cost inflation. These results show that the substitution effect of the credit tax towards more leisure and fewer goods ends up affecting only the marginal utility of income and is of less importance for cases of moderate sustained inflation. The dominant effect of the credit tax is left as the efficient gain back to society of the resources spent avoiding the inflation tax.

5.3.3 The second-best credit tax given the inflation rate

A way to determine the net welfare effect of a small increase in the credit tax and the second-best optimum is to compute a function giving the welfare cost of a given inflation rate for variable credit tax rates. To derive such a welfare cost, substitute the equilibrium goods and leisure from Appendix 5.A into the utility function and set the utility level in the equilibrium (with i given and $a = 0$) equal to the utility level at the first-best optimum (with $i = 0$). Then solve for a from this equation. With $\upsilon(\bullet)$ denoting the indirect utility function, this equation is $\upsilon(i, a, t_e, \bullet) = \upsilon(0, 0, t_e, \bullet)$. Normalizing by the Becker (1965) "full" income of $1 \bullet w$ (the time endowment equals 1), and given $\bar{s} = 1 - (i - t_e)/(Aw)$, the cost function is

$$\frac{a}{w} = \left[\left(\frac{1+i}{1+t_e}\right)^{(1+t_e)/Aw} \Big/ \frac{e^{(1-\bar{s})}}{(1+t_e)}\right]^{1/(1+a)}$$

$$\times\left[1 - \frac{1}{1+a}\left(\frac{i\bar{s}}{1+i} + t_e \ln\left(\frac{1+i}{1+t_e}\right)\Big/Aw\right)\right] - 1. \qquad (11)$$

The first bracketed term contains the effect of substitution between goods and leisure, and the second bracketed term contains the effect of the marginal utility of income, including the tax transfers. Specifying the parameters as $Aw = 0.54$, $a = 2.27$ and $\beta = 1/1.03$ (Gillman, 1993), the graph of equation (10) in Figure 5.1 illustrates how the welfare cost locus monotonically shifts down towards its minimum as t_e rises and approaches i. The ridge of optimality in Figure 5.1 at $t_e = i$ shows the second-best optimal locus. To indicate in Figure 5.1 the infeasibility of $t_e > i$ where $\bar{s} > 1$, welfare costs are set equal to zero for $t_e > i$.

5.3.4 Sensitivity and robustness of the results

The second-best result of $t_e = i$ is robust to any specification of $a < \infty$ and $Aw < 0$, given the restriction of $Aw > i - t_e$ that keeps the $\bar{s}$ within range. As a goes to zero, the credit tax induces a proportionately larger gain in welfare. For large values of a, the gain from a credit tax is proportionately less. At $a = 0$, the first-best and second-best optima are the same, since in this case the credit tax induces no inefficient goods-to-leisure substitution. As Aw goes to its minimum allowable value, the benefit of the credit tax is proportionately

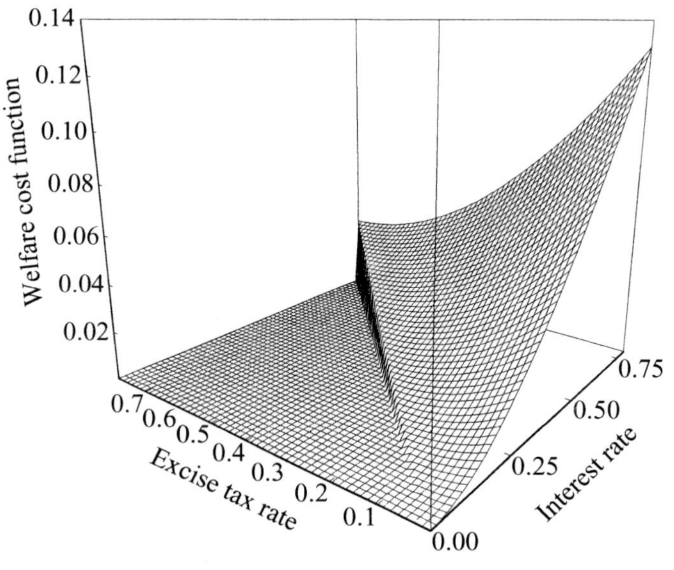

Figure 5.1 The cost of inflation: the credit goods tax.

greater; as Aw approaches infinity, the gain from the credit tax goes to zero. The credit tax is most important when leisure preference is small and the cost of credit low. The actual value of the leisure preference tends to be calibrated at low levels, near 2, and the technological advance in the banking sector suggests that the cost of credit appears to be falling. If the productivity in credit production outpaces the economy-wide productivity increase (if A falls faster than w rises), then the cost of credit will trend downwards and the gain from the credit tax will rise.

With this log-utility example, leisure demand depends on its own shadow price w, α and the marginal utility of income (see Appendix 5A). More generally, leisure can also depend positively on the shadow price of the credit good, including the credit tax. Then the credit tax induces more leisure, and it is possible that $i = t_e$ may not be second-best. Further, when the credit tax causes additional negative income results, it can be suboptimal. Destruction of the credit tax revenues, as occurs typically with a regulation rather than an explicit tax, can make the credit tax decrease welfare, as can a cost of tax collection (Gillman, 1987). These results compare to the suboptimality of the reserve requirements in Lucas (1993a) where there is even less efficient tax avoidance activity. With log utility, and leaving aside such negative income effects, the optimality of an effectively prohibitive credit restriction is robust to alternative forms of the restriction. It is second-best optimal to set to infinity a tax on time in credit activity (like an income tax on the bank sector profits), and to set to zero a ceiling on the interest rate that credit funds can earn (see Gillman, 1987). However, introducing a benefit to credit use changes the optimum from restricting all inflation tax avoidance to trading off such restrictions against fewer benefits.

5.4 Restricting credit when it has other benefits

Many attribute an increase in the capital stock to the development of the financial intermediation sector. This generally would increase the economy's marginal product of labour. In the labour-only economy of Section 5.2, this can be captured by assuming that the marginal product of labour depends linearly on the degree to which credit is used on average in the economy. In particular, let $w(t) = w(\bar{s}_a, t)$, where $w_1(\bar{s}_a, t) < 0$. The example used is $w(s_a) = \hat{w} + n(1 - \bar{s}_a)$, where $\hat{w}, n \in R_+$. In equilibrium, $\bar{s} = \bar{s}_a$; the agent recognizes the external effect of average credit use in solving the equilibrium.[5] The marginal rate of substitution between any money good and a credit good at store s now equals $(1 + i)/[1 + t_e + A(\hat{w} + n[1 - \bar{s}])(1 - s)]$. The credit tax still directly raises the shadow price of credit goods but also now indirectly lowers the shadow price through the term that contains the fraction of stores using credit $(1 - \bar{s})$.

5.4.1 The theory of second best and the optimum quantity of money

The construction of a welfare cost function again allows the net effect of the tax to be determined, although now this is less standard because of the externality. The planner solves for the real goods endowment a from the utility equation $\upsilon(i, a, t_e, \bullet) = \upsilon(0, 0, t_e, \bullet)$ and the normalized welfare cost of inflation $a/w(\bar{s}_a)$ is given in Appendix A. The Friedman optimum of $i = 0$ no longer by itself gives the minimum of this function because of the marginal external benefit of credit use. It is still part of the first-best optimum, as the marginal social cost of money is still equal to zero. Now, in addition, the marginal social cost and marginal social benefit of credit must be equalized. This marginal social cost equals the marginal private cost, which equals the supply price of credit, or the nominal interest rate net of the credit tax. The marginal social benefit is the rate of gain that comes from the economy-wide productivity increase. Call this rate b, and then the first-best optimum occurs when $i = 0$ and $i - t_e = b$, or when $t_e = -b$. This means that the first-best optimum includes credit subsidization through a negative credit tax rate. The rate b varies with the economy's parameters, especially n. In the second-best optimum b also varies with t_e and i. When the nominal interest rate is given at a rate above the Friedman optimum, say at $\bar{\imath}$, then the second-best optimum is achieved with a credit tax rate of $t_e = \bar{\imath} - b(\bar{\imath})$. When the credit tax rate is given at a rate above its first-best subsidy rate, say at $\hat{t}_e$, then the second-best optimum is achieved with a nominal interest rate of $i = \hat{t}_e + b(\hat{t}_e)$.

5.4.2 The results

The results are shown in Figure 5.2 and Table 5.1. In Figure 5.2, $n = 0.09$, $\alpha = 2.27$, $A = 1$, $\hat{w} = 1$ and $\beta = 1/1.03$. The first-best is the minimum of the cost function in Figure 5.2 at $i = 0$, and $t_e = -0.107$ ($\bar{s} = 0.895$). The external benefit causes the cost function to lose its monotonicity with respect to the interest rate and the credit tax rate. When $\bar{\imath} > b(\bar{\imath})$, credit taxes are beneficial up to the second-best rate of $t_e = \bar{\imath} - b(\bar{\imath})$. For $\bar{\imath} < b(\bar{\imath})$, credit subsidies are beneficial up to a rate of $-t_e = -(\bar{\imath} - b(\bar{\imath}))$. Figure 5.2 shows the trough along which lies the minimum welfare cost locus that corresponds to the optimal credit tax for each given level of the interest rate, and the optimal interest rate for each given level of the credit tax. Table 5.1 shows how the results vary with parameter values. Changes in the external factor n cause a smaller effect as the leisure preference parameter α rises. Marginal changes in A and $\hat{w}$ have little effect.

Consider a case that might apply to industrial nations. Let the inflation rate be set by policy at zero. With a rate of time preference of $(1/\beta) - 1 \equiv \rho = 0.03$, the nominal interest rate is $i = 0.03$. Because of its developed state, let the external factor n be relatively low at $n = 0.03$, and let $\alpha = 2.27$ as calibrated for the United States (Gillman, 1993). Then the optimal credit tax is zero (not reported in Table 5.1). But if there is a greater external effect of credit use,

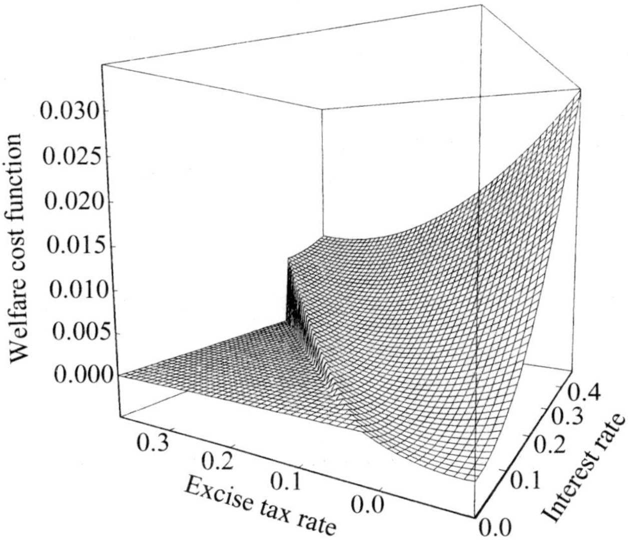

Figure 5.2 The productivity effect and the credit goods tax.

then the implied policy is a subsidization of credit use, perhaps through government supply of bank and capital market oversight, business practice codification or even insurance coverage.

Or consider being given a moderately high inflation rate in a developed economy, say with $i = 0.10$, $n = 0.03$ and $a = 2.27$. A credit tax of 6.7% would be optimal because it would deter excessive avoidance of the inflation tax (see Table 5.1).

Lastly, consider a case that might apply to developing or transition

Table 5.1 The optimal policies under different parameters

	Optimal credit tax t_e					*Optimal nominal interest rate i*			
n	$A = 1$ $i = 0$	*1* *0.5*	*1* *0.1*	*0.1* *0.1*	n	$A = 1$ $t_e = -0.05$	*1* *0*	*1* *0.05*	*2* *0.05*
$a = 0$									
0.00	0.00	0.05	0.10	0.10	0.00	0.0*	0.0	0.0	0.0
0.03	−0.030	0.021	0.071	0.071	0.03	0.0*	0.029	0.079	0.079
0.06	−0.057	−0.007	0.043	0.042	0.06	0.007	0.057	0.107	0.107
0.09	−0.083	−0.033	0.016	0.015	0.09	0.033	0.084	0.134	0.134
$a = 2.27$									
0.00	0.00	0.05	0.10	0.10	0.00	0.0*	0.0	0.0	0.0
0.03	−0.029	0.019	0.067	0.067	0.03	0*	0.018	0.05*	0.05*
0.06	−0.056	−0.010	0.036	0.037	0.06	0.005	0.037	0.069	0.05*
0.09	−0.082	−0.038	0.007	0.011	0.09	0.023	0.057	0.090	0.063

* The optimum is a boundary point constrained either by $i \geq 0$ or $\bar{s} \in (0, 1]$.

countries. Let the implicit tax rate on credit use be given at 0.05 because of inefficient govenment control of intermediation. With emerging credit markets, the external effect might be relatively high, say with $n = 0.06$. With $a = 2.27$ and $\rho = 0.03$, the optimal interest rate is about 0.07, implying an inflation rate of about 4% (see Table 5.1). With other examples of the specification of $w(\bar{s}_a)$, it is conceivable that there are multiple ranges of the inflation tax in which credit taxes or subsidies are efficient.

5.5 Endogenous growth and the credit tax

An endogenous growth setting distinguishes between the growth and level effects of the credit taxation. Assume the same production of credit services using only labour, and let credit use initially allow avoidance of the inflation tax without other benefits. Assume a Cobb-Douglas production of goods with physical and human capital, denoted k and h respectively, as in Lucas (1988b) but without an external effect from average human capital: $y = Bk^{\gamma}(lh)^{1-\gamma}$, with $B \in R_{++}$, $\gamma \in (0, 1)$. Time spent in human capital accumulation is the endowment of one minus labour time, denoted l, leisure, and time spent in providing credit services: $1 - l - x - \int_{\bar{s}}^{1} A(1-s)c(s)\,\mathrm{d}s$. With c denoting the sum of all consumption goods ($c \equiv \int_{\bar{s}}^{1} c(s,\ t)\,\mathrm{d}s$) along the balanced growth path, the growth rates of y, c, M/P, k and h are the same and the levels of c/k, c/h, h/k, x, l and $\bar{s}$ are stationary. With ϕ the efficacy factor of human capital investment, and ρ the rate of time preference, the growth rate of consumption g is $g = \phi - \rho$. See Appendix 5B for these and the following results.

5.5.1 Without leisure

When the preference parameter for leisure is zero, the growth rate g is unaffected by the inflation rate. And it is unaffected by the credit tax. Time is used up in avoiding the inflation tax by increasing the production of credit services. But rather than this credit time being taken away from human capital production, it comes one-for-one from goods production, because the return on human capital and time invested in human capital remains unchanged. Increases in the money supply growth rate cause a rise in the inflation rate and a decrease in the amount of goods produced for consumption and investment: labour hours l falls, the ratio c/h falls and the ratio h/k rises. In a sense, inflation induces a less efficient use of human capital. The imposition of a credit tax t_e offsets this distortion. The credit tax leaves unchanged the growth rate of consumption, causes l and c/h to rise, and h/k to fall, and so induces a lesser waste of tax avoidance time and a greater production of goods. The maximum c/h occurs at $t_e = i$ similar to the optimality results in the Section 5.2 model.

5.5.2 With leisure

With a positive preference for leisure (x), the return on human capital investment becomes $\phi(1 - x)$. The more time that the agent puts into leisure, the less is the return on the human capital investment. The growth rate of consumption becomes $\phi(1 - x) - \rho$ and falls correspondingly when leisure increases. The inflation rate equals $\sigma - [\phi(1 - x) - \rho]$ and rises as leisure rises. An increase in t_e that decreases leisure will raise the growth rate of consumption, lower the inflation rate and increase c/k. However, since the credit tax increases substitution from goods to leisure in the base model of Sections 3.2–4, a decrease in leisure may be unlikely; this is a topic for further research.

5.5.3 With the effect of intermediation of capital

Now consider letting the capital stock k rise with the average degree of financial intermediation, $1 - \bar{s}_a$, so that $k = k(\bar{s}_a)$ and $k'(\bar{s}_a) < 0$. For example with $k(\bar{s}_a) = k(2 - \bar{s}_a)$, k is unchanged when $(1 - \bar{s}_a) = 0$ (only money use), and k is doubled when $(1 - \bar{s}_a) = 1$ (only credit use). An increase in the average extra-marginal credit use raises the capital stock in equilibrium, where $\bar{s}_a = \bar{s}$ and the other equilibrium conditions are unchanged. In the economy without leisure, the balanced path growth rate is unchanged, as are the ratios c/k and hl/k. Other variables and ratios are affected and the full balanced-path solution requires numerical techniques. The effect of an external capital stock increase resulting from greater credit use also depends upon the transitional dynamics. However, it can be shown that a small increase in credit use decreases the amount of labour hours when the economy's credit market is "emerging" (a nominal interest rate near to zero, or a credit tax rate near to the nominal interest rate). In this case, the level of human capital rises with the external increases in the capital stock. And the level of productivity, in terms of the ratio of goods to labour hours c/l, rises as a result of the expansion of credit use. In this sense, the external increase in labour productivity in the labour-only model of Section 5.4 can be thought of as an abstraction of this more involved economy. Both models involve a tradeoff between productivity benefits of credit use and lost resources in inflation-tax avoidance, which a credit restriction must balance in the optimum. With the insight of the endogenous balanced growth path, the tradeoff now can be characterized as weighing the human capital inefficiency that comes from inflation tax avoidance against the productivity benefits of capital enhancement. With positive levels of leisure, the tradeoff affects the growth rate.

5.6 Conclusion

Focusing initially on inflation tax avoidance through the use of exchange credit, the chapter finds a robustness in the second-best credit restrictions in the face of a given nonoptimal inflation. In a cash-in-advance model with an explicit bank sector, the chapter presents excise-type taxes on credit goods that need to be of a level proportional to the interest rate in order to achieve a second-best prohibitive optimum that is characterized by a uniform "rainbow" consumption across the continuum. It derives the market price of the credit service and uses it to build intuition for this result on the margins, through elasticities, and in a welfare cost function. It then includes a positive external effect of credit use on the marginal product of labour and shows a locus of second-best optimal money and credit taxes that balance inflation tax avoidance and productivity effects. The intuition of the optima is extended to an endogenous growth model. Given that inflation affects the growth rate through its effect on leisure, the chapter suggests determining through further research whether restricting credit use eliminates wasteful credit use but causes an even greater use of leisure and a lower growth rate. Related research might incorporate an intertemporal function for exchange credit through a Kiyotaki (1998) type credit constraint.

Appendix 5.A: base model

First-order conditions and equilibrium solution

First-order conditions

$$[\beta^t/c(s,t)] - \beta^t \lambda(t) P(t) = 0, \quad \text{for } 0 < s \leq \bar{s}(t); \tag{A1}$$

$$[\beta^t/c(s,t)] - \mu q^t P(t)[wA(1-s) + 1 + t_e] = 0, \quad \text{for } \bar{s} < s \leq 1; \tag{A2}$$

$$\beta^t \int_0^1 (a/x(t))\, \mathrm{d}s - \mu q^t P(t) w = 0; \tag{A3}$$

$$-\beta^t \lambda(t) P(t) c(\bar{s},t) + \mu q^t P(t) c(\bar{s},t)[wA(1-\bar{s}) + 1 + t_e] = 0; \tag{A4}$$

$$\beta^t \lambda(t) - \mu q^{t-1} = 0. \tag{A5}$$

Equilibrium solution

$$c^*(s) = (w+a)/[(1+i)(1+a-[1/(1+i)][1-(i-t_e)/(Aw)]$$
$$- t_e[\ln(1+i) - t_e \ln(1+t_e)]/(Aw)], \quad \text{for } 0 < s \leq \bar{s}(t);$$

$$\bar{s} = 1 - [(i-t_e)/Aw];$$

$$\lambda(t) P(t) = 1/c^*, \quad \text{for } \bar{s}(t) < s \leq 1,\ c(s,t) = (1+i)/$$
$$\{[1 + t_e + Aw(1-s)]\lambda(t)P(t)\};$$

$x = a/(w\lambda(t)P(t))$; $M(t)/P(t) = \bar{s}/[\lambda(t)P(t)]$, or

$$\frac{M(t)}{P(t)} =$$

$$\frac{1 - [(i - t_e)/(Aw)])(w + a)}{[(1 + i)(1 + a - [1/(1 + i)][1 - (i - t_e)/(Aw)] - t_e[\ln(1 + i) - t_e \ln(1 + t_e)]/(Aw))]}. \tag{A6}$$

Productivity effect of credit use

With $w(\bar{s}) = \hat{w} + n(1 - \bar{s})$,

$$c^* = [a + \hat{w} + n(1 - \bar{s})]/[(1 + i)(1 + a - [i\bar{s}/(1 + i)]$$
$$- t_e \ln[(1 + i)/(1 + t_e)]/(A[\hat{w} + n(1 - \bar{s})]))];$$
$$\bar{s} = 1 - (\hat{w}/2n) + [(\hat{w}^2/4n^2) + (1 - t_e)/(An)]^{0.5};$$

the rest of the solution is then is above.

Welfare cost function

$$\frac{a}{w(\bar{s})} = \left[\frac{[(1 + i)/(1 + t_e)]^{(1 + \{(1 + t_e)/A[\hat{w} + n(1 - \bar{s})]\})}}{e^{(1 - \bar{s})}[1 + n(1 - \bar{s})/\hat{w}]/(1 + t_e)}\right]^{1/(1 + a)}$$
$$\times \left[1 - \frac{1}{1 + a}\left(\frac{i\bar{s}}{1 + i} + \frac{t_e \ln[(1 + i)/(1 + t_e)]}{A[\hat{w} + n(1 - \bar{s})]}\right)\right] - 1.$$

Appendix 5.B: endogenous growth

The bank problem here is made implicit as in Gillman (1993) (rather than *ex*plicit, as in Section 5.2), with no effect on the first-order conditions, and continuous time is used, both for ease of presentation. Let d denote the nominal sum of the money and capital assets, let r and w denote the marginal products of capital and effective labour, let the utility function be modified for balanced growth, and let $1/(1 + \rho) \equiv \beta$. Human capital investment function depends linearly on time spent in human capital accumulation:

$$\dot{h} = \phi\left[1 - l - x - \int_{\bar{s}}^{1} A(1 - s)c(s)\, \mathrm{d}s\right] h,$$

where $\phi \in R_+$, is the efficacy parameter. The following Hamiltonian extends the base model:

$$\max_{c_1(0 < s \leq \bar{s}), c_2(\bar{s} < s \leq 1), \bar{s}, M, k, d, h, l} \mathcal{H} = \int_0^{\infty} e^{-\rho t} \left[\ln \int_0^1 c(s)\, ds + \beta(x^{1-\theta} - 1)/(1-\theta) \right] dt$$

$$+ \lambda \left[Pkr + Plhw - P \int_0^{\bar{s}} c(s)\, ds - P(1 + t_e) \int_{\bar{s}}^1 c(s)\, ds + V + G + \dot{P}k \right]$$

$$+ \mu\phi h \left[1 - l - x - \int_{\bar{s}}^1 A(1 - s)c(s)\, ds \right] + \gamma[d - M - Pk]$$

$$+ \delta \left[M - P \int_0^{\bar{s}} c(s)\, ds \right].$$

The solution

$\dot{c}/c = g = \phi - \rho$; $r = \phi$; $w = (1 - \gamma)(k/lh)^{\gamma}$;

$lh/k = (\phi/\gamma)^{1/(1-\gamma)}$; $c/k = (\phi/\gamma) - g$; $\bar{s} = 1 - [(i - t_e)/Aw]$;

$l = [1 - g/\phi]/[1 + (c_1/k)(k/lh)(1 + i)[(1 + t_e) \ln([1 + t_e]/[1 + i]) + i - t_e]/ Aww]$;

$c/h = (c/k)(k/hl)\, l$.

The credit tax t_e affects only l and c/h. Given the restrictions in Section 5.2 ($t_e \leq i < Aw$; $s \in (0, 1]$), the following comparative statics can be shown:

$\partial l/\partial i < 0$; $\partial l/\partial t_e > 0$; $\partial(c/h)/\partial i < 0$; $\partial(c/h)/\partial t_e > 0$; $\partial(k/h)/\partial i < 0$; $\partial(k/h)/\partial t_e > 0$.

With leisure (x), $\dot{c}/c = g = \phi(1 - x) - \rho$; $r = \phi(1 - x)$; $lh/k = [\phi(1 - x)/\gamma]^{1/(1-\gamma)}$; and $c/k = [\phi(1 - x)/\gamma] - g$.

Notes

* Gillman, Max, 2000, 'On The Optimality of Restricting Credit: Inflation-Avoidance and Productivity', *Japanese Economic Review*, 51(3), September, 375–390.

† I thank Michal Kejak, Lance Fisher, Glenn Boyle, Dorian Owen, seminar participants at the Center for Economic Research and Graduate Education – Economics Institute, University of Otago, University of Waikato, Victoria University of Wellington, the 21st Conference of Economists, and the Armidale Australasian Meeting of the Econometric Society.

1 See Hartley (1998) for related work in which the credit good is specified through preferences.

2 Excluding $s = 0$ precludes a credit-only economy in which the price level is not well defined.

3 For comparison to the standard cash-in-advance economies with credit (as in Lucas and Stokey, 1983, and Englund and Svensson, 1988), each money good can be thought of as $c_1(s, t)$ on the lower part of the (0, 1] continuum, and each credit good as $c_2(s, t)$, on the upper part of the store continuum.

4 The Bailey link is shown to be valid in Gillman (1995) for general equilibrium as well as for partial equilibrium.
5 See Lucas (1988b) for a similar treatment of the effect of external human capital.

6 Ramsey-Friedman optimality with banking time*

Max Gillman and Oleg Yerokhin

Summary

This chapter conducts a Ramsey analysis within an endogenous growth cash-in-advance economy with policy commitment. Credit and money are alternative payment mechanisms that act as inputs into the household production of exchange. The credit is produced with a diminishing returns technology with Inada conditions that implies along the balanced-growth path a degree one homogeneity of effective banking time. This tightens the restrictions found within shopping time economies while providing a production basis for the Ramsey-Friedman optimum that suggests a special case of Diamond and Mirrlees (1971).

6.1 Introduction

Homogeneity of the shopping time function in Correia and Teles (1999) is necessary for Ramsey (1927) optimality of the Friedman (1969) rule. This second-best Friedman optimum is an interesting result in that it occurs in one of the most standard exchange economies in use today. However the required homogeneity of the arguments in the shopping time function is difficult to interpret since this is a general transactions cost technology, involving the input of the consumer's shopping time as derived from some combination of real money and consumption. One interpretation is supplied by Lucas (2000). In specifying the shopping time model, he chooses a functional form that makes shopping time inversely proportional to the consumption velocity of real money demand (see also Canzoneri and Diba, 2005). This implies a money demand interest elasticity of – 0.5 as in Baumol (1952) and a unitary income elasticity, while implying a shopping time function that is homogenous of degree one in real money and consumption goods. More generally, Correia and Teles (1999) do not impose a unitary income elasticity of money demand and find that any degree of homogeneity is sufficient for the Friedman rule to be Ramsey optimal, although here the implications for the underlying money demand function are not drawn out.

This chapter contributes a different approach that offers a new derivation and interpretation of the homogeneity result. Alternatively it can be viewed as a more restrictive approach that focuses like Lucas (2000) on the resulting money demand function. The model imposes restrictions on the transactions technology by assuming that credit is produced with diminishing returns to labor. It is assumed that exchange credit is produced using labor time (or "banking time") and goods in a Cobb-Douglas fashion, where the credit serves as a costly way to buy goods without using interest-foregoing money. This results in a money demand function with an interest elasticity similar to Cagan's in that it rises with the inflation rate; and it has a unitary consumption elasticity.

The credit production specification also yields a restriction equivalent to homogeneity of degree one on effective time used in exchange in a way that is comparable to a special case of a shopping time function. The credit production specification is partly restricted by the need of its endogenous growth setting to have all variables in the economy grow at the same rate on the balanced-growth path (BGP) equilibrium. This means that money and consumption must grow at the same rate, and consumption velocity must be stable, giving a unitary consumption elasticity of money demand. This in turn restricts the homogeneity on the time spent in transactions.

The key necessary condition for Ramsey (1927) optimality of the Friedman rule is that the marginal productivity of the banking time in producing credit must be driven to infinity. At this point, with only an assumption of diminishing returns in producing credit per unit of consumption, credit production is indeed zero and only money is used by the consumer for exchange. In contrast, the Ramsey (1927) optimality condition within the shopping time economy requires that there is "satiation" of real money balances so that there is no use of shopping time required once this particular satiation level of money demand is reached. This also involves the additional assumption that the change in shopping time with respect to money is equal to zero at that point, a differentiability required for the Ramsey optimum. The banking time model instead substitutes zero credit use for the satiation point and substitutes a diminishing marginal product of labor in credit production with Inada conditions for the differentiability of the shopping time function.

The resulting Ramsey (1927) optimality of the Friedman (1969) optimum can be interpreted as a special case of Diamond and Mirrlees (1971): credit is specified as an alternative input into producing exchange, along with money, making it an intermediate good within a Becker (1975) household production economy. The consumer needs not only the good, but also the exchange means to get the good, either money or credit.[1] This is why the shadow price of consumption contains a shadow goods cost component (one) plus a shadow exchange cost component (a weighted average of the cost of using cash and of using credit). The shadow costs reflect a Becker (1975)- like interpretation of money and credit as inputs, and this provides the second-best intuition: intermediate goods with CRS production functions are not to be taxed because it distorts the production margins (the input allocations) as well as the consumption margins (goods versus leisure), as long as the goods output is also CRS produced (Diamond and Mirrlees 1971). The Ramsey-Diamond-Mirrless result in the economy implies that money as an input to exchange should not be taxed when other taxes are available that do not distort the exchange production margin; otherwise the efficient production of exchange is needlessly distorted towards wasteful inflation-tax avoiding credit use. Zero credit production is second-best optimal because it avoids unnecessary distortions to production efficiency.

6.2 The "banking time" economy

6.2.1 The consumer problem

The representative consumer's time period t utility function depends on consumption goods and leisure, and is given by $u(c_t, x_t)$, with the assumed Inada conditions with respect to c_t and x_t. Discounted by the time preference rate $\rho \in (0, 1)$ the utility stream is

$$\int_0^\infty e^{-\rho t} u(c_t, x_t)\, dt. \tag{1}$$

The consumer divides an endowment of 1 unit of time between working to produce goods output, l_t, working to produce credit, l_{dt}, investing in human capital production, l_{ht}, and taking leisure, x_t. The allocation of time constraint can be written as

$$1 = l_t + l_{dt} + l_{ht} + x_t. \tag{2}$$

6.2.1.1 Production technology

Consumption with goods and exchange Consider a Becker (1975)-type household production economy as extended to include exchange activity as part of household production, and also including human capital (Lucas 1988b). The consumer engages in household production of exchange, using money and credit, and of the consumption good using goods output and exchange. The good that the agent consumes is the aggregate consumption good, denoted c_t. This is produced using the aggregate output y_t that is devoted to consumption goods, denoted by y_{ct}, and an amount of exchange that is needed to purchase the good, denoted by y_{et}. Note here that only consumption goods are assumed to require exchange; capital and labor markets do not require exchange. Let the production of the consumption good be Leontieff in terms of the goods output and the exchange. Whereas Aiyagari, Braun, and Eckstein (1998) use a Leontieff technology to produce the credit good at each store of a continuum of stores, here the approach is extended by having an aggregate good combined with exchange, either cash or credit, in Leontieff fashion to produce the Becker (1975)-type consumption good:

$$c_t = \min(y_{ct}, y_{et}). \tag{3}$$

Only the efficient frontier of the Leontieff production of the consumption good will be utilized, this being a ray from the origin in isoquant space, if the relative price of the output of goods to the exchange means for goods is between zero and infinity. Here the assumption is that the slope is one. This means simply that the amount of goods bought corresponds directly to the amount of money or credit paid for the goods, in a one-to-one fashion.[2] This implies that along the ray

$$c_t = y_{ct}; \tag{4}$$

$$c_t = y_{et}. \tag{5}$$

The production of output y_t is a standard constant returns to scale function in capital, k_t, and effective labor, the human capital, h_t, factored by the labor supply, l_t:

$$y_t = f(k_t, l_t h_t) = Ak_t^a (l_t h_t)^{1-a}. \tag{6}$$

The production of human capital is given by the function $H(\cdot)$ that has as its only argument l_{ht}:

$$\dot{h}_t = h_t\, H(l_{ht}). \tag{7}$$

It is assumed that $H'(l_{ht}) > 0$, and $H''(l_{ht}) < 0$.

The production of exchange requires inputs of real money balances and/or real credit. Denote the real money balances as $m_t \equiv M_t / P_t$, with M_t denoting the nominal money stock, and P_t denoting the price of the aggregate consumption good. And let real credit be denoted by d_t. The production of exchange is assumed to be homogeneous of degree one in m_t and d_t. In general it given as

$$y_{et} = f_e(m_t, d_t). \tag{8}$$

Specifically, assume that real money and credit are perfect substitutes, so that

$$y_{et} = m_t + d_t. \tag{9}$$

Credit The credit technology is a costly self-produced means of purchasing goods instead of using money. This might be thought of as an abstraction from a world with payment uncertainty, where for example, the agent produces information about his purchase and payment history that enables credit to be issued just as a credit agency might. Here there is not a decentralized credit market, but rather the representative agent simply acts in part as a bank, producing what can be called exchange credit.[3]

The specification is that the effective labor per unit of consumption produces the share of credit in total purchases with a diminishing marginal productivity. In particular, from equations (4), (5), and (9), $d_t/c_t = 1 - (m_t/c_t)$. Define the share

$$a_t \equiv m_t/c_t. \tag{10}$$

Then $d_t = c_t(1 - a_t)$ is the total credit used. Specify the production of this credit, with $\gamma \in (0, 1)$, as

$$d_t = c_t A_{dt} (l_{dt} h_t/c_t)^\gamma = A_d (l_{dt} h_t)^\gamma c_t^{1-\gamma}, \tag{11}$$

or in terms of the share a_t:

$$1 - a_t = A_d (l_{dt} h_t/c_t)^\gamma \tag{12}$$

The diminishing returns technology implies that the marginal cost per unit of consumption is an upward sloping curve that depends on the parameter γ. This marginal cost (MC_t) can be defined as the marginal factor cost divided by the marginal factor product, or, with w_t denoting the marginal labor cost, $MC_t \equiv (w_t/\gamma) A_d^{-1/\gamma} (d_t/c_t)^{(1-\gamma)/\gamma}$ (this definition instead can be derived from the BGP equilibrium conditions below, as in equation (49), where $R_t = MC_t$). With $\gamma = 0.5$, this marginal cost curve slopes upward with a straight line; with $\gamma < 0.5$ it exhibits an upward sloping convex marginal cost curve that entails an increasing marginal cost as output of credit per unit of consumption increases. This (0, 0.5) range is the most plausible for γ since it produces the typically shaped marginal cost curve; for the (0.5, 1) range the marginal costs rise at a decreasing rate.

6.2.1.2 Total income

The consumer buys and sells nominal government bonds, denoted by B_t, which earn the nominal interest rate of R_t. The change over time in the real bond purchases is $\dot{B}_t/P_t$ and the real value of the interest is $R_t B_t/P_t$. This net purchase of bonds, plus the consumer's real goods purchases y_{ct}, equal to c_t by equation (4), plus the capital investment, denoted by $\dot{k}_t$, and investment in real money $\dot{M}_t/P_t$ are equal to the after tax return to labor and capital rentals plus the bond income. With W_t and r_t denoting the rental prices of labor and capital, denote the after tax real wage and interest rental rates as

$$\tilde{w}_t \equiv (1 - \tau_t^l)w_t, \tag{13}$$

$$\tilde{r}_t \equiv (1 - \tau_t^k)r_t. \tag{14}$$

The consumer budget constraint is

$$c_t + \dot{k}_t + \dot{M}_t/P_t + \dot{B}_t/P_t = \tilde{w}_t l_t h_t + \tilde{r}_t k_t + R_t B_t/P_t. \tag{15}$$

The money investment can be written as

$$\dot{M}_t/P_t = \dot{m}_t + m_t \pi_t, \tag{16}$$

and inserted into equation (15) to give

$$c_t + \dot{k}_t + \dot{m}_t + m_t \pi_t + \dot{B}_t/P_t = \tilde{w}_t l_t h_t + \tilde{r}_t k_t + R_t B_t/P_t. \tag{17}$$

The consumer problem could now be stated in a Hamiltonian form (see for example Turnovsky (1997)) as the maximization of utility (1) subject to the allocation of time constraint (2), the human capital investment constraint (7), the income constraint (17) and the money and credit constraints (10), (11) and (12). The choice variables would be m_t, d_t, and a_t plus all of the time allocations, the goods consumption, and the physical and human capital levels. A reduced set of constraints results by eliminating a_t by combining the money and credit constraints into one constraint of $c_t = d_t + m_t$. The credit output d_t can be eliminated by substituting in from the credit technology equation (11) so that the constraints are now $c_t A_d (l_{dt} h_t / c_t)^\gamma = c_t + m_t$, plus the human capital investment, allocation of time, and income constraints. A further reduced set of constraints, of human capital investment, allocation of time, and income, can result by eliminating the banking time l_{dt} by solving for it in terms of c_t, m_t, and h_t and substituting this into the allocation of time constraint (see equation (31) below).

Note that in the Hamiltonian, differentiating with respect to the physical capital level and the nominal bond level B_t, yields the Fisher equation

$$R_t = \pi_t + \tilde{r}_t. \tag{18}$$

This gets suppressed when using the wealth constraint approach below with Ricardian equivalence.

6.2.2 The goods producer problem

The goods producer rents labor and capital from the consumer, taking the competitive real prices of labor and capital as given. The firm's first-order conditions, using equation (6), are

$$w_t = (1 - a)\left(\frac{k_t}{l_t h_t}\right)^a = f_{lh}\,(k_t, l_t h_t), \tag{19}$$

$$r_t = a\left(\frac{k_t}{l_t h_t}\right)^{a-1} = f_k\,(k_t, l_t h_t), \tag{20}$$

and the CRS production function implies that there are zero profits.

6.2.3 Government budget constraint

The government has no access to lump sum taxes and finances its expenditure g_t partly with flat proportional taxes on labor and capital income. With these tax rates at time t denoted by τ_t^l and τ_t^k, this real tax income is $\tau_t^k r_t k_t + \tau_t^l w_t l_t h_t$. Added to this is the net proceeds of new bond issues $(\dot{B}_t - R_t B_t)/P_t$, and proceeds from new money printing $(M_{t+1} - M_t)/P_t$, where the nominal money supply is assumed to exogenously grow at a constant rate σ through open market operations, and where the consumer is already given the initial stock $M_0 > 0$. The government budget constraint is given by

$$\tau_t^k r_t k_t + \tau_t^l w_t l_t h_t + \left(\dot{B}_t - R_t B_t\right)/P_t + \dot{M}_t/P_t = g_t. \tag{21}$$

6.2.4 Resource constraint

Writing out the consumer's income constraint (17) by using that $\tilde{w}_t \equiv (1 - \tau_t^l)w_t$, and $\tilde{r}_t \equiv (1 - \tau_t^k)r_t$ (equations 13 and 14), so that

$$c_t + \dot{k}_t + \dot{M}_t/P_t + \dot{B}_t/P_t = (1 - \tau_t^l)w_t l_t h_t + (1 - \tau_t^k)r_t k_t + R_t B_t/P_t,$$

and substituting in for $\tau_t^k r_t k_t + \tau_t^l w_t l_t h_t$ from the government budget constraint (21), gives that

$$c_t + \dot{k}_t + g_t = w_t l_t h_t + r_t k_t.$$

Using the CRS property of goods production, whereby

$$w_t l_t h_t + r_t k_t = A k_t^a\,(l_t h_t)^{1-a},$$

this then reduces to the resource constraint of

$$c_t + \dot{k}_t + g_t = A k_t^a\,(l_t h_t)^{1-a}. \tag{22}$$

6.3 Equilibrium

6.3.1 The wealth constraint

A formulation convenient for the Ramsey (1927) problem is to construct the wealth constraint from the income flow constraint (17). Define real wealth, denoted as W_t, by the sum of physical capital and the real money stock:

$$W_t = k_t + m_t + B_t/P_t. \tag{23}$$

Then from equations (17), (23), and using the Fisher identity in (18) that $R_t = \pi_t + \tilde{r}_t$, it follows that

$$\dot{W}_t = \tilde{r}_t\,(k_t + m_t + B_t/P_t) + \tilde{w}_t h_t l_t - c_t - R_t m_t. \tag{24}$$

Note that it is assumed that $R_t \geq 0$ so that the wealth constraint is not unbounded (see for example Ljungqvist and Sargent (2000)).

Given the initial period m_0 and k_0, integrating over the infinite horizon, and imposing the transversality conditions,

$$\lim_{t\to\infty} m_t e^{-\int_0^t \tilde{r}_s ds} = 0; \tag{25}$$

$$\lim_{t\to\infty} k_t e^{-\int_0^t \tilde{r}_s ds} = 0; \tag{26}$$

$$\lim_{t\to\infty} (B_t/P_t)\, e^{-\int_0^t \tilde{r}_s ds} = 0; \tag{27}$$

the wealth constraint (see Appendix 6.A.1) is

$$\int_0^\infty e^{-\int_0^t \tilde{r}_s ds}\,[c_t + R_t m_t - \tilde{w}_t h_t l_t]\, dt = m_0 + k_0 + B_0/P_0. \tag{28}$$

Constraint (28) is a dynamic version of the income constraint of Mulligan and Sala-I-Martin (1997) (see equation 2, p.7).

The consumer problem can be stated as the maximization of utility (equation 1) subject to equations (2), (7), (10), (12) and (28), the allocation of time, human capital investment, money, credit and wealth constraints, with respect to c_t, x_t, l_t, l_{ht}, l_{dt}, a_t, m_t, k_t, and h_t.

6.3.2 Definition of equilibrium

The competitive equilibrium consists of a time path for the allocation $\{yct, y_{et}, d_t, c_t, x_t, l_t, l_{ht}, l_{dt}, m_t, k_t, h_t\}_{t=0}^{\infty}$ given the input prices $\{w_t, r_t\}_{t=0}^{\infty}$, tax rates $\{\tau_t^l, \tau_t^k\}_{t=0}^{\infty}$, government spending $\{g_t\}_{t=0}^{\infty}$, and the initial period k_0, M_0, B_0 and

P_0 (normalized to one), such that $\{c_t, x_t, l_t, l_{ht}, m_t, k_t, h_t, B_t/P_t\}_{t=0}^{\infty}$ maximizes (1) subject to constraints (2), (7), (10), (12) and (28), and such that $\{\tau_t^l, \tau_t^k\}_{t=0}^{\infty}$, and $\{k_t, l_t, h_t, r_t, w_t\}_{t=0}^{\infty}$, satisfy the constraints (6), (19), (20), (21) and (22), and that constraints (4), (5), (9), and (11) are satisfied.

6.3.3 Characterization of equilibrium

The effective labor in credit production, which in equilibrium can be thought of as the derived demand, can be solved from equations (10) and (12) as

$$l_{dt}\, h_t = (A_d)^{-1/\gamma}\, c_t\,]1 - (m_t/c_t)]^{1/\gamma}. \tag{29}$$

Equation (29) is mathematically analogous to a special case of the McCallum and Goodfriend (1987) shopping time economy (Walsh 1998) as extended to endogenous growth. But here instead the concept is banking time that is used to produce an intermediate good, credit, that in turn is combined with money to produce another intermediate good, exchange, which finally is combined in Leontieff fashion with goods output to produce consumption goods.

Solving for l_{dt} and defining it as $b(c_t, m_t, h_t)$,

$$l_{dt} = \left(A_d^{-1/\gamma}\, c_t\, [1 - (m_t/c_t)]^{1/\gamma}\right)/h_t \equiv b(c_t, m_t, h_t), \tag{30}$$

where $b_c > 0$, $b_m < 0$, $b_h < 0$, this raw *banking time* can be substituted directly into the allocation of time constraint (2):

$$1 = l_t + b(c_t, m_t, h_t) + l_{ht} + x_t, \tag{31}$$

while $l_{dt}h_t$ is the effective banking time. The function $b(c_t, m_t, h_t)$ of equation (30) exhibits homogeneity of degree one in c_t and m_t as in equation (29), and exhibits homogeneity of degree zero (HD0) in its three arguments.

The present value Hamiltonian for the consumer problem can then be written as

$$\begin{aligned}\mathcal{H} = {} & e^{-\rho t}u(c_t, x_t) + \mu_t h_t H(l_{ht}) + \theta_t\,[1 - x_t - b\,(c_t, m_t, h_t) - l_t - l_{ht}] \\ & + \lambda\left[m_0 + k_0 + B_0/P_0 + \int_0^{\infty} e^{-\int_0^t \tilde{r}_s ds}\,(\tilde{w}_t h_t l_t - c_t - R_t m_t)\, dt\right].\end{aligned} \tag{32}$$

The first-order conditions are

$$e^{-\rho t}u_c(c_t, x_t) - \lambda e^{-\int_0^t \tilde{r}_s ds} - \theta_t b_c(c_t, m_t, h_t) = 0; \tag{33}$$

$$e^{-\rho t}u_x(c_t, x_t) - \theta_t = 0; \tag{34}$$

$$\lambda e^{-\int_0^t \tilde{r}_s ds}\, \tilde{w}_t h_t - \theta_t = 0; \tag{35}$$

$$\mu_t h_t H'(l_{ht}) - \theta_t = 0; \tag{36}$$

$$-\lambda e^{-\int_0^t \tilde{r}_s ds} R_t - \theta_t b_m(c_t, m_t, h_t) = 0; \tag{37}$$

$$\mu_t H(l_{ht}) + \lambda e^{-\int_0^t \tilde{r}_s ds} \tilde{w}_t l_t - \theta_t b_h(c_t, m_t, h_t) = -\dot{\mu}_t. \tag{38}$$

Combining equations (35) and (38) to get

$$\mu_t H(l_{ht}) + \lambda e^{-\int_0^t \tilde{r}_s ds} \tilde{w}_t [l_t - h_s b_h(c_t, m_t, h_t)] = -\dot{\mu}_t; \tag{39}$$

multiplying through by h_t and substituting in equation (7) gives

$$\dot{\mu}_t h_t + \mu_t \dot{h}_t = -\lambda e^{-\int_0^t \tilde{r}_s ds} \tilde{w}_t h_t [l_t - h_s b_h(c_t, m_t, h_t)]. \tag{40}$$

This can be written as

$$\frac{d}{ds}(\mu_s h_s) = -\lambda e^{-\int_0^s \tilde{r}_\xi d\xi} \tilde{w}_s h_s [l_s - h_s b_h(c_s, m_s, h_s)]. \tag{41}$$

Integrating both sides from t to ∞ and imposing the transversality condition

$$\lim_{s \to \infty} \mu_s h_s = 0, \tag{42}$$

gives that

$$\mu_t h_t = \lambda e^{-\int_0^t \tilde{r}_\xi d\xi} \int_t^\infty e^{-\int_t^s \tilde{r}_\xi d\xi} \tilde{w}_s h_s [l_s - h_s b_h(c_s, m_s, h_s)]. \tag{43}$$

Substituting in equations (35) and (36), and using the fact that

$$-h_t b_h(c_t, m_t, h_t) = b_c(c_t, m_t, h_t)c_t + b_m(c_t, m_t, h_t)m_t = b(c_t, m_t, h_t), \tag{44}$$

gives the Becker (1975)-type [p. 68, equation (63)] margin of human capital accmulation, stated as

$$\tilde{w}_t h_t = H'(l_{ht}) \int_t^\infty e^{-\int_t^s \tilde{r}_\xi d\xi} \tilde{w}_s h_s [l_s + b(c_s, m_s, h_s)] ds. \tag{45}$$

Equation (45) is the Euler equation for the motion of human capital in the economy with banking time. The left-hand side is the workers earnings if a unit of time is spent in the production of goods. The right-hand side is the product of two terms: the percentage increase in human capital if a unit of time is spent in human capital accumulation, and the discounted value of increased earnings flow that this additional human capital will yield. Alternatively this condition can be written as

$$e^{-\rho t} u_x(c_t, x_t) = \lambda \left(e^{-\int_0^t \tilde{r}_\xi d\xi} H'(l_{ht}) \int_t^\infty e^{-\int_t^s \tilde{r}_\xi d\xi} \tilde{w}_s h_s [l_s + b(c_s, m_s, h_s)] \, ds \right), \quad (46)$$

defining the margin of leisure time versus time spent in human capital accumulation. The left-hand side is the utility value of a unit of time devoted to leisure in period t from the point of view of period 0. The right-hand side is the same value of time in human capital accumulation as in equation (45), now discounted back to period zero and converted to its utility value through multiplication by the shadow value of wealth.

From equations (33) and (35), the intertemporal consumption marginal rate of substitution between dates 0 and t is

$$\frac{e^{-\rho t} u_c(c_t, x_t)}{u_c(c_0, x_0)} = \frac{e^{-\int_0^t \tilde{r}_s ds} [1 + \tilde{w}_t h_t b_c(c_t, m_t, h_t)]}{1 + \tilde{w}_0 h_0 b_c(c_0, m_0, h_0, B_0/P_0)}. \quad (47)$$

Equation (33), (34) and (35) imply that the marginal rate of substitution between consumption and leisure is

$$\frac{u_c(c_t, x_t)}{u_x(c_t, x_t)} = \frac{1 + \tilde{w}_t h_t b_c(c_t, m_t, h_t)}{\tilde{w}_t h_t}, \quad (48)$$

being equal to the ratio of the shadow prices of consumption and leisure, comparable to, for example, Walsh's (1998) shopping time model, where 1 is the goods cost and $\tilde{w}_t h_t b_c(c_t, m_t, h_t)$ the exchange cost. Since $\tilde{w}_t h_t b_c (c_t, m_t, h_t) < \infty$, there is a solution at the corner of the square Leontieff isoquant in equation (3). In particular, the slope along the Leontieff isoquant is either zero or infinity. Thus if there is a relative cost of goods versus exchange which is between zero and infinity, then this guarantees that the slope of the isocost line is between zero and infinity and touches the isoquant at its corner. Here being in a "corner" is good. It produces an interior solution that guarantees that the consumer indeed chooses to combine an equal amount of goods and exchange in order to "produce" the consumption good from these two inputs.

Also note the alternative interpretation of the shadow exchange cost of goods, $\tilde{w}_t h_t b_c$. It can be shown that in equilibrium $\tilde{w}_t h_t b_c = a_t R_t + (1 - a_t)\gamma R_t$. The term $a_t R_t + (1 - a_t)\gamma R_t$ is a weighted average of the average costs of money and credit. The average cost of credit γR_t is less than the average cost of money R_t since $\gamma < 1$. This means that although the marginal cost of credit is equal to R_t in equilibrium, its average cost is less and so the consumer saves by using credit.

To see that the marginal cost of credit is equal to the nominal interest rate, use equations (35) and (37) to write

$$\tilde{w}_t h_t b_m = R_t. \tag{49}$$

This is the analogue to the original equilibrium condition in Baumol (1952) from minimizing the costs of using money or going to the bank. The condition (49) similarly equalizes the marginal cost of the alternative exchange means. This follows by using equations (10), (11), (12) and (30) to show that $b_m = 1/[\partial d_t / \partial(l_{dt})]$, so that $\tilde{w}_t h_t b_m = \tilde{w}_t h_t / [\partial d_t / \partial(l_{dt})]$. This latter term is the marginal factor cost divided by the marginal factor product, which by microeconomic theory is equal to the marginal cost of the output d_t. This relation implies that R_t is equal to the marginal cost of credit.

6.3.4 Money and banking

The condition (49) that equalizes the marginal costs of exchange, along with equations (10) (11), and (12), also yields the solution for a_t, the money demand function, and the consumption velocity:

$$R_t = \tilde{w}_t h_t b_m(c_t, m_t, h_t) = \tilde{w}_t A_d^{1/\gamma} [1 - (m_t/c_t)]^{(1/\gamma)-1}/\gamma; \tag{50}$$

$$a_t = 1 - \left[A_d^{1/(1-\gamma)} (R_t \gamma / \tilde{w}_t)^{\gamma/(1-\gamma)} \right]; \tag{51}$$

$$m_t = c_t \left(1 - \left[A_d^{1/(1-\gamma)} (R_t \gamma / \tilde{w}_t)^{\gamma/(1-\gamma)} \right] \right). \tag{52}$$

The consumption velocity is $c_t/m_t = 1/\{1 - [(R_t\gamma)/(\tilde{w}_t A_d)]^{\gamma/(1-\gamma)}\}$; it is constant on the balanced-growth path. This results because the wage rate of effective labor, $w_t = (1 - a)\left(\frac{k_t}{l_t h_t}\right)^a$, depends on the capital to effective labor ratio; k_t and h_t grow at the same rate on the balanced-growth path, and the labor share l_t is constant on the balanced-growth path. Since $\tilde{w}_t \equiv (1 - \tau_s^l) w_t$, and given that the labor and capital tax rates are also constant on the balanced-growth path, so $\tilde{w}_t$ is also constant. With $\tilde{r}_t$ constant as well, the nominal interest rate is constant on the balanced-growth path, and so is the consumption velocity. This also gives a unitary consumption elasticity.

The banking time is also constant on the balanced-growth path. From equation (30), $l_{dt} = A_d^{-1/\gamma} (c_t/h_t) [1 - (m_t/c_t)]^{1/\gamma}$. With c_t and h_t growing at the same rate on the balanced-growth path, and with m_t/c_t also constant, so is the banking time. These balanced-growth conditions also make the banking time homogeneous of degree one with respect to m_t and c_t.

The interest elasticity of m_t/c_t, or of the money demand normalized by consumption, is denoted by η_a^R, and given by $\eta_a^R = -[\gamma/(1-\gamma)](1 - a_t)/a_t$. As the interest rises, the credit to cash ratio, $(1 - a_t)/a_t$, rises and the normalized interest elasticity becomes more negative: $\partial\eta_a^R/\partial R_t = -R_t[\gamma/(1-\gamma)]^2(1-a_t)/(a_t)^2 < 0$. Its increasing elasticity with inflation is similar to that in the Cagan (1956) model. Or another way to see the interest elasticity is to write it in terms of the elasticity of substitution between the two inputs money and credit, denoted by ε. Following Gillman and Kejak (2005b), define this as $\in \equiv \left[\partial\left(\frac{ac}{(1-a)c}\right)/\partial\left(\frac{R}{\tilde{w}_t/\gamma A_d^{1/\gamma}}\right)\right]\left[\left(\frac{R}{\tilde{w}_t/\gamma A_d^{1/\gamma}}\right)/\left(\frac{ac}{(1-a)c}\right)\right]$, which is solved as $\in = -[\gamma/(1-\gamma)]/a$. Then with η_a^R denoting the interest elasticity of money demand (not normalized) and η_c^R *denoting the interest elasticity of consumption*, the interest elasticity of money can be written as a sum of the share of the substitute factor, credit, factored by the elasticity of substitution between money and credit, plus a scale effect:

$$\eta_m^R = (1-a) \in +\eta_c^R. \tag{53}$$

And at $R = 0$, the interest elasticity is zero since by equation (49) $l_d = 0$ and $\eta_c^R = [1/(1-\gamma)]\,(\tilde{w}_t l_d h c)/(1 + \tilde{w}_t l_d h/c) = 0$ and the share of credit is zero. As the nominal interest rate rises from zero the interest elasticity gradually rises in magnitude from zero.

6.4 The Ramsey optimum

Here the primal approach to optimal taxation (Ljungqvist and Sargent 2000) is used to express time t prices in terms of allocations (see Appendix 6.A.2).

From equations (34), (35), and (37)

$$\tilde{w}_t h_t = \frac{u_x(c_t, x_t)}{u_c(c_t, x_t) - u_x(c_t, x_t)b_c(c_t, m_t, h_t)}. \tag{54}$$

Equations (33), (34), and (37) imply that

$$R_t = \frac{u_x(c_t, x_t)b_m(c_t, m_t, h_t)}{u_x(c_t, x_t)b_c(c_t, m_t, h_t) - u_c(c_t, x_t)}. \tag{55}$$

From equations (34) and (35), and given that λ is constant for all t, it follows that $\lambda = u_x(c_0, x_0)/\tilde{w}_0 h_0$, and that, with equations (33) and (34),

$$e^{-\int_0^t \tilde{r}_s ds} = \frac{\tilde{w}_0 h_0}{u_x(c_0, x_0)} e^{-\rho t}[u_c(c_t, x_t) - u_x(c_t, x_t)b_c(c_t, m_t, h_t)]. \tag{56}$$

Assuming that $\tau_0^k = \tau_0^l = 0$, and using equations (19) and (20), this expression can be written as

$$e^{-\int_0^t f_k(k_s,\, l_s h_s)ds} = \frac{f_{lh}(k_0,\, l_0 h_0)h_0}{u_x(c_0,\, x_0)} e^{-\rho t}[u_c(c_t,\, x_t) - u_x(c_t,\, x_t)b_c(c_t,\, m_t,\, h_t)]. \tag{57}$$

Substituting equations (54), (55) and (57) into equations (28) and (46), and using the homogeneity properties of credit time function as given in equation (30), the implementability constraints can be derived as

$$\frac{u_x(c_0,\, x_0)[k_0 + m_0]}{f_{lh}(k_0,\, l_0 h_0)h_0} = \int_0^\infty e^{-\rho t}\, \{u_c(c_t,\, x_t)c_t - u_x(c_t,\, x_t)[l_t + b(c_t,\, m_t,\, h_t)]\}\, dt, \tag{58}$$

$$u_x(c_t,\, x_t) = H'(l_{ht}) \int_t^\infty e^{-\rho(s-t)} u_x(c_s,\, x_s)[l_s + b(c_s,\, m_s,\, h_s)]ds. \tag{59}$$

Equation (58) is the consumer's budget constraint with prices expressed in terms of allocations. The use of human capital accumulation constraint (59) is motivated by the fact that human capital accumulation occurs outside of the market and cannot be taxed. There is no tax instrument that can be used to make this Euler equation hold for an arbitrary allocation, and consequently it constitutes a constraint on the set of competitive allocations. One way to approach this problem was suggested by Jones, Manuelli, and Rossi (1997), who solve for the Ramsey (1927) plan without including this constraint and then check to see if it is satisfied by the first-order conditions to the planner's problem in the steady-state (see also Ljungqvist and Sargent (2000)). Alternatively, here the constraint is included in the maximization problem explicitly.

The Ramsey (1927) problem can be formulated as the social planner's maximization of the representative agent's utility (1) subject to the implementability constraints (58), (59) and the goods and time resource constraints. The goods resource constraint (22) can be combined with the time constraint (31) to give

$$Ak_t^a([1 - x_t - l_{ht} - b(c_s,\, m_s,\, h_s)]h_t)^{1-a} - c_t - \dot{k}_t - g_t = 0. \tag{60}$$

This gives the Ramsey problem of

$$\underset{c_t,\, x_t,\, m_t,\, l_t,\, l_{ht},\, h_t,\, k_t}{Max} \quad \mathcal{H} = \int_0^\infty u(c_t,\, x_t)dt \tag{61}$$

$$+\varphi_t\{Ak_t^a([1 - x_t - l_{ht} - b(c_t,\, m_t,\, h_t)]h_t)^{1-a} - c_t - \dot{k}_t - g_t\}$$

$$+ \Phi\left(\frac{u_x(c_0,\, x_0)[k_0 + m_0 + B_0/P_0]}{f_{lh}(k_0,\, l_0 h_0)h_0} - \right.$$

$$\left.\int_0^\infty e^{-\rho t}\{u_c(c_t,\, x_t)c_t - u_x(c_t,\, x_t)[l_t + b(c_t,\, m_t,\, h_t)]\}dt\right)$$

$$+ \Lambda_t \left(u_x(c_t, x_t) - H'(l_{ht}) \int_t^{\infty} e^{-\rho(s-t)} u_x(c_s, x_s)[l_s + b(c_s, m_s, h_s)]ds \right).$$

Lemma 1 *With positive resources, the optimum monetary policy in the endogenous growth economy with a "banking time" specification of the transaction costs function, is satisfied only if*

$$b_m(c_t, m_t, h_t) = 0. \quad (62)$$

proof. The first-order condition of the problem in equation (61) with respect to m_t is

$$b_m(c_t, m_t, h_t)\{-\varphi_t f_{lh}(k_t, l_t h_t)h_t + [\Phi e^{-\rho t} - \Lambda H'(l_{ht})]u_x(c_t, x_t)\} = 0. \quad (63)$$

The first-order conditions with respect to l_t is

$$[\Phi e^{-\rho t} - \Lambda H'(l_{ht})]u_x(c_t, x_t) = 0, \quad (64)$$

which can be substituted into equation (63) to give that

$$b_m(c_t, m_t, h_t)\varphi_t f_{lh}(k_t, l_t h_t)h_t = 0. \quad (65)$$

Case 1. Suppose that $b_m(c_s, m_s, h_s) \neq 0$. Then it would be true that

$$\varphi_t f_{lh}(k_t, l_t h_t)h_t = 0. \quad (66)$$

By equation (19) and the facts that labor and capital are limited, that k_t and h_t are growing at the balanced path growth rate, and that $c_t > 0$ because of Inada conditions on the utility function, so that l_t must be positive, it follows that $f_{lh}(k_t, l_t h_t) > 0$ and $h_t > 0$. And the shadow price of the real resource constraint must be positive since there are positive resources, as in equation (2), and insatiable utility, so that $\varphi_t > 0$. Thus this leads to a contradiction.

Case 2. $b_m(c_s, m_s, h_s) = 0$. Equation (30) implies that $b_m = A_{st}c_t(1/\gamma)[1 - (m_t/c_t)]^{(1/\gamma)-1}/h_t$. With $\gamma \in (0, 1)$, this case is satisfied when $m_t/c_t = a_t = 1$, which is feasible.

Corollary 1 *The Friedman rule of $R_t = 0$ holds at the Ramsey optimum.*

proof. By Lemma 1 $b_m(c_s, m_s, h_s) = 0$. This can be written as $b_m = -b/[(1 - a_t)c_t\gamma] = 0$. And since $(1 - a_t)c_t = d_t$ by equation (11), and $b(c_s, m_s, h_s) = l_{dt}$, then by equation (30), $b_m = -1/(\partial d_t/\partial l_{dt}) = 0$. This is the (negative) inverse of the marginal product of labor in the credit production. The Inada condition on credit production, $\lim_{l_{dt} \to 0} \partial d_t/\partial l_{dt} = \infty$, applies to equation (30) and so implies the satisfaction of the condition $b_m(c_s, m_s, h_s) = 0$ at $l_{dt} = 0$. With no labor in credit production, there is zero credit produced, and this implies by equation (5), (9), (10), and (11) that $a_t = 1$. In turn $a_t = 1$ implies by equations (10) and (50) that $R_t = 0$.

At the Friedman (1969) optimum, the amount of credit services provided (and inflation-tax avoidance) is zero. This in turn implies that Friedman optimum is part of the Ramsey (1927) optimal solution.

6.5 Discussion

In order for the Friedman (1969) rule to be Ramsey (1927) optimal the production of credit must show diminishing returns in terms of the labor input into the credit production function, or, of the banking time. The Inada conditions allow the marginal product to go to infinity as the labor time goes to zero.

The result is not sensitive to non-extreme values of the parameters of the variable cost credit technology. Extreme values of γ and A_d present corner solutions and equilibrium uniqueness problems. If the diminishing returns parameter is given by $\gamma = 1$, then the credit has a constant marginal cost equal to its average cost, and this would be equivalent to a linear production of credit with A_d equal to the constant marginal product of labor. Then there may be no unique equilibrium. If the nominal interest rate coincides with the marginal cost of credit, so that $R_t = w_t/A_d$, then the consumer's equilibrium choice between money and credit is arbitrary. If $R_t < w_t/A_d$, then the consumer uses only money; and if $R_t > w_t/A_d$, the consumer uses only credit and nominal prices are not well-defined. The Friedman (1969) rule would still be first best in these cases, since it would save on resources used in exchange (except when $A_d = \infty$ and credit is free of use as implicitly is the case in Lucas and Stokey (1983)). But if A_d is near zero in the CRS case, it is similar to making credit prohibitively expensive so that the economy is similar to the cash-only Lucas (1980) model. With no viable substitutes to money, the inflation tax then only distorts the consumption margin of goods to leisure and is no worse than a value-added tax on goods purchases.

Money demand is affected by γ and A_d in terms of how interest elastic it is. The effect of γ on the interest elasticity is ambiguous in general, while a higher A_d unambiguously makes the money demand more interest elastic at all inflation rates. Regardless of the particular non-extreme values of γ and A_d, the money demand still exhibits an increasing interest elasticity as the inflation rate rises, as in Cagan (1956), and as is critical in explaining a certain nonlinearity in the inflation-growth effect of the model and as in evidence (Gillman and Kejak 2005b). But the different non-extreme γ and A_d values do not affect the Ramsey (1927) analysis.

6.6 Conclusion

The chapter derives optimal monetary policy with commitment in an endogenous growth economy using an approach based on a price-theoretic description of money and credit. More explicit than the shopping time model in these connections, the consumer uses both credit and money as intermediate goods in producing the household consumption good. The production of credit allows us to relate the conditions for optimality of the Friedman (1969) rule to the underlying credit production technology. The optimality conditions are related directly to conditions for balanced growth (see also Alvarez, Kehoe, and Neumeyer (2004)); the consumption velocity of credit must also be constant on the balanced-growth path. Shifts in the parameters determining the credit velocity, such as in the productivity of credit during financial deregulation, can shift the credit velocity but do not affect the Ramsey analysis.

The chapter gives new intuition to the homogeneity assumption for Ramsey (1927) optimality of the Friedman (1969) rule. Credit use is zero in the optimum and the marginal productivity of credit is infinite at this point, although this is productivity only in avoiding the inflation tax. This bases the proof of the Friedman rule as Ramsey optimal upon the Inada conditions on the production function of credit while giving the intuition that there is no proclivity of the consumer to substitute towards credit at this point, since the interest elasticity of money demand is zero at the optimum.

The money demand implied by the credit technology has been supported with empirical evidence (see Mark and Sul, 2003 and Gillman and Otto, 2002) and is consistent with facets of the inflation experience along the balanced-growth path that also have empirical support (Gillman and Kejak, 2005b, Gillman, Harris, and Matyas, 2004, Gillman and Nakov, 2003).[4] This consistency strengthens the paper's intuition.

Appendix 6.A: derivation of equations

6.A.1 Wealth constraint (28)

From equation (17), add and subtract $r_t\, m_t$ to the RHS and solve for $\dot{k}_t + \dot{m}_t$. With the Fisher equation of interest rates this gives equation (24). Multiply both sides by $e^{-\int_0^t \tilde{r}_s ds}$ and integrate both sides over the infinite horizon:

$$e^{-\int_0^t \tilde{r}_s ds}[\dot{W}_t - \tilde{r}_t W_t]dt = e^{-\int_0^t \tilde{r}_s ds}[c_t + R_t m_t - \tilde{w}_t h_t l_t]dt. \tag{67}$$

The LHS of this equation can be written as

$$\begin{aligned}\int_0^\infty (e^{-\int_0^t \tilde{r}_s ds} W_t)dt &= \lim_{t\to\infty}(e^{-\int_0^t \tilde{r}_s ds} W_t) - e^{-\int_0^0 \tilde{r}_s ds} W_0 \\ &= \lim_{t\to\infty} e^{-\int_0^t \tilde{r}_s ds} m_t + \lim_{t\to\infty} e^{-\int_0^t \tilde{r}_s ds} k_t - (k_0 + m_0 + B_0/P_0). \end{aligned} \tag{68}$$

Imposing the transversality conditions (25) and (26) gives the wealth constraint (28).

6.A.2 Implementability conditions

Equations (33), (34) and (35) imply that

$$w_t h_t = \frac{e^{-\rho t} u_x(t)}{e^{-\rho t}[u_c(t) - u_x(t) b_c(t)]}, \tag{69}$$

which gives the equation (54).

Equation (34), (35), and (37) imply equation (55).

Equation (33), (34) and (36) imply that

$$\lambda = \frac{e^{-\rho t} u_x(t)}{e^{-\int_0^t \tilde{r}_s ds} w_t h_t}. \tag{70}$$

At time 0, the constant λ is given by

$$\lambda = \frac{u_x(0)}{w_0 h_0}. \tag{71}$$

This implies equation (56):

$$e^{-\int_0^t \tilde{r}_s ds} = \frac{w_0 h_0}{u_x(0)} e^{-\rho t}[u_c(t) - u_x(t) b_c(t)]. \tag{72}$$

To get equation (59), take equation (45) and substitute in for prices from the from equations (54), (55), and (57). Also note that $e^{-\int_t^s \tilde{r}_\xi d\xi} = (e^{-\int_s^t \tilde{r}_\xi d\xi})^{-1}$. Then from equation (56),

$$e^{-\int_t^s \tilde{r}_\xi d\xi} = (e^{-\int_s^t \tilde{r}_\xi d\xi})^{-1} = \frac{u_x(s)}{w_s h_s} e^{-(s-t)\rho} \frac{1}{u_c(t) - u_x(t) b_c(t)}; \tag{73}$$

and this gives that

$$\frac{u_x(t)}{u_c(t) - u_x(t) b_c(t)} = H'(l_{ht}) \int_t^\infty \{\frac{u_x(s)}{w_s h_s} e^{-\rho(s-t)} \frac{w_s h_s [l_s + b_s]}{u_c(t) - u_x(t) b_c(t)}\} ds. \tag{74}$$

And that implies equation (59).

Notes

* Gillman, Max, and Oleg Yerokhin (2005). 'Ramsey-Friedman Optimality in a Banking Time Economy', *Berkeley Electronic Journals in Macroeconomics: Topics*, 5(1), article 16.

1 The framework is developed in Gillman and Kejak (2005b).
2 In Aiyagari, Braun, and Eckstein (1998) the ray is assumed to have a slope not necessarily equal to one; this is crucial for their imposition in equilibrium of an exogenous money demand function.
3 It is a Hicks (1935) suggestion to have the agent "act in part as a bank".
4 See also Aiyagari, Braun, and Eckstein (1998) and Eckstein and Leiderman (1992) who use a Cagan money demand to explain banking and seignoirage respectively.

Part II

Money demand and velocity

7 The demand for bank reserves and other monetary aggregates*

Max Gillman and Michal Kejak†

Summary

The chapter starts with Haslag's (1998) model of the bank's demand for reserves and reformulates it with a cash-in-advance approach for both financial intermediary and consumer. This gives a demand for a base of cash plus reserves that is not sensitive to who gets the inflation tax transfer. It extends the model to formulate a demand for demand deposits, yielding an M1-type demand, and then includes exchange credit, yielding an M2-type demand. Based on the comparative statics of the model, it provides an interpretation of the evidence on monetary aggregates. This explanation relies on the nominal interest as well as technology factors of the banking sector. (JEL E31, E13, O42)

7.1 Introduction

Modeling the monetary aggregates in general equilibrium has been a challenge. There are some examples such as Chari et al. (1996), and Gordon et al. (1998), who present models that are compared to Base money. Ireland (1995) presents one that he relates to M1-A velocity. These models have been employed as ways to explain the actual monetary aggregate time-series evidence. However, McGrattan (1998), for example, argues that the simple linear econometric model in which velocity depends negatively on the nominal interest rate may do just as well or better in explaining the evidence.

The article here takes up the topic by modeling a nesting of the aggregates that uses a set of factors that expands from the nominal interest rate by including the production of banking services. Through this approach the productivity factor of banking enters, as well as a cost to using money, sometimes thought of as a convenience cost. With this general equilibrium model, and its comparative statics, an explanation of velocity is provided that depends in part on the nominal interest rate, similar in spirit to McGrattan (1998). Also using technology factors, we explain U.S. evidence on monetary base velocity, M1 velocity, and M2 velocity, as well as for the ratios of various aggregates. This more extended explanation than previous work highlights the limits to a nominal interest rate story, while revealing a plausible role of technological factors in determining the aggregate mix.

The original literature on the welfare cost of inflation, well-represented by Bailey (1992), assumes no cost to banks in increasing their exchange services as consumers flee from currency during increasing inflations.[1] Similarly, Johnson (1969) and Marty (1969) assume no real costs for banks in producing "inside money."[2] The approach here builds on the more recent literature of Gillman (1993), Aiyagari et al. (1998), and Lucas (2000) that assumes resource costs to avoiding the inflation tax by using alternative exchange means. In particular, we specify production functions for banking instruments, both demand deposits (inside money) and credit, that require real resource use. This gives rise to the role of banking productivity factors in explaining the movement of aggregates.[3]

The next section reviews Haslag's (1998) model and shows how it is sensitive to the distribution of the lump sum inflation proceeds. This sensitivity makes tentative the growth effect of inflation with the model. The demand for reserves can be made insensitive to the distribution of the inflation tax transfer by framing it within a model in which the bank must hold money in advance as in the timing of transactions that is pioneered in Lucas (1980). This is done in section 7.3 using Haslag's (1998) notation, Ak production technology, and full savings intermediation. The resulting real interest rate depends negatively on the nominal interest rate, so inflation negatively affects the growth rate, similar in fashion to the central result of Haslag (1998). A parallel consumer cash-in-advance demand for goods is also added, as in Chari et al. (1996), to give a model of reserves plus currency.

The chapter then expands the model to give a formulation of the demand for the base plus non-interest-bearing demand deposits, or an aggregate similar to M1.[4] Following a credit production approach used in a series of related works (see Gillman and Kejak 2002; Gillman et al. 2004; Gillman and Nakov 2003), we then add credit, or interest-bearing demand deposits, to give a formulation for an aggregate similar to M2.

7.2 Sensitivity to lump transfers

In Haslag (1998), all savings funds are costlessly intermediated into investment by the bank. The bank must hold reserves in the form of money. This gives rise to a bank demand for money to meet reserve requirements on the savings deposits. The consumer-agent does not use money, although the lump sum inflation tax is transferred to the agent. Instead the agent simply holds savings deposits at the bank and earns interest as the bank intermediates all investment. The bank's return is lowered by the need to use money for reserves. Further, the timing of the model is such that inflation decreases the real return to depositors, and therefore also the growth rate, through the requirement that reserves be held as money.

The following model gives the reported result in Haslag (1998).[5]

With the gross return on invested capital being $1 + A - \delta$, as in an Ak model, with the time t capital stock denoted by k_t, the savings deposits denoted by d_t, the nominal money stock by M_t, the price level by P_t, and the net return paid on deposits denoted by r_t, the nominal profits are given as

$$\Pi_t = P_t(1 + A - \delta)k_t + M_{t-1} - P_t(1 + r_t)d_t. \tag{1}$$

This is stated as a maximization problem with respect to k_t, M_{t-1}, d_t and subject to two constraints. The constraints (with equality imposed) are that the sum of capital and last periods real balances equals deposits:

$$k_t + M_{t-1}/P_{t-1} = d_t, \tag{2}$$

and that a fraction γ_{t-1}, given in the last period, of time t deposits is held as real money balances in time $t - 1$:

$$M_{t-1}/P_{t-1} = \gamma_{t-1}d_t. \tag{3}$$

Assuming zero profit, this yields through simple substitution the return reported by Haslag (1998):

$$1 + r_t = (1 + A - \delta)(1 - \gamma_{t-1}) + \gamma_{t-1}(P_{t-1}/P_t). \tag{4}$$

The result is sensitive to who gets the lumpsum cash transfer from the government. If the transfer instead goes to the bank, the only user of money in the model, then there is no growth effect of inflation. This can be seen in the following way: Let the money supply process be given as in Haslag (1998) as $M_t = M_{t-1} + H_{t-1}$, where H_{t-1} is the lump-sum transfer by the government. With the transfer given to the bank, the profit of equation (1) becomes

$$\Pi_t = P_t(1 + A - \delta)k_t + M_{t-1} + H_{t-1} - P_t(1 + r_t)d_t. \tag{5}$$

Let the balanced growth rate of the economy be denoted by g_t, and the consumer's time preference by ρ, whereby the consumer's problem in Haslag (1998) with log utility gives that $1 + g_t = (1 + r_t)/(1 + \rho)$. With this growth rate in mind, the zero profit equilibrium now gives a rate of return to depositors of

$$1 + r_t = (1 + A - \delta)(1 - \gamma_{t-1}) + \gamma_t(1 + g_t), \tag{6}$$

and there is no inflation tax on the return or on the growth rate.

Alternatively let the profit function be given as equation (5). Then assume that the stock and reserve constraints, equations (2) and (3), are all in terms of current period variables, as in a standard cash-in-advance economy where here the reserve constraint now would look like a Clower (1967) type of constraint. Substituting in M_t for $M_{t-1} + H_{t-1}$, then, the model is exactly as in Chari et al. (1996). This gives the result, also found in Einarsson and Marquis (2001), that

$$1 + r_t = (1 + A - \delta)(1 - \gamma_t) + \gamma_t. \tag{7}$$

The return is lowered because reserves are idle, but there is no inflation tax.

7.3 Models of monetary aggregates

7.3.1 Monetary base

The financial intermediary has a demand for nominal money, denoted by M_t^r, as created by the need for reserves, with the reserve ratio denoted by $\gamma \in [0, 1]$. But here, as in Chari et al. (1996), the reserve constraint is considered as the bank's Clower (1967) constraint and structured accordingly in a fashion parallel to the consumer's, being that

$$M_t^r = \gamma P_t d_t. \tag{8}$$

In addition, the asset constraint adds together the current period real money stock with the current period capital stock to get the current period real deposits. In real terms this is written as

$$k_t + M_t^r / P_t = d_t. \tag{9}$$

Unlike Chari et al. (1996), the bank has to set aside cash-in-advance of the next period's accounting of the reserve requirement to meet any increase in its reserve requirements. The bank has revenue from its return on investment and costs from payment of interest to depositors, and from any increase in money holdings for reserves.

The technology for the output of goods, as in Haslag (1998), is an *AK* production function, making the current period profit function:

$$\Pi_t^r = P_t(1 + A - \delta)k_t + M_t^r - M_{t+1}^r - P_t d_t (1 + r_t). \tag{10}$$

The profit maximization problem is dynamic because of the way money enters the bank's profit function in two different periods, the same dynamic feature of the consumer problem. The competitive bank discounts the nominal profit stream by the nominal rate of interest, and maximizes the time 0 discounted stream, denoted by $\hat{\Pi}_0^r$, with respect to the real capital stock, k_t, the real deposits, d_t, and the money stock used for reserves, denoted by M_{t+1}^r, and subject to the Clower (1967) type of reserve and asset stock constraints of equations (8) and (9):

$$\underset{d_t, M^r_{t+1}, k_t}{Max}\ \hat{\Pi}^r_0 = \sum_{t=0}^{\infty} \prod_{i=1}^{t} (1/[1 + R_i])^t \{[P_t(1 + A - \delta)k_t$$

$$+ M^r_t - M^r_{t+1} - P_t(1 + r_t)d_t] + \lambda_t[P_t d_t - M^r_t - P_t k_t]$$

$$+ \mu_t[M^r_t - \gamma P_t d_t]\}. \tag{11}$$

Assuming a constant money supply growth rate, so that the nominal interest rate is constant over time, the first-order conditions imply that the rate of return is

$$1 + r = (1 + A - \delta)(1 - \gamma) - \gamma R. \tag{12}$$

Using the Fisher equation of nominal interest rates (presented in [17]), with equation (12) shows that there is a negative effect of inflation on the return. Combined with the consumer's problem and the derivation of the balanced-growth rate as depending on the real interest rate, inflation therefore causes a negative effect on the balanced-path growth rate.

The bank does not receive any lump-sum transfer from the government; the consumer-agent receives it all. However, the distribution only affects how much profit the intermediary makes. Because the profit is transferred to the consumer, just as is the lump-sum transfer of inflation proceeds, the distribution of the inflation proceeds between the bank and the consumer can be changed without affecting the allocation of resources in the economy. For example, if the intermediary gets part of the inflation proceeds transfer, by an amount at time t equal to $M^r_{t+1} - M^r_t$, then in equilibrium the money terms cancel from the profit function, and $\Pi^r_t/(P_t k_k) = R[\gamma/(1 - \gamma)]$. At the Friedman optimum, this profit is zero.[6]

Consider a consumer problem as in Haslag (1998) except that now the consumer uses cash, as in Lucas (1980). The problem then includes the setting aside of the consumer's cash-in-advance of trading in the next period, denoted by M^c_{t+1}, and the receipt of the lump-sum government transfer of inflation proceeds, denoted by H_t.

The consumer's Clower (1967) constraint is

$$M^c_t = P_t c_t. \tag{13}$$

The consumer also makes real (time) deposits, denoted by d_t, with the real return, denoted by r_t, as the form of all savings and wholly intermediated through banks, as in Haslag (1998). This involves choosing the next period deposits d_{t+1} and receiving as real income $(1 + r_t)d_t$. The nominal current period profit of the intermediation bank, Π^r_t, is received by the consumer each period as a lump-sum income source. This makes the consumer current period budget constraint of income minus expenditures as in the following:

$$P_t(1 + r_t)d_t + H_t + \Pi^r_t + M^c_t - M^c_{t+1} - P_tc_t - P_td_{t+1} = 0. \tag{14}$$

The problem is to maximize the time preference discounted stream of current period utility, where $\beta \equiv 1/(1 + \rho)$ denotes the discount factor, subject to the income and Clower (1967) constraints:

$$\underset{c_t, d_{t+1}, M^c_{t+1}}{Max} \; L = \sum_{t=0}^{\infty} \beta^t \{u(c_t) + \lambda_t [P_t(1 + r_t)d_t$$

$$+ H_t + \Pi^r_t + M^c_t - M^c_{t+1} - P_tc_t - P_td_{t+1}] + \mu_t [M^c_t - P_tc_t]\}. \tag{15}$$

The first-order conditions are

$$u_{c_t} = \lambda_t P_t(1 + \mu_t/\lambda_t), \tag{16}$$

$$\lambda_t/(\lambda_{t+1}\beta) = (1 + r_{t+1})(1 + \pi_{t+1}) \equiv (1 + R_{t+1}),^7 \tag{17}$$

$$\lambda_t/(\lambda_{t+1}\beta) = 1 + \mu_{t+1}/\lambda_{t+1}. \tag{18}$$

These imply that

$$u_{c_t} = \lambda_t P_t(1 + R_t), \tag{19}$$

so that the nominal interest rate is the shadow exchange cost of buying a unit's worth of consumption. Using this latter equation to form an Euler equation, then along the balanced-growth equilibrium with log utility it follows that the growth rate of consumption, where $1 + g_{t+1} = c_{t+1} / c_t$, is constant and given by

$$1 + g = (1 + r)/(1 + \rho). \tag{20}$$

The demand for money is given by the Clower (1967) constraint, $M^c_t = P_tc_t$. This standard Lucas (1980) demand function can be thought of as a demand for "currency," in this, the simplest version of the model.

The total demand for money is the sum of the bank's and the consumer's, and this is set equal to the total money supply as a condition of market clearing in equilibrium:

$$M^r_t + M^c_t \equiv M^b_t. \tag{21}$$

The total money supply equation is that this period's money base, denoted by M^b_t, plus the lump-sum transfer equal next period's base supply of money:

$$M_t^b + H_t = M_{t+1}^b. \tag{22}$$

Assume that the money supply growth rate is constant at σ, where $\sigma \equiv H_t / M_t^b$.

7.3.2 M1

Now consider an extension in which the consumer suffers a nominal cost of using money that is proportional to the amount of cash used to make purchases. This can be thought of as the convenience cost of using money. This can be related to the average amount stolen in robberies by pick-pockets, lost by carelessness, and spent on protection against crime and carelessness. It can also be Karni's (1974) time costs or Baumol's (1952) shoe-leather costs. These costs can be affected by the availability of bank locations, and now ATM locations.[8] Let this amount be given by ϕM_t^c, with $\phi \in [0, 1]$. Second, assume that a second bank exists, a bank that supplies only non-interest-bearing deposits, denoted by $M_t^{dd,s}$ that can be used in exchange. This money can be thought of demand deposits as in the United States or as a debit card as is more common in Europe.[9] The bank charges a nominal fee of P_t^{dd} per unit of real deposits, so that it receives from the consumer total such receipts equal to $P_t^{dd}\ (M_t^{dd,s}/P_t)$; and the bank produces these non-interest-bearing deposits through a production process. The consumer receives from the deposit bank its nominal profit, denoted by Π_t^{dd}, the profit from the intermediation bank, and the lump-sum inflation tax transfer from the government. The consumer's demand for the real non-interest-bearing deposits is denoted by M_t^{dd}/P_t. Also, the consumer invests in capital that is rented out by the demand deposit bank at the rate of r_t, with this capital denoted by k_t^{dd}. This makes the bank similar to a "mutual" customer-owned bank, and its capital does not get intermediated through the savings deposit bank. The depreciation rate on this capital is assumed to be zero, so that the consumer invests in this capital each period by the amount of $k_{t+1}^{dd} - k_t^{dd}$.

The consumer chooses what fraction of purchases to be made with cash, denoted by $a_t^c \in [0, 1]$, and what fraction to be made with noninterest demand deposits, $a_t^{dd} \in [0, 1]$; where

$$a_t^c + a_t^{dd} = 1. \tag{23}$$

The Clower (1967) constraints become

$$M_t^c = a_t^c P_t c_t; \tag{24}$$

$$M_t^{dd} = (1 - a_t^c) P_t c_t. \tag{25}$$

The consumer problem now is

$$\underset{c_t, d_{t+1}, k_{t+1}^{dd}, M_{t+1}^c, M_{t+1}^{dd}, a_t^c}{Max} \quad L = \sum_{t=0}^{\infty} \beta^t \{u(c_t) + \lambda_t [P_t(1+r_t)d_t + H_t$$
$$+ \Pi_t^r + \Pi_t^{dd} + M_t^c + M_t^{dd} - M_{t+1}^c - \phi M_t^c - M_{t+1}^{dd} - (P_t^{dd}/P_t)M_t^{dd}$$
$$- P_t c_t - P_t d_{t+1} - P_t k_{t+1}^{dd} + P_t k_t^{dd}(1+r_t)] + \mu_t^u[M_t^c - a_t^c P_t c_t]$$
$$+ \mu_t^{dd}[M_t^{dd} - (1-a_t^c)P_t c_t]\}. \tag{26}$$

The first-order condition with respect to a_t^c gives that $\mu_t^{dd} = \mu_t^c$. In combination with the first-order conditions with respect to the two money stocks, M_{t+1}^c and M_{t+1}^{dd}, this implies that the interior solution satisfies

$$P_t^{dd}/P_t = \phi. \tag{27}$$

Note that the shadow cost of buying goods with cash is given by the marginal condition

$$u_{c_t} = \lambda_t P_t(1 + R_t + \phi), \tag{28}$$

so that the shadow exchange cost now is equal to $R_t + \phi$ instead of only R_t, as in the previous subsection.

The demands for the cash and for the demand deposits are given by the Clower (1967) constraints in equilibrium, where the a_t^c variable is determined by finding the equilibrium bank supply of demand deposits and setting this equal to the demand for demand deposits.

The original bank, the capital intermediation bank, has the same problem as stated previously. Now consider the specification for the production function of the new bank. This bank uses real resources in the process of producing demand deposits and so is costly, unlike the intermediation bank. With an $\hat{A}K$ type production function for the non-interest-bearing demand-deposit bank, it can be shown that the equilibrium would not be well defined. If the $\hat{A}$ parameter equals ϕ, then there is no unique equilibrium; and if $\hat{A}$ equals any other value, there is an equilibrium either with no demand for cash or with no demand for credit. A unique equilibrium is satisfied by specifying a diminishing returns technology whereby there is a margin at which the fixed ϕ is equal to the variable marginal cost of producing the demand deposits. Initially assume that the new demand deposit bank faces the following production function that is diminishing in its capital input. Denoting the shift parameter by $\hat{A}_{dd}$ and the capital input by k_t^{dd}, and with $a \in (0, 1)$, let the function be specified as

$$M_t^{dd,s}/P_t = \hat{A}_{dd}(k_t^{dd})^a. \tag{29}$$

The demand deposit bank gets revenue from "printing" new demand deposits, $M_{t+1}^{dd} - M_t^{dd}$, and from the fee the consumer pays for the services, and on the cost side rents capital from the consumer at the market real interest rate of r_t. The current period profit, Π_t^{dd}, is given as the revenue minus the costs,

$$\Pi_t^{dd} = (P_t^{dd}/P_t)M_t^{dd} - P_t r_t k_t^{dd} + M_{t+1}^{dd} - M_t^{dd}. \tag{30}$$

With a constant money supply growth rate, the nominal interest rate is constant at R and the deposit bank faces the following dynamic profit maximization problem:

$$\underset{d_t, M_{t+1}^{dd}, k_t}{Max} \ \hat{\Pi}_0^r = \sum_{t=0}^{\infty} \Pi_{i=1}^t (1/[1+R_i])^t\{[(P_t^{dd}/P_t)$$

$$\times M_t^{dd} - P_t r_t k_t^{dd} + M_{t+1}^{dd} - M_t^{dd}] + \lambda_t[P_t \hat{A}_{dd}(k_t^{dd})^a - M_t^{dd}]\}.$$

The first-order conditions imply that

$$R + (P_t^{dd}/P_t) = r_t/[\hat{A}_{dd}\alpha(k_t^{dd})^{a-1}], \tag{31}$$

which, when combined with the consumer's equilibrium condition (27), gives that

$$R + \phi = r_t/[\hat{A}_{dd}\alpha(k_t^{dd})^{a-1}]. \tag{32}$$

This equation sets the marginal cost of demand deposits to the marginal cost of capital divided by the marginal product of capital in producing demand deposits, a standard microeconomic pricing condition.[10]

Solving for the equilibrium capital stock,

$$k_t^{dd} = [\hat{A}_{dd}\alpha(R+\phi)/r_t]^{1/(1-a)}, \tag{33}$$

and substituting this into equation (29) gives the supply of demand deposits as

$$M_t^{dd,s}/P_t = \hat{A}_{dd}^{1/(1-a)}[a(R+\phi)/r_t]^{a/(1-a)}. \tag{34}$$

As the cost of using money $R + \phi$ falls due to a nominal interest falling toward $R = 0$, there is still production due to cost ϕ. If in addition ϕ goes to zero, the capital used in produced non-interest-bearing deposits, and the output also goes to zero, and then the consumer uses only cash.

Here $M_t^{dd,s}/P_t = M_t^{dd}/P_t$ and the M1 aggregate can be represented as follows:

$$M_t^c + M_t^{dd} \equiv M1_t. \tag{35}$$

The problem with this specification is that in the equilibrium, with a positive growth rate g_t, the ratio of M_t^c/M_t^{dd} is increasing toward infinity. Although there may be some trend in this ratio empirically, it should be explainable by changes in other exogenous factors that determine the ratio; with constant exogenous factors, theoretically the trend should be stable on the balanced growth path. To see that the ratio is not stable, equations (24) and (25) imply that $M_t^c/M_t^{dd} = a_t^c/(1 - a_t^c)$. The solution for a_t^c is found by setting equal the supply and demand from equations (25) and (34), giving that $a_t^c = 1 - [(\hat{A}_{dd}^{1/(1-a)}[a(R+\phi)/r_t]^{a/(1-a)})/c_t]$, with $r_t = (1 + A - \delta)(1 - \gamma) - \gamma R - 1$ by equation (12). This implies that $a_t^c/(1 - a_t^c) = \{1 - [(\hat{A}_{dd}^{1/(1-a)}[a(R+\phi)/r_t]^{a/(1-a)})/c_t]\}/\{\hat{A}_{dd}^{1/(1-a)}[a(R+\phi)/r_t]^{a/(1-a)}/c_t\}$, or $a_t^c/(1 - a_t^c) = \{c_t/(\hat{A}_{dd}^{1/(1-a)}[a(R+\phi)/r_t]^{a/(1-a)})\} - 1$. By inspection it is clear that with c_t rising when there is positive growth on the equilibrium path, and with the real interest rate being stable given that there is a stationary inflation rate, the ratio $a_t^c/(1 - a_t^c)$ also rises toward infinity toward a cash-only solution with no demand deposits.

An alternative production function that gives a stationary ratio of M_t^c/M_t^{dd} is one that includes an externality that affects the shift parameter $\hat{A}_{dd}$. In particular let $\hat{A}_{dd} = A_{dd}c_t^{1-a}$, so that the production function is CRS in terms of capital and goods consumption:

$$M_t^{dd,s}/P_t = A_{dd}c_t^{1-a}(k_t^{dd})^a. \tag{36}$$

This function is a type of positive externality in which the goods output is complementary to the bank's output; see also Romer (1986). It has the property that the share of goods bought with demand deposits, a_t^{dd}, is a function of the capital to goods ratio; by equations (23), (25), and (36),

$$a_t^{dd} = A_{dd}(k_t^{dd}/c_t)^a. \tag{37}$$

This means that the bank takes the aggregate consumption as given and demands capital and produces demand deposits in proportion to the aggregate consumption. Substituting the alternative production function into the profit maximization problem of equation (30), with $\hat{A}_{dd} = A_{dd}c_t^{1-a}$, the solution is

$$k_t^{dd}/c_t = [A_{dd}\,a\,(R+\phi)/r_t]^{1/(1-a)}. \tag{38}$$

From equations (37) and (38), the solution for the equilibrium share of demand deposits is

$$a_t^{dd} = A_{dd}^{1/(1-a)}[a(R+\phi)/r_t]^{a/(1-a)}.\text{[11]} \tag{39}$$

Figure 7.1 graphs the equilibrium for the demand deposit bank. To graph this, the current period profit function was solved along the balanced growth path. The dynamic nature of the bank problem brings the growth rate into the equilibrium profit function, which is substituted in for using equation (20). The resulting profit solution can be written as

$$\Pi_t^{dd}/[P_t\, c_t\, (\sigma + \phi)] = M_t^{dd}/(P_t c_t) - r(k_t^{dd}/c_t)/(\sigma + \phi), \tag{40}$$

which is graphed as the straight line in Figure 7.1.

With the production function of equation (36), the balanced-growth path exists and the ratio M_t^c/M_t^{dd} is stationary along it. Stationarity of M_t^c/M_t^{dd} follows directly, where it is shown that $M_t^c/M_t^{dd} = a_t^c/(1 - a_t^c)$. By equation (23) this can be written as $M_t^c/M_t^{dd} = (1 - a_t^{dd})/a_t^{dd}$ and by inspection of equation (39) can be seen to be stationary.

7.3.3 M2

The model can be expanded to its full form by allowing the agent the choice of using costly credit to make purchases, or "exchange credit," along with cash or non-interest-bearing demand deposits. Here the credit is like a credit card, such as the American Express card, rather than a debit card. The agent must pay a fee for this service that is proportional to the amount of the exchange credit; this is like the percentage fee paid by stores using the American Express card (without a rollover debt feature). Denoting the time t nominal amount of exchange credit demanded by the consumer by M_t^{cd}, and the nominal fee by P_t^{cd}, the consumer's expenditure on such fees is given by $(P_t^{cd}/P_t)M_t^{cd}$. The consumer again owns the exchange credit bank, receives the nominal profit, denoted by Π_t^{cd}, and rents nondepreciating capital k_t^{cd} and

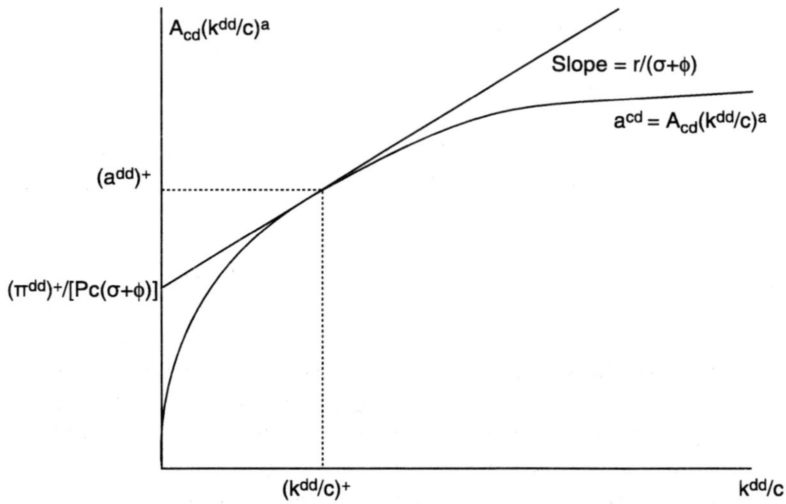

Figure 7.1 Equilibrium in the demand deposit bank sector.

invests in the capital each period by an amount $k^{cd}_{t+1} - k^{cd}_t$. The consumer must pay off the debt incurred using the exchange credit at the end of the period. But this credit saves the agent from having to set aside money in advance of trading, and so allows avoidance of the inflation tax. Now with three types of exchange, let the share of consumption good purchases made by cash and by non-interest-bearing demand deposits remain notated by a^c_t, and a^{dd}_t, and the share of consumption good purchases made by exchange credit by a^{cd}_t, where the shares sum to one:

$$a^c_t + a^{dd}_t + a^{cd}_t = 1 \tag{41}$$

This adds a third Clower (1967) constraint to the consumer's problem, allowing the three constraints to be written as

$$M^c_t = P_t c_t a^c_t, \tag{42}$$

$$M^{dd}_t = P_t c_t a^{dd}_t, \tag{43}$$

$$M^{cd}_t = P_t c_t (1 - a^c_t - a^{dd}_t). \tag{44}$$

The consumer problem now buys goods with cash or demand deposits as before, but also has a debit of $a^{cd}_t P_t c_t$ for credit purchases, and has a debit of $(P^{cd}_t / P_t) M^{cd}_t$ due to the credit fee.

This makes the consumer problem

$$\underset{c_t, d_{t+1}, k^{dd}_{t+1}, k^{cd}_{t+1}, M^c_{t+1}, M^{dd}_{t+1}, M^{cd}_t, a^c_t, a^{dd}_t}{Max} \quad L$$

$$\begin{aligned} = \sum_{t=0}^{\infty} \beta^t \{ & u(c_t) + \lambda_t [P_t(1 + r_t) d_t + H_t + \Pi^r_t + \Pi^{dd}_t + \Pi^{cd}_t + M^c_t + M^{dd}_t \\ & - M^c_{t+1} - P_t k^{dd}_{t+1} + P_t k^{dd}_t (1 + r_t) - P_t k^{cd}_{t+1} + P_t k^{cd}_t (1 + r_t) - \phi M^c_t \\ & - M^{dd}_{t+1} - (P^{dd}_t / P_t) M^{dd}_t - (P^{cd}_t / P_t) M^{cd}_t - P_t c_t - P_t d_{t+1}] \\ & + \mu^c_t [M^c_t - a^c_t P_t c_t] + \mu^{dd}_t [M^{dd}_t - a^{dd}_t P_t c_t] \\ & + \mu^{cd}_t [M^{cd}_t - (1 - a^c_t - a^{dd}_t) P_t c_t] \}. \end{aligned} \tag{45}$$

The first-order conditions imply that the interior solution satisfies

$$P^{dd}_t / P_t = \phi \tag{46}$$

$$P^{cd}_t / P_t = R + \phi, \tag{47}$$

and the shadow cost goods is again, as in the last section, given by

$$u_{c_t} = \lambda_t P_t (1 + R_t + \phi). \tag{48}$$

Denote the name for the exchange credit banking firm as Amex. Amex is assumed to supply the exchange credit, denoted by $M_t^{cd,s}$ using only capital, denoted by k_t^{cd} in a diminishing returns fashion similar to the technology for the demand deposit bank. Although this technology could be given as $(M_t^{cd,s}/P_t) = \hat{A}_{cd}(k_t^{cd})^{\theta}$, where $\hat{A}_{cd} > 0$ and $\theta \in (0, 1)$, for a general diminishing returns case, the problem would arise that the equilibrium share of the Amex credit would trend down toward zero if there was a positive growth rate g_t, making infeasible the existence of a balanced-growth path. Therefore consider a technology similar to equation (36), which gives a stable share of exchange credit in purchases. In particular, let the function be specified with a complementary goods externality that affects the shift parameter $\hat{A}_{cd}$, whereby $\hat{A}_{cd} = A_{cd}c^{1-\theta}$, so that

$$M_t^{cd,s}/P_t = A_{cd}c_t^{1-\theta}(k_t^{cd})^{\theta}. \tag{49}$$

The profit maximization problem is static and given by

$$\underset{k_t^{cd}}{Max}\ \Pi_t^{cd} = P_t^{cd}\ A_{cd}c_t^{1-\theta}\ (k_t^{cd})^{\theta} - P_t r_t k_t^{cd}. \tag{50}$$

The equilibrium conditions of the consumer and Amex bank imply that

$$R_t + \phi = P_t^{cd}/P_t = r_t/[A_{cd}\theta(k_t^{cd}/c_t)^{\theta-1}]; \tag{51}$$

$$k_t^{cd}/c_t = [A_{cd}\theta(R_t + \phi)/r_t]^{1/(1-\theta)}. \tag{52}$$

This means that as the nominal interest rate rises, the Amex bank expands credit supply and k_t^{cd}/c_t rises in equilibrium. *It means that the marginal costs of exchange are equated to* $R + \phi$ *across all of the different forms of exchange*, being cash, demand deposits, or credit. This equalization of the marginal costs of the various means of exchange, the basis of Baumol's (1952) equilibrium, is one of the most important features of the general equilibrium.

Equating the supply and demand for the Amex credit, from equations (44) and (49), and using equation (51), the share of exchange credit can be found to be

$$a_t^{cd} = A_{cd}^{1/(1-\theta)}\ [\theta(R_t + \phi)/r_t]^{\theta/(1-\theta)}, \tag{53}$$

also rising as the nominal interest rate goes up. Note that by substituting equation (53) into equation (41), so that $1 - a_t^{cd} = a_t^{c} + a_t^{dd}$, and then substituting in equation (39), the solution for a_t^c is found.[12]

Figure 7.2 illustrates the equilibrium for the credit bank. At the Friedman optimum of $R = 0$, some credit would still be provided as long as $\phi > 0$. This use of credit at $R = 0$ contrasts to zero such use of credit in Gillman (1993), Ireland (1994b), and Gillman and Kejak (2002).

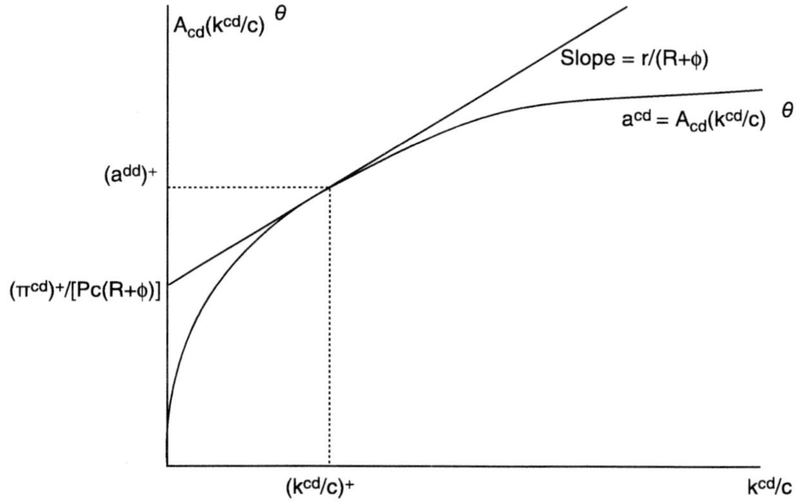

Figure 7.2 Equilibrium in the credit bank sector.

The money market clearing condition here is that the demand for the exchange credit equals the supply of the exchange credit. This can also be further aggregated to

$$M_t^c + M_t^{dd} + M_t^{cd} \equiv M2_t, \tag{54}$$

and can be considered an aggregate like M2. It includes the monetary base, demand deposits, plus the exchange credit that allows funds to collect interest during the period, as do certificates of deposit, and is then paid off with "money market mutual funds" invested in short-term government securities. So it is a mixed set of non-interest-bearing aggregates that suffer the inflation tax and are traditionally thought of as money-like in nature, and of the Amex credit and money market accounts that avoid the inflation tax, unlike "money."

7.4 Changes in aggregates over time

The model of M2 can be used to analyze how subsets of aggregates change according to changes in exogenous factors. In particular the focus is on changes in the money supply growth rate, σ, or more simply in the nominal rate of interest because this is given by $R = \sigma + \rho + \rho\sigma$. Also the focus is on changes in the banking productivity parameters A_{dd} and A_{cd}, and the banking cost parameter ϕ. Comparative statics of these factors are then applied to explain the actual profiles of the velocity of monetary aggregates, and the profiles of their ratios.

The explanation of the aggregates relies on changes in productivity that result from changes in U.S. bank law. This approach can be formalized by adding a proportional tax to the credit firm's proceeds from selling the credit, denoted by τ, whereby the price received by the firm is $P_{cd}(1 - \tau)$. Now assume that the tax proceeds are destroyed, as regulations sometimes are modeled. Then the equilibrium is such that in equation (51) the productivity factor is factored by $(1 - \tau)$. An increase in regulations makes τ bigger, and effective (net) productivity smaller, whereas deregulation causes τ to decrease and effective (net) productivity to increase. The same regulations can likewise affect A_{dd}. Now consider the following brief review of major U.S. deregulatory laws in banking to indicate how and when the effective productivity factor might shift.

7.4.1 Financial deregulation and increases in bank productivity

Significant U.S. financial deregulation manifested with the Depository Institutions Deregulation and Monetary Control Act of 1980, the Garn-St. Germain Financial Modernization Act of 1982, the Riegle-Neal Interstate Banking and Branching Efficiency Act of 1994, and the Gramm-Leach-Bliley Act of 1999. The 1980 law phased out interest ceilings and allowed banks to pay more interest on deposits. The 1982 law allowed banks to offer money market accounts to compete with mutual funds. The 1994 act allowed national bank branching and consolidation:

> Congress passed significant reform legislation in the 1990s. In 1994, the Riegle-Neal interstate Banking and Branching Efficiency Act repealed the McFadden Act of 1927 and Douglas Amendments of 1970, which had curtailed interstate banking. In particular, the McFadden Act, seeking to level the playing field between national and state banks with respect to branching, had effectively prohibited interstate branch banking. Starting in 1997, banks were allowed to own and operate branches in different states. This immediately triggered a dramatic increase in mergers and acquisitions. The banking system began to consolidate and for the first time form true national banking institutions, such as Bank of America, formed via the merger of BankAmerica and NationsBank.
>
> (Guzman 2003).

The 1999 law permitted mergers between banks, brokerage houses, and insurance companies, "allowing banking organizations to merge with other types of financial institutions under a financial holding company structure" (Hoenig 2000).

7.4.2 Comparative statics and comparison to the evidence

The income velocity of money is defined as income divided by a particular monetary aggregate. The income in the economy comes from the goods production function; this makes it equal to $(A - \delta)k_t$, which equals $(A - \delta)(1 - \gamma)d_t$. The velocity of the monetary aggregates can then be defined as $(A - \delta)(1 - \gamma)d_t/M_t^b$.

PROPOSITION 1. *Given* $g = 0$, *and along the balanced growth path, the base money velocity rises with the nominal interest rate, or*

$$\partial[(A - \delta)(1 - \gamma)d_t/M_t^b]/\partial R > 0.$$

Proof. The solution for the base velocity is

$$(A - \delta)(1 - \gamma)d_t/M_t^b = [(A - \delta)(1 - \gamma)(d_t/c_t)]/[1 - a^{dd} - a^{cd} + \gamma(d_t/c_t)],$$

where $a^{dd} = A_{dd}^{1/(1-\alpha)}[\alpha(R + \phi)/r]^{\alpha/(1-\alpha)}$, $a^{cd} = A_{cd}^{1/(1-\theta)}[\theta(R + \phi)/r]^{\theta/(1-\theta)}$, $r = (A - \delta)(1 - \gamma) - \gamma(1 + R)$, $(1 + g) = (1 + r)/(1 + \rho)$, and $d_t/c_t = [1 + \phi(1 - a^{dd} - a^{cd}) + g(k_t^{dd} + k_t^{cd})/c_t]/[(A - \delta)(1 - \gamma) - g - \gamma]$. At $g = 0$, $d_t/c_t = [1 + \phi(1 - a^{dd} - a^{cd})]/[(A - \delta)(1 - \gamma) - \gamma]$ and $(A - \delta)(1 - \gamma)d_t/M_t^b = (A - \delta)(1 - \gamma)/\{[(A - \delta)(1 - \gamma) + \gamma]/([1/(1 - a^{dd} - a^{cd})] + \phi) + \gamma\}$.

Substituting in for a^{dd}, a^{cd}, it can be seen that $\partial[(A - \delta)(1 - \gamma)d_t/M_t^b]/\partial R > 0$.

Note that the solution of d_t/c_t, requires substituting into the budget constraint of the problem in equation (45), using equations (10), (30), (41), (42), (50).

Figure 7.3 shows the post-1959 U.S. base money velocity and the 10-year bond, U.S. Treasury, interest rate. McGrattan (1998) presents such a graph and argues, in her comment on Gordon et al. (1998), that the nominal interest rate goes a long way to explaining base money velocity.[13] And this is implication of the result of Proposition 1. The difference from McGrattan (1998) is that she uses a simple linear econometric equation, as found in Meltzer (1963) and Lucas (1988a), to argue that the nominal interest rate has a direct effect on velocity. Here the velocity is derived analytically to make the point from the general equilibrium perspective.[14]

Comparative statics for the other factors, A_{cd}, A_{dd}, and ϕ, are ambiguous in general because of the d_t/c_t, factor, but holding d_t/c_t constant then all three factor have a positive effect on base velocity. This positive direction of the effect of these factors is also readily apparent in calibrations. Although these other factors do not provide any obvious help in interpreting base velocity empirical evidence, they do provide an explanation as based on the model of the evidence on the ratio of reserves to currency.

Figure 7.4 shows the post-1959 U.S. reserves/currency ratio against the long-term interest rate. There is a marked trend down, with a flattening out

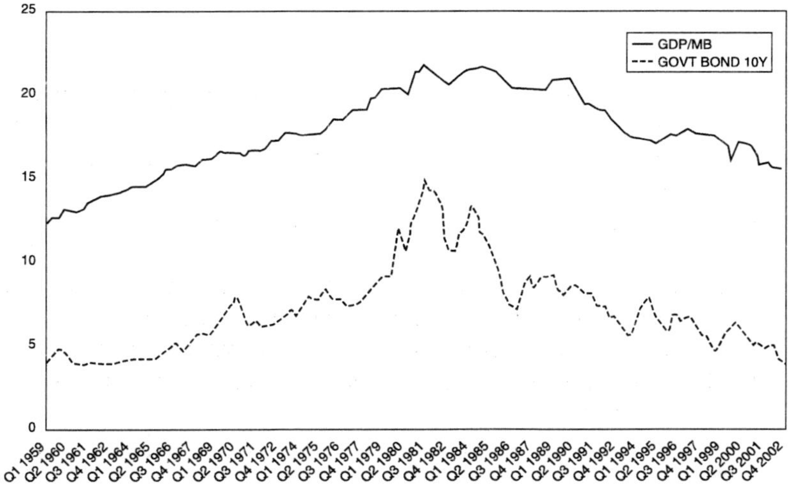

Figure 7.3 U.S. base velocity and nominal interest rates: 1959–2003.

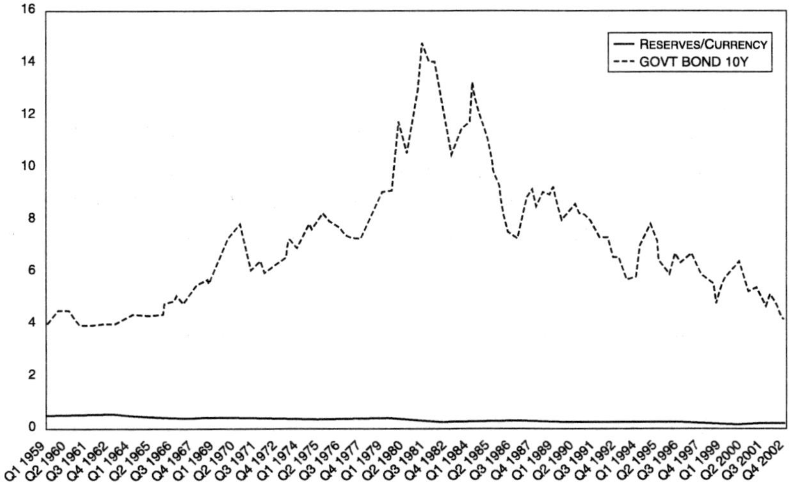

Figure 7.4 U.S. reserves to currency ratio and interest rates: 1959–2003.

period during the 1980s, and a rather more pronounced downward direction after 1994. In the model, M_t^r / M_t^c is the notation for the reserves to currency ratio and is given $M_t^r / M_t^c = \gamma d_t / c_t / (1 - a^{dd} - a^{cd})$. With d_t / c_t held constant, the reserves to currency ratio rises with increases in each R, ϕ, A_{dd}, and A_{cd}. Because the U.S. reserves/currency trend is downward and the effect of the nominal interest is upward in the 1959–81 period, it appears that the nominal interest plays no role in explaining this ratio. In contrast, the hypothesis of a downward trend in the cost of using money, ϕ, serves well to explain the evidence.

M1 velocity is defined by $(A-\delta)(1-\gamma)\ d_t/M1_t = [(A-\delta)(1-\gamma)(d_t/c_t)]/(1-a_t^{cd})$. With d_t/c_t held constant, along the balanced growth path, M1 velocity rises with the nominal interest rate because a_t^{cd} rises. Similarly, an increase in A_{cd} and ϕ cause M1 velocity to go up.

Figure 7.5 shows the U.S. M1 velocity and the 10-year U.S. Treasury interest rate from 1959 to 2003. The rise in velocity from 1959 to 1981 is consistent with the rise in the nominal interest rate. While still following changes in the nominal interest rate in the 1980s, M1 velocity appears to level off rather than fall during this period by as much as would be expected from the decrease in the nominal interest rate. Deregulation of the 1980s, and an associated increase in A_{cd} presents an explanation of the leveling off of velocity in the 1980s. The striking trend upward in velocity after 1994 is consistent with an accelerated increase in A_{cd} that can be from the deregulation of interstate branching that led to national branching and the diffusion of ATMs, as well as the banking consolidation because of the 1999 act. Thus the two factors of the nominal interest rates and the banking productivity each play a distinct role in this explanation.[15]

A way to see further into the M1 velocity profile is to look at the ratio of its components, currency and demand deposits. Analytically the demand deposit to currency ratio in the model is M^{dd}/M^c.

PROPOSITION 2. *The demand deposit to currency ratio, M_t^{dd}/M_t^c, rises with increases in each R, ϕ, A_{dd}, and A_{cd}.*

Proof. From equations (39), (41), (42), (43), (44), and (53), $M_t^{dd}/M_t^c = (A_{dd}^{1/(1-\alpha)}[\alpha(R+\phi)/r]^{\alpha/(1-\alpha)})/(1 - A_{dd}^{1/(1-\alpha)}[\alpha(R+\phi)/r]^{\alpha/(1-\alpha)} - A_{cd}^{1/(1-\theta)}[\theta(R+\phi)/r_t]^{\theta/(1-\theta)})$,

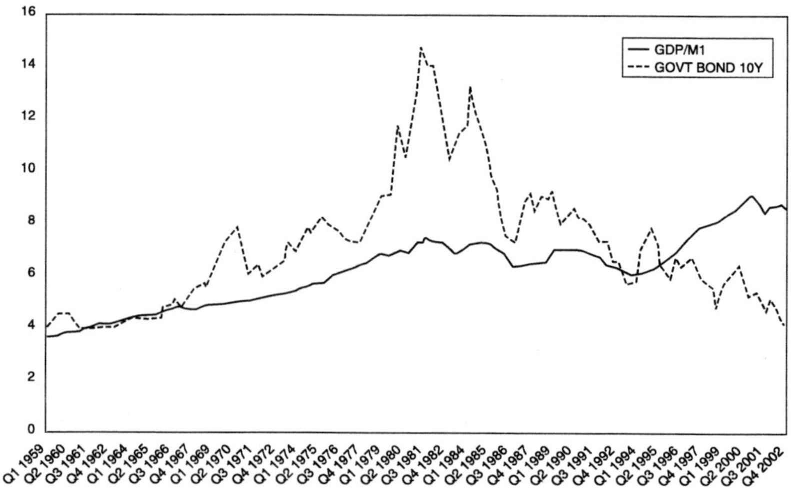

Figure 7.5 U.S. M1 velocity and nominal interest rates: 1959–2003.

and $\partial(M_t^{dd}/M_t^c)/\partial R > 0$, $\partial(M_t^{dd}/M_t^c)/\partial A_{cd} > 0$, $\partial(M_t^{dd}/M_t^c/\partial A_{dd} > 0$, and $\partial(M_t^{dd}/M_t^c)/\partial\phi > 0$.

Figure 7.6 shows the U.S. demand deposit to currency ratio and the 10-year U.S. Treasury interest rate for the same 1959–2003 period. In a first look, the ratio simply trends down. But looking more closely shows a simple trend down, from 1959 to 1981, that levels off in the 1980s, as with M1 velocity, and then moves down steadily post-1994 at an accelerated rate compared to the earlier period.

A downward trend in ϕ well explains the downward trend in the demand deposit to currency ratio in a way the nominal interest rate's pre-1981 upward trend and a possible upward trend in A_{cd} and A_{dd} cannot. However, the role of A_{cd} and A_{dd} again emerges as the only way to explain the leveling off of the trend in demand deposits to currency in the 1980s, when there was financial deregulation and a surge in A_{cd} and A_{dd}. Furthermore, the accelerated downward trend in the ratio after 1994 is consistent with an accelerated decrease in ϕ because of the ATM diffusion.[16]

Now consider the velocity of the broader aggregate M2. In the model, M2 velocity is defined by $(A-\delta)(1-\gamma)d_t/M2_t$. This is given by $(A-\delta)(1-\gamma)d/M2_t = (A-\delta)(1-\gamma)d_t/[c_t(a_t^c + a_t^{dd} + a_t^{cd})] = (A-\delta)(1-\gamma)(d_t/c_t)$.Thecomparative statics of the M2 velocity are therefore as the comparative statics of the ratio of savings to consumption. The effects of R, A_{cd}, A_{dd}, and ϕ are ambiguous in general, although with $g = 0$, it is true as shown that $\partial(d_t/c_t)/\partial R > 0$. But the (d_t/c_t) factor does not appear to play any significant role in the explanation of base or M1 velocity. Figure 7.7 indeed shows that U.S. M2 velocity has been remarkably constant relative to the 10-year U.S. Treasury bond rate. Thus the explanation from the model is that the magnitude of

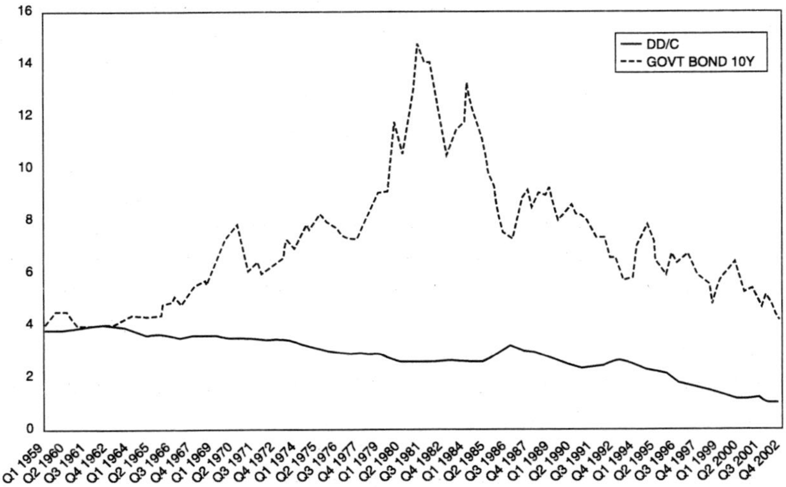

Figure 7.6 U.S. demand deposits to currency ratio and interest rates: 1959–2003.

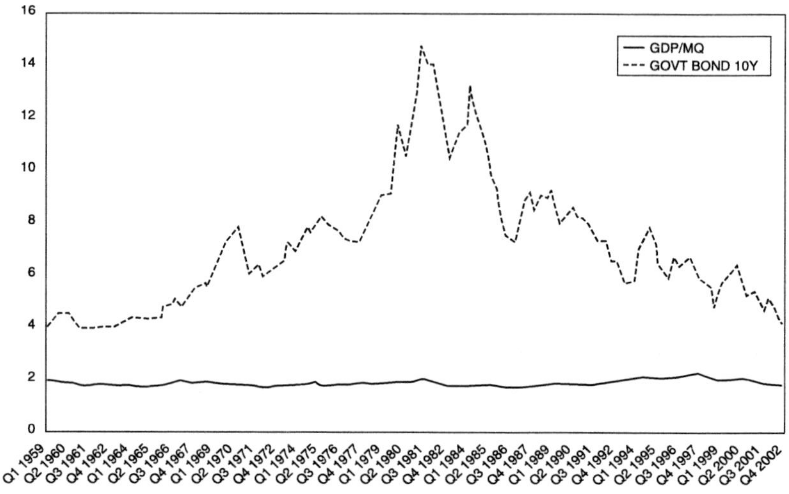

Figure 7.7 U.S. M2 velocity and nominal interest rates: 1959–2003.

changes in (d_t/c_t), because of the factors considered here, is small. It is easy to confirm this with calibrations, although this exercise is not reported. However, one aspect of this is worth noting. With a relatively unchanging d_t/c_t as the explanation for a stable M2 velocity, it is internally consistent with the previous analysis that the comparative statics of A_{cd}, A_{dd}, and ϕ, with d_t/c_t held constant, can be used to explain base and M1 velocity.

Breaking down the components of M2 is more revealing. Consider the ratio of M2 to M1. In the model this is given by $M2_t/M1_t = 1/[1 - A_{cd}^{1/(1-\theta)}[\theta(R+\phi)/r]^{\theta/(1-\theta)}]$.

PROPOSITION 3. *Along the balanced growth path, the ratio $M2_t/M1_t$ rises with an increase in the nominal interest rate, or $\partial(M2_t/M1_t)/\partial R > 0$.*

Proof. $\partial([1 - A_{cd}^{1/(1-\theta)}[\theta(R+\phi)/r]^{\theta/(1-\theta)}])/\partial R > 0$.

The other comparative statics with respect to A_{cd} and ϕ are ambiguous because of the d_t/c_t factor; holding d_t/c_t constant, the ratio $M2_t/M1_t$ rises with each of these. Now consider Figure 7.8, which shows the U.S. ratio of M2 to M1 from 1959 to 2003, along with the 10-year U.S. Treasury bond rate. Proposition 3 provides a way to explain the upward trend in M2/M1 from 1959 to 1981, and perhaps the fall in M2/M1 from 1990 to 1994. The leveling off of M2/M1 in the 1980s can be explained by financial deregulation and increases in A_{cd}; note that the downward change in R during this period, and a downward trend in ϕ during this period cannot explain the leveling off of M2/M1, because these factors work to make the ratio go down. The trend upward after 1994 again can be explained by upward increases in A_{cd} because of national branching being allowed, ATM diffusion, and consolidation.

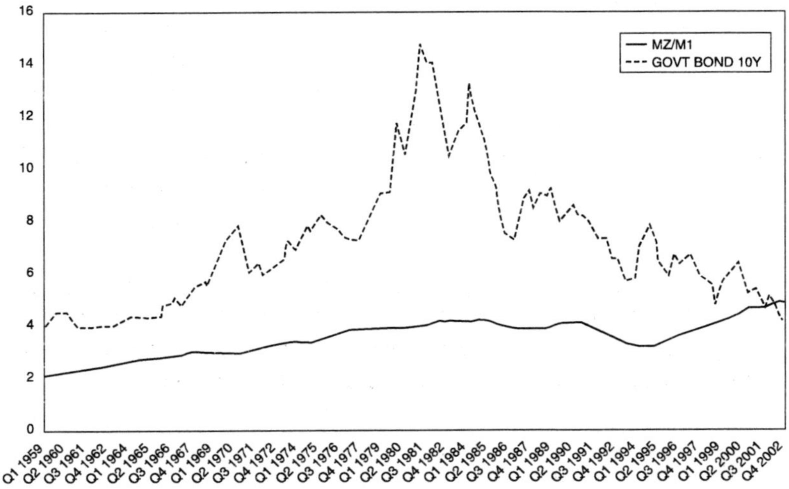

Figure 7.8 U.S. ratio of M2 to M1 and interest rates: 1959–2003.

7.5 Discussion

The demand for bank reserves that Haslag (1998) put forth helps pave the way for modeling the demand for a range of monetary aggregates. The model as revised here acts as a missing link that ties together conventional money demand functions from the cash-in-advance approach with an analog to the monetary aggregates widely studied, by adding a bank's demand for cash reserve. An inflation tax on the deposit rate of return results because, as in the cash-in-advance economies, the intermediation bank must in effect put aside cash-in-advance to meet the demands of the reserve requirement. This is similar to Stockman (1981) in which the Clower (1967) constraint is applied to all investment; here however, the intermediation bank's Clower (1967) constraint applies only to the reserve fraction of the investment.

On the basis of the intermediation bank's demand for reserves plus the imposition of a standard Clower (1967) constraint on the consumer's purchase of goods, the demand for an aggregate similar to the monetary base, reserves plus currency (cash), is constructed whereby the inflation rate can affect the real return to intermediated investment under an AK technology because of the need to hold cash reserves. This model is extended to include non-interest-bearing deposits, unlike previous work, and in a way that gives an aggregate analogous to $M1$. The model further is extended to include exchange credit, to give an aggregate analogous to $M2$. In this fully extended model comparative statics are presented for base, M1, and M2 velocity and the ratios of demand deposits to reserves, demand deposits to currency, and M2/M1. With these analytics the empirical evidence on both the velocities and various ratios of the aggregates are explained in an internally consistent way. This requires more than only the nominal interest rate. In addition the productivity of the credit bank sector plays a critical role in explaining aggregate movement during the financial deregulation era. The convenience cost of using money has a unique role in explaining the trends in the reserve to currency and in the demand deposit to currency ratios.

The models here enable the consumer to choose the least expensive source of exchange means. As a result, the Clower (1967) constraints are not "exogenously" imposed on the consumer but rather left as a consumer choice to bind certain fractions of purchases to particular exchange means only to the extent that the particular exchange means is efficient for the consumer to use. This consumer choice among alternative means of exchange might be seen as ameliorating the strength of the criticism of the "deep" models of money that the Clower (1967) constraint is exogenously imposed, or even as offering an alternative approach to the search for deep models.[17]

Note that the model of the exchange credit sets the quantity of credit that is produced equal to the value of the output of the consumption good that is being bought on credit. Aiyagari et al. (1998) instead model credit as a service that is produced, and then enters as an input into a production function for credit goods. The credit goods production is Leontieff in its inputs of the credit service and of the value of the consumption goods being bought with the credit. This Leontieff technology in equilibrium implies as a special case the condition that the credit services output equals the value of the consumption goods being bought with the credit.[18] In this article, as in the continuum-of-stores approach in Gillman (1993), Ireland (1994b), and Erosa and Ventura (2000), there are no credit or cash goods per se, only the consumption good that can be bought with cash or credit. This, in a sense, can be thought of as collapsing the Aiyagari et al. (1998) type of credit goods and credit services into a single technology called credit, whereby the equilibrium condition that is implied by the special case of the Leontieff technology of Aiyagari, et al. (1998) is implicitly applied. The advantage of the model here over the continuum-of-stores approach is that here the velocity can be solved more simply.

The model's implications for growth are that inflation lowers growth because it lowers the real interest rate, a result supported in Ahmed and Rogers (2000). However, this feature combined with an *Ak* goods production technology cannot account for the substitution from effective labor to capital, as induced by inflation, that Chari et al. (1996) describe and that Gillman and Nakov (2003) further elaborate; Gillman and Nakov (2003) find evidence in support of this substitution for the postwar U.S. and U.K. data. Thus, although the *Ak* model provides easier analytic tractability, a goods production function with both labor and capital as in Gomme (1993) and Gillman and Kejak (2002) also can account for a negative effect of inflation on growth (see also Jones and Manuelli 1995). Because this approach also involves the inflation-induced labor to capital substitution, it may be useful to nest the models of monetary aggregates within the Gomme (1993) framework.[19]

Gillman and Kejak (2002) go partly in this direction by extending Gomme (1993) so as to include credit, as in section 7.3 of this article. One advantage of having monetary aggregates more fully embedded in the King and Rebelo (1990) type of endogenous growth model is that this provides the leisure channel by which to substitute away from inflation and so make the inflation tax less burdensome to the individual consumer. As Gillman and Otto (2002) show, the Gillman and Kejak (2002) model with leisure and the credit substitute in addition creates an interest elasticity of money demand that rises significantly in magnitude with inflation. This feature also exists in our model, and this is the central feature of the Cagan (1956) model. Or, as Martin Bailey (1992) put it, "Cagan's principal conclusion, indeed, is that the demand for real cash balances . . . has a higher and higher elasticity at higher and higher rates of inflation." Mark and Sul (2003) report recent international panel evidence in support of the Cagan (1956) money demand function. Only with such an elasticity, within the general equilibrium money demand function, are Gillman et al. (2004) able to explain international evidence on inflation and growth.[20]

The current *Ak* model of this article implies that an increase in the nominal interest rate causes the same degree of a growth rate decrease, no matter what the level of the nominal interest rate. But rather than this linear relation, the evidence shows a high degree of nonlinearity, with stronger negative inflation effects at low inflation rate levels. An inflation-induced rising interest elasticity makes substitution toward leisure less and toward credit more, making the decrease in the growth rate less. Therefore, as inflation rises, the additional leisure and credit channels help explain both effective-labor-to-capital substitution and a rising interest elasticity that leads to a falling magnitude of the marginal decrease in the growth rate.

Acknowledgements

We are grateful to participants at a seminar in CERGE-EI, Prague, and at the 2003 North American Econometric Society Summer Meetings; also to Toni Braun, Mark Harris, Bee Jeong, Jan Kmenta, Rowena Pecchenino and Sergey Slobodyan. Excellent research assistance by Szilárd Benk is also appreciated. Gillman also thanks Central European University, Budapest for research grant support.

Notes

* Gillman, Max, and Michal Kejak (2004). 'The Demand for Bank Reserves and Other Monetary Aggregates', *Economic Inquiry*, 42(3), 518–533.

† We are grateful to participants at a seminar in CERGE-EI, Prague, and at the 2003 North American Econometric Society Summer Meetings; also to Toni Braun, Mark Harris, Bee Jeong, Jan Kmenta, Rowena Pecchenino and Sergey Slobodyan. Excellent research assistance by Szilárd Benk is also appreciated. Gillman also thanks Central European University, Budapest for research grant support.

1 "The presence of the banking system has no real effect whatever but merely alters the nominal rate of inflation necessary to achieve a given real size of the government budget" (Bailey 1992, 234); in the model here the latter statement is true, but not the former because capital is used up in banking activities and because reserve requirements affect the real interest rate when there is a non-Friedman optimum rate of interest.

2 Johnson (1969, 32), for example, writes that "a banking organization could issue non-interest-bearing deposites, assumed to be costless to administer." Marty (1969, 106) discusses demand deposits and assumes that "the cost of setting up and running a bank is zero." Here both authors are focusing on the wealth effects of inside and outside money.

3 Hicks (1935) seeks a theory of money based on marginal utility, with cash held in advance of purchases, as Lucas (1980) follows. Hicks shunts aside both Keynes's alternative to Fisher's quantity theory as found in his *Treatise* (see Gillman 2002 on flaws in this theory), and considers "Velocities of Circulation" as in Fisher's quantity theory an "evasion." He reasons that money use suggests the existence of a friction and that "we have to look the friction in the face." The "most obvious sort of friction" is "the cost of transfering assets from one form to another." Hicks says that we should consider "every individual in the community as being, on a small scale, a bank. Monetary theory becomes a sort of generalisation of banking theory." In alignment with Hicks, the agent in this article acts as a bank in part, and the bank has costs from creating new instruments, such as demand deposits and credit. But in contrast, here velocity is endogenously determined as a fundamental part of the resulting equilibrium. Hicks's and Lucas's approaches converge with Fisher's.

4 This abstracts from the interest that is earned on some demand deposit accounts included in the U.S. M1 aggregate, because this interest tends to be of nominal amounts compared to the savings accounts included in M2.

5 However, to get this result, three changes were made to the model actually published in Haslag (1998), indicating incidental errors in the published paper: The money stock in the profit equation (1) is in time $t - 1$, instead of t as published; and the money stock and the price level in equation (2) are in time $t - 1$ instead of time t as published. The actual return in the article as published is that $r_t = (A - \delta)[1 - \gamma_t(1 + g_t)$, where g_t denotes the balanced-path growth rate; it is independent of the inflation rate.

6 See Bailey (1992) for an early discussion of intermediary earnings during inflation. If current period non-negative profit is required for the bank intermediary to exist, then a transfer to the bank as in the above-described transfer scheme, with $\Pi'_t/(P_t k_t) = R_t[\gamma/(1 - \gamma)]$, would satisfy this at all inflation rates.

7 Including the market for nominal bonds as in Lucas and Stokey (1987) would give R_t as the price of the bonds and would explicitly derive the Fisher equation.

8 We are indebted to Bob Lucas for originally suggesting the concept of the cost from crime and to Rowena Pecchenino for comments on this. Note that these costs are on the consumer side of the problem, while costs of alternative instruments for exchange are on the banking firm side of the problem. The so-called shopping time costs (Lucas 2000) actually compare better to the bank firm costs in this problem, as is shown in note 12. Karni's and Baumol's costs are a story more about the costs on the consumer side. The diffusion of ATMs plausibly affects both banking productivity and the consumer's cost of using money.

9 In Russia, after losing confidence in the bank sector during its collapse in 1997, people are again starting to use banks to hold cash. " 'I'm used to carrying all my cash with me, but with a [debit] card it's easier,' said Denis Tafintsev, a 25-year-old warehouse manager. 'If you lose your card you don't lose your money.' " ("Retail Banking Grows in Russia", *Wall Street Journal Europe*, 28 May 2003, p. M1).

10 This result extends the traditional literature, such as Marty (1969, 105), who postulates that "if bank money were the only money, competitively produced bank money not subject to outside constraints will result in equality of the price of money with its cost of production. Since these costs are zero, the price of money would in equilibrium be zero." Here with positive production costs, the marginal cost in equilibrium is equal to the cost of the substitute, cash, which is $R + \phi$. This can be zero only at the Friedman optimum of $R = 0$ combined with the case that $\phi = 0$, in which case there will be no demand for demand deposits.

11 Note that if $a_t^{dd} = 1$, and so $a_t^c, = 0$ there would be no consumer demand for cash. The monetary equilibrium would still have well-defined nominal prices as long as $\gamma > 0$, so that there was a reserves demand for cash by the intermediation bank. This could then be characterized solely as a legal restrictions demand for money. At $a_t^c = 0$, and $\gamma = 0$, and with a positive supply of money, prices may not be well defined.

12 Alternatively, the exchange credit sector can be kept implicit by having the consumer engage in "self-production" of the exchange credit. This can be done by constraining the consumer's problem by the technology constraint (49), combining this constraint with equation (44), solving for a_t^{cd}, and using this to substitute in for a_t^{cd} in the consumer problem (45), with the consumer now choosing k_t^{cd} instead of a_t^{cd}. This approach would make the revised Clower contraint (44) equal to $M_t^{cd} = P_t A_{cd} c^{1-\theta}(k_t^{cd})^{\theta}$. Setting $\gamma = 0$ and $\phi = 0$, then $M_t^c/(P_t c_t) = 1 - a_t^{cd} = a_t^c$, and only this one Clower constraint would be necessary. Now solve this constraint for k_t^{cd}, and it would take a form exactly analogous to a special case of the McCallum and Goodfriend (1987) shopping time constraint, but in capital instead of time, that depends on real money balances and goods in the same direction: $k_t^{cd} = c_t [1 - (M_t^c / P_t) / c_t]^{1/\theta}(1/A_{cd})^{1/\theta}$; with $\partial k_t^{cd}/\partial(M_t^c/P_t) < 0$, and $\partial k_t^{cd}/\partial c_t > 0$ (see Walsh 1998, on shopping time models).

13 McGrattan (1998) argues that the long-term rate is better to use than the short-term rate that Gordon et al. (1998) use. "Low frequency movements in velocity are well-explained by low frequency movements in observed interest rates."

14 Note that Gillman and Otto (2002) take the time series approach of Meltzer (1963) and Lucas (1988) while including a data series on the productivity in banking to capture changes in productivity. They find cointegration of money demand with the productivity series, but without it the money demand appears to be instable. Or as Parry (2000) asserts, "Once deposit interest rates began to vary with market rates, the demands for M1 and M2—the primary guides to monetary policy—became unstable."

15 Ireland (1995) compares U.S. M1–A velocity with six-month Treasury bill interest rates. He explains velocity as following a continuous upward trend due to financial innovation.

16 Note that stable deposit to currency ratios were reported by Cagan (1956) for the hyperinflations he studied (an exception was post-WWII Hungary that Cagan suggests is due to data problems). This indicates a small role of the nominal interest rate in causing changes in this ratio and is consistent with the small role given here to the nominal interest rate in explaining the U.S. ratio's postwar movement.

17 See Bullard and Smith (2001), and Azariadis et al. (2000), for example, for an alternative approach to modeling "inside" money, based on a three-period model. They apply this to analyze the optimality of restricting inside money; Gillman (2000) analyzes the optimality of such restrictions in a model similar to the paper here.

18 The case is that $q = 1$ in Aiyagari et al. (1998) model, using their notation.

19 Changes in the real interest rate in the *Ak* model presented here occur only through changes in the inflation rate and are discussed in this fashion. In a

model with labor and capital, the real interest rate could move endogenously with velocity. At business cycle frequencies, this simultaneity may be interesting to investigate.

20 Paal and Smith (2000) offer an overlapping generations model in which low inflation can cause a positive effect on growth, while higher inflation causes a negative level. This is supported in the panel evidence of Ghosh and Phillips (1998), Khan and Senhadji (2001), Judson and Orphanides (1999), and Gillman et al. (2004) in which a threshold level of inflation is found after which the inflation-growth effect is negative. However the positive effect at low inflation rates is found to be insignificant in these works. Gillman et al. (2004) show that using instrumental variables, the effect of inflation on growth is negative for all positive levels of inflation, across both OECD and APEC regions, as well as in the full sample; Ghosh and Phillips (1998) also find this for a full sample.

8 Money velocity with costly credit*

Max Gillman, Pierre L. Siklos, and J. Lew Silver

Summary

The chapter functionally describes the income velocity of money by including the cost of a key substitute to money: exchange credit. Financial innovation causes the cost of credit to fall, the quantity of money demanded to fall, and the velocity to rise, all without shifting the money demand function. The chapter derives a general equilibrium money demand function, specifies a parametric equation of the income velocity of money from the model, and finds cointegration between the relevant variables in an expanded velocity equation which also produces consistent dynamics. It explains U.S. post-war long-run velocity through only the substitution effects from the relative cost of exchange by money versus credit. It explains short run dynamics with the same substitution effect. In addition, evidence suggests that an income effect helps explain the dynamics as predicted by an application of the permanent income hypothesis.

8.1 Introduction

Some authors view the fundamental proposition of monetarism as being consistent with the notion that the income velocity of money is stable and predictable. Keynes (1930) interpreted velocity as predictable, with the implication, for example, that money supply control for the purposes of achieving price stability is feasible. Meltzer (1987) and McCallum (1990) propose similar rules for money supply growth that account for velocity changes. Ireland (1996) examines rules of money growth in the presence of shocks with velocity treated as being exogenous. Our paper complements Ireland by explaining such shifts endogenously.

Evidence of a stable conventional money demand function has been mixed. This paper advances new evidence as based on a theoretically derived velocity function. For annual US postwar data, we find cointegration by including a measure of the cost of credit. In addition, we find that an income effect related to Cochrane's (1994) ratio of non-durable consumption to GDP helps explain the error correction of the velocity equation. Our model suggests that money demand depends not only on the own price, the interest rate, and income, but also on the price of the main substitute. We are, therefore, able to derive a money demand function that equates the price of the closest substitute to the cost of exchange credit.[1] As financial innovation occurs, the time per unit of output in finance falls, the cost of credit falls, and the quantity of money demanded falls – all without shifting the money demand function.

The exchange approach to modelling money demand differs from the asset approach emphasized by Keynes (1936), Friedman (1956), Wallace (1980), and Hoffman and Rasche (1991). In their approaches, financial and physical capital constitute the substitute for money, and the interest rate captures the cost of foregoing these assets in order to hold money. The approach in this chapter instead follows the money and banking view of Fisher (1911), Hicks (1935), Baumol (1952), Lucas and Stokey (1983), and Lucas (1993a). It makes exchange credit rather than asset capital the substitute to money. Moreover, it defines money as that which foregoes the interest on capital while being set aside for exchange, and it defines credit as an exchange device that enables funds to keep earning interest but that costs real time to produce.

The exchange approach not only precisely specifies money demand, but also implies which monetary aggregate to use in estimation, namely that which includes all non-interest bearing exchange means. Cash and zero-interest demand deposits fit this definition of money, even though one is public debt and one is private debt. Deposits earning market interest rates do not fit the definition. The paper uses the M1 money aggregate although this does contain some low-interest bearing assets. The "checkable" market-interest-earning items beyond M1 that constitute M2 and M3 fit the chapter's definition of exchange credit. Examples include American Express and Visa cards paid off after approximately 30 days by check drawn on M2-type (consumer) or on M3-type (firm) money market accounts.

By functionally encompassing financial innovation, long-run velocity behaviour can be explained on the basis of the substitution term of the money demand function. Also in contrast to conventional estimates of money demand we find a higher interest elasticity of money demand. The chapter describes how this is to be expected because exchange credit acts as a near substitute that makes money demand more own-price elastic. By capturing cyclical fluctuations in temporary income, we are also able to explain the short-run dynamics of velocity through an income effect as well as substitution effects. Applying the permanent income hypothesis to money demand (see Friedman, 1959, Meltzer, 1963, Lucas, 1988a) is interpreted here to mean that the ratio of permanent to current income should help explain velocity dynamics. We conclude that cointegration between the relevant variables in an expanded velocity equation which also produces consistent dynamics, via the estimation of error correction models, explains velocity through elemental substitution effects and also corroborate evidence of the predicted income effect.

The chapter is organized as follows. The model is set out and its trade-offs in general equilibrium in section 8.2. Next, we formulate the agent's theoretical income velocity of money demand, and specify a parametric velocity equation for estimation (section 8.3).[2] The data are described in section 8.4, the empirical results in section 8.5, and the paper concludes with a summary in section 8.6.

8.2 The representative agent economy

The paper modifies Gillman's (1993) cash-in-advance economy so that velocity simply equals the inverse of the fraction of goods bought with cash. The consumer chooses this fraction, defined $A(t) \in (0,1]$, as based on the Baumolian (1952) relative cost of cash versus exchange credit. Denoting goods at time t by $c(t)$, the price of goods as $P(t)$, and cash holdings as $M(t)$, the consumer constrains cash expenditures below cash holdings:

$$A(t) \bullet P(t)c(t) \leq M(t). \tag{1}$$

And the consumer receives end-of-period lump sum cash transfers $H(t)$:

$$M(t+1) = M(t) + H(t). \tag{2}$$

The consumer also purchases a fraction $1 - A(t)$ of the consumption basket with credit. This avoids the interest cost of cash but requires time to produce the credit. Let $\tau(A,t)$ be the time required per unit of good purchased by credit, and let $\partial\tau(A,t)/\partial A < 0$ so that increases in the fraction bought with credit, $1 - A(t)$, coincide with increases in the time cost per good bought with credit. This gives an increasing marginal cost of credit use. Multiplying the amount of goods purchased with credit, $[1 - A(t)]\, c(s,t)$, by the time per good, $\tau(A,t)$, gives the total time used up in credit activity: $[1 - A(t)]\, c(s,t)\tau(A,t)$.

The consumer's resource constraint shows how the time in credit production subtracts from labour time. With a linear competitive production of goods using labour, goods output $c(t)$ equals the constant marginal product of labour, denoted $w(t)$, factored by labour time. Labour residually equals the endowment of 1 after subtraction of the leisure time, denoted $x(t)$, and the credit time $[1 - A(t)]\, c(s,t)\tau(A,t)$. This makes the resource constraint:

$$c(t) = w(t)[1 - x(t) - (1 - A(t))\tau(A,t)c(t)]. \tag{3}$$

The consumer finds the resource constraint embodied in the wealth constraint. At the end of each period, the consumer receives nominal wages $w(t)P(t)[1 - x(t) - (1 - A(t))\tau(A,t)c(t)]$ and the cash transfer $H(t)$. For expenditures, the consumer sets aside cash-in-advance of trading in the next period, $M(t+1)$, and pays off the credit debt, $[1 - A(t)]P(t)c(t)$. Discounting by the market rate $q^t \in (0,1]$, net wealth is

$$\sum_{t=0}^{\infty} q^t < w(t)P(t)[1x(t)(1 - A(t))\tau(A,t)c(t)] + H(t)$$
$$- M(t+1)\ [1A(t)]P(t)c(t) > \geq 0. \tag{4}$$

Substituting for $H(t)$ from equation (2), and then for $M(t)$ from equation (1), gives back the net-wealth form of the social resource constraint in equation (3).

Given $\tau(A,t)$, $w(t)$, $H(t)$, q^t and $a \geq 0$, the consumer maximizes a discounted log-utility function subject to the cash and wealth constraints of equations (1) and (4):

$$\text{Max } L = \sum_{t=0}^{\infty} \beta^t \{ \ln [c(t)] + a \ln [x(t)]$$
$$\{c(t), x(t),$$
$$M(t), A(t)\}$$
$$t = 0, \ldots, \infty$$
$$+ \lambda(t)[M(t) - A(t)P(t)c(t)] \}$$

$$+ \mu \{ \sum_{t=0}^{\infty} q^t [w(t)P(t)[1x(t)(1 - A(t))\tau(A, t)c(t)]$$
$$+ H(t) - M(t+1)(1A(t))P(t)c(t)\ ] \}. \tag{5}$$

The consumer reaches equilibrium at the set $\{c^*(t), x^*(t), A^*(t), M^*(t), P^*(t), \lambda^*(t), \mu^*\}_{t=0,\ldots,infinity}$ that satisfies equation (5), the cash market clearing equation (2), the nonnegativity constraints, and the $0 - 1$ bounds on $A(t)$.

From equation (1), equilibrium money demand is $M^*(t)/P^*(t) = A^*(t)c^*(t)$; money demand depends on the proportion of goods bought with cash and on the goods demand. Goods demand depends on the marginal rate of substitution between goods and leisure. Denoting this margin by $MRS_{c,x}$, denoting the nominal interest rate by $i(t)$, and defining $q^t \equiv 1/[(1 + i[1])(1 + i[2])\cdots(1 + i[t])]$, equations (20–23) of Appendix 8.A imply that this marginal rate equals the ratio of the shadow cost of goods to the shadow cost of time:

$$MRS_{c,x} = \frac{1 + A(t)i(t) + (1 - A(t))w(t)\tau(A, t)}{w(t)}. \tag{6}$$

The shadow cost of goods equals the real goods cost of one, plus the per unit exchange cost. The exchange cost equals an average of the cash cost and the credit cost, as weighted by $A(t)$. If the inflation rate rises, for example, then the shadow cost of exchange by cash rises and the consumer substitutes from goods to leisure. But because of the consumer's production of credit, the

$$V^*(t) \equiv \frac{c^*(t)}{M^*(t)/P^*(t)} = \frac{1}{A^*(t)}. \tag{7}$$

Specifying the consumer's production of exchange credit shows exactly how the cash fraction $A^*(t)$ depends on the relative cost of exchange. With $\zeta(t) \geq 1$ denoting a technological shift factor in credit production, and with $\gamma \in (0,1)$ representing a decreasing returns coefficient, let the production of the share of exchange credit in total purchases be given by $(1 - A) = \zeta \tau^{\gamma}$: increasing the time spent increases the share of credit purchases at a diminishing rate. Then the Baumolian margin in equation (7) becomes $i = w\tau[(1 + \gamma)/\gamma]$, where $\tau = (1 - A)^{1/\gamma} \zeta^{-1/\gamma}$. Solving for $A^*(t)$:

$$A^* = 1 - \zeta\left(\frac{i}{w}\right)^{\gamma} \left(\frac{\gamma}{1 + \gamma}\right)^{\gamma}. \tag{8}$$

The solution implies that velocity depends positively on the interest/wage ratio, and on the credit sector's productivity ζ. More generally we can write a function $f(.)$ where $A^* = f(i,w,1/\zeta)$ and $f_1 < 0, f_2 > 0, f_3 > 0$. We can use the equilibrium conditions to write this as $A^* = f(i/w,1/\zeta)$ with $f_1 < 0, f_2 > 0$. The higher is the real wage, the higher is the value of time used in credit production, the higher is the cost of credit and the higher is the fraction of purchases made with money. Similarly, the higher the time required to produce (and use) credit, the higher is the cost of credit, and the higher is the demand for money.

We formulate our income velocity function as current real income, divided by current real money demand. Denoting this velocity as v, then $v = y/m$. Suppose we just say that $m^* = A^*c^*$, that c equals current real income y, and that we can write v as $v = y/(A^*y)$. Then velocity equals just the inverse of A^*. This is the methodology derivative from Hofman and Raasche (1991) whom explain money demand as a function of the nominal interest rate and current real income. They impose a unitary income elasticity in order to find cointegration. Our function A^* would then simply be $f(i)$, $f' < 0$. And our velocity with the unitary income elasticity of money demand imposed would be just $1/f(i)$.

Our theory differs not only by adding in additional variables in the $f(.)$ to capture the cost of credit. Also at this step we are careful to distinguish between current income and permanent income. From this distinction we are able to hypothesise the existence of an income effect on velocity over the business cycle. The measure of income by which we define velocity is current income. For the income upon which real money demand depends, it is actually c^*. With homothetic utility, we can write c^* as a function $g(.)y_P$ where y_P is permanent income. From the example in Gillman (1993) or in a standard way, we can argue that g depends on the interest rate and the real wage, or the ratio i/w, so that $c^* = g(i/w)y_P$. By the substitution effect of $g(.)$, equilibrium consumption falls with an interest rate increase and rises with a real wage increase. These changes may also alter permanent income y_P. Then we can consider real money demand to be given by $m^* = A^*c^* = f(i/w, 1/\zeta)g(i/w)y_P$ or, $m^* = h(i/w, 1/\zeta)y_P$, where $h(.) = f(.)g(.)$. The first and second arguments of $h(.)$ have negative and positive signs, and so we have that the substitution term $h(.)$ has the same arguments as in $f(.)$; the other term that is permanent income gives us the income term.

We therefore are invoking the permanent income hypothesis as applied to money demand (see Friedman, 1959). First, consider that money demand like consumption demand depends on permanent income for its scale effect rather than depending on current income since $m^* = h(.)y_P$. Second, we use the equilibrium money demand m^*, which is a type of fixed point solution to the dynamic optimisation problem, as the permanent component of money demand. This is exactly as Friedman (1957) chose his equilibrium c^* that resulted as the solution to his Fisherian intertemporal optimisation problem. He set this to be equal to the permanent component of consumption. Friedman further specifies a temporary component of consumption that acts as a noisy error term in his study of the ratio of c/y. He also specifies a temporary income component and this is a focus of his study.

Applying the permanent income hypothesis to money demand uses the same device of temporary and permanent components of money, instead of consumption, and of income. Note that the cash-in-advance economy allows this application because money is used for current consumption. We define current real money demand m to be the product of permanent money demand m^* and temporary money demand denoted as m_T: $m = m^*m_T$ where m_T is defined as a white noise variable with mean 1. We define current income y as the product of permanent income and temporary income denoted as y_T: $y = y_P y_T$ where y_T is a normal random variable with mean 1. Then the current income velocity of current real money demand is given by $v = y/(m^*m_T) = y/(A^*c^*m_T) = (1/A^*)(y/c^*)(1/m_T)$. Taking logs we get

$$\begin{aligned} \ln(v) &= -\ln(A^*) + \ln(y/c^*) + \ln(m_T) \\ &= -\ln[f(i, w, 1/\zeta)] + \ln(y/c^*) + e \end{aligned} \tag{9}$$

where $e \equiv \ln(m_T)$. We then specify our equation for estimation as

$$\ln(v) = a_1 + a_2(i) + a_3(w) + a_4(1/\zeta) + a_5 \ln(y/c^*) + e \tag{10}$$

with a constant a_1, with $a_2 > 0, a_3 < 0, a_4 < 0, a_5 > 0$ and with $a_2 = a_3$ because the nominal interest rate and the real wage actually enter f as the ratio (i/w). We could also test to see if a_4. Here we specify c^* as the the consumption of non-durables and services. This should capture the maintanence of and flow of services from durables.

If technological change in the finance sector trends upward at a faster rate than the technological change in the general economy, then $[1/\zeta(t)]$ would fall by more than the average product $w(t)$ would rise. This would cause the cost of credit to trend downwards and velocity to trend upwards, a trend that the velocity equation (10) can capture empirically. This result relies on $\gamma < 1$ as specified in the model and this translates into the further parameter restriction that $a_4 > a_3 = -a_2$.

We construct a testable equation of the log of the GDP velocity of a narrow M1-type aggregate. The question for the other variables is whether they enter the equation in logs or levels. Entering these other variables in logs implies a "log-log" estimation that gives a constant velocity elasticity with respect to each of the variables. Entering these other variables in levels implies a constant velocity semi-elasticity with respect to each variable. The cash-in-advance economy that Gillman (1993) extends to include costly credit implies that the money demand elasticity with respect to the interest rate rises as the level of the interest rate rises. This suggests a specification of the interest rate in levels, which gives in combination with the log velocity a constant semi-interest elasticity. Since the interest elasticity equals the product of the semi elasticity and the interest rate, this makes the interest elasticity increase with the interest rate as Gillman suggests. The idea is that the money demand function becomes more price elastic as the price rises.

However note that Lucas (1994) compares "log-log" and "log-level" money demand functions with respect to the interest rate in OLS regressions and finds a better fit for the log-log at low interest rates. Therefore we try both log and level interest rate specifications. And we do the same for the other variables.

We expect that the income term (y/c^*) will have no effect on the trend of velocity and that the trend is described entirely by the substitution variables. We do expect the income term to effect the dynamics over the business cycle and therefore to be significant in the error correction. This is because the model can of velocity can be written as $v = y/m = y/[h(.)y_P m_T]$. Decomposing the current income term, this makes the velocity function: $v = y_P y_T / [h(.)y_P m_T] = y_T / [h(.)m_T]$. The permanent income components cancel out of the velocity function, leaving the velocity as the product of $[1/h(.)]$ and the ratio of the temporary income to the temporary money variables. Over the trend both of these are expected to have no effect. But just as the temporary income plays the key role in its effect on the c/y ratio in Friedman (1957) across groups of people (when they might have positive or negative income shocks), so it can play a key role over the business cycle when there are positive and negative temporary income shocks. The remaining temporary money shock can be given less importance as part of the random error as in Friedman's (1957) treatment of the temporary consumption shock. Thus both temporary components are part of the random error, but over the cycle we expect the temporary component to behave in a predictable way. And this is what we want to incorporate in the error-correction.

8.2.1 Dynamics: the income effect

The dynamic income effect can be intuitively explained through different perspectives of the permanent income hypothesis. Consider, as Friedman (1959) explains, that in an expansion, temporary income tends to be positive, while permanent income may also rise but by less. Money demand may increase because of an increase in permanent income, but money demand does not increase by as much as does current income. This makes the current income velocity of money rise in an expansion and conversely fall in a contraction. The temporary income makes velocity procyclical.

The temporary income effect on money velocity can also be thought of in terms of durable goods purchases. During an expansion, investment in firm and household durables increases. This expenditure sources from retained earnings and household savings. Such cyclical investment funds tend to be placed in short-term interest bearing accounts until being spent. And because of the large nature of these purchases, there is an incentive to make such transactions with credit rather than money so as to keep earning interest on the funds for as long as possible. This means that the exchange for durables can be to some extent thought of as a credit-type transaction drawn upon interest bearing funds. And it implies that total transactions rise by more than money demand during expansions, again implying the pro-cyclic movement of velocity. Conversely in the downturn, firm "restructuring" and household disinvestment occur through a decrease in maintenance expenditure on durables. This makes total transactions fall by more than does money demand; the current income velocity would then fall in the contraction. This latter durable good approach can be thought of as explaining the "transactions" velocity of money that mirrors the income velocity of money.

Third, the short run dynamics of the income effect can also be put in the perspective of real business cycle (RBC) theory. The main driving stochastic process in RBC models is the shock to economy-wide productivity (the "technology shock") that can raise or lower social resources. The permanent part of the shock is typically a unit root or near unit root process. An independent temporary shock to income comes through a simple case of specifying the "government shock" to resources as a zero-persistence, temporary process. Further the government shock can have serial correlation. Then the shock process can be decomposed by a Kalman filter, unobserved variables approach, or alternatively by a Beverage-Nelson ARIMA process of permanent and temporary components. These permanent and temporary decompositions of income are either independent as in the Kalman filter decomposition or perfectly correlated as in the Beverage-Nelson decomposition.

The representative agent's demand for real money in an RBC model would be expected to co-move with the permanent component of the technology shock because the agent bases expectations of social resources upon the degree of persistence of the shock. The agents expectations would be independent of the temporary effect because of its lack of persistence. With money demand dependent on the persistent parts of the shock, and with current income rising because of positive permanent and positive temporary shocks (this assumes a positive covariance of the permanent and temporary shocks), then the current income velocity of money demand would be expected to be procyclic. In an RBC model with a standard cash-in-advance economy without costly credit, Cooley and Hansen(1995) do find velocity to be highly correlated with current output in their simulated model and in their actual data. However this could be due to cyclic income or substitution effects.

8.2.2 Dynamics: the substitution effects

The real business cycle approach also leads to a way to frame the substitution effects that we expect to comprise the error-correction dynamics. Cooley and Hansen (1995), like Friedman (1959), point out that velocity tends to peak somewhat before output and so leads the output fluctuation. Friedman explains the dynamics over the business as primarily due to the the income effect through application of the permanent income hypothesis, and secondarily through an effect on the timing of the velocity peaks through the relative prices that effect the substitution term affecting real money demand. Friedman finds the interest rate the primary effect here and he also mentions a possible influence of the real wage. In the RBC context, a substitution effect on consumption demand can be due to the real interest rate and the real wage rate movements. Adding in money as in Cooley and Hansen, the inflation rate through the nominal interest rate also affects money demand. In our money demand theory the nominal interest rate negatively affects money demand while the real wage rate is part of the time cost of credit and so positively effects money demand. Therefore, as the ratio of the interest rate to the real wage rises, as it typically does before the peak of the business cycle, money demand would fall and velocity would rise by this substitution effect. If the ratio of the nominal interest rate to the real wage peaks before the output peak, then this substitution effect would pressure velocity towards peaking first.

The substitution dynamics, from the effect of the ratio of the nominal interest rate to the real wage, also combine with the effect of the finance sector productivity. However the inclusion of money demand within the RBC approach as in Cooley and Hansen still relies mainly on standard cash-in-advance economies without costly credit and without an associated exchange technology of credit production. This makes it difficult to ascertain the effect of credit technology shocks. To the extent that such shocks move credit productivity in line with the economy-wide RBC technology shocks, then we would expect this to make velocity even more procyclic by the substitution effect. This is because as the cost of credit falls due to financial technological increase, then the money demand falls as credit demand rises, and velocity increases.

8.3 Data

Finding a time series proxy for the cost of credit poses some difficulties. As in Karni (1974), we use the wage rate in estimating a velocity function. Our model suggests defining the cost of credit as the value of time factored by the time per unit of output in exchange credit and, in estimating equation (10), the parameters a_3 and a_4 are the relevant ones for testing the importance of exchange credit in money demand. Following the calibration of the cost of credit in Gillman (1993), the estimation assumes that the Finance, Insurance, and Real Estate (FIR) sector captures the economy's exchange credit. As a broader sector than just exchange credit, this choice assumes that wage rates and labour productivities in exchange credit parallel those of the sector.

Our model equates the real wage in goods production with that which values time in credit production. Without a theoretical distinction between the two, the estimation experiments with both the average real wage rate in all manufacturing (as in, for example, Karni, 1974) and the average real wage rate in FIR. For the measure of time per unit of output in FIR, which equals the inverse of labour productivity in FIR, the estimated series equals the labour hours in FIR divided by real GDP in FIR. We proxy total labour hours by using the annual number of full and part time employees in FIR, multiplied by the number of hours worked per full and part time employee in FIR. All years in the data set were assumed to consist of 52 weeks.

A second data source exists that measures a combined cost of credit variable. This alternative requires that equality holds between the wage rate parameter and the time cost parameter: $a_3 = a_4$. However, this is contrary to the model's restriction that $a_4 > a_3$ (see equation (10)). Nevertheless, since a_4 theoretically may be close to a_3, and as a type of robustness check, we also experimented with the combined cost-of-credit variable. It is defined as the annual total wages in FIR divided by the real GDP in FIR. From a constant-returns-to-scale perspective, this alternative equates the cost of credit to the share of labour in output. Multiplication of the wage rate by labour hours per unit of output in FIR gives a proxy similar to the first construct just described, but, as pointed our above, provides an alternative combined cost-of-credit measure.

The Treasury bill rate (TBR) and, alternatively, the Commercial Paper rate (CPR), serve as proxies for the opportunity cost of holding money. We also experimented with the 3–5 year Treasury bond rate and the Triple-A long term bond rate as proxies for the cost of holding money.

Using GNP always as a measure of current income, three alternative proxies for the ratio of permanent income were considered for the income ratio variable. They are: (1) the Friedman (1957)-type distributed lag, as in Bordo and Jonung (1987), Siklos (1993) and Bordo, Jonung and Siklos (1997); (2) consumption, as in Cochrane (1994) and as implied by the model, except that consumption here is lagged one period while GNP is contemporaneous;[3] and (3) an approximate measure of expected income using a simple Kuznets (1941)-type of decomposition of national income. Motivated by Knight (1922), Fama and French (1988), and Quah (1992), the third measure defines expected income as wages, salaries, rental income and interest; adding the rest of income, corporate profits plus proprietors' income, we obtain national income. The first four components of the decomposition of national income capture a notion of expected income, while the last two components capture a notion of pure economic profit.

The *National Income and Product Accounts, 1929–1982*, with updates from the *Survey of Current Business*, provides all the data series except for M1, the interest rate, and the implicit price deflator series, which are obtained from the *Economic Report of the President*. The requirement of a consistent time series restricts our annual sample to the 1948–1990 period. Relevant data from the finance sector begin in 1948, although some of the time series can be traced back to 1929. The replacement of these data series by the recent chain-weighted data restricts our sample to end with the 1990 annual observation. If we were instead to use the historical chain-weighted revisions (see *Survey of Current Business* 1996) this would deleteriously restrict the sample to begin in 1959 only. The older series gives an additional 12 observations at the cost of some more recent data.[4]

8.4 Results

The results we report for equation (10), reflect considerable experimentation with alternative variable specifications.[5] Each series in log levels is found to be $I(1)$, that is, non-stationary, except the proxies for permanent to current income which are $I(0)$. Plots of the time series reveal, and the results assume, that each of the series also contains an underlying linear deterministic trend. If cointegrated, then the variables of equation (1) describe a long-run velocity function. The estimation strategy consists in testing for cointegration using the so-called Johansen method in a VAR framework (see Johansen (1995), and Hamilton (1994) for details).

Cointegration testing also requires specification of the VAR lag length. Both the Akaike Information Criterion (AIC) and Schwarz's Criterion (SC) give a relevant selection basis. The former tends to select longer lags than the latter and, consequently, makes the residuals white noise with a higher probability. By contrast, the SC criterion preserves precious degrees of freedom. Generally, the results found adequate a lag of one or two years in the VARs. Note also that, with annual data, a lag of 1 translates into 4 lags at the quarterly frequency, well within the findings of quarterly studies of U.S. money demand (e.g., Hafer and Jansen, 1991). In most cases, both the AIC and SC criteria selected one lag as optimal.

To highlight the contrast of the cointegration results with conventional specifications, Table 8.1 presents cointegration tests for a velocity function that depends on an interest rate variable and a measure of income or permanent income. GNP measures current income, and the Friedman-type series as well as a wages and salaries series each measure permanent income. For 1929–1990 data, the results detect no long-run relationship, except possibly when augmenting the equation with a dummy variable for the oil price shocks of the 1970s. The conventional specifications are unable to support the finding of a long-run equilibrium relationship among the variables in question. Unreported results for the 1948–1990 data lead to the same conclusion.

We can, therefore, now focus the discussion on the ability of the cost of credit to "repair" the velocity function. Table 8.2 shows the results of various cointegration tests. It reports two alternative interest rate measures, the commercial paper rate in cases 1 and 2, and the Treasury Bill rate in cases 3 and 4. The wage rate and the time per unit of finance output enter as separate variables in cases 1 and 3, and combined in cases 2 and 4. The null of a single cointegrating vector cannot be rejected. The commercial paper rate gives this result more strongly than does the Treasury bill rate, and both short-term rates gave stronger results than when the long-term rates were used. In case 1, there is the possibility, at the 5% level of significance, of three cointegrating vectors, that is, of one common stochastic trend. Subsequent testing, however, identifies only a single cointegrating vector.[6] Tables 8.2A and 8.2B provide additional tests. Table 8.2A shows that using a broader wage measure does not affect the finding of cointegration; Table 8.2B shows that omission of the cost of credit variable results in the breakdown of the cointegration property.[7]

Table 8.3 provides estimates of the long-run coefficients, their standard errors, and the results of tests of the restriction for the equivalence of the interest and the negative real-wage elasticities, $a_2 = - a_3$. As shown, all the substitution variables are of the correct sign and are statistically significant; the income ration term was not significant and is not reported. In cases 1 and 3, estimates of the interest rate elasticities a_2 range from .249 to .330, and the null hypothesis that $a_2 = - a_3$ cannot be rejected. These results also confirm that $a_4 > a_3$. Results with the combined cost-of-credit specification in cases 2 and 4, under which $a_3 = a_4$ is imposed, show a higher interest elasticity for both of the alternative measures. The table also reports the results with the measure given by the wages and salaries divided by output in the finance sector.

Table 8.4 reports, for comparison purposes, the impact of scaling velocity by consumption defined as nondurables consumption. Note that these estimates are not based on the implications from our model, but address some of the relevant issues raised by Mankiw and Summers (1987). Further experiments used both full consumption and the 1992 NIPA revisions of

Table 8.1 Cointegration tests: conventional specifications

Case 1: v(t),I(t), y(t); I(t)=CPR; **sample:** 1929–1990	
No. Of Cointegrating Vectors	Test Statistic: λ max
r=0	29.34
r≤1	13.61
r≤2	0.11
Lags= 1	
Case 2: v(t), I(t), y(t); I(t) = TBR; **sample=** 1929–1990	
r=0	29.25
r≤1	13.40
r≤2	0.01
Lags=1	
Case 3: v(t), I(t), y(t); I(t)= CPR, **sample=** 1929–1990	
r=0	23.34
r≤1	5.26
r≤2	0.04
Lags=2	
Case 4: v(t), I(t), y(t) +BREAKS; I(t)= TBR,; **sample=** 1929–90	
r=0	47.67*
r≤1	17.03
r≤2	3.84
Lags=1	
Case 5: v(t), I(t), y*(t); I(t) = CPR; **sample=**1929–90	
r=0	42.14
r≤1	21.79
r≤2	9.43
Lags=2	
Case 6: v(t), I(t), y*(t)+BREAKS; I(t) = TBR; **sample=** 1929–90	
r=0	43.13*
r≤1	25.06
r≤2	11.33

Notes: All the variables are as defined in the text, except for y(t), and y*(t) which are the two proxies for permanent income. y(t) is the proxy based on wages and salaries while y*(t) is the proxy for permanent income first used by Bordo and Jonung (1987). * indicates statistical significance at the 5% level; r refers to the number of cointegrating vectors. BREAKS= dummy variable (=1) for 1973–74 and 1979–80 oil price shocks.

Table 8.2 Cointegration tests: equation (10)[1]

Case 1	Series: v(t), I(t), w(t), [1/ζ(t)]; I(t)=CPR Test Statistics (sample: 1948–90)	
	No. of CI Vectors	λ_{max}
	r=0	108.46*
	r≤1	57.08*
	r≤2	30.63*
	r≤3	11.22
	LAGS=1	
Case 2	Series: v(t), I(t), w(t)·[1/ζ(t)]; I(t)=CPR Tests Statistics (Sample: 1948–90)	
	No. of CI vectors	λ_{max}
	r=0	43.73*
	r≤1	24.47
	r≤2	7.44
	LAGS=1	
Case 3	Series: v(t), I(t), w(t), [1/ζ(t)]; I(t)=TBR Test Statistics (Sample: 1948–90)	
	No. of CI Vectors	λ_{max}
	r=0	102.25**
	r≤1	56.16
	r≤2	27.63
	r≤3	10.98
	LAGS=1	
Case 4	Series: v(t), I(t), w(t)·[1/ζ(t)]; I(t)=TBR Test Statistics (Sample: 1948–90)	
	No. of CI Vectors	λ_{max}
	r=0	42.40*
	r≤1	22.90
	r≤2	7.51
	LAGS=1	

Notes:

1. The tests assume that a linear deterministic trend is present in the data.

** signifies that the null is rejected at the 1% level; * means rejection at the 5% level and + means rejection at the 10% level.

Table 8.2A The effect of using a different wage proxy

Case 1: v(t), I(t), w(t), [1/ζ(t)]; I(t) = CPR; **sample=** 1948–90	
No. Of Cointegrating Vectors	Test Statistic: λ max
r=0	54.97**
r≤1	24.74
r≤2	7.93
r≤3	.004
Lags=1	
Case 3: v(t), I(t), w(t), [1/ζ(t)]; I(t) = TBR; **sample=** 1948–90	
r=0	74.63**
r≤1	38.58
r≤2	19.87
r≤3	7.71
Lags=1	

Table 8.2B The effect of omitting [1/ζ(t)]

Case 1: v(t), I(t), w(t); I(t)= CPR; **sample=** 1948–1990	
No. Of Cointegrating Vectors	Test Statistic: λ max
r=0	24.53
r≤1	9.82
r≤2	.55
Lags = 2	
Case 3: v(t), I(t), w(t); I(t)= CPR; **sample=** 1948–90	
r=0	24.53
r≤1	9.82
r≤2	0.55
Lags=2	

Notes: w(t) in Table 8.2A uses manfucturing wages instead of wages in the FIR sector. In Table 8.2B we exclude ζ(t), in effect imposing a zero restriction on the cost of credit variable.

Table 8.3 Long-run coefficients

Case 1	a_2=+.330 (.078)* a_3= −.692 (.165)* a_4= −1.148 (.414)**
	Test of a_2=a_3, $\chi(1)$=.042[.838]
Case 2	a_2= .548 (.046) a_3= {w(t)·[1/ζ(t)]}= −.106 (.596)
Case 3	a_2= .249 (.056)* a_3= −.697 (.166)* a_4= −1.068 (.391)**
	Test of a_2=a_3, $\chi(1)$= .0224[.900]
Case 4	a_2= .315 (.020)* a_3= {w(t)·[1/ζ(t)]}= −.445 (.940)*

Note: The cases and variables referred to are the ones listed in Table 8.2. The coefficients are those in equation (10). Standard errors are in parenthesis. * indicates statistically significant at the 10% level; ** at the 5% level.

consumption. Generally, more cointegration, that is, fewer common stochastic trends, and, therefore, more system stability results. However, when a single cointegrating vector is found it is at a lower significance level than in the results reported in Table 8.2. The conclusions regarding the cost of credit and the interest elasticity generally carry over but, as the model under the permanent income hypothesis stipulates that a current income measure should scale velocity, Table 8.4 omits a fuller analysis of the kind considered in Tables 8.2A, 8.2B, and 8.3.

Cointegration requires that the coefficients of the lagged residuals from the cointegrating regression be statistically significant and negative in the error correction representation (see Engle and Granger, 1987). For cases 1 and 3 of Table 8.2, Table 8.5 presents estimates of the reduced-form velocity equation. The highly significant error correction term confirms the existence of an equilibrium relationship between velocity, the commercial paper rate, the wage rate, and the time per unit of finance output (case 1). And this term implies that disequilibria correct within approximately six years. Case 1 passes all the diagnostic tests. In case 3, there is evidence of ARCH type effects and estimates of a GARCH(1,1) model (results not shown) render the EC term insignificant. The results accept without reservation case 1 with the commercial paper interest rate. For the unreported cases with a combined cost of credit variable, the error-correction term could not pass all the diagnostics.

To investigate further the short-run dynamics, three alternatives were considered. For all three alternatives, the results show the correct sign;

Table 8.4 Cointegration tests: the effect of scale variables

Velocity Scaled by non-durables consumption/Sample = 1948–1990		
	No. Of Cointegrating Vectors	Test statistic: λ *max*
Case 1	r=0	98.77**
	r≤1	59.81*
	r≤2	30.46*
	r≤3	10.48
	Lags=2	
Case 2	r=0	62.57**
	r≤1	34.19**
	r≤2	10.19
	Lags=2	
Velocity scaled by total consumption / sample = 1948–1990		
Case 1	r=0	62.57**
	r≤1	66.18**
	r≤2	32.22**
	r≤3	11.36
	Lags=1	
Case 2	r=0	55.81**
	r≤1	18.43
	r≤2	4.74
Velocity scaled by 1992 Comprehensive NIPA revision/ sample= 1948–1990		
Case 1	r=0	94.68**
	r≤1	51.35**
	r≤2	24.41
	r≤3	9.71
	Lags =1	
Case 2	r=0	55.30**
	r≤1	16.37
	r≤2	3.66
	Lags =1	

Note: The cases refer to those listed in Table 8.2. See Table 8.2 for significance level symbols.

Table 8.5 Error correction estimates of the velocity equation (10)

	Dependent Variable: Log Difference M1 Velocity	
Independent Variables	*Case 1 sample 1948–90; I=CPR Coefficients (std error)*	*Case 3 sample 1948–90; I=TBR Coefficients (std error)*
Constant	.068(3.949)**	−.012(.412)
Δv(t-1)	.388(2.517)*	.422(2.265)*
Δv(t-2)	−.245(1.613)	−.092(.524)
Δi(t-1)	−.049(3.113)**	.002(.011)
Δi(t-2)	.010(0.706)	.016(.927)
Δw(t-1)	−.361(1.397)	.579(1.830)+
Δw(t-2)	−.601(2.822)**	−.171(.556)
Δ[1/ζ(t-1)]	−.296(1.962)+	.058(.349)
Δ[1/ζ(t-2)]	−.182(1.290)	−.032(.197)
EC(t-1)	−.17(3.913)**	−.006(1.867)+
Diagnostics:		
Adj- R^2	.454	.249
F-Statistic	4.510(.00)	2.437(.032)
Serial Corr Q(1)	4.19(.52)	8.664(.032)*
Jarque-Bera (Norm)	.96(.62)	2.094(.351)
ARCH(1)- F Statistic	.69(.41)	13.186(.001)**
White (heterosk.) F	1.33(.27)	3.535(.003)**

Notes:
EC refers to the error correction term derived from the estimates of the relevant cointegrating vector. Cases are those listed in Table 8.2. All variable definitions are as in the text. The Δ symbol is the first difference operator. t-statistics in parenthesis. * signifies statistically significant at the 5% level; ** at the 1% level; + at the 10% level.

because we estimated the ratio as permanent income over current income following Cochrane (1994), the expected sign is negative rather than positive as in equation (10), that is, $a_5 < 0$ (not all results shown). As predicted, none of the measures of the income ratio show the ratio significant in the long-run cointegration vector. In the error-correction, the Bordo and Jonung (1987) type measure, based on Friedman (1957), gives an insignificant t-statistic; the Cochrane (1994) and expected income type measures both give significant t-statistics. Focusing on the Cochrane-type measure, because it represents a possibly new standard in the application of the permanent income hypothesis and is implied directly by the model, Table 8.6 reports the relevant error-correction results. Inclusion of this ratio makes the error-correction term more significant and produces some changes in the

Table 8.6 Revised error correction estimates of velocity equation (11)

Independent Variables	*Case 1* I=CPR	*Case 3* I=TBR
Constant	−.294(−1.665)+	−.320(−2.266)*
Δv(t−1)	.323(1.883)*	.467(2.604)**
Δv(t−2)	−.484(−2.847)**	−.383(−2.314)**
Δi(t−1)	−.067(−2.303)**	−.010(−.355)
Δi(t−2)	.023(.849)	.040(1.465)
Δw(t−1)	−.128(−.280)	.216(.892)
Δw(t−2)	−.348(−.816)	.258(1.062)
Δ[1/ζ(t−1)]	−.205(−.787)	1.031(2.263)**
Δ[1/ζ(t−2)]	.073(.288)	.390(.824)
c(t−1)/y	−.625(−2.456)**	−.475(−2.214)**
EC(t−1)	−.191(−2.559)**	−.012(−2.431)*
Adj R squared	.509	.478
F	4.946(.0003)**	4.578(.001)**
Q(5)	4.255(.513)	1.835(.871)
SC(1)	6.101(.02)*	.363(.218)
ARCH (1)	.257(.616)	.018(.895)
White	1.139(.394)	.872(.619)

Notes:
Column (1) uses the commercial paper rate; column (2) uses the Treasury bill rate; * signifies statistically significant at the 5% level; ** at the 1% level; + at the 10% level. t-statistics are in parenthesis.

substitution terms as when compared with the results in Table 8.5. Use of contemporaneous consumption instead of lagged consumption gives similar results, except that the ratio term itself lacks statistical significance, although it has the hypothesized negative sign. The significance of (lagged) consumption)/GNP and the increased significance of the error-correction term imply that the ratio term explains unanticipated effects otherwise left as residuals.

8.5 Conclusion

This chapter specifies the equilibrium velocity of money demand from a Baumolian (1952)-type cash-in-advance economy with costly credit. Interpreting this velocity as long-run velocity, we find cointegration among GNP/M1, the interest rate, the real wage, and the time per unit of finance sector output. The significance of the latter two variables verifies that inclusion of the cost of credit produces a stable velocity function. Increased financial innovation arising out of deregulation influences velocity via a lower cost of credit, a lower quantity demanded of money compared to exchange credit, resulting in higher velocity. Long-run velocity is explained only through these substitution terms of the money demand function.

Other studies of money demand may find cointegration without a credit cost but these are often estimated when little financial innovation has taken place and the cost of credit has varied little. Thus, for example, Arrau, De Gregorio, Reinhart and Wickham (1996) cannot find cointegration for data from Chile and Mexico because a proxy for financial innovation is excluded. Turning to studies for developed economies excluding the cost of credit would be unlikely to result in the cointegration property where major financial deregulation has occurred, or where major financial innovation has evolved in part to avoid a sustained high inflation-tax. For example, during the "missing money" period of the early 1980's, Friedman and Kuttner (1992) find a break in cointegration in U.S. data when financial deregulation occurred during a high inflation period, and Butkiewicz and McConnell (1995) find parameter instability in U.S. money demand due to financial deregulation. Examples from other countries also attest as to the general nature of the phenomenon considered in this paper.

Our results show that including the cost of credit raises the interest elasticity of money demand. To see intuitively why this should occur, consider a credit-cash perspective: denoting the interest elasticity of real money by η_i^m and the interest elasticity of income by η_i^c, then $\eta_i^m = \gamma(1\ A^*)/(A^*) + \eta_i^c$. With a small interest elasticity of income, the theoretical interest elasticity of money demand rises approximately proportionately with the credit-cash ratio. With cash only and $A^* = 1$, η_i^m reduces to η_i^c. But, as the consumer substitutes to credit, and as the share of credit rises from zero, the money demand elasticity becomes more negative. Consider instead a velocity perspective: including exchange credit in the economy raises $1/A^*$ up from 1, and so increases the interest elasticity of money demand. Going one step further in price-theoretic intuition, consider the elasticity of substitution between cash and credit. Denoting this inverse curvature measure by σ and specifying $\zeta^{(1/\gamma)}(i/w)$ as the relative price of cash purchases to credit purchases, then $\sigma = -\gamma/A^*$. The elasticity of substitution equals a factor of velocity. It also forms a central part of the own-price elasticity, which can be written as $\eta_i^m = \sigma(1 - A^*) + \eta_i^c$. The greater the substitutability between cash and credit, the higher the interest elasticity of money demand. And, as the solution for A^* suggests, with the cost of credit trending down, the elasticity of substitution and the interest elasticity will trend up. This leads us to expect that our estimated parameter a_2, is not only comparatively higher, but also trending upwards in time.

The results presented in this chapter verify the finding of a relatively higher interest elasticity. For example, when cointegration is found in a conventional specification (see Table 8.1), interest elasticity estimates range from −.078 to −.085, as compared to −.25 to −.33 (see Table 8.3) when conditioning on the costs of credit. Gillman (1993) predicts this theoretically; Siklos (1993, Table 8.3) reports higher interest elasticities for most tested countries in a model augmented with proxies for changes in the financial system; and Melnick (1995) finds a semi-inflation-rate elasticity for Israel that increases from −1.00 to −1.83 when adding proxies for financial innovation.

Finally, our results explain the short-run velocity dynamics through the same substitution term, plus an income effect as predicted by Friedman (1959) and Cochrane (1994). The ratio of permanent to current income essentially represents a proxy that otherwise could be captured by a conventional error-correction term found in conventional specifications of money demand. We thus present evidence that supports an application of the permanent income hypothesis to money demand, while explaining long-run velocity through the relative price of money to exchange credit. Extensions of our approach could, for example, posit that the technological shift factor in banking (ζ) become endogenous and be used to explain Friedman and Schwartz (1982)- type differences in velocity among countries partly through different finance sector productivities, as well as be used to identify the underlying differences through factor endowments (as in Lucas, 1993b) and tax structures (as in King and Rebelo, 1990).

Our model represents an attempt at identifying a stable money demand function for the U.S. which conventional specifications have trouble finding. Another way to test robustness is to apply the theory in other countries. Preliminary evidence for Australia, on a quarterly basis from 1975–1996, has found cointegration of velocity where other studies have not been able to find a stable function.

Appendix 8.A: first-order conditions of equilibrium

$$[\beta^t/c(t)] - \beta^t\lambda(t)A(t)P(t)$$

$$- \mu q^t w(t)P(t)\tau(A, t)(1 - A(t)) - \mu q^t P(t)(1 - A(t)) = 0;$$

$$[\beta^t/x(t)] - \mu q^t w(t)P(t) = 0;$$

$$\beta^t \lambda(t) - \mu q^{t-1} = 0;$$

$$- \beta^t \lambda(t)P(t)c(t) + \mu q^t [P(t)\tau(t)c(t)$$

$$- w(t)P(t)(1 - A(t))\, \tau_A(A, t)\, c(t)]$$

$$+ \mu q^t P(t)c(t) = 0.$$

Appendix 8.B: additional estimation details

Error Correction Estimates with combined cost of credit

Independent Variables	*(1)*	*(2)*	*(3)*	*(5)*
Constant	–.259(–2.475)	–.266 (–2.559)	.011(1.679)	.010(1.389)
Δv(t–1)	.072(.370)	.022(.113)	.205(.794)	.216(1.391)
Δv(t–2)	–.369(–1.873)	–.399(–2.014)		
Δi(t–1)	.034(.813)	.048(1.209)	–.007(.329)	–.015(.658)
Δi(t–2)	.077(1.883)	.069(1.971)		
Δ[w ζ] (t–1)	.108(.316)	.127(.374)	–1.58(.722)	–.183(.881)
Δ[w ζ] (t–2)	.260(.773)	.260(.784)		
c(t–1)/y	–.549(–2.984)	–.567(–3.127)		
EC(t–1)	.255(2.122)	.300(2.153)	.072(1.384)	.052(.976)
Adj. R squared	.337	.334	.040	.052
F	3.536(.005)	3.511(.005)	1.428(.244)	1.564(.204)
Q(5)	3.887(.566)	4.045(.543)	1.341(.931)	1.686(.891)
SC(1)	15.85(.0004)	10.638(.003)		
ARCH (1)	.307(.583)	.711(.404)	12.543(.000)	11.037(.001)
White	1.244(.307)	1.171(.355)	13.721(.471)	15.087(.372)

Note: In columns (1) and (3), Interest rate = commercial paper rate.

Cointegration test

Consumption of non-durables and services vs. GNP both in 1986 $ based on the 1992 NIPA comprehensive revision

No. Of Vectors	*λ max statistic*
$r = 0$	28.50*
$r \leq 1$	2.50

Cointegrating vector: [1, –1.07(.012)], standard error in parenthesis.

Notes: The vector means that $c(t) - 1.07\, y(t)$ is stationary at the 1% level of significance. Alternatively, the null of a unit root in c/y is also rejected at the 1% level based on the Augmented Dickey-Fuller test with 1 lag in the AR part of the test equation ($ lags were tried but only lag 1 was statistically significant at the 10% level).

Notes

* Gillman, Max, Pierre L. Siklos and J. Lew Silver (1997). 'Money Velocity with Costly Credit', *Journal of Economic Research*, 2(1), 179–207.

1 This is consistent with Duca and Whitesell (1995).

2 The microfoundations approach here responds to the call made by King (1988) for an estimation of long-run velocity that uses cash-in-advance economies with a more variable velocity function than standard cash-in-advance models. Hodrick, Kocherlakota and Lucas (1991) buttress the need for better model velocity results with their simulation of the Lucas-Stokey (1987) cash-in-advance/credit economy, from which they conclude that the model cannot successfully capture the velocity series.

3 While tests also investigated contemporaneous consumption, the lag anticipates the consumer's prediction of permanent income on the basis of last period's consumption.

4 The choice to use the 1948-1990 data (similar to that of Bordo and Jonung 1987, Siklos 1993, and Bordo, Jonung and Siklos 1997) means that velocity rises by more after WWII until the late 1970's here as compared to the chain-weighted revisions of the NIPA (SCB 1996), since updated.

5 Granger and Swanson (1996) point out that cointegration is more easily found when the series are in log levels rather than in levels.

6 The other two cointegrating vectors were found to have incorrect signs and their residuals were found to be non-stationary. Johansen (1995) also uses this approach to eliminate some cointegrating vectors from consideration.

7 Siklos and Granger (1996) argue that cointegration can be turned "on" or "off" by the addition of some common stochastic trend.

9 Money demand in general equilibrium endogenous growth

Estimating the role of a variable interest elasticity*

Max Gillman and Glenn Otto

Summary

The chapter presents and tests a theory of the demand for money that is derived from a general equilibrium, endogenous growth economy, which in effect combines a special case of the shopping time exchange economy with the cash-in-advance framework. The model predicts that both higher inflation and financial innovation – that reduces the cost of credit – induce agents to substitute away from money towards exchange credit. The implied interest elasticity of money demand rises with the inflation rate and financial innovation rather than being constant as is typical in shopping time specifications. Using quarterly data for the US and Australia, we find evidence of cointegration for the money demand model. This money demand stability results because of the extra series that capture financial innovation; included are robustness checks and comparison to a standard money demand specification.

9.1 Introduction

The chapter offers a test of the money demand function, as derived from a general equilibrium endogenous growth model that includes financial sector productivity (Gillman and Kejak, 2005b). This model explains inflation as having a negative but diminishing effect on growth as the inflation rate is raised. Underlying the result is that the consumer becomes increasingly sensitive to inflation, as this tax is increased, substituting more from money to credit, and less from goods to leisure. Since the human capital utilization rate decreases as leisure use increases, the growth rate falls, but falls by lesser amounts as inflation increases. The implied money demand function is similar to a Cagan (1956) function, with a constant "semi-interest" elasticity, or rather an elasticity that rises in magnitude as the inflation rate rises.

An additional feature of the money demand is that its interest elasticity also rises with productivity increases in the credit production sector that outstrip aggregate productivity increases that are reflected in the real wage. This means that during a period of financial deregulation, as occurred in the US and Australia, starting in the late 1970s and early 1980s, the interest elasticity ceteris paribus would be expected to rise in magnitude due to the less expensive credit that acted as an alternative means of exchange. Decreases in the nominal interest rates that occurred during the later part of the deregulatory period, due to falling inflation, would cause by themselves the interest elasticity to decrease in magnitude. The net effect of these two opposing factors in a sense can be hinted at by what happened to velocity during this period. For example for the US, the income velocity of money continued to rise even after the fall in nominal interest rates. This is explained by the financial sector productivity increases dominating the nominal interest rate decreases, in Gillman and Kejak (2004). From this velocity experience, then, it would be expected that the interest elasticity would rise over the period.

This gives two central hypotheses for the paper. One, that a stable money demand function can be found for the Cagan-like model that also explains the inflation-growth profile (Gillman and Kejak, 2005b), as based on the inclusion of an "additional variable", reflecting financial sector productivity, as compared to standard money demand models. Second, that the interest elasticity as estimated would be found to rise over the period because of the importance of the post-deregulation productivity in financial services. Note that the deregulation generally took place in phases, with a series of banking laws that each contributed productivity shocks (see Benk, Gillman, and Kejak, 2005). Thus the financial productivity variable would be expected to reflect these increases over a period of time, thereby affecting the stationary estimation rather than being confined to a jump that could be netted out of the estimation using various procedures.

In Section 9.2, the general equilibrium money demand is presented, and in Section 9.3 a testable model is derived. Section 9.4 describes the data to be used in the study. Section 9.5 provides empirical results for US and Australian money demand. Section 9.6 presents evidence of the robustness of the results. Discussion and conclusions follow in Sections 9.7 and 9.8, respectively.

9.2 Representative agent economy

Consider a representative agent who as consumer likes goods c_t and leisure x_t, and has a current period utility function given by

$$u = \ln c_t + \alpha \ln x_t. \tag{1}$$

The consumer can purchase the good using either money, denoted by M_t, or with exchange-credit. Letting a_t denoted the fraction of purchases of the aggregate consumption good that the agent chooses to make with money, and with P_t as the goods nominal price, the cash-in-advance, or exchange technology, constraint is

$$M_t = a_t c_t P_t. \tag{2}$$

It is apparent that the model predicts a unitary consumption elasticity and a (variable) consumption velocity of money equal to $1/a_t$. Total exchange is equal to both money and credit purchases of the consumption goods. With q_t denoting the real quantity of credit used, the exchange constraint can be expressed as

$$M_t + P_t q_t = P_t c_t, \tag{3}$$

and combining equations (2) and (3),

$$q_t = (1 - a_t)\, c_t. \tag{4}$$

The fraction of time spent in each activity sums to one. With l_{Gt}, l_{Ft}, and l_{Ht} denoting the time spent in goods production, credit production, and human capital investment production, respectively,

$$1 = x_t + l_t + l_{Ft} + l_{Ht}. \tag{5}$$

Credit services are produced using only effective labour and total deposited funds, a constant returns to scale (CRS) function that follows the standard banking literature begun with the seminal contributions of Clark (1984) and Hancock (1985), except that there is no physical capital as an input, for simplification.[1] The total funds deposited, if the financial intermediary is decentralized, are the money and credit given in equation (3); the deposited funds are set equal to c_t.[2] With h_t denoting the stock of human capital, the effective labor used in producing credit is $l_{Ft}h_t$; this can be thought of as the banking time of the agent. With $A_F \in R_+$, the CRS credit services production technology is given as

$$q_t = A_F\,(l_{Ft}h_t)^{\gamma}\, c_t^{\,1-\gamma}. \tag{6}$$

Solving for a_t in equations (4) and (6), and substituting this into the exchange constraint (2), the money constraint can be written in a way that includes the credit production technology:

$$M_t = [1 - A_F\,(l_{Ft}h_t/c_t)^{\gamma}]\, P_t c_t. \tag{7}$$

This version of the Clower constraint can be shown to be equivalent to a special case of the shopping time constraint, if the effective banking time $l_{Ft}h_t$ is solved for; then this banking time rises with c_t, and falls with M_t/P_t, just as does shopping time. But whereas in the typical shopping time specification, the interest elasticity is constant by design, here in contrast the CRS production function for credit crucially implies an equilibrium money demand interest elasticity that rises in magnitude with the inflation rate.

The consumer accumulates both human capital h_t and physical capital, denoted by k_t, renting both to the goods producer. The rate of human capital investment is assumed to be proportional to the effective time spent in human capital accumulation $l_{Ht}h_t$, as in Lucas (1988b). With $A_H \in R_{++}$ and the depreciation rate δ_h,

$$\dot{h}_t = A_H l_{Ht} h_t - \delta_h h_t. \tag{8}$$

Physical capital investment i_t, given the depreciation rate δ_k, is given by

$$\dot{k}_t = i_t - \delta_k k_t. \tag{9}$$

The nominal value of the financial capital stock, denoted by Q_t, equals the sum of the money stock and the nominal value of the physical capital stock. It is given by

$$Q_t = M_t + P_t k_t, \tag{10}$$

making the flow of nominal financial wealth:

$$\dot{Q}_t = \dot{M}_t + P_t \dot{k}_t + \dot{P}_t k_t. \tag{11}$$

By the social resource constraint, or the allocation of goods constraint that is similar to the allocation of time constraint in equation (5), income is equal to investment plus consumption expenditures. With the real interest rate and real wage rate denoted by r_t and w_t, this can be written by solving for nominal investment as

$$P_t i_t = r_t P_t k_t + w_t P_t l_t h_t - P_t c_t. \tag{12}$$

Substituting from equations (9) and (11) into equation (12), the flow constraint (11) can be written as

$$\dot{Q}_t = r_t P_t k_t + w_t P_t l_t h_t - P_t c_t + \dot{M}_t + \dot{P}_t k_t - \delta_k k_t. \tag{13}$$

9.2.1 Goods producer problem

Goods are produced, by the representative agent acting as a producer, with a Cobb-Douglas technology involving physical capital, k_t, and effective labour, which equals the human capital stock, h_t, factored by the fraction of time spent in goods production. With $A_G \in R_{++}$ a shift parameter, $\beta \in (0, 1)$, and y_t denoting the total output of goods that can be converted costlessly to capital, production of goods is given by

$$y_t = A_G (l_t h_t)^{\beta} k_t^{1-\beta}. \tag{14}$$

The firm maximizes the standard profit subject to rental capital and labor inputs, with the first-order conditions that

$$w = \beta A_G (l_t h_t)^{\beta - 1} k_t^{1-\beta}, \tag{15}$$

$$r = (1 - \beta) A_G (l_t h_t)^{\beta} k_t^{-\beta}. \tag{16}$$

9.2.2 Government

It is assumed that the government supplies money through lump sum transfers V_t to the agent,

$$\dot{M}_t = V_t, \tag{17}$$

where $V_t = \sigma M_t$, so that the rate of money growth is constant at σ.

9.2.3 Equilibrium

Equilibrium is characterized by the firm's conditions (15) and (16), the money supply condition (17), and the consumer's equilibrium conditions from the following Hamiltonian problem: the consumer maximizes the present value of utility given by (1) subject to the constraints (7), (8), (10) and (13) with respect to c_t, x_t, l_t, l_{Ft}, h_t, k_t, and M_t:

$$\begin{aligned} H = {} & e^{-\rho t} (\ln c_t + a \ln x_t) \\ & + \mu_t \{M_t - [1 - A_F (l_{Ft} h_t / c_t)^{\gamma}] P_t c_t\} \\ & + \varphi_t (Q_t - M_t - P_t k_t) \\ & + \lambda_t (r_t P_t k_t + w_t P_t l_t h_t - P_t c_t + V_t + \dot{P}_t k_t - \delta_k k_t) \\ & + \phi_t [A_H (1 - x_t - l_t - l_{Ft}) h_t - \delta_h h_t]. \end{aligned} \tag{18}$$

9.2.4 Balanced growth path

The agent's equilibrium conditions along the balanced growth path can be expressed, with the time subscripts dropped, with g denoting the balanced-path growth rate, and with R denoting the nominal interest rate (made explicitly the interest rate for nominal bonds, if bonds are included in the problem), as

$$\frac{x}{ac} = \frac{1 + aR + \gamma (1 - a) R}{wh}, \tag{19}$$

$$g = r - \delta_K - \rho, \tag{20}$$

$$-\dot{\phi}_t / \phi_t = A_H (1 - x) - \delta_H = r - \delta_K, \tag{21}$$

$$-\dot{\lambda}_t/\lambda_t = r + \dot{P}/P \equiv R, \tag{22}$$

$$w = \beta A_G [A_H (1 - x)/(1 - \beta)]^{-(1-\beta)/\beta}, \tag{23}$$

$$R = w/[\gamma A_F (l_F h/c)^{\gamma - 1}]. \tag{24}$$

The first equilibrium equation (19) describes substitution between goods c and leisure x, as being dependent on the real wage w as discounted the by nominal interest rate R, whereby the discount is smaller the greater is the use of credit (a larger $1 - a$); put differently, a rise in R causes substitution from goods to leisure. The second condition (20) gives the balanced growth rate g as being equal to the return on physical capital $r - \delta_K$ minus time preference ρ, as well as equaling, by the third equation (21), the return on human capital minus time preference ρ; human capital's utilization rate $(1 - x)$ goes down, and the growth rate goes down, when leisure x goes up because of inflation. Equation (22) presents a form of the Fisher equation of interest rates, by which the real interest rate and the inflation rate sum up to the nominal interest rate; while equation (23) from the producer problem shows that the real wage rises with an increase in leisure when inflation increases.

9.2.4.1 Money demand

Equations (23) and (24) describe the standard input price relations in the goods and credit service sectors, with the price of labor equaling its marginal product in (23), and with the marginal cost of credit equaling the ratio of the marginal factor price w to the marginal factor product $\gamma A_F (l_F h/c)^{\gamma - 1}$ in (24). From this latter equation, and the exchange constraint (7), the agent's real money demand can be derived as

$$M/P = m = \left[1 - \left(\frac{\gamma R}{w}\right)^{\gamma/(1-\gamma)} A_F^{1/(1-\gamma)}\right] c. \tag{25}$$

Writing money demand in terms of its inverse income velocity,

$$m/y = \left[1 - \left(\frac{\gamma R}{w}\right)^{\gamma/(1-\gamma)} A_F^{1/(1-\gamma)}\right] (c/y). \tag{26}$$

The solution for c/y follows from

$$c/y = 1 - (i/y) = 1 - \left(\dot{k}_t + \delta_K k_t\right)/y = \left(\dot{k}/k + \delta_K\right)(k/y) = 1 - [(g + \delta_K) \cdot (k/y)].$$

Since k/y is the inverse of the average product of capital in the Cobb-Douglas production of goods, $k/y = (1 - \beta)/r$. Using this relation and substituting in for g from equation (20) gives that $c/y = \beta + (\rho/r)(1 - \beta)$, so that

$$m/y = \left[1 - \left(\frac{\gamma R}{w}\right)^{\gamma/(1-\gamma)} A_F^{1/(1-\gamma)}\right] [\beta + (\rho/r)(1 - \beta)]. \tag{27}$$

The money demand per output depends negatively on the nominal interest rate R, positively on the real wage w (as in Karni, 1974, Dowd, 1990, and Goodfriend, 1997), and negatively on the level of productivity in the credit sector A_F. Although financial innovation has been considered as a factor of money demand in various ways, for example in Friedman and Schwartz (1982), Orden and Fisher (1993), and Collins and Anderson (1998), the inclusion of A_F is more novel as a time series variable. An increase in A_F increases the productivity of credit services and so decreases the demand for real money balances. The parameter γ determines the degree of diminishing returns to effective labor per unit of consumption in the credit sector, a measure of development that changes only gradually over long periods of time and that is treated as a constant for the money demand estimation.

9.2.4.2 *Interest elasticity*

From equations (2) and (27), the interest elasticity of m/y, denoted by $\eta_R^{m/y}$, is

$$\eta_R^{m/y} = -\left(\frac{\gamma}{1-\gamma}\right)\left(\frac{1-a}{a}\right)$$

$$= -\left(\frac{\gamma}{1-\gamma}\right)\left(\frac{\left(\frac{\gamma R}{w}\right)^{\gamma/(1-\gamma)} A_F^{1/(1-\gamma)}}{1 - \left(\frac{\gamma R}{w}\right)^{\gamma/(1-\gamma)} A_F^{1/(1-\gamma)}}\right).$$

It is immediately clear that $\partial \mid \eta_R^{m/y} \mid / \partial R > 0$; given the Fisher equation (22), this implies that the elasticity increases as inflation goes up. Increases in credit productivity, A_F, similarly increase the elasticity magnitude.

9.2.5 *Basis for testing*

The nature of the interest elasticity will be tested by an approximation to the money demand in (27). The second factor in equation (27), $[\beta + (\rho/r)(1 - \beta)]$, which depends on the real interest rate, will be assumed to be constant. This assumption effectively is ignoring cyclical income effects on inverse income velocity coming through changes in consumption relative to income as a result of temporary income effects.[3] Here, with an emphasis on the trends in the interest elasticity over time, the assumption that this term is constant implies that temporary income effects are absent, as is consistent with the model's deterministic setting.[4]

9.3 Econometric model specification

Applying the approximation $(1 - z) = -\ln z$ to equation (27), a more tractable form for estimation is

$$m/y = -B\ \{[\gamma/(1-\gamma)]\ (1 + \ln R - \ln w) + (1/\gamma) \ln A_F\}, \tag{28}$$

where $B \equiv [\beta + (\rho/r)(1-\beta)] \leq 1$, for $g \geq 0$, is treated as a constant.[5]

9.3.1 Baseline money demand specification

From the equilibrium money demand approximation in equation (28), the model for estimation can be directly expressed as

$$(m_t/y_t) = a_0 + a_1 \ln R_t + a_2 \ln w_t + a_3 \ln A_{Ft} + u_{1t}. \tag{29}$$

u_{1t} is assumed to be a stationary error term, which reflects dynamic adjustment, measurement errors and (stationary) omitted variables. As described in the Data section below and in the Appendix, the nominal interest rate is measured by the government short term interest rate, the real wage is measured by the economy-wide hourly wage rate, and the productivity in the credit sector is measured by either the output divided by hours worked in the Finance sector, or by the real wage in the Finance sector; real GDP is used for output, a narrow measure of M1 is used as the baseline money stock measure, and broader monetary aggregates are also employed in the robustness analysis.

The comparative statics of equation (28) impose the following general sign restrictions on the parameters for the variables in (29):

$$a_1 < 0,\ a_2 > 0,\ a_3 < 0. \tag{30}$$

Equation (28) and the Cobb-Douglas specification for the credit production imply the additional variable restrictions:

$$-a_1 = a_2 = \gamma/(1-\gamma),\ a_3 = (1/\gamma)\ a_2,\ \gamma < 1. \tag{31}$$

9.3.2 Alternative standard money demand specification

As an alternative to equation (29) we also consider a standard constant interest elasticity model for money demand:

$$\ln(m_t/y_t) = \beta_0 + \beta_1 \ln i_t + \beta_2 \ln y_t + u_{2t}. \tag{32}$$

This is similar to the form estimated by Hoffman, Rasche, and Tieslau (1995), except that for comparability with (29) our dependent variable is inverse velocity. From standard theory we expect $\beta_1 < 0$, as it measures the interest elasticity of money demand, while the magnitude and sign of β_2 is ambiguous as it depends on whether the income elasticity of money demand is greater or less than one. A unitary income elasticity (as implied by the exchange credit model) makes $\beta_2 = 0$, while an income elasticity, for example, of less than one makes β_2 negative.

The key feature of this conventional specification is that it does not allow for the effect of changes in the cost of exchange credit on the demand for money. If for example the 1980s and 1990s represent a period during which the relative price of exchange credit fell sharply, due to the effects of deregulation and rapid technological progress in the financial sector, then according to the banking time model, the conventional specification should not be an adequate model of the demand for cash.

9.4 Data

A quarterly data set is constructed for the United States from 1976:1 to 1998:2 and for Australia from 1975:1 to 1996:2. These are periods when both of these countries experienced relatively high inflation, deregulation of the financial system and the growth of interest bearing exchange credit. The majority of series used in the paper are produced by government departments and official statistical agencies. However for some series we are forced to extrapolate or interpolate the available data. Definitions of the series used are provided in Appendix A, while the full data set and the primary sources are available from the authors on request.

Two comments about the variables used in the paper are in order. In the theoretical model, money is a non-interest bearing means of payment that is costless to produce. Therefore in the empirical analysis we use a narrower monetary aggregate than M1 or M2, both of which have been widely used in previous empirical studies. These monetary aggregates include assets that we consider more like credit than our model's concept of money. The model suggests the use of a narrow monetary aggregate, which we measure as currency plus non-interest bearing bank deposits.

One problem that we face in estimating equation (29) for Australia is the lack of a useful measure of labour productivity in the finance sector. In Australia the official measure of aggregate output in the finance sector aggregate is obtained adding the value of inputs and assuming a zero growth rate for labour productivity. In the absence of a direct productivity measure for the Australian finance sector we use the real wage for that sector as a proxy. Provided factor markets are reasonably competitive, changes in the real wage will reflect productivity changes. It is apparent from equation (6) that the marginal product of labour in credit production depends on A_F. Lowe (1995) provides some empirical evidence, which suggests that the real wage in the Australian financial sector is a plausible indicator of productivity in that sector.

9.5 Results

The two models that we consider are given by equations (29) and (32). We view these models as alternative equilibrium relationships that potentially describe the long-run influences on money holdings. It is apparent from looking at plots of the variables that the series are non-stationary. Moreover the augmented Dickey-Fuller test for a unit root implies that it is not unreasonable to characterise the variables in the two models as integrated of order one. Given the non-stationary nature of the data, our econometric strategy is to employ the cointegration techniques developed by Johansen and Juselius (1990) and Johansen (1995) to estimate the two alternative models.

9.5.1 Baseline model

Tables 9.1 and 9.2 present the results for United States and Australian data obtained from estimation of the banking time model using the Johansen procedure. The results for both countries are based on a VAR in levels with four lags, however (as indicated below) our results are not particularly sensitive to choice of lag length.[6] The trace and the λ-max statistics are used to test for the number of cointegrating vectors. Using a 5 percent level of significance the trace test points to a single cointegrating relationship among the four variables in the banking time model for both the United States and

Table 9.1 Banking time model 1976: 1 – 1998: 2 – United States

Hypothesis	*Trace*	*λ-max*
$p \leq 3$	0.36	0.36
$p \leq 2$	9.84	9.48
$p \leq 1$	24.09	14.25
$p = 0$	49.36*	25.27

Unrestricted Estimates: Point and 95 percent Interval Estimates

a_1	a_2	a_3
–0.23 (–0.62 to 0.16)	0.34 (–0.48 to 1.17)	–0.18 (–0.57 to –0.21)

Restriction: $-a_1 = a_2$

Likelihood Ratio Test of Restriction:

LR = 0.04

Restricted Estimates: Point and 95 percent Interval Estimates

a_1	a_2	a_3
–0.26 (–0.63 to 0.12)	0.26 (–0.12 to 0.63)	–0.22 (–0.47 to 0.04)

Notes
Critical values for the Trace and λ-max test statistics are from Johansen and Juselius (1990. Table A2). A * indicates the null hypothesis can be rejected at the 5 percent level of significance. The LR test of the coefficient restriction is distributed as a Chi-squared with one degree of freedom.

Table 9.2 Banking time model 1975: 1 – 1996: 2 – Australia

Hypothesis	*Trace*	*λ-max*
$\rho \leq 3$	1.05	1.05
$\rho \leq 2$	7.59	6.54
$\rho \leq 1$	18.28	10.69
$\rho = 0$	49.11*	30.83*

Unrestricted Estimates: Point and 95 percent Interval Estimates

a_1	a_2	a_3
–0.49 (–0.93 to 0.04)	1.31 (–1.13 to 3.76)	–4.30 (–8.18 to –0.42)

Restriction: $-a_1 = a_2$

Likelihood Ratio Test of Restriction:

LR = 0.75

Restricted Estimates: Point and 95 percent Interval Estimates

a_1	a_2	a_3
–0.36 (–0.53 to –0.18)	0.36 (0.18 to 0.53)	–2.98 (–4.06 to –1.89)

Notes: Critical values for the Trace and λ-max test statistics are from Johansen and Juselius (1990). Table A2). A * indicates the null hypothesis can be rejected at the 5 percent level of significance. The LR test of the coefficient restriction is distributed as a Chi-squared with one degree of freedom.

Australian data. The λ-max test is consistent with this finding for Australia, but provides slightly weaker support for a cointegrating vector for the United States (about the 10 percent level). However, on balance there seems to be reasonable evidence of a cointegrating relationship among the four variables in the banking time model for both countries.

Conditional on the existence of a single cointegrating vector we normalize by setting the coefficient on m/y equal to unity and then interpret the other coefficient estimates in the vector as the long-run coefficients in equation (29). The unrestricted point estimates of the a coefficients along with 95 percent confidence intervals are reported in the tables. For both countries the signs of the unrestricted point estimates are consistent with the predictions of the model. Equilibrium holdings of money are negatively related to the nominal interest rate and to productivity in the credit sector, while they are positively related to the aggregate real wage rate. However one problem with the unrestricted estimates for both countries is that the estimated standard errors are large. This can be seen from the reported 95 percent confidence intervals, which typically include zero.

9.5.1.1 Restrictions

More precise estimates can be obtained by imposing the restriction on the cointegrating vector that

$$-a_1 = a_2. \tag{33}$$

A likelihood ratio test indicates that this restriction is not rejected by the data for either country and the respective restricted estimates are reported in Tables 9.1 and 9.2. For Australia the coefficient estimates for the restricted model are all statistically significant. From equation (31), $|a_1| = a_2 = \gamma/(1-\gamma)$, and the implied point estimate of γ is 0.26. For the United States data imposing the restriction reduces the coverage of the 95 percent interval estimate, but all intervals still include zero. The implied point estimate on the interest rate and real wage is $\gamma = 0.21$. These point estimates of γ for both countries provide strong empirical support for the assumption of decreasing marginal returns to time spent in credit production.

The estimated coefficients on the measure of productivity in the credit sector are negative for both sets of data. This is consistent with model's prediction that productivity improvements in the credit sector will lower the price of credit (as a means of exchange) and result in substitution away from cash. One difference between the point estimates for the United States and Australia is the absolute magnitude of the coefficients. In fact the results for Australia provide greater support for our particular parameterization of the banking time model than those for the United States. Since equation (31) implies that $a_3 = -[1/(1-\gamma)]$, another estimate of γ can be recovered from the point estimate of a_3. For Australia the implied value of γ is 0.66, which is within the (0, 1) assumed bounds; however for the United States the implied value for γ is negative, which violates the bounds. This forces reliance only upon the estimate of γ as given by the a_1 and a_2 joint estimate.

9.5.1.2 Interest elasticity estimate

From equation (29) it is apparent that the (approximate) interest elasticity implied by our specification of the banking time model is given by $-[\gamma/(1-\gamma)]$ (m/y). Thus the interest elasticity of money is time varying and given the time series properties of m/y is actually non-stationary. Figure 9.1 presents a plot of the interest elasticity for the United States and Australia implied by the restricted estimates. In both countries the demand for money has tended to become more elastic over time.

The results in Tables 9.1 and 9.2 suggest that the baseline model is able to capture key aspects of the long run behaviour of the non-interest bearing money in the United States and Australia. In particular, productivity growth in exchange credit production and the consequent fall in the cost of exchange credit services appear to be important influences on the transactions demand for cash.

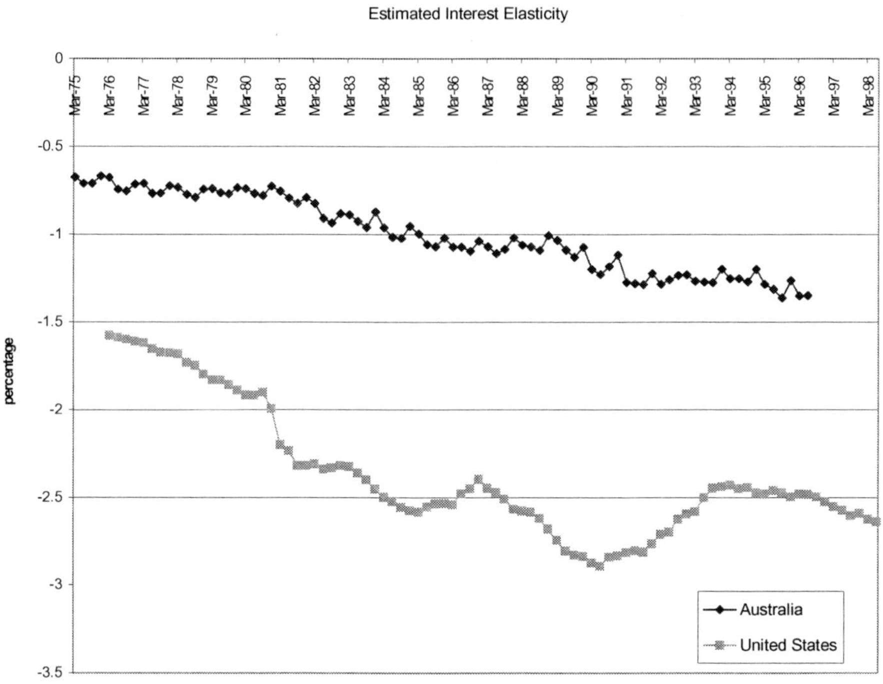

Figure 9.1 Interest elasticity for the United States and Australia.

9.5.2 Conventional model

If the cost of credit services is an important determinant of the demand for money, then a conventional money demand should not be able to explain the trend behaviour of cash. We now examine this hypothesis formally by estimating equation (32). This specification is equivalent to the model for log-velocity that has been estimated by Hoffman, Rasche, and Tieslau (1995) for a number of countries. The results are reported in Tables 9.3 and 9.4.

For the United States both the trace and the λ-max test point to the existence of a single cointegrating vector, however the estimated long run interest elasticity is positive. The Australian results provide even less support for the conventional model, since there is strong evidence that the velocity of money is not cointegrated with real income and the nominal interest rate. What these results indicate is that real income and nominal interest rates are not sufficient to explain the trend behaviour of money in the United States and Australia over the last twenty-five years.

Table 9.3 Conventional model 1976: 1 – 1998: 2 – United States

Hypothesis	*Trace*	*λ-max*
$\rho \leq 2$	0.03	0.05
$\rho \leq 1$	10.27	10.21
$\rho = 0$	30.73*	20.46*

Unrestricted Estimates: Point and 95 percent Interval Estimates

β_1	β_2
2.41 (–4.98 to 9.80)	1.82 (–6.01 to 9.65)

Note: See Table 9.1.

Table 9.4 Conventional model 1975: 1 – 1996: 2 – Australia

Hypothesis	*Trace*	*λ-max*
$\rho \leq 2$	0.44	0.44
$\rho \leq 1$	7.80	7.80
$\rho = 0$	19.06	11.25

Unrestricted Estimates: Point and 95 percent Interval Estimates

β_1	β_2
0.09 (–0.02 to 0.19)	1.13 (0.94 to 1.31)

Note: See Table 9.1.

9.6 Robustness

9.6.1 Sensitivity of the estimates of the baseline model

While the results reported in Tables 9.1 and 9.2 provide prima facie support for the predictions of the banking time model it is important to provide some evidence of the robustness of our estimates. To do this we consider how the results obtained from estimating equation (29) change as we vary first the sample size and then the number of lags of the VAR model (Hoffman, Rasche, and Tieslau, 1995). Tables 9.5 and 9.6 present some recursive estimates for equation (29). These are obtained by fixing the starting point of the sample and then estimating the model over progressively longer sample periods. Each set of estimates adds an extra four quarters. All of the recursive estimates are based on VAR with four lags.

For each of the recursive estimates we report the trace statistic for testing the null of no cointegration, the unrestricted estimates of (29), the likelihood ratio statistic for testing $-a_1 = a_2$, and the restricted estimates. The results suggest that there is strong evidence of at least one cointegrating vector for all

Table 9.5 Recursive estimates of the banking time model – United States

	Unrestricted Estimates				*Restricted Estimates*		
Sample End	*Trace*	a_1	a_2	a_3	*LR*	γ	a_3
91:2	52.10*	0.00	1.23	0.15	6.72*	0.74	1.17
92:2	59.16*	−0.01	1.14	0.10	8.93*	0.12	−0.29
93:2	50.43*	−0.06	0.89	0.00	4.96*	0.09	−0.25
94:2	56.07*	−0.09	0.52	−0.11	1.00	0.11	−0.25
95:2	50.58*	−0.46	−3.88	−1.66	1.55	0.25	−0.22
96:2	51.71*	−0.27	0.23	−0.23	0.00	0.21	−0.22
97:2	50.80*	−0.26	0.17	−0.25	0.00	0.19	−0.22
98:2	49.36*	−0.23	0.34	−0.18	0.04	0.20	−0.22

Notes: See Table 9.1. All samples in the recursive models end in the year and quarter indicated.

Table 9.6 Recursive estimates of the banking time model – Australia

	Unrestricted Estimates				*Restricted Estimates*		
Sample End	*Trace*	a_1	a_2	a_3	*LR*	γ	a_3
89:2	52.58*	−0.19	−0.33	0.94	0.52	0.22	−1.55
90:2	51.54*	−0.44	0.95	−2.31	1.02	0.26	−1.53
91:2	50.64*	−0.55	1.76	−4.47	2.12	0.25	−2.61
92:2	50.33*	−0.64	2.70	−7.07	3.04	0.24	−3.37
93:2	50.86*	−0.63	2.52	−6.80	2.73	0.24	−3.39
94:2	52.61*	−0.59	2.14	−5.87	2.24	0.26	−3.18
95:2	53.67*	−0.59	2.14	−5.75	2.34	0.26	−3.12
96:2	49.11*	−0.49	1.31	−4.30	0.75	0.26	−2.97

Notes: See Table 9.1 All samples in the recursive models end in the year and quarter indicated.

of the sample lengths considered. In addition the parameter estimates, particularly the restricted estimates, are quite robust to the changes in the sample size considered, particularly for the Australian data. In the restricted model for Australia the point estimate of λ varies from 0.22 to 0.26, while the estimate of ranges from −3.39 to −1.53. Overall these recursive estimates suggest that our theory yields a relatively stable model for money in Australia. With the United States data there is somewhat more variation in both the restricted and unrestricted estimates, until about 1995.

Finally we consider the sensitivity of our estimates of (γ) to changing the lag length of the VAR model used in the Johansen estimator. Table 9.7 presents a comparison of the results obtained from estimation of equation (29) for VAR models with lags lengths of 3, 4 and 5. The results for the United States are quite robust to this variation in lag length. For Australia with the VAR(3) and VAR(5) specifications there is considerably less support for a cointegrating relationship, although the coefficient estimates obtained from these specifications are consistent with the predictions of the

Table 9.7 Estimates of the banking time model for alternative lag lengths

	Unrestricted Estimates				*Restricted Estimates*		
VAR(k)	*Trace*	a_0	a_1	a_2	*LR*	γ	a_2
United States							
k=3	50.33*	−0.32	0.76	−0.09	0.38	0.40	−0.28
k=4	49.36*	−0.23	0.34	−0.18	0.04	0.20	−0.22
k=5	47.47*	−0.30	0.15	−0.24	0.08	0.21	−0.20
Australia							
k=3	31.20	−0.59	1.15	−4.68	0.08	0.32	−3.67
k=4	49.11*	−0.49	1.31	−4.30	0.75	0.26	−2.98
k=5	41.35	−1.46	5.24	−11.96	1.30	0.38	−4.45

Note: See Table 9.1.

Table 9.8 Dynamic banking time model – United States

	Dependent Variable: $\Delta(m_t/y_t)$	
	Unrestricted Model	*Restricted Model*
Constant	0.003 (1.54)	0.004 (1.63)
$\Delta\ (m_{t-1}/y_{t-1})$	0.288 (2.49)	0.290 (2.48)
$\Delta \ln i_{t-1}$	−0.007 (3.87)	−0.007 (3.84)
ΔA_{Ft-1}	0.026 (3.17)	0.026 (3.17)
ECM_{t-1}	−0.005 (1.87)	−0.005 (1.87)
$\bar{R}^2$	0.484	0.483
LM1 (5)	0.114	0.112
LM2 (5)	0.515	0.530

Notes: The t-statistics are computed using White's (1980) heteroscedasticity-consistent covariance matrix estimator. LM1 is a Lagrange multiplier test for serial correlation and LM2 is a test for ARCH effects. Both allow for possible effects up to fifth order.

banking time model and are qualitatively similar to those from the VAR(4) model.

9.6.2 Short run dynamics

The cointegration analysis is concerned with testing for long run relationships and estimating the long run coefficients. We now consider the short run dynamics. Given the existence of a cointegrating relationship we can model the dynamic behaviour of money by an error correction model. Tables 9.8 and 9.9 report our attempts to obtain a relatively parsimonious error correction model for money. The models are obtained by the usual general-to-specific strategy. Initial models included two lags of the following variables: $\Delta(m/y)$, $\Delta(\ln w)$, $\Delta(\ln A_F)$, and the error correction mechanism lagged once.

Table 9.9 Dynamic banking time model – Australia

	Dependent Variable: $\Delta\ (m_t/y_t)$	
	Unrestricted Model	*Restricted Model*
Constant	0.236 (3.58)	0.260 (3.51)
$\Delta\ (m_{t-1}/y_{t-1})$	−0.182 (2.04)	−0.184 (2.04)
$\Delta\ (m_{t-2}/y_{t-2})$	−0.295 (2.94)	−0.302 (3.00)
$\Delta \ln i_{t-1}$	−0.010 (1.37)	−0.010 (1.30)
ECM_{t-1}	−0.026 (3.79)	−0.033 (3.60)
$\bar{R}^2$	0.737	0.736
LM1 (5)	0.548	0.439
LM2 (5)	0.817	0.754

Notes: The t-statistics are computed using White's (1980) heteroscedasticity-consistent covariance matrix estimator. LM1 is a Lagrange multiplier test for serial correlation and LM2 is a test for ARCH effects. Both allow for possible effects up to fifth order.

When statistically insignificant variables were omitted, on the basis of t-tests, we are left with the models reported in Table 9.8 and 9.9. For both countries a reasonably parsimonious dynamic model can be obtained. Diagnostic tests on the residuals of the models indicate no evidence of serial correlation or ARCH effects up to five lags. To ensure that our inference is robust to the presence of heteroskedasticity, the reported t-statistics are computed using White (1980) heteroskedasticity-consistent covariance matrix estimator.

For Australia the dynamic model explains about 75 percent of the variation in $\Delta\ (m/y)$. The significant variables are two lags of $\Delta\ (m/y)$, the lagged change in the interest rate and the error correction term. Notice the error correction term is the most significant of all the variables in the dynamic model, providing some additional evidence that the banking time model is a valid cointegrating relationship. Lagged changes in the economy-wide real wage and in the finance sector real wage are not important in explaining $\Delta\ (m/y)$ despite their key role in explaining the trend in non-interest bearing money. For the United States the dynamic model explains about half the variation in $\Delta\ (m/y)$. In this case $\Delta\ (\ln A_{Ft} - 1)$ is found to be a significant explanatory variable.

9.6.3 M1, M2, and M3 estimation results

As a final test of the banking time model we estimated it using broader some measures of money. While we have not included tables of the results in this paper the main findings can be summarised as follows. We estimate the model using M1 for both the United States and Australia and using M2 for the United States and M3 for Australia. All of the measures of money provide some support for the existence of at least one cointegrating vector. However in the case of M1 the restriction, $-a_1 = a_2$, is strongly rejected for both countries, while the unrestricted coefficient estimates typically have the wrong signs. For the broader aggregates M2 and M3 the coefficient restriction is not rejected, but the estimated coefficient on productivity is found to be small and statistically insignificant.

9.7 Discussion

In the cash-in-advance models, money is a non-interest bearing means of payment that is costless to produce. We therefore use, as our baseline aggregate for the theory, money plus non-interest bearing demand deposits, assuming away the cost of such deposits. In addition to this definition of money as non-interest bearing instruments, we investigate whether the theory might unexpectedly also explain the broader aggregates, of M1 and M2, and even M3, but do not report the results here. These broad aggregates contain features of both the non-interest bearing aggregates that in our model acts as money as well as the interest-bearing aggregates that in our model acts as exchange credit, and so are not as well-suited to being explained by standard exchange-based general equilibrium monetary models. Including the productivity of the finance sector is expected to capture the shift away from non-interest bearing money into interest-bearing aggregates. So it is not surprising that it does not help to explain, for example, Australian M3 demand, which includes interest-bearing aggregates. The M3 results do indicate cointegration with significance for the real wage, also a theorized cost of using exchange credit.

Alternatively, a contrasting approach to estimating money demand is to change the definition of the monetary aggregate so that it contains the non-interest bearing elements of all of the monetary instruments. Barnett (1980) does this with the "Divisia" application of index theory to monetary aggregates, and Lucas (2000) suggests this may be a useful direction. Here when a shift in the price of interest-bearing credit activity leads to a different relative usage of the various monetary instruments, the definition of the Divisia aggregate is changed to re-weight the different instruments in reflection of their new usage. For example, a lowering of the cost of interest bearing accounts, like "checkable" interest-bearing money market accounts, may induce an increased use of such accounts. During the moderately high-inflation and financial-deregulation environment of the industrial countries in the 1980s, the Divisia index increased the weight of such partially interest-bearing aggregates in the Divisia aggregate, while reducing the weight given to aggregates like currency. Changing the definition of the aggregate so that it captures the non-interest bearing parts of all of the monetary instruments can enable the aggregate to remain responsive only to the nominal interest rate, the own-price of money, in a stable function. It avoids a shift in its demand during changes in the substitute prices, such as in the cost of the interest-bearing instruments, by instead shifting the weights that define the aggregate.

However, central banks engaged in inflation-rate targeting may need to understand the demand for the very narrowly defined money that they actually supply and how it can shift when inflation variability induces financial innovations. The Divisia approach provides a brilliant exposition of how the nominal interest rate acts as the own-price of money. But it cannot explain the demand for narrowly defined money. Dixon (1997) suggests that Barnett (1997) "makes a strong case for the Divisia approach as the only model that can successfully provide a stable money demand based on indisputably rigorous microeconomics". The chapter offers up a demand for money derived from a fairly fully specified model, including one based upon the microeconomic structure of banking services production. Modelling the banking sector is our key to finding a stable money demand without "missing money" and without changing the definition of the aggregate in order to do so.

Money demand is another facet of general equilibrium models that can be tested. If they cannot explain money demand when deregulation in the financial sector occurs, then they would seem to require extension so that they can internalise such related factors within the money demand function. This is a central argument of the chapter. The chapter provides a micro-founded paradigm of banking time as a special case of shopping time, with the result being an interest elasticity that varies significantly with the inflation rate in a way similar to the Cagan (1956) model. And it gives less free money demand parameters as compared to shopping time models, money-in-the-utility function models, and cash-good, credit-good models, in the sense that there are no unrestricted utility and "transactions cost function" parameters; Indeed it is the attempt to restrict such free utility parameters with some basis in outside data that has led researchers to impose a constant interest elasticity within the shopping time framework. Such parameters here are replaced by only the technology parameters of the credit production function that follows the intermediation literature of Clark (1984). By using a time series for a measure of the productivity of the credit services sector, the estimation implies an estimate of the degree of diminishing returns. This gives an estimated technology parameter that is constant, while the behavioural "parameter" of the interest elasticity is allowed to vary endogenously.

9.8 Conclusion

The finding of a stable money demand compares to Mark and Sul (2003), who find a cointegrated Cagan money demand function for individual countries and in a panel. In contrast, is the constant interest elasticity assumption in the exogenous growth, general equilibrium, shopping time models of, for example, Goodfriend (1997), Lucas (2000), and Dittmar, Gavin, and Kydland (2005). The difference is important in that the inflation-growth profile has been shown to be replicated in general equilibrium only with a variable interest elasticity, which rises in magnitude with the interest rate and with productivity increases in credit supply. The rising interest elasticity, in response to the inflation tax rising, may be part of a broader phenomena of greater price sensitivity as tax rates increase, with the results of negative but diminishing growth effects. And such increasing price elasticities also means that tax revenues, inflation, labor or capital taxes, will go up at a decreasing rate as the taxes increase, making such increases less efficacious.

Greater inflation tax sensitivity adds support to the agenda of low inflation from the growth perspective, and may help explain the global move towards inflation targeting at low levels of inflation, while seeking high-growth economic policies. As Gillman and Kejak (2005b) illustrate, there can be bigger increases in growth as the inflation rate is knocked downwards; and as extended to other taxes, this suggests that a low inflation and low flat tax regime is useful in achieving high growth.

Appendix 9.A: data description

Money. Non-interest bearing money is measured as currency plus non-interest bearing current deposits and M1 is the sum of currency and total current deposits. United States: Money is measured as M1 less other checkable deposits. Australia: Data on currency holdings (not seasonally adjusted) are available from 1975:1. The Reserve Bank of Australia publishes a series for total current (ie. demand) deposits with banks over the same period, however a decomposition of this series into interest and non-interest bearing components is only available from 1984:3 to 1996:2. An estimate of non-interest bearing deposits for the period 1975:1 to 1984:2 is obtained by simply extrapolating interest bearing deposits from 1984:2 back to 1975:1 (assuming a constant growth rate of 10 percent per quarter) and subtracting these from total current deposits.

Real income. United States: Constant price income in 1992 prices is measured as nominal GDP deflated by the price index for GDP. Australia: Constant price income in 1989–90 prices is measured as nominal GDP deflated by the implicit price deflator for GDP.

Nominal interest rate. United States: The interest rate is the 3 month T-bill rate. Australia: The interest rate used is the 90 day bank-accepted bill rate.

Economy-wide real wage. United States: The economy-wide real wage is measured as total private sector average hourly earnings in 1982 dollars. Australia: The economy-wide hourly wage rate is obtained by dividing average weekly earnings of males in all industries by the average weekly hours by males in all industries. This is deflated by the implicit price deflator for GDP to obtain a real hourly wage rate.

Productivity in credit production. United States: An index of productivity in finance is computed as constant price GDP in the Finance, Insurance and Real Estate (FIR) sector divided by total hours worked in FIR. Australia: In the absence of a suitable productivity measure for the credit sector, the real wage in credit production is used as a proxy for labour productivity. This is measured as the nominal hourly wage in the Finance and Insurance (FI) sector. It is computed by dividing average weekly earnings in FI by average weekly hours in FI and deflating by implicit price deflator for GDP. We note that quarterly data for the average weekly earnings per employee in FI is available only from 1984:4. For the period 1975:1 to 1984:3 we interpolate annual data for this series to get a quarterly series. Quarterly data on average weekly hours is based on the numbers for the FI sub-sector from 1984:4 to 1996:2. For the earlier period 1975:4 to 1983:3 quarterly hours data are only available for the sector the more general sector Finance, Insurance, Property, and Business Services (FIRB). Finally for the three quarters 1975:1 to 1975:3 we interpolate from annual data for the FIPB sector.

Acknowledgements

We thank Bruce Felmingham, Eva-Ulrike Fieber, Lance Fisher, Geoffrey Kingston, By Jeong, Michal Kejak, Jan Kmenta, Adrian Pagan, Andreas Schabert, Graham Voss and seminar participants at Australian National University, CERGE-EI of Prague, the University of New South Wales, University of Melbourne, the Third Macroeconomics Workshop at the University of Tasmania, the EEA Annual Meetings at Toulouse, the National Bank of Hungary, and the Monetary Economics Workshop HWWA Hamburg, for helpful comments.

Notes

* Gillman, Max, and Glenn Otto (2007). 'Money Demand in General Equilibrium Endogenous Growth: Estimating the Role of a Variable Interest Elasticity', *Quantitative and Qualitative Analysis*, 1(1), 1–25.

1 See Gillman and Kejak (2005a) for specifications with capital.

2 In a decentralized model, with bank deposits denoted by d_t, consider requiring that d_t is equal to the sum of money and credit, so that all means of exchange come from the bank deposits; then $d_t = a_t c_t + (1 - a_t)\ c_t = c_t$. And let the Clark (1984) production function be $q_t = A_F(l_{Ft}h_t)^{\gamma}\ d_t^{1-\gamma}$; then in equilibrium $c_t = d_t$ and equation (6) results.

3 Such changes are possible and dealt with in Friedman (1959), Friedman and Schwartz (1963b), and Benk, Gillman, and Kejak (2008), in which an increase in temporary income causes an increase in velocity in a procyclic fashion; and this is investigated econometrically in Gillman, Siklos, and Silver (1997).

4 Note that other major dimensions of this model have been tested. Gillman and Nakov (2004) find support for the implied general equilibrium Tobin effect, whereby inflation causes the capital to effective labor ratios across sectors to rise, because of a higher input price ratio of w/r; Gillman, Harris, and Matyas (2004) find support for the negative effect of inflation on growth.

5 This approximation is best for low values of the variables in the (0,1) range; and all variables are less than 0.15, allowing for a good approximation.

6 There is an unrestricted intercept, with drift in the levels.

10 Money demand in an EU accession country

A VECM Study of Croatia*

Dario Cziráky and Max Gillman†

Summary

The chapter estimates the money demand in Croatia using monthly data from 1994 to 2002. A failure of the Fisher equation is found, and adjustment to the standard money-demand function is made to include the inflation rate as well as the nominal interest rate. In a two-equation cointegrated system, a stable money demand shows rapid convergence back to equilibrium after shocks. This function performs better than an alternative using the exchange rate instead of the inflation rate as in the 'pass-through' literature on exchange rates. The results provide a basis for inflation rate forecasting and suggest the ability to use inflation targeting goals in transition countries during the EU accession process. Finding a stable money demand also limits the scope for central bank 'inflation bias'.

10.1 Introduction

Neoclassical money-demand functions underlie much theoretical and empirical work. Typically, the nominal interest rate is the price of money, and the income velocity of money moves in conjunction with this rate. This is as in Friedman's (1956) restatement of money-demand theory, although it contrasts with the institutionally fixed velocity in Fisher's (1911) quantity theory. Similar to Fisher, velocity has often been assumed to be exogenous (Lucas, 1980; Ireland, 1996; Alvarez et al., 2001). Similar to Friedman, others have endeavoured to explain velocity and related phenomena within the model (Hodrick et al., 1991; Eckstein and Leiderman, 1992; Ireland, 1995; Lucas, 2000; Gillman and Kejak, 2004, 2005b).

Empirical work on money demand has focused on interest rate explanations as in the constant semi-interest elasticity model of Cagan (1956) (Eckstein and Leiderman, 1992; Mark and Sul, 2003) or the constant interest elasticity model of Baumol (1952) (Hoffman and Rasche, 1991; Hoffman et al., 1995; Lucas, 2000). Apparent instability in empirical money-demand functions was found because of 'shifts' in demand in the 1980s; for example, Friedman and Kuttner (1992) found a break in cointegration around 1980. This instability literature was met with an effort to include, within the money-demand function, the prices of substitutes for money that may have been subjected to large changes and that may have caused money demand without these substitute prices to appear unstable. In particular, interest earning accounts with demand deposits that could be used in exchange, or 'exchange credit', were used to avoid the high inflation tax of the 1980s and seemed to cause a shift in money demand. Including proxies for financial service innovation led to renewed results of stable money-demand functions, even including the period of the big financial deregulations (Friedman and Schwartz, 1982; Gillman et al., 1997; Gillman and Otto, 2007).

Money demand has become less visible in the policy debate because of interest in Taylor (1999)-type rules. The focus on nominal interest rate instruments has bred the perception of policy irrelevance of money-demand theory and the use of monetary aggregates. However, McCallum (1999) has disputed such conclusions by emphasizing that money demand and the use of rules based partly on money aggregates are being disregarded to the detriment of the ultimate monetary policy results. Alvarez et al. (2001) further advance the importance of money aggregates by providing a general equilibrium basis for the equivalence between interest rate rules and money supply rules. Similarly, Schabert (2005) establishes a liquidity effect in a general equilibrium neoclassical monetary model, in which there is also a direct relation between the money supply growth rate and the nominal interest rate. And empirical money-demand work has recently become more prominent in the central banks of developed nations (e.g., the euro-area studies of Brand and Cassola, 2004; Brand et al., 2002; Kontolemis, 2002).

Developing nations tend to rely more on discretion rather than rules and often justify this just as central banks in developed nations did in the past: the money-demand function is unstable. This sort of discretion instead of rules can lead to an 'inflation bias' of the type described by Kydland and Prescott (1977). Empirically, evaluating the stability of money demand still remains a challenge in developing countries because of lack of confidence in the data quality and because of the many major changes that continue to occur in such economies.

In this chapter, the key extension to a standard money-demand function results from an investigation of whether the Fisher equation of interest rates holds.[1] The myriad ways in which an unexpected acceleration or deceleration of the inflation rate can affect the real interest rate makes suspect the standard Fisher (1930) relation that underlies classical money-demand functions. In those, changes in the inflation rate are directly reflected in the nominal interest rate. But if this is not true, which can be a likely scenario in a transition country, then the standard money-demand function requires modification from only including the nominal interest rate as the price of money.

With an extended money-demand specification, the chapter shows that a stable money-demand function can be found for Croatia, despite tumultuous changes there over the transition period. This presents a good case study in that the finding of a stable money demand may be surprising. Both the emphasis of the Croatian central bank on the exchange rate in its monetary policy and the high fraction of private foreign exchange use in the country have led to the expectation that Croatian money demand is unstable (see Kraft, 2003). However, with a money demand that accounts for failure of the Fisher relation, a stable function is estimated with vector error correction model (VECM) techniques using monthly International Financial Statistics (IFS) data from 1994 to 2002. Over this period the data are reliable, and several robustness checks are conducted, including a focus on exchange rates within the money-demand function.

The data begin only after the Croatian hyperinflation of 1993 and near to the beginning of the issuing of the new Croatian currency, providing confidence in the data. The data's stationarity and seasonal properties are tested carefully (Section 10.3). After finding the Croatian income velocity of money non-stationary (Section 10.4.1), in contrast to Fisher's (1911) concept, the paper focuses on whether the Fisher (1930) equation of interest rates holds in Croatia. Researchers such as Baba et al. (1992) have included the inflation rate as well as the nominal interest rate in the money-demand function. This strategy is justified here in that evidence suggests a failure of the long-run Fisher relation in which the nominal interest rate and inflation rate move together and are interchangeable in the money-demand function (Section 10.4.2). This extension of money demand to include the inflation rate along with the nominal interest rate, and hence capture deviations from the Fisher equation, constitutes the baseline model (Section 10.4.3).

Petrovic and Mladenovic (2000) estimate Yugoslavian money demand using the exchange rate rather than the inflation rate or the nominal interest rate. The idea is that exchange rates reflect the inflation rate changes as in the uncovered interest rate parity concept (see, for example, Walsh, 2003). This approach to money demand is sometimes used to support a monetary policy of exchange rate targeting even when the goal is to decrease the inflation rate. As part of the robustness investigation, the paper compares this alternative money-demand approach to the baseline model (Section 10.4.3.2).

While data limitations in terms of the length of the time series are an important qualification, implications can still be cautiously deduced. A stable money demand is useful because it suggests the variables that can be used to forecast inflation. And all central banks appear to engage in inflation rate forecasting as one of their crucial tasks. Croatia in 2001, along with Hungary in 2001 and Poland in 1997, established new central bank chartering acts that state price stability as the primary goal of the central bank. Croatia has recently had very low inflation, and low inflation in Croatia remains the goal, even if it may be using the exchange rate as its primary instrument.

The results show that the inflation rate enters a stable money-demand function that exhibits fast readjustment to shocks. This suggests that an inflation targeting policy (Svensson, 1999) will not 'de-stabilize' money demand. In contrast to the baseline model, including the exchange rate instead of the inflation rate yields a near-zero adjustment to shocks. This implies that an exchange rate targeting strategy may induce a perceived instability in the money-demand function if, for example, such a policy results in substantial inflation-rate volatility that keeps the money demand constantly readjusting (Section 10.5).

10.2 Croatian money, policy and banking background

We first consider some descriptive facts about Croatian real money use, nominal interest rates and the inflation rate over the 1994–2002 period. These help indicate whether it is likely that a classic money-demand function will be operative. The money aggregate M1 comprises the new Croatian kuna currency, as of 30 May 1994, and kuna-denominated demand deposits.[2] Figure 10.1 shows that the quantity of real money (M/P), defined here in terms of M1, and the nominal interest rate (money market rate (MM)) move inversely as in a classical money-demand function. However, the figure also shows that the inflation rate and nominal interest rate do not move together as in a Fisher equation.

Between 1994 and 2001, the inflation rate was fairly stable around 5 percent; it then moved downwards steadily towards very low levels by 2003, and it has remained in the 1.5 percent range. With such low rates, the Croatian National Bank has begun succeeding in its 'primary objective to achieve and maintain price stability' (2001 National Bank Act). This low inflation has been

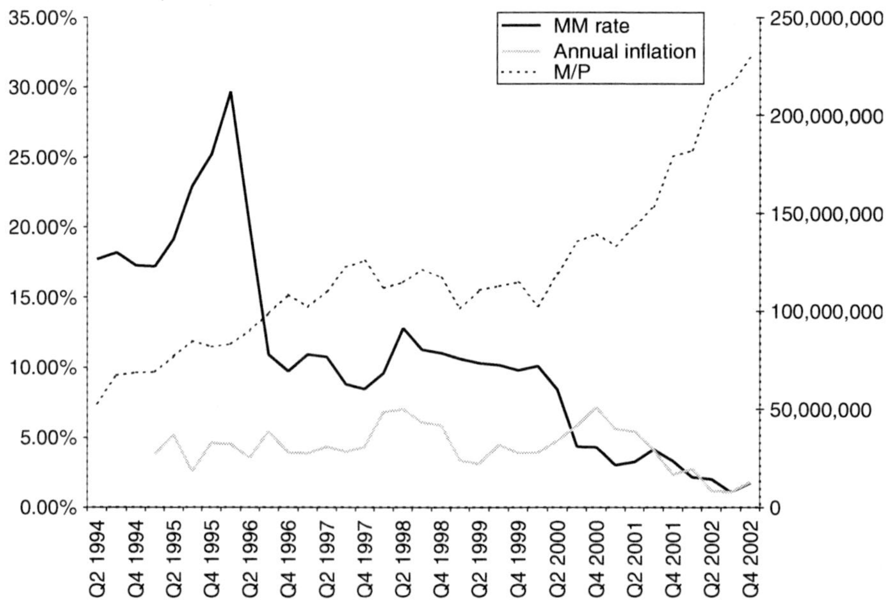

Figure 10.1 Real money, inflation and nominal interest rate.

achieved while the Bank has been described as being engaged in 'strict exchange rate targeting' (Billmeier and Bonato, 2004). Or as Kraft (2003) puts it, 'The main intermediate target is the exchange rate, not any monetary aggregate. In that respect, Croatia's monetary policy resembles an exchange rate fix more than a float of any sort' (p. 14). These different perspectives suggest that the exchange rate may have been an important instrument in the Bank's realization of its low inflation goal.

An interesting banking aspect of the M1 aggregate can be seen in Figure 10.2. Currency constitutes the lion's share of M1. The demand deposit to currency ratio averages well below 1. In comparison, for example, the US demand deposit to currency ratio has trended downwards steadily from 4 in 1959 to near 1 in 2002. Low- or non-interest-bearing demand deposits have been used significantly less in Croatia than in the USA.

Another banking feature is that there have been significant foreign-currency-denominated deposits, now primarily in euros. These deposits have accounted for some 75 percent of total new deposits (Kraft, 2003). Kraft suggests that these holdings may imply a 'lack of credible monetary policy', adding that Croatians have a 'habit of saving in foreign exchange' (p. 4). Such a habit can be because of inflation avoidance and, in addition, may reflect a lesser use of banking for exchange purposes.

The commercial bank sector has seen significant turmoil. The banks started out as state owned and have gradually become privatized in the face of many disruptions to activity. Stringent restrictions have been imposed on the banks at times, for example, with reserve requirements as high as 31 percent during the war period of 1995 and with punitive levels of reserves if bank credit exceeded a certain threshold in recent years. Deregulation and liberalization started in earnest in 1996, when the government received an investment grade rating on its debt and a large commercial bank consolidation took place. A crisis occurred in 1998–99 with some bank insolvencies, and

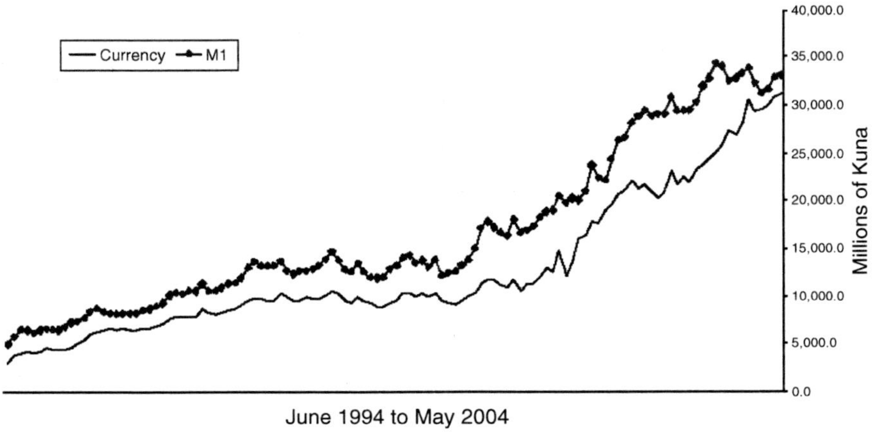

Figure 10.2 Croatian monetary aggregates.

bank reform acts were passed in 1999 and 2002. Restructuring and privatization were largely finished by 2001.[3]

A weak, gradually reforming commercial bank sector could help explain the greater use of currency and foreign-exchange-denominated deposits. But a lesser use of banking does not necessarily threaten the stability of money demand. The main factors that have caused large shifts in money demand in developed countries have been the big, sudden financial deregulations of the 1980s (Gillman and Kejak, 2004; Benk et al., 2005). Such changes in financial sector productivity can be incorporated in money-demand functions to stabilize an otherwise seemingly unstable money-demand function, as Gillman and Otto (2003) show in time series estimations for the USA and Australia. However, deregulation has been gradual in Croatia and inclusion of financial sector variables in the money-demand function appears less necessary.

10.3 Data and descriptive analysis

The data used in the estimation are IFS time series with monthly frequency and seasonal adjustment: industrial production for the output variable, M1 money, consumer prices, a Croatian kuna (HRK)–euro exchange rate and the money market interest rate (Table 10.1).

The variables are in natural logarithms of the indices with base year 1995. The data span is from April 1994 till August 2002 for all series, which are plotted in Figure 10.3 along with velocity (output divided by real money).

10.3.1 Seasonal unit root tests

To ensure that the use of seasonally adjusted data is appropriate, we first consider Figure 10.4, which compares seasonally unadjusted series with seasonally adjusted series. Only modest differences emerge. However, it is useful to test whether explicit modelling of seasonality is requisite. In particular, if the series are stochastic and there exist seasonal unit roots, then these unit roots would need to be adjusted for through seasonal differencing (Davidson

Table 10.1 Definition of variables

Symbol	*Definition*
i_t	Industrial production
m_t	Money
$(m-p)_t$	Real money
p_t	CPI prices
Δp_t	Inflation
ex_t	HRK-euro exchange rate
r_t	Money market interest rate
v_t	Money velocity $(p_t + y_t - m_t)$

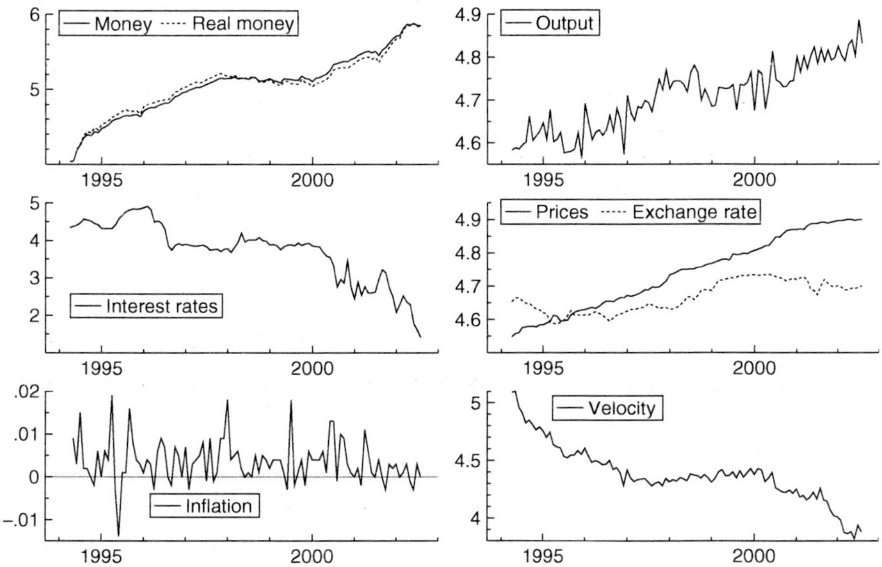

Figure 10.3 Money-demand variables.

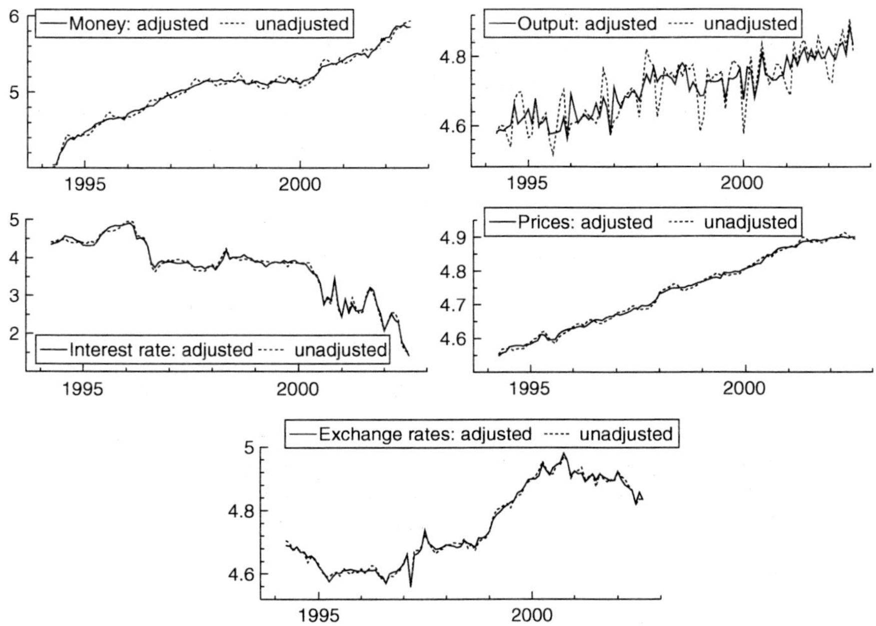

Figure 10.4 The effect of seasonal adjustment.

et al., 1978; Dickey et al., 1984; Beaulieu and Miron, 1993; Canova and Hansen, 1995).

The particular test used for seasonal unit roots is that of Hylleberg et al. (1990) as adapted to monthly data by Franses (1990), based on the following ordinary least squares (OLS) regression:

$$\begin{aligned}\Delta_{12}y_t = {} & \pi_1 y_{1,t-1} + \pi_2 y_{2,t-1} + \pi_3 y_{3,t-1} + \pi_4 y_{3,t-2} + \pi_5 y_{4,t-1} \\ & + \pi_6 y_{4,t-2} + \pi_7 y_{5,t-1} + \pi_8 y_{5,t-2} + \pi_9 y_{6,t-1} + \pi_{10} y_{6,t-2} \\ & + \pi_{11} y_{7,t-1} + \pi_{12} y_{7,t-2} + \sum_{i=1}^{12} a_i D_{it} + \gamma t + u_t,\end{aligned}$$

where

$$\begin{aligned} y_{1,t} &= (1+L)(1+L^2)(1+L^4+L^8)y_t, \\ y_{2,t} &= -(1-L)(1+L^2)(1+L^4+L^8)y_t, \\ y_{3,t} &= -(1-L^2)(1+L^4+L^8)y_t, \\ y_{4,t} &= -(1-L^4)(1-\sqrt{3}L+L^2)(1+L^2+L^4)y_t, \\ y_{5,t} &= -(1-L^4)(1+\sqrt{3}L+L^2)(1+L^2+L^4)y_t, \\ y_{6,t} &= -(1-L^4)(1-L^2+L^4)(1-L+L^2)y_t, \\ y_{7,t} &= -(1-L^4)(1-L^2+L^4)(1+L+L^2)y_t. \end{aligned}$$

The t-tests for the significance of the coefficients are given in Table 10.2, which can be compared to the critical values tabulated by Franses (1990). The

Table 10.2 Seasonal unit root tests (t-values)

Coefficient	m_t	p_t	i_t	ex_t	r_t
π_1	−2.997	−1.647	−1.798	−1.685	−1.891
π_2	−4.963	−4.069	−1.536	−4.959	−3.392
π_3	−2.649	−2.584	−3.845	−2.653	−2.097
π_4	−5.337	−4.693	−3.967	−3.419	−3.392
π_5	−11.503	−8.545	−6.766	−10.734	−8.241
π_6	−5.393	−4.171	−3.356	−3.230	−4.063
π_7	−3.640	−3.709	−5.500	−5.289	−3.634
π_8	−12.289	−9.077	−6.733	−11.215	−8.508
π_9	−8.902	−6.795	−5.670	−8.720	−6.821
π_{10}	−4.684	−3.728	−2.932	−4.827	−3.607
π_{11}	−4.500	−4.257	−5.303	−5.577	−4.343
π_{12}	−12.729	−8.328	−4.694	−11.143	−7.838

π_1 coefficients are below their 95 percent critical values indicating that a unit root hypothesis cannot be rejected at the zero frequency, using the standard Dickey–Fuller tests. Yet the existence of seasonal unit roots is rejected for all π_i coefficients. Note that seasonal dummies and a time trend are included in the test regressions. These results together indicate that there is a stochastic trend within the series and that seasonality is deterministic. This means that seasonality need not be modelled explicitly. Using seasonally adjusted data directly, without having to remove any seasonal unit roots, allows us to save degrees of freedom with a limited data set.

10.3.2 Unit root tests of seasonally adjusted series

Augmented Dickey–Fuller (ADF) unit root tests for the order of integration (Table 10.3) do not reject the hypothesis that the tested series have a unit root and are thus I(1). The ADF tests were performed by considering all options regarding deterministic components (i.e., trend and constant), and in all cases the unit root hypothesis could not be rejected. Additional ADF tests on first differences find strong rejection of the unit root null in all series.

The inflation rate series deserves careful consideration, in that evidence on the integration order of the inflation rate tends to be mixed between unit root and stationarity findings (Culver and Papell, 1997; Benati and Kapetanios, 2003). Perron (1989)-type tests for structural breaks can indicate if an apparent unit root is break-adjusted stationary. While such an investigation is limited within the short time periods available for transition countries, the Croatian inflation rate (Δp_t) does not appear to be trending (Figure 10.1). The visual impression is further confirmed by the unit root tests (Table 10.3),

Table 10.3 Augmented Dickey–Fuller unit root tests

Variable	*t-ADF*	$\beta(y_{t-1})$	$\hat{\sigma}$	j*	$t-\Delta y_{t-j}$	*p value*
†m_t	−1.815	0.937	0.026	9	3.333	0.001
‡m_t	0.166	1.002	0.026	9	3.029	0.003
†p_t	−1.542	0.883	0.005	5	−1.847	0.068
‡p_t	−1.018	0.995	0.005	4	−1.847	0.068
†i_t	−2.326	0.589	0.032	9	2.097	0.039
‡i_t	−0.644	0.966	0.033	2	−4.708	0.000
†$(m-p)_t$	−1.794	0.939	0.026	9	3.623	0.001
‡$(m-p)_t$	0.113	1.002	0.026	9	3.299	0.002
‡Δp_t	−6.999	0.038	0.005	1	−0.125	0.901
†ex_t	−1.033	0.966	0.007	2	−2.183	0.032
‡ex_t	−1.725	0.971	0.007	2	−2.333	0.022
†r_t	−1.485	0.893	0.195	5	1.975	0.052
‡r_t	0.713	1.023	0.199	5	1.707	0.092

* Highest significant lag in the ADF regression.
† Trend and constant included; 5% c.v. = −3.461, 1% c.v. = −4.066.
‡ Constant included; 5% c.v. = −2.895, 1% c.v. = −3.507.

which strongly reject the null up to the fifth lag in the ADF regression (as no lagged differences are significant, a simple DF test suffices; the t-DF value is –9.653, with $\beta(y_{t-1}) = 0.026$).

10.4 Econometric modelling

10.4.1 The income velocity of money

The observed downward trend in velocity in Figure 10.3 may be deterministic or stochastic. A stochastic trend can be tested for using an unrestricted vector autoregression (VAR) in levels. The resulting VECM system is given in equation (1), and the results are summarized in Table 10.4.[4]

$$\begin{pmatrix} \Delta m_t \\ \Delta y_t \end{pmatrix} = \begin{pmatrix} \mu_1 \\ \mu_2 \end{pmatrix} + \sum_{i=1}^{11} \begin{pmatrix} \gamma_{11}^{(i)} & \gamma_{12}^{(i)} \\ \gamma_{21}^{(i)} & \gamma_{22}^{(i)} \end{pmatrix} \begin{pmatrix} \Delta m_{t-i} \\ \Delta y_{t-i} \end{pmatrix} + \begin{pmatrix} a_{11} & a_{12} \\ a_{21} & a_{22} \end{pmatrix} \begin{pmatrix} \beta_{11} & \beta_{12} \\ \beta_{21} & \beta_{22} \end{pmatrix}' \begin{pmatrix} m_t \\ y_t \end{pmatrix} + \begin{pmatrix} \varepsilon_{1t} \\ \varepsilon_{2t} \end{pmatrix}. \quad (1)$$

The Johansen (1995) cointegration tests suggest that there is one cointegrating vector between money and output. Both λ-max and λ-trace statistics are above their 95 percent critical values with λ-max being significant at the 1 percent level. The (first) cointegrating vector including coefficients of m_t, y_t and t (a time trend) is estimated as $\boldsymbol{\beta}' = (1, -6.6, 0.01)$ with the accompanying adjustment coefficient vector $a = (0.05, -0.02)$. This implies a long-run relationship $p_t + 6.6y_t - m_t$. Imposing the restriction[5] $\boldsymbol{\beta}' = (1, -1, *)$ results in the estimated trend coefficient of –0.05 and $a = (-0.03, 0.1)$, which, however, is strongly rejected by the likelihood ratio (LR) $\chi^2_{(2)}$ of 22.3. It is clear then that the restriction $\boldsymbol{\beta}' = (1, -1, 0)$, being even more restricted, cannot hold either (which is confirmed by the highly significant LR $\chi^2_{(2)}$ test of 24.64).

The findings imply that $\upsilon_t \sim I(1)$ regardless of the presence of a deterministic trend in the cointegration space. That is, an apparently systematic decline in the money velocity is in fact stochastic, and no fixed per annum percent decline or deterministic downward trend can be claimed. It follows that long-run stability of the money-demand equation requires consideration of additional variables such as the interest, inflation or exchange rates.

Table 10.4 Johansen cointegration tests: *VAR(11) with* $y' = (m_t, y_t)^*$

H_0: $r = p$	*λ-max*	*95% CV*	*λ-trace*	*95% CV*
$p = 0$	29.53	19.0	25.79	25.3
$p \leq 1$	4.60	12.3	4.60	12.3

* Eigenvalues: $\lambda_1 = 0.280$, $\lambda_2 = 0.050$.

10.4.2 The Fisher equation

Denoting the nominal interest rate in period t by r_t, the real interest rate by ρ_t and inflation by Π_t, the Fisher equation (Dimand, 1999; see also Fisher, 1930) can be written as $r_t = \rho_t + \Pi_t$. With the additional assumption that $\rho_t = \hat{\alpha} + \hat{\varepsilon}_t$ (i.e., real interest rate is constant), where $\hat{\varepsilon}_t$ is independently and identically distributed (i.i.d.), the Fisher equation becomes $r_t = \hat{\alpha} + \Pi_t + \hat{\varepsilon}_t$, which implies independence of the real interest rate and inflation. The equation is usually estimated in log levels as $\ln(r_t) = \hat{\beta}_0 + \hat{\beta}_1 \ln(\Pi_t) + \hat{u}_t$, and a test of the restriction $\hat{\beta}_1 = 1$ is taken to be the test of the (long-run) validity of the Fisher equation. The constant $\hat{\beta}_0$ can be interpreted as the long-run equilibrium real rate of interest. Note that when the variables are in logarithms, inflation measured as $\ln(\Pi_t) = \ln(p_t/p_{t-1})$ is equivalent to a simple difference in the log of the price index, i.e., $\Delta\ln(p_t)$. Hence, the Fisher equation can be stated as[6]

$$\ln(r_t) = \hat{\beta}_0 + \hat{\beta}_1 \, \Delta \ln(p_t) + \hat{u}_t, \quad \hat{u}_t \sim \text{i.i.d.}, \quad \hat{\beta}_1 = 1. \tag{2}$$

Initially ignoring the order of integration, the estimated equation is

$$\ln(r_t) = \underset{(0.10)}{3.65} + \underset{(15.46)}{20.03} \, \Delta \ln(p_t),$$

where standard errors are in parentheses and $R^2 = 0.017$, $\hat{\sigma} = 0.783$ and $DW = 0.081$. It is evident that the null hypothesis H_0: $\hat{\beta}_1 = 0$ cannot be rejected, and in addition a low Durbin–Watson statistic implies dynamic misspecification. The ADF unit root test on $\hat{u}_t$ produced a t-value of 0.519 where the highest significant lag is 4, which clearly cannot reject that $\hat{u}_t \sim I(1)$. Note that this can also be inferred from the fact that $\ln(r_t) \sim I(1)$ while $\Delta\ln(p_t) \sim I(0)$; therefore, it must be that, for all γ, $\ln(r_t) - \gamma\Delta\ln(p_t) \sim I(1)$.

Alternatively, estimation of Sargent's (1972) extended Fisher equation, with $n = m = 3$, yields

$$\begin{aligned}\ln(r_t) = {} & \underset{(0.45)}{13.74} - \underset{(1.15)}{2.17} \ln(m_t) - \underset{(1.62)}{2.16} \ln(m_{t-1}) - \underset{(1.61)}{1.08} \ln(m_{t-2}) + \underset{(1.05)}{3.46} \ln(m_{t-3}) \\ & + \underset{(6.23)}{6.44} \, \Delta \ln(p_t) + \underset{(6.12)}{0.74} \, \Delta \ln(p_{t-1}) + \underset{(6.13)}{0.70} \, \Delta \ln(p_{t-2}) - \underset{(6.15)}{2.68} \, \Delta \ln(p_{t-3})\end{aligned}$$

with $R^2 = 0.863$, $\sigma = 0.305$ and $DW = 0.570$. Here, while the Durbin–Watson statistic is still indicative of some remaining residual autocorrelation, the fit is improved and the residuals are close to stationary.[7] However, inflation is not significant at any lag. This is also seen in the long-run solution

$$\ln(r_t) = \underset{(0.45)}{13.74} - \underset{(0.08)}{1.95} \ln(m_t) + \underset{(12.95)}{5.19} \, \Delta \ln(p_t),$$

where Wald $\chi^2_{(2)} = 548.32$, which is highly significant. Individually, only the money variable is significant; inflation is not. Similar results are obtained by estimating the distributed lag version of the Fisher equation (Sargent, 1973), which is specified as a special case of the 'extended' equation, i.e., $\ln(r_t) = \tilde{a} + \sum_{i=1}^{m} \tilde{\nu}_i \Delta \ln(p_{t-i}) + \breve{\varepsilon}_t$. Estimation of this equation produces insignificant coefficients of inflation at all lags (including up to 12 lags) and similarly insignificant long-run coefficients (not shown). In addition, the residuals are non-stationary which confirms the previous conclusion about the integration orders.

Alternatively, following Crowder and Hoffman (1996) and Crowder (1997), we can consider a bivariate VECM system using the Johansen technique. The specification is

$$\begin{pmatrix} \Delta r_t \\ \Delta^2 p_t \end{pmatrix} = \begin{pmatrix} \tau_1 \\ \tau_2 \end{pmatrix} + \sum_{i=1}^{11} \begin{pmatrix} k_{11}^{(i)} & k_{12}^{(i)} \\ k_{21}^{(i)} & k_{22}^{(i)} \end{pmatrix} \begin{pmatrix} \Delta r_{t-i} \\ \Delta^2 p_{t-i} \end{pmatrix}$$

$$+ \begin{pmatrix} \chi_{11} & \chi_{12} \\ \chi_{21} & \chi_{22} \end{pmatrix} \begin{pmatrix} \theta_{11} & \theta_{12} \\ \theta_{21} & \theta_{22} \end{pmatrix}' \begin{pmatrix} r_{t-1} \\ \Delta^2 p_{t-1} \end{pmatrix} + \begin{pmatrix} \eta_{1t} \\ \eta_{2t} \end{pmatrix}.$$

Estimation of this system produces eigenvalues of $\lambda_1 = 0.109$ and $\lambda_2 = 0.055$; the λ-max and λ-trace statistics are 10.31 and 15.38, respectively, which are well below their 95 percent critical values of 19 and 25.3.[8] These results imply that the interest rate and the inflation rate are not cointegrated. The long-run Fisher equation does not hold.

The above approaches to testing the Fisher equation have the problem of the integration order of interest rates and inflation variables, because the Croatian inflation is I(0).[9] To avoid the integration order problems and consistently estimate $\hat{\beta}_1$ from the Fisher equation, $\ln(r_t) = \hat{\beta}_0 + \hat{\beta}_1 \Delta \ln(p_t) + \hat{u}_t$, consider the OLS estimator[10]

$$\tilde{\beta}_1 = \frac{\sum_{t=1}^{T} \Delta^2 \ln(p_t) \Delta \ln(r_t)}{\sum_{t=1}^{T} [\Delta^2 \ln(p_t)]^2}.$$

It can be shown that $\tilde{\beta}_1$ is asymptotically normally distributed, because $\ln(r_t \sim I(1) \Rightarrow \Delta \ln(r_t) \sim I(0)$, while $\Delta \ln(p_t) \sim I(0) \Rightarrow \Delta^2 \ln(p_t \sim I(0)$; this estimator uses only I(0) variables and the standard distribution theory applies.[11] Estimation produces the following results:

$$\Delta \ln(r_t) = \underset{(2.69)}{3.56}\, \Delta^2 \ln(p_t),$$

where $R^2 = 0.018$, $\sigma = 0.190$ and DW = 2.04. These results allow correct statistical inference on the estimated coefficients to be drawn, and also the Durbin–Watson statistic is indicative of no remaining autocorrelation in the residuals. However, the standard error of the $\tilde{\beta}_1$ coefficient is 2.69, which gives a t-ratio of 1.33. The null hypothesis H_0: $\tilde{\beta}_1 = 0$ cannot be rejected. This result again implies that the Fisher equation does not hold in Croatia. Thus, it may be that the inflation rate enters the long-run money-demand relation as a separate variable along with the interest rate.

10.4.3 Money demand estimation

Following Baba *et al.* (1992), the baseline real money demand, or $(m-p)_t$, is specified so as to include real income y_t, the nominal interest rate r_t and the inflation rate Δp_t. Within a multivariate cointegration framework, the order of the estimated VECM needs to be properly specified in terms of the lag-length selection before commencing with the cointegration analysis. Formal tests of the system's reduction validity, progressively reducing the number of lags in the system, reject all reductions beyond VAR(12), making the model a VECM with $\Delta z_t = [\Delta(m-p)_t, \Delta y_t, \Delta^2 p_t, \Delta r_t]$, and using 12 lags. The four-variable system is specified as

$$\begin{pmatrix} \Delta(m-p)_t \\ \Delta y_t \\ \Delta^2 p_t \\ \Delta r_t \end{pmatrix} = \begin{pmatrix} \omega_1 \\ \omega_2 \\ \omega_3 \\ \omega_4 \end{pmatrix} + \sum_{i=1}^{12} \begin{pmatrix} \phi_{11}^{(i)} & \phi_{12}^{(i)} & \phi_{13}^{(i)} & \phi_{14}^{(i)} \\ \phi_{21}^{(i)} & \phi_{22}^{(i)} & \phi_{23}^{(i)} & \phi_{24}^{(i)} \\ \phi_{31}^{(i)} & \phi_{32}^{(i)} & \phi_{33}^{(i)} & \phi_{34}^{(i)} \\ \phi_{41}^{(i)} & \phi_{42}^{(i)} & \phi_{43}^{(i)} & \phi_{44}^{(i)} \end{pmatrix} \begin{pmatrix} \Delta(m-p)_{t-i} \\ \Delta y_{t-i} \\ \Delta^2 p_{t-i} \\ \Delta r_{t-i} \end{pmatrix}$$

$$+ \begin{pmatrix} \psi_{11} & \psi_{12} & \psi_{13} & \psi_{14} \\ \psi_{21} & \psi_{22} & \psi_{23} & \psi_{24} \\ \psi_{31} & \psi_{32} & \psi_{33} & \psi_{34} \\ \psi_{41} & \psi_{42} & \psi_{43} & \psi_{44} \end{pmatrix} \begin{pmatrix} \xi_{11} & \xi_{12} & \xi_{13} & \xi_{14} \\ \xi_{21} & \xi_{22} & \xi_{23} & \xi_{24} \\ \xi_{31} & \xi_{32} & \xi_{33} & \xi_{34} \\ \xi_{41} & \xi_{42} & \xi_{43} & \xi_{44} \end{pmatrix} \begin{pmatrix} (m-p)_{t-1} \\ y_{t-1} \\ \Delta p_{t-1} \\ r_{t-1} \\ t \end{pmatrix}$$

$$+ \begin{pmatrix} \iota_{1t} \\ \iota_{2t} \\ \iota_{3t} \\ \iota_{4t} \end{pmatrix}.$$

Estimation using the Johansen maximum likelihood technique indicates two stationary combinations among (real) money, output, the interest rate and inflation rate variables (Table 10.5).[12] In particular, the restricted estimation where the rank condition ($r = 2$) and weak exogeneity of inflation were jointly imposed produced an LR $\chi^2_{(2)}$ test of 3.733 ($p = 0.155$). Thus, the joint hypothesis that $r = 2$ and that inflation is weakly exogenous with respect to the long-run parameters cannot be rejected.

Table 10.5 Johansen cointegration tests: $z = [(m-p)_t, y_t, \Delta p_t, r_t]$*

H_0: $r = p$	λ-*max*	*95% CV*	λ-*trace*	*95% CV*
$p = 0$	66.11	31.5	124.50	63.0
$p \leq 1$	36.03	25.5	58.40	42.4
$p \leq 2$	15.48	19.0	22.37	25.3
$p \leq 3$	6.89	12.3	6.89	12.3

* Eigenvalues: $\lambda_1 = 0.528$, $\lambda_2 = 0.336$, $\lambda_3 = 0.161$, $\lambda_4 = 0.075$.

The ξ' and ψ are estimated as

$$\xi' = \begin{pmatrix} 1.00 & -2.66 & 17.00 & 0.36 & 0.0079 \\ -0.02 & 1.00 & -3.40 & 0.09 & -0.0002 \\ 0.00 & -0.01 & 1.00 & -0.00 & -0.000 \\ 18.45 & -15.30 & -147.46 & 1.00 & -0.1223 \end{pmatrix}$$

$$\psi = \begin{pmatrix} 0.09 & -0.58 & -4.93 & -0.0023 \\ 0.20 & -0.99 & 0.23 & 0.0025 \\ -0.02 & 0.02 & -1.18 & 0.0005 \\ -2.42 & -3.34 & 15.53 & 0.0027 \end{pmatrix}.$$

Imposing the rank restrictions, the estimates of ξ' and ψ are

$$\xi' = \begin{pmatrix} -0.23 & 0.59 & -3.04 & -0.08 & -0.0018 \\ -0.02 & 0.67 & -2.06 & 0.06 & -0.0002 \end{pmatrix}$$

$$\psi = \begin{pmatrix} -0.37 & -0.86 \\ -0.99 & -1.51 \\ - & - \\ 10.71 & -4.97 \end{pmatrix}.$$

The adjustment coefficients for the money-demand relation are large and negative (– 0.37 and – 0.86), which indicates fast adjustment to the long run. Normalizing the first cointegrating relation to $(m-p)_t$ and the second one to y_t and writing the long-run relationships in equation format, the long-run money demand and income determination equations are

$$(m-p)_t = 2.57y_t - 13.22\Delta p_t - 0.35r_t - 0.01t,$$

$$y_t = 0.03(m-p)_t + 3.07\Delta p_t - 0.09r_t + 0.003t.$$

The latter relation can be interpreted as a small real balance effect on output (see, for example, Ireland, 2005, on this effect) or as indicating a Phillips curve relation.

One-step and breakpoint Chow tests were conducted for the individual equations and for the entire system. Stability of the system is indicated by the fact that the recursive breakpoint Chow tests generally fall below the 95 percent critical value. The one-step Chow tests detect an outlier in March 2000.

10.4.3.1 Money demand without the inflation rate

As part of the robustness check of the baseline model, the money demand is also estimated with the assumption that the Fisher equation holds, and hence the inclusion of the inflation rate is not necessary. The estimation of the system without the inflation rate term requires a three-variable VECM instead of the four-variable one for the baseline. Experiments here find three cointegrating vectors with two of the three eigenvalues significant on the basis of both λ-max and λ-trace statistics (Table 10.6). This suggests that the third vector is apparently non-stationary, or I(1), while the estimates of the cointegrating vectors and their adjustment coefficients are similar in both the models. The money-demand cointegrating vector is $(m_t - p_t) = 2.25y_t - 0.44r_t - 0.01t$.

Additional tests are made for the reduced rank $r = 2$ and (jointly) for the exclusion of the deterministic trend from the cointegrating space. The exclusion of the trend is strongly rejected by the LR test statistic: $\chi^2_{(2)} = 25.36$. A significant problem with the reduced rank model emerges from one-step and breakpoint Chow tests. These tests are failed, which indicates a lack of parameter stability (or constancy) that may be causing instability of the entire system.

10.4.3.2 Money demand with exchange rates

As another alternative that checks the robustness of the baseline specification, we consider Petrovic and Mladenovic's (2000) model of money demand which includes exchange rates in lieu of a nominal interest rate or an inflation rate. This approach is based on 'dollarization' or 'fear of floating' arguments (Calvo and Reinhart, 2002), although note that Taylor (2001) is more circumspect about what role exchange rates might play during an inflation targeting regime. To test the exchange rate approach, money demand is re-estimated

Table 10.6 Johansen cointegration tests: *VAR (11)*: $z = [(m-p)_t, y_t, r_t]$*

H_0: $r = p$	*λ-max*	*95% CV*	*λ-trace*	*95% CV*
$p = 0$	48.90	25.5	79.80	42.4
$p \leq 1$	26.25	19.0	30.90	25.3
$p \leq 2$	4.65	12.3	4.65	12.3

* Eigenvalues: $\lambda_1 = 0.419$, $\lambda_2 = 0.253$, $\lambda_3 = 0.050$.

with the exchange rate (ex_t) replacing the inflation rate; the nominal interest rate is kept in the system. The VECM system is then $\Delta\hat{z}_t = [\Delta(m-p)_t, \Delta y_t, \Delta ex_t, \Delta r_t]$, and the results of the cointegration tests are presented in Table 10.7. They indicate as many as three cointegrating vectors.

The unrestricted estimates of the ξ' and $\hat{\psi}$ matrices are similar to the baseline model. Restricting the cointegrating rank to $r = 2$ and imposing weak exogeneity of the exchange rate gives the following estimates:

$$\xi' = \begin{pmatrix} -0.48 & 1.69 & 0.10 & -0.17 & -0.005 \\ -0.16 & 1.62 & -0.30 & 0.20 & -0.004 \end{pmatrix}$$

$$\hat{\psi} = \begin{pmatrix} -0.03 & -0.02 \\ -0.30 & -0.72 \\ - & - \\ 3.10 & -2.65 \end{pmatrix}.$$

The LR test for the imposed restrictions has a $\chi^2_{(2)}$ of 2.226 ($p = 0.329$), which does not reject the joint restriction that $r = 2$ and that the exchange rate is weakly exogenous for the long-run parameters. A notable difference, however, is in the near-zero values for the adjustment parameters in the money-demand equation (– 0.03 and – 0.02). Including the exchange rate in place of the inflation rate causes the model to lose completely the fast short-run adjustment property of the baseline model. The adjustment would take place almost never, making the exchange rate model unable to explain a stable money demand in the face of shocks.

10.5 Conclusion

The chapter presents a rigorous model of money demand for an EU accession country, Croatia, during its transition years. First, it examines whether the classical Fisher equation of interest rates holds, whereby the nominal interest rate should move together with the inflation rate. Transition/EU-accession countries such as Croatia are perhaps especially likely to be undergoing changes in inflation rate policy that produce unexpected inflation rates. This can lead to a failure of the nominal interest rate and the inflation rate to move together. Finding no evidence in support of the Fisher interest

Table 10.7 Johansen cointegration tests: $\hat{z} = [(m-p)_t, y_t, ex_t, r_t]$*

H_0: $r = p$	λ-*max*	*95% CV*	λ-*trace*	*95% CV*
$p = 0$	60.62	31.5	149.00	63.0
$p \leq 1$	49.96	25.5	88.37	42.4
$p \leq 2$	26.32	19.0	38.41	25.3
$p \leq 3$	12.09	12.3	12.09	12.3

* Eigenvalues: $\lambda_1 = 0.498$, $\lambda_2 = 0.430$, $\lambda_3 = 0.256$, $\lambda_4 = 0.127$.

equation for Croatia, using a battery of tests, the chapter then specifies the baseline model as a classical money-demand function extended to include the inflation rate. With vector error correction methods, a cointegrated money-demand function results with both parameter stability and timely dynamic re-equilibration to shocks.

For robustness, the baseline model specification is compared to likely alternative specifications. First examined is the baseline without the inflation rate, this being the standard, classic, money-demand function. This alternative exhibits parameter instability. Second, the exchange rate is substituted into the baseline model in place of the inflation rate. This reflects a theme of the transition money-demand literature that the exchange rate acts as the inflation rate in the money-demand function, because the inflation rate is fully 'passed through' to exchange rate changes. This specification shows long-run cointegration but no timely dynamic adjustment to shocks. The lack of short-run adjustment makes it an inferior alternative. The robustness of the baseline model relative to the main alternatives allows for some confidence in the results.

Interpretation requires caution because of the data limitations that characterize all transition country studies. Starting the data series for Croatia only in 1994 avoids a hyperinflation that peeked at around a 1500 percent annual rate in 1993; after this, a new currency was introduced. Given the data qualification, the results can be interpreted first as showing that a stable money demand exists despite a less than calm period economically and politically.

Second, the analysis suggests that a policy that causes gradual changes in the inflation rate is unlikely to disrupt the baseline money-demand function because it includes the inflation rate as a variable. This means that a policy of maintaining a low inflation rate, or even gradually reducing the inflation rate if it were at a higher level as in Hungary, is not likely to induce an apparent instability in the estimated money-demand function. In turn, the inflation rate should be able to be more easily forecasted using variables that enter the money-demand function. Then the forecasts can be used by the central bank to continue to act to stabilize the inflation rate, a type of self-reinforcing interaction of policy with the behaviour of consumers.[13]

In contrast, a policy for example that targets the exchange rate without regard to the inflation rate could induce unexpected jumps in the inflation rate that cause apparent 'shifts' in the money-demand function. This can lead to the belief that money demand is unstable, and justify further discretion from the central bank to offset the apparently unstable money-demand function. This circle of interaction between policy and the consumer is less appealing in that the ultimate policy would probably be less efficacious and could lead to an 'inflation bias'. This is not to argue that exchange rate targeting is necessarily worse than inflation rate targeting. It does suggest that the use of exchange rate instruments in Croatia may *de facto* be part of a policy of inflation rate targeting.

Policy-consumer interaction is an important factor in the ultimate efficaciousness of policy, as emphasized by Lucas's (1976) 'critique'. The nature of such interaction in general is not regime or consumer-behaviour dependent, given the usual assumption of rationality of the agents. The specifics of the policy 'function' that incorporates the consumer behavioural reactions will certainly change with the particular policy employed. Some policies will be less wasteful of societal resources than others. Arguably, a stable money-demand function combined with inflation rate goals results in a rather efficacious interaction. And it is of some interest to see such a stable money-demand function arising in a dynamic economy like Croatia that has an explicit price stability goal set out in its central bank act.

Notes

* Cziraky, D., and M. Gillman (2006). 'Money Demand in an European Union Accession Country: A Vector-Error Correction Study of Croatia', *Bulletin of Economic Research*, 58(2), 105–127.

† We are grateful to Central European University and the Open Society Institute for grant support and thank Szilard Benk and Tony Nakov suggestions.

1 For example, see Crowder's (2003) panel testing of this equation; see also Brand and Cassola (2004) for an alternative multi-equation money-demand approach that includes a Fisher equation.

2 The kuna replaced the Croatian dinar that had been introduced on 23 December 1991, when Croatia became an independent state.

3 For example, three banks, Bjelovarska Banka, Trgovacka Banka and Cakovecka Banka, were merged into Erste and Sleiermarkische Bank in September 2000 to make one of the ten largest banks in Croatia. Erste then bought 85 percent of Rijecka Banka in April 2002 and merged it with Erste and Sleiermarkische Bank in August 2003 to make the third largest bank group in Croatia. Another example is Slavoska Banka, which started in 1955 and sold some 35 percent of its shares in 1999 to the EBRD and Hypo Alpe Adria Bank. Zagrebacka Banka was the first Croatian bank to be registered as a joint stock company, with limited liability, in 1989, the first bank rated by the three major international rating companies in 1997, and a bank that recently accounted for 25 percent of total Croatian banking assets. It partnered internationally in 2002, with UniCredito Italiano and Allianz.

4 The lag length of the VAR was determined by sequential testing for the validity of the system's reduction, starting with 12 lags (i.e., 1 year of data) and reducing one lag at a time. The reduction from 12 to 11 lags was not rejected, while all further reductions were strongly rejected by the system reduction *F*-tests.

5 The asterisk implies an unrestricted coefficient.

6 An alternative version of the Fisher equation, given constant money velocity, is $\Delta m_t = \Delta p_t$ (see, for example, Monnet and Weber, 2001). This, however, is not suitable for the cases where velocity is not constant.

7 The ADF *t*-value was –2.637 with seven lags included in the regression, which is above the 1 percent critical value of –2.591 for the regression without trend or constant.

8 A linear trend was included in the cointegrating space.

9 However, Sargent's (1972) extension that includes levels of money will yield valid inference, given that money is I(1) and cointegrated with interest rates; hence, the I(0) inflation would enter merely as an additional stationary regressor.

10 We assume the variables are measured as deviations from the means.

11 To see that $\tilde{\beta}_1$ is a consistent estimator of $\hat{\beta}_1$, observe that

$$\ln(r_t) - \ln(r_{t-1}) = \hat{\beta}_0 + \hat{\beta}_1 \Delta \ln(p_t) + \hat{u}_t - [\hat{\beta}_0 + \hat{\beta}_1 \Delta \ln(p_{t-1}) + \hat{u}_{t-1}]$$
$$\Rightarrow \Delta \ln(r_t) = \hat{\beta}_1 \Delta^2 \ln(p_t) + \check{u}_t$$

where $\Delta^2 \ln(p_t) \equiv \Delta \ln(p_t) - \Delta \ln(p_{t-1}) = \ln(p_t) - 2 \ln(p_{t-1}) + \ln(p_{t-2})$ and $\check{u}_t \equiv \hat{u}_t - \hat{u}_{t-1}$. However, the $\hat{\beta}_0$ coefficient from $\ln(r_t) = \hat{\beta}_0 + \hat{\beta}_1 \Delta \ln(p_t) + \hat{u}_t$, i.e., the long-run equilibrium real rate of interest, cannot be estimated.

12 See also Cziráky (2002).

13 In discussing inflation forecasting, Balfoussia and Wickens (2005) note that 'Although there is no necessary reason for a good forecasting model to have theoretical underpinnings, theory may still be able to help in the choice of the model to use' (p. 1).

Part III

Inflation and growth

11 Inflation and balanced-path growth with alternative payment mechanisms*

Max Gillman and Michal Kejak[†]

Summary

The chapter shows that contrary to conventional wisdom an endogenous growth economy with human capital and alternative payment mechanisms can robustly explain major facets of the long-run inflation experience. A negative inflation-growth relation is explained, including a striking nonlinearity found repeatedly in empirical studies. A set of Tobin (1965) effects are also explained and, further, linked in magnitude to the growth effects through the interest elasticity of money demand. Undisclosed previously, this link helps fill out the intuition of how the inflation experience can be plausibly explained in a robust fashion with a model extended to include credit as a payment mechanism.

The evidence on the effect of inflation on growth has continued to show a strong negative relation. Recent panel studies report strong inflation effects, both for developed and developing country samples. Further, evidence has emerged of a striking nonlinearity in this effect. There is a stronger negative effect of inflation at lower rates of inflation, which becomes weaker as the inflation rate rises. This still makes for a rising cumulative effect of inflation rate increases but for a significantly weaker, negative, marginal effect on growth as the rate of inflation becomes higher.[1]

The achievement of the theoretical literature in replicating such results has been more mixed. It has been unclear whether a monetary general equilibrium economy with a payments technology can explain the evidence of how inflation affects economic growth and other related activity. One emphasis has been on calibrating the marginal effect on growth of an increase in the inflation rate, from a level typically of 10%, and then matching that to the average estimates in the empirical literature. A variety of endogenous growth models have been offered in this regard, with widely varying results. For example, both Chari et al. (1996), using human capital, and Dotsey and Sarte (2000), using an AK model with uncertainty, present endogenous growth models with cash-in-advance technologies in which inflation has an insignificant effect on growth. In contrast, for example, both Gomme (1993), in a human capital model with a cash-in-advance constraint, and Haslag (1998), in an AK model with money used for bank reserves, find a significant effect of inflation on growth.[2] Thus these models have been ambivalent. In focusing on just one level of the inflation rate, this literature has begged the question of how inflation affects growth over a wide range of inflation rates, and of whether the models can replicate the nonlinear profile of the inflation–growth effect. Also, after a strong appearance in the older exogenous growth literature, the recent growth literature has largely ignored the issue of whether the models generate empirically consistent Tobin (1965) effects.[3]

The main contribution of the chapter here is that it presents a model in which a reasonable calibration can account for the empirical evidence, across the range of inflation rates, on inflation and growth. It does this in a robust fashion, and with an extension of a standard model using human capital and cash-in-advance. The chapter also shows that the inflation–growth explanation is fully consistent with evidence on the existence of the Tobin (1965) style effects, including a rise in output per effective labour, even as the balanced-path growth rate declines as a result of an inflation rate increase.[4] Further it presents a novel, systemic, link between the strength of the growth effect and the strength of the Tobin (1965) evidence. This fills another gap in the theoretical literature and opens up a new line of model predictions that have yet to be empirically examined: that the magnitude of the Tobin (1965) effect is roughly proportional to the magnitude of the growth effect and that these magnitudes vary monotonically from higher to lower as the inflation rate increases.

The key mechanism that gives our model the added flexibility to explain the evidence is the ability of the representative consumer to choose between competing payment mechanisms, money and credit, so that in equilibrium the marginal cost of each is equal. With such credit available to purchase the good, the nonlinearity is greatly magnified. When inflation rises, the exchange cost of goods rises but with credit available it rises by less than otherwise. So the consumer substitutes from goods to leisure but uses credit to decrease the amount of substitution towards leisure. This credit is relied upon increasingly as the inflation rate goes up and leisure is relied upon increasingly less as a substitution channel. This is because the marginal utility of goods gets increasingly high as fewer goods are consumed, while the marginal utility of leisure becomes increasingly lower as more leisure is consumed. This inflation-induced distortion in the marginal rate of substitution between goods and leisure is alleviated by the consumer's use of credit, so credit gets used more as the distortion gets bigger. This occurs despite the increasing marginal cost of credit use and in a way that is robust to the nature of the marginal cost specification. Because credit gets used increasingly and leisure is used increasingly less as a substitution channel, the inflation–growth nonlinearity results. Leisure plays a key role in determining the growth rate: increased leisure use causes a lower return on human capital and a lower growth rate. So the increasingly lower use of leisure makes the decrease in the growth rate be increasingly smaller, as the inflation rate rises. The resulting inflation–growth profile is shown to be very nonlinear compared to the model without credit and it qualitatively matches the profile in the evidence, unlike in the previous literature.

The use of credit has a residual implication for the use of money. And the nature of the model's money demand function is an alternative way to explain the basis for the inflation–growth nonlinearity. The money demand can be described as being similar to a general equilibrium version of the Cagan (1956) function, in that it has an approximately constant semi-interest elasticity. This means that as the inflation rate rises, the interest elasticity increases substantially. This is because of the decreasing use of real money, as credit is instead used to ameliorate the rising goods-to-leisure inflation-induced distortion, as the inflation rate rises. As part of this increasing interest elasticity, in the model with credit, the use of money is much more interest elastic at all levels of the inflation rate relative to the same model without credit available.[5] And the approximate semi-interest elasticity is a testable model implication that has substantial support, such as in recent international panel evidence by Mark and Sul (2003). It thereby provides a parallel dimension to the nonlinear inflation–growth evidence.[6]

In particular, the rising interest elasticity and its correspondence to the nonlinearity of the inflation–growth profile involves a previously unreported systemic link between the strength of the growth and of the Tobin (1965) effects: when the inflation rate is low and the money demand function is in the relatively inelastic range, the growth and Tobin (1965) effects are both marginally stronger, that is, larger. When the inflation rate is relatively high and money demand is in a relatively elastic range, these effects are weak. Credit, instead of leisure, takes most of the substitution burden of an increase in the inflation rate when the level of the inflation rate is already high. This results in less growth and capital reallocation effects in re-equilibrating the return on human and physical capital at a lower rate of return.

Alternative solutions to the problem, of explaining the inflation experience, that rely on popular existing payment mechanisms all face inadequacies. The Lucas (1988b) model with a standard payment mechanism can potentially produce both significant calibrated effect of the inflation–growth effect as well as the Tobin (1965) effects, but it yields a weakly nonlinear inflation–growth profile that is strained to match the evidence. Models with Lucas and Stokey (1983) cash goods and credit goods, but without a payments mechanism specified for credit, can only explain the effects of inflation through the agent's preference for credit goods versus cash goods. The lack of microeconomic evidence for this dichotomy makes the model difficult to calibrate in a non-arbitrary way. While it has been common to interpret leisure as the credit good, making leisure the credit good in the endogenous growth models simply reduces the model back to the cash-only model with goods and leisure in the utility function.[7] Shopping time economies, a now commonly used alternative approach, in one sense improve on other standard payments mechanisms by allowing time to be used as a substitute to using money. But it is unclear what this shopping time is meant to represent, as it has no obvious market analogy. With little to guide the specification, the fashion has been to use a constant interest elasticity to set the shopping time parameters, similar to how the preference-for-money parameters have been set in the money-in-the-utility function approach.[8] Some have interpreted shopping time as banking time but have not taken the approach of modelling any part of banking. This is precisely what we do with our credit sector. And the result is a Cagan (1956)-like strongly rising interest elasticity, not a constant one, that is robust to a range of credit production function parameters and is key to explaining the nonlinear nature of the evidence.

11.1 The economy with goods, human capital and exchange production

11.1.1 The consumer problem

The representative consumer's utility at time t depends on goods consumption, c_t, and leisure, x_t, in the constant elasticity form. Lifetime utility is

$$U_0 = \int_0^{\infty} e^{-\rho t} \frac{c_t^{1-\theta} x_t^{\alpha(1-\theta)}}{1-\theta} dt. \tag{1}$$

Output of goods, denoted by y_t, can be turned costlessly into physical capital. Both goods output and human capital are produced with physical capital and human capital-indexed labour in constant-returns-to-scale functions. Let k_t and h_t denote the stocks of physical capital and human capital, with the fixed depreciation rate of the capital stocks denoted by δ_k and δ_h. Let s_{Gt}, and s_{Ht} denote the fraction of capital that the agent uses in the goods production and human capital production, whereby

$$s_{Gt} + s_{Ht} = 1, \tag{2}$$

and $s_{Gt}k_t$, and $s_{Ht}k_t$ are the amounts of capital used in each sector. Similarly, let l_{Gt}, l_{Ht}, and l_{Ft} denote the fraction of time the agent uses in the goods, human capital, and credit sectors. This makes the allocation of time constraint

$$l_{Gt} + l_{Ht} + l_{Ft} = 1 - x_t, \tag{3}$$

and making $l_{Gt}h_t$, $l_{Ht}h_t$, and $l_{Ft}h_t$ the effective labour in each sector.

With β, $\varepsilon \in [0, 1]$ and A_G and A_H being positive shift parameters, the goods production function is

$$y_t = A_G (s_{Gt}k_t)^{1-\beta} (l_{Gt}h_t)^{\beta}. \tag{4}$$

The marginal product of capital $s_{Gt}k_t$, denoted by r_t, and the marginal product of effective labour $l_{Gt}h_t$, denoted by w_t, are

$$r_t = (1-\beta)\, A_G (s_{Gt}k_t)^{-\beta} (l_{Gt}h_t)^{\beta}, \tag{5}$$

$$w_t = \beta A_G (s_{Gt}k_t)^{1-\beta} (l_{Gt}h_t)^{\beta-1}. \tag{6}$$

The human capital equation of motion, given $h_0 > 0$, is

$$\dot{h}_t = A_H [(1 - s_{Gt})\, k_t]^{1-\varepsilon} [(1 - l_{Gt} - l_{Ft} - x_t)\, h]^{\varepsilon} - \delta_h h_t. \tag{7}$$

Note that this human capital investment equation is the same as in Lucas (1988b) except that there is also physical capital used as an input along with the effective labour. This follows the King and Rebelo (1990) extension of the Lucas (1988b) model which makes it more suitable for calibration purposes. While in the Lucas (1988b) model the growth rate of human capital is proportional to the labour time devoted to human capital accumulation, or to 'learning', here the growth rate is a combination of the fraction of time and the fraction of capital devoted to human capital accumulation. In both the Lucas (1988b) model and this extension, the balanced-path growth rate equals the human capital stock growth rate and both are reduced when leisure time increases.

The goods output forms an input into the Becker (1965) household production of the consumption good c_t. The goods used as an input for producing the consumption are denoted by y_{ct}. The other input is exchange, denoted by y_{et}, which enters the production function $f_c(\cdot)$:

$$c_t = f_c(y_{ct}, y_{et}). \tag{8}$$

The production function for the consumption good is assumed to be Leontieff, with the isoquant ray from the origin having a slope of one:

$$c_t = y_{ct}, \tag{9}$$

$$c_t = y_{et}. \tag{10}$$

This technology ensures that the amount of consumption goods equals the amount of physical goods and that the value of the physical goods is equal to the value of the amount that is paid (or exchanged) for the goods. This one-to-one relation is the most intuitively appealing; other specifications are possible but would require some extended justification.

The exchange in turn is produced using two inputs: real money balances, denoted by m_t, and real credit, denoted by d_t. These inputs are perfect substitutes, implying that

$$y_{et} = m_t + d_t. \tag{11}$$

Real money balances are defined as the nominal money stock, denoted by M_t, divided by the nominal price of goods output, denoted by P_t; $m_t \equiv M_t/P_t$. The initial nominal money stock M_0 is given to the consumer. Additional money stock is transferred to the consumer exogenously in a lump sum fashion by an amount V_t. The consumer uses the money to buy some fraction of the output goods with money and the rest with credit. Let $a_t \in (0, 1]$ denote the fraction of output goods bought with money.[9] Then the agents demand for money is constrained to be this fraction of goods purchased. In real terms,

$$m_t = a_t y_{ct}. \tag{12}$$

Substitution from (9) gives a Clower (1967) constraint:

$$m_t = a_t c_t; \tag{13}$$

$$M_t = P_t a_t c_t. \tag{14}$$

Credit demand is the residual fraction of output goods purchases,

$$d_t = (1 - a_t)\, y_{ct}, \tag{15}$$

or substituting from (9),

$$d_t = (1 - a_t)\, c_t. \tag{16}$$

With $\gamma \in (0, 1)$, and A_F a shift parameter, the credit production function is specified as

$$d_t = A_F (l_{Ft} h_t)^{\gamma} c_t^{1-\gamma}. \tag{17}$$

This function can be interpreted using duality. Because the total cost of production in the credit sector is the wage bill of the effective labour, $w_t l_{Ft} h_t$, (17) implies the marginal cost (MC_t) function

$$MC_t = (w_t/\gamma)\, A_F^{-1/\gamma} (d_t/c_t)^{(1-\gamma)/\gamma}. \tag{18}$$

With $\gamma < 0.5$, this gives a marginal cost of credit output, per unit of consumption, that rises at an increasing rate as in a traditional U-shaped cost curve. Figure 11.1 graphs the three cases of $\gamma = 0.3$ (thicker line), $\gamma = 0.5$ (middle, straight, line) and $\gamma = 0.7$ (and with $w_t = A_F = 0.2$).

A rising marginal cost function per unit of consumption is the same device used in Gillman (1993). The difference is that in that model there was a continuum of goods and of stores each with a different time cost of supplying

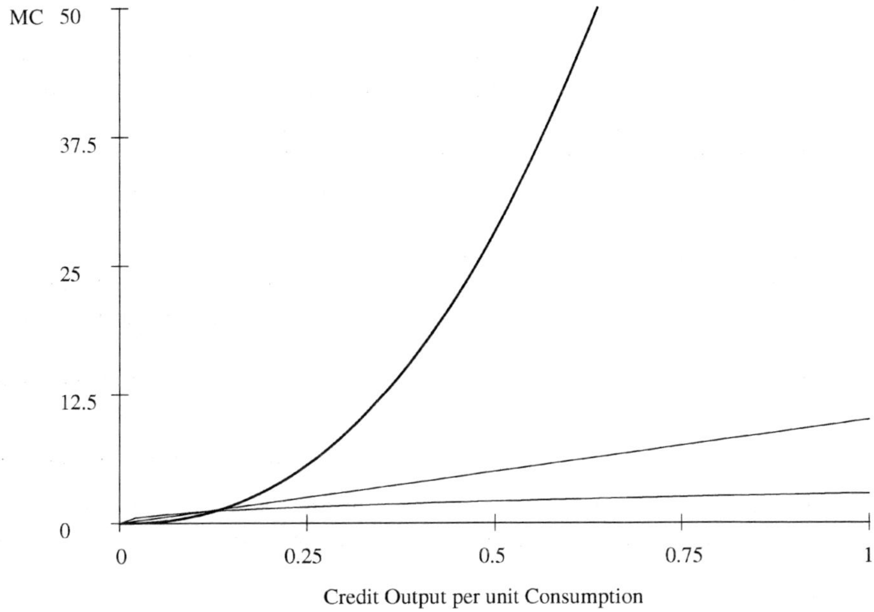

Figure 11.1 Marginal cost of credit.

credit to buy their good. In aggregate the stores present an upward sloping marginal cost curve, so that a unique equilibrium with the nominal interest exists at each nominal interest rate. However here there is only one consumption good and one credit production function, with γ being the diminishing returns parameter that determines the shape of the curve; the unique equilibrium results as long as $\gamma < 1$, although $\gamma > 0.5$ seems unlikely in that they indicate a marginal cost that rises at a decreasing rate in contrast to typical industrial organisation evidence.

The upward sloping cost curve, for example, with $\gamma = 0.3$ as in Figure 11.1, can also be interpreted in terms of the value-added of the credit sector. This requires an explicit price for the credit service through a decentralisation of the sector.[10] Given the decentralisation, it is found that the price of the credit service is the nominal interest rate. In market clearing equilibrium, this price equals the marginal cost given above. And indeed the equality of the nominal interest rate and the marginal cost of credit is one of the key equilibrium conditions (32). This 'price' can also be used to define the value-added, or total revenues as in national accounts, of the credit sector; this equals the nominal interest rate factored by the quantity of the credit supplied. Given the assumed production function, in equilibrium it can be shown that this value-added is proportional to the cost of production ($[Rc(1-a)]/(wl_F h) = 1/\gamma$). This gives another way to interpret the assumed production specification. Even simpler, the specification implies that the per unit marginal cost is higher than average cost by a fixed proportion for all levels of credit output, resulting in a constant profit rate. Thus the assumption is the same as assuming an upward sloping marginal cost curve, proportional to average cost, with a constant profit rate, which has its intuition based firmly in standard price theory.

Note that the output of such a service sector is necessarily proportional to aggregate consumption. Factoring out this proportionality factor to determine what is being produced gives the share of the output for which the service is provided. If it is also assumed that the production function has diminishing returns, then the production of the share necessarily includes an 'externality' effect from the aggregate consumption. Where constant returns to scale are specified for the service, while at the same time there is a substitute price that exhibits a constant marginal cost, which is what the nominal interest rate presents for the marginal cost of real money, then there is no unique equilibrium between the two alternatives. Thus the production function for credit must be specified with diminishing returns in order to have a unique equilibrium and, as a service proportional to aggregate consumption, it must include the externality effect. However, consider an illustration of what this really means in the model economy. A credit card company such as American Express, in a decentralised setting, would maximise profit while taking as given how much is spent on goods for consumption. American Express would not try to change this goods expenditure but must consider it in making its optimal credit supply available to the consumer. By making its inputs grow as the consumption of goods grows, it can maintain its share of supplying credit. This simply means that if the aggregate consumption increases and the credit sector does not increase its effective labour proportionally, then it will lose its share of output for which it provides the service.

Setting credit demand equal to credit supply, in (16) and (17),

$$(1 - a_t) = A_F \left(l_{Ft} h_t / c_t\right)^{\gamma}. \tag{19}$$

Substituting into (14) for a_t from (19), the money and credit constraints can be written as

$$M_t = \left[1 - A_F\left(\frac{l_{Ft} h_t}{c_t}\right)^{\gamma}\right] P_t c_t. \tag{20}$$

11.1.2 Government money supply

The initial money stock M_0 is given to the representative agent and the only role of the government is to change the money supply from its initial value. To do this, each period the government transfers to the consumer an exogenous lump sum money supply of V_t at a constant rate of σ;

$$\dot{M}_t = V_t = \sigma M_t. \tag{21}$$

The stock V_t is the inflation 'proceeds' that result when the government buys output/capital (they are costlessly interchangeable) with freshly printed fiat and then gives this (thereby producing real money) to the consumer as an income transfer. Net government spending equals zero and is omitted for notational simplification. The only effect of such 'Production' is a relative price distortion if the inflation rate ends up non-optimal.

In real terms, dividing (21) by P_t implies that the government's investment rate in real money is the supply growth rate minus the inflation-based depreciation of $\pi \equiv \dot{P}_t/P_t$:

$$\dot{m}_t = (\sigma - \pi) m_t. \tag{22}$$

11.1.3 Definition of Equilibrium

The consumer's total nominal financial wealth, denoted by Q_t, is the sum of the money stock M_t and the nominal value of the physical capital stock $P_t k_t$:

$$Q_t = M_t + P_t k_t; \tag{23}$$

$$\dot{Q}_t = \dot{M}_t + P_t \dot{k}_t + \dot{P}_t k_t. \tag{24}$$

The consumer's change in the financial wealth over time, $\dot{Q}_t$, is equal to the sum of V_t by (21), plus the nominal value of the change in physical capital, $P_t \dot{k}_t$, and plus the nominal price appreciation factor $\dot{P}_t k_t$. The $P_t \dot{k}_t$ term is the output of goods, which can be written in terms of marginal products using (5) and (6), minus the output of goods that are purchased for consumption, which by (9) equals $P_t c_t$, and minus capital depreciation $P_t \delta_k k_t$. This gives

$$\dot{Q}_t = P_t r_t s_{Gt} k_t + P_t w_t l_{Gt} h_t + V_t - P_t c_t - P_t \delta_k k_t + \dot{P}_t k_t. \tag{25}$$

Equations (4), (5), (6), (25) and (21) imply the social resource constraint

$$y_t = c_t + \dot{k}_t + \delta_k k_t. \tag{26}$$

Given M_0, k_0, h_0, and the normalisation of $P_0 = 1$, equilibrium consists of the values of the prices $\{r_t, w_t, P_t\}_{t=0}^{\infty}$ and the allocations $\{c_t, x_t, s_{Gt}, l_{Gt}, l_{Ft}, M_t, Q_t, k_t\}_{t=0}^{\infty}$ that satisfy

(*i*) the representative consumer's maximisation of lifetime utility (1) subject to the constraints in equations (7), (20), (23), and (25), taking as given the prices and the transfer V_t,
(*ii*) the firm's maximisation problem taking prices as given,
(*iii*) the government supply of money in (21), and

(*iv*) the clearing of all markets in the economy, with (26) for the goods market.

11.1.4 Balanced-Growth Path

On the balanced-growth path, c_t, k_t, h_t, m_t and y_t grow at the same rate, denoted by g. The variables x_t, l_{Gt}, l_{Ft}, l_{Ht}, s_{Gt}, s_{Ht}, w_t, r_t are stationary.

A balanced-growth path reduced set of equilibrium conditions are set out below, with time subscripts dropped and assuming $\delta_k = \delta_h$:

$$\frac{u_c(c,x)}{u_x(c,x)} = \frac{x}{\alpha c} = \frac{1 + aR + wl_F h/c}{wh}, \tag{27}$$

$$\frac{w}{r} = \frac{\beta}{1-\beta}\frac{s_G k}{l_G h} = \frac{\varepsilon}{1-\varepsilon}\frac{s_H k}{l_H h}, \tag{28}$$

$$g \equiv \frac{\dot{c}}{c} = \frac{\dot{k}}{k} = \frac{\dot{h}}{h} = \frac{\dot{m}}{m} = \frac{r - \delta_k - \rho}{\theta} \tag{29}$$

$$= \frac{\varepsilon(1-x)A_H[(s_{Ht}k_t)/(l_{Ht}h_t)]^{1-\varepsilon} - \delta_h - \rho}{\theta}, \tag{30}$$

$$r - \delta_k + \frac{\dot{P}}{P} \equiv R, \tag{31}$$

$$R = w/\left[\gamma A_F\left(\frac{l_{Ft}h_t}{c_t}\right)^{\gamma-1}\right]. \tag{32}$$

Because of the novel nature of the credit sector, a focus on this last equation (32) helps describe the model. In the Baumol (1952) model, the consumer chooses between two payment mechanisms: the use of money and the use of banking in which interest is earned on the income. The banking of these models is similar to the credit in the model here. Also similar is that the consumer optimally chooses between the two according to the cost of each relative to the other. This choice yields the only equilibrium condition in Baumol (1952). There is no such margin in the standard cash-only Lucas (1980) or Lucas and Stokey (1983) economies. The model here follows Baumol (1952) and adds this as an additional margin relative to the standard cash-in-advance economy with the following equilibrium condition. The cost of money, R, equals the marginal cost of credit, which is the marginal factor cost of effective labour in the credit sector, w_t, divided by the marginal product of labour in the credit sector. This is a standard microeconomic pricing condition for factor market equilibrium. The existence of this condition, not found in Baumol (1952), takes the important margin that Baumol (1952) develops and places it securely within microeconomic theory, while using the single-good standard neoclassical growth framework.[11] This makes standard monetary theory tractable back to the production structure of credit, unlike in Baumol (1952).

The marginal rate of substitution of goods relative to leisure is given by (27), and can be understood as the ratio of the shadow price of the consumption good to leisure. The shadow price of consumption goods is one, the goods cost, plus the exchange cost of $aR + wl_F h/c$ per unit. If only money is used in exchange, this is just the nominal interest R. But with credit also used this exchange cost is less than R and can be expressed as a weighted average of money and credit use, or $1 + aR + (1 - a)\gamma R$. Or with a focus on a, this can be written as $1 + \gamma R + aR(1 - \gamma)$. When the inflation rate goes up the cost of exchange rises. But because of substitution towards credit, the cash share a falls, the shadow exchange price rises by less than proportionately to R, and so it rises by less than in the cash-only model. Thus there is substitution towards leisure as in the cash-only model but less of it.

Other balanced-growth path equilibrium conditions here show that the growth rate equals the return on capital minus the time preference rate, in the log-utility case, and that the returns of human and physical capital are equal; with equal depreciation rates, $r = \varepsilon(1 - x) A_H[(s_{Ht} k_t) / (l_{Ht} h_t)]^{1-\varepsilon}$. This last expression highlights how the increased leisure can decrease the growth rate, while the Tobin (1965) effect towards greater capital intensity in both goods and human capital sectors, as w/r increases because of an inflation increase, can partially offset the decrease in the growth rate.

11.1.5 Effect of inflation on balanced-growth path

Technically, the effect of a change in the inflation rate on the balanced-growth path equilibrium can be solved analytically for certain parameter specifications by solving all equations in terms of leisure and then solving for the change in leisure from one implicit equation in terms of only leisure. Then the main results follow and can be summarised in the following two Lemmas. For analytic tractability, log-utility is assumed and in addition no physical capital is assumed for the second lemma and its two corollaries. These assumptions are relaxed in the calibration.

Note that the results state what happens when there is an increase in the money supply growth rate. The inflation rate, as in all such models, increases because the exogenous rate of money supply growth is assumed to increase. The inflation rate goes up a bit more than the money supply growth rate increase, because the balanced-path growth rate falls somewhat, while the sum of the inflation rate and the balanced-path growth rate are constrained to equal the money supply growth rate; from (22), $\pi = \sigma - g$. So while this is generally thought of as the effect of inflation on growth in such models and this is the usage made in this paper, the inflation–growth relation is more precisely a result of the money supply changes.

LEMMA 1 *An increase in the money supply growth rate σ causes an increase in* *leisure time, a decrease in the real interest rate, an increase in the capital to effective labour ratio in the goods and human capital production sectors, an increase in the goods capital to output ratio and a decrease in the balanced-growth path growth rate. It is assumed that $\theta = 1$, $\beta = \varepsilon = \gamma = 0.5$, $A_G = A_H$, and that the change in the money supply growth rate is evaluated at the Friedman optimum of $R = 0$.*

Proof. Please see Appendix 11.A.1.

The increase in the exchange cost of goods causes a relative decrease in the opportunity cost of leisure, thereby inducing a shift back in the supply of labour for goods production, while there is a shift of labour into credit production. The real wage rises (by less than does the exchange cost of goods) in order to clear the labour market, inducing firms to realign inputs towards capital and away from labour. The increase in the capital to effective labour ratios, across both goods and human capital production sectors, lowers the marginal product of capital and the real interest rate.[12] Here the rising capital to effective labour effect marks the Tobin (1965) effect in the human capital model, rather than the rising capital per worker as in the Solow exogenous growth model without leisure. Output per effective unit of labour also goes up in a way similar to Tobin (1965). A lower real interest rate from an inflation increase can be viewed as part of this Tobin (1965) effect but, unlike in Tobin (1965), here the growth rate goes down.

Note that in the Lucas (1988b) model, only effective labour is used in human capital accumulation and there is no leisure in the utility function; in this case the rate of return on human capital in equilibrium is just proportional to the time spent accumulating human capital, or $A_H l_H$. When the time spent in human capital production goes down, the growth rate goes down. In the monetary extension of the human capital growth model, leisure plays a critical role with respect to inflation. For example, with no physical capital and log-utility (as assumed in the next Lemma), the rate of return on human capital is proportional to the time spent working in all sectors, or $A_H(1 - x)$. In this case the change in the total time spent working $(1 - x)$ (in all three sectors) is exactly equal to the change in the time spent in human capital accumulation l_H; here the Lucas (1988b) explanation of the growth rate, as being proportional to the time spent in human capital accumulation, is perfectly interchangeable with the time spent working. With physical capital the growth rate more generally depends on the rate of return to human capital, in which a falling amount of leisure time because of inflation is the primary effect, while an increase in the capital to effective labour ratio is of secondary magnitude, moderating the decrease in the growth rate.

LEMMA 2 *The magnitude of the change in the balanced-growth path growth rate, from a change in the money supply growth rate, is determined inversely by the magnitude of the interest elasticity of money demand, given that*

$\beta = \varepsilon = \theta = 1$ and given that the interest elasticity is less than one in magnitude. Further with a cash-only restriction ($a \equiv 1$), the inflation–growth profile is exactly linear.

Proof. Please see Appendix 11.A.2.

This is the log-utility and no physical capital case. At the Friedman (1969) optimum of $R = 0$, the marginal rate of substitution between goods and leisure is undistorted and leisure is a close substitute for goods because there is no tax wedge to force their marginal utilities to diverge. As the inflation rate rises from the optimal rate, leisure tends to be used readily to avoid the inflation tax, while credit use is relegated to a secondary role in avoiding inflation, despite the fact that the marginal cost of credit is relatively low at low inflation rates since there is a rising marginal cost curve. However at higher rates of inflation, the inflation tax wedge makes the use of more leisure increasingly less attractive relative to the use of more credit because leisure's diminishing marginal utility and goods' increasing marginal utility, in effect, dominate the rising cost of the credit. Credit is used increasingly more and therefore the interest elasticity of money demand is increasingly high. Because the growth rate effect is dependent directly on how much leisure is used when inflation rises, this effect is strongest when the inflation rate is rising from the optimum and the wedge in the goods-leisure rate of substitution is at its smallest. The growth rate falls by increasingly less as the inflation rate rises and the interest elasticity of money demand rises in magnitude.

At a unitary interest elasticity, the growth rate stops falling and actually begins to rise. However the baseline calibration puts this juncture at a hyperinflation rate of inflation, above which the government makes less seigniorage anyway. This suggests that only the range of the inflation rate that induces a less than unitary elasticity is likely to be empirically relevant. Note the relation of this result to Eckstein and Leiderman (1992). They find that seigniorage in Israel rises at a steadily decreasing rate, which they model with a money demand derived from putting real money balances in the utility function. Our nonlinear inflation–growth profile and the rising magnitude of interest elasticity correspond directly to a seigniorage that rises at a diminishing rate. As in the Cagan (1956) model but unlike that of Eckstein and Leiderman (1992), the total seigniorage would begin to fall once the interest elasticity rose above one in magnitude but we suggest that this is not an empirically relevant long-run range for the elasticity.

COROLLARY 1 *The magnitude of the interest elasticity of the goods-normalised money demand rises with an increase in the inflation rate because the magnitude of the elasticity of substitution between money and credit, and the share of credit in purchases, each rise with an increase in the nominal interest rate.*

Proof. Please see Appendix 11.A.3.

A standard factor-price elasticity of substitution between real money and credit, as the two inputs into producing exchange, can be defined as the percentage change in inputs over the percentage change in marginal products. Then the interest elasticity of money demand can be expressed as a price elasticity of the derived input demand, in terms of the elasticity of substitution. In particular, the interest elasticity of money demand (η_m^R) equals the (negative) share of the other input credit $(1 - a)$ as factored by the elasticity of substitution between money and credit (ε), plus a scale effect (η_c^R); or $\eta_m^R = (1 - a)\varepsilon + \eta_c^R$.[13] The scale effect is of secondary importance in terms of magnitude and, when normalising the money demand by consumption, this term drops out (this is the only term in the cash-only economy). As the inflation rate rises, leisure becomes a worse substitute, even while money and credit remain perfect technical substitutes (11). This increases the two-factor elasticity of substitution; the share of credit $1 - a$ also rises unambiguously. Note that the isoquant for producing exchange is not linear because of the role of leisure.[14]

The result is insensitive to the specification of the parameters in the credit production function. Given that $\gamma \in (0, 1)$ and $A_F > 0$, there is a rising marginal cost of credit, as the credit use per unit of consumption increases. The degree of diminishing returns, γ, affects shape of the marginal cost curve in an unambiguous way but affects the normalised interest elasticity in an ambiguous fashion that depends on the calibration; the shift parameter A_F does has a clear effect on the magnitude of the normalised interest elasticity (as indicated in the next Corollary). But regardless of these specifications, it is the fact of the existence of the credit (with a rising marginal cost), combined with the nature of the goods to leisure marginal rate of substitution, that produces the Corollary results, of an increasing interest elasticity with inflation rate increases. This can alternatively be seen by writing the normalised elasticity as $(1 - a)\varepsilon = -[\gamma/(1 - \gamma)][(1 - a)/a]$. All that is necessary for this elasticity to rise in magnitude is that the normalised money usage (a) falls as the inflation rate rises.

COROLLARY 2 *The magnitude of the interest elasticity of the goods-normalised money demand rises with an increase in productivity in the credit sector, as indicated by an increase in the total factor productivity A_F of the credit production function.*

Proof. Please see Appendix 11.A.4.

This Corollary brings in one additional factor, the productivity of the credit sector. This can be important for example in analysing changes in financial regulation. A deregulation is similar to a decrease in the implicit tax on the credit sector that has the effect of shifting up the productivity parameter A_F. Continuing the example, deregulation here has the effect on increasing the demand for credit at each nominal interest rate, making the demand for money in effect more interest elastic. The fall in the price of a substitute to money causes a shift back in the money demand function. Given the same nominal interest rate, this moves the consumer 'up' the money demand function to a more interest elastic point.

11.2 Calibration

The analytic results of the Lemmas and Corollaries, on how inflation affects the balanced-growth equilibrium, are shown to apply as well in the general model through its calibration. The calibration makes clear that the model produces a significant effect of inflation on growth, within the range of empirical estimates reviewed for example by Chari et al. (1996), while showing the nonlinearity of this effect, the existence of Tobin (1965) effects, and the link between the magnitude of the growth and Tobin (1965) effects. Also the calibration shows the robustness of the results to a full range of alternative specifications of the parameters of the credit production function.

11.2.1 Assumed parameter values

Standard parameters values are assumed as in the literature. Table 11.1 presents the assumed values for the baseline calibration. Leisure is set as in Jones et al. (1997); risk aversion and Cobb-Douglas parameters for goods and human capital sectors as in Gomme (1993); depreciation rates as in King and Rebelo (1990); the growth rate as in Chari et al. (1996); the share of cash is similar to Dotsey and Ireland (1996); leisure preference is set within the range in the literature. For the credit sector technology, the degree of diminishing returns is set to 0.2, as based on the estimated value of this parameter that is found for the US in the money demand estimation of Gillman and Otto (2002), a companion paper. This parameter is varied below in Table 4 and a fuller set of such variations can be found in Gillman and Kejak (2002).

11.2.2 The results

Table 11.2 shows that the baseline calibration for the negative growth rate effect of a 10% point increase in the inflation rate is a –0.23 percentage point

Table 11.1 Baseline parameter and variable values

Parameters	ρ	δ_h	δ_k	θ	β	ε	α	γ	A_G	A_H	A_F
	0.04	0.1	0.1	1.5	0.64	0.64	4.692	0.2	1	0.581	0.801

Variables	a	x	g	π	l_G	l_H	l_F
	0.7	0.7	0.02	0.05	0.1635	0.1355	0.00098

Table 11.2 Baseline calibration of the effect of increasing the inflation rate

	Inflation rate change		
Baseline change in variable	*5 → 15%*	*15 → 25%*	*25 → 35%*
Growth Rate g	–0.00232	–0.00199	–0.00173
Leisure x	0.00878	0.00824	0.00705
Real Interest Rate r	–0.00320	–0.00304	–0.00263
Real Wage w	0.01054	0.01029	0.00914
Capit/Lab Gds $(s_G k)/(l_G h)$	0.09800	0.09753	0.08810
Capit/Lab Hum $(s_H k)/(l_H h)$	0.09800	0.09753	0.08810
Capit/Output $(s_G k)/y$	0.04086	0.04023	0.03599
Output/Eff.Labour $y/(l_G h)$	0.01647	0.01608	0.01428
Money/Consumption-Goods a	–0.04187	–0.03310	–0.02586
Point Est of Int Elast η^m_R	–0.12757	–0.17570	–0.22204

change in the growth rate of output, comparable to the range in Chari et al. (1996). Note that the –0.23 indicates that starting from a baseline of 0.02% growth (a 2% growth rate) at an inflation rate of 0.05, the growth rate falls to 0.0177 when the inflation rate rises to 0.15. Figure 11.2*a* simulates this in the solid line. The negative growth effect falls in magnitude as the inflation rate rises. This non-linear relation, of a marginally decreasing magnitude of the negative growth effect, has been found empirically in many studies. This occurs even while the Tobin (1965) effect is present through a higher output to effective labour ratio (Figure 11.2*b*).

Figure 11.2*a* also includes for contrast a dashed line for the cash-only economy that is almost linear, contrary to evidence. Additionally for the economy of Lemma 2, in which there is no physical capital, Figure 11.2*c* shows that the inflation growth profile is perfectly linear for the cash-only economy (dashed line) versus the nonlinear Section 11.2 model with credit (solid line).

Table 11.2 also shows how leisure rises with inflation (Figure 11.3*a*), the real interest rate falls (Figure 11.3*b*), the real effective wage rises (Figure 11.3*c*), and the capital to effective labour ratio in the goods sector and the capital to output ratio rise (Figure 11.3*d,e*). The sectorial reallocations are supported empirically in Gillman and Nakov (2003), while supporting evidence for the positive investment rate effect and negative real interest rate effect are found in Ahmed and Rogers (2000). Figure 11.3*f* simulates the money demand per unit of consumption goods; this is the inverse, endogenous, consumption velocity and it contrasts for example to the assumption in Alvarez et al. (2001) that velocity is exogenous. In addition, Table 11.2 shows the link among the magnitude of the growth and Tobin (1965) effects and the magnitude of the interest elasticity of money demand.

Table 11.3 provides a calibration with the goods sector's capital intensity increased above that of the human capital production sector, with $\beta = 0.50$,

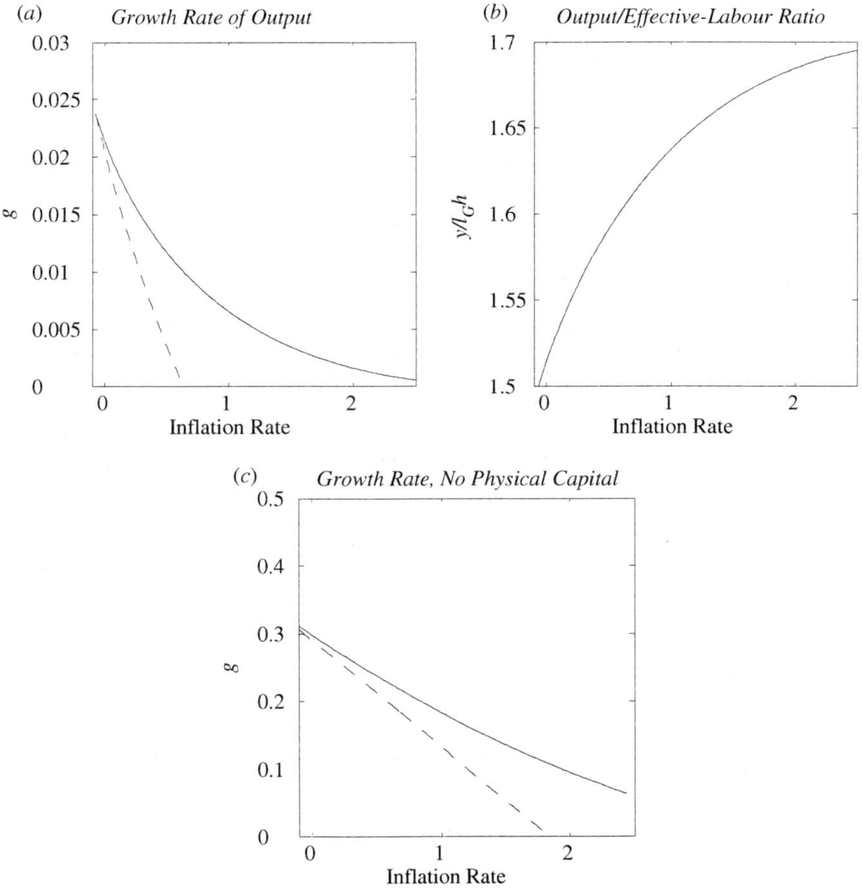

Figure 11.2 Inflation with growth and output per unit of effective labour credit; cash-only (dashed).

instead of $\beta = 0.64$ as in the baseline. This shows that with a greater goods sector capital intensity, the inflation-induced substitution from labour to capital is marginally greater, and the Tobin (1965) and growth effects stronger, relative to the baseline, while the interest elasticity is of smaller magnitude. This acts to shift up the inflation–growth profile marginally; Figure 11.3*g* shows this with the solid line being the baseline and with the dashed line having $\beta = 0.50$ and all other parameters as in the baseline.

Table 11.4 shows the effect of increasing the parameter that indicates the degree of diminishing returns in the credit sector from its baseline value. It shows that such increases cause larger growth and Tobin (1965) effects and a smaller interest elasticity. This calibration is done for a neighbourhood of the baseline calibration with respect to changes in γ. Simulation of the inflation–growth effect with a larger γ show that this acts to pivot down the

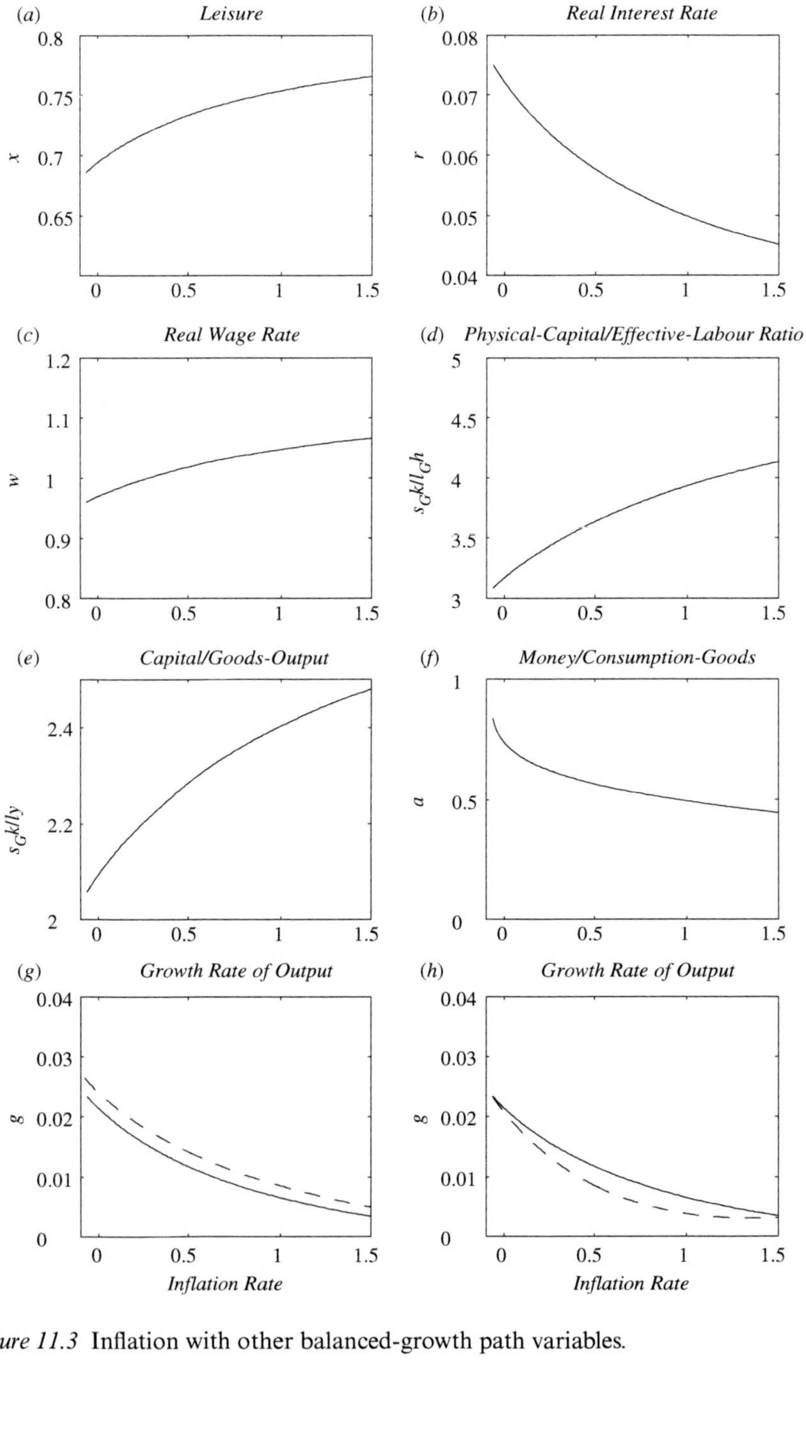

Figure 11.3 Inflation with other balanced-growth path variables.

Table 11.3 Baseline calibration except for an increase in the capital intensity in goods production

	Inflation rate change		
Baseline except $\beta = 0.50$ change in variable	*5 → 15%*	*15 → 25%*	*25 → 35%*
Growth Rate g	−0.00234	−0.00206	−0.00179
Leisure x	0.00926	0.00805	0.00691
Real Interest Rate Rt r	−0.00351	−0.00308	−0.00269
Real Wage w	0.02967	0.02699	0.02437
Capit/Lab Gds $(s_G k)/(l_G h)$	0.34530	0.31929	0.29365
Capit/Lab Hum $(s_H k)/(l_H h)$	0.19423	0.17960	0.16518
Capit/Output $(s_G k/y$	0.05935	0.05397	0.04974
Output/Eff. Labour $y/(l_G h)$	0.05735	0.05397	0.04874
Money/Consumption-Goods a	−0.03933	−0.02915	−0.02228
Point Est of Int Elast η^m_R	−0.10536	−0.17436	−0.18526

Table 11.4 The inflation effects when increasing the degree of diminishing returns in credit production

	Degree of diminishing returns in credit production		
Baseline: inflation rate 5 → 15% change in variable	$\gamma = 0.2$	$\gamma = 0.3$	$\gamma = 0.5$
Growth Rate g	−0.00232	−0.00273	−0.00338
Leisure x	0.00878	0.01148	0.01423
Real Interest Rate r	−0.00320	−0.00421	−0.00524
Real Wage w	0.01054	0.01398	0.01769
Capit/Lab Gds $(s_G k)/(l_G h)$	0.09800	0.13083	0.16724
Capit/Lab Hum $(s_H k)/(l_H h)$	0.09800	0.13083	0.16724
Capit/Output $(S_G k/y$	0.04091	0.04866	0.06908
Output/Eff.Labour $y/(l_G h)$	0.01647	0.02184	0.02764
Money/Consumption-Goods a	−0.04187	−0.05434	−0.03080
Point Est of Int Elast η^m_R	−0.12757	−0.11737	−0.08745

inflation–growth profile. Figure 11.3*h* shows this with the solid line being the baseline and with the dashed line having $\gamma = 0.25$ and all other parameters as in the baseline.

While the role of financial development on the inflation–growth effect has been little studied (although there are sizeable literatures on each the inflation and growth relation, and the financial development and growth relation), Gillman et al. (2004) present evidence of differences in the inflation–growth profile for APEC and OECD samples. The profiles compare closely to Figure 11.3*h* in that APEC's profile is less steep at every rate of inflation, while the profile starts at about the same point, so that the APEC profile appears pivoted up relative to the OECD profile. The model thus suggests a comparatively greater degree of diminishing returns in credit production and a more steeply rising marginal cost curve, in the APEC region. This offers one explanation consistent with the different inflation–growth results that cannot be provided with the standard cash-only cash-in-advance exchange technology.

11.3. Comparison to other payment mechanisms

One type of comparison that can be further detailed is to use the same human capital model but with different payment mechanisms.

11.3.1 Cash-only Economy

The most standard is the cash-only economy of Lucas (1980). Here the consumer can use only money to buy goods. This case results from the Section 11.1 model when $a \equiv 1$ is imposed. Or this can be derived by having credit be prohibitively expensive (A_F close to zero). Figure 11.2*a* (dashed line) shows the resulting inflation–growth profile with the baseline calibration. The almost linear profile indicates that the growth rate becomes negative quickly as the inflation rate rises, contrary to evidence. The cash-only model overstates the inflation effect on growth at every level of the inflation rate for $R > 0$, in comparison to the Section 11.1 model. The reason is that when inflation increases, with cash-only the consumer can only substitute towards leisure and so uses more leisure for each marginal increase in the inflation rate than if credit were available. So instead of having much smaller leisure increases as the inflation rate goes higher, which is what happens when credit is available, the increases in leisure only decrease in magnitude slightly.

11.3.2 The Shopping Time Economy

The Lucas (2000) shopping time model focuses on the use of resources in exchange activity. Calling this activity ‘shopping time’ after McCallum and Goodfriend (1987), and showing the sense in which it exactly equals the welfare cost of inflation in the economy (with no leisure), he specifies the shopping time exchange constraint so as to induce a constant interest elasticity. This strategy of specifying the exchange technology so as to have a constant interest elasticity is also used in Goodfriend (1997), who cites an earlier version of the Lucas (2000) paper, and in Gavin and Kydland (1999).

By assuming a constant interest elasticity, the free parameters of the shopping time function can be constrained in a non-arbitrary way. However the problem with the constant interest elasticity assumption is that it is in conflict with the evidence. Lucas (2000) describes how a constant-like interest elasticity model seems to breakdown for US data during the 1980s, after which he concludes that a constant semi-interest elasticity model seems to be the preferred model. Mark and Sul (2003) find substantial cointegration panel data evidence in support of the constant semi-interest elasticity model.

If in fact a constant semi-interest elasticity is the appropriate model, then the key fact here is that the interest elasticity rises as the interest rate rises, rather than remaining constant as in the shopping time models. In this case the shopping time models are forcing an undue lack of nonlinearity upon the inflation effects with respect to growth and Tobin (1965) variables. This means that the constant interest elasticity will make the effects too weak for low values of the inflation rate and too strong for higher values of the inflation rate, depending on the particulars of which constant interest elasticity is chosen.

The model of Section 11.1 can in fact be viewed as a special case of the shopping time economy. The special case is that the shopping time of the McCallum and Goodfriend (1987) exchange constraint becomes instead the banking time of an explicit credit production technology.[15] The credit technology parameters determine only how quickly the interest elasticity of money demand rises with the inflation rate. Corollary 1 explains why a rising interest elasticity with inflation does not depend on the exact specification of these parameters, a result confirmed with calibration. Rather through their effect on the interest elasticity they determine the degree of nonlinearity of the inflation–growth profile. Extreme values can reproduce the cash-only economy ($A_F = 0$ or $\gamma = 0$).

11.4 Conclusion

The chapter shows that, contrary to what has become generally accepted, growth models with Lucas (1988b) human capital and well-defined payments mechanisms can successfully explain major facets of how inflation affects long-run economic activity. First it makes clear that point estimates, of significant magnitude, of the negative effect of inflation on the balanced-path growth rate can be found with a standard calibration that is robust to varying the parameters of the credit production function. Second the credit allows the consumer to use less leisure as inflation increases, so that the economy exhibits a significantly nonlinear inflation–growth relation, as has been found repeatedly in empirical studies. Third the model shows that related Tobin (1965) effects are at work in the economy, with a decrease in the real interest rate to the real wage ratio, an increase in the capital to effective labour ratios across sectors, and a rise in the output per unit of effective labour input. This inflation-tax-induced increase in the output per effective labour hour is a result of the household trying to moderate the growth rate decrease by realigning inputs towards capital as labour becomes scarce and leisure in greater use.

The model has household production of consumption using goods and exchange. The exchange is produced interchangeably with money or a credit sector. This offers a direction alternative to general transaction cost models such as the shopping time models. The approach is related to the cash-credit framework of Aiyagari et al. (1998), who assume a constant semi-interest elasticity of money demand. Here such a money demand is generated endogenously as the consumer equalises the marginal cost of alternative payment mechanisms. As a result, links between the money demand function and the inflation effects are pervasive and, unlike previous work, are made explicit. The money demand's interest elasticity inversely determines the strength of the growth and Tobin (1965) effects in a way that fills out intuition of these events. This presents also an alternative research strategy towards further developing and calibrating such models: to use structural parameters of the credit production technology in addition to so-called behavioural parameters of the partial equilibrium money demand functions. This may further advance understanding of how inflation affects international growth and other aspects of the structure of the economy.

Appendix 11.A

11.A.1 Proof of Lemma 1

The equilibrium conditions, including the marginal product definitions in (5) and (6), imply that the balanced-growth solution of all of the variables of the economy can be written in terms of $1 - x$, in addition is an implicit equation in $1 - x$. The implicit equation, derived from $1 - x = l_F + l_G + l_H$, is

$$1 - x = \frac{r^{(1-\varepsilon)/\beta}}{A_H\,[A_G(1-\beta)]^{(1-\varepsilon)/\beta}} \frac{\left[A_G\left(\frac{l_G h}{s_G k}\right)^{\beta}(r-\rho) + A_H\left(\frac{c}{h}\right)\left(\frac{l_H h}{s_H k}\right)^{\varepsilon}\right]}{\beta A_G\left(\frac{l_G h}{s_G k}\right)^{\beta} + \rho}$$
$$+ \frac{w^{\gamma/(\gamma-1)}\,x}{a(\gamma A_F R)^{1/(\gamma-1)}\left[1 + aR + w\left(\frac{l_F h}{c}\right)\right]}.$$

With $\varepsilon = \beta = \gamma = 0.5$, and $A_G = A_H = 1$ this gives the following polynomial in $z \equiv (1 - x)^{0.5}$, where $\Omega \equiv [A_F(\sigma + \rho)]^2$.

$$0 = -\,0.5\Omega z^3 + [2a\rho\Omega - (1 + \rho\Omega)]z^2 - [4a\rho(1 + \sigma + \rho) - 0.5\Omega]\,z + 1 + \rho\Omega. \qquad (33)$$

Differentiating with respect to σ and z, and solving for $\partial z/\partial\sigma$, we have

$$\frac{\partial z}{\partial \sigma} = \frac{(\partial\Omega/\partial\sigma)\,[-\,0.5z^3 + \rho(2a-1)z^2 + 0.5z + \rho] - 4a\rho}{\Omega\,[1.5z^2 - 2\rho(2a-1)z + 0.5] + 2z + 4a\rho(1 + \sigma + \rho)},$$

where $\partial\Omega/\partial\sigma = 2A_F^2(\sigma + \rho)$. Evaluating $\partial z/\partial\sigma$ at the optimum of $\sigma + \rho = 0$, implies that $\partial z/\partial\sigma = -2a\rho/(z + 2a\rho)$. Since $a, \rho > 0$ and $z = 1 - x \in (0, 1)$, $\partial z/\partial\sigma = \partial(1 - x)/\partial\sigma < 0$. Then the equilibrium values of all variables can be examined in terms of their change with respect to $1 - x$ and σ. With the above parameter restrictions these are given by $r = 0.5(1 - x)^{0.5}$, with $\partial r/\partial(1 - x) > 0$, and $\partial r/\partial\sigma < 0$; $w = 0.5(1 - x)^{-0.5}$, $\partial w/\partial(1 - x) < 0$; $\partial w/\partial\sigma > 0$; $s_G k/l_G h = s_H k/l_H h = (1 - x)^{-1}$; $\partial(s_G k/l_G h)/\partial\sigma < 0$; $(s_G k)/y = 1/[r(1 - \beta)]$, $\partial[(s_G k)/y]/\partial\sigma > 0$; $g = r - \delta_k - \rho$, $\partial g/\partial\sigma < 0$.

Finally we derive the unique solution for x at the optimum. Evaluating (33) at the optimum of $\sigma + \rho = 0$, implies that $z^2 + 4a\rho z - 1 = 0$. The quadratic equation has two solutions: $z_{1,2} = 2a\rho\,[-1 \pm \sqrt{1 + 1/(4a^2\rho^2)}]$. One solution gives a negative x, outside its feasible range. And it can be shown that the unique solution for leisure, $x \in [0, 1]$, is $1 - 4a^2\rho^2[-1 + \sqrt{1 + 1/(4a^2\rho^2)}\,]^2$.

11.A.2 Proof of Lemma 2

Under the assumptions of $\beta = \varepsilon = \theta = 1$ the economy uses no physical capital and has logutility. Here the growth rate is determined by the marginal product of human capital and is given by $g = A_H(1 - x) - \delta_h$, and $\partial g/\partial\sigma = -A_H\partial x/\partial\sigma$. The economy has a closed form solution and $x = (\rho a/A_H)\,[(1 + aR + A_G l_F h/c)]\,/\,(1 + A_G l_F h/c)$. Since $R = \sigma + \rho$, it follows that $\partial g/\partial\sigma = \partial g/\partial R$. Using this fact and the expression for x, $\partial g/\partial\sigma$ can be written as $\partial g/\partial R = -a\rho[a/(1 + A_G l_F h/c)][1 + \eta_R^a - \eta_R^{l_F h/c}(A_G l_F h/c)/(1 + A_G l_F h/c)]$, where η_R^a is the elasticity of a with respect to R and is given by $\eta_R^a = -[\gamma/(1 - \gamma)]\,[(1 - a)/a]$, and $\eta_R^{l_F h/c}$ is a similar elasticity given by $\eta_R^{l_F h/c} = 1/(1 - \gamma)$. Further, $-\eta_R^{l_F h/c}(A_G l_F h/c)/(1 + A_G l_F h/c) = \eta_R^c$, and so $1 + \eta_R^a - \eta_R^{l_F h/c}(A_G l_F h/c)/(1 + A_G l_F h/c) = 1 + \eta_R^a + \eta_R^c = 1 + \eta_R^m$, where $\eta_R^m \leq 0$ is the interest elasticity of money demand in (13). Therefore $\partial g/\partial R = -a\rho\,[a/(1 + A_G l_F h/c)]\,(1 + \eta_R^m)$. At $R = 0$, $\eta_R^m = 0$. As R rises the elasticity becomes increasingly negative, and $1 + \eta_R^m$ gets smaller. Because it can be shown that the other term also falls unambiguously as R rises, that is $\partial[a/(1 + A_G l_F h/c)]/\partial R < 0$, the growth rate decrease that occurs for $\eta_R^m \geq -1$ becomes increasingly smaller as R increases; and its decrease is made directly less by the rising interest elasticity of money demand and the falling magnitude of the $1 + \eta_R^m$. Now if $a \equiv 1$, then from above it is clear that $\partial g/\partial R = -a\rho$, which implies a linear inflation-growth relation.

11.A.3 Proof of Corollary 1

Define the elasticity of substitution between cash and credit as

$$\varepsilon \equiv \partial\left[\frac{ac}{(1 - a)c}\right] / \partial\left(\frac{R}{A_G/\gamma A_F^{1/\gamma}}\right)\left\{\left(\frac{R}{A_G/\gamma A_F^{1/\gamma}}\right) / \left[\frac{ac}{(1 - a)\,c}\right]\right\},$$

which is solved as $\varepsilon = -[\gamma/(1 - \gamma)]/a$. In turn the interest elasticity of money is

$\eta_R^m = \eta_R^a + \eta_R^c$, and this can be written as $\eta_R^m = (1 - a)\varepsilon + \eta_R^c$. Normalising the money demand m by dividing by the goods consumed, c, gives $m/c = a$, $\eta_R^a = (1 - a)\varepsilon$. Since $1 - a = A_F^{1/(1-\gamma)} (R\gamma/A_G)^{\gamma/(1-\gamma)}$, by (19) and (32), then $\partial(1 - a)/\partial R \geq 0$, $\partial\,|\varepsilon|/\partial R \geq 0$, and so $\partial\eta_R^a/\partial R \leq 0$; for $R > 0$, $\partial\eta_R^a/\partial R < 0$.

11.A.4 Proof of Corollary 2

By Lemma 2 and Corollary 1, $\eta_R^a = -[\gamma/(1-\gamma)][(1-a)/a] = -[\gamma/(1-\gamma)][A_F^{1/(1-\gamma)} (R\gamma/A_G)^{\gamma/(1-\gamma)}]/[1 - A_F^{1/(1-\gamma)} (R\gamma/A_G)^{\gamma/(1-\gamma)}]$, and $\partial\eta_R^a/\partial A_F \leq 0$ so that the magnitude of η_R^a rises as A_F rises.

Notes

* Gillman, Max, and Michal Kejak (2005). 'Inflation and Balanced-path Growth with Alternative Payment Mechanism', *Economic Journal*, 115(500), 247–270.

† We are especially grateful to Akos Valentinyi, Szilard Benk, Glenn Boyle, Toni Braun, Mark Harris, Bee Jeoug, Tony Nakov, and Sergey Slobodyan. We thank conference participants at LACEA Madrid, EEA Laussanne, NASMES Los Angeles, MMF Belfast, Midwest Macro Pittsburg, T2M Nice and seminar groups at the IAS Vienna, IIES University of Stockholm, University of Tokyo, Stockholm School of Economics, University College, Dublin, University of Manchester, Comenius University, CEU and CERGE-EI. The first author is grateful for research grants from the Central European University.

1 A debate has arisen on the effects of inflation below certain 'threshold' rates of inflation, with some findings of insignificant inflation effects at inflation rates below the threshold. But this rate has been found to be close to 0 for developed country samples. In developing country samples, the threshold tends to be higher, near 10%, but a strong negative effect is typically re-established at all rates of inflation in all samples when instrumental variables are used, as in Ghosh and Phillips (1998) and in Gillman et al. (2004). These studies also find the marked nonlinearity, as do Khan and Senhadji (2001) and Judson and Orphanides (1999). Bruno and Easterly (1998) provide statistical averages of high inflation episodes whereby high inflation is correlated with lower growth rates than both before and after the episode; Gylfason and Herbertsson (2001) and Chari et al. (1996) provide reviews of earlier evidence of a negative inflation effect; Barro (2001) finds a significant negative effect while emphasising human capital.

2 Dotsey and Sarte (2000) also present a deterministic AK version of the Stockman (1981) model in which there is a significant negative effect. And in a more robust reformulation of the Haslag (1998) model, using a cash-in-advance approach instead, Gillman and Kejak (2004*b*) also find this strong negative effect. For a comparison of such models, see Gillman and Kejak (2004*a*).

3 For example, neither Dotsey and Ireland (1996), Aiyagari et al. (1998), nor Gomme (1993) indicate Tobin type results, although Gomme (1993) is clearly consistent with them. The original Tobin (1965) effect is within an exogenous growth model in which an increase in the inflation rate causes an increase in the capital to labour ratio and in per capita output; see Walsh (1998) for a review. Ahmed and Rogers (2000) compare the Tobin (1965) effect across various exogenous growth models. Gillman and Kejak (2004*a*) compare Tobin-like effects across endogenous growth models.

4 Ahmed and Rogers (2000) report long-run US evidence showing that inflation has had a negative effect on the real interest rate historically, which would be

expected if inflation causes the capital to effective labour ratio to rise as in the Tobin (1965) effect. Gillman and Nakov (2003) report long-run US and UK evidence of an increase in the capital to effective labour ratio as a result of inflation.

5 As shown in a related model in Gillman (1993).

6 Another testable hypothesis here is the models ability to explain velocity; in a closely related model, Gillman and Kejak (2004*b*) are able to explain velocity trends for an array of monetary aggregates.

7 Hodrick et al. (1991) found a Lucas and Stokey (1983)-type economy unable to explain velocity movements.

8 See Goodfriend (1997), Lucas (2000) and Gavin and Kydland (1999).

9 An equilibrium with $a = 0$ does not have well-defined nominal prices.

10 See Gillman and Kejak (2004*b*).

11 One comparison in the literature to (32) can be found in an innovative paper by Canzoneri and Diba (2005); it follows more of the Tobin (1956) approach by specifying bonds that back up a non-money exchange service (not dissimilar to credit), and it uses this to solve the price indeterminacy problem.

12 We thank an anonymous referee for a suggested description here.

13 See for example Marshall (1920) or a standard microeconomic text on derived demand elasticiticies.

14 See Gillman (2000) for another example of the input price elasticity as applied to real money, in a model using the store continuum as in Gillman (1993), Dotsey and Ireland (1996) and Aiyagari et al. (1998). Such a curved isoquant between real money and credit in general equilibrium is graphed in Gillman (1995).

15 In a related paper, Gillman and Yerokhin (2005) detail this connection. One implication is that shopping time function in an endogenous growth setting should include human capital in its specification, unlike in Love and Wen (1999).

12 Contrasting models of the effect of inflation on growth*

Max Gillman and Michal Kejak

Summary

The chapter formulates a nesting model for studying the theoretical literature on inflation and endogenous growth. It analyses different classes of endogenous growth models, with different usage of physical and human capital, with different exchange technologies. First, the chapter shows that a broad array of models can all generate significant negative effects of inflation on growth. Second, it shows that these models can be differentiated primarily by the fact whether there is a Tobin-type effect of inflation and also whether the inflation–growth effect becomes weaker as the inflation rate rises, a non-linearity, or stays essentially constant over the range of inflation rates. The chapter compares these features of the models to empirical evidence as a way to summarize the efficacy of the models.

12.1 Introduction

There are three main controversies in the literature on the long-run effect of inflation on growth. First is whether models can exhibit a significant negative effect of stationary inflation on the balanced-path growth rate. Second is the nature of the inflation–growth effect across the whole range of the levels of inflation rate. Third is whether the inflation–growth models and evidence can at the same time be consistent with evidence of Tobin-type (1965) effects.

The contribution of the chapter is to first bring together for comparison several main approaches to modelling the inflation–growth effect by nesting them within a general model. This shows what factors determine the magnitude of the inflation–growth effect across these different approaches and it yields the following notable result: a robustness for the ability to generate a strong magnitude of the inflation–growth effect. In addition, the chapter explains the source of the effect by showing that the key distinguishing feature of competing approaches is whether inflation acts mainly as a tax on physical capital or on human capital. The outcome of this determines whether the inflation–growth effect accompanies an inverse or positive Tobin (1965) effect. Finally, evidence on the growth and Tobin (1965) effects is brought to bear on these competing models, as a way to lend support to favouring one approach over another.

The chapter's approach to explaining this literature is to allow for a mix of physical and human capital in the production of goods and for a mix of exchange means, money and credit, in buying the goods. The general model starts with an exchange technology extended from the standard cash-in-advance genre using microfoundations in such a way that it also encompasses a special case of the shopping time model. The extension specifies the production of credit, which is used as an alternative to money. This helps distinguish the overall inflation–growth effect in terms of its theoretical characteristics over the range of (non-hyperinflation) inflation rates, as well as some additional 'money and banking' facts.

Starting with Ireland's (1994b) 'Money and Growth: An Alternative Approach' that compares to transitional inflation–growth effects found in Sidrauski's (1967), the chapter sets out a model that puts Ireland's (1994b) approach within an aggregate consumption good setting. From this capital-only economy that includes credit, the paper next covers a case of Stockman's (1981) capital-only economy with investment as a 'cash good'; this model with uncertainty added is used in Dotsey and Sarte (2000).[1] The paper then turns to human capital-only models that compare to Gillman et al. (1999) and Stokey and Lucas (1987) (section 5.8). Then the chapter sets out models with both types of capital that compare to Gomme (1993) and to the capital accumulation process of Chari et al. (1996). Finally, an extension to Gomme (1993) is put forth that includes credit, as in Gillman and Kejak (2002, 2005b).

Most evidence finds a negative inflation–growth effect. For example, by way of large changes in the inflation rate, Gylfason and Herbertsson (2001) list some 17 studies for which all but one find a significant decrease in the growth rate from increasing the inflation rate from 5 to 50%. More by the way of a marginal increase in the inflation rate, Chari *et al.* (1996) review the empirical results from increasing the inflation rate from 10 to 20%; they report a significant fall in the growth rate within a range of 0.2–0.7%; for example, the growth rate falls from an initial level of 3% at a 10% inflation rate to between 2.8 and 2.3% at a 20% inflation rate. Recent findings, for example, of Barro (2001) compound the evidence of a strongly significant negative effect of inflation on growth.

In addition, evidence suggests that the negative effect is marginally stronger at low inflation rates and marginally weaker as the inflation rate rises. This negative and highly non-linear effect is strongly supported in Judson and Orphanides (1999), Ghosh and Phillips (1998), Khan and Senhadji (2001) and Gillman et al. (2004). Some evidence is qualified by findings of a 'threshold' rate of inflation, above which the effect is strongly significant and negative, but below which the effect is insignificant and positive. For industrialized country samples, this threshold level has been tested for and found to be very low, at a 1% inflation rate (Khan and Senhadji,

2001), although others have assumed (without such testing) higher thresholds of 2.5% (Ghosh and Phillips, 1998) or 10% (Judson and Orphanides, 1999). The 'threshold' for developing country samples has been found through testing to be at 11% (Khan and Senhadji, 2001), below which again the inflation–growth effect is insignificant and positive. However, when using instrumental variables in order to adjust for possible inflation–growth endogeneity bias, the negative non-linear inflation–growth effect has been reinstated at all positive inflation rate levels for both developed and developing country samples (Ghosh and Phillips, 1998; Gillman et al., 2004). This suggests no inconsistency in a modelling approach that focuses only on a negative effect of inflation on growth.[2]

Tobin (1965) evidence includes an inflation-induced decrease in the real interest rate, an increase in the average investment level and decline in the consumption level, normalized by output, and a rise in the aggregate capital-to-effective-labour ratio. Ahmed and Rogers (2000) find a variety of Tobin (1965) long-run evidence for the US, including a decrease in the real interest rate because of permanent inflation increases. Similarly, Rapach (2003) finds that permanent inflation increases lower the long-run real interest rate in 14 out of 14 countries studied. There is also the related evidence in Gillman and Nakov (2004) of inflation Granger-causing increases in the capital-to-effective-labour ratios in the US and UK postwar data, which is consistent with a Tobin (1965) effect of increased capital intensity.

The literature on how to model such evidence extends the traditional Tobin (1965) modification of the Solow exogenous growth model, whereby money is introduced as an alternative to capital. Similar to the original IS-LM model, in the Tobin (1965) model, an increase in the money-supply growth rate, or in the inflation rate, causes investment, capital and output to rise. But the growth rate is exogenous and so is unaffected by the inflation rate. The extensions from the Tobin (1965) framework are classes of the Cass-Koopman neoclassical model that endogenizes the savings rate of the exogenous Solow growth model through utility maximization; this gives the Euler equation results whereby the growth rate equals the marginal product of capital, net of time preference, and (for CES [constant elasticity of substitution] utility) normalized by a utility parameter. Furthermore, the extensions are of the endogenous growth genre as extended to a monetary setting, whereby the rate of return on real money, being based on the inflation rate, can affect the marginal product of capital and the growth rate. In the endogenous growth models, inflation typically causes the growth rate to fall, while the output as a balanced-growth-path ratio relative to different variables can rise or fall, resulting in either Tobin (1965) effects or inverse Tobin (1965) effects. The idea of an inverse Tobin (1965) effect follows from Stockman (1981), whereby the inflation rate increase causes a capital stock decrease.

Therefore, in the endogenous growth models, the inflation rate affects the growth rate because it affects the marginal product of capital, either that of physical capital as in *Ak* models, or that of human capital as in *Ah* models, or that of both physical and human capital in combined capital models. Some models have produced insignificant long-run inflation–growth effects, for example, the *Ak* models of Ireland (1994b) and Dotsey and Sarte (2000) and the physical and human capital model of Chari et al. (1996), while at least equally diverse models have produced significant and negative inflation–growth effects, including the *Ak* models of Haslag (1998) and Gillman and Kejak (2004), the *Ah* model of Gillman et al. (1999), Gylfason and Herbertsson's (2001) model with money in the goods production function, Gomme's (1993) physical and human capital model and Gillman and Kejak's (2002, 2005b) extension of Gomme (1993). Using a nesting as based on *Ak*, *Ah* or a combination of physical and human capital can illustrate the results from most of the models, and hence this is the approach taken here.

Note that these are balanced-path, stationary-state, results. And it is actually the rate of money-supply growth in these models that is exogenous, changes in which 'cause' changes in the stationary inflation rate and simultaneously cause changes in the output growth rate. However, because, for example, long-run evidence finds that money Granger causes inflation (Crowder, 1998), and because some evidence also finds that inflation Granger causes the output growth rate (Gillman and Nakov, 2004; Gillman and Wallace, 2003; Cziraky and Gillman, 2006), this literature on inflation and growth tends to discuss how inflation affects the output growth rate. This convention is also used here. Furthermore, with logutility as we assume throughout the chapter, the nominal interest rate depends on only the money-supply growth rate and the rate of time preference, so that we can calibrate how increases in the nominal interest rate affect the economy in a way equivalent to a money-supply acceleration.

The calibration strategy is to examine the change in the nominal interest rate on the balanced-path growth rate, the real interest rate and the capital-to-labour ratio in the goods sector across the different models. For all models, the growth rate and the real interest rate are fixed at the same values at the optimum, of 3% for the growth rate and 6% for the real interest rate (nine for the gross real interest rate). Given the greater number of degrees of freedom in the more complicated models relative to the simpler models, calibrating them so that they have a common point at the optimum allows for a normalized comparison of how inflation affects the economies as it rises up from its optimal level.

12.2 The general monetary endogenous growth economy

The nesting model has three sectors that each uses both physical capital-indexed and human capital-indexed labour: goods production, human capital investment and credit production. The notation, parameter assumptions and production specifications are presented in the Table 12.1.

Table 12.1 Notation and assumptions

Variables		*Parameters*
Real	l_{Ht}: HC share, HC	$\beta \in [0,1]$
y_t: Goods output	l_{Ft}: Credit share, HC	$\varepsilon \in [0,1]$
c_t: Consumption goods	r_t: Interest rate	$\gamma_1, \gamma_2 \in [0,1]$
x_t: Leisure time	w_t: Effective wage rate	$A_G > 0$
k_t: Physical capital (PC)	Nominal	$A_H > 0$
h_t: Human capital (HC)	M_t: Money stock	$A_F > 0$
i_t: PC investment	P_t: Goods price	$\delta_K \geq 0$
i_{Ht}: HC investment	V_t: Money transfer	$\delta_H \geq 0$
s_{Gt}: Goods share, PC	Definitions	$\alpha > 0$
s_{Ht}: HC share, PC	$m_t \equiv M_t / P_t$	$\sigma \geq -\rho$
s_{Ft}: Credit share, PC	$a_t \equiv m_t / c_t$	$\rho \in (0,1)$
l_{Gt}: Goods share, HC	$d_t \equiv (1 - a_t)\, c_t$	$a_2 \in [0,1]$
	Production functions	
Goods	Human capital investment	Credit
$y_t = A_G (s_{Gt} k_t)^{\beta} (l_{Gt} h_t)^{1-\beta}$	$i_{Ht} = A_H (s_{Ht} k_t)^{\varepsilon} (l_{Ht} h_t)^{1-\varepsilon}$	$d_t / c_t = A_F (s_{Ft} k_t / c_t)^{\gamma 1} (l_{Ft} h_t / c_t)^{\gamma 2}$

Current period utility is of the constant elasticity of substitution form, whereby

$$u(c_t, x_t) = \ln c_t + \alpha \ln x_t \tag{1}$$

The consumer allocates time to labour supplied to the goods producer, to self-production of human capital and to self-production of credit. With an endowment of one unit of time, the time constraint is similar to an adding-up-of-shares constraint:

$$1 = x_t + l_{Ft} + l_{Gt} + l_{Ht} \tag{2}$$

Similarly, a share of the capital stock is used potentially in each of the three production functions, and the shares must add to one:

$$1 = s_{Gt} + s_{Ht} + s_{Ft} \tag{3}$$

The physical capital investment equation is standard in its assumption of no costs of adding to the capital stock except the actual capital:

$$k_{t+1} = k_t(1 - \delta_K) + i_t \tag{4}$$

The human capital investment technology function follows Becker (1975). The equation for motion of the accumulation is $h_t + 1 = h_t(1 - \delta_H) + i_{Ht}$. The investment in human capital i_{Ht} requires effective labour and capital whereby

$$h_{t+1} = h_t(1 - \delta_H) + A_H(s_{Ht}k_t)^{\varepsilon}(l_{Ht}h_t)^{1-\varepsilon} \tag{5}$$

The consumer receives income from the human capital augmented labour for goods production and from the rental of capital to the goods producer; there is also the lump-sum transfer of money V_t from the government that the consumer receives. Given the consumer's endowment of initial money stock M_0, and dividing the income between goods purchases and investment, the equation of motion for the consumer's nominal income, or the income constraint, can be put in terms of the change in the nominal money stock:

$$M_{t+1} - M_t = P_t w_t l_{Gt} h_t + P_t r_t s_{Gt} k_t - P_t c_t - P_t k_{t+1} + P_t k_t (1 - \delta_K) + V_t \tag{6}$$

The consumer can buy the consumption good at a price of P_t either using the money (carried over from the end of the last period) or using the credit. The fraction of goods bought with money can vary between zero and one, with $a_t \in [0,1]$, and with $1 - a_t$ being the residual fraction of goods that is bought with credit. A fixed fraction $a_2 \in [0,1]$ of physical capital investment is also bought with money. The rest of the investment is a 'costless' credit good requiring neither money nor credit as is standard in this literature (think of retained earnings). This makes the so-called Clower (1967) constraint

$$M_t = a_t P_t c_t + a_2 P_t i_t, \tag{7}$$

which is that of Stockman (1981) if $a_t = a_2 = 1$.

The consumer's choice of a_t is determined by how much labour the agent decides to spend supplying the alternative to money, this being the credit. Here, the total real credit d_t equals the residual real amount of consumption goods not bought with money, or $d_t \equiv c_t(1 - a_t)$, and is given as

$$d_t = c_t A_F \left(\frac{s_{Ft}k_t}{c_t}\right)^{\gamma_1} \left(\frac{l_{Ft}h_t}{c_t}\right)^{\gamma_2} \tag{8}$$

This exhibits constant returns to scale in its three factors, c_t, $s_{Ft}k_t/c_t$ and $l_{Ft}h_t/c_t$, resulting in an upward sloping marginal cost of credit supply per unit of consumption as long as $\gamma_1 + \gamma_2 < 1$. With $\gamma_1 + \gamma_2 < 1$ the consumption velocity of money, the inverse of a_t, is stationary along the balanced growth path as in the evidence. The Cobb-Douglas case of $\gamma_1 + \gamma_2 = 1$ is problematic because it creates an equilibrium that is not well defined because then both money and credit have a constant marginal cost, and also velocity would not be stationary. Dividing the above equation by c_t and using the definition $d_t \equiv c_t(1 - a_t)$, the share of credit in purchases $(1 - a_t)$ can be written as

$$(1 - a_t) = A_F \left(\frac{s_{Ft}k_t}{c_t}\right)^{\gamma_1} \left(\frac{l_{Ft}h_t}{c_t}\right)^{\gamma_2} \tag{9}$$

In this specification, the effective labour and capital inputs are proportional to total consumption, so that the share of credit use remains constant when consumption is growing only if the effective labour and capital inputs grow at the same rate.

A combined exchange constraint for money and credit, which are perfect substitutes, results by solving for a_t from (9) and substituting this into (7):

$$M_t = P_t\left[c_t - A_F\left(\frac{s_{Ft}k_t}{c_t}\right)^{\gamma_1}\left(\frac{l_{Ft}h_t}{c_t}\right)^{\gamma_2} c_t + a_2 i_t\right] \tag{10}$$

This results in the standard (Lucas, 1980) 'cash-only' Clower (1967) constraint when $a_2 = 0$ and $A_F = 0$, so that credit is prohibitively costly to produce.

The goods producer maximizes profit subject to the CRS (constant returns to scale) production technology, with the following first-order conditions, and zero profit in equilibrium:

$$w_t = (1-\beta)A_G(s_{Gt}k_t)^{\beta}(l_{Gt}h_t)^{-\beta}; \tag{11}$$

$$r_t = \beta A_G(s_{Gt}k_t)^{\beta-1}(l_{Gt}h_t)^{1-\beta} \tag{12}$$

The government supplies nominal money through the lump-sum transfer V_t at a steady rate σ, whereby

$$M_{t+1} = M_t + V_t \equiv M_t(1+\sigma) \tag{13}$$

This money supply process is used without alteration in all models of the paper.

With social resources being that output is divided between consumption and investment, the social resource constraint can be found to be

$$y_t = c_t + i_t \tag{14}$$

This resource constraint holds for all of the calibrated models below.

The consumer maximizes the preference-discounted stream of utility in (1) subject to the constraints (5), (6) and (10), with respect to c_t, x_t, M_{t+1}, k_{t+1}, h_{t+1}, s_{Gt}, l_{Gt}, s_{Ft} and l_{Ft}. The first-order conditions are presented in Appendix. The stationary variables on the balanced growth path are the shares l_G, l_H, l_F x, s_G, s_H and s_F, while the variables that grow at the rate g are c_t, $m_t = M_t/P_t$, k_t, h_t, i_t, i_{Ht}. Equilibrium can be characterized by the marginal rate of substitution between goods and leisure, the balanced-path growth rate, the equivalence between the returns on physical and human capital, and the marginal condition between credit and money use, made known by Baumol (1952).

The goods-leisure marginal rate of substitution is

$$\frac{ax}{c_t} = \frac{1 + aR + w\left(\frac{l_F h}{c}\right) + r\left(\frac{s_F k}{c}\right)}{wh_t} = \frac{1 + aR + (1 - a)\,(\gamma_1 + \gamma_2)\,R}{wh_t} \tag{15}$$

This rate equals the ratio of the shadow price of goods to that of leisure. The goods shadow cost is one plus the shadow cost of exchange, $aR + w(l_F h/c) + r(s_F k/c)$ with $w(l_F h/c) + r(s_F k/c)$ being a real resource cost of inflation avoidance through credit activity. Or the shadow cost can be written equivalently as the weighted average of cash and credit $aR + (1 - a)(\gamma_1 + \gamma_2)R$.

The balanced-path growth rate can be expressed by

$$1 + g = \frac{1 + \frac{r}{1 + a_2 R} - \delta_K}{1 + \rho} = \frac{1 + (1 - \varepsilon)\, A_H \left(\frac{l_H h}{s_H k}\right)^{-\varepsilon} (1 - x) - \delta_H}{1 + \rho} \tag{16}$$

The growth rate is decreased because of the a_2 factor if $R > 0$, where the need to use money to buy investment goods acts as a tax, as in Stockman (1981). And here, given that $\delta_K = \delta_H$, the return on physical capital $r/(1 + a_2 R)$ is equal to the return on human capital $(1 - \varepsilon)A_H(l_H h/s_H k)^{-\varepsilon}(1 - x)$. An increase in leisure works directly to bring down the human capital return.

The linkage between R, σ and π along the BGP (balanced growth path) in all of the models is first through the Fisher equation,

$$1 + R \equiv (1 + \pi)\left(1 + \frac{r}{(1 + a_2 R)} - \delta_K\right), \tag{17}$$

that can be derived by introducing government bonds.[3] Second, using the Fisher equation plus Clower (1967) constraint (7) and the growth rate (16), the nominal interest rate and money growth rate are related by

$$1 + R = (1 + \sigma)(1 + \rho) \tag{18}$$

Changes in the nominal interest rate are directly caused by changes in the money-supply growth rate. And in response to an increase in σ, and in R, it is important to realize that the gross real interest rate r falls, even as π rises. The change in r is emphasized throughout the paper as part of the Tobin (1965) effect and is simultaneous with an increasing capital-to-effective-labour ratio across sectors as a result of a higher σ.

The factor input ratios in the goods and human capital sectors are given by

$$\frac{r}{w} = \left(\frac{\beta}{1 - \beta}\right)\left(\frac{l_G h_t}{s_G k_t}\right) = \left(\frac{\varepsilon}{1 - \varepsilon}\right)\left(\frac{l_H h_t}{s_H k_t}\right) \tag{19}$$

The credit sector input equilibrium is determined by the Baumol-type (1952) conditions:

$$R = \frac{w}{\gamma_2 A_F \left(\frac{l_F h_t}{c_t}\right)^{\gamma_2 - 1} \left(\frac{s_F k_t}{c_t}\right)^{\gamma_1}}; \tag{20}$$

$$R = \frac{r}{\gamma_1 A_F \left(\frac{l_F h_t}{c_t}\right)^{\gamma_2} \left(\frac{s_F k_t}{c_t}\right)^{\gamma_1 - 1}} \tag{21}$$

Each of the above two exchange conditions set the marginal cost of money, R, equal to the marginal factor cost divided by the marginal factor product in producing credit. With this general equilibrium setting for the Baumol (1952) condition, combined with the existence of an explicit credit sector, these conditions are nothing more than a standard microeconomic sectoral condition whereby the marginal cost of output equals the factor price divided by its marginal product. This implies, in equalizing the marginal costs of different exchange means as in the original Baumol (1952) model, that the marginal cost of credit is the nominal interest rate; it is verified with a decentralized formalization for an explicit credit sector, and an explicit price of the credit service, that the price of credit is the nominal interest rate in Gillman and Kejak (2004) and Gillman (2000).

The Baumol (1952) conditions determine the equilibrium demand for money and its interest elasticity. For example, when only money is used, such as in the standard Lucas (1980) cash-in-advance model, then $m = c$, and the interest elasticity of money demand is simply the interest elasticity of consumption. Gillman (1993) shows in a related economy that this type of model gives a very low magnitude of the interest elasticity of money, while when credit is produced to avoid the inflation, the interest elasticity rises in magnitude by several-fold. Gillman and Kejak (2002, 2005b) show that the higher is the interest elasticity in magnitude the lower is the inflation–growth effect in magnitude, along with the Tobin-type (1965) effects. And a substantially rising interest elasticity as inflation increases produces a highly non-linear inflation–growth profile as is similar to evidence.

12.3 Physical capital only models

12.3.1 Ireland (1994b)

Ireland (1994b) uses only physical capital in an aggregate production function with a constant marginal product of capital: the Ak model. In addition, the consumer avoids inflation through a sector that provides credit for buying goods instead of using money. The credit is produced using only goods and is used across a continuum of stores, selling a continuum of goods, with a different monotonically changing cost of credit at each store. As the inflation rate goes up, credit is used at more stores, with each marginally added store having a somewhat higher cost of producing the credit. This has the effect in aggregate of establishing a rising marginal cost of credit as more credit is used to avoid inflation.

Such a continuum of stores, with a continuum of goods and each with a different cost of credit that can be used to buy the goods, is also found in Gillman (1993), Gillman (2000), Aiyagari et al. (1998) and Erosa and Ventura (2002). The credit supply in these models is therefore very similar except that they use time, rather than goods or capital as in Ireland (1994b), to provide the credit. To illustrate Ireland's (1994b) model in a way compatible with the standard neoclassical growth and business-cycle paradigm, consider using a single aggregate consumption good as in the section 12.2 model. Here, the production function for credit explicitly has an increasing marginal cost, rather than this resulting in aggregate from a continuum of stores. And because goods are costlessly convertible into capital in the Ireland (1994b) economy, here it can be assumed that capital is used (rather than goods) in the production of the credit.

Assume the following special case of the section 12.2 economy. Let there be a zero, instead of one, time endowment. Set the utility value of leisure to zero; $\alpha = 0$. Assume there is no human capital investment, including that $h_0 = 0$ and $A_H = 0$. Also with only physical capital being used, $\beta = 1$, goods output is CRS, and this gives the Ak function. Also, here the money is used only for consumption goods, so that $a_2 = 0$. For the credit production, let $\gamma_2 = 0$ so that there is only capital used with diminishing returns and an increasing marginal cost (Table 12.2).

The credit production function then is given by $(1 - a_t)c_t = A_F(s_{Ft}k_t/c_t)^{\gamma_1}c_t$, and the shares of capital add to one, $s_{Gt} + s_{Ft} = 1$. The Clower (1967) constraint (7) with $a_2 = 0$ is $M_t = a_t\ P_tc_t$. The Clower (1967) constraint can be combined with the credit production function to make the combined exchange constraint (10) now as given by $M_t = P_tc_t - P_tA_F(s_{Ft}k_t)^{\gamma_1}c_t^{1-\gamma_1}$. In the above equation, when $s_{Ft}k_t = 0$ so that no credit is produced, the standard 'cash-only' Clower (1967) constraint results in which $a_t = 1$. Note also that the amount of resources that the consumer willingly uses in credit production

Table 12.2 Assumptions for special case: Ireland (1994b) economy

Parameters	*Production functions*
$\alpha = h_0 = A_H = \gamma_2 = a_2 = 0$; $\beta = 1$	$y_t = A_G s_{Gt} k_t$; $d_t = A_F\left(\frac{s_{Ft}k_t}{c_t}\right)^{\gamma_1} c_t$

to avoid inflation is the capital $s_{Ft}k_t$. The rental value of this capital is the amount that corresponds precisely to Lucas (2000) measure of the welfare cost of inflation. However, where that cost was the value of the shopping time spent, here the welfare cost is the rental value of the capital used in credit production. Solving for credit capital $s_{Ft}k_t$ from the last equation gives $s_{Ft}k_{Ft} = [(1 - (m_t/c_t))/A_F]^{1/\gamma_1}c_t$. Analogous to the shopping time model, the credit capital falls with increases in m_t and with decreases in c_t.

With $a = h_0 = A_H = \gamma_2 = a_2 = 0$ and $\beta = 1$, the consumer maximizes the preference-discounted stream of utility in (1) subject to the constraints (6) and (10), with respect to c_t, M_{t+1}, k_{t+1} and s_{Gt}. The real interest rate from the firm problem is $r = A_G$. The balanced-growth rate is constant, as given by $1 + g = (1 + A_G - \delta_K)/(1 + \rho)$.

The shadow price of goods is $1 + R - R(1 - \gamma_1)A_F(s_Fk_t/^{\gamma_1}$, showing that credit use decreases the shadow exchange cost of goods below R as it would be with only money. The single Baumol (1952) condition, comparable to (21), is $R = A_G/[\gamma_1 A_F\ (s_{Ft}k_t/c_t)^{\gamma - 1}]$. This condition implies that capital in credit production, relative to consumption, rises as the nominal interest rate rises. This gives the diversion of capital from goods production when the inflation rate rises, one of Ireland's (1994) main results.[4]

The 'great ratios' can be found to equal as $c_t/y_t = (\rho/A_G)(1 + A_G - \delta_K)/[(1 + \rho) + [A_G - \rho(1 - \delta_K)](R\gamma_1\ A_F/A_G)^{1/(1-\gamma_1)}]$, $i_t/y_t = 1 - c_t/y_t$, $c_t/k_t = [\rho/(1 + \rho)](1 + A_G - \delta_K)/[1 + A_G(R\gamma_1 A_F/A_G)^{1/(1-\gamma_1)}]$ and $y_t/k_t = c_t/k_t + (A_G - \rho\ (1 - \delta_K))/(1 + \rho)$. When the nominal interest rate R rises, c_t/y_t, c_t/k_t and y_t/k_t fall, while i_t/y_t rises, similar to Tobin (1965). However, the real interest rate r is constant while the Gillman and Nakov (2003) evidence indicates that r falls with increases in inflation in the long run.

The solution for the share of money usage is $a = 1 - [(R\gamma_1/A_G)^{\gamma_1/(1-\gamma_1)} A^{1/(1-\gamma_1)}_F]$. Because both a and c_t/k_t fall with an increase in R, it can be seen that the money-to-capital ratio also falls with an increase in the nominal interest rate, in that $m_t/k_t = ac_t/k_t$. This indicates substitution from real money to capital when inflation rises, again as in Tobin (1965).

Ireland (1994b) demonstrates how the increase in capital coming from the diversion of capital into banking decreases the growth rate along the transition, but not in the stationary state at the limiting end of the transition. In the model above also there is no long-run growth effect of inflation, contrary to evidence. However, in this model and in Ireland's (1994b) are some of the empirically supported Tobin (1965) effects.

12.3.2 Stockman / Dotsey and Sarte

A special case of the Stockman (1981) economy, also used in Dotsey and Sarte (2000), results by assuming only a goods sector, with no human capital and no credit production, and by assuming a constant marginal product of capital, whereby $y = A_Gk_G$. This is the same Ak production function as in the last section except that now $s_G = 1$. With only money used in exchange, $a_t = 1$.

Also as in Stockman (1981), let investment be purchased with money as well as goods, so that $a_t = a_2 = 1$. By using the Ak function, this puts the Stockman model in an endogenous growth setting.

The assumptions are summarized in Table 12.3.

With $a = h_0 = A_H = A_F = 0$ and $a_t = a_2 = s_G = \beta = 1$, the consumer maximizes the preference-discounted stream of utility in (1) subject to the constraints (6) and (10), with respect to c_t, M_{t+1} and k_{t+1}. The balanced-path solution has a growth rate of $1 + g = [1 + (A_G/(1 + R)) - \delta_K]/(1 + \rho)$, so that an increase in the nominal interest rate lowers the growth rate. The after-inflation-tax marginal product of capital $A_G/(1 + R)$ falls because investment must be purchased with money. The shadow price of goods is $1 + R$, and the rest of the solution is $c_t/y_t = 1 - ((g + \delta_K)/A_G)$, $i_t/y_t = (g + \delta_k)/A_G$ and $m_t/k_t = A_G$.

An increase in the nominal interest rate causes the growth rate to fall and c/y to rise and i/y to fall, which as Stockman (1981) noted is similar to an 'inverse' Tobin (1965) effect; r is constant. Furthermore, with m/k constant, there is no substitution between money and capital as in Ireland's (1994b) and Tobin's (1965) model. In fact, there is no possibility to avoid the inflation tax as there is only one good produced, one means of exchange and one input to utility.

However, the calibration along the balanced-growth path, given in Table 12.3 and graphed in Figure 12.1, shows that a significant negative growth effect can result robustly in this model. Note that Figure 12.1, as well as the subsequent Figure 12.2, graphs the nominal interest rate against the growth rate, rather than the inflation rate, because the analytic solution for R vs. g is simple while that solution for π and g is quite complex.

The inflation–growth effect, of –0.67% in Table 12.3, falls within the Chari et al. (1996) range. But over the whole range of inflation rates, there is only a marginal non-linearity resulting in a counter-empirical negative growth rate as inflation gets above 50%.

Table 12.3 Assumptions for special case: Stockman (1981) economy

Assumptions		*Production functions*
$a = h_0 = A_H = A_F = 0$; $a_t = a_2 = s_G = \beta = 1$		$y = A_G k_G$
	Calibration	
Parameters		Variables
$\rho = \delta_k = 0.03$, $A_G = 0.0909$		$R = 0$, $g = 0.03$, $r = 0.0909$
Δ Nominal interest rate	Δ Growth rate	Δ Real interest rate
0.00→0.10	–0.0080	0
0.10→0.20	–0.0067	0

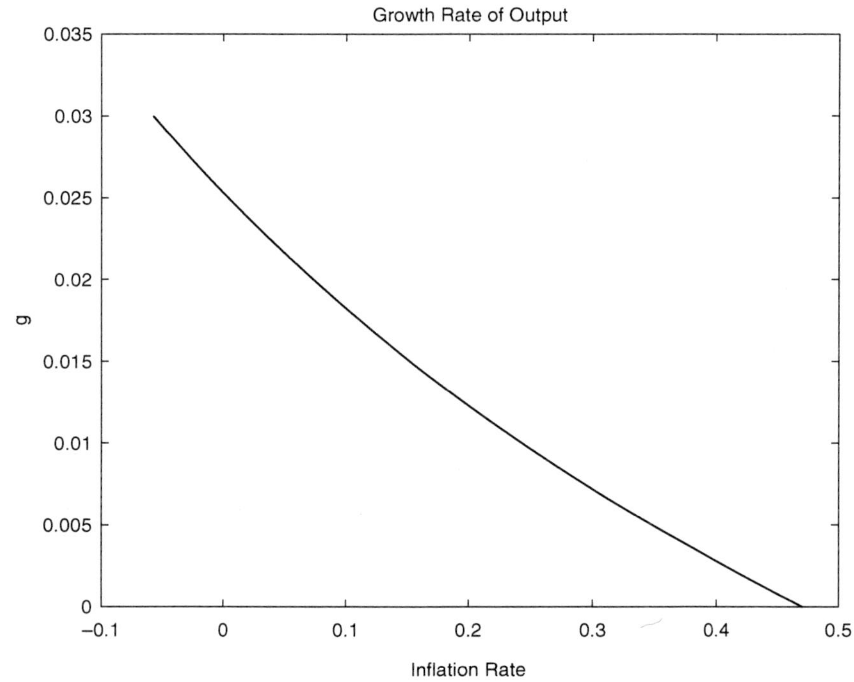

Figure 12.1 Model 12.3.2 inflation and growth calibration.

12.4 Human capital only models

Two models using only human capital are reviewed here. Both use a linear production of goods using only human capital-indexed labour. The difference is in the nature of the human capital investment function. This function can be 'costless' in the sense that a certain amount of output can be costlessly transformed into human capital; this is the analogue to the standard physical capital investment accumulation (4). Or the human capital investment can be 'costly', as in Becker (1975) and Lucas (1988b), whereby labour time and possibly physical capital inputs with diminishing returns to each input are transformed into human capital; King and Rebelo (1990) describe this as the analogue of costly physical capital investment, such as the 'adjustment cost' in Lucas (1967).

Table 12.4 summarizes the specification of costly human capital model 4.1. And here, define the gross marginal product of capital as $\tilde{r} \equiv A_H(1 - x)$. With $a = k_0 = A_F = a_2 = \beta = \varepsilon = 0$, the consumer maximizes the preference-discounted stream of utility in (1) subject to (5), (6) and (10), with respect to c_t, x_t, M_{t+1}, h_{t+1}, and l_{Gt}. The real wage rate from the firm problem is given by $w = A_G$, while the growth rate is expressed as $1 + g = (1 + A_H(1 - x) - \delta_H)/(1 + \rho)$. The negative effect of inflation comes through its induced decrease in

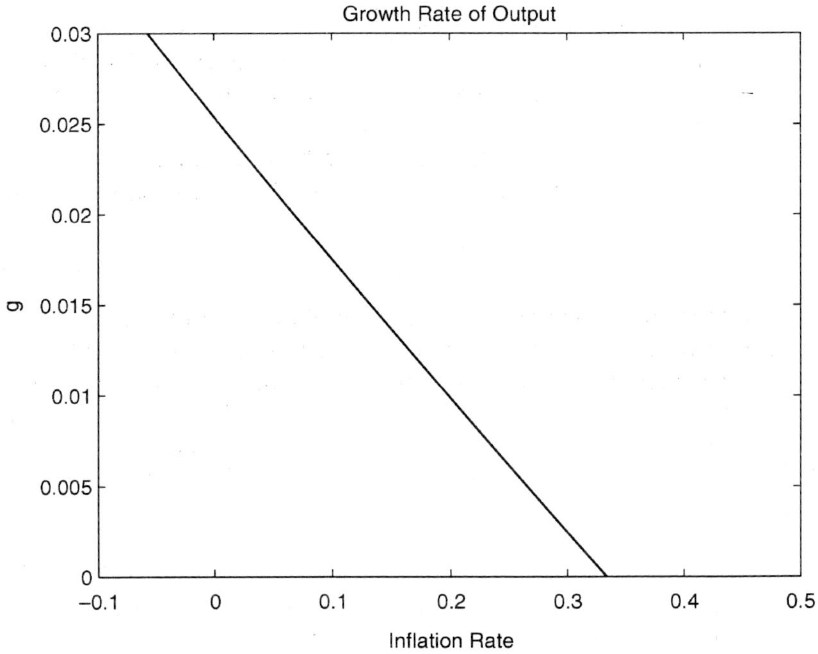

Figure 12.2 Model 12.4.1 inflation and growth calibration.

Table 12.4 Assumptions for special case: 4.1 economy

Parameters		*Production functions*
$a = k_0 = A_F = a_2 = \beta = \varepsilon = 0$; $a_t = 1$		$y_t = A_G l_{Gt} h_t$; $i_{Ht} = A_H (1 - x_t - l_{Gt}) h_t$
	I. Baseline calibration	
Parameters $\rho = \delta_H = 0.03$, $a = 3$, $A_G = 0.1836$, $A_H = 0.1836$		Variables $R = 0$, $g = 0.03$, $\tilde{r} = 0.0909$
	II. Calibration	
$a = 2$, $A_G = 0.1836$, $A_H = 0.1527$		$R = 0$, $g = 0.03$, $\tilde{r} = 0.0909$
	I	II
Δ Nominal interest rate	Δ Growth rate	Δ Growth rate
0.00→0.10	−0.0082	−0.0056
0.10→0.20	−0.0081	−0.0056

leisure time and the resulting change in the marginal product of human capital. The marginal rate of substitution between goods and leisure is $x/(ac_t) = (1 + R)/(A_G h_t$, and the closed-form solution of the economy is $c_t/h_t = \rho A_G(1 + A_H - \delta_H)/[A_H(1 + \rho[1 + a(1 + R)])]$, $x = \rho a(1 + R)(1 + A_H - \delta_H)/[A_H(1 + \rho[1 + a(1 + R)])]$ and $1 + g = (1 + A_H - \delta_H)/[1 + \rho[1 + a(1 + R)]]$.

Table 12.4 summarizes a significant negative inflation–growth effect, of 0.81%. Instead of the baseline value of $a = 3$ and $A_H = 0.1836$, this growth effect becomes smaller in magnitude, 0.56% when a is set equal to 2, and A_H recalibrated to 0.1527. This shows sensitivity but still robustness in generating a large magnitude. But as Figure 12.2 shows that the inflation–growth profile is almost linear, and the growth rate becomes negative at a relatively low inflation rate, while in the long-run evidence, the growth rate stays positive for all inflation rates.

Note how this compares to a similar but non-nested model 12.4.2. Continue to assume that $\beta = \varepsilon = 0$ and that $A_F = 0$, so that only human capital is used in production and there is no credit available. But now assume also that $A_H = 0$, so that human capital investment does not take place through a production process. Instead, in a slight deviation from the section 12.2 model, assume that goods output can be costlessly turned into human capital, as compared to assuming that goods output can be turned into physical capital in the section 2 model. With $\tilde{\imath}_{Ht}$ denoting these goods that become human capital, the social resource constraint becomes $y_t = c_t + \tilde{\imath}_{Ht}$. Table 12.5 summarizes the specification.

The human capital accumulation equation is $h_{t+1} = h_t\,(1 - \delta_H) + \tilde{\imath}_{Ht}$. This accumulation equation is the approach taken in Chari et al. (1996), although there, physical capital also is used. With no time in human capital accumulation, the time constraint simplifies even further from that of the last subsection to $1 = x_t + l_{Gt}$.

With $A_F = A_H = a_2 = \beta = 0$, the consumer maximizes the preference-discounted stream of utility in (1) subject to (5), (6) and (10), with respect to c_t, x_t, M_{t+1}, h_{t+1} and $\tilde{\imath}_{Ht}$. The first-order conditions imply that the solution for the growth rate in terms of leisure is $1 + g = (1 + A_G(1 - x) - \delta_H)/(1 + \rho)$, where $x = a\rho(1 + R)(1 + A_G - \delta_H)/(A_G(1 + \rho[1 + a(1 + R)]))$ and $c_t/h_t = \rho[1 + A_G - \delta_H)/(1 + \rho[1 + a](1 + R)])$. This makes the growth rate equal

Table 12.5 Assumptions for special case 4.2 economy

Assumptions	*Production functions*
$A_F = A_H = a_2 = \beta = 0$; $a_t = 1$	$y_t = A_G l_G h_t$
Calibration	
Parameters: $\rho = \delta_H = 0.03$, $A_G = 0.1836$	Variables: $R = 0$, g $= 0.03$, $r = 0.0909$

$1 + g = (1 + A_G - \delta_H)/(1 + \rho[1 + a(1 + R)])$. The growth rate is identical to the previous model of section 12.4.1 if $A_G = A_H$, with the same calibration.

The singularity of the two models can also be viewed as implying that both models have two sectors, although the latter model has a simple technology for the human capital sector that is usually viewed as being a one-sector model only in goods production. And it means that the non-nested model here can be made equivalent to the nested model of section 12.4.1.

12.5 Models with physical and human capital

In a model with both physical and human capital, a standard Clower (1967) constraint, and with human capital as the source of endogenous growth, the inflation effect on growth depends on the nature of the human capital investment function. The differences are shown by examining a model with a simple accumulation equation (Chari et al., 1996) vs. one with a Becker (1975)-King and Rebelo (1990) human capital investment function.

12.5.1 Simple human capital accumulation

The simple human capital accumulation equation, in which say $\tilde{i}_{ht} = h_{t+1} - h_t(1 - \delta_H)$, sidesteps the traditional literature on human capital in which time is involved in human capital accumulation (Schultz, 1964; Becker, 1975). An approach sympathetic with this simple accumulation equation, but still fully nested within the Becker (1975) human capital investment function, is to assume that the production function for the human capital investment uses only capital and no labour. Here, instead of assuming that $\tilde{i}_{ht}$ is transformed goods output, assume instead that the Becker (1975) human capital function has the form of (5) but assumes that $\varepsilon = 0$ and that A_H equals 1, so that only physical capital is used to produce the human capital. Because goods output can be costlessly transformed into physical capital in these models, the use of physical capital instead of goods output allows for a nesting of this modified simple accumulation equation.[5] Table 12.6 provides the specification details.

Comparing the two definitions, of $\tilde{i}_{Ht}$ from the last section 12.4 and i_{Ht} in this section, it could be stated that $\tilde{i}_{Ht} = s_{Ht}k_t$, just as physical capital instead of goods are used in the section 12.3.1 model that compares to Ireland (1994). The human capital accumulation process now becomes $h_{t+1} = h_t(1 - \delta_H) + s_{Ht}k_t$ and the accounting of the shares of human and physical capital are now $1 = s_{Gt} + s_{Ht}$ and $1 = x_t + l_{Gt}$. The resource constraint is the same as in section 12.2, in (4) and (14).

With $A_F = a_2 = 0$ and $a_t = A_H = \varepsilon = 1$, the consumer maximizes the preference-discounted stream of utility in (1) subject to (5), (6) and (10), with respect to c_t, x_t, M_{t+1}, k_{t+1}, h_{t+1} and s_{Gt}. The growth rate is given by

$$1+g=\frac{1+r-\delta_K}{1+\rho}=\frac{1+\dfrac{w}{r}(1-x)-\delta_H}{1+\rho}, \tag{22}$$

whereby balanced growth implies an equivalence of the marginal products of physical capital and human capital.

Solving the economy numerically, the baseline calibration of the change in the growth rate is given in Table 12.6. The growth rate decreases are significant and within the range of empirical estimates. A problem, however, is that with human capital so productive relative to goods production, in that $A_H = 1$ and $A_G = 0.0877$, most of the capital is directed to human capital. The capital-to-effective-labour ratio at the optimum of $R = 0$ is only $(s_G k / l_G H) = 0.0184$. This is not a very plausible ratio and represents an indication of the problem with the general specification. However, qualitatively, the calibration shows the positive Tobin (1965) effect of a rising capital-to-effective-labour ratio as the nominal interest rate rises, while the growth rate falls.

Figure 12.3 graphs the inflation–growth profile over a range of inflation rates. The line representing the model is the dot-dash one. It shows a marginal degree of non-linearity that tends to be much less than found empirically. Although there is no exact empirical measure for the degree of non-linearity, evidence indicates that the growth rate never becomes negative, while in the model here, it does become negative.

The model with the alternate assumption of using goods in the simple human capital accumulation equation was also calibrated, but is not shown here as it is not nested. The results for the growth rate are quite similar, and hence, in this respect, the models compare closely. In both, the model of this section and the alternate, the effect of inflation on growth is about half the magnitude of that effect when the human capital function also includes time, as in the next section.[6]

Table 12.6 Calibration for section 12.5.1 economy

Assumptions			*Production functions*
$A_F = a_2 = 0$; $a_t = A_H = \varepsilon = 1$			$y_t = A_G(s_{Gt}k_t)^{\beta}(l_{Gt}h_t)^{1-\beta}$; $i_{Ht} = s_{Ht}k_t$
	Baseline calibration		
Parameters			Variables
$\rho = \delta_H = \delta_k = 0.03, \beta = 0.4,$ $A_G = 0.0877$			$R = 0, g = 0.03, r = 0.0909$; $s_G k / l_G h = 0.0184$
Δ Nominal interest rate	Δ Growth rate	Δ Real interest rate	Δ Capital–labour ratio
0.00→0.10	–0.00281	–0.00298	0.01167
0.00→0.20	–0.00258	–0.00273	0.01167

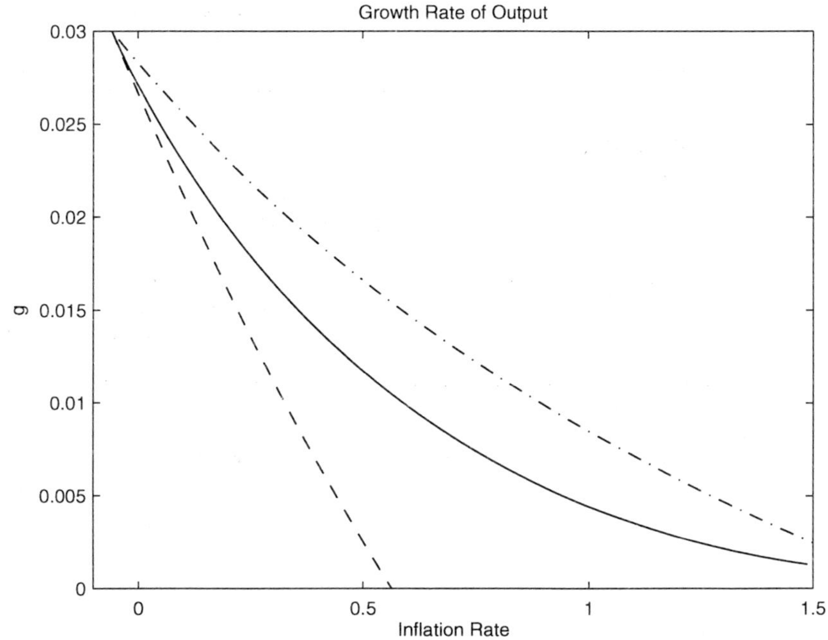

Figure 12.3 Calibration of inflation and growth: section 5 models.

12.5.2 Becker–Lucas model

Using a more general Becker (1975) function as in the section 2 model relaxes the constraint on A_H and ε, as in Gillman and Kejak (2002). The human capital investment function uses both effective labour and capital. Table 12.7 summarizes the specification.

With $A_F = a_2 = 0$ and $a_t = 1$, the consumer maximizes the preference-discounted stream of utility in (1) subject to (5), (6) and (10), with respect to c_t, x_t, M_{t+1}, k_{t+1}, h_{t+1}, s_{Gt} and l_{Gt}. The balanced-path growth rate can be expressed as $1 + g = (1 + \beta A_G(l_G h/s_G k)^{1-\beta} - \delta_k)/(1 + \rho) = (1 + (1 - x)(1 - \varepsilon)A_H(s_H k/l_H h)^{\varepsilon} - \delta_H)/(1 + \rho)$.

Solving for this system numerically, the baseline calibration is given in Table 12.7. The general nature of the human capital investment function makes the magnitude about double of the previous model in section 12.5.1. The only significant problem here in matching the evidence is the marginal degree of non-linearity in the inflation–growth effect. The inflation–growth profile is graphed in Figure 12.3 as the dashed line. It is nearly linear and indicates a negative growth rate as inflation increases contrary to evidence.

Table 12.7 Calibration for section 12.5.2 economy

Assumptions			*Production functions*	
$A_F = a_2 = 0$ $a_t = 1$			$y_t = A_G (s_{Gt} k_t)^{\beta} (l_{Gt} h_t)^{1-\beta}$ $i_{Ht} = A_H (s_{Ht} k_t)^{\varepsilon} (l_{Ht} h_t)^{1-\varepsilon}$	
Parameters			Variables	
		I. Baseline calibration		
$\rho = \delta_H = \delta_K = 0.03, \beta = 0.4, \varepsilon = 0.3, a = 3,$ $A_G = 0.3110, A_H = 0.2609$			$R = 0, g = 0.03, r = 0.0909$	
		II. Calibration		
$\varepsilon = 0.4, A_G = 0.3110, A_H = 0.3318$			$R = 0, g = 0.03, r = 0.0909$	
		III. Calibration		
$a = 2, A_G = 0.3110, A_H = 0.2609$			$R = 0, g = 0.03, r = 0.0909$	
		I	II. $\varepsilon = 0.4$	III. $a = 2$
Δ Nominal interest rate	Δ Growth rate	Δ Real interest rate	Δ Growth rate	Δ Growth rate
0.00→0.10	–0.00572	–0.00607	–0.00492	–0.00439
0.00→0.20	–0.00538	–0.00570	–0.00459	–0.00420

12.5.3 Becker–Lucas model with a credit sector

Finally, consider adding a credit sector to the model of section 12.5.2. This adds one more margin to the consumer and yields considerable flexibility to avoid the inflation tax. This gives the model the ability to explain not only a significant inflation–growth effect, and Tobin (1965) effects, but also the non-linearity of the inflation–growth effect. In addition, while not detailed here (Gillman et al., 2003), it can show differences in the inflation–growth effect across regions as based on financial development. Here, a credit sector is added using only effective labour, in contrast to the capital-only model of section 12.3.1. The assumptions are given in Table 12.8.

With $a_2 = \gamma_1 = 0$, the consumer maximizes the preference-discounted stream of utility in (1) subject to (5), (6) and (10), with respect to c_t, x_t, M_{t+1}, k_{t+1}, h_{t+1}, s_{Gt}, l_{Gt} and l_{Ft}. The added first-order condition is the Baumol (1952) equation $R = w/[\gamma_2 A_F (l_F h_t/c_t)^{\gamma_2 - 1}]$.

The calibration results are reported in Table 12.8, and details of similar calibrations can be found in Gillman and Kejak (2002, 2005b). Figure 12.3 graphs the inflation–growth profile in the solid line. This conforms roughly to evidence on the shape of the non-linearity (Gillman et al., 2004), in which the growth rate does not become negative as the inflation rate increases.

Table 12.8 Calibration for section 12.5.3 economy

Assumptions			*Production functions*
$a_2 = \gamma_1 = 0$;			$y_t = A_G (s_{Gt} k_t)^{\beta} (l_{Gt} h_t)^{1-\beta}$ $i_{Ht} = A_H (s_{Ht} k_t)^{\varepsilon} (l_{Ht} h_t)^{1-\varepsilon}$ $d_t = (1 - a_t) = A_F (l_{Ft} h_t / c_t)^{\gamma_2} c_t$
	Baseline calibration		
Parameters $\rho = \delta_H = \delta_K = 0.03, \beta = 0.4$ $\varepsilon = 0.3, a = 3, \gamma_2 = 0.3, A_F = 0.5184$ $A_G = 0.3110, A_H = 0.3279,$			Variables $R = 0, g = 0.03, r = 0.0909$ $s_G k / l_G h = 1.6871$
Δ Nominal interest rate	Δ Growth rate	Δ Real interest rate	Δ Capital–labour ratio
0.00→0.10	–0.00472	–0.00500	0.16696
0.00→0.20	–0.00381	–0.00401	0.15398

12.6 Comparison of models

Table 12.9 summarizes the findings across the different models. The table summarizes, in its second column, that all models but the first have inflation–growth effects close to the Chari et al. (1996) range of –0.2 to –0.7% for a change in the inflation rate from 10 to 20% (although here we report the results for similar changes in R). While some of the models have calibrations that are a bit high, none are too low. This establishes clearly a robust significant negative inflation–growth effect across a range of models. Distinguishing further among the models requires use of the third and fourth columns, on non-linearity and Tobin-type (1965) effects. With growing evidence of a strong non-linearity, whereby the inflation–growth effect is marginally weaker as higher levels of the inflation rate, and on positive Tobin-type (1965) effects, only two models, 12.5.1 and 12.5.3, meet all criterion. The model of section 12.5.1, however, does not provide a sense of plausibility, in that the parameter assumption of $A_H = 1$ leads to a nearly insignificant capital-to-effective-labour ratio. Also, its non-linearity is only marginal and generates negative levels of the growth rate. The model of section 12.5.3 has no such plausibility problems and has a strong non-linearity without negative levels of the growth rate.

Only the last model also is jointly consistent with the Aiyagari et al. (1998) money and banking findings that the banking sector expands in size in conjunction with the level of the inflation rate. Furthermore, Gillman and Kejak (2002, 2005b) show that this section 12.5.3 model yields a money demand closely comparable to a Cagan-type (1956) constant semi-interest elasticity model for which Mark and Sul (2003) find recent broad-based cointegration support.

Table 12.9 Summary of growth and Tobin effects

	BGP inflation–growth decrease			
Models of section	*R: 0→0.10*	*R: 0.10→0.20*	*Non-linearity*	*Tobin effect*
3.1	0	0	NA	Positive
3.2	–0.0080	–0.0067	Marginal	Inverse
4.1	–0.0082	–0.0081	Near linear	None
5.1	–0.0028	–0.0026	Marginal	Positive
5.2	–0.0057	–0.0054	Near linear	Positive
5.3	–0.0047	–0.0038	High	Positive

12.7. Conclusions

The chapter presents a general monetary endogenous growth model with both human and physical capital, and then categorizes a set of models as being nested within this model. The first subset of models considered are *Ak* models in which inflation acts as a tax on physical capital with a negative long-run Tobin-type (1965) effect. Next presented are *Ah* models in which inflation acts as a tax on human capital and there is a positive Tobin (1965) effect. Then come the more general models with human and physical capital, in which inflation acts more as a tax on human capital and there is a positive Tobin (1965) effect.

While there is no unemployment *per se* in any of these three classes of models, the employment rate moves in the opposite direction of the inflation rate in the models with human capital. This direction and causality of the employment effect is not inconsistent with evidence in Shadman-Mehta (2001). They find cointegration of inflation and unemployment for historical UK data, including Phillips original sample period, and that inflation Granger causes unemployment in the long run.

The reviewed models show a strong linkage between the magnitude of the inflation–growth and the Tobin-type (1965) effects, and between the non-linearity of both of these effects. The growth rate decrease, when the inflation rate rises from 0 to 10% and then to 20%, is proportional in its strength of magnitude and its degree of non-linerity directly to the real interest rate decrease and the capital-to-effective-labour rate increase. This linkage is a general characteristic across models that act as a key distinguishing feature. If the non-linearity is in fact significant, as evidence suggests, then models without this overstate significantly the inflation effects for rates of inflation above the baseline level. The explanation of this non-linearity comes back to the money demand elasticity that underlies the model. A rising interest elasticity, with inflation rising, leads to easier substitution away from inflation and causes the non-linearity. A near-constant interest elasticity money demand, as in the standard cash-in-advance model, leads to a near-linear response.

Debate on the monetary growth models and on the existence within these models of Tobin-type (1965) effects on the real interest rate and the Great Ratios, c/y and i/y, goes back to when monetary growth models used the Solow model as modified by Tobin (1965) to include money as the basis of debates (Johnson, 1969; Niehans, 1969). The advent of endogenous growth theory as ushered in by Lucas (1988b) marked a substantial leap in progress that reframed this debate once money was included within these models using the Lucas (1980) approach (Gomme, 1993). The resulting endogeneity of the growth rate relative to changes in the inflation rate, as working through the labour-leisure channel, allowed for calibration of the inflation–growth effect within the estimated empirical range. However, the *Ak* models also have been able to accomplish the same feat, making unclear what approach is more advantageous. Updating the traditional focus on the Great Ratios has allowed for a re-focusing on how these models can be differentiated. The Gomme-type (1993) models capture general equilibrium decreases in the real interest rate and the consumption-to-output ratio, and increases in the investment-to-out-put ratios, all as a result of inflation and as consistent with evidence. This makes the simpler *Ak* models more dated, in that they cannot so easily, if at all, achieve similar results. A further distinguishing factor, going beyond the magnitude of the inflation–growth effect, and beyond the direction of the Tobin-type (1965) effects, is how these effects behave over the range of inflation rate levels. Evidence shows a strong non-linearity in the inflation–growth effect. And the Lucas (1988b)-Gomme (1993) model that is extended to include credit production as a substitute to cash, in a Baumol-type (1952) fashion, can account for this non-linearity by producing an implied interest elasticity of money demand that rises in magnitude with the inflation rate, as in the successful Cagan (1956) model. There are currently few such models that link the evidence in favour of near-constant semi-interest elasticities of money demand, with the non-linearity of the inflation–growth effect, along with a significant negative magnitude of this effect, while also capturing the Tobin-type (1965) effects.

Appendix 12.A: section 12.2 first-order conditions

Define η_t, λ_t and μ_t as the Lagrangian multipliers for the human capital, income and money constraints, respectively, of equations. The first-order conditions of the section 12.2 model are:

$$c_t : \frac{1}{c_t} = \lambda_t P_t \left\{ 1 + \left(\frac{\mu_t}{\lambda_t}\right) \left[\gamma_1 + \gamma_2 + (1 - \gamma_1 - \gamma_2) \left(1 - A_F \left(\frac{s_{Ft} k_t}{c_t}\right)^{\gamma_1} \left(\frac{l_{Ft} h_t}{c_t}\right)^{\gamma_2} \right) \right] \right\};$$

$$x_t : \frac{a}{x_t} = \eta_t A_H (1 - \varepsilon) h_t \, (s_{Ht} k_t)^{\varepsilon} \, (l_{Ht} h_t)^{-\varepsilon} \, h_t;$$

$$M_{t+1}: -\lambda_t + \left(\frac{1}{1+\rho}\right)(\lambda_{t+1} + \mu_{t+1}) = 0;$$

$$k_{t+1}: -\lambda_t P_t - \mu_t P_t a_2 + \left(\frac{1}{1+\rho}\right) P_{t+1} r_{t+1} s_{Gt+1} + \left(\frac{1}{1+\rho}\right) P_{t+1}(1-\delta_K)$$

$$+ \left(\frac{1}{1+\rho}\right) \mu_{t+1} a_2 (1-\delta_K) P_{t+1} + \left(\frac{1}{1+\rho}\right) \mu_{t+1} \gamma_1 \frac{s_{Ft+1}}{c_{t+1}} P_{t+1} A_F \left(\frac{s_{Ft+1} k_{t+1}}{c_{t+1}}\right)^{\gamma_1 - 1}$$

$$\left(\frac{l_{Ft+1} h_{t+1}}{c_{t+1}}\right)^{\gamma_2} c_{t+1} + \left(\frac{1}{1+\rho}\right) \eta_{t+1} \varepsilon (s_{Ht+1}) A_H (s_{Ht+1} k_{t+1})^{\varepsilon - 1} (l_{Ht+1} h_{t+1})^{1-\varepsilon} = 0;$$

$$h_{t+1}: -\eta_t + \left(\frac{1}{1+\rho}\right) \lambda_{t+1} P_{t+1} w_{t+1} l_{Gt+1} + \left(\frac{1}{1+\rho}\right) \eta_{t+1} (1-\delta_H)$$

$$+ \left(\frac{1}{1+\rho}\right) \mu_{t+1} P_{t+1} \gamma_2 l_{Ft+1} A_F \left(\frac{s_{Ft+1} k_{t+1}}{c_{t+1}}\right)^{\gamma_1} \left(\frac{l_{Ft+1} h_{t+1}}{c_{t+1}}\right)^{\gamma_2 - 1}$$

$$+ \left(\frac{1}{1+\rho}\right) \eta_{t+1} (1-\varepsilon) l_{Ht+1} A_H (s_{Ht+1} k_{t+1})^{\varepsilon} (l_{Ht+1} h_{t+1})^{-\varepsilon} = 0;$$

$$s_{Gt}: \lambda_t P_t r_t - \eta_t \varepsilon A_H \left(\frac{l_{Ht} h_t}{s_{Ht} k_t}\right)^{1-\varepsilon} = 0;$$

$$l_{Gt}: \lambda_t P_t w_t - \eta_t (1-\varepsilon) A_H \left(\frac{l_{Ht} h_t}{s_{Ht} k_t}\right)^{-e} = 0;$$

$$s_{Ft}: \mu_t \gamma_1 P_t A_F \left(\frac{s_{Ft+1} k_{t+1}}{c_{t+1}}\right)^{\gamma_1 - 1} \left(\frac{l_{Ft+1} h_{t+1}}{c_{t+1}}\right)^{\gamma_2} - \eta_t \varepsilon A_H \left(\frac{l_{Ht} h_t}{s_{Ht} k_t}\right)^{1-e} = 0;$$

$$l_{Ft}: \mu_t \gamma_2 P_t A_F \left(\frac{s_{Ft+1} k_{t+1}}{c_{t+1}}\right)^{\gamma_1} \left(\frac{l_{Ft+1} h_{t+1}}{c_{t+1}}\right)^{\gamma_2 - 1} - \eta_t (1-\varepsilon) A_H \left(\frac{l_{Ht} h_t}{s_{Ht} k_t}\right)^{-e} = 0.$$

Acknowledgements

We thank Tony Braun, Bee Jeong, Jan Kmenta and seminar participants at CERGE-EI. Max Gillman is grateful for research grants from Central European University. Michael Kejak is grateful for research grants from CERGE-EI (Centre of Economic Research and Graduate Education – Economics Institute) in Prague.

Notes

* Gillman, Max, and Michal Kejak (2005). 'Contrasting Models of the Effect of Inflation on Growth', *Journal of Economic Surveys*, 19(1), 113–136.

1 See also Haslag (1998) for *Ak* economies in which money is required as bank reserves; these models have negative inflation–growth effects in a way similar to Stockman's (1981) model.

2 As an exception, Paal and Smith (2000) present an overlapping generations model in which a threshold inflation rate exists.

3 Denote nominal discount bonds that are purchased at time t by B_{t+1}, and their price by q_{t+1}. Then the receipts B_t and costs $-q_{t+1}B_{t+1}$ are added to the income constraint in equation (6), and the derivative with respect to B_{t+1} gives that $(1 + R_{t+1}) \equiv (1/q_{t+1}) = (1 + g_{t+1})(1 + \pi_{t+1})(1 + \rho)$. This combined with equation (16) gives the Fisher equation (17).

4 See Otto and Crosby (2000) for some related empirical work.

5 For an alternative view, see Barro and Sala-i-Martin (1995), footnote 13, page 181.

6 Chari et al. (1996) use a Lucas and Stokey (1983) cash-good, credit-good, preference function, which cannot be nested in the section 2 model of this paper, and report an insignificant inflation–growth effect. It is possible that if the Lucas and Stokey (1983) preference parameters are specified so that cash and credit goods are near-perfect substitutes, while at the same time, there is no real resource cost to using the credit, which is true in the Lucas and Stokey (1983) model, then inflation can cause near-perfect substitution to the credit good, with close to zero increase in leisure, resulting in an insignificant growth effect.

13 A revised Tobin effect from inflation

Relative input price and capital ratio realignments, USA and UK, 1959–1999*

Max Gillman and Anton Nakov

Summary

The chapter studies the realignments induced by inflation within an endogenous growth monetary economy. Accelerating inflation raises the ratio of the real wage to the real interest rate, and so raises the use of physical capital relative to human capital across all sectors. We find cointegration evidence for the US and UK economies consistent with a general equilibrium, Tobin-type, effect of inflation on input prices and capital intensity, even while the growth rate of output is reduced by inflation.

13.1 Introduction

Non-neutralities of long-term inflation have been identified as a key topic in macroeconomic research such as Lucas (1996). The Tobin (1965) effect is a long studied type of inflation non-neutrality. As Walsh (1998) details, Tobin looks at what happens, in an exogenous growth Solow economy with a fixed savings rate, to the use of physical capital when inflation increases. Money serves no useful role other than as a financial capital asset like physical capital. Assuming *ad hoc* that the money–capital ratio depends negatively on the inflation rate, an increase in the inflation rate causes a greater holding of capital relative to money. Output and consumption therefore rise in the steady state. This very simple model gives this result easily because there is no cost arising from using less money. It is an improvement on earlier models in that it gives us the basic asset stock and asset flow constraints for a model that includes money and capital as assets.

Using the similar stock and flow constraints as in Tobin's asset approach, Sidrauski (1967b) lets the agent optimize with money entering the utility function. Deriving the marginal product of capital, he finds that it does not in fact depend on the inflation rate. This is a result that continues to hold in all subsequent models with such stock and flow constraints.[1] With goods and money in the utility function (MIUF), inflation decreases utility by taxing money and inducing the agent to substitute goods consumption for money;

money and goods are necessarily substitutes, with only two goods in the utility function. But steady-state output and consumption remain unaffected. The only result is that the demand for money goes down. Walsh (1998) analyses the transition dynamics of such a MIUF model, and shows that inflation can induce more consumption, and so requires more capital accumulation to produce that consumption along the path. Thus, the Tobin effect is only transitional here.

The more recent cash-in-advance approach to the Tobin-type effect dates back to Stockman (1981). He requires capital as well as consumption goods to be bought with cash, so that inflation has a negative effect on physical capital and the level of output, the opposite of the Tobin result. Ireland (1994b) employs a linear, capital-only model, the so-called 'AK' model, with a cash-in-advance constraint on consumption. However, the agent can avoid inflation by using credit for exchange, on condition that capital is employed in providing the credit services. This causes a speed-up of capital accumulation along the transition path. The growth rate of output in the AK setting is unaffected. This represents a transitional Tobin-type effect similar to that of Walsh (1998). Dotsey and Sarte (2000), in a similar AK model, find no growth effect of inflation in the deterministic case. Ahmed and Rogers (2000) review other variations of Tobin-type effects within exogenous-growth, representative-agent monetary models.

In this chapter we present an endogenous-growth, cash-in-advance model with striking Tobin-type effects in general equilibrium. The model redefines the Tobin effect in a way very sympathetic to the original work. Here it is the realignment of factor inputs whereby an increase in the inflation rate increases the physical capital-effective labour ratios across sectors. The savings rate rises as well. These are permanent effects on the new balanced-growth path.

The rationale for this new-style Tobin effect is based on the effect that inflation has on the return to capital, as well as on the real wage—i.e. the factor prices. An inflation rate increase induces substitution from (exchange) goods to (non-exchange) leisure. This leisure increase drives the results. First, the 'leakage' of time through more leisure reduces the return on *human* capital.[2] Since all capital earns the same return in equilibrium, the real interest, i.e. the return on physical capital, must also fall. Meanwhile, labour is diverted in the model towards credit services, similar to how Ireland (1994b) diverts capital for this purpose, and so the real wage rises.[3] The growth rate falls because the return on all capital falls. The capital–effective labour ratios are increased, because of the rise in the real wage relative to the real interest rate, thereby allowing the decrease both in the return to capital and in the growth rate to be slightly mitigated. So, while the 'Tobin effect' of the capital–effective labour reallocation does not increase output or the growth rate of output, the better allocation of inputs in the face of the inflation tax does lessen the fall in the growth rate.

The Kormendi–Meguire (1985) negative effect of inflation on growth has recently been found to be robust empirically by Ghosh and Phillips (1998), Khan and Senhadji (2001) and Gillman et al. (2004) using advanced panel data estimation methods. These papers clarify how, for developing countries, the inflation–growth effect can be positive at low ranges of the inflation rate. But for high ranges of the inflation rate for developing countries, and for all (positive) inflation rates for developed countries, the effect is negative. Further, a nonlinearity in the inflation–growth effect is identified theoretically in Chari et al. (1996), explained theoretically in Gillman and Kejak (2002), and found econometrically in the above-mentioned three empirical papers. For example, Gillman et al. identify the nonlinearity by segmenting a postwar OECD panel into three average inflation rate ranges of 0–10%, 10%–20% and above 20%. They find the highest magnitude of the negative inflation–growth effect in the low inflation rate range of 0–10%, and the smallest magnitude in the high range of above 20%. Thus, the nonlinearity is that the negative inflation – growth effect gets weaker as the level of the inflation rate rises.

In this chapter we continue to extend this literature on the effects of inflation by giving a theoretical statement of the Tobin-style effect as derived from the Gillman–Kejak (2002) model.[4] We then test it with time-series evidence for two of the most developed, lowest-inflation countries, the United States and the United Kingdom. For these countries both the inflation–growth effect and the Tobin-type effect of factor allocation should be strongest, in that evidence suggests that the strongest, negative, inflation–growth effect is in industrial countries. The strength of the growth effect translates through to the strength of the Tobin-type effect, according to calibrations by Gillman and Kejak (2002). They show that the strength of the inflation–growth effect and the input reallocation effects are part of the same set of adjustments, and so are related in the magnitude of their effects. The Tobin-type input reallocation is just another side of the inflation–growth effect. On this basis, the United States and the United Kingdom should be fertile ground for finding evidence of Tobin-style input reallocations.

We present the monetary model in Section 13.2 and discuss the equilibrium link of the Tobin effect and the growth effect. We discuss the quarterly data and present unit root, causality and cointegration results in Section 13.3. We conclude, in Section 13.4, that this adds significant new evidence in support of this new style of Tobin effect.

13.2 Endogenous growth, cash-in-advance model

The model is that of Gillman and Kejak (2002), and our restatement of it will focus on details relating to the factor reallocation effects of inflation. It is an endogenous-growth, cash-in-advance model with human and physical capital, and with a finance sector producing credit services that are used to avoid the inflation tax. Utility at time t depends on goods, c_t, and leisure, x_t, in the CES form:

$$U = \int_0^\infty e^{-\rho t} [c_t^{1-\theta} x^{a(1-\theta)} / (1-\theta)] dt. \tag{1}$$

Goods and human capital are produced with physical capital and effective labour, each through a Cobb–Douglas production function. With h_t and k_t denoting the stock of human and physical capital, and l_{Gt} and s_{Gt} the share of raw labour and physical capital used in goods production, with $\beta \in (0, 1)$, and with A_{Gt} a productivity shift parameter, the output y_t of goods is given by

$$y_t = A_G(s_{Gt}k_t)^{1-\beta} (l_{Gt}h_t)^{\beta}. \tag{2}$$

With similar notation, using H for the human capital sector, with $\eta \in (0, 1)$, and with the depreciation rate given by $\delta_h \in \mathbb{R}_+$, the change in the human capital stock is given by

$$\dot{h}_t = A_H(s_{Ht}k_t)^{1-\eta} (l_{Ht}h_t)^{\eta} - \delta_h h_t. \tag{3}$$

The share of goods bought with currency is an endogenous fraction $a_t \in (0, 1]$ and the share of goods bought with credit residually is $(1 - a_t)$. The share of credit is produced using only the effective labour per unit of goods consumption, with diminishing returns. Let l_{Ft} denote the fraction of raw labour devoted to credit service production and assume that $\gamma \in (0, 1)$. The production function is

$$(1 - a_t) = A_F(l_{Ft}h_t/c_t)^{\gamma}. \tag{4}$$

Money purchases are constrained by the nominal money balances in a Clower-type constraint,

$$M_t = a_t P_t c_t, \tag{5}$$

which can be restated with substitution from (4) as

$$M_t = [1 - A_F(l_{Ft}h_t/c_t)^{\gamma}]P_t c_t. \tag{6}$$

Money is supplied by the government at a constant rate $\sigma \in \mathbb{R}$ each period through a lump-sum cash transfer of V_t, so that $\dot{M}_t = V_t \equiv \sigma M_t$.

The total financial wealth, denoted by Q_t, is the sum of the money stock M_t and the nominal value of the physical capital stock:

$$Q_t = M_t + P_t k_t. \tag{7}$$

The output of goods is divided between consumption and investment net of capital depreciation:

$$c_t + \dot{k}_t - \delta_k k_t = A_G(s_{Gt}k_t)^{1-\beta}(l_{Gt}h_t)^{\beta}. \tag{8}$$

The nominal capital and labour income from goods production is the nominal value of the marginal products factored by the capital and effective labour used in production. Let r_t be the marginal product of capital ($s_{Gt}k_t$), and w_t be the marginal product of effective labour ($l_{Gt}h_t$). The change over time in the agent's financial capital $\dot{Q}_t$ equals the income net of expenditure and depreciation, plus the term $\dot{P}_t k_t$ to account for the change in nominal value of physical capital:

$$\dot{Q}_t = \dot{M}_t + P_t\dot{k}_t + \dot{P}_t k_t = r_t P_t s_{Gt} k_t + w_t P_t l_{Gt} h_t + V_t - P_t c_t - \delta_k P_t k_t + \dot{P}_t k_t. \tag{9}$$

13.2.1 Equilibrium

The agent maximizes utility in (1) subject to the stock constraints (6) and (7) and the flow constraints (3) and (9) with respect to c_t, x_t, s_{Gt}, l_{GT}, l_{Ft}, M_t, Q_t, k_t and h_t. Using a Becker (1965)-type allocation of time constraint, $1 = x_t + l_{Gt} + l_{Ht} + l_{Ft}$, and the constraint $1 = s_{Gt} + s_{Ht}$, the problem can be stated as follows:

$$\begin{aligned} \text{Max} \sim \boldsymbol{H} = {} & e^{-\rho t} c_t^{1-\theta} x_t^{\alpha(1-\theta)}/(1-\theta) \\ & + \eta_t(M_t - [1 - A_F(l_{Ft}h_t/c_t)^{\gamma}]P_t c_t) \\ & + \varphi_t(Q_t - M_t - P_t k_t) \\ & + \lambda_t(r_t P_t s_{Gt} k_t + w_t P_t l_{Gt} h_t - P_t c_t + V_t - \delta_k k_t + \dot{P}_t k_t) \\ & + \mu_t(A_H[(1 - s_{Ft} - s_{Gt})k_t]^{1-\eta}[(1 - x_t - l_{Ft} - l_{Gt})h_t]^{\eta} - \delta_h h_t). \end{aligned} \tag{10}$$

The first-order equilibrium conditions are:

$$u_c/u_x = x/(\alpha c) = [1 + aR + (1-a)\gamma R]/wh; \tag{11}$$

$$-\dot{\lambda}/\lambda \equiv R = r + \dot{P}/P; \tag{12}$$

$$R = (w/[A_F\gamma(s_F k/l_F h)^{1-\gamma}]); \tag{13}$$

$$w/r = (s_G k/l_G h)(\beta/[1-\beta]) = (s_H k/l_H h)(\eta/[1-\eta]); \tag{14}$$

$$\begin{aligned} g \equiv \dot{c}/c = \dot{k}/k = \dot{h}/h &= [r - \rho]/\theta \\ &= [(1-x)A_H\beta(s_H k/l_H h)^{1-\eta} - \rho]/\theta. \end{aligned} \tag{15}$$

By (11), the marginal rate of substitution between leisure and goods per unit of human capital equals the ratio of the shadow price of leisure to goods. As the inflation rate increases, the nominal interest rate R rises and induces substitution on the utility side from c/h to x. Gillman and Kejak (2002) show that the nominal interest rate, which by (13) equals the marginal factor cost divided by the marginal factor input, represents the marginal cost of credit services, a generalization of the Baumol (1952) model.

Further, calibrations in Gillman and Kejak (2002) show that the inflation-induced reallocation of time into credit services and leisure, away from goods production and human capital accumulation, raises the real wage w. On the other hand, by taxing goods consumption, inflation reduces the return on both physical and human capital in goods production, which is reflected in a lower real interest rate r and confirmed by calibration in Gillman and Kejak. The combined effect is that the input price ratio of the net real wage to the net real interest rate rises and the capital–labour ratio rises as well (equation 14), also confirmed by calibration.

Finally, by (15), the steady-state growth rate equals the return on physical capital, or the return on human capital net of leisure leakage, minus the subjective rate of time preference, all normalized by θ. The reduction in the return on capital, as a result of an increased inflation tax, causes a lower growth rate. The advantage of this model is that some of the burden of inflation avoidance that otherwise falls on substitution from goods to leisure is now taken over by reallocation of time into credit services. This produces a realistically large fall in growth, and one that becomes smaller as the inflation rate increases, which matches the nonlinearity of the negative inflation–growth evidence. In addition, (14) and (15) imply that the fall in the growth rate is also mitigated by the reallocations of inputs, in Tobin fashion, in that a rise in the capital–effective labour ratios across sectors will make the growth rate decline less than otherwise.

13.2.2 A test of first-order conditions

Gillman et al. (2004) use equation (15) as the basis for a test of the determinants of economic growth. They use postwar panel data, adjusted for fixed country and time effects, for OECD and APEC countries and find a strong negative, nonlinear, growth effect of inflation on growth for the OECD countries, whereby the marginal effect of inflation rate increases is highest at the lowest levels of the inflation rate. The primary relation tested below is instead the little studied factor input reallocation that is induced by the inflation distortion, as given in (14). In particular, the ratio of the real wage to the real interest rate determines the capital intensity across sectors. Since calibrations in Gillman and Kejak (2002) show a robust positive effect of the inflation rate on the real wage–real interest rate ratio, there is *a direct relation between the three sets of variables*, i.e. the inflation rate, the real wage–real interest rate ratio and the capital–effective labour ratio, in the goods and human capital sectors.

To see the effect of inflation on the total capital–effective labour ratio, and not just on each of the goods and human capital sectors, we need to sum up across the three sectors including credit services. As this sector uses only effective labour in the model, the effect of inflation on the total capital to total effective labour is a priori ambiguous, since the inflation rate has a positive effect on the labour used in credit services. Because of the small size of the credit services sector, calibrations in Gillman and Kejak (2002) find that the total capital–total effective labour ratio across all sectors similarly rises with the inflation rate, as does each of the goods and human capital sectors. Thus, we are able to proceed to test, based on the model, the effect of inflation on the input–price ratio and the capital–effective labour ratio.

13.3 Empirical methodology and results

The empirical analysis uses seasonally adjusted quarterly data for the United States and the United Kingdom from 1950(I) to 1999(IV). These economies traditionally have had the highest-quality data and also are candidates for operating close to the steady state. For both countries, data on inflation, the interest rate, wages and GDP are obtained from *International Financial Statistics* (February 2000), published by the IMF. For the United States the series for the unemployment rate, productivity and hours worked are from the Bureau of Labor Statistics online database. For the United Kingdom the series for the unemployment rate and productivity are obtained from the National Statistics online databank. The capital stock series for both countries are those constructed by Easterly and Levine (2002). We use variables definitions and notation as set out in Table 13.A1 in the Appendix.

Testing for the existence of statistical relationships among the variables is conducted in three steps. The first step is to verify the order of integration of the variables, to determine which of them may enter into stable equilibrium relationships. The second step establishes such relationships through cointegration testing, using both the Engle–Granger (1987) two-step procedure and the Johansen maximum likelihood approach (Johansen 1995; Johansen and Juselius 1990). And in the third step we test for causality in the Granger (1969) sense, applying the procedure of Mosconi and Giannini (1992) for causality testing in cointegrated systems.

13.3.1 Unit root tests

We apply three tests for unit root: the augmented Dickey–Fuller (ADF) (1979), the Phillips–Perron (1988) and the KPSS (Kwiatkowski et al. 1992). The first two tests have as null hypothesis that of non-stationarity, and we use the t-statistic with critical values calculated by MacKinnon (1991). In the ADF test the order of autoregression in the test equation is determined in two ways: (i) by adding lagged difference terms until error autocorrelation (measured by the Breusch–Godfrey LM test) is removed (see Godfrey 1988); and (ii) by starting with a sufficiently large number of lags and reducing them until all lagged differences become significant at 5%. Since these two methods sometimes produce a different number of lags for inclusion into the test equation, we also apply the Phillips–Perron test with a standard lag truncation of 4.

Furthermore, we test the converse null hypothesis, that of stationarity, by applying the KPSS test. That test requires a consistent estimate of the error variance, and we use the Newey–West HAC estimator (Newey and West 1987) with a Bartlett kernel of width from 1 to 4.

The results from testing the null of unit root (see Table 13.1) are very similar for the United States and the United Kingdom and show that all series are non-stationary at the standard 5% significance level except perhaps the inflation rate, which is a controversial case. The augmented Dickey–Fuller test for inflation is sensitive to the order of autoregression: with one lagged difference the null hypothesis of unit root is rejected at 5%, while with more lags it cannot be rejected even at 10%. While the LM test indicates that more lags are necessary in order to remove residual autocorrelation, suggesting that inflation is non-stationary, the Phillips–Perron test rejects non-stationarity. On the other hand, testing for stationarity with the KPSS yields a rejection of the null hypothesis for all variables except possibly the US effective capital – labour ratio. We accept the combined results as sufficient evidence for the presence of unit root in all series and proceed with that hypothesis.

13.3.2 Cointegration

In this section we perform tests for pairwise cointegration of inflation with the real wage–real interest rate ratio, the capital–effective labour ratio, and between the real wage–real interest rate ratio and the capital–effective labour ratio. Theoretically, if cointegration exists in two of the pairs, it should be present also in the third pair.

Table 13.1 Unit root tests

Series	*ADF*	*Phillips-Perron*	*1%**	*5%**	*10%**	*KPSS 1 lag*	*KPSS 4 lags*	*5%***	*Order of integration*
UK									
INFL	−2.56	−6.98	−3.47	−2.88	−2.58	1.10	0.54	0.46	I(1)
KLH	−2.25	−2.21	−3.47	−2.88	−2.58	5.10	2.10	0.46	I(1)
WR	−2.68	−2.78	−3.48	−2.88	−2.58	1.46	0.65	0.46	I(1)
M0	2.94	4.86	−3.48	−2.89	−2.58	6.06	2.50	0.46	I(1)
USA									
INFL	−2.07	−3.65	−3.47	−2.88	−2.58	1.16	0.52	0.46	I(1)
KLH	−2.92	−2.81	−3.48	−2.88	−2.58	0.43	0.20	0.46	I(1)
WR	−1.85	−1.90	−3.47	−2.88	−2.58	1.74	0.72	0.46	I(1)
M1	2.24	3.71	−3.47	−2.88	−2.58	7.77	3.17	0.46	I(1)

* MacKinnon (1991) critical values for rejection of the hypothesis of unit root.
** Sephton (1995) critical value for rejection of the hypothesis of stationarity.

The pairwise cointegration tests are performed applying both the Engle–Granger (EG)(1987) method and the Johansen (1991) maximum likelihood procedure. In the EG approach we check the residual for stationarity, applying the ADF test with critical values calculated according to MacKinnon (1991). We look also at the cointegrating regression Durbin–Watson statistic (CRDW).

We run the following diagnostic tests: (i) the Breusch–Godfrey LM test, which is the appropriate serial correlation test when a lagged dependent variable is a regressor; (ii) Ramsey's (1969) RESET test for specification errors such as omitted variables, incorrect functional form or correlation of the regressors with the disturbance term; and (iii) the CUSUM of squares test, which indicates parameter or variance instability when the plot of the test statistic moves outside the critical lines.

We find very strong evidence of cointegration between inflation and the real wage–real interest rate ratio, in both US and UK data, and applying both the Engle–Granger method and Johansen's procedure. In the US data, in which the null hypothesis of 'no cointegration' is rejected at 1% with both methods, inflation appears to explain a larger part of the variation in the real wage–real interest rate ratio compared with the UK data.

Evidence of cointegration between inflation and the capital–effective labour ratio is also good, though less compelling: in the UK data cointegration is found at 5% with Johansen's procedure and at 1% with the EG method, while in the US data it is found at 5% with Johansen's procedure but only at 10% with the EG method. In the UK data inflation is found to explain a larger part of the variation in the capital–effective labour ratio compared to the US data.

Next, we find evidence of cointegration directly between the capital–effective labour ratio and the real wage–real interest rate ratio: in the US data cointegration is found at 5% with both methods, while in the UK the hypothesis of 'no cointegration' can be rejected at 5% with Johansen's procedure but cannot be rejected with the EG method at reasonable levels of significance. Interestingly, applying the EG test for the UK in the opposite direction—putting the capital–effective labour ratio as explanatory variable and the real wage–real interest rate ratio as dependent variable—results in rejection of the null of 'no cointegration' at 10%. Finally, in both US and UK data, money supply and the respective consumer price indexes are found to be cointegrated at the 1% significance level applying Johansen's test.

13.3.3 Granger causality

The Granger (1969) causality test is performed on the basis of Mosconi and Giannini (1992), which is appropriate for cointegrated systems. Let $z_t = (\text{INFL, KLH, WR})$ be a three-dimensional vector partitioned into $y_t = \text{INFL}$ and $x_t = (\text{KLH, WR})$. The hypothesis to be tested is that y_t does not Granger-cause x_t. Formally, given the ECM representation of the system,

$$\Delta z_t = \Gamma_1 \Delta z_{t-1} + \ldots + \Gamma_{k-1} \Delta z_{t-k+1} + \Pi z_{t-k} + e_t,$$

the hypothesis under test is

$$H_0(r_1, r_2)\text{: } \alpha = [U_{\perp} a_1 \mid a_2], \quad \beta = [b_1 \mid U b_2], \quad U' \Gamma_i V = 0, \quad i = 1, \ldots, k-1,$$

where

$$U_{\perp} = \begin{bmatrix} 1 \\ 0 \\ 0 \end{bmatrix}, \quad U = \begin{bmatrix} 0 & 0 \\ 1 & 0 \\ 0 & 0 \end{bmatrix}, \quad V = I_{k-1} \otimes U_{\perp},$$

$$\Gamma = [\Gamma_1, \ldots, \Gamma_{k-1}], \quad \Pi = \alpha\beta',$$

a_1 is a $1 \times r_1$ vector of unknown constants, a_2 is a $3 \times r_2$ matrix of unknown constants, b_1 is a $3 \times r_1$ matrix of unknown constants, and b_2 is a $2 \times r_2$ matrix of unknown constants. The interpretation of r_1 and r_2 is discussed in Mosconi and Giannini (1992). Under the null hypothesis, the matrices Π and Γ_i, $(i = 1, \ldots, k-1)$ should be upper-block triangular so that the variables in the first subset (y_t) do not Granger-cause the variables in the second (x_t). In order to reject non-causality, we need to reject the null hypothesis for all pairs (r_1, r_2) satisfying

$$r_1 + r_2 = r, \quad 0 \le r_1 \le 1, \quad 0 \le r_2 \le 2,$$

where r is the cointegration rank of the system (in our case, 2). The likelihood ratio test is distributed X^2 with $3r - r_1 - 2r_2 - r_1 r_2 + 2(k-1)$ degrees of freedom.

The test was computed for different lag specifications from 1 to 8. In all cases the result was a strong rejection (at 1%) of the null hypothesis that inflation does not Granger-cause the input price ratio and the capital ratio. The output from the test for $k = 3$ is presented in Table 13.2. Notice that non-causality is rejected when the significance level is less than 0.05 for all possible combinations of r_1 and r_2.

Table 13.2 Granger causality test

	r_1	r_2	*No. of iterations*	*Converge*	*Log-L.*	*Test*	*DGF*	*Signif.*	*Akaike*
UK	0	2	2000	Yes	735.4	66.896	6	0.0000.	−13.080
	1	1	2000	Yes	746.0	45.771	6	0.000	−13.272
USA	0	2	2000	Yes	2634.1	47.835	6	0.0000	−39.076
	1	1	2000	Yes	2643.5	29.000	6	0.0001	−39.216

13.4 Conclusions and qualifications

Our results provide support for the model that there is an active Tobin-type realignment of inputs as part of the equilibrium response to changes in the expected inflation rate. This research aims to help fill out the broader effects of inflation in the postwar industrial economies and so enables us to understand better the rise and fall of stagflation. An increasing real wage–real interest rate ratio, and an aggregate physical capital–effective labour ratio, are candidate components of the effects of accelerating inflation. While motivated analytically by Tobin, the general equilibrium presentation of this input response is one involving both capital and labour and not just capital, as in Tobin. Further, it is a reallocation that coincides with a decrease in the growth rate within the model, as some evidence suggests, rather than an increase in the growth rate or no growth effect, as suggested by Ahmed and Rogers (2000) and Dotsey and Sarte (2000). This contribution represents a preliminary beginning of what could be a more extensive investigation into such input realignments internationally.

Appendix 13.A: description of the data set

The paper uses seasonally adjusted quarterly data for the United States and the United Kingdom from 1950(I) to 1999(IV). For both countries, data on inflation, the interest rate, wages and GDP are obtained from *International Financial Statistics*, published by IMF. For the United States the series for the unemployment rate, productivity and hours worked are from the Bureau of Labor Statistics online database. For the United Kingdom the series for the unemployment rate and productivity are obtained from the National Statistics online database. The capital stock series are obtained from Easterly and Levine (1999), calculated on the basis of disaggregated investment. We use variables definition and notation as presented in Table 13.A1.

Table 13.A1 Variables definition and notation

Variables	*Definition*	*Notation*
Inflation	Quarterly % change in the Consumer Price Index	INFL
Money stock	M1 for the USA, M0 for the UK	M1, M0
Capital–effective labour ratio	Capital stock per skilled labour is the ratio of capital stock to the number of workers, adjusted by a productivity index as a proxy for human capital	KLH
Real wage–real interest rate ratio	Real wage is the nominal wage in production divided by CPI. The real 'raw' wage is the real wage divided by an index of productivity as a proxy for human capital. Real interest rate is the yield on government bonds less inflation. For the UK, *w*/*r* is the ratio between the real raw wage and the real interest rate. For the USA, where productivity gains are not reflected in a rising real wage, *w*/*r* is just the ratio of the real wage to the real interest rate.	WR

Acknowledgements

We are grateful to Michal Kejak and Laszlo Matyas for comments and to participants at seminars at Central European University and the Stockholm School of Economics.

Notes

* Gillman, Max, and Anton Nakov (2003). 'A Revised Tobin Effect from Inflation: Relative Input Prices and Capital Ratio Realignments, US and UK, 1959–1999', *Economica*, 70(279), 439–450.

1 However, with capital taxes inflation can induce a higher effective tax rate on corporate profits, e.g. through an increase in tax liabilities due to inventory accounting methods, and the erosion of depreciation allowances (Feldstein 1982). Jones et al. (1993) also show that, with nominally fixed depreciation allowances, inflation increases the effective tax on investment.

2 Boskin et al. (1980) and Leijonhufvud (1977) show how inflation can reduce work effort.

3 Baumol (1952) argues that the using up of resources in non-productive inflation tax-avoidance represents a loss.

4 See Einarsson and Marquis (1999) for a related model.

14 Inflation and growth

Explaining a negative effect*

Max Gillman, Mark N. Harris and László Mátyás

Summary

The chapter presents a monetary model of endogenous growth and specifies an econometric model consistent with it. The economic model suggests a negative inflation-growth effect, and one that is stronger at lower levels of inflation. Empirical evaluation of the model is based on a large panel of OECD and APEC member countries over the years 1961–1997. The hypothesized negative inflation effect is found comprehensively for the OECD countries to be significant and, as in the theory, to increase marginally as the inflation rate falls. For APEC countries, the results from using instrumental variables also show significant evidence of a similar behavior. The nature of the inflation-growth profile and differences in this between the regions are interpreted with the credit production technology of the model in a way not possible with a standard cash-only economy.

14.1 Introduction

Kormendi and McGuire (1985) document a negative effect of inflation on economic growth for a cross-section of 47 countries during the period 1950–1977. Recent panel evidence such as Barro's (2001) strengthens the support for such a negative effect. In qualification, Khan and Senhadji (2001), Ghosh and Phillips (1998), and Judson and Orphanides (1996) all find a significant negative inflation-growth effect above a certain "threshold" value of the inflation rate, and no significant effect below the threshold value, without using instrumental variables and with differences found between less and more developed country samples. Further the above-threshold negative effect that they find is significantly non-linear whereby the marginal effect is stronger at lower inflation rates than at higher ones; see also Fischer (1993).

Linking such evidence with a theoretical model has been somewhat tenuous. The Tobin (1965) paper concerns the induced increase in the capital stock within a Solow exogenous growth model. Stockman (1981) demonstrates a reverse Tobin effect of inflation on capital by applying Lucas's (1980) Clower constraint to investment as well as consumption purchases, but does not explicitly deal with the balanced-growth rate of output.[1] Sidrauski's (1967b) money-in-the-utility function model and Ireland's (1994b) AK model derive only a transitional effect of inflation on the growth rate. Dotsey and Sarte (2000) use an AK-type model, apply the Clower constraint to investment as in Stockman (1981), add uncertainty, and calibrate a negligibly small negative effect of inflation on the balanced-growth rate. Chari, Jones and Manuelli (1996) calibrate, in an endogenous growth model with human capital, a negative effect of inflation on the balanced-growth rate, but one of a magnitude far below what they consider to be within the estimated range found in empirical studies.

However, it has sometimes been overlooked that Gomme's (1993) endogenous growth framework, with a somewhat extended model relative to Chari et al. (1996), uses a Lucas (1988b) type production function for human capital investment and produces a significant negative calibrated effect of inflation on growth. Because this model produces effects that are within the range of the significant negative effects found in recent panel estimates (see Gillman and Kejak 2002), it is a plausible candidate for a theory of the inflation-growth effect.

The contribution of the chapter here is that we extend a Gomme (1993)-type model, and apply the extension to guide and interpret the estimation of the inflation-growth effect in a comprehensive way. This produces a simple way to understand the effect of inflation on growth, and a linked way to estimate this effect that is not inconsistent with previous work. However, the empirical results differ somewhat in that the effect of inflation is found to be significant and negative at all positive levels of the inflation rate, when using instrumental variables for both developed and less developed country samples. Together with the model this offers a novel combination of a fully supported theory of the inflation-growth effect.

The extension made to the Gomme (1993)–type model concerns the exchange technology. Instead of a cash-only economy, here as in Gillman and Kejak (2002) both money and credit can be used to buy the consumption good. The credit production function is specified explicitly in an additional layer of "micro-foundations". This allows interpretation of different results between OECD and APEC samples using differences in the credit technology, or in the "financial development".

The model-based explanation is that inflation lowers the rate of return on capital, both human and physical. Ever since the Ramsey-Cass-Koopmans theory endogenized the savings rate of the Solow model by using utility optimization, the growth rate has depended on one variable: the rate of return to capital. Taxes that decrease that rate of return decrease the growth rate. Models that explain growth endogenously, with a Lucas (1988b) human capital accumulation, further develop the theory by implying that the growth rate depends on the rate of return to human capital as well as physical capital, whereby the rate of return on all forms of capital must be equal in the balanced-growth equilibrium.[2] A tax on either form of capital induces a lower return in equilibrium on all forms of capital. When such endogenous growth models are set within a monetary exchange framework, such as those of Lucas (1980), Lucas and Stokey (1987), or McCallum and Goodfriend (1987), the inflation tax also will affect the rate of return on capital. In particular, as Chari et al. (1996) discuss, the inflation tax induces goods to leisure substitution that lowers the return to human capital, and the growth rate.

With a parsimonious empirical theory, the chapter here explains growth through factors that reflect the return to physical and human capital in terms of easily measurable variables. The real interest rate, a measure of the return to physical capital, is proxied with the investment rate in a way suggested by the theory. Any further changes across countries to this real rate, for example as caused by differing tax regimes, are accounted for via use of fixed country specific effects within the econometric model. This is important in that the model implies (see King and Rebelo 1990), that a tax on capital income directly reduces the growth rate; a tax on labor income can also affect the growth rate for example if there is any kind of tax or subsidy to the human capital investment sector. The inflation rate enters the econometric specification as the one systematic, easily measured, tax on human capital within each country that is suggested by the theory.

Another aspect of the empirical work here is that time effects are conditioned upon, as fixed parameters in the econometric model, and interpreted as being related to unexpected international changes in the inflation rate.

The model also includes a variable designed to capture transitional dynamics. There are several potential sources of transitional dynamics in the model. For one, note that in the Lucas (1988b) human capital model, without the assumption of a human capital externality, the human capital index acts to explain endogenously the original Solow exogenous technological change, or "total factor productivity" shift parameter. Further, Solow-like transitional dynamics exist when the model includes physical capital in the production of human capital, as in King and Rebelo (1990) and as in this paper. Thus there are the Solow-like transitional dynamics whereby a below-balanced-path-equilibrium amount of capital, now human as well as physical, leads to increases in capital and income levels on the transition towards the stationary state. Applying this representative agent model to a panel suggests that countries within an interlinked group, or "growth club", will converge to the same balanced-growth path, as in Barro (1997) for example. Therefore including the ratio of income in each country relative to that of the balanced-path "leader", for example the US, can capture the effect of the transitional dynamics on the growth rate.

Second, Einarsson and Marquis (1999) present transitional dynamics for a Gomme (1993)-type model and indicate how the income variable moves transitionally with changes in the inflation rate, as a result of changes in the exogenous rate of money supply growth. This suggests that should the leader of a growth club have an influence on the inflation rates of the other countries in the club, the other countries in the club would have transitional effects on income that would be relative to the leader to some extent. For these two sources of transitional dynamics, and assuming the US as the lead country, we follow the older exogenous Solow-growth literature (Kormendi and Meguire 1985), and the new endogenous growth literature (Barro 2001), and include as a variable the ratio of the level of income in the US to the level of income in each other country.

Instrumental variables (IV's), to test for possible endogeneity of the inflation and growth rates, are little used in the literature cited above. We test for such endogeneity and report results for all samples using an instrument suggested directly by the theoretical model. The paper follows the model's implication that the money supply is exogenous and largely determines the inflation rate along the balanced growth rate. Further, there is evidence that finds that the money supply growth rate Granger-causes the inflation rate, while the inflation rate in turn Granger causes the output growth rate, such as in Nakov and Gillman (2004). This suggests the use of money as an instrument for the inflation rate in a way consistent with the model.

Also, note that the theoretical model predicts a non-linearity in the inflation-growth effect, whereby the effect is marginally stronger at lower inflation rates than at higher ones, but negative everywhere. So at the Friedman optimum of a zero nominal interest rate the effect is marginally the strongest, and monotonically weaker thereafter. This non-linearity is explored using alternative specifications, these being the natural logarithm, quadratic, and spline functions.

Finally, it is noted that the optimization model does not dismiss the Tobin (1965) effect, but rather re-states it in general equilibrium terms. Here, in contrast to Stockman (1981), there is a positive Tobin-type effect. The endogenous growth, cash-in-advance, setting implies that the inflation tax reduces the return on human capital, and that the return on physical capital must adjust downwards in equilibrium. This adjustment requires an increased investment and an increased capital/labor usage across all sectors. This input realignment slightly mitigates the degree to which the return on human capital and physical capital must fall as a result of an increase in the inflation rate. Thus the Tobin effect here is the more efficient use of inputs given the higher tax on labor relative to leisure that results from an inflation rate increase. It means a higher physical capital usage relative to effective labor, and a slightly smaller decline in the balanced-path growth rate. However, the effect of inflation on the balanced-growth rate is still negative, in contrast to the exogenous growth, monetary, model of Tobin, or related models reviewed by Ahmed and Rogers (2000).

14.2 Endogenous growth monetary framework

The representative agent works in a constant-returns-to-scale (CRS) goods sector that employs physical capital and effective labor. Effective labor is defined as raw labor factored by the human capital (quality indexed). The agent also devotes recourses to two additional, implicit price, sectors. These are the CRS human capital production that involves the investment of capital and effective labor, and a credit services sector that involves only effective labor in a diminishing returns technology. The agent faces four constraints on the maximization of utility over goods and leisure in terms of the flow of human capital; the flow of financial capital that is comprised of money and physical capital; the stock of financial capital; and the exchange technology. The technology of the credit services sector is built into the cash-in-advance constraint.

At time t, denote the real quantities of output and consumption goods by y_t and c_t, and the fraction of time spent in leisure, in credit services production, and in goods production by x_t, l_{Ft}, and l_{Gt}. The share of physical capital in goods production is given by s_{Gt}. The stocks of physical and human capital and their depreciation rates are given by k_t, h_t, δ_k, and δ_h respectively. Denote the input prices of capital and effective labor by r_t, the real interest rate, and w_t, the real wage. The positive shift parameters of the production functions of goods, credit services, and human capital are A_G, A_F, and A_H. Nominal variables are the price of goods P_t, the stock of nominal financial capital Q_t, the stock of money M_t, and the lump sum government transfer of cash V_t that is a constant fraction σ of the money stock. In addition denote by d_t the amount of real credit used in making purchases. Given parameters ρ, β, ε, and γ are in the (0,1) interval, and $a > 0$, and $\theta > 0$.

14.2.1 The goods producer

Let the output of goods be produced by the function

$$y_t = A_G (s_{Gt}k_t)^{1-\beta} (l_{Gt}h_t)^{\beta}. \tag{1}$$

The firm's first-order conditions set the market's real interest rate and real wage equal to the marginal products:

$$r_t = (1 - \beta)A_G [(s_{Gt}k_t) / (l_{Gt}h_t)]^{-\beta}, \tag{2}$$

$$w_t = \beta A_G [(s_{Gt}k_t) / (l_{Gt}h_t)]^{1-\beta}. \tag{3}$$

14.2.2 The consumer problem

The consumer's current period utility function is given by

$$u(c_t, x_t) = c_t^{1-\theta} x_t^{a(1-\theta)} / (1 - \theta). \tag{4}$$

14.2.2.1 Income and human capital constraints

The nominal financial capital constraint is

$$Q_t = M_t + P_t k_t. \tag{5}$$

The nominal income constraint derives from setting the change in financial capital to zero. This sets income of $r_t P_t s_{Gt} k_t + w_t P_t l_{Gt} h_t + V_t + P_t k_t$ minus expenditure of $P_t c_t + \delta_K P_t k_t$ equal to zero:

$$\dot{Q}_t = r_t P_t s_{Gt} k_t + w_t P_t l_{Gt} h_t + V_t + \dot{P}_t k_t - \delta_K P_t k_t - P_t c_t = 0. \tag{6}$$

Human capital is CRS produced, with capital not used in goods production $(1 - s_{Gt})k_t$ and time not used in leisure, credit services production, or goods production $(1 - x_t - l_{Gt} - l_{Ft})$. The investment in human capital is given by

$$\dot{h} = A_H (1 - x_t - l_{Gt} - l_{Ft})^{\delta} h_t (1 - s_{Gt})^{1-\delta} k_t - \delta_h h_t. \tag{7}$$

14.2.2.2 Exchange technology

Money and credit are perfect substitutes in purchasing the consumption good. This can be expressed by equating the sum of real money balances and total real credit to the aggregate consumption:

$$(M_t / P_t) + d_t = c_t. \tag{8}$$

Define by $a_t \in (0,1)$ the fraction of purchases made with cash, so that

$$[(M_t / P_t) / c_t] + (d_t / c_t) \equiv a_t + (d_t / c_t) = 1. \tag{9}$$

This makes the so-called cash-in-advance, Lucas's (1980) "Clower constraint", merely a part of the description of the perfect substitutability of money and credit:

$$M_t = a_t P_t c_t. \tag{10}$$

The money supply progresses through the government transfer, which is assumed to be made at a constant rate σ:

$$M_{t+1} = M_t + V_t = M_t (1 + \sigma). \tag{11}$$

From Eq. (9), it is clear that the share of purchases made by credit is given by $1 - a_t$. Or the total amount of credit used can be expressed as

$$d_t = (1 - a_t) c_t. \tag{12}$$

Consider specifying the production of this credit using an effective-labor only technology, with diminishing returns, whereby $\tilde{A}_F$ is a function that depends on the level of consumption c_t:

$$d_t = \tilde{A}_F\,[c_t]\,(l_{Ft}h_t)^{\gamma}. \tag{13}$$

With the shift parameter containing this dependence upon c_t, the function $\tilde{A}_F$ is specified as $\tilde{A}_F = A_F c_t^{1-\gamma}$, and the credit production function is Cobb-Douglas in $l_{Ft}h_t$ and c_t:

$$d_t = A_F(l_{Ft}h_t)^{\gamma}\, c_t^{1-\gamma}, \tag{14}$$

which can be written using equation (12) as

$$(1 - a_t)c_t = A_F(l_{Ft}h_t)^{\gamma}\, c_t^{1-\gamma}. \tag{15}$$

The rationale of the introduction of c_t into the total productivity factor is that the credit supplier, which in a decentralized framework can be thought of as a hypothetical firm similar to American Express, must take total economic activity as a given. The credit supplier can only hope to increase its share of the total activity that is being exchanged with credit.[3]

The nature of the externality is chosen by restricting the consumption velocity of money to be stable on the balanced growth path, as evidence suggests allowing for shifts due to financial innovation. Rewriting the Eq. (15) as

$$1/a_t = 1/[1 - A_F(l_{Ft}h_t/c_t)^{\gamma}], \tag{16}$$

velocity $1/a_t$ is stationary because l_{Ft} and c_t/h_t are each stationary. Balanced-path changes in velocity, such as increases that result from deregulation and innovation in the Finance sector, are captured when A_F exogenously increases.[4]

Solving for a_t from Eq. (16), and substituting into Eq. (10),

$$M_t = [1 - A_F(l_{Ft}h_t/c_t)^{\gamma}]\,P_t c_t, \tag{17}$$

gives the constraint that enters the consumer maximization problem, which can be found presented in full in the Appendix in Gillman et al. (2001).

Note that Eq. (17) can be solved for l_{Ft}, the total time devoted by the consumer in the role as credit producer. This "banking time" solution of the constraint presents an exchange constraint that can be viewed as being equivalent to a special case of the shopping-time economy, as for example in Lucas (2000). Except here the time spent in exchange activity is only that time that enters into the credit production function.[5] The advantage of this over the shopping time models is that those models are typically, as in Lucas

(2000), calibrated so as to yield a constant interest elasticity of money. Here the interest elasticity rises in magnitude as the inflation rate goes up, as consistent with evidence (see Mark and Sul 2003); the rising elasticity constitutes the central feature used to explain the non-linear nature of the inflation-growth effect.

14.2.3 The effect of inflation on the balanced-growth path

The representative agent maximizes the discounted stream of the period utility of Eq. (4), subject to Eqs. (5), (6), (7), and (17).[6] The marginal rate of substitution between goods and leisure is

$$ac/xh = w/(1 + aR + wl_F h/c), \tag{18}$$

where R is defined as the nominal interest rate. The marginal rate equals the shadow price of leisure w divided by the shadow price of goods, $1 + aR + wl_F h/c$. The goods shadow price includes a goods price of 1 and a cost of exchange that is the sum of the average cash cost aR, and the average credit cost $wl_F h/c$. This relation shows that an increase in the inflation rate, which increases R directly, goes in the direction of causing c/h to fall relative to leisure, x, by a first-order effect. There are second-order changes of lesser magnitude that go in the opposite direction. In particular, a falls and w rises as the inflation rate goes up, but calibrations in Gillman and Kejak (2002) show that the rise in R ends up being dominant for levels of the inflation rate below hyperinflation, as typically defined, and the substitution goes from goods (normalized by human capital) to leisure.[7]

The equilibrium balanced-path growth rate g is characterized by

$$g \equiv \dot{c}/c = \dot{k}/k = \dot{h}/h = [r - \rho]/\theta, \tag{19}$$

and by the equality of the return of physical capital in goods production to the return on effective labor in human capital production:

$$r = (1 - x) A_H \beta (s_H k / l_H h)^{1-\beta} - \delta_h. \tag{20}$$

Equations (19) and (20) suggest that an increase in leisure x may have a significant effect on decreasing r and the growth rate.[8] With Eq. (18), these equations show how inflation can cause a negative growth effect through the increase in leisure.

Calibrations in Gillman and Kejak (2002) show that this negative effect is very significant and robust. It occurs for a wide range of parameters around the baseline, which is set by using standard values from the literature. For the non-standard parameters, mainly $\gamma \in (0, 1)$ of the credit production sector, the full range of values was experimented with and all yield the negative inflation-growth effect. For example, with $\gamma = 0.2$ (the baseline value as based on evidence in Gillman and Otto, 2002), an increase in the inflation rate from 5 to 15% causes a decrease in the growth rate by 0.27%. The non-linear nature of the inflation-growth effect is illustrated by increasing the inflation rate further from 15 to 25%; this causes a smaller decrease in the growth rate of 0.22%. Such a decreasing magnitude continues to result with continued inflation rate increases.

The non-linearity implies that the inflation-growth effect falls towards zero at high inflation rates. Depending on the calibration, for standard parameters the inflation rate at which the growth rate decrease becomes zero is between 100 and 200%. This is effectively above any stationary (non-hyperinflation) rate of inflation likely to be experienced in any given country.

14.2.3.1 Non-linearity of the inflation-growth effect

The intuition for the non-linearity derives from the exchange technology. When the inflation rate is at a low level, the consumer uses mainly money and just a little amount of credit. The theory implies that the interest elasticity of money demand is very low in absolute value, or "inelastic", at low inflation rates, and that it becomes increasingly more elastic (more negative) as the inflation rate rises and the agent substitutes towards credit. With an inelastic money demand, the agent substitutes from goods to leisure, and a bit from money to credit when the inflation rate goes up. As the interest elasticity increases with increases in the inflation rate, the agent still substitutes from goods to leisure but increasingly substitutes towards the use of credit away from money. The rising interest elasticity, and the emergence of increasing substitution towards credit as the primary substitution channel, means that the agent relies less on the goods to leisure channel. Therefore leisure increases at a decreasing rate, and the growth rate falls by increasingly smaller amounts. The bigger increases in credit and the smaller increases in leisure, as the inflation rate rises, explains why the inflation-growth effect is of smaller magnitude at higher inflation rates.

However, note that if no credit is available, then $a = 1$ in the model and the interest elasticity of money remains low in magnitude even as the inflation rate rises. This gives a more linear inflation-growth effect whereby the decrease in the growth rate from increased inflation remains large even at very high inflation rates. Below such a case is considered as an alternative for explaining the evidence

14.2.3.2 Tobin effect and the savings rate

The Tobin effect here is a general equilibrium one along the balanced growth path whereby an increase in the inflation rate causes an increase in the input price ratio, w/r, and in the capital to effective labor ratio in both goods and human capital production. Calibrations show that the inflation rate robustly causes a decrease in the return to capital, r, as the return on human capital is forced down, and an increase in the real wage w, as a result mainly of the consumer using more leisure. This induces substitution from effective labor to capital, and produces the model's Tobin-type increase in capital intensity, even while causing a decrease in the growth rate.

The savings rate is shown in this model, in Gillman et al. (2001), to depend on the input price ratio, w/r, on leisure, and on the nominal interest rate. The effect of an increase in the real interest rate r is to increase the savings rate. And in equilibrium the savings rate equals the investment rate. It is on this basis that we proxy the effect of the real interest rate on the growth rate through the use of the investment rate. This abstracts from other effects such as the real wage, and so makes the investment rate an imperfect proxy of the real interest rate.

14.2.3.3 Financial development

The credit production function depends primarily on the degree of diminishing returns parameter γ. Calibrations show that as γ decreases from its baseline value, the inflation-growth effect is less. With the interpretation that less developed countries have a greater degree of such diminishing returns, then the inflation-growth effect is pivoted up for developing versus developed countries, as in Figure 14.1 (see Section 14.6).

14.3 The data

Three panels of countries are examined. The first consists of 29 OECD countries; the second panel consists of 18 APEC members (six of them jointly belonging to the OECD); and the third panel includes all 41 countries.

The data are from *EconData* and *World Bank World Tables*. The data set comprises annual measures on the following four variables: Per capita GDP, 1995 $US million; average annual growth rate of real GDP, percent per annum; GDP deflator, percent per annum inflation rate; and the proportion of gross domestic investment in GDP, percent (these series have the following

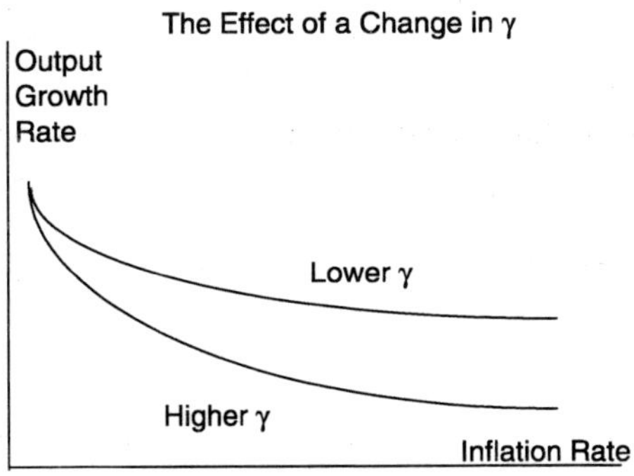

Figure 14.1 Comparative statics of the credit production function.

names: PCGDP, GDPGR, GDPDEF, INVPGDP respectively). The money stock data series is that listed as "money" in the online International Financial Statistics, or as M1 for some countries with multiple monetary aggregate listings; these generally correspond to the M1 aggregate.

The original sample period is 1961–1997 for all countries, except the Czech Republic (1985–1997), Germany (1992–1997), Turkey (1969–1997), Poland (1985–1997), Russia (1990–1997) and Vietnam (1986–1997).

Data is smoothed by setting each 5-year period as one averaged observation, as for example in Ghosh and Phillips (1998).

There appears to be no one definitive measure of the variable that represents the "inflation rate" in the literature. For example, Barro (1995) uses the inflation rate level, π; while Judson and Orphanides (1999) use the logarithm form, $\log(1 + \pi)$. Ghosh and Phillips (1998) use four measures: π; $\pi/(1 + \pi)$, $\log(1 + \pi)$ and a non-monotonic transformation, $(1/(1 - \gamma))\, \pi^{(1-\gamma)}$; Khan and Senhadji (2001) use $\log(\pi)$. In the raw data, inflation rates range from −11% to over 6,000%. To avoid hyperinflation measures, the data alternatively is capped at an inflation rate of 50, 100, and 150%, whereby values with higher rates are dropped from the sample. Also the few negative observations are dropped. Examination of the distributions shows that substantial outliers are still heavily skewing the distribution of the level of the inflation rate, such that this may bias the estimated inflation effect. The $\log(1 + \pi)$ has a more normal distribution of inflation rates.

14.4 The econometric model

The economic model derived in Section 14.2, leads to the following econometric specification

$$y_{it} = a_i + \lambda_t + \beta_g g(\pi_{it}) + \beta_{I/y} \ln(I_{it}/y_{it}) + \beta_{y/y} \ln(y_{USA,t}/y_{it}) + u_{it} \qquad (21)$$

where: y_{it} is the average annual growth rate (% pa) in GDP at constant prices, of country i in year t; β the vector of unknown coefficients; $g(\pi_{it})$ a non-linear function of the annual rate of inflation; I_{it}/y_{it} the proportion of gross domestic investment in GDP (equal to the savings rate in the representative agent framework); $y_{USA,t}/y_{it}$ the ratio of US output to country i output; a_i the country specific, time invariant, effect which captures unobserved country heterogeneity, such as physical tax rates (conditioning on such, allows long-run growth rates to differ across countries, irrespective of their observed heterogeneity); λ_t the country invariant time effects, which account for any trend-deviation effects; and u_{it} the disturbance term. Signs on the investment/saving rate and on the ratio of incomes are predicted to be positive, while the inflation effect is predicted to be negative.

A fixed effects approach is followed in the estimations, as in Matyas and Sevestre (1996), to avoid any potential biases arising from correlations between the included variables and the unobserved effects.

14.4.1 Modeling the inflation-growth non-linearity

Several variants of the non-linear relationship between π and growth, $g(\pi_{it})$, were estimated. First, as in Judson and Orphanides (1999) and Ghosh and Phillips (1998), the relation is specified as $g(\pi_{it}) = \log(1 + \pi_{it})$. In addition, a "tied" spline is constructed. For the log specification, the spline is $g(\pi_{it}) = \sum_{j=1}^{3} D_j\beta_j \log(1 + \pi_{it})$, where D_j are three dummy variables, with D_1 representing "low", D_2 "medium," and D_3 "high" inflation. Restrictions are imposed on the parameters to ensure that the spline functions are continuous at the spline knots. In addition to these two specifications for the logarithmic function, there is an instrumental variables estimation using the money stock as the instrument.[9]

14.4.2 Robustness and endogeneity

Experiments were conducted regarding the robustness of the specification of the econometric model, the cut-off point for inflation rate outliers, and possible endogeneity bias from any simultaneity of growth and infaltion. In terms of the robustness of the conditioning variables, the literature reports experiments with a variety of conditioning sets. That is, in addition to inflation, different sets of explanatory variables are included in the econometric specification (for example human capital variables). The different conditioning sets tend to be insignificant in terms of their effect on the inflation-growth relationship (see, for example, Khan and Senhadji, 2001). While also experimented with here, such additional variables were not found to be significant and such results are not reported.

Negligible differences were found when using the different inflation rate truncation points of 50%, 100% and 150%. Given the traditional (Cagan 1956) hyperinflation definition of rates over 50%, the base specifications reported below use the 50% cut-off point.

The inflation rate enters the econometric model of Eq. (21) under the assumption that it is an exogenous variable relative to the output growth rate. To try to eliminate potential endogeneity bias, the model is re-estimated by the use of instrumental variables. Ghosh and Phillips (1998) use three alternatives: central bank independence, the exchange regime, and central bank governor turnover. They find a negative significant inflation-growth effect for the first two of these and insignificance for the latter. The approach here is to use current and lagged values of the money supply as instruments for inflation. This is suggested from the Sect. 2 model's balanced-growth equilibrium in which the money supply is exogenous and causes changes in the inflation rate.[10]

14.5 Results

The results reported in Table 14.1 are with data observations dropped from the sample if the inflation rates are above 50%. The table reports the

Table 14.1 Logarithm of inflation, logarithm of inflation – IVs and spline function in the logarithm of inflation

	OECD coefficient	*FULL coefficient*	*APEC coefficient*
Specification A: *Within* Estimation; $g(\pi_{it}) = \ln(1 + \pi_{it})$			
$\ln(I_{it}/y_{it})$	0.260 (0.026)*	0.220 (0.020)*	0.232 (0.031)*
$\ln(y_{it}^{USA}/y_{it})$	3.059 (1.654)**	2.196 (1.185)**	3.168 (1.589)*
$\ln(1 + \pi_{it})$	−0.774 (0.132)*	−0.427 (0.123)*	−0.060 (0.218)
Constant	−1.717 (0.837)*	−1.180 (0.896)***	−2.668 (1.786)***
$\bar{R}^2$	47%	48%	43%
F-test	9.254*	8.598*	4.775*
NT	932	1,253	528
Hausman	3.813*	6.176*	5.162*
Specification B: IV *Within* Estimation; $g(\pi_{it}) = \ln(1 + \pi_{it})$			
$\ln(I_{it}/y_{it})$	2.255 (0.487)*	2.765 (0.428)*	3.289 (0.607)*
$\ln(y_{it}^{USA}/y_{it})$	−5.190 (1.541)*	−3.939 (1.146)*	−2.010 (1.585)***
$\ln(1 + \pi_{it})$	−0.922 (0.168)*	−0.617 (0.147)*	−0.448 (0.236)**
Constant	2.120 (0.944)*	1.720 (0.897)**	1.287 (1.435)
$\bar{R}^2$	44%	46%	46%
NT	835	1,086	458
Specification C: *Within* Estimation of the Spl ine Function; $g(\pi_{it}) = \sum_{j=1}^{3} D_j\beta_j \log(1 + \pi_{it})$			
$\ln(I_{it}/y_{it})$	0.258 (0.026)*	0.213 (0.020)*	0.219 (0.031)*
$\ln(y_{it}^{USA}/y_{it})$	3.635 (1.674)*	2.532 (1.190)*	3.347 (1.590)*
π_{it}	−0.567 (0.164)*	−0.182 (0.155)	0.222 (0.272)
$(\ln[1 + \pi_{it}] - \ln[10]) \times 1(\pi_{it} > 10)$	−1.053 (0.565)**	−1.117 (0.544)*	−0.912 (0.971)
$(\ln[1 + \pi_{it}] - \ln[20]) \times 1(\pi_{it} > 20)$	0.589 (1.153)	0.297 (1.039)	−0.849 (1.767)
Constant	−2.037 (0.849)*	−1.431 (0.901)***	−2.827 (1.789)***
$\bar{R}^2$	47%	48%	43%
F-test	9.024*	8.588*	4.856*
NT	932	1,253	528

Notes

p-value of *F*-test for joint significance of all of the unobserved (fixed) effects (null model, are jointly zero); *Hausman* is the Hausman test for endogeneity of the inflation variable (null model is of exogeneity); robust standard errors in parentheses.

* Reject (two-sided) null hypothesis at 5% size.

** Reject (two-sided) null hypothesis at 10% size.

*** Reject (one-sided) null hypothesis at 10% size.

results for the case when the inflation rate enters in the log form, $\ln(1 + \pi_{it})$ (Specification A), for the IV version of the log specification (Specification B), and for the spline approximation of a non-linear relationship in the log function without IVs (Specification C). Figures 14.2–14.4 illustrate the results, with the "growth" label referring to Specification A, the "IVs" label to Specification B and the "Spline" label to Specification C.

Robust standard errors are reported in each case. In all specifications one rejects the null hypothesis that the individual and time effects are jointly zero. The direction and shape of the inflation effect in Table 14.1 is clear for Specifications A and B. A negative effect on the variable log $(1 + \pi)$ implies a non-linear negative relationship. For the spline, the results can be readily interpreted in terms of the implied inflation-growth profiles, in Figures 14.2–14.4. Here the splines are represented according to their various implied marginal effects with all other variables evaluated at appropriate sample means.

For the OECD group of countries, there exists a striking amount of consensus of the non-linear negative inflation effect, irrespective of the estimation technique and the specification of the inflation effect in the estimated equation. Figure 14.2 shows that the marginal negative effect of inflation on growth is greatest at low levels of inflation – in particular at levels below around 10%. Moreover, in each of the separate splines, the inflation effects are individually significant, at least at the 10% level, with one exception being the high inflation section of the spline function in the log specification. Instrumental variables estimation gives an almost identical result to those without instruments, suggesting little effect on the inflation rate coefficient of any endogeneity between inflation and growth.

When only APEC countries are considered, illustrated in Figure 14.3, further reductions in significance levels are witnessed, and the expected non-linear relationship is only somewhat evident in the logarithm specification. The only significant inflation effect comes with the IVs estimation, with a negative inflation-growth effect at all levels of the inflation rate. Here the

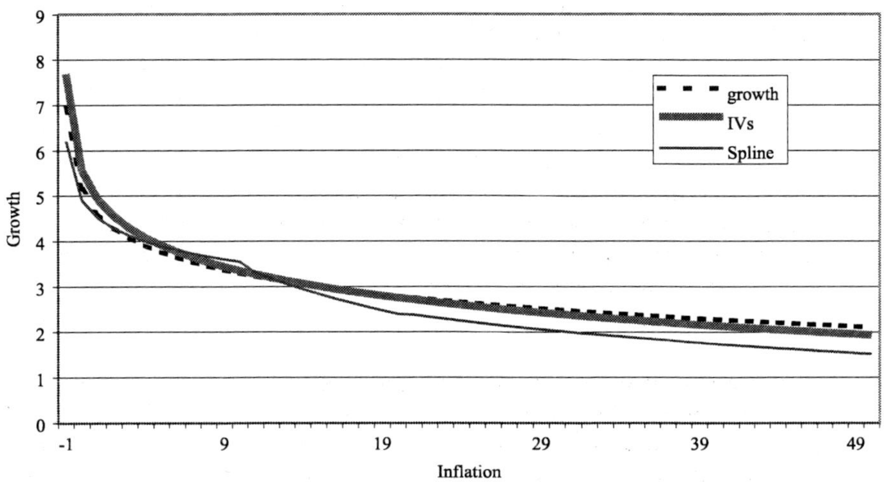

Figure 14.2 Inflation-growth relationship, OECD, inflation < 50%.

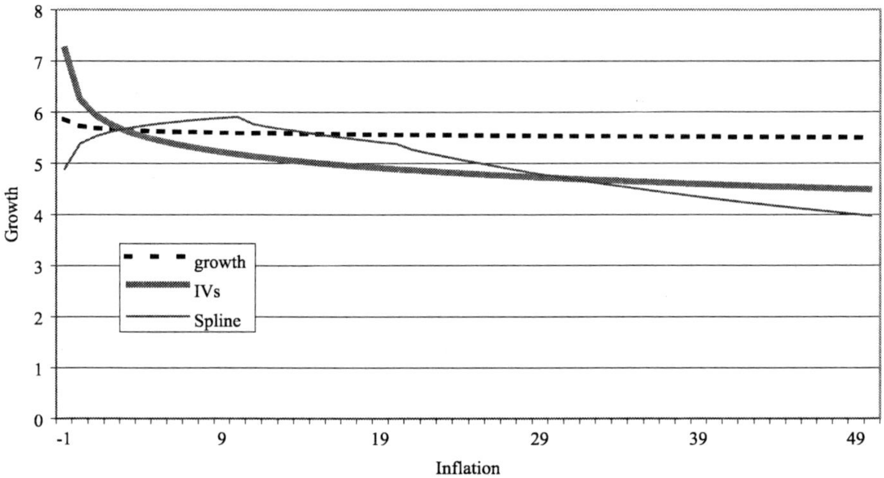

Figure 14.3 Inflation-growth relationship, APEC, inflation < 50%.

coefficient is about half of that of the OECD inflation-growth effect. For the splines estimation, in Figure 14.3, there is a positive but insignificant effect at low levels of inflation. This insignificant effect is increasingly negative at levels of inflation in excess of 10%.

The full sample results in Table 14.1 show a lower significance level than the OECD results, for the inflation variables, in one case. This is for the spline results in the range of the lowest infaltion rates. It reflects the APEC positive but insignificant results in this range. Also, the full sample coefficient of the inflation effect in the IVs estimation is about halfway between the level of the OECD and APEC coefficients. These results can be summarized as saying that the OECD results show up in the entire sample, but with less robustness. The non-linearity still emerges in all three specifications, as shown in Figure 14.4, with it most pronounced in the logarithm specification.

Taken together, the results show the importance of separating out the OECD from the APEC countries, in the sense that the negative effect of the inflation rate is more robust and stronger in the separate OECD sample. However, instrumental variable estimation finds that the theoretically-predicted effect still is operative in the generally less financially-developed APEC group.

14.6 Discussion of results

14.6.1 Comparison

The results compare closely to those of Khan and Senhadji (2001), Judson and Orphanides (1999), and Ghosh and Phillips (1998). First, our use of the logarithm specification has support in Ghosh and Phillips (1998) who find

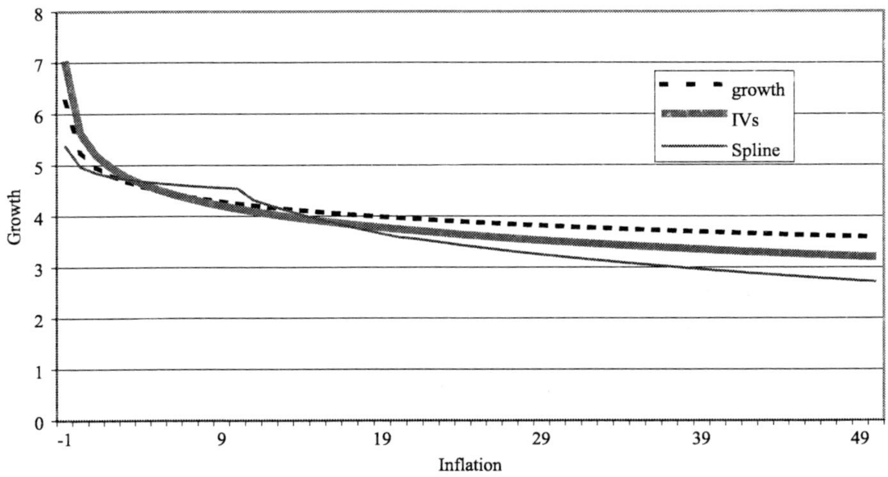

Figure 14.4 Inflation-growth relationship, full sample, inflation < 50%.

this specification to have the best fit in non-linear models, while finding that the alternative linear specification is biased. Second, all of these studies above find significant negative inflation-growth results for rates above their chosen threshold values, for all samples. Third, for rates of inflation below the threshold values, using splines and no instrumental variables, all three report a positive but insignificant effect of inflation on growth for non-OECD (or lower income) samples, and a negative inflation-growth effect for OECD (or high income, or developed) country sub-samples.

Khan and Senhadji (2001) find an optimal threshold value inflation rate for developing nations sample of 11% with a positive and insignificant inflation-growth effect for rates below the threshold, without using instrumental variables. This corresponds to our spline results in Figure 14.3, which show a somewhat positive but statistically insignificant effect of inflation for inflation rates 10% or below. Khan and Senhadji (2001) further find a significant negative effect for all inflation rates above one percent for developed countries, similar to both our non-instrumented and instrumented results in Figure 14.2. Judson and Orphanides (1999) use a 10% threshold value below which they find positive and insignificant effects for their non-OECD sub-samples, similar to our Figure 14.3 spline results. And for the OECD at inflation rates below the threshold, they find a negative insignificant inflation-growth value; this compares to our Figure 14.2 spline except that our results are significant.[11]

Ghosh and Phillips (1998) pick a two and a half percent inflation rate as the threshold value and find a positive inflation-growth effect for lower income sub-samples of countries, and a negative inflation-growth effect for an upper income sub-sample; again these non-instrumented results compare directly to our APEC and OECD log specification splines. When they use exchange rate and central bank independence instrumental variables, they report significant negative inflation-growth effects for their full sample (subsamples not reported); this compares to our negative IV effects in all log specifications.

14.6.2 Characterization

To interpret the results, first consider their characterization. Consider a comparison of any of the three alternative OECD log specifications in Figure 14.2 relative to the APEC IV log specification in Figure 14.3. The initial slope of the APEC profile, at the lowest inflation rate, is not as steep as the comparable OECD slope. And while both the APEC and OECD slopes show significant non-linearity, it can be seen that the slope of the APEC profile is flatter at all inflation rates. Thus the APEC profile is less non-linear and similar to a "pivoting up" of the OECD profile.

14.6.3 Interpretation

There are two dimensions of the credit model that aid in the interpretation of these results. First is the general extension of the cash-only model. To see this, consider an explanation 1) using the cash-only economy which is the special case of $a = 1$, and 2) the extended model of Section 14.2 with credit being produced. Calibrations in Gillman and Kejak (2002) show that the model with cash-only has a bigger inflation-growth effect but a substantially more linear one, unlike any of the profiles in Figure 14.2. When the inflation rate rises, in the cash-only model the magnitude of the interest elasticity rises slightly, while with the provision of credit in the model the magnitude of the interest elasticity of money rises much more quickly, making the inflation-growth effect increasingly much smaller, as in Figure 14.2. A simulated cash-only economy inflation-growth profile, as based on a calibration such as in Gillman and Kejak (2002), if superimposed on those profiles of Figure 14.2, would "cross" the other lines at moderately high levels of the inflation rate because the growth rate would fall too quickly relative to the evidence. In contrast the credit model simulation shows a profile that tapers out towards a zero inflation-growth effect, as in Figure 14.2.

Second, the use of the credit production model has the additional advantage in that the nature of financial development within the economy can be described, and the interest elasticity determined, by the credit technology parameters. This allows differences in such parameters to be used to potentially explain differences in the inflation-growth profiles between the OECD and APEC results. Figure 14.1, showing two inflation-growth profiles with a different degree of the diminishing returns parameter, γ, corresponds well to the differences found between the OECD and APEC profiles with IV. Since $\gamma = 1$ is the case of constant returns to scale, a smaller γ indicates a greater degree of diminishing returns. It is plausible that the less developed economies would have a greater degree of diminishing returns, which would suggest assigning a lower value of γ to APEC than to the OECD. Calibrations in Gillman and Kejak (2002) show that a smaller γ implies a higher level of the interest elasticity of money. So as the inflation rate rises from low levels, the initial decrease in growth would not be as severe. And as inflation continued to rise, the higher interest elasticity would make the profile for APEC have a flatter slope at all levels of the inflation rate, as in the IV estimation of Figure 14.3.

14.7 Conclusion

Our results confirm findings in the literature of a significant negative inflation-growth effect. Further our non-instrumented results replicate the insignificant positive inflation growth effect at low inflation rates for developing countries. Use of instrumental variables is not common in literature. Ghosh and Phillips (1998) report the use of IVs for one sample and find significant negative inflation-growth effects, but do not distinguish between regions. Our results suggest that the instrumental variables make a difference for the APEC but not the OECD sample. And these instrumented results show a negative inflation-growth effect at all levels of the inflation rate in all samples.

The results indicate interesting differences between regions that we interpret through the use of the endogenous growth human capital economy, with credit production explicitly modeled. With the advantage of the additional credit sector microfoundations, the paper presents a way to explain comprehensively the inflation-growth empirical evidence with a theoretical model. In particular, the inflation tax causes substitution to leisure at a decreasing rate as the inflation rate rises and the magnitude of the interest elasticity of money likewise rises. This causes a decreasing negative inflation-growth effect, at all levels of the inflation rate, and causes its highly non-linear inflation-growth profile. This is a human capital driven growth model, as in Lucas (1988b) and as used extensively in the macroeconomic literature, but the paper's contribution is to use it to generate and interpret the inflation-growth profile.

The theory is consistent with a positive realignment towards a higher capital to effective labor ratio as a result of inflation, what we consider to be a generalized Tobin effect. This occurs even while the growth rate goes down. Such realignment has found empirical support in Gillman and Nakov (2003), for the postwar US and UK; see also Ahmed and Rogers (2000) for additional long term US evidence in support of a Tobin effect. The growth evidence of this paper, given its theoretical model, makes it a complement to the Tobin evidence.

The model also attributes a significant role to the leisure substitution away from employment as a result of inflation. While there is no unemployment per se in the model, the change in employment makes this relation similar in some ways to a reverse long-run Phillips curve. Further, there is evidence that is consistent with this. Ireland (1999) finds that inflation and unemployment are cointegrated, while testing a Barro-Gordon hypothesis that unemployment causes inflation. However he presents no evidence on causality and so these results equally support the model here in which inflation (really an increase in the money supply growth rate) causes a decrease in employment. Further, Shadman-Mehta (2001) finds similar inflation and unemployment cointegration, and also presents evidence that inflation Granger causes unemployment. This study uses long historical series for the UK including Phillips's original sample sub-period. Parallel to the growth and Tobin- type evidence, the employment aspect of the model could be further investigated for example by using the theory to give the structural VAR in Shadman-Mehta (2001) even more structure, and by also studying other countries ideally within a panel.

Acknowledgements

Research assistance by László Konya, Rezida Zakirova, and Anton Nakov and comments by Michal Kejak, Myles Wallace and Toni Braun are kindly acknowledged, along with comments from the 17th European Economic Association Meetings, Venice, and the 10th International Panel Data Conference, Berlin. The first author is grateful to the Central European University for research funds.

Notes

* Gillman, Max, Mark Harris and László Mátyás (2004). 'Inflation and Growth: Explaining a Negative Effect', *Empirical Economics*, 29(1), 149–167.

1 However the Stockman (1981) model can produce a negative effect on inflation on the balanced-growth path for the special case of an "AK" production function; see also Haslag (1998) who uses a Stockman-related approach with growth effects.

2 In contrast the balanced-growth path return on capital is fixed at A in AK models, and inflation effects this return and the growth rate only through devices that somehow put capital under the cash-in-advance constraint, such as in Stockman (1981), Haslag (1998) and Dotsey and Sarte (2000); but then these have non-empirically consistent reverse-Tobin type effects whereby inflation causes substitution away from capital because inflation lowers its return directly.

3 Gillman and Yerokhin (2005) detail how this model is equivalent to an interpretation of an Beckerian household production economy with a production of exchange using the intermediate goods of money and credit; the exchange is itself also and intermediate good that is then combined with the goods output to yield the Beckerian household consumption good.

4 See Gillman and Otto (2002) for an empirical investigation of velocity as given by this model.

5 See Gillman and Yerokhin (2005) for a proof of the shopping-time/banking-time equivalence and for further discussion.

6 Details of the equilibrium conditions for this economy are found in Gillman and

Kejak (2002); existence and uniqueness of the equilibrium is proved in the case of no physical capital in Gillman et al. (1999).

7 See Gillman et al. (1999) for a human-capital only version of the model, which enables a closed-form solution, and details of how the inflation-growth effect turns positive only for rates of inflation above the level at which the magnitude of the interest elasticity equals one.

8 Long run evidence presented in Ahmed and Rogers (2000) supports a decrease in the real interest rate as a result of an increase in the inflation rate.

9 Extending the linear model, a quadratic form was also estimated whereby a squared term is included in π. Here $g(\pi_{it}) = \sum_{j=1}^{2} \beta_j \pi_{it}^j$ so that $g(\pi_{it})$ is a quadratic in the level of inflation. For this, the spline specification is $g(\pi_{it}) = \sum_{j=1}^{3} D_j \beta_j \pi_{it}$. The results did not improve upon the logarithmic specification and are not reported here but can be found in the working paper, Gillman et al. (2001).

10 As there were more missing values in these series, the IV versions generally have smaller sample size. Sargan-like tests for the appropriateness of such instruments are difficult to implement in fixed effects models, and are not reported for example in Ghosh and Phillips (1998) IV estimation (Table 5).

11 Khan and Senhadji (2001) note in their conclusions specifically that the inflation and output growth rates may be endogenous, so that non-instrumented results may entail biased estimate coefficients.

15 Granger causality of the inflation–growth mirror in accession countries

*Max Gillman and Anton Nakov**

Summary

The chapter presents a model in which the exogenous money supply causes changes in the inflation rate and the output growth rate. While inflation and growth rate changes occur simultaneously, the inflation acts as a tax on the return to human capital and in this sense induces the growth rate decrease. Shifts in the model's credit sector productivity cause shifts in the income velocity of money that can break the otherwise stable relationship between money, inflation, and output growth. Applied to two accession countries, Hungary and Poland, a VAR system is estimated for each that incorporates endogenously determined multiple structural breaks. Results indicate Granger causality positively from money to inflation and negatively from inflation to growth for both Hungary and Poland, as suggested by the model, although there is some feedback to money for Poland. Three structural breaks are found for each country that are linked to changes in velocity trends, and to the breaks found in the other country.

15.1 Introduction

Research has investigated both the cause of inflation in transition and the effect of inflation on output and its growth. For example Ross (2000) finds evidence of Granger causality from money to inflation in Slovenia; Nikolic (2000) finds a money-price link in Russia; Hernandez-Cata's (1999) regression analysis of 26 CEE and CIS countries finds that while price decontrol has a one-time effect on the price level, monetary expansion has been the fundamental determinant of inflation; and Sahay and Vegh (1995) find that the market economy relation, whereby money is the main factor in inflation, also applies to transition countries.[1] In terms of inflation and growth, in transitional countries inflation has been found to negatively affect output growth for inflation rates above a threshold rate (Christoffersen and Doyle, 2000), to relate negatively with output growth in four Asian transition economies (including China), and to relate negatively to output growth in 26 transition countries (Lougani and Sheets, 1995). Or as Wyplosz (2000) finds, '*inflation has been found to be incompatible with growth . . . and the choice of the exchange rate regime, another of the early controversies, appears as secondary to the adherence of a strict monetary policy*'.

This chapter contributes a VAR analysis of money, prices, and output, from which Granger causality is examined from money to inflation and from inflation to output growth in two accession countries, Hungary and Poland. The empirical investigation is based on an analytic model of money, inflation, and growth in which the income velocity of money is endogenously determined by the relative cost of money versus the cost of credit that is produced in a separate 'banking' sector. In the model, money supply increases cause inflation. Inflation lowers the return to human capital and decreases the growth rate. The empirical results find strong evidence of Granger causality from money to inflation and from inflation to growth for Hungary and for Poland as is suggested by the equilibrium balanced-growth path of the model. Polish results, however, additionally indicate some feedback to the money supply. Several structural breaks are found for both countries. These are explained by shifts in the income velocity of money that 'break' the otherwise stable relation between money, inflation and output growth.

Figures 15.1–15.4 present data which suggest a close relation between money, inflation and growth in four transition countries. During certain periods, the inflation data almost mirror the output growth data, a phenomenon we call the 'transition mirror'. The data are for the growth rate of the (CPI) price index, of the real GDP or the industrial production index, and of the money supply (all measured in one year percentage changes) for four EU accession countries. These are two 'first wave' countries, Hungary and Poland, and two 'second wave' countries, Romania and Bulgaria. These countries are chosen on the basis of having the longest IMF compiled data series within the *International Financial Statistics* (2002) on-line data-base;

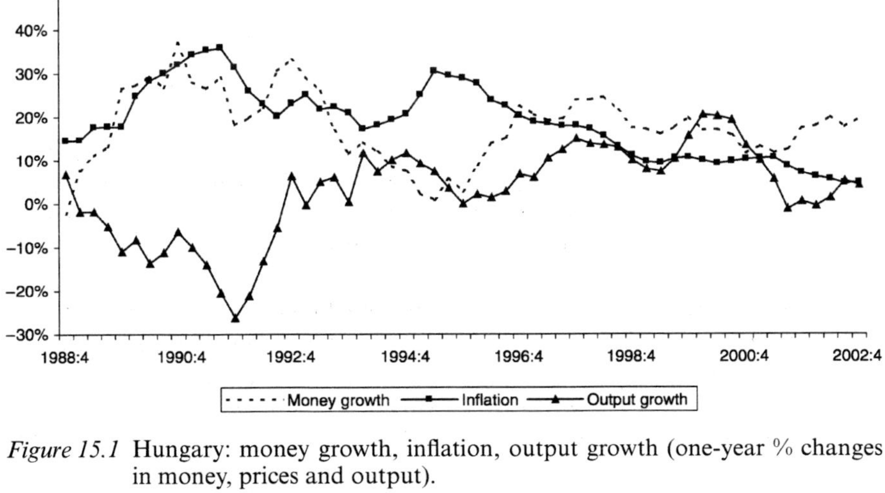

Figure 15.1 Hungary: money growth, inflation, output growth (one-year % changes in money, prices and output).

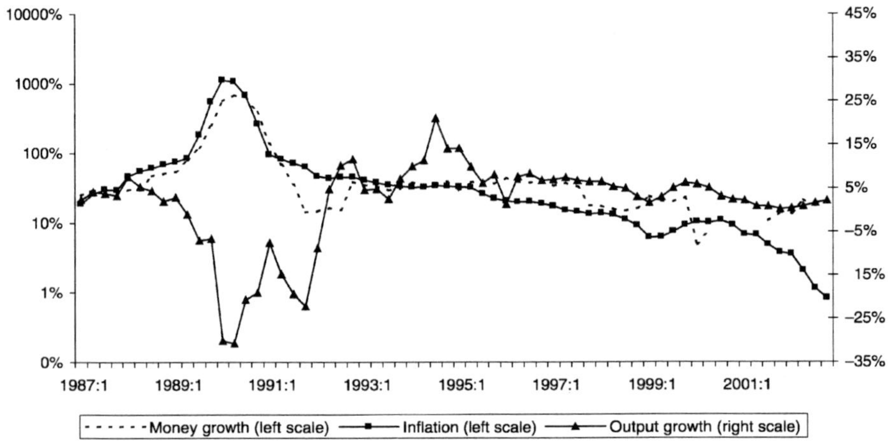

Figure 15.2 Poland: money growth, inflation, output growth.

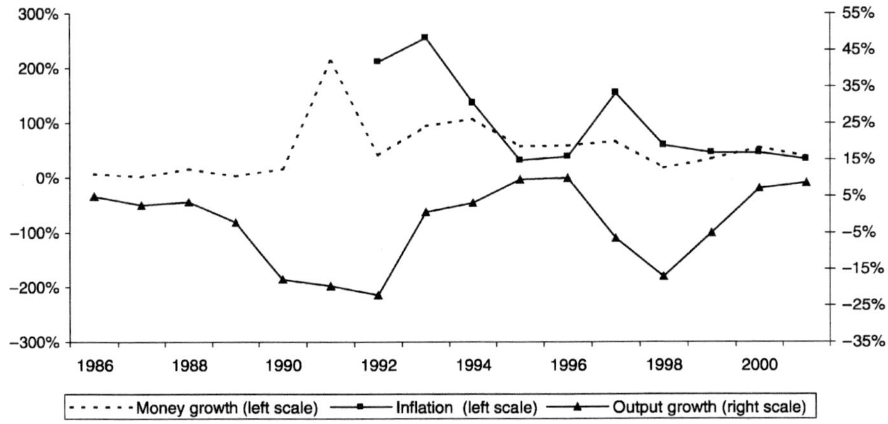

Figure 15.3 Romania: money growth, inflation, output growth.

quarterly data starting in 1987 are provided for Hungary and Poland, and annual data starting in 1986 for Romania and Bulgaria. In all four countries there is an association of high money growth with inflation. And there is a strong negative correlation between the inflation rate and the growth rate; for example, in Figure 15.1, Hungary shows this strikingly from 1988 to 1998.

Romania and Bulgaria cannot be tested econometrically because of the paucity of quarterly data. However, some fifteen years of quarterly data exist for Hungary and Poland. Regression analysis, including Granger causality testing, for transition economies requires an important allowance for 'structural breaks' that might affect the relationships among variables; otherwise the regression results can be misleading when assuming parameter constancy over time. In particular, ignoring significant breaks affects both the coefficient

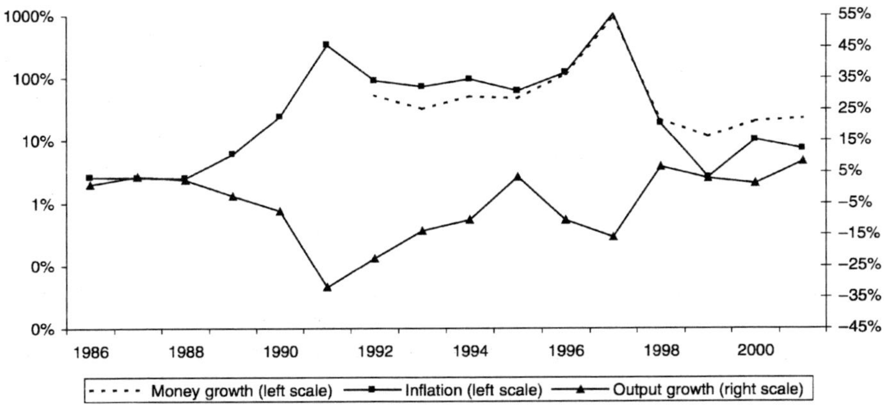

Figure 15.4 Bulgaria: money growth, inflation, output growth.

estimates and the estimated standard errors, which leads to invalid inference due to model misspecification. To establish the nature of Granger causality in the systems for Hungary and Poland, as based on the monetary endogenous growth economy, we conduct a VAR analysis of money growth, inflation, and output growth. We incorporate endogenously determined multiple structural breaks, estimate the coefficients of the money growth-inflation and inflation-output growth links, and test these relationships for Granger causality. The results offer support for the model and suggest that monetary factors have influenced the course of inflation and growth during the transition stabilization period.

15.2 The model

The model is an endogenous growth monetary model with growth driven by Lucas type human capital accumulation (Lucas, 1988b), and money employed through a modified cash-in-advance (Lucas, 1980) transactions technology that includes credit as an exchange alternative. It is an extension of the Gillman and Kejak (2005b) economy, with two main differences. First physical capital is used in goods production, but not in human capital production as in Gillman and Kejak (2005b), to make human capital production of a simpler linear form as in Lucas (1988b). Second, credit is used not only for consumption, as in Gillman and Kejak (2005b), but also for investment. Here it is assumed that the same fraction of both consumption goods and investment goods are bought with credit, where the fraction is determined endogenously within the model in a way similar to Gillman and Kejak (2005b). This allows the income velocity of money to be expressed with a closed-form solution, while only the consumption velocity is solved as a closed-form solution in Gillman and Kejak (2005b). This extension is important because the income velocity of money plays an important role in explaining structural breaks found in the empirical evidence. Having a closed-form solution of income velocity allows us to explain the breaks with shifts in the parameters affecting velocity.

15.2.1 Consumer problem

Let the representative consumer's current period utility function be given by the log form:

$$u_t = \ln c_t + \alpha \ln x_t. \tag{1}$$

The consumer allocates time fractionally between working in the goods production sector, l_t, working to produce human capital, l_{ht}, working to produce credit, l_{dt} (we will call this 'banking time') and spending time in leisure, x_t. The allocation of time constraint is:

$$1 = l_t + l_{ht} + l_{dt} + x_t. \tag{2}$$

The consumer accumulates physical capital k_t and rents it to the goods producer, earning a real rental income of $r_t k_t$. Along with the real wage income from effective labour of $w_t l_t h_t$, where h_t is the human capital stock, the consumer spends the income on consumption of goods c_t, on physical capital investment $\dot{k}_t + \delta_k k_t$, and on money stock investment, denoted in nominal terms by $\dot{M}_t$, or in real terms by $\dot{M}_t / P_t$ with P_t denoting the price of the consumption good. A real lump sum transfer from the government adds to the consumer's income, this being the inflation tax proceeds as denoted by V_t / P_t. In real terms we can define $m_t \equiv M_t / P_t$ and $v_t \equiv V_t / P_t$, and can define the inflation rate as $\pi_t = \dot{P}_t / P_t$, and then write $\dot{M}_t / P_t = \dot{m}_t + \pi_t m_t$. This makes the income constraint equal to:

$$r_t k_t + w_t l_t h_t + v_t - c_t - \dot{k}_t - \delta_k k_t - \dot{m}_t - \pi_t m_t = 0. \tag{3}$$

The consumer accumulates human capital, net of the depreciation $\delta_h h_t$, with a function that is linear in the effective time spent in human capital investment, $l_{ht} h_t$. Given the shift parameter $A_h > 0$, and $\delta_h \in [0, 1]$,

$$\dot{h}_t = (1 - \delta_h) h_t + A_h l_{ht} h_t. \tag{4}$$

And the consumer buys the total output, $y_t = c_t + \dot{k}_t + \delta_k k_t$, using either money or credit. The real credit purchases, denoted by d_t, plus the real money purchases m_t, sum to give the total output:

$$m_t + d_t = y_t. \tag{5}$$

The credit is produced by the consumer using the following technology

$$d_t = A_{dt}(l_{dt}h_t)^{\gamma} y_t^{1-\gamma}. \tag{6}$$

This means for example that as the economy progresses along the balanced growth path, with human capital and output growing at the same rate, an increase in the share of goods bought with credit, that is of d_t/y_t, requires an increase in the labour time l_{dt} allocated to credit production. This increase in the share occurs with diminishing returns to labour time, which implies an upward sloping marginal cost curve in producing the share d_t/y_t. The diminishing returns parameter γ determines the convexity of the marginal cost curve, with $\gamma \in (0, 0.5)$ implying a conventional convex marginal cost that rises as the output share rises.

Defining the share of purchases made with money as $a_t \equiv m_t/y_t$, the 'Clower constraint' can be written as

$$m_t = a_t y_t. \tag{7}$$

Substituting Equations (6) and (7) into (5), the credit share is

$$(1 - a_t) = A_{dt}(l_{dt}h_t/y_t)^{\gamma}. \tag{8}$$

Solving for a_t from Equation (8) and substituting this into Equation (7) gives the revised Clower constraint of

$$m_t = [1 - A_{dt}(l_{dt}h_t/y_t)^{\gamma}]y_t. \tag{9}$$

This contains the credit technology. With this as an additional constraint on the optimization problem, like the Clower constraint in monetary economies, the consumer's choice of its banking time will yield a Baumol-type equalization of the marginal cost of money and of credit in equilibrium that in turn determines money demand and velocity (Baumol, 1952). Altogether the consumer's utility maximization is subject to the income (3), human capital (4), and exchange (9) constraints with respect to goods, leisure, goods labour time, human capital time, banking time, and money, human, and physical capital stock levels.[2]

15.2.2 Goods producer problem

The goods production technology is assumed to be constant returns to scale in effective labour and physical capital. With A_g a shift parameter and $\beta \in (0, 1)$,

$$y_t = A_g(l_t h_t)^{\beta}(k_t)^{1-\beta}. \tag{10}$$

The first-order conditions of the standard profit maximization problem give that

$$w_t = \beta A_g(l_t h_t)^{\beta-1}(k_t)^{1-\beta}, \tag{11}$$

$$r_t = (1-\beta)A_g(l_t h_t)^{\beta}(k_t)^{-\beta}. \tag{12}$$

15.2.3 Government money supply

The government supplies new money through lump sum transfers V_t to the consumer so that the money supply evolves as

$$\dot{M}_t = V_t. \tag{13}$$

This occurs at an assumed constant rate σ, where $\dot{M}_t/M_t = V_t/P_t = \sigma$.

15.2.4 Equilibrium

The consumer's problem can be expressed as a current period Hamiltonian, with maximization with respect to c_t, x_t, l_t, l_{dt}, m_t, k_t, h_t:

$$\begin{aligned} H = {} & e^{-\rho t}(\ln c_t + \alpha \ln x_t) \\ & + \lambda_t(r_t k_t + w_t l_t h_t + v_t - c_t - \dot{k}_t - \delta_k k_t - \dot{m}_t - \pi_t m_t) \\ & + \eta_t[A_h(1 - l_t - l_{dt} - x_t)h_t - \delta_h h_t - \dot{h}_t] \\ & + \mu_t\{m_t - [1 - A_{dt}\,(l_{dt}h_t/[A_g\,(l_t h_t)^{\beta}(k_t)^{1-\beta}])^{\gamma}]A_g(l_t h_t)^{\beta}(k_t)^{1-\beta}\} \end{aligned} \tag{14}$$

The equilibrium conditions can be expressed as a reduced set of equations along the balanced-growth path that describe a certain marginal rate of substitution between goods and leisure, an equalization of the return on human capital to the return on physical capital, a balanced-path growth rate denoted by g, an implicit Fisherian equation of the nominal interest rate, denoted by R_t, a closed-form solution for a_t, and the demand for money. These conditions respectively are:

$$\frac{x_t}{\alpha c_t} = \frac{1 + R_t[\gamma + a_t(1-\gamma)]}{w_t h_t} \tag{15}$$

$$\begin{aligned} -\frac{\dot{\mu}_t}{\mu_t} &= A_h(1 - x_t) - \delta_h \\ &= r_t\left\{1 - \frac{a_t R_t}{1 + R_t[\gamma + a_t(1-\gamma)]}\right\} - \delta_k = -\frac{\dot{\lambda}_t}{\lambda_t} \end{aligned} \tag{16}$$

$$\begin{aligned} g &= A_h(1 - x_t) - \delta_h - \rho \\ &= r_t\left\{1 - \frac{a_t R_t}{1 + R_t[\gamma + a_t(1-\gamma)]}\right\} - \delta_k - \rho \end{aligned} \tag{17}$$

$$R_t = r_t - \frac{a_t R_t r_t}{1 + R_t[\gamma + a_t(1 - \gamma)]} - \delta_k + \pi_t \tag{18}$$

$$m_t = [1 - A_d^{1/(1-\gamma)}(\gamma R_t / w_t)^{\gamma/(1-\gamma)}]y_t \tag{19}$$

$$a_t = 1 - A_d^{1/(1-\gamma)}(\gamma R_t / w_t)^{\gamma/(1-\gamma)} \tag{20}$$

From these conditions we can fully describe the economics of the model. First note that in the marginal rate of substitution Equation (15), if $a_t = 1$ so that it is a money-only economy, this rate is similar to a Stockman (1981) model extended with human capital. Then the shadow price of goods is 1 plus the nominal interest rate R_t for all purchases. With credit, the exchange cost is less than R_t in general, equal instead to a weighted average of money and credit exchange costs, or $R_t[\gamma + a_t(1 - \gamma)]$, which is also equivalent to $a_t R_t + (1 - a_t)\gamma R_t$. The average cost of money is R_t and that of credit is γR_t, and the weights are a_t and $(1 - a_t)$. When inflation goes up, the nominal interest rate rises, and while a_t falls (see Equation (20)) so that less money and more credit is used, the cost of goods relative to leisure still rises; the agent then substitutes from goods to leisure. This substitution towards leisure causes the return on human capital (Equation (16)) to fall and the growth rate to fall (Equation (17)). There is a subsidiary effect of an increased capital to effective labour ratio in both goods and human capital sectors, a Tobin (1965) effect (see Gillman and Nakov, 2003), until the real return on physical capital falls sufficiently to reestablish equilibrium with the return to human capital.[3] This reallocation of inputs mitigates the fall in the growth rate because of inflation, but is a second-order effect that leaves the growth rate still lower as a result of inflation.

Note that the nominal interest rate R_t is affected by the Stockman (1981) result whereby investment as well as consumption is purchased by money, as shown in the cash in advance constraint. The difference here from Stockman is that only the endogenous fraction a_t of investment is subject to this. This makes the real return to capital contain the inflation tax, and with $a_t = 1$ the exact Stockman result ensues, that $R_t = \frac{r_t}{1 + R_t} - \delta_k + \pi_t$. Therefore the equilibrium more generally with $a_t \leq 1$ represents an extension of Stockman.

Inflation lowers the growth rate by inducing a lower rate of return to capital.[4] This creates the main link between inflation and growth. The inflation also increases the income velocity of money, y_t/m_t, as seen in Equation (19). Other exogenous factors can also cause a shift in velocity. This is the focus of Gillman and Kejak (2004) who explain changes in the trends in velocity of various US monetary aggregates on the basis of changes in inflation, and in particular changes in the productivity of banking as a result of deregulation. Here bank deregulation is captured by an increase in the productivity parameter A_{dt}. The steady relation between money, inflation, and output found in the money demand Equation (19), which might be estimated in a VAR, can be broken with a sudden shift in A_{dt}.

15.3 Data and empirical methodology

We use quarterly data for Poland from 1986:1 to 2002:4 (68 obs.) and Hungary from 1987:4 to 2002:4 (61 obs.) from the *International Financial Statistics* (2002), IMF. Table 15.1 describes the data.

Formal testing of the relationships among the variables described in the introduction and backed by our theoretical model takes the following steps. First, we check the order of integration of the series to determine which of them may enter into stable relationships. In these tests we allow for the possibility of structural breaks as opposed to a stochastic trend in the series. Next, we test for cointegration among the I(1) variables using Johansen's maximum likelihood procedure (Johansen and Juselius, 1990). In the absence of cointegration among the I(1) variables, we estimate stationary VAR models with the log-differenced series, allowing for multiple structural breaks in the relationships. We test for Granger-causality (Granger, 1969), show impulse-responses and comment on the variance decompositions.

15.4 Empirical results

We begin the analysis by examining the univariate statistical properties of the series. We start by applying two standard unit root tests: the Augmented Dickey and Fuller (1979), and the Phillips and Perron (1988), also known as the ADF t and Phillips Z_t tests, respectively. These tests have as null hypothesis that of non-stationarity and the critical values are provided by MacKinnon (1991). As the column labeled 'Standard ADF' of Table 15.2 shows, on the basis of the conventional ADF test, it appears that the levels of prices and output in Hungary and of output in Poland are I(2) because their first differences appear to have unit roots. Likewise, judging by the standard Phillips Z_t test, money and prices in Poland seem to display I(2) behaviour.

Recent literature has argued that economic time series are unlikely to have such highly non-stationary behaviour. Since Perron (1989), a number of studies have emphasized that rather than possessing a unit root many economic time series may be 'broken-trend stationary'. Perron (1989) showed through a Monte-Carlo experiment that if the magnitude of a discreet shift in the series

Table 15.1 Data series

Variable	*Notation*	*Definition*	*IFS series code*
Money	m	National Currency	9.434 . . . ZF . . .
Prices	p	Consumer Price Index (1995 = 100)	9.464 . . . ZF . . .
Output	y	Industrial Production or GDP Volume (both 1995 = 100)	9.466 . . . ZF . . .

Notes
The output series for Poland is obtained by splicing Industrial Production, which is available only through 1995, with GDP Volume (IFS code 96499B . . . ZF . . .). We apply 'Census X12' additive seasonal adjustment to the level series.

Table 15.2 Unit root tests

Variable	*ADF t*		*Phillips Z_t*	*Order of integration*
	Standard	*With break*		
Hungary				
Money	1.60	−3.34	2.53	I(1)
Money growth	−7.02**	−8.27**	−7.07**	I(0)
Prices	−2.23	−2.87	−3.36	I(1)
Inflation	−2.87	−5.51*	−4.50**	I(0)
Output	−2.12	−4.60	−1.14	I(1)
Output growth	−3.45	−8.55**	−5.92**	I(0)
Poland				
Money	−1.44	−5.50*	−0.85	I(1)
Money growth	−3.93*	−6.12**	−3.41	I(0)
Prices	−1.46	−9.25**	−0.68	I(1)
Inflation	−4.72**	−8.32**	−3.22	I(0)
Output	−2.25	−7.99**	−1.31	I(1)
Output growth	−2.51	−8.63**	−6.41**	I(0)

Notes
*(**) denotes significance at 5%(1%). The 5%(1%) MacKinnon (1991) critical values for the standard ADF *t* and Phillips Z_t tests including constant and trend are −3.49(−4.12). The 5%(1%) Zivot and Andrews (1992) critical values for the ADF test with break in the level and the trend are −5.08(−5.57). The reported ADF *t* statistics are for downward-t-chosen autoregressive lag length, while the Phillips Z_t tests use Bartlett kernel with Newey-West lag truncation.

is significant, standard unit root tests such as ADF *t* fail to reject the null of non-stationarity even if the series are stationary with a broken trend and *iid* disturbances.

Indeed, pre-testing our series with three standard tests for structural break – the Quandt–Andrews *SupF* test (Quandt, 1960; Andrews, 1993), and the *ExpF* and *AveF* tests of Andrews (1993) and Andrews and Ploberger (1994) using the *p*-values of Hansen (1997), we find strong evidence of discrete shifts in each of the series for both countries. In light of this finding, we repeat the ADF unit root test, this time allowing for a single structural break in the level and trend of each series. We follow the procedure of Zivot and Andrews (1992), estimating the breakpoint from the data, searching for the minimum ADF *t* statistic over all possible break dates. In the column labeled 'ADF with break', Table 2 juxtaposes the results of these tests to the conventional ones.

Notice that money growth, inflation and output growth in Hungary all test stationary when applying the ADF test with break, while the levels of money, prices and output for this country all test I(1).[5] These results for Hungary are confirmed by the Phillips Z_t test, which uses a non-parametric approach to controlling for serial correlation.

Interestingly, for Poland the ADF *t* test with break indicates that all series – levels and growth rates – are broken-trend stationary. However, this (which may be a result of the near-hyperinflation in Poland) is not confirmed by the Phillips Z_t test, which, like the standard ADF test, suggests that the levels are I(1), while the growth rates are stationary.

On the whole we conclude in the last column of Table 15.2 that while the level series are more likely to be non-stationary, the rate-of-change series are better described as containing discrete shifts rather than stochastic trends. In any case, we are interested in estimating the growth effects of inflation, and establishing stationarity of the growth rates was necessary for correct inference based on a VAR in first differences. Before we proceed with the estimation, following the standard methodology, we test for cointegration among the I(1) levels to see if we should include error-correction terms in the VAR system. Table 15.3 shows the results from these cointegration tests.

Using the Bayesian information criterion (BIC) as a model selection tool, we fail to find compelling evidence of cointegration among the levels of the three variables. Indeed, while for some of the richer lag specifications BIC indicates the presence of one cointegrating vector, in general the criterion is minimized with fewer lags and under the assumption of no cointegration. For example, among the models for Hungary in Table 15.3, the model with three lags, a quadratic trend in the data (notice the U-shape of output in Hungary) and no cointegration yields the minimum Bayesian information criterion.

Absence of cointegration is consistent with the notion of an unstable real-money/real income relationship during the transition. In fact, forcing cointegration among the levels of output, prices and money implies imposing a stationary velocity of money. The following Figure 15.5, which depicts the velocity series for Hungary and Poland (defined as output over real money, normalized into standard deviations from the mean), suggests that the latter is unlikely during the period of transition. Formal unit root tests confirm this conjecture: the ADF t and Phillips Z_t statistics for money velocity in Hungary are –0.92 and –0.67 respectively, while for Poland they are –2.37 and –2.25, pointing to non-stationarity in both cases.

Table 15.3 Cointegration ranks of the systems in levels

Data trend: *Coint. vector:*	*None no c, no trend*	*None c, no trend*	*Linear c, no trend*	*Linear c, trend*	*Quadratic c, trend*
	Number of cointegration relationships chosen by BIC				
Hungary					
3 lags	0	0	0	0	0*
4 lags	0	0	0	0	0
5 lags	1	1	1	0	0
Poland					
3 lags	0	0	0	0	0
4 lags	1	1	0	0	0*
5 lags	1	1	1	1	1

Note: (*) denotes the model which minimizes BIC among the listed models for each country.

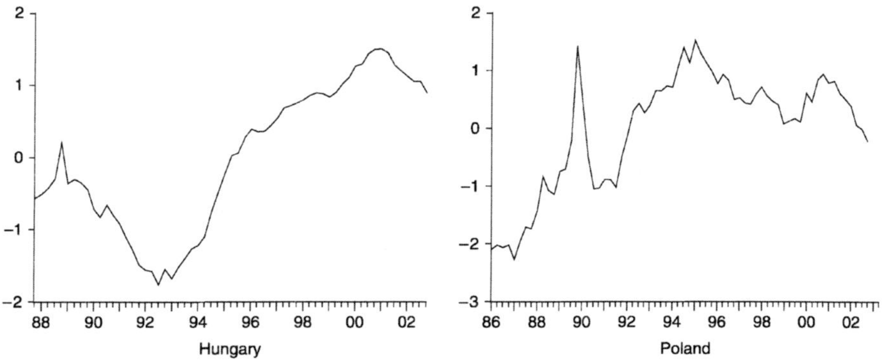

Figure 15.5 Non-stationary money velocity in Hungary and Poland (normalized data).

We therefore proceed under the more realistic assumption that the levels of money, prices and output are not cointegrated. This means that we can estimate VAR systems in the stationary growth rates of the three variables without including any error correction terms, a task to which we turn next.

Since the pioneering work of Chow (1960) and Quandt (1960), a number of economists have emphasized the possibility that structural changes may affect the relationships among key economic variables. Such structural breaks are very likely to occur during the transition from a centrally-planned to a market-oriented economy, and may reflect major changes in regulation, the break-up of the CMEA trading system, exchange rate regime shifts, or even changes in the methodology for compiling statistical data, to name a few. In order to account for this possibility, we allow for the existence of multiple structural breaks in the stationary VAR systems. At this point, we consider only partial breaks in the intercepts because allowing for breaks in the slope coefficients too would result in a substantial loss of degrees of freedom given the relatively small sample sizes and the fact that we want to allow many breaks. Nevertheless, our parsimonious approach turns out to provide significant gains in the descriptive power of the models and results in specifications which pass a large number of diagnostic tests.

In general, breaks in the VAR structure need not coincide in time with breaks in the individual series found at the stage of univariate unit root testing. To detect the break dates in the model's relationships, rather than specify them using *a priori* information, we first test each of the VAR equations, applying the full battery of tests developed in Bai and Perron (1998), with issues related to their practical application covered by Bai and Perron (2003). These tests include a *SupF*-type test against a fixed number of breaks, the so-called *double maximum tests, UDmax* and *WDmax*, against an unknown number of breaks, a procedure of global minimization of the sum of squared residuals and a sequential procedure using the $SupF(l + 1 \mid l)$ test, as well as the *repartition method* of Bai (1997).[6] To resolve potential discrepancies among the different procedures, we use the Bayesian information criterion for selecting the best model among the models with different numbers of breaks.

While the breaks found in one equation need not coincide with breaks in the other two, adding a potentially insignificant break in a VAR equation is safer than omitting a significant one. Therefore, in the next stage, we augment each equation of the VAR system by the break dummies found in all three equations. This preserves the symmetry of the system and the equivalence between efficient maximum-likelihood and least-squares estimation of an unrestricted VAR.

In this way, we find three structural breaks for Hungary: H-1993:2, H-1996:2 and H-2001:1, and three breaks for Poland: P-1989:3, P-1992:3 and P-1998:3. These are discussed at length and relative to the Section 15.2 model in the subsequent Section 15.5.

An alternative way to establish the breakpoints is to estimate them directly from the velocity series, which summarizes the *contemporaneous* relationship among the *levels* of money, prices and output. From this perspective, breaks in the *trend* of velocity correspond to breaks in the *contemporaneous* relationship among the *growth rates* of money, prices and output. Estimating the breaks in the trend of velocity and comparing them with the breaks estimated from the VARs we find surprisingly, that the breakpoints estimated from the velocity series and from the VAR coincide exactly for Hungary but differ for Poland. This is demonstrated in Figure 15.6, which plots the velocity series together with the break dates shown as vertical lines. In the case of Hungary, estimating the breaks from the VAR yields the same breakpoints as estimating them from a regression of the velocity series on a broken trend, which can be verified visually by the excellent fit of the broken-trend line with the actual velocity series. In the case of Poland, however, we find three breaks in the VAR but four in the velocity series. We attribute this difference to the near-hyperinflation experience in Poland, which makes the contemporaneous relationship (velocity) less stable than the dynamic relationship (captured by the VAR) in which lagged effects play an important role. Since our primary interest is to estimate the dynamic effects of inflation on growth, we choose to work with the VAR-established break dates for Poland.

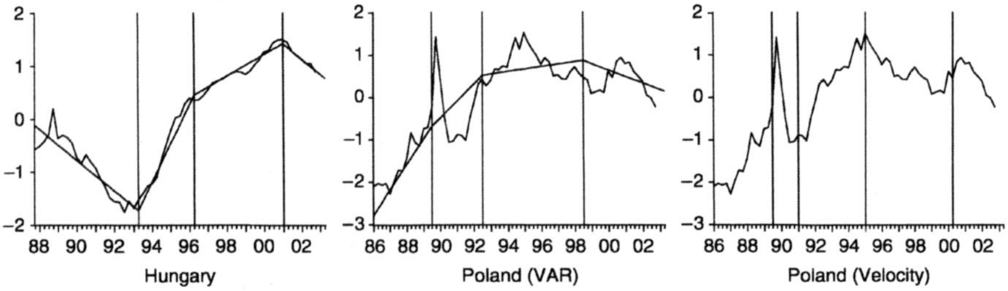

Figure 15.6 Breaks in the VAR vs breaks in velocity.

15.4.1 Granger causality results

Having determined the break dates T^k, where T^k is the time of the kth *structural break, we turn to the estimation of the two break-augmented VAR systems. In particular, we are interested in the cumulative effects and Granger causality of inflation in the output growth equation and of money growth in the inflation equation for each country. Formally, the two VARs that we estimate are:*

$$\begin{bmatrix} \Delta m_t \\ \Delta p_t \\ \Delta y_t \end{bmatrix} = \sum_{k=0}^{3} \begin{bmatrix} a_m^k \\ a_p^k \\ a_y^k \end{bmatrix} D_t^k + \sum_{q=1}^{4} \begin{bmatrix} \beta_{mm}^q & \beta_{mp}^q & \beta_{my}^q \\ \beta_{pm}^q & \beta_{pp}^q & \beta_{py}^q \\ \beta_{ym}^q & \beta_{yp}^q & \beta_{yy}^q \end{bmatrix} \begin{bmatrix} \Delta m_{t-q} \\ \Delta p_{t-q} \\ \Delta y_{t-q} \end{bmatrix} + \begin{bmatrix} \varepsilon_t^m \\ \varepsilon_t^p \\ \varepsilon_t^y \end{bmatrix}$$

where $D_t^0 = 1, \forall t$, gives the constant, and $D_t^k = \begin{cases} 1 & \text{if } t > T^k \\ 0 & \text{otherwise.} \end{cases}$

Except for the break dummies D_t^k, the above VAR model is standard in the empirical monetary economics literature, as described in Chapter 1 of Walsh (2003). Our tests for Granger causality are in the spirit of Sims (1972). However, because of the issue of non-stationarity, rather than estimating the VAR in levels like Sims (1972), we estimate it in the stationary growth rates like Eichenbaum and Singleton (1986). Our analysis is related also to Stock and Watson (1989) and Sims, Stock and Watson (1990) in that we study extensively the stochastic properties of the series to ensure that standard distribution theory can be used to interpret the Granger causality tests.

At the same time, by including multiple structural breaks in our VAR system, we relax the extreme assumption of full parameter constancy over time, made implicitly by other studies of the money-growth link in transition economies (Ross, 2000). In this, our approach is similar to Estrella and Fuhrer (2003) who apply Bai's (1997) test for multiple breaks to a single-equation policy reaction function model, and to Vilasuso (2000) who uses the procedure of Bai and Perron (1998) to establish Granger causality from detrended money to output in the US postwar experience.

We next present the results of the VAR estimation, together with Granger causality tests, in Tables 15.4, 15.5, and 15.6, and plot the dynamic impulse-responses in Figures 15.7 and 15.8. Tables 15.4 and 15.5 summarize the estimation results for the conventional VAR(4) systems for Hungary and Poland in terms of the cumulative coefficients of each endogenous variable in each equation, together with the probability values of the F tests for joint significance of the estimated coefficients on lags 1 to 4. Thus, for Hungary we find in Table 15.4 that inflation has a negative cumulative coefficient in the growth equation, estimated at –1.37. Since the p-value of the F test for joint significance of past inflation in the growth equation is well below 0.05, we discover that there is strong evidence of Granger causality running from inflation to growth. At the same time, money growth has a positive cumulative coefficient in the inflation equation, estimated at 0.14. In addition, the F test of joint

Table 15.4 VAR(4) estimates and Granger causality, Hungary

Equation	*Growth* (Δy_t) $i \equiv y$	*Inflation* (Δp_t) $i \equiv p$	*Money* (Δm_t) $i \equiv m$
$\Sigma_{q=1}^{4}(\beta_{iy}^{q})$-growth	−0.725**	0.062	−0.462
p-value of F-stat	(0.002)	(0.904)	(0.102)
$\Sigma_{q=1}^{4}(\beta_{ip}^{q})$-inflation	−1.371**	0.659**	−0.144
p-value of F-stat	(0.000)	(0.000)	(0.795)
$\Sigma_{q=1}^{4}(\beta_{im}^{q})$-money	0.104	0.139*	−0.402
p-value of F-stat	(0.470)	(0.028)	(0.071)
a_i^0	0.022	0.013	0.079**
p-value of t-stat	(0.223)	(0.147)	(0.000)
a_i^1 (1993:2)	0.077**	0.002	−0.038*
p-value of t-stat	(0.000)	(0.781)	(0.018)
a_i^2 (1996:2)	−0.009	−0.014*	0.038**
p-value of t-stat	(0.419)	(0.012)	(0.002)
a_i^3 (2001:1)	−0.053**	−0.003	−0.010
p-value of t-stat	(0.000)	(0.667)	(0.442)
R^2	0.736	0.799	0.502

Note:*(**) denotes significance at 5%(1%), respectively.

Table 15.5 VAR(4) estimates and Granger causality, Poland

Equation	*Growth* (Δy_t) $i \equiv y$	*Inflation* (Δp_t) $i \equiv p$	*Money* (Δm_t) $i \equiv m$
$\Sigma_{q=1}^{4}(\beta_{iy}^{q})$-growth	−0.886**	2.654**	1.429**
p-value of F-stat	(0.000)	(0.000)	(0.001)
$\Sigma_{q=1}^{4}(\beta_{ip}^{q})$-inflation	−0.112**	0.091**	0.330**
p-value of F-stat	(0.000)	(0.000)	(0.000)
$\Sigma_{q=1}^{4}(\beta_{im}^{q})$-money	−0.178	0.460**	0.387*
p-value of F-stat	(0.181)	(0.002)	(0.024)
a_i^0	0.043**	0.044	0.014
p-value of t-stat	(0.000)	(0.064)	(0.498)
a_i^1 (1989:3)	−0.039	0.235**	0.091*
p-value of t-stat	(0.067)	(0.000)	(0.048)
a_i^2 (1992:3)	0.050*	−0.316**	−0.109*
p-value of t-stat	(0.040)	(0.000)	(0.036)
a_i^3 (1998:3)	−0.035**	0.015	0.006
p-value of t-stat	(0.000)	(0.486)	(0.765)
R^2	0.780	0.906	0.888

Note: *(**) denotes significance at 5%(1%), respectively.

Table 15.6 VAR(q) Granger causality tests, q = 3,4,5

Null hypothesis		*VAR lag length in quarters*		
		[3]	*[4]*	*[5]*
Hungary				
Money Growth ↛ Inflation	F-statistic	3.659*	3.044*	1.027
	p-value	0.019	0.028	0.416
Inflation ↛ Growth	F-statistic	5.102**	6.797**	5.711**
	p-value	0.004	0.000	0.000
Growth and Inflation ↛ Money	F-statistic	0.924	1.063	1.273
	p-value	0.487	0.408	0.282
Poland				
Money Growth ↛ Inflation	F-statistic	5.781**	4.908**	2.044
	p-value	0.002	0.002	0.091
Inflation ↛ Growth	F-statistic	11.51**	11.91**	11.64**
	p-value	0.000	0.000	0.000
Growth and Inflation ↛ Money	F-statistic	12.99**	10.61**	8.855**
	p-value	0.000	0.000	0.000

Note: 'No Granger causality' is rejected at 5%(1%) when the p-value is less than 0.05 (0.01), respectively. BIC chooses VAR(3) for Hungary and VAR(4) for Poland.

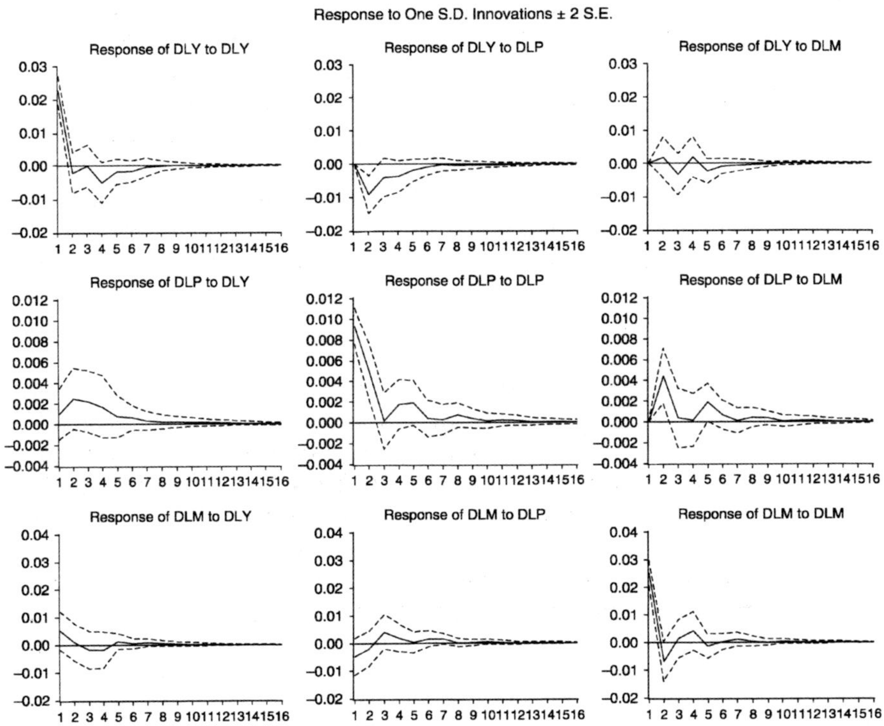

Figure 15.7 VAR impulse-responses: Hungary.

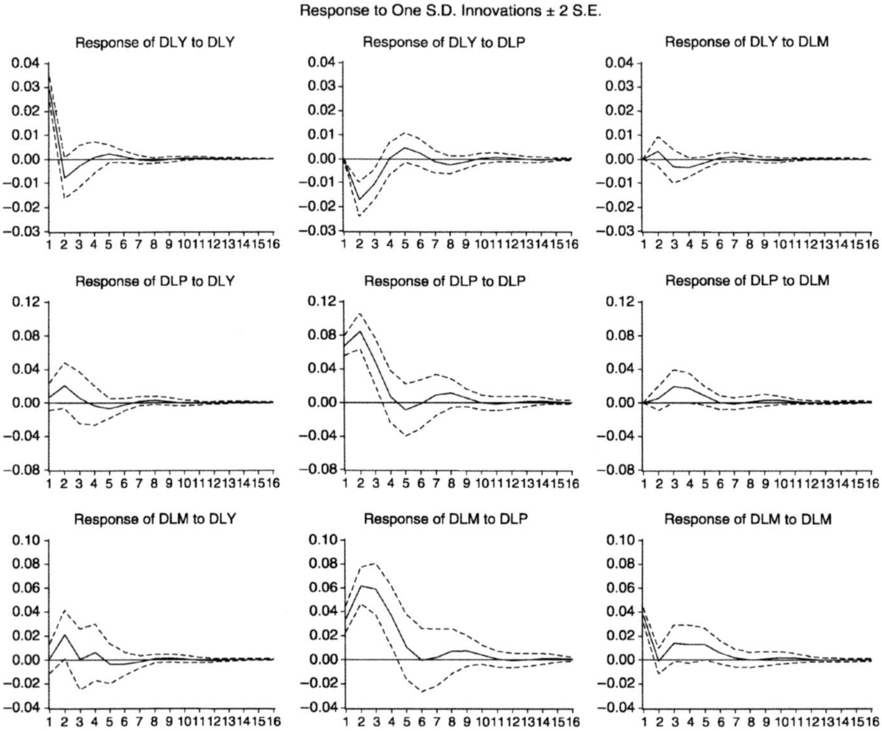

Figure 15.8 VAR impulse-responses: Poland.

significance of past money growth on inflation rejects Granger non-causality at the standard 5 percent level. On the other hand, neither past output growth, nor past inflation are significant at 5 percent in explaining money growth, supporting the hypothesis of exogeneity of the growth rate of money supply in the system including the three variables. Furthermore, we find no evidence that output growth Granger-causes inflation, or that money growth directly Granger-causes output growth in the Hungarian transition experience.

Turning to Poland, Table 15.5 shows that in this country, too, money growth Granger-causes inflation, with an estimated cumulative coefficient of 0.46 for the standard VAR(4). As in Hungary, inflation in Poland also affects output growth negatively, with an estimated cumulative coefficient of –0.11. However, in contrast to Hungary, in the case of Poland we reject money growth exogeneity in light of evidence of Granger causality running also from output growth and inflation to money growth, possibly reflecting the reaction of the monetary authority during the period of hyperinflation.

The above results are not very sensitive to changes in the VAR lag specification. For example, the estimated cumulative coefficient of inflation on growth in Hungary lies between –1.13 for VAR(3) and –1.57 for VAR(5) and

Table 15.6 shows that in each case the *F* test finds strong evidence of Granger causality from inflation to growth.

Likewise, the estimated cumulative coefficient of inflation on growth in Poland is in the range between –0.11 and –0.27 and Granger non-causality is rejected strongly with three and five lags as well. Note that our choice of lag length is supported formally by the Bayesian information criterion, which selects three lags in Hungary and four lags in Poland. Moreover, these parsimonious specifications pass a number of diagnostic tests such as (vector) Portmanteau, error autocorrelation, normality and heteroskedasticity tests.

15.4.2 Impulse responses and variance decomposition

Finally, in Figures 15.7 and 15.8 we show the dynamic impulse-responses of the VAR systems for Hungary and Poland, using the orthogonal Cholesky decomposition to identify the shocks. Since we have found that cross-correlation among the VAR residuals is quite small, the resulting impulse-responses are not sensitive to the ordering of the variables in the systems. The responses to a shock in any of the variables die out in less than four years, which is consistent with our conjecture of stationarity of the system. In particular, the negative response of growth to a single one-standard-deviation shock in inflation lasts for about 8–10 quarters in Hungary and Poland. Similarly, the positive response of inflation to a single one-standard-deviation shock in money growth dies out in about two years in both countries. Finally, observe in the third row that money growth essentially does not respond to either inflation or output growth shocks in Hungary but it does respond to inflation shocks in Poland.

In terms of variance decomposition, in Hungary a shock to money growth accounts for about 15 percent of the variation in inflation in four years' time, while an inflation innovation contributes up to 19 percent of the output growth variation over the same period. In Poland, the contribution of a money growth shock to inflation variation in four years' time is about 26 percent, while the share of variance in output growth due to a four-years old inflation innovation is about 33 percent.

To summarize, we find Granger causality with a positive effect running from the money growth rate to inflation, and Granger causality with a negative effect running from inflation to output growth in the transition experience of both Hungary and Poland. We take this econometric evidence as strong support for the existence of a positive link from money growth to inflation and a negative link from inflation to output growth, in line with the theoretical prediction of Section 15.2. We attribute the feedback from output to money and to inflation in Poland to the near-hyperinflation experience of this country.

15.5 Structural breaks in Hungary and Poland

The breaks reported in Section 15.4 are found to correspond to changes in the velocity trends. And surprisingly there are three similar events that happened in each country at different times. This gives a pairwise explanation with three events.

15.5.1 Hungary

Before detailing our explanation of the breaks consider the contrast between the velocity graphs in Figure 15.5 and 15.6 with the inflation graphs in Figures 15.1 and 15.2. Consider Hungary first. The inflation rate rose and then fell from 1988 to 1993 roughly similar to the rise and fall in velocity over the same period. In 1993 the inflation rate starting rising again, but only for some six quarters before resuming a permanent trend downwards. In contrast the velocity of money graph shows a rapid climb that continues right up until 2001. This upward trend shows a break to a less steep trend in 1996, but it remains a period of strong velocity increases until 2001. This is completely at odds with the movement of the inflation rate, which by itself would induce a downward trend in velocity. A candidate explanation from the Section 2 model is that the productivity of banking shifted upwards because of deregulation; this would cause velocity to increase. Indeed there were major financial sector deregulations that occurred in 1993 and in 1996.

A major bank refinancing of bad loans started in late 1992 and continued until 2000 with a cost of approximately 13 percent of GDP. The consolidation and restructuring of the bank sector took place in stages. This included 'cleaning' the portfolios of the banking sector, where in the second half of 1993 certain large state-owned firms had their bad debts taken off the books of banks in exchange for government bonds. A dramatic drop in non-performing loans as a percentage of total loans took place: from 30 percent in 1993 to 20 percent in 1994, and down to close to 10 percent in 1995, with gradual decreases in all but one year thereafter to below 5 percent by 2000. This ushered in a new era of creating acceptable capital adequacy ratios that enabled banks to move towards the international standards of a competitively functioning bank sector.

Another major event occurred at the end of 1995, the privatization of the bank sector. This began with the selling of six state-owned banks, with a 31 percent market share, to foreign banks. The largest Hungarian bank, the NSB with a 29 percent market share before privatization, was privatized through the stock exchange. State ownership continued to drop until by 1997 it was only 20 percent of the banking sector's capital. Szapary (2001) details these changes in the Hungarian banking sector.

The two Hungarian episodes of major bank deregulation each represent shifts upward in bank sector productivity, A_{dt} in the theoretical model, that cause upwards shifts in the velocity. Thus we explain the first two Hungarian shifts in H-1993:3 and H-1996:2 in this way.

A different radical change occurred in the Hungarian banking sector with the passage of a new Central Bank Act in July 2001. This was a reform of the Hungarian central bank, the National Bank of Hungary, via a new charter that instituted inflation rate targeting instead of the previous practice of exchange rate targeting. This aimed to reduce the variance of the inflation rate and to lower its level down towards the 0–2 percent international norm among central banks that target the inflation rate. A dramatically lower expected variance in the inflation rate is outside of the theoretical framework of the Section 15.2 model, which is deterministic. In a stylized way within the model, this lower variance can act as a negative shock to the productivity of the private bank sector in our model, in that banks would no longer play as large a role in allowing agents to avoid fluctuations in the inflation tax. The inflation rate did begin falling in 2001, but it was only a gradual fall, while the velocity abruptly began trending downwards in a way that cannot be explained only by the change in the average inflation rate. A dramatic shift down in the expected variance, acting as a decrease in the bank productivity shift factor, offers an explanation of this velocity shift, and thus we explain the shift H-2001:1 in this way.

15.5.2 Poland

Velocity versus the inflation trends in Poland were similar to those of Hungary with respect to the times at which the empirically identified structural breaks occurred, although as Figure 15.6 shows there are some differences related to the hyperinflation. At the end of 1989, the inflation rate peaked and began falling rapidly, and trended downwards mostly from then onwards. This would suggest that velocity would also fall rapidly and then trend downwards as based on an explanation using only the inflation rate. Velocity did initially fall as hyperinflation receded, but it then levelled off and began rising in 1991. As inflation continued steadily downwards in the 1992 to 1994 period, the velocity again acted in the opposite direction as expected from the inflation data alone, with a further steady shift upwards from 1992 to 1995. After that, velocity trended down as did the inflation rate, until the end of 1998. Then Poland experienced an initial increase in the inflation rate for almost two years, before inflation finally steadily moved down towards one percent. Velocity shifted up as did the inflation rate in 1999–2000 and then began a sharp downwards movement.

The divergences of velocity trends from the inflation rate path, near to the break periods of P-1989:3 and P-1992:3, is markedly similar to the experience in Hungary, near to the breaks of H-1993:2 and H-1996:2. The Section 15.2 model suggests that a candidate explanation for these divergences is shifts in the banking sector productivity parameter. And the following description supports the conclusion that the empirically identified shifts occur largely in line with banking sector deregulations.

On January 1 1989, Poland passed the Banking Act and the National Bank of Poland Act that separated from the central bank nine commercial banks, thereby creating the 'two-tier' model of banking. Also legislation was introduced in 1989 that allowed individuals, including foreigners, to form new banks as limited stock companies, with some 70 licences issued from 1989 to 1991. This deregulation continued with privatization of the Export Development Bank in October 1991, and with the nine state-owned commercial banks transformed into limited stock companies. These events effectuated a massive deregulation of banking that started in 1989.

Another banking act was passed in March 1992 that allowed for standard enforcement of capital adequacy and loss provisions. Also a programme with the IMF and World Bank was established for 'twinning' whereby Western banking methods were introduced into the Polish bank sector. In November 1992, the central bank required banks to provision fully against loans, and in March 1993 an Enterprise and Bank Restructuring Program was begun to recapitalize bad loans. This involved a one-time recapitalization of $520 million of the bank sector. Together these regulatory changes resulted in a recapitalization of the bad loans of the banking system, in a fashion similar to what happened in Hungary. Gray and Holle (1996) and Mondschean and Opiela (1997) provide extensive details of these two different types of Polish bank restructurings that began in 1989 and 1992.

August 1997 brought a new central bank independence act, the National Bank of Poland Act, that established inflation rate targeting, or 'price stability', as its main objective. In November 1998 the complimentary Public Finances Act was passed that prohibits funding of the public sector by the central bank. Initially this could be considered as acting as a decrease in the expected variance of the inflation rate that, in the terms of our model, might be described as a shift down in the productivity of banking in avoiding inflation tax. As with Hungary, this is how we explain the break here, but it is less clearly visible for Poland in that the new inflation targeting policy in Poland appears to have been less credible initially since the inflation rate rose at first. This makes it less discernible to what extent velocity may have risen by less and then fallen by more, as a result of the new policy, than could be readily explained by inflation changes alone.

15.5.3 Pairwise breaks in Hungary and Poland

To summarize:

1 The H-1993:3 and P-1992:3 breaks correspond to a massive refinancing of the bad loans in the state-owned banks. This involved restructuring and consolidation of the banks, and allowed the banks to go forward on a more internationally competitive basis after that point. This acted as

a shift up in the productivity of the banking sector that pressured velocity upwards even though inflation rates were increasing.

2 The H-1996:2 and P-1989:3 breaks correspond to major bank privatization laws. These also pressured velocity upwards because of a shift upwards in bank productivity.

3 The H-2001:1 and P-1998:3 breaks correspond to new national bank acts in which inflation targeting was adopted by law. This can be thought of as bringing about a significant change in the expected variance and mean of the inflation rate. Such a reduction in inflation uncertainty can act like a shift down in the banks productivity in producing exchange credit, or other instruments that can be used to avoid the inflation tax, since the value of this avoidance becomes lower as the variance of inflation falls.

15.6 Discussion

Two points are especially worth discussing further. One issue is whether the model is appropriate for analysing periods of hyperinflation, and a second is whether other factors unrelated to credit sector productivity may be the cause of the structural shifts found in the empirical results. The Cagan (1956) model of money explains hyperinflation as part of a stable money demand function. Since it is not derived from a dynamic general equilibrium model, we cannot really say if it is a long-run or short-run model. But we can see that others have found this model a reasonable description of long-run stable money behaviour. For example Mark and Sul (2003) provide strong evidence of a stable Cagan (1956) money demand for an international panel dataset in which they find a cointegrated money demand function with an income elasticity of 1.08 and a semi-interest elasticity of –0.02.

The model presented here provides a general equilibrium version of a model that is similar to the Cagan (1956) model. In particular, as Gillman and Kejak (2002) show through calibration of a closely related model, as the nominal interest rate rises the magnitude of the interest elasticity rises nearly in proportion to it. The calibrated semi-interest elasticity is nearly constant, depending on the specifics of the calibration. One difference relative to the Cagan (1956) model concerns the paradox, pointed out by Cagan (1956) and Lucas (2000): Cagan (1956) finds a seigniorage-revenue maximizing rate of inflation at $R^* = -1/b$, where b is the estimated constant semi-interest elasticity, while the hyperinflation rates actually observed were clearly above this level.

The paradox is offered a resolution by Marcet and Nicolini (2003). They assume a Cagan-type model of money demand, rationalized by an overlapping generations economy, but suggest a learning process whereby agents can shift their expectations from an adaptive process that is a simple average of past inflation rates to one that more fully understands the onset of a hyperinflation. This 'tracking' model weighs the most recent inflation rates most heavily, with the result that the seigniorage path continues to rise slightly even as the inflation rate rises exponentially. Such a gradually rising seigniorage is also found in Eckstein and Leiderman (1992), in their Sidrauski (1967b)-based explanation of Israeli seigniorage.

In the model presented here, the magnitude of the interest elasticity of money starts at zero and rises steadily as the inflation rate rises. But it does not reach one in magnitude, the revenue maximizing point, until very high levels, typically hyperinflation levels depending on the calibration. Thus the model of this paper, like Marcet and Nicolini (2003), does explain a stable money process during hyperinflation, *when the hyperinflation is expected.* And like Eckstein and Leiderman (1992), it is consistent with a seigniorage that approaches a levelling off as the inflation rate rises, even up to hyperinflation rates of inflation. However, it does not explain unexpected surges in inflation.

The paper is potentially able to explain the full Polish experience given that the hyperinflation was expected, and this is possible given the budget deficits being experienced at the time. However the result that Granger causality evidence was also found from output growth and inflation to money for Poland indicates some feedback that may have been a result of the hyperinflation. In particular, if some of the hyperinflation experience were not fully anticipated, possible Phillips curve effects may arise initially that can conceivably lead to such feedback. For example in Poland there may have been an initially delayed shift in the 'tracking' expectations regime that Marcet and Nicolini (2003) describe.

It may also be possible that the breaks in velocity were caused by other factors than shifts in the productivity of the finance sector, A_d. For example, keeping in mind the typical sources of shocks found in the real business cycle literature, the total productivity factor of goods output A_g may have been a source of structural breaks, or even the productivity factor for the human capital production sector, A_h. To consider what effects these may have had consider the equilibrium conditions of the model.

Equation (20) gives the solution for the inverse of the income velocity of real money demand, which is defined by the three variables entering the VAR: the money stock, aggregate price and real output. Should there be a productivity shock through A_g, then inverse velocity is affected through the real wage and real interest rates of Equations (11) and (12). These enter Equation (20) through the ratio of the nominal interest rate to the real wage, R/w. Using the Fisher equation of interest rates, this ratio can be written as $(r + \pi)/w$.[7] A shift in A_d would effectively cancel out for the r/w part of this, leaving it to affect only π/w in the equation; and in this way a positive shock could decrease velocity ($1/a$). Such an effect is possible but difficult to uncover because of a lack of evidence on total factor productivity in Hungary and Poland.

A shock from the A_h factor for the productivity of human capital investment cannot easily be tracked in Equation (20), as it would enter only indirectly through the capital to effective labour ratios that enter Equations (11) and (12). And such evidence on A_h would seemingly be even more difficult to uncover than for A_g.

Thus while other factors may be behind the VAR structural breaks, corroborating evidence is presented for the shift being from the A_d factor. Further, other studies have found structural breaks that are not inconsistent with this explanation. Using similar Bai and Perron (1998) techniques as in this paper to find structural breaks in inflation series, Benati and Kapetanios (2003) for example find breaks in New Zealand in 1989, in Canada in 1991 and in the UK in 1991 which are interpreted as being due to those countries' adoption of inflation rate targeting. And such inflation rate targeting was described as being related to one of the structural breaks for both Hungary and Poland. Also with the same Bai and Perron (1998) techniques, Vilasuso (2000) examines a money and output VAR for the US from 1960 to 1997 and finds causality from money to output with two structural breaks, in 1984 and 1991. Benk, Gillman and Kejak (2005) identify business cycle shocks from the credit sector for US data in the 1983–85 and the 1990–92 periods that they associate with changes that followed new banking laws. In particular these were the Garn – St. Germain Act of 1982 that significantly deregulated the banking sector and the Financial Institutions Reform, Recovery and Enforcement Act of 1989 that was designed to clean up the bad loans of the savings and loans industry. A bank deregulation and bad loan clean-up are also associated with the two other structural breaks found for both Hungary and Poland in this paper.

15.7 Conclusion

The chapter presents a dynamic general equilibrium monetary economy with a closed form solution for the income velocity of real money demand. The economy includes the production of credit that enables the consumer to avoid inflation tax. This formulation makes money demand and its velocity depend on structural parameters of credit technology rather than utility parameters as in the Sidrauski (1967b) approach or the Lucas and Stokey (1987) approach, or transaction cost parameters in shopping time economies. Unlike these other approaches, here productivity shifts in the production of credit can shift the velocity of money demand. The model also shows how the money supply side of the money market affects the economy through its imposition of inflation tax. This implicit tax reduces the return on human capital and the economy's growth rate. And when there are changes on the money demand side, from changes in productivity in the credit sector, the effect of inflation tax on growth is altered.

Empirical models of the effect of money on inflation and of inflation on growth can as a result be affected by shifts in velocity. This appears to be reflected in the results presented here on structural breaks in the VAR systems. These breaks are explained in terms of shifts in velocity caused by major changes in banking laws.

With the structural breaks, evidence supports Granger causality from money growth to inflation and from inflation to output growth for both

Hungary and Poland, leading accession countries. Such evidence provides support for the endogenous growth model in which increases in the money supply growth rate cause the inflation rate to go up, which in turn acts as a tax that causes the output growth rate to fall. For Poland there is also Granger causality of output growth and of inflation on money, which is not explained by the model. A difference between the two countries is that Poland experienced hyperinflation while Hungary did not. Some of the hyperinflation in Poland may have been unanticipated and part of a feedback process between money and output.

The strong results provide support for a monetary-type explanation for part of the transitional recessions experienced in these countries. This may warrant investigating such possibilities in other transition countries, especially as the data become more available; data limitations currently constrain such a broader inquiry. The thesis is meant as an addition to the other hypotheses in the literature that attempt to explain the transitional recessions, as well as indicating the potential importance for developing countries to have low, stationary, inflation rates.

Acknowledgements

The authors are grateful to Szilard Benk, Tony Braun, Marek Dabrowski, Zsolt Darvas, Stanislaw Gomulka, Jacek Rostowski, Janos Vincze and Myles Wallace for comments, and to the Central European University for research grants.

Notes

* Gillman, Max, and Anton Nakov (2004). ‘Causality of the Inflation-Growth Mirror in Accession Countries’, *Economics of Transition*, 12(4), 653–682.

1 For an example within industrial countries, see Crowder (1998) for evidence of Granger causality from money to inflation for US data.

2 The credit technology is very similar to that in Li (2000), except that Li includes a mechanism designed to induce a liquidity effect. Note that while Li specifies that both labour and capital enter the production of the credit, capital is assumed to be fixed; this is analogous to the assumptions made here, with the fixed capital set equal to one.

3 Rapach (2003) finds evidence of a long-run reduction in the real interest rate as caused by inflation in each of 14 industrial countries.

4 This type of model and its negative effect of inflation on growth is supported empirically by Gillman, Harris and Matyas (2004).

5 Even though the ADF test statistics ‘with break’ are uniformly smaller (more negative) than the standard ones by construction, the critical values for the ADF test with break are substantially smaller than those for the standard ADF test.

6 The procedures, limiting distributions of the estimators and test statistics for all these tests are described in detail in Bai and Perron (1998).

7 The Fisher equation can be derived formally within the model by including nominal bonds, but this is suppressed to economize on notation.

Part IV

Monetary business cycles

16 Keynes's *Treatise*: aggregate price theory for modern analysis?*

Max Gillman†

Summary

The chapter explores the theory of the aggregate price, profit, and business fluctuations in Keynes's *Treatise* for its implications for modern macro-economic analysis. As in the *Treatise*, profits are first defined within a theory of the aggregate price level, as aggregate investment minus saving. Deriving aggregate total revenue and aggregate total cost from this price theory, the paper shows how to construct a version of the Keynesian cross diagram. The cross construction suggests an important qualification for fiscal policy, that total cost does not shift. Then, using a neoclassical definition of profit and the total-cost/total-revenue approach, the paper derives aggregate supply, and then adds aggregate demand in an integrated framework. Comparative statics of the AS-AD analysis and the central role of profit in the *Treatise* suggest that a focus on profit might be useful in identifying exogenous technology shocks of real business cycle theory.

16.1 The *Treatise*'s theory of the aggregate price

Keynes's (1930) *Treatise on Money* contains an interesting although flawed theory of the aggregate price. The flaw, relative to neoclassical theory, is its definition of profit. By showing the implications of the theory, both with and without the flaw, the analysis suggests a qualification to fiscal policy results, a clarification of AS-AD analysis, and a possible direction for current aggregate analysis. This gives a modern resonance for Keynes's price theory.

Keynes (1930) begins his *Treatise*'s analysis of the aggregate price level with Fisher's (1911) quantity theory. Use of this theory found precedence in Keynes's (1923) *Tract on Monetary Reform*. There he recommends a policy of price stability on the basis of the quantity theory, whereby anticipated velocity movements are offset by changes in money supply growth rates. However, as a theory of the aggregate price level, Keynes in the *Treastise* expresses dissatisfaction with the quantity theory.[1] He proceeds explicitly to replace its determination of the price with a Marshallian cost-of-production approach. This approach can also be thought of as a real, cost-based, rather than a nominal, money-based, approach. Keynes develops and rationalizes this theory in a dynamic context, linking fluctuations in the aggregate price level to the fluctuations in the aggregate business cycle. The main 'propagation mechanism', to borrow a real business cycle term that originates with Ragner Frisch, is changes in the exogenous, 'windfall' profit residual.

The *Treatise* posits that the aggregate price of output is the average cost of aggregate output plus the average aggregate 'windfall' profit. This can be viewed as an aggregation based on the Marshallian theory of the firm.[2] And in fact, besides applying it to the aggregate, the only *prima facie* difference in the *Treatise*'s price theory from standard neoclassical price theory is the definition of profit. This definition follows an involved discussion of profit in the *Treatise*, that is defended against critics in the *General Theory*.[3] In particular, aggregate 'windfall' profits are defined to equal aggregate investment minus savings, and per unit 'windfall' profit is the aggregate profit normalized by output.[4] Within this definition, Keynes's concept of windfall profit might be viewed as the amount of earnings above the competitive return to capital. Keynes sometimes drops the term 'windfall' and uses just the term 'profit', and this convention will be used in this paper (with further discussion of profit below in section 16.6).[5]

Consistent with the price theory Keynes defines long-run equilibrium and how departures from it describe business cycle fluctuations. In long-run equilibrium, profit is zero when investment equals savings. In the short run, when investment demand exceeds savings supply profit is positive and so output expands. When savings supply exceeds investment demand profit is negative and so output contracts.[6] This theory is developed as a business cycle description that is consistent with the *Treatise*'s theory of the aggregate price.[7] Formally the *Treatise*'s price theory can be stated as the following. With P denoting the aggregate price level, y denoting real aggregate output, I denoting nominal aggregate investment, S denoting nominal aggregate savings, and AC denoting the average cost of aggregate output,

$$P = AC + [(I - S)/y].^{8} \tag{1}$$

At the long-run equilibrium, $P = AC$. During departures from this, there is a mark-up from positive profit with $I > S$, and a mark-down from negative profit with $I < S$, giving a procyclic aggregate price. Thus the Marshallian, market-clearing, scarcity rent from demand in the short run here takes the form of investment in excess of savings.[9]

The next section shows that the *Treatise*'s price theory forms a basis for one way to construct and interpret the so-called 'Keynesian cross'. Standard fiscal policy results within the cross reconstruction, as developed in section 16.3, require the assumption that the total cost schedule does not shift when total revenue does shift. Then the chapter replaces the *Treatise*'s definition of profit with the Marshallian definition in section 16.4 and again it is necessary to assume no total cost shift in order to get standard fiscal policy results. The

Marshallian version is consistent with the representative agent, neo-classical, theory of aggregate supply and demand that underlies modern real business cycle theory, as shown in section 16.5. In turn this suggests that the role of profit in the *Treatise* may be a valuable way to analyse cyclic shocks to productivity, as discussed in section 16.6. The last section 16.7 qualifies the conclusions and speculates in a *Treatise* motivated way about identifying shocks to business cycles.

16.2 Construction of a Keynesian cross

Darity and Young (1995) discuss generations of the Keynesian 45 degree diagram, with the name 'Keynesian cross' attributed to Fusfeld (1985). A version of the cross, perhaps most similar to Bishop (1948),[10] can be constructed from equation (1) in combination with other assumptions. Consider simply multiplying the price equation through by real output y. The product of the price of output and the quantity of real output is an aggregate version of total revenues (TR), or nominal output, and equation (1) gives this as

$$TR \equiv Py = (AC)y + (I - S). \tag{1}$$

Now consider adding an accounting proposition in which the total firm revenues Py, or 'proceeds', are defined as equal to nominal consumption C plus investment:[11]

$$TR \equiv Py = C + I. \tag{2}$$

Equations (1) and (2) imply that $C + I = Py = (AC)y + I - S$. Solving for total costs (TC),

$$TC \equiv (AC)y = C + S. \tag{3}$$

In sum, assuming that aggregate total revenues (TR) are given as in equation (2), and combining this with the *Treatise*'s price theory of equation (1), implies the aggregate total cost formula of equation (3).

A cross diagram can be constructed from the aggregate total revenue and cost equations with additional assumptions. On the nature of C and I, the *General Theory* has been widely interpreted as letting C be a line with a slope positive but less than one in magnitude, and with a positive vertical-axis intercept. This will be assumed here for C and investment I will be assumed to be independent of y, as is typical for the cross diagrams. Then the aggregate total revenue line of $C + I$ is also a line with a slope positive but less than one, and with a positive vertical-axis intercept.

On the nature of total cost, assume that this cost reflects the long run. Taking the *Treatise*'s case of a long run with zero profit as in classical theory, the horizontal, coinciding, marginal and average cost curves are plausible choices for this representation. And these imply a simple upward-sloping total cost line. More precisely, to go from the production function of the representative firm to an aggregate linear total cost curve requires particular assumptions not only about production but also about factor markets. A constant returns to scale production function in capital and labour, and no adjustment cost to adding capital or labor, gives an individual firm a flat marginal and average cost schedule, assuming factor prices are given as a constant. But in aggregate, factor supplies tend to be limited. Thus an important assumption for the linearity of the total cost curve is that factors remain in relatively unlimited supply around the neighbourhood of the equilibrium. This is not innocuous but can be taken as a qualified assumption for now (section 16.5 relaxes this assumption). Then, aggregating the firm's cost under unlimited factor supply conditions, the total cost curve indeed is a straight, upward-sloping line, out of the origin. To get a 45 degree line, the aggregate price is assumed equal to one. More formally, the aggregate real output can be described as the aggregate consumption basket, where this basket is the numeraire good. With CRS, constant factor prices, and $P = 1$, the constant slope of the total cost curve is one: $[(Wl + Rk)/y] = Py/y = 1$, where Wl and Rk denote the nominal aggregate costs of labour and capital.

The resulting standard-looking cross diagram is shown in Figure 16.1. The difference is that here the cross lines are interpreted as aggregate total cost

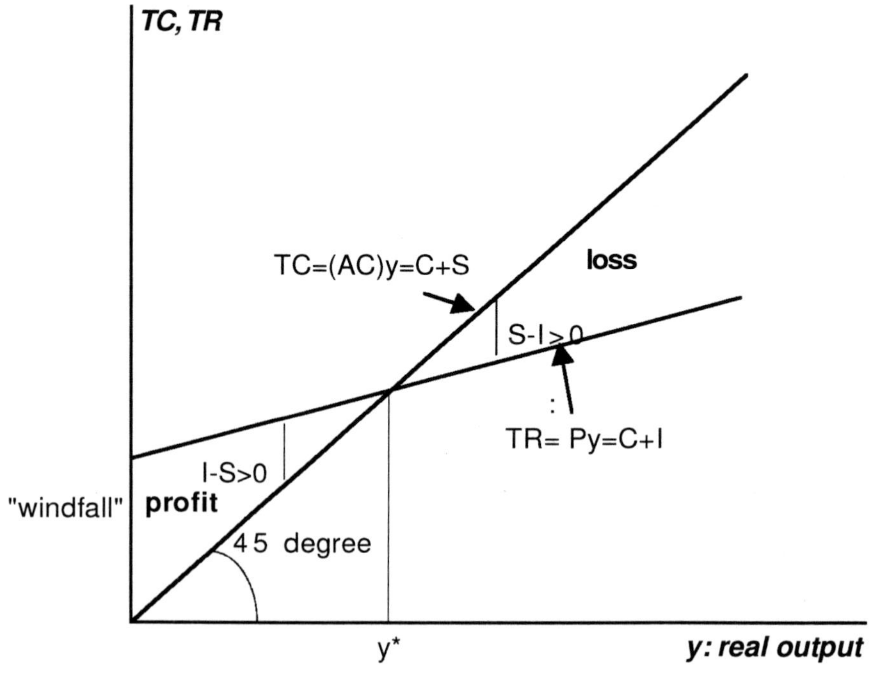

Figure 16.1 Total cost and total revenue construction of a Keynesian cross.

and total revenue. Further, the relationship between these schedules is consistent with the relationship between the aggregate total cost and total revenue equations that are derived from the equation (1). Because of the additional *General Theory*-type assumptions for total revenue, and the CRS and factor supply assumptions for total cost, the total cost line cuts the total revenue line from below.[12]

Examining Figure 16.1, the question of equilibrium immediately arises. At the intersection, *Treatise*-defined profit of $I - S$ is zero since at that point $TR = TC$. Is it correct to interpret this as the equilibrium? Through equations and discussion the *Treatise* argues specifically that when $I = S$ the economy is at its long run equilibrium. This suggests the same concept for the crossing point of Figure 16.1. This means that when the economy is not at the crossing point, it is in 'disequilibrium', or on some short run transition part to the long run equilibrium, as in the *Treatise*. The cross diagram and equation (1) in particular can mutually support such an explanation of the dynamics of the contraction and expansion of output, based on exogenous-type shocks to profit. When $I > S$, the aggregate price P is higher than in the long run equilibrium. And aggregate profit is, by definition, positive and above that of the long run equilibrium. The *Treatise* argues that the incentive motive of firms turns the profit into the force that pushes output upwards. And this profit is simply a market outcome that was not anticipated a priori. In this way it acts as an exogenous factor relative to the firm that in aggregate acts to force the economy back towards its long run equilibrium. It is an equilibrium process similar in ways to the transition to the balanced growth path in neoclassical growth theory, whereby high marginal products of capital induce an increase in capital stock.[13]

Moving along both total cost and total revenue lines in Figure 16.1, when starting to the left of the crossing point, the profits begin to decrease as output expands and I becomes closer in magnitude to S. The output increase causes the economy to move towards the intersection of TC and TR, thereby creating a type of dynamic equilibrium, or disequilibrium, adjustment. When $S > I$, the aggregate price is below it's long run equilibrium. The economy's output is to the left of the intersection, total cost exceeds total revenue, and profit is negative. By the same reasoning, the *Treatise* argues that this creates an incentive for firms to exit the market or reduce output while staying in the market. The unanticipated losses again create an exogenous type of effect that causes output to decrease. As output contracts, the economy symmetrically moves towards the intersection of TC and TR as in a dynamic equilibrium adjustment.

Put differently, not only can the *Treatise*'s theory of the aggregate price be used to construct the cross-type diagram of Figure 16.1, but also this diagram can be used to construct a *Treatise*-type theory of an equilibrium business cycle. This suggests an internal consistency. It also presents a way in which the profit acts as an exogenous 'propagation mechanism' at the firm level that causes a disequilibrium adjustment or transition to the long run aggregate equilibrium, as an interpretation of the *Treatise*'s theory of business fluctuations. This marks quite a cohesive theory so far.

16.3 A qualification about fiscal policy from this interpretation

The *Treatise*'s postulate of how investment can be different from savings in a closed economy model as part of a disequilibrium was taken up by contemporaries of Keynes in building the blocks of the IS-LM framework. Hicks (1950) creates an accounting identity between S and I that still preserves a way in which cyclic investment can fall short of savings. Hicks posits that there is long-term investment that is not designed to yield profit in the current business cycle and that fills the so-called savings-investment gap. With A denoting some type of 'autonomous', long-run, investment, and I' denoting shorter-term investment, Hicks considers the equation:

$$S = I' + A = I. \tag{4}$$

Such a definition, of $S - I' \equiv A$, is not exactly the same as defining the gap between savings and investment as losses. But it may not be entirely inconsistent with a profit/loss definition if the argument is that long-run investment of savings can yield a loss in a downturn (for example, high fixed costs), a gain in the upturn, and no profit over the competitive long run.[14]

However consider the changes, to my interpretation of the theory of the *Treatise*, that this approach makes when it is framed within the constructed cross diagram of Figure 16.1. If $S = I' + A = I$ and $Py = C + I$, then $Py = C + I' + A$, and we have the ability to shift up the total revenue line in figure 16.1 by increasing autonomous investment. However, the effect of an increase on total costs from an increase in A must also be considered. If it is assumed *ad hoc* that total costs do not shift per unit of output, then the total revenue curve shifts up along the stationary total cost curve. The total-revenue/total-cost construction of equations (1) to (4), plus the assumption that total costs do not change when A increases, allows for the fiscal policy results that output increases if the government increases long term A. Setting $A \equiv G$, letting G denote government expenditure, keeping G independent of y, and suppressing the total-revenue/total-cost concepts, gives a version of the cross diagram that is usually found in modern textbooks, starting as early as Samuelson (1951). The total revenue line might be called the income line, and the total cost might be called just the 45 degree line, or the words 'aggregate demand' and 'aggregate supply' might be used. Regardless, an increase in government spending causes output to increase, as in the standard Keynesian cross analysis of fiscal policy.

Generally, if the government increases long-term investment in physical or human capital, for example a new highway system or education system, the taxes must be raised to finance this. Barring lump sum taxes and imposing Ricardian equivalence of debt into future taxes, the cost of production must rise because of increased taxes on exchange, output, and/or labour and capital inputs. This would cause the total cost curve to shift (or pivot) up for a given level of output. For example, initially let $TC = C + S$ and $TR = C + I$. Then increase TR by $\bar{G}$, so that $TR = C + I + \bar{G}$. Also let this government spending be financed by taxes that add to the total factor cost of production by an equal amount $\bar{G}$. Then $TC = C + S = rPk + wPl + \bar{G}$ and the average cost, TC/y, becomes $1 + \bar{G}/y$ as the TC line pivots up. Bishop (1948) shows how such a balanced budget experiment implies no change in output.[15]

In a general equilibrium with rational expectations, no shift up in the total cost curve would appear very difficult to maintain. The cross reconstruction clarifies that its fiscal policy result, that of an increase in output from an increase in government spending, rests on no shift in the cost of production. That total cost does not shift up when deriving the standard fiscal policy result is an important qualification raised by the cross reconstruction.

There may be other ways to justify the assumption of no cost schedule shift. It might be said that there exists excess saving that has already been incurred as part of total cost, but has not been turned into investment, which is a part of total revenue. For example, if the private banking system collapses, saving already allocated to financial intermediation sector cannot be easily processed into intertemporal investment. And if the government can somehow act as the intermediary of this unallocated saving in place of the private intermediaries, then the investment schedule may shift up while the saving schedule remains fixed. Some might suggest that this is the case that occurred during the Great Depression. It is true that internalizing a bank contagion externality through the establishment of federal deposit insurance may involve little cost. But long-term government programmes like re-capitalization of banks during a prolonged banking crisis, 'public works' infrastructure construction, unemployment insurance, or even a war that results in opening up markets all have significant costs.

Accepting that government spending replaces the profit definition of I-S, and accepting that this spending does not shift up in the cost curve, the analysis becomes different from that of the *Treatise*. Before the model was of profit and loss, of disequilibrium readjustment along the total cost and total revenue lines, and of reestablishment of an equilibrium price with no extra profit, all within the private sector. Now the model becomes that increased government spending can shift up the total revenue line, move the equilibrium to a new position along the total cost line, and raise output, with the profit-induced dynamic adjustment within a business cycle no longer a part of the model. This also results in a jump in the analysis from positing temporary losses that coincide with savings in excess of investment in a downturn, to finding that an increase in output can result through long-term government spending at any time.

The qualification that total cost does not shift up in the fiscal policy exercise with the cross is a qualification that also can be viewed as applying to the IS-LM analysis, despite having discarded the direct link to the total-cost/total-revenue framework. To see this, consider construction of the standard IS-LM analysis, starting from equations (2) and (4). Denote Py as nominal income Y instead of as total revenue (TR), so that $Y \equiv Py = C + I' + A$. Then an IS model can be constructed by letting R denote the interest rate, letting C be specified for example as $C = a + bR + cY$, with $b < 0$ and $c < 1$, and letting $I' = d + eR + fY$, with e < 0 and f = 0. The last restriction of $f = 0$ is consistent with the modern cross diagram in which I' does not depend on Y, and it guarantees a downward sloping IS curve under the assumption that S is dependent on income.[16] With $S = I' + A$ of equation (4) as the only other equation, S is not specified but typically is assumed to be a vertical curve that is independent of the interest rate, and dependent on Y. Then as Y exogenously increases, S shifts out, I does not shift, and a downward sloping IS curve is traced out in the plane of Y and R. For fiscal policy as in equation (4), an increase in A can be graphed in the capital market as a parallel shift out of the downward-sloping investment schedule I', with the horizontal-axis intercept rising by A. This causes a shift up in the IS curve and, with a standard LM curve, causes an increase in Y (see Figure 16.2).

Mathematically, computation of the multipliers for C and for I also shows that an increase in $A \equiv G$ causes an increase in output. But an examination of the multiplier suggests the interpretation of how costs are kept constant when G increases. With $I = d + eR$, an increase in G from 0 to $\bar{G}$ means that savings ($S = I + G$) rises in tandem by $\bar{G}$, that output ($Y = C + I + G$) initially rises in tandem by $\bar{G}$, and then that output rises again because C rises. Consider that solving for C from $Y = C + I + G$ implies that $C = [cI + cG + a + bR]/[1 - c]$. With the increase in G from 0 to $\bar{G}$, the consumption solution gives an extra $c/(1 - c)$ increase in C. The total increase in Y is then $\bar{G} + c\bar{G}/(1 - c) = \bar{G}/(1 - c)$, the standard IS multiplier. However the decomposition into the above two components can be interpreted as a result of two perfectly elastic

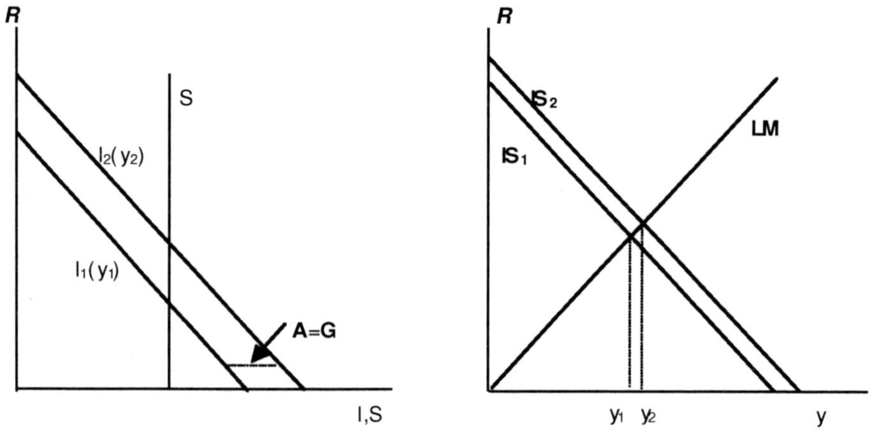

Figure 16.2 Investment, savings, government spending, and IS-LM.

supplies, of savings and output. If the downward-sloping demand for capital shifts out $\bar{G}$ by when government spending rises by $\bar{G}$, and the equilibrium investment rises by $\bar{G}$, then the savings curve appears to be a horizontal line. And if the demand for output shifts out by $\bar{G}/(1 - c)$ because the investment shifts by an increase of $\bar{G}$ and consumption by the increase $c\bar{G}/(1 - c)$, then apparently the output supply curve is a horizontal line. This implies that the multiplier increase in Y results from turning G amount of the unlimited savings at the given interest rate into more Y directly, and from the consumption out of income, along a flat marginal-cost-of-income line, that has initially increased by G. A horizontal S curve implies the notion of excess, unused, savings that is found in the literature. And the flat marginal cost of output schedule is as in the cross reconstruction. This bolsters the interpretation that the multiplier results because of the lack of scarcity in savings and income, in the sense of horizontal savings and output supply curves.[17] And a horizontal output schedule is a marginal/average cost schedule that remains fixed only if the cost schedules do not shift up when spending increases.

Now consider when there are additional costs in terms of higher taxes. Let the agent's income constraint find an increase in government spending but also an equal decrease in wages from higher taxes, as in standard general equilibrium neoclassical models. Starting from $Y = C + I$, $C = a + bR + cY$ and $I = d + eR + fY$, suppose that now that $Y' = C' + I + G - tY$, $C' = a + bR + c(Y - tY + G)$, $I' = d + eR + fY'$, and $G = tY$, where t is an income tax rate. Government spending is a wash; and $Y' = Y = C + I$. While such a 'wash' has been emphasized by 'Ricardians', and found by Bishop (1948), here the point is to view this as a cost increase in the IS-LM analysis that is comparable to a cost increase in the cross construction of section 16.2, both with the result that fiscal policy does not effect output. With distortionary taxes, output in general would fall.

In sum, adding equation (4) to the total revenue and total cost equations, as constructed from the *Treatise*'s price theory, replaces the profit notion implicit in equation (1) with autonomous investment. Further keeping total costs constant as autonomous investment rises allows conversion of the cross diagram of total revenue and total cost into a textbook-type cross in terms of fiscal policy results. And with equation (4) and no allowable cost schedule shifts, the IS model can give the same fiscal policy results when combined with a flat or upward-sloping LM schedule. To both the cross and IS-LM constructions, the qualification of no shift in the total cost schedule appears to be necessary for the standard increase in output from an increase in government spending. And both the price theory and the business cycle theory of the *Treatise* are lost in this revision of the total-cost/total-revenue framework.

16.4 Modification with a neoclassical definition of profit

The *Treatise*'s price theory is innovative with its use of ('windfall') profit to construct a cohesive theory of business fluctuations, and notable for its ability to form a basis for the modern cross model. However by equating ('windfall') profit with the difference between investment and saving, it departs from generally accepted neoclassical macroeconomic theory. Neoclassical theory lets investment exceed saving when a country borrows capital from abroad (Obstfeld and Rogoff 1996), which Keynes in the *Treatise* actually discusses,[18] but this borrowed capital is not equated with aggregate profit (although it may lead to an increase in the nation's permanent income stream).

Neoclassical, Marshallian, profit can be expressed in a form relative to equation (1). Looking at the marginal and average cost curves of a competitive firm, per unit profit at the equilibrium output is given by the marginal cost minus the average cost. And the competitive price as applied to an aggregate consumption basket, instead of equation (1), is:

$$P = AC + (MC - AC), \tag{5}$$

or just $P = MC$. Consider a reconstruction of a cross diagram from equation (5). Multiplying equation (5) through by y, and again setting $TR = C + I$, implies that $C + I = Py = (MC)y$, which is correct if $TR = C + I$. But unlike when the same operations were conducted with equation (1), this gives no information on total costs in general. And consider the classical long run. If $AC = MC$ and $P = AC$, then $TR \equiv C + I = (AC)y \equiv TC$. There is no implication that $TC = C + S$, although total cost can still be graphed as a 45 degree line by assuming constant returns to scale, unlimited factor supplies, and $P = 1$. And the business cycle explanation based on differences between I and S is no longer implied. However the Hicks-type equation of $S = I' + A = I$ still can be inserted so that $Y = C + I' + A$ and A has a role.

If the government or private sector increases long-run investment, then the purchases show up as increases in total revenue, or current dollar GDP. However without any equivalence of total costs with $C + S$, or any special role of savings in total cost, then total costs presumably shift up as well when A goes up. There is no description of S; it need not be horizontal or vertical. Any increase in Y by government action in general would require some conversion of scarce debt or tax revenue, either explicit current taxes, or increases in future taxes, or seigniorage, into something greater than it would otherwise yield. This could happen in general for example if the government taxing and spending activity more efficiently lowers transaction costs in markets than can the private sector.

16.5 Total revenue, total cost, and AS-AD analysis

Substituting in the neoclassical definition of profit, the *Treatise*'s theory of aggregate price becomes in a sense only a shell for modern macroeconomic analysis as based on a representative consumer/firm. But with this shell, it is possible to derive aggregate supply and to add onto this the derivation of aggregate demand, yielding an AS-AD analysis that is derived from a general equilibrium economy.[19] Consider the following simple example, in which there is no investment, but rather only the aggregate good y and leisure $100 - l$, where l is the time spent working. With s and d superscripts denoting supply and demand, utility is defined as $u = \ln y^d + \alpha \ln (100 - l^s)$. The production technology is $y^s = A(1^d)\gamma$, where $\gamma \varepsilon (0,1)$, and A is a technological shift parameter. The optimization problem can be divided into consumer and firm parts. With Π denoting nominal firm profit, W denoting the nominal wage and P denoting the nominal price of the aggregate good, the consumer maximizes u subject to $Py^d = \Pi + Wl^s$, with respect to the demand for output and the supply of labour. And the firm maximizes $\Pi = Py^s + Wl^d$ subject to the production technology, with respect to the supply of output and the demand for labour. The supply and demand for goods and labour can be solved as can the profit and the equilibrium wage.

On the firm side, and as in the *Treatise*, nominal profit can be expressed as total revenue minus total cost. The example implies that these are given as $TR \equiv Pt^s$ and $TC \equiv Wl^d$. In equilibrium, it can be found that the aggregate supply curve (AS) is $y^s = (A^{1/\gamma}\gamma P/W)^{\gamma/(1-\gamma)}$. Solving for P this can be written as $P = W(y^s)^{(1-\gamma)/\gamma}/(\gamma A^{1/\gamma})$. Deriving the same AS schedule is possible also by deriving the labour demand, total cost, and then the marginal cost. It can be found that $l^d = (y^s/A);^{1/\gamma}$, and so $TC \equiv Wl^d = W(y^s/A)^{1/\gamma}$. Then marginal cost is given by $MC \equiv \partial(TC)/\partial y^s = W(y^s)^{(1-\gamma)/\gamma}/\ (\gamma A^{1/\gamma})$, and this is the same AS function. Thus $P = MC$ is the AS function and the AS can be derived from the equilibrium total cost function as an application of Sheppard's lemma. Using the $P = MC$ equation, equilibrium TR can be expressed in terms of output: $TR \equiv Py^s = W(y^s)^{1/\gamma}/\ (\gamma A^{1/\gamma})$. Therefore along with the AS graph, the TC and TR can be graphed as functions of y^s, with each rising monotonically with y^s and the real profit per unit of goods constant at $(1 - \gamma)$.[20] Expressing each the AS, TC, and TR functions in real terms by dividing through by the nominal wage W, they are graphed in Figure 16.3, with the parameters are set at $\gamma = 0.5$ and $A = 1$. The relative price of real output in the AS function is $P/W \equiv 1/w$, the inverse of the real wage.

The equilibrium quantity of goods that are supplied and the equilibrium price can be determined with the addition of aggregate demand. While perhaps tempted to derive this from the total revenue function, just as aggregate supply was derived from the total cost function, this would be fallacious. Total revenue, a part of the profit function, is a simple function of aggregate supply. Instead aggregate demand, the marginal benefit function, can be derived from the equilibrium total benefit (*TB*) function by using the envelope theorem. The total benefit is the indirect utility normalized by the marginal utility of income. Indirect utility is given in the economy as $u^* = \ln [y^d]^* + \alpha \ln [100 - (l^s)^*]$, where * denotes equilibrium. Divide this by the equilibrium marginal utility of income, which is the value of the Lagrangian multiplier, here denoted by λ, of the above consumer maximization of u subject to the income constraint. Then the total benefit can be expressed as $TB \equiv u^*/\lambda$. By the envelope theorem the derivative of TB with respect to the

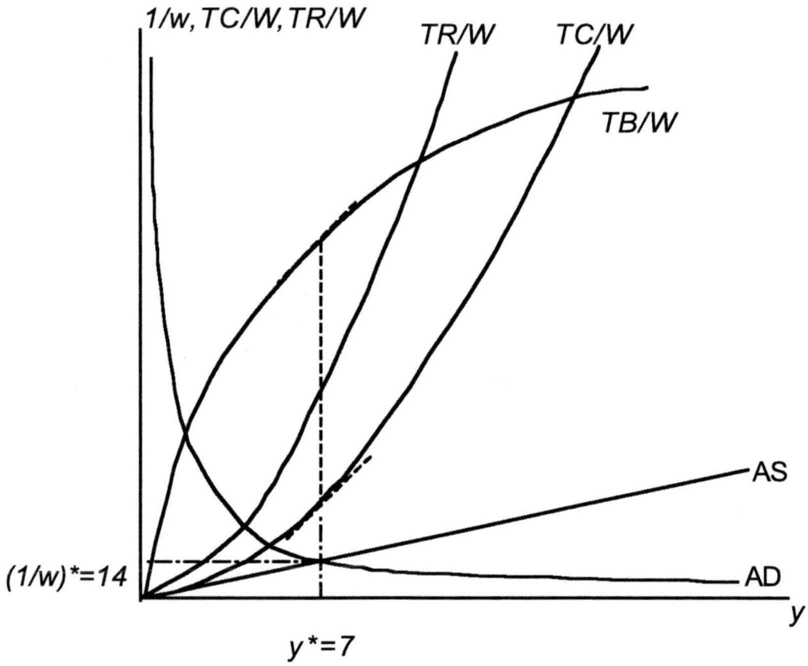

Figure 16.3 Derivation of AS-AD from TC and TB with $y = a = 0.5$, $A = 1$.

quantity of goods demanded is equal to the marginal utility divided by λ, which in turn can be defined as the marginal benefit (*MB*) function; or $\partial(TB)/\partial y^d = (\partial u^*/\partial y^d)/\lambda \equiv MB$. From the first-order conditions of the consumer problem, the marginal benefit equals the price of the consumption good $([\partial u^*/\partial y^d]/\lambda = P$ and this equation of $MB = P$ is the aggregate demand (AD) function. It can be shown in equilibrium that $y^d = (\Pi + 100W)/[P(1 + a)]$. Solving for P, the AD function can be expressed as $MB = P = (\Pi + 100W)/[y^d(1 + a)]$. In real terms the AD function is $P/W = 1/w = [(\Pi/P) + 100w]/[y^d(1 + a)]$ with $\gamma = a = 0.5$ and substituting in the equilibrium value of Π/P, which can be found to be $\Pi/P = A^2/(4w)$, the AD function can be written as $y^d = (2/3)[100w + A^2/(4w]$. This is also graphed in Figure 16.3. The intersection of the AS and AD occurs at the equilibrium quantity of goods where the slopes of the *TC* and *TB* curves are equal. This is also where $MB = MC$ and where by welfare theorems (not proved here) the distance between the *TB* and *TC* curves is at a maximum (not where *TR* and *TC* interest as in Figure 16.1).

Derivation of the AS and AD functions allows for comparative statics that represent the essence of the propagation mechanism of real business cycle: exogenous shocks to productivity. This can be illustrated by a change in the production shift parameter A in the example economy. Figure 16.4 shows, for $\gamma = a = 0.5$, that when the parameter A doubles in value from 1 to 2, the AS and AD curves both shift out. Supply pivots out because of higher

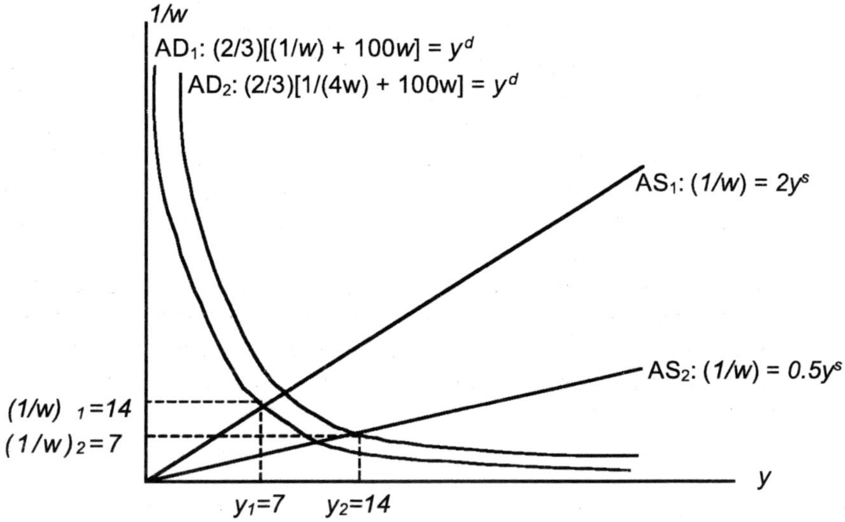

Figure 16.4 Comparative statics of an increase in productivity from A = 1 to A = 2.

productivity and demand pivots out because of higher income from a higher profit. Also the demand for labour shifts out because of higher productivity and the supply of labour pivots up because of the income effect of the higher profit. The equilibrium real wage rises, so that the relative price $1/w$ falls, as supply shifts out by more than demand. The fall in $1/w$ is consistent with a cyclic upturn and with a secular growth trend, described here by a supply that shifts out faster than demand (see Harberger 1998, for a focus on secularly falling cost).[21]

The simple economy can conceivably be expanded into a fuller model with physical capital and constant returns to scale, and even two-sectors with a market and non-market good. Then the 'price' against which the AS-AD curves is graphed can be the ratio of the real interest rate to the real wage, which is generally thought to be pro-cyclic, rather than only the inverse of the real wage as above. Exploring how the ratio of the real interest rate to the real wage moves over the business cycle in response to shocks that shift AS and AD would not only further the development of AS-AD analysis but may also enrich the real business cycle literature by bringing out the AS-AD analysis that is implicit in it.

16.6 Discussion and comparison of the analysis

The preceding sections argue that the *Treatise* is important historically for laying a foundation for modern cross and even IS-LM analysis. But further, the *Treatise's* theory of price and business cycles, based on exogenous profit shocks that change productivity, can be seen as a basis for modern AS-AD analysis. In particular, the AS-AD analysis and modified total-cost/total-revenue analysis presented here clearly lie at the basis of both the neoclassical growth and business cycle models, although they are rarely drawn out. And therefore the *Treatise's* message, that profit is a shock driving the business cycle, may be equally valid and worth investigating.

Such a constructive view of the *Treatise* stands a bit at odds with, for example, Patinkin (1976) and Dimand (1988). Patinkin (p. 25) writes that the *Treatise* is only of historical interest and does not much underlie the *GT*.[22] Dimand perhaps gives the *Treatise* more stature as being a force that is extended into the *GT*.[23] Both argue that a difference between the two works is that the marginal propensity to consume is implicitly assumed to be one in the *Treatise* and less than one in the *GT*. But putting aside how much the *Treatise* underlies the *GT*, the main difference of the perspective of these well-known writers from the point of view of this paper is the investigation of the 'fundamental equations' on price, and the implication arising from this. Patinkin and Dimand both consider Keynes's definition of profit a tautology,[24] while this paper points out the definition's inconsistency with neoclassical theory. And while it might be possible somehow to interpret Keynes's definition of I and S so that I-S is equivalent to MC-AC, that is an exercise not attempted here. And so this paper stands in contrast because it says that the price theory requires correction. With this correction, and with cost increases allowed when there is government spending, the standard fiscal policy results of the cross and IS-LM do not apply. But with the correction, the *Treatise's* theory points to a seemingly unjustly ignored aspect that may be crucial in advancing the neoclassical growth and business cycle theory: the potential role of profits as the exogenous shock that may underlie the productivity shock of neoclassical theory.

The *Treatise's* discussion of profit therefore in itself is of some interest, in particular because it shows a genesis of how Keynes distinguished between analysing the business cycle and determining how to induce changes in the business cycle. Keynes describes investment and profit as increasing for example when banks increase lending to firms with savings unchanged, causing the real interest rate to fall.[25] Keynes's business cycle theory is that when profit rises so does the aggregate price, and so does investment. This is arguably consistent with modern facts (see Den Haan, 2000, for evidence of a pro-cyclic aggregate price). The difficulty occurs when Keynes talks of an injection of money into the banking system that lowers the real interest rate, raises investment, increases 'windfall' profits, and increases output. As Patinkin (p. 47) points out, this type of analysis is found as early as Marshall's evidence before the Gold and Silver Commission of 1887. It is closely related to a Phillips-curve type increase in output, rather than a normal, or 'spontaneous' in Keynes's words, exogenous profit-shock induced type of business cycle. What alerts the reader to the incompatibility of this phenomenon with 'long-term' business cycle 'facts', is that here the real interest rate moves conter-cyclically rather than pro-cyclically as in the facts. Thus

Keynes's discussion of profits in the *Treatise* gives the readers a fine line that is easily crossed,[26] that of considering how to induce continually an increase in profits with a money supply or government spending increase, versus an understanding that profits can act as the exogenous shock that drive real business cycles. And here, it almost seems, is found the key to a mystery that Lucas (1976: 104) lamented: 'The inference that permanent inflation will therefore induce a permanent economic high is no doubt equally ancient, yet it is only recently that this notion has undergone the mysterious transformation from obvious fallacy to cornerstone of the theory of economic policy.'

Keynes's discussion of price, profit, and how the cycle might be propagated also relates to the price stability goals of modern central bankers (and of Keynes in the *Tract*). Patinkin argues that the *Treatise* implies that price stability results by letting the interest rate follow its natural path.[27] And indeed this is the same intuition behind today's widespread confirmation of the applicability of the Taylor (1993) rule, and the increasingly global use of inflation-rate targeting. While outside the scope of this paper, it can be shown that the central bank model of the Taylor rule can be interpreted so as to imply that price stability results if the central bank allows the real interest rate to rise and fall as does the output growth rate. This appears consistent with Patinkin's conclusion from the *Treatise*, and it suggests that Keynes's price and business cycle analysis has some consistency not only with the neoclassical real business cycle theory but also with the recent neo-classical policy prescriptions for the supply of money.

16.7 Conclusions and qualifications

The chapter contributes a *Treatise*-motivated construction of a cross analysis that frames the *Treatise*'s equilibrium theory of business cycles. The fiscal policy of this construction shows that income rises when government spending increases as in the standard cross analysis only if it is assumed that the total cost schedule does not pivot up. This qualification is argued also to be applicable to the *IS-LM* fiscal policy results. Then the chapter replaces the *Treatise*'s specification of profit with a Marshallian definition. While lacking any of the standard cross-type fiscal policy results, this allows derivation of AS-AD from an extended total-revenue/total-cost framework, and of comparative statics of a change in productivity as in a business cycle. The total cost/total revenue approach also suggests investigating whether profit constitutes the exogenous technology shock in cycle theory.

The chapter stands in contrast to the discussion of Keynes's concepts in Patinkin (1976: 8), who wants to 'try to avoid the temptation to translate them into modern concepts'. And while Patinkin at the same time argues that Keynes focuses ineffectively on the fundamental equations in the *Treatise*,[28] here an attempt to develop relevance for modern concepts is derived from a focus on Keynes's equation for the theory of aggregate price. Such a focus on the mathematical structure of a theory can be particularly worthwhile because it forces clarification of the issues to such a point that they can more easily be advanced. And here the advancement is that the *Treatise*'s theory when corrected seems to contain an insufficiently explored element of neoclassical analysis. In the neoclassical real business cycle theory there generally is no profit *per se* because of the constant-returns-to-scale assumption for production. There is only an increase and decrease in the marginal products of factors, leading Mankiw (1989) to suggest that such negative shocks other than oil shocks have never been seen.[29] But clearly negative profits have always been seen and continue to be identified. And a profit increase is the manifestation of how capital has a higher yield, while 'restructuring' that writes off capital losses is the manifestation of how capital has a lower yield. Therefore it remains a potentially worthwhile endeavour to sort out the profit contribution to the marginal product change. In a way that seems suggested by the *Treatise*, it may entail endogenizing the exogenous productivity change so that instead there is the exogenous profit shock that induces the productivity change.

The shift of cash into loans, as in the *Treatise* and as Patinkin (1976: 45, for example) discusses, may certainly be a part of the process of a profit increase. However other than being induced by government injections of money, this might occur competitively within banking as investment is shifted from low-risk, low yield, sectors into higher risk, higher yield, sectors. And it may be that realistic changes in expectations of the future flow of profit constitute a shock that pushes the cycle up or down. Further, it may not be a far-fetched speculation that the underlying element of such shifts in expectations of profit may simply be changes in the implicit and explicit taxes of operating in markets. For example the information technology sector recently began its collapse after the change in the regulatory environment as signalled by the Microsoft antitrust case. Or take the expansion of markets as induced by less restrictive democratic governments coming to power in Eastern Europe, Russia, and China. Or consider Ireland's dramatic reduction in the corporate income tax and its subsequent growth-induced upturn; the mid 1980s US reduction in corporate and personal taxes and its subsequent growth; or the recent Russian dramatic reduction in personal income taxes to 13 per cent, and the recent Russian-proposed reduction in corporate taxes to 24 per cent. This view, about the effects of changes in policy, suggests that changes that affect the aggregate cost of production may lead to large changes in profits and output. This would bring the analysis full circle, from the implicit assumption in the paper's cross construction that costs are held fixed to the view that policy induced changes in aggregate cost may shock business cycles. And such policy-induced changes are identifiable at the aggregate level.

Notes

* Max Gillman (2002). 'Keynes's [Treatise]: Aggregate Price Theory for Modern Analysis?', *European Journal of The History of Economic Thought*, 9(3), 430–451.

† This paper was developed partly while a fellow at the University of New South Wales, Sydney. For helpful comments I thank the referees of this journal, Antoin Murphy, John Neville, Glenn Otto, Geoffrey Harcourt, Lance Fisher, and Jacek Rostowski. I am also grateful to participants at the seminars of the University of New South Wales and the University of Sydney, and at the Workshop on the Globalisation of the World Economy at the University cf Wollongong.

1 'The fundamental problem of monetary theory is not merely to establish identities or statical equations relating (e.g.) the turnover of monetary instruments to the turnover of things traded for money. The real task of such a theory is to treat the problem dynamically, analysing the different elements involved, in such a manner as to exhibit the causal process by which the price level is determined, and the method of transition from one position of equilibrium to another. The forms of the quantity theory, however, on which we have all been brought up – I shall give an account of them in detail in chapter 14 – are but ill adapted for this purpose. . . . they do not, any of them, have the advantage of separating out those factors through which, in a modern economic system, the causal process actually operates during a period of change' (Keynes 1930, vol.1: 133). Or as Patinkin 1976: 18) put it 'In the *Treatise* . . . he continued to maintain the quantity theory in a macroeconomic (though not microeconomic) context, but critized it as being restricted in its validity to comparative-statics analysis; accordingly Keynes considered its supplementation by an appropriate dynamic analysis to be one of his major objectives in the book.'

2 Contemporaneously Marshall (1920: 264–5) also could be said to have ventured towards aggregate analysis on the basis of the theory of the firm with his discussion of the representative, or average, firm: 'We shall have to analyse carefully the normal cost of producing a commodity, relatively to a given aggregate volume of production; and for this purpose we shall have to study *the expenses of a representative producer* for that aggregate volume' (italics in original).

3 Keynes (1936: 77–81).

4 'Profits (Q) are . . . Q = I – S so that entrepreneurs make a profit or a loss according as the money value of current investment exceeds or falls short of current savings' (Keynes 1930, vol. 1: 151); 'the reader will appreciate that the condition of zero profits means that *aggregate* profits are zero' (italics in original, Keynes 1930, vol.1: 152).

5 'It has been suggested to me . . . that it might be better to employ *Windfalls* for what I call here *Profits*. It may help some readers mentally to substitute this term; but for my own part I prefer the term *Profits* as carrying with it on the whole the most helpful penumbra of suggestion' (Keynes, 1930, vol. 1: 125).

6 'If producers as a whole are making a profit, individual producers will seek to enlarge their output so as to make more profit . . . by employing more of the factors of production . . . Thus we may conclude that, as a rule, the existence of profit will provide a tendency toward a higher rate of employment and of remuneration for the factors of production; and *vice versa*' (italics in original, Keynes, 1930, vol.2: 163). See also Keynes (1930, vol.1: 136–65).

7 Patinkin (1976) and Dimand (1988) both criticize the *Treatise* for not going further in bringing out its theory of output and employment, which they argue the *General Theory* remedies.

8 In the book III, *The Fundamental Equations*, Keynes (1930, vol.1: 136–8) describes the equation $\Pi = (E/O) + [(I - S)/O]$, where Π is 'the price level of output as a whole', O is 'the total output of goods' E is the 'earnings of the community' or the factors of production, E/O is 'rate of earnings of the factors of production', and (I – S)/O is 'the rate of profits per unit of output'. Note that O is real output rather than nominal output as Keynes (p. 135) also uses it in the Fisher (1911) equation that he writes as 'PO = M1V1.' Meltzer (1988: 63–4) also

interprets this equation of Keynes, stating that 'The point of the fundamental equations is to show that when price differ from costs of production, investment and saving differ. . . . The deviation of prices from long-run equilibrium is equal to the difference between investment I and saving S per unit of real product.' However Patinkin (1976: 45–6) also notes how Keynes views his price theory as reducing to Fisher's (1911) quantity theory when I = S; this requires that total costs equal M1V1, which can conceivably hold with a constant returns to scale production function within a cash-in-advance economy, but with zero profits at all time.

9 A modern version of this scarcity rent can be found in Topel and Rosen (1988) in which the price of housing services equals the long run marginal cost plus a short run factor due to costly adjustment of the stock of housing.

10 I thank anonymous referees for pointing this out.

11 Keynes (1930, vol.1: 135) has an equation similar to this, whereby real output equals the sum of the 'volume of liquid consumption goods and services' plus 'the net increment of investment'; also arguably found in the Keynes (1936: 29).

12 Bishop (1948) does not construct his cross diagram in this fashion, and uses the terms 'aggregate demand' and 'aggregate supply'; nonetheless, he does appear to be using the concepts analogous to total revenue and total cost.

13 'Thus – generally speaking – every change towards a new equilibrium price level is initiated by a departure of profits from zero' (Keynes, 1930, vol.1: 158). 'Thus when I say that the disequilibrium between saving and investment is the mainspring of change, I do not mean to deny that the behavior of entrepreneurs at any given moment is based on a mixture of experience and anticipation' (Keynes, 1930, vol.1: 160). 'It must be enough to repeat here the indication already given on p.125, that we do not require for the purposes of the present analysis to make any particular assumptions as to the time which has to elapse before losses (or profits), actual or anticipated, produce their full reaction on the behavior of entrepreneurs. It is sufficient that the general tendency of a disequilibrium between saving and investment is in the sense described, and that, if the cause persists, the tendency must materialise sooner or later. Nor do any of the qualifications of this section affect in any way the rigour or the validity of our conclusions as to the quantitative effect of divergences between saving and investment on the price levels ruling in the market' (Keynes, 1930, vol.1: 161).

14 Closer to the *Treatise*, Dimand (1988) interprets this equation as $I \equiv S + Q$ where Q is windfall profit.

15 Bishop (1948) analyses this case of a 'balanced increase in government expenditures and taxes' and finds 'a peculiarly precise conclusion' of no change in output, in his cross construction.

16 Keynes (1936) and Hicks (1937) use the demand for investment and the supply of savings to construct the (first) IS diagrams with investment and savings on one axis and the interest rate on the other axis. See also note 27.

17 Colander (1995) also explores the lack of scarcity in the Keynesian framework.

18 Keynes (1930, vol.1: 161–6).

19 See King (1995) and Neville and Rao (1996) for an explanation of AS-AD analysis in the Keynesian framework.

20 The constancy of the real profit follows from the nature of the example Cobb-Douglas-type production function, in which both the labour share and the profit share are fixed.

21 Note that in this example, behind the AS-AD shifts, TB/W pivots up because the marginal utility of income $W\lambda$, which in equilibrium is given by $W\lambda = 1.5/\{A^2/(4W) + 100\}$, falls as the increase in A causes an increase in profit. This makes the slope of *TB*/Whigher for each y and this corresponds to a higher price $1/w$ for each y^d along the new AD curve. The TC/W curve pivots down, making the slope lower for each y and this corresponds to a lower price $1/w$ for each y^s along the *AS* curve.

The curve TR/W also pivots down whereby the real profit per unit of output, $\Pi/(Py)$, remains the same at 0.5.

22 Patinkin (1976: 25): 'From the substantive viewpoint, all of these volumes are now in the domain of the history of monetary doctrine: their basic scientific contributions have long since been incorporated in the current macroeconomic literature . . . of importance only to students of this history.' '. . . the recent revival in the *Treatise* not-withstanding, I can (from the viewpoint of macroeconomic theory) see little profit (and certainly no pleasure) in reading it today. . . . it contributes little toward an understanding of the substance of the [GT] theory itself, which differs so fundamentally from that of the *Treatise*.'

23 Dimand (1988: 22) writes 'Keynes' reliance on disequilibrium analysis in the *Treatise* and his insistence on the continual evolution of his thought indicate that these disequilibrium interpretations of the *General Theory* are not simply pulled out of thin air. A close reading of the *Treatise*, in fact, shows that they were part and parcel of Keynes' thought for at least a decade. . . . The disequilibrium interpretation of the *General Theory* suggests that the methodological break between that book and the *Treatise* was not as sharp as has usually been supposed.'

24 Patinkin (1976: 35): 'Thus all that fundamental equation (i) consists of is the quite obvious statement that the change (with respect to the base period) in the price of consumption goods equals the change in per-unit costs of production of these goods plus the change in per-unit profits (assumed zero in the base period); and equation (ii) makes a correspondingly obvious statement for output as a whole . . . (p. 36) Keynes was fully aware of the triviality of these conclusions per se. . . . (p. 51) in reading the *Treatise* I have had the uncomfortable feeling that Keynes was so enthusiastic about what he felt were the new truths revealed by his fundamental equations that he all too frequently shifted unawares across the slippery line that lies between 'tracing cause and effect' and simply repeating the tautologies inherent in these equations. . . . and even when this is done in a way which succeeds in escaping the tautologies of the fundamental equations, Keynes' argument at these points reduces to an extremely mechanical application of these equations'. Dimand (1988: 23–4) reverberates that 'Keynes' two Fundamental Equations for the price level of consumption goods and for the price level of output as a whole are tautologies, but are converted into equilibrium conditions by the imposition of behavioral constraints on the variables in the equations.'

25 See Patinkin (pp. 36–7). Note that while the argument here is that investment increases when banks lend out more, an increase in lending out of reserves can be consistent with only a change in the composition of investment, as funds are shifted from low interest government-type securities to higher yield corporate lending.

26 Patinkin seems to allude to this conundrum; see note 24.

27 Patinkin (1976: 37): 'It follows that if there are no 'spontaneous' changes in these rates of earnings – and for the most part Keynes was not concerned with such changes – then a necessary and sufficient condition for price stability is that the market rate of interest equal the natural rate . . . (p. 47) the natural rate was in his view not a separate analytical entity, but a certain value of the market rate; namely, that value at which savings and investment are equal.'

28 Patinkin (1976: 23–4) '. . . the mathematical analysis that appears in these [GT] chapters is not only not essential to the argument but is also problematic. And this fact – together with the effectualness of the 'fundamental equations' of the *Treatise* – makes it clear that whatever may have been Keynes's attitude towards the proper role of mathematical methods in economic analysis, his strength did not lie in the use of such methods.'

29 We argue in Gillman and Nakov (2001) that oil 'shocks' were merely a reflection of the acceleration of the US inflation rate, and so were monetary phenomenon rather than supply side shocks.

17 Credit shocks in the financial deregulatory era

Not the usual suspects*

Szilárd Benk, Max Gillman and Michal Kejak

Summary

The chapter constructs credit shocks using data and the solution to a monetary business cycle model. The model extends the standard stochastic cash-in-advance economy by including the production of credit that serves as an alternative to money in exchange. Shocks to goods productivity, money, and credit productivity are constructed robustly using the solution to the model and quarterly US data on key variables. The contribution of the credit shock to US GDP movements is found, and this is interpreted in terms of changes in banking legislation during the US financial deregulation era. The results put forth the credit shock as a candidate shock that matters in determining GDP, including in the sense of Uhlig [What moves real GNP, Manuscript, Humbolt University, Berlin, 2003].

17.1 Introduction

Identifying the sources of shocks that influence the real business cycle has become the focus of recent research. Chari et al. (2007) and Kehoe and Prescott (2002) consider how policy may explain capital, labor and goods distortions that contribute to business cycle fluctuations. Uhlig (2004) in contrast takes an atheoretical approach to decomposing fluctuations into certain candidate shocks, finding that a medium range output productivity shock and a shorter range less discernible shock together explain a good portion of the fluctuations. Meanwhile, Espino and Hintermaier (2004) extend Kocherlakota's (2000) formulation of the Kiyotaki and Moore (1997) intertemporal credit shock by constructing a real business cycle with credit constraints.

A credit shock may make a viable candidate for causing some of the output fluctuations, although this still remains little explored within the business cycle framework. One alternative to intertemporal credit is the use of credit for exchange purposes, where the credit is produced in a banking sector using real resources. With this production of credit approach, Einarsson and Marquis (2001) examine the movements of credit aggregates in a monetary business cycle model with banking, while Li (2000) presents a credit model that exhibits some of the classic liquidity effects when open market operations must pass through financial intermediaries. While neither of the latter two papers introduce a shock to the credit sector, there is a separate literature on banking as a source of innovations. This includes Berger (2003), who documents technological progress in the banking sector, and Strahan (2003), who presents econometric evidence of how US bank deregulation has acted as a positive shock that has contributed to GDP increases. Strahan (2003) estimates how asset structures in the banking industry changed significantly after branching and interstate banking deregulations, how the bank profit rate became sharply more correlated with its subsequent asset growth following the 1980s deregulation, and how US state panel data show that the states' growth rate of personal income accelerated by 0.56 percentage points following branching deregulation.[1] Thus bank law deregulations have been specifically linked to structural change in the banking industry and US output growth rate increases.

The chapter here contributes a study of how credit shocks affect output in a credit production framework. The model includes credit as an alternative to money in a stochastic exogenous growth version of Gillman and Kejak (2005b), with shocks to the productivity of credit along with the more traditional shocks to output productivity and to money supply. From the solution to the monetary business cycle model, the credit shock is constructed each year using data as in Parkin (1988) and Ingram et al. (1994, 1997). Then the contribution of the shock to GDP changes is estimated. Further the chapter follows the spirit of Kehoe and Prescott (2002) by attributing the source of the shocks to changes in legislation, specifically banking legislation. The shocks are compared to the major law changes during the national US financial deregulation that occurred in the 1980s and 1990s. A significant ability to correlate the shock-induced GDP movements with the deregulation is found.

The model's recursive solution is used along with US data to construct the shocks in a robust fashion. The profile of the credit shock is found to be stable under some six different ways of estimating it. Along with the model's solution, at least three variables need to be assigned values with time series data in order to minimally identify the three shocks. Five such variables are found to be available and all are used for the baseline, by employing an estimation procedure to identify the three shocks from five equations. Alternative constructions are also made for robustness; it is found that the nearly identical shock profile results in all cases when variables associated with sectors in which the three shocks occur in the model are included in the construction. And this includes two cases in which there is exact identification of the shocks. Other representations of the shocks are possible, such as through the methods of Chari et al. (2007), but are left for future work.

As an added characterization of the credit shock, its contribution to the variance of the output is also presented. This variance is found to vary widely, a verification of the Ingram et al. (1994) finding that the contribution of an individual shock to variance can have a wide range of values, depending for example on its ordering in the VAR. However, since the shock construction procedure uses only the autocorrelation coefficients of the shock processes, this uncertain variance decomposition does not affect the construction. Further, the estimated autocorrelation that results from the time series for the constructed credit shock is close in value to the assumed value used in the construction, a feature that adds validation.

The chapter therefore presents a rigorous testing of the hypothesis that shocks to credit technology may play a role in explaining the output fluctuations during certain historical episodes. Although it does not go as far as to combine an intertemporal credit role with the exchange credit function in the model, the paper shows that the exchange credit function itself may be important during periods when the use of credit for exchange is significantly shocked. For example, consider the lifting of Regulation Q. The unrestricted ability to write checks on money market mutual funds that are invested in short term government treasury securities allowed the consumer a greater chance to earn interest during the period while purchasing goods with credit, instead of using cash. Such an efficiency increase can induce the investment of more funds during each period rather than keeping them idle as cash, and cause a jolt to GDP.

The approach of linking a change in policies with the source of shocks is consistent with a growing literature on decomposing total factor productivity changes. Examples are found in Hopenhayn and Neumeyer (2002), Cole and Ohanian (2002) and Kehoe and Prescott (2002). And finally the paper is able to show that several of the features of Uhlig's (2004) second, unidentified, shorter term shock are satisfied by the credit shock of our model. Taken together, the construction of the shock and its effect on GDP, the link of the shock to certain policy changes, and its partial conformity with the atheoretical shock identified by Uhlig (2004), allows the conclusion that the credit shock is a viable, previously unidentified, candidate shock that can significantly affect output during certain periods.

17.2 The credit model

The representative agent self produces credit with labor only and buys the aggregate consumption good with a combination of money and credit, whereby the marginal cost of money (the nominal interest rate) equals the marginal cost of credit (the real wage divided by the marginal product of labor in credit production). The credit production exhibits a rising marginal cost as the share of credit used in exchange goes up. The particular form of the credit production function is equivalent to the assumption that the value-added from the credit service is proportional to the cost of production.

With an explicit price for the credit service as in Gillman and Kejak (2004), it can be shown that this assumption implies that the total revenue from selling the credit service (the value-added) is proportional to the wage cost, leaving a constant rate of profit. This proportionality of the value added with the total cost implies that as total consumption rises, so must the labor input into credit services in order to keep constant the share of credit in exchange. Then the implied production function can be written simply in terms of the share of credit being equal to a diminishing function of the ratio of labor in credit production relative to the total good consumption.

The credit production specification allows for an additional productivity shock. Instead of just good productivity and money shocks, there are three shocks also including one to the productivity of credit.

Consider a representative consumer that maximizes over an infinite horizon its expected lifetime utility over consumption c_t and leisure x_t. Utility is given by:

$$U = E_0 \sum_{t=0}^{\infty} \beta^t (\log c_t + \Psi \log x_t), \quad 0 < \beta < 1. \tag{1}$$

The consumer can purchase the goods by using either money or credit services. Let $a_t \in (0, 1]$ denote the fraction of consumption goods that are purchased with money. Then the consumer's cash-in-advance constraint will have the form:

$$M_{t-1} + T_t \geq a_t P_t c_t, \tag{2}$$

where M_{t-1} is the money stock carried from the previous period, T_t is the nominal lumpsum money transfer received from the government and P_t denotes the current price level. It is assumed that the government policy includes sequences of nominal transfers which satisfy:

$$T_t = \Theta_t M_{t-1} = (\Theta^* + e^{u_t} - 1) M_{t-1}, \tag{3}$$

where Θ_t is the growth rate of money and Θ^* is the stationary growth rate of money. Transfer is subject to random shocks u_t which follow the autoregressive process:

$$u_t = \varphi_u u_{t-1} + \varepsilon_{ut}, \quad \varepsilon_{ut} \sim N(0, \sigma_{\varepsilon u}^2),\ 0 < \varphi_u < 1. \tag{4}$$

The amount of credit used is equal to $c_t (1 - a_t)$. The production function for this amount of credit is given by

$$c_t(1 - a_t) = A_F e^{v_t} \left(\frac{l_{Ft}}{c_t}\right)^{\gamma} c_t, \quad A_F > 0,\ \gamma \in (0, 1).$$

This can be written as

$$1 - a_t = A_F e^{v_t} \left(\frac{l_{Ft}}{c_t}\right)^{\gamma}, \tag{5}$$

where $1 - a_t$ is the share of goods bought with credit, $A_F e^{v_t}$ is the productivity shift parameter and l_{Ft} is the labor time spent in producing credit services. There exist productivity shocks that follow an autocorrelated process:

$$v_t = \varphi_v v_{t-1} + \varepsilon_{vt}, \quad \varepsilon_{vt} \sim N(0, \sigma_{\varepsilon v}^2), 0 < \varphi_v < 1. \tag{6}$$

Assume a total time endowment of 1, which is divided among time spent working, leisure and time spent in credit service production:

$$n_t + x_t + l_{Ft} = 1. \tag{7}$$

Output y_t is produced by the agent, acting in part as the representative firm, from capital accumulated in the previous period k_{t-1} and current labor n_t using a Cobb-Douglas CRS production function which is subject to technology shocks z_t:

$$y_t = e^{z_t} k_{t-1}^{a} n_t^{1-a}, \tag{8}$$

$$z_t = \varphi_z Z_{t-1} + \varepsilon_{zt}, \quad \varepsilon_{zt} \sim N(0, \sigma_{\varepsilon v}^2), 0 < \varphi_z < 1. \tag{9}$$

The part of output that is not consumed is invested in physical capital. Current investment i_t together with depreciated capital form the capital stock used for production in the next period:

$$k_t = (1 - \delta)k_{t-1} + i_t. \tag{10}$$

Firms maximize their profits $y_t - r_t k_{t-1} - w_t n_t + (1 - \delta)k_{t-1}$, which yield the following functions for w_t, the real wage rate and r_t, the gross real rate of return, net of depreciation δ:

$$w_t = (1 - a)e^{z_t} k_{t-1}^{a} n_t^{-a}, \tag{11}$$

$$r_t = a e^{z_t} k_{t-1}^{a-1} n_t^{1-a} + 1 - \delta. \tag{12}$$

Current income from labor, capital, money balances and lump-sum transfers are spent on consumption, new capital formation and the accumulation of real balances. The period t budget constraint of the representative consumer is given by:

$$w_t P_t (1 - x_t - l_{Ft}) + P_t r_t k_{t-1} + T_t + M_{t-1} \geq P_t c_t + P_t k_t + M_t. \tag{13}$$

The consumer chooses consumption, leisure, time spent in credit service production, capital stock, the share of purchases made with cash, and the money stock $\{c_t, x_t, l_{Ft}, k_t, a_t, M_t\}_{t=0}^{\infty}$ to maximize lifetime utility (1) subject to the cash-in-advance constraint (2), budget constraint (13) and credit service technology (5).

17.2.1 Equilibrium

Dividing Eqs. (2) and (13) by the price level and substituting l_{Ft} expressed from (5), the Lagrangian of the maximization problem of the household is

$$L = E\sum_{t=0}^{\infty} \beta^t \Bigg\{(\log c_t + \Psi \log x_t) + \lambda_t \left[\frac{M_{t-1} + T_t}{P_t} - a_t c_t\right]$$
$$+ \mu_t \Bigg[w_t \left(1 - x_t - \left(\frac{1 - a_t}{A_F \mathrm{e}^{v_t}}\right)^{1/\gamma} c_t\right)$$
$$+ r_t k_{t-1} + \frac{M_{t-1} + T_t}{P_t} - c_t - k_t - \frac{M_t}{P_t}\Bigg]\Bigg\}. \tag{14}$$

The first-order conditions with respect to c_t, x_t, k_t, a_t, M_t are

$$\frac{1}{c_t} - \lambda_t a_t - \mu_t w_t \left(\frac{1 - a_t}{A_F \mathrm{e}^{v_t}}\right)^{1/\gamma} - \mu_t = 0, \tag{15}$$

$$\frac{\Psi}{x_t} - \mu_t w_t = 0, \tag{16}$$

$$-\mu_t + \beta E_t \{\mu_{t+1} r_{t+1}\} = 0, \tag{17}$$

$$-\lambda_t c_t + \mu_t w_t c_t \frac{1}{\gamma A_F \mathrm{e}^{v_t}} \left(\frac{1 - a_t}{A_F \mathrm{e}^{v_t}}\right)^{1/\gamma - 1} = 0, \tag{18}$$

$$\frac{-\mu_t}{P_t} + \beta E_t \left\{\frac{\lambda_{t+1} + \mu_{t+1}}{P_{t+1}}\right\} = 0. \tag{19}$$

A competitive equilibrium for this economy consists of a set of allocations $\{c_t, x_t, l_t, n_t, k_t, a_t, M_t\}_{t=0}^{\infty}$, a set of prices $\{w_t, r_t\}_{t=0}^{\infty}$, exogenous shock processes $\{z_t, v_t, u_t\}_{t=0}^{\infty}$, money supply process and initial conditions k_{-1} and M_{-1} such that given the prices, shocks and government transfers, the allocations solve the consumer's utility maximization problem, solve the firm's profit maximization problem and the goods and labor and money markets clear.

In a stationary deterministic steady state we use the transformation $P_t = P_t / M_t$ (and also denote real money balances by $m_t = M_t / P_t$). There is no uncertainty and time indices can be dropped, denoting by (*) the steady-state values and by $R^* = r^*\ (\Theta^* + 1)$ the steady-state interest factor. In the equilibrium, inflation equals the growth rate of the money supply. The first order conditions (15)–(19) can be simplified to:

$$R^* - 1 = \frac{w^*}{\gamma^* A_F^*}\left(\frac{1-a^*}{A_F^*}\right)^{1/\gamma - 1}, \tag{20}$$

$$\frac{x_t}{\Psi_{c_t}} = \frac{1 + a^*(R^* - 1) + w^*((1-a^*)/A_F^*)^{1/\gamma}}{w^*}, \tag{21}$$

$$r^* = \frac{1}{\beta}. \tag{22}$$

Equations (20)–(22) together with the steady-state versions of Eqs. (2)–(9) and (11)–(13) define the steady state of the system.

17.2.2. Calibration and numerical dynamics solution

The model is solved by using the log-linearization technique of King et al. (1987), Campbell (1994) and Uhlig (1995). A first-order Taylor approximation of the log variables around the steady state results in 12 equations for the first-order conditions of the consumer and firm, and the constraints, together with the productivity and money supply shocks processes (4), (6) and (9).[2] This gives a system of linear stochastic difference equations in the log-linearized endogenous state variable $\hat{k}_t$, the exogenous state variables z_t, v_t, u_t, and the log-linearized control and other endogenous variables, $\hat{c}_t$, $\hat{x}_t$, $\hat{n}_t$, $\hat{l}_{Ft}$, $\hat{a}_t$, $\hat{w}_t$, $\hat{r}_t$, $\hat{y}_t$, $\hat{p}_t$, and shadow prices $\hat{\lambda}_t$, $\hat{\mu}_t$.

Solving the stochastic difference equations system above means determining a recursive equilibrium law of motion of the endogenous variable $\mathbf{X}'_t = [\hat{k}_t]$ and $\mathbf{Y}'_t = [\hat{c}_t\ \hat{x}_t\ \hat{n}_t\ \hat{l}_{Ft}\ \hat{a}_t\ \hat{w}_t\ \hat{r}_t\ \hat{y}_t\ \hat{p}_t]$ on the lagged values of the endogenous state variable $\mathbf{X}'_{t-1} = [\hat{k}_{t-1}]$ and on the current values of the exogenous state variables $\mathbf{Z}'_t\,[z_t\ v_t\ u_t]$. The solution has the form:

$$\mathbf{X}_t = P\,P\,\mathbf{X}_{t-1} + Q\,Q\mathbf{Z}_t, \tag{23}$$

$$\mathbf{Y}_t = R\,R\,\mathbf{X}_{t-1} + S\,S\,\mathbf{Z}_t, \tag{24}$$

where $P\,P$, QQ, RR, SS are coefficient matrixes.

The US economy is the benchmark for calibration of parameters, which are chosen as close as possible to the values in the literature (Cooley and Hansen, 1989, 1995; Gillman and Kejak, 2005b). The length of a period is assumed to be one quarter. The quarterly discount factor is assumed to be $\beta = 0.99$. This implies through Eq. (22) a quarterly net real return of 1%. The depreciation rate is set equal to $\delta = 0.025$ and the share of capital input is set equal to $a = 0.36$.

Regarding the parameters of the exchange technology, the degree of diminishing return in the credit sector is set to $\lambda = 0.21$, which is Gillman and Otto's (2003) time series estimate of γ in a related model for the US (values of $\gamma \in (0, 0.5)$ give a convex, upwards-loping, marginal cost curve). The share of cash purchases is fixed at $a = 0.7$ as in Gillman and Kejak (2005b). With a baseline nominal interest rate of 2.25%, explained below, the productivity parameter A_F is then implied to be 1.422.

The baseline proportion of time allocated to leisure is set at $x_t = 0.7055$, similar to the 0.7 in Gillman and Kejak (2005b) and the 0.69 in Jones et al. (1993). Then, the steady-state first order conditions imply the fraction of hours spent in credit services production, which is $l_F = 0.00049$, as compared to 0.0014 in Gillman and Kejak (2005b).

For the shock processes, the standard deviations and autocorrelations need values. The standard deviation of disturbances to the goods production technology is calibrated so that the standard deviation of the simulated output series is near to the standard deviation of the US output, giving $\sigma_{\in z} = 0.0075$ (as compared to 0.00721 in Cooley and Hansen, 1989). Persistence is set equal to $\varphi_z = 0.95$, as is common.

The money supply process is calibrated so that the M1 money aggregate varies in a way that is consistent with the US experience between 1959–2000. Following Cooley and Hansen (1989, 1995) the persistence and the variance of the money supply is estimated from the following regression for the money supply growth (standard errors in parentheses):

$$\Delta \log M_t = \underset{(0.0011)}{0.005139} + \underset{(0.065)}{0.576748}\, \Delta \log M_{t-1} + \varepsilon_t, \quad \sigma_\varepsilon = 0.010022. \tag{25}$$

This implies $\varphi_u = 0.58$, $\sigma_{\varepsilon u} = 0.01$, close to Cooley and Hansen's (1995) estimates of 0.49 and 0.0089 for the period 1954–1991. The regression above also implies an average growth rate of money ($E\,\Delta \log M_t$) of 1.23% per quarter, which is around 5% per year. And a 1.23% quarterly inflation rate plus a 1% real interest rate implies a 2.25% quarterly nominal interest rate.

Finally, values for the credit shock generation process are required. While the persistence of the aggregate output is typically estimated from the Solow residual, this is more difficult to do for a specific sector, such as the credit sector. Instead, it is assumed that the credit shock process has the same standard deviation and autocorrelation as in the aggregate goods sector, or that $\sigma_{\varepsilon v} = 0.0075$ and $\varphi_v = 0.95$. This assumption proves reasonable as is seen below in that the estimated autocorrelation is close to the assumed value.

Given the values for the parameters and the steady state variables, the recursive system of linear stochastic difference equations is solved using the methods of Uhlig (1995). Here the MATLAB program provided online by Uhlig is adapted for our model, and the solution given by Eqs. (23) and (24) takes the form

$$\hat{k}_t = 0.953\hat{k}_{t-1} + 0.117z_t - 0.0003v_t + 0.007u_t, \tag{26}$$

$$\begin{bmatrix} \hat{c}_t \\ \hat{x}_t \\ \hat{n}_t \\ \hat{l}_{Ft} \\ \hat{a}_t \\ \hat{w}_t \\ \hat{r}_t \\ \hat{p}_t \\ \hat{y}_t \end{bmatrix} = \begin{bmatrix} 0.564 \\ 0.110 \\ -0.265 \\ 0.100 \\ 0.042 \\ 0.456 \\ -0.028 \\ -0.606 \\ 0.190 \end{bmatrix} [\hat{k}_{t-1}] + \begin{bmatrix} 0.399 & 0.014 & -0.120 \\ -0.321 & -0.005 & 0.002 \\ 0.772 & 0.011 & -0.023 \\ -0.551 & 0.056 & 10.430 \\ 0.085 & -0.432 & -0.949 \\ 0.722 & -0.004 & 0.008 \\ 0.052 & 0.0002 & -0.001 \\ -0.485 & 0.4184 & 1.068 \\ 1.494 & 0.007 & -0.015 \end{bmatrix} \begin{bmatrix} z_t \\ v_t \\ u_t \end{bmatrix}. \tag{27}$$

17.2.3 Impulse responses of the credit shock

The recursive equilibrium laws of motion determined in the previous section permit computation of the impulse responses of shocks on the variables of the model. Figure 17.1 illustrates the impulse responses of the credit economy when faced with a 1% shock to the productivity of the banking sector. Intuitively, financial innovation and productivity growth in the banking sector decreases the cost of using credit relative to cash, inducing an increase in demand for credit and a decrease in the demand for cash. The share of cash purchases falls by 0.43% while the real money demand drops by 0.42%, this

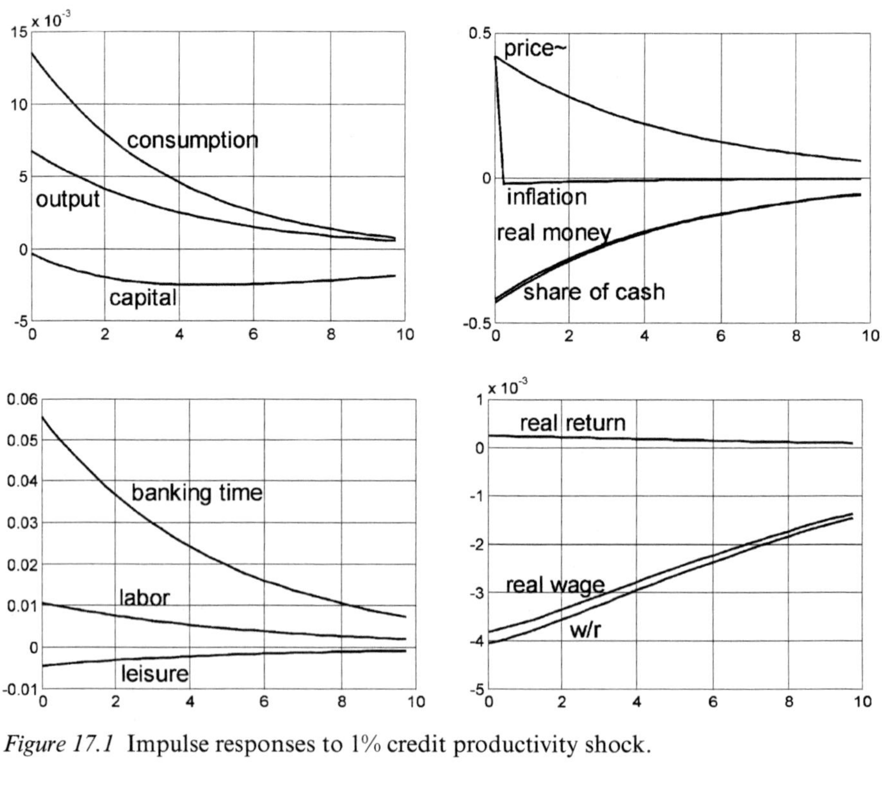

Figure 17.1 Impulse responses to 1% credit productivity shock.

drop being equivalent with an immediate upward jump in the nominal price level. The price level jumps up, given that there is the same money supply and less money demand, and adjusts back to its long-run growth path after the shock. This causes inflation to converge from below to its long-run level.

The fall in the cost of credit lowers the shadow exchange cost of consumption goods relative to leisure and induces substitution to consumption from leisure. This involves an increase in consumption of 0.014% and a decrease in leisure of 0.005%. With more efficient labor in the credit sector, and less leisure, labor in the goods sector increases by 0.01%. The modestly increased labor supply somewhat lowers the real wage and the input price ratio (w/r) by about 0.004%. This results in a decrease in the capital to labor ratio, in contrast to a Tobin (1965) type effect. The time spent in the banking sector increases by 0.056%. However note that if the credit productivity parameter is calibrated to be large enough, then the time spent in banking can potentially decrease. This results when there is a large enough shift out in the credit services output, from the productivity boost, that less labor is required in the end.

In sum, a positive credit productivity shock sees the economy have increased work, consumption, output, prices and banking, with less leisure, capital, and real money use.

17.3 Results: the construction of credit shocks

The effects of the changes in banking laws on the business cycle can be studied by identifying the magnitude of the credit shocks, and their effects on output, and then by comparing these effects with the chronology of the deregulation. First is the construction of the three shocks, z_t, v_t and u_t, in each period from 1972:1 to 2000:4. This is done by assigning values to certain control and state variables, using US quarterly data, substituting the values back into the solution to the recursive equilibrium system given in Eqs. (26) and (27), and then solving for z_t, v_t and u_t. The choice of the control variables that are assigned values using data is made on the simple basis of using as many variables for which there is reliable data, while trying to include key variables like labor hours in banking. The banking hours is the limiting factor in the data range, beginning only in 1972. The result is five variables: output, consumption, investment, banking hours and real money.[3] Having five equations in the three unknown shocks gives an overidentification of the shocks, while in contrast with only three equations there would be an exact identification. Overidentification still allows for a unique determination of the three shocks through an estimation procedure. This is done with ordinary least squares as described below.

Given the five control variables with values from US data, the log-deviations of these variables $\hat{y}_t$, $\hat{c}_t$, $\hat{\imath}_t$, $\hat{l}_{Ft}$ and $\hat{m}_t$ are defined as the percentage deviations of the variables in each period relative to their H-P filtered trend. Next is the construction of the state variable, the capital stock. Following Chari et al. (2007), this variable is constructed by using the capital accumulation equation, the investment data, and an assumed value for the initial capital stock. With the data on investment used to compute $\hat{l}_t$, the cyclical component of the H-P filtered series, the initial value choice of the log-linearized capital stock $\hat{k}_{-1}$ is set equal to 0. Then the log-linearization of the capital accumulation equation (10) is used to generate $\hat{k}_t$.

The five equations with the now given values for $\hat{y}_t$, $\hat{c}_t$, $\hat{\imath}_t$, $\hat{l}_{Ft}$, $\hat{m}_t$, and $\hat{k}_t$, allow for the ordinary least squares estimation of the three unknown shocks, z_t, v_t and u_t. To illustrate this, rewrite Eq. (27) in matrix form as

$$X_t = A[\hat{k}_{t-1}] + B\,E_t,$$

where A and B are the coefficient matrices from Eq. (27), and

$$X_t = [\hat{y}_t \quad \hat{c}_t \quad \hat{\imath}_t \quad \hat{l}_{Ft} \quad \hat{m}_t]', \quad E_t = [z_t \quad v_t \quad u_t]'.$$

For this system of five linear equations in three unknowns, for each t the ordinary least squares estimate of $\tilde{E}_t$ is found from the formula:

$$\tilde{E}_t = (B'\,B)^{-1}\,B'\,(X_t - A[\hat{k}_{t-1}]). \tag{28}$$

The magnitudes of the shocks are plotted in Figure 17.2.

The estimated autocorrelation coefficients, with ρ denoting estimated values, are $\rho_z = 0.9203$, $\rho_v = 0.9362$, and $\rho_u = 0.6564$, which are found by fitting an AR(1) model to the shocks and which compare well to the assumed values of $\varphi_z = 0.95$, $\varphi_v = 0.95$, and $\varphi_u = 0.57$. The variance of credit shocks appears to be larger than the variance of the productivity shocks, while the assumption is that they are the same. The difference can be because the aggregation of the sectoral shocks into a cumulative shock z_t results in the smoothing of idiosyncratic sectoral shocks, and a smaller variance relative to some individual sectors such as the credit sector. Using the larger estimated variance for the credit shock in simulations results in somewhat altered

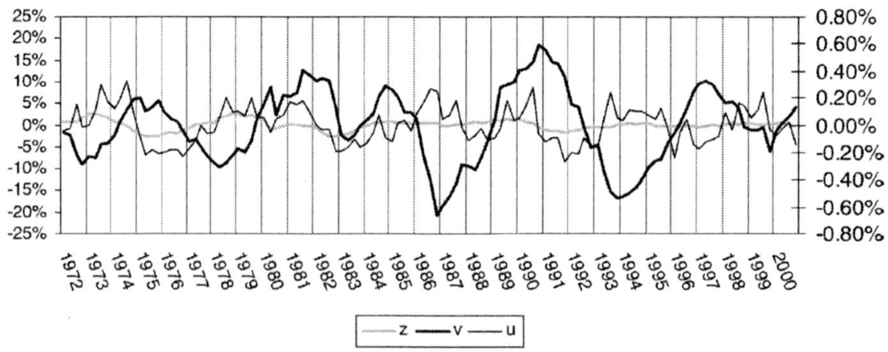

Figure 17.2 Evolution of productivity (z), credit (v) and money (u) shocks (u on the right axis).

correlations amongst variables, but does not affect the construction of the magnitude of the shock or its effect on GDP.

17.3.1 Effect of the credit shock on output

Given the construction of v_t, two measures can be determined that help illustrate how the credit shock effects the economy. These are the period-by-period innovations to the credit shock process (ε_{vt}), and a measure of the effect of the credit shock on GDP. The innovations are computed directly from Eq. (6) by substituting in the values for v_t and the estimated value for the autocorrelation parameter, $\rho_v = 0.9362$. These are graphed in Figure 17.3, plotted on the left axis, along with the v_t themselves.

Second, consider defining a measure of the effect of credit shocks on GDP that uses the ratio of the actual GDP to the simulated GDP when it is assumed that the credit shocks v_t are each equal to zero. Taking this ratio and subtracting one gives the percentage deviation of actual GDP from the simulated GDP with no credit shocks, or $GDP_{\text{actual}}/GDP|_{v=0} - 1$. The result is a measure of how much higher GDP was during the period as a result of the credit shocks taking on the values that are estimated in Eq. (28). This is graphed also in Figure 17.3, plotted on the right axis. The graphs show that the individual credit shock innovations tend to bunch up in positive and negative directions and so cumulate to create the shocks v_t and the cyclical changes in output with some lag.

17.3.2 Robustness of the credit shock construction

The construction of the economy's three shocks uses five variables in the baseline calculation. Alternatively the combinations of five variables taken four at a time, and five taken three at a time, allow for 15 more possible ways to construct the credit shock v_t. All fifteen of these were computed, and Figure 17.4 graphs six of these along with the baseline. The results show that

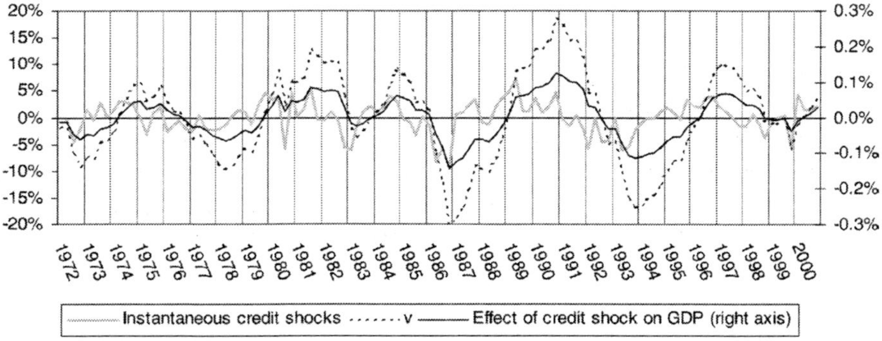

Figure 17.3 Credit innovations ($\hat{\varepsilon}_{vt}$), the credit shock (v_t), and the effect of credit shocks on GDP ($GDP_{\text{actual}}/GDP|_{v=0} - 1$).

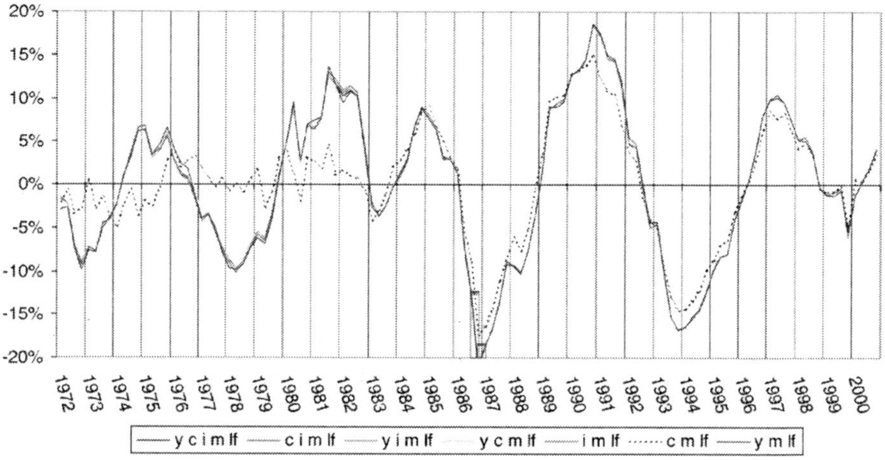

Figure 17.4 The credit shock under alternative identifications.

all variable combinations that include real money, labor hours in banking, and either output or investment, generate nearly the same figure. The other combination presented in Figure 17.4 is money, banking hours and consumption, which shows conformity in the second part of the period but appears rather random in the first part of the period. Other combinations show such randomness and a lack of conformity for the whole period.

The interpretation of these results is that as long as the variables are included that correspond to the model's sectors in which the three shocks occur, then the results have a non-random form that allow for further interpretation. In particular, the real money, banking hours and output variables correspond directly to the sectors in which the money, credit and output shocks occur. As a qualification, the investment variable instead of output gives similar results. Given the standard business cycle evidence of how investment reflects well the goods sector productivity shock, this substitutability of investment for output is not surprising. Further, because it is also well known that the consumption series does not reflect as well the output productivity shock, it is not surprising that substitution of consumption for both output and investment gives a more random result.

Thus the construction is robust within six different alternatives for variable combinations, these being $\hat{y}_t$, $\hat{c}_t$, $\hat{\imath}_t$, $\hat{l}_{Ft}$, $\hat{m}_t$; $\hat{y}_t$, $\hat{c}_t$, $\hat{l}_{Ft}$, $\hat{m}_t$; $\hat{y}_t$, $\hat{\imath}_t$, $\hat{l}_{Ft}$, $\hat{m}_t$; $\hat{c}_t$, $\hat{\imath}_t$, $\hat{l}_{Ft}$, $\hat{m}_t$; $\hat{y}_t$, $\hat{l}_{Ft}$, $\hat{m}_t$; and $\hat{\imath}_t$, $\hat{l}_{Ft}$, $\hat{m}_t$. The latter two constructions are exact identifications that are made without estimation.

17.3.3 Variance decomposition

The construction of the credit shock makes use of the autocorrelation coefficient φ_v, for the credit shock process given in Eq. (6), when it uses the recursive equilibrium solution found in Eqs. (26) and (27). This coefficient is then estimated from an AR(1) process for the resulting credit shock series v_t. And then the shock innovations ε_{vt} are computed with the time series v_t and its estimated autocorrelation. The closeness in value between the autocorrelation coefficient that is assumed in the construction ($\varphi_v = 0.95$) and its estimated value using the constructed shock ($\rho_v = 0.9362$) is in a sense a further check on the consistency of the credit shock construction.

The standard deviation of the shock processes is not used in the shock construction, although it is used in simulations of the economy for the impulse responses. As an additional step to characterize the credit shock process, the results are presented here of a study of the contribution of the shocks to the variance of the output. Ingram et al. (1994) show that the contribution to the variance of output from a particular shock can vary widely depending on its VAR ordering. Results for the Section 17.2 economy confirm this. Alternative variance decompositions of the three shocks were made using all possible alternative constructions of the shocks, and under all possible VAR orderings. The distribution of these variances varies significantly with each of the three possible VAR orderings. The distributions presented in Figure 17.5 are for the credit shock when ordered first (left-hand side) and second, using the alternative constructions with all possible combinations of the five variables ($\hat{y}_t$, $\hat{c}_t$, $\hat{\imath}_t$, $\hat{l}_{Ft}$, $\hat{\mathrm{m}}_t$) that contain at least the real money, banking hours and either output and investment (a total of 12 observations for each VAR ordering). The credit shock shows some bunching around 10%.

Ingram et al. (1994) point out that only when shocks are completely uncorrelated with each other will the variance decomposition be unique. Table 17.1 illustrates for example the non-zero correlations between the output and credit sector shocks for the baseline construction. They range from positive to negative, over the one-period lag and one-period lead. This is the correlation that gives rise to the variation in the variance decomposition. However, despite finding such variation in the fraction of the variance of output explained by the credit shock, it is important to note that the credit shock construction remains unaffected by this variation.

17.4 Credit shocks and banking deregulation

The credit shock innovations and their effect on GDP, graphed in Figure 17.3, appear to have some significant chronological conformity to the timing of banking reform legislation during the period. To see this, consider first an outline of the deregulatory era and its major acts, the timing of the business cycles during the period, how the acts fall within the cycles, and finally the degree to which the credit shocks appear to coincide with the acts.

17.4.1 Legislative events

The US banking crises of the 1930s in the US led to regulations designed to increase the soundness of the banking system. This restricted the scope of

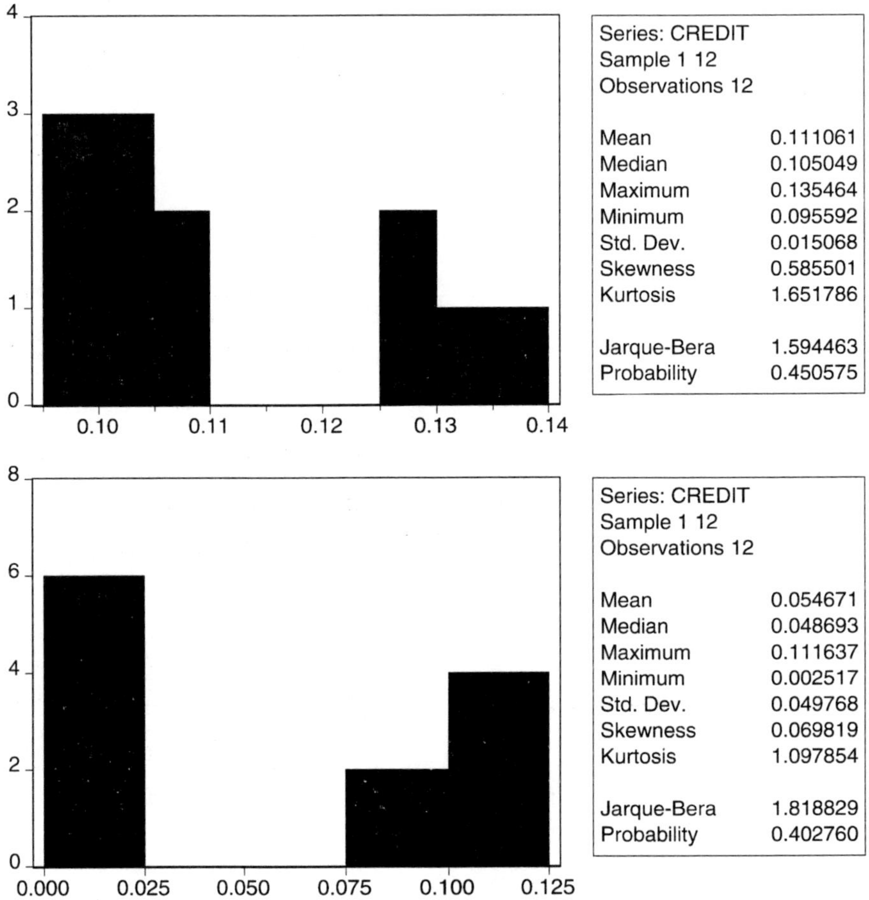

Figure 17.5 Distribution of the variance decompositions of the credit shock, with 1st and 2nd orderings.

banking geographically and vertically, while prohibiting the payment of interest on demand deposits and putting a ceiling on interest rates payable on time deposits (The Banking Acts of 1933 and 1935, Regulation Q). High inflation during the 1960s and 1970s caused interest rates to rise above the ceilings, made it difficult for banks to compete for deposit funds, and led to the expansion of unregulated money market funds. This created pressure to deregulate.

There were five major acts during this period, with a sixth falling at the end of the period under study. The Depository Institutions Deregulation and Monetary Control Act (DIDMCA) of 1980 phased out the deposit interest rate ceilings and allowed checkable deposits that paid a market interest rate. A second major step in the deregulatory process was the Garn-St Germain Act of 1982, which authorized banks and other depository institutions to

Table 17.1 Cross-correlations between the output sector and credit sector shocks

i	$corr(z(t), v(t-i))$ *lags*	$corr(z(t), v(t+i))$ *leads*
0	−0.2859	−0.2859
1	−0.3869	−0.1614
2	−0.4487	−0.0574
3	−0.4721	−0.0439
4	−0.4627	0.1308
5	−0.4327	0.2087
6	−0.3788	0.2682
7	−0.3075	0.3107
8	−0.2228	0.3388
9	−0.1385	0.3585
10	−0.0548	0.3929

offer money market deposit accounts that could compete with money market mutual funds.[4]

The end of the 1980s brought a crisis to the savings and loan sector in the US, apparently a fall-out of the innovation in the other parts of the banking sector and of the 1986 repeal of highly favorable tax write-offs for real estate limited partnerships that were enacted in the major tax act of 1981. The Financial Institutions Reform, Recovery and Enforcement Act of 1989 (FIREA) and the Federal Deposit Insurance Corporation Improvement Act of 1991 (FDICIA) provided for a restructuring of the savings and loan sector that enabled it to compete anew on a more level basis with the rest of the financial industry. The FIRREA created the Resolution Trust Company (RTC) which made closure easier, equalized rules for savings and loans relative to banks, extended FDIC insurance to savings and loans, and facilitated the conversion of savings and loans to banks. The FDICIA in contrast increased the cost of deposit insurance with risk-based premiums and allowed savings and loans to fail more easily by discouraging bail-outs.[5]

The 1990s saw the elimination of most of the remaining restrictions from the 1930s regulatory acts. The Riegle–Neal Interstate Banking and Branching Efficiency Act of 1994 repealed the McFadden Act and allowed interstate bank branching and consolidation. The Gramm–Leach–Bliley Act of 1999 repealed the Glass–Steagall Act and allowed mergers between commercial banks, insurance companies and investment banks. Together these Acts evidently increased competition, generated greater efficiencies and increased the productivity in the banking sector.[6]

17.4.2 Correlation of shock-induced GDP movements with law changes

The effect of the deregulatory acts can be viewed within the business cycle framework. Consider first a definition of the cycles during the period 1972:1 to 2000:4, using the Bry and Boschan (1971) technique, and their brief characterization. Table 17.2 reports the duration (quarters) and amplitude (percent of GDP) of the cycles, as well as Harding and Pagan (2002) measures of the cumulative movements (total gain/loss during the cycle, in percent) and excess movements (the deviation of the cumulative movements from its approximation by a triangle, in percent). The first column reports the averages of these measures for the postwar US data, and the other columns report the particular values for the cycles of the period. The results show for example a longer than average duration, a higher than average amplitude, and a greater cumulative total for the expansions starting in 1982 and in 1991, during which time most of the major financial deregulations occurred. Also in evidence is a stronger expansion (more cumulative GDP increase) for the short one starting in 1980: III and the longer one starting in 1982:III, as implied by a lower excess measure as compared to the average.

The dating of the cycles and their characterization are consistent with the possibility that the major financial deregulations of the early 1980s and early to mid 1990s helped boost output. Analysis of the credit shock innovations strengthens the evidence that the banking legislation contributed to the source of the increases in GDP during these expansions. Figure 17.3 shows a positive credit shock lasting from 1980 to 1983, and another from 1983 to 1986; the innovations to the credit shocks show spikes that correspond to the period following the introduction of the two early 1980s deregulatory acts. Similar positive innovation spikes and credit shocks follow the 1989 and 1994

Table 17.2 Cycle characteristics: post-war averages, and individual cycle values

	US avg.	*1973:IV ↘ 1975:I ↗*	*1980:I ↘ 1980:III ↗*	*1981:III ↘ 1982:III ↗*	*1990:II ↘ 1991:I ↗*
Duration					
Peak ↘ Trough	3.17	5	2	4	3
Trough ↗ Peak	24	20	4	31	39
Amplitude					
Peak ↘ Trough	−2.02	−3.40	−2.19	−2.86	−1.49
Trough ↗ Peak	28.87	23.66	4.26	37.04	39.39
Cumulation					
Peak ↘ Trough	−2.65	−5.06	−2.04	−6.40	−1.19
Trough ↗ Peak	423.79	252.43	8.57	603.20	668.06
Excess					
Peak ↘ Trough	−0.58	−1.04	−0.62	−0.19	−0.60
Trough ↗ Peak	1.02	−0.20	0.51	−0.34	3.07

acts. Thus these four acts coincide closely with the four positive credit shocks that increased GDP during this period. The 1999 act also correlates closely to an innovation spike seen to occur at the end of the period.

Also of interest are the negative effects of the credit shocks on GDP. There are three larger such effects, occurring from 1976 to 1980, 1986 to 1989, and from 1992 to 1996, caused by innovations somewhat preceding these periods. In terms of the acts, the enactment of the 1991 FDICIA act is followed by some negative spikes that caused the 1986 to 1989 negative effect of the credit shock. The 1991 act increased costs to the savings and loans, while allowing for easier closures, and there was a significant consolidation of the savings and loans sector following this act, involving the many closures; these effects may have caused an initially negative effect on output.

The negative shock of 1976 to 1980 is interpreted as being a result of the banks bumping up against restrictive financial industry regulation. In particular, in 1976 to 1980 banks faced binding constraints from Regulation Q, as the inflation rate shot up, that suddenly inhibited their intermediation ability. This could have created the negative spikes at that time. The negative credit shock from 1986 to 1989 conceivably is related to the ending in 1986 of a highly favorable tax treatment for the real estate industry. The Tax Reform Act of 1986 repealed the limited partnership write-offs for real estate investments through which limited partners could get (from unused write-offs of general partners) up to eight times the value of their investment in write-offs that directly reduced their taxable income. This allowed for economically unattractive investment projects to be attractive nonetheless because of the tax law. The 1986 act was viewed as "bursting a bubble" in real estate investment. With the savings and loans' returns propped up by assets weighted heavily in such real estate, this 1986 reform may have triggered the collapse of the savings and loans and its subsequent reform and deregulation. In evidence in 1986 is a strong negative credit shock innovation that preceded the 1986 to 1989 negative effect on GDP of the credit shock, and that coincides in time to the 1986 law change.

17.5 Discussion

Uhlig (2004), taking an atheoretical approach, finds two main shocks which are able to explain more than 90% of the movements in US GDP. He interprets these shocks in terms of a list of the "prime suspects" of business cycle propagation. One of these is a medium-run shock that is found to be similar to the typical output productivity shock. The other is a shorter term shock that he finds does not fit well the characteristics of any of the shocks on his list of candidate shocks. A comparison shows that the credit shock of our model has several similar features of Uhlig's (2004) short-term shock.

In particular, the real side of the economy compares closely while the nominal side shows less congruence. On the real side, the impulse responses of output, consumption, labor hours are similar for the Section 17.2 model's credit shock and for Uhlig's (2004) short-term shock. The real wage rate response to the credit shock can be compared to the labor productivity response for the short term shock in Uhlig (2004). Both fall after the shock and then gradually adjust back; the pattern of the credit shock is especially similar in the decomposition case in Uhlig (2004) for which θ is equal to 150. Note however that while the credit shock impulse responses die out by construction, there is some persistence evident in the Uhlig (2004) short-term shock.

On the nominal side, the model's inflation rate response matches the short term shock response of Uhlig (2004) to some degree. The pattern of the model's inflation rate from the second period on is very similar to that of Uhlig's (2004) PPI inflation. And the pattern of the model's inflation rate impulse response to the credit shock is similar to the Uhlig's (2004) CPI inflation impulse response in that in both there is a positive jump that then turns negative. However, in the model the jump is immediate and in Uhlig (2004) it is gradual, possibly explained by a lack of price stickiness in the credit model; and the model's nominal interest rate response compares less well with the federal funds response in Uhlig (2004), possibly for a related reason.

17.6 Conclusions

The chapter analyzes a stochastic version of the Gillman and Kejak (2005b) monetary economy with a payments technology for exchange credit. Deterministically this credit technology has been useful in explaining the effect of inflation on growth (Gillman and Kejak, 2005b), the role of financial development in the inflation-growth evidence (Gillman et al., 2004), and in explaining Tobin (1965) evidence (Gillman and Nakov, 2003), as well as for allowing for a liquidity effect to be postulated Li (2000). Applied to the business cycle, a shock to credit productivity allows for a new focus on shocks besides the goods productivity and money supply shocks. The chapter constructs the credit shock by solving the recursive equilibrium system, substituting in data for the endogenous variables in the equilibrium solution, and then either estimating or solving for each of the three shocks, in a procedure related to Parkin (1988) and Ingram et al. (1994, 1997). The construction is found to be robust to the use of several different data sets, with the condition that data for variables from the sectors being shocked needs to be included in the construction. The credit shock innovations show congruence with change in US banking laws during the financial deregulatory era of the 1980s and 1990s. The idea that a credit shock can affect aggregate productivity and be linked to changes in government policy is not inconsistent with the conclusions of Kehoe and Prescott (2002) that depressions across the world have resulted from shocks to productivity related to government policy changes. Indeed it would be interesting to apply the analysis of the chapter to the US 1930s depression period, although data on the bank sector may be a constraining factor.

The credit shock also shows similar features to a key shock identified by Uhlig (2005). He finds that two shocks explain the majority of the movements in GNP: a medium-run one similar to the goods productivity shock, and another shorter term one that lacks similarities with the candidate shocks that Uhlig (2005) considers. The credit shock of this model parallels the effect of this second shorter term shock on the real side of the economy. This strengthens the case for considering the credit shock as a potentially important candidate shock that can contribute significantly to business cycle movements.

Another approach in the business cycle literature is that of Chari et al. (2007) who decompose the shocks into different sources of marginal distortions. How the credit shock identified here may fit into their productivity, labor tax, and capital tax wedges may be worth further study. Since their labor tax distorts the leisure-labor margin in a way similar to the inflation tax in a monetary model, and both the cost of credit and the cost of money affect this margin in the model of this chapter, the credit shocks might partly be accounted for through this wedge.

Acknowledgements

The second author is grateful to Central European University for grant support, and the second and third authors are also supported by a grant from the World Bank Global Development Network.

Notes

* Benk, Szilárd, Max Gillman and Michal Kejak (2005). 'Credit Shocks in the Financial Deregulatory Era: Not the Usual Suspects', *Review of Economic Dynamics*, 8(3), 668–687.

1 This updates a previous study by Jayaratne and Strahan (1996) that finds that the states' growth rate accelerated by 0.5 to 1 percentage points following deregulation during the 1972 to 1992 period.

2 The details of the log-linearization can be found in Benk et al. (2004).

3 The data sources is the IMF online IFS database for all variables except the hours in banking, which is from the online Bureau of Labor Statistics. For this series, the Commercial Banks sector is used, where the hour series is the product of the two series, "average weekly hours of production workers" and "production workers, thousands." This data is at a monthly frequency, and it is converted to a quarterly basis using a simple three-month average.

4 For more detailed explanations regarding banking legislation, see Mishkin (1997).

5 See Hanc (1998) for a detailed analysis.

6 See Guzman (2003) for details on financial deregulations in the 1990s. Strahan (2003) documents other US changes. Cetorelli (2004) finds evidence of greater competition in banking in the EU following deregulation of the finance sector.

18 A comparison of exchange economies within a monetary business cycle*

Szilárd Benk, Max Gillman and Michal Kejak†

Summary

The chapter sets out a monetary business cycle model with three alternative exchange technologies: the cash-only, shopping time and credit production models. The goods productivity and money shocks affect all three models, while the credit model has in addition a credit productivity shock. The chapter compares the performance of the models in explaining the puzzles of the monetary business cycle theory. The credit model improves the ability to explain the procyclic movement of monetary aggregates, inflation and the nominal interest rate.

18.1 Introduction

The contribution of monetary factors to business cycle movements has been studied using the general equilibrium approach in the cash-in-advance economies of Cooley and Hansen (1989, 1995, 1998) and the shopping time model of Gavin and Kydland (1999) and Dittmar et al. (2005). While money supply shocks have been found to have little effect on business cycles, supported also in Ireland (2004) and Benk et al. (2005), there are still many nominal features that present a challenge for general equilibrium monetary modeling. For example, inflation persistence results in the model of Dittmar et al. (2005) through the use of Taylor rules of money rather than simple growth rate rules. Liquidity features have not been well explained in the 'inflation tax' models although recent work has brought a rudimentary liquidity effect into otherwise standard exchange-based economies without imposing nominal rigidities; this is through the use of a credit production sector in Li (2000). Explaining procyclic monetary aggregates and inflation rate movements has been even more elusive. A procyclic inflation movement is found only in Dittmar et al. (2005) when there is negative or near-zero feedback from output in the Taylor rule, whereas this feedback parameter is typically estimated at higher positive levels.

Extending the exchange economy by allowing for the production of credit as an alternative to cash, while maintaining a simple money supply growth rule, has found success in other related areas besides the liquidity effect.

These include the modeling of the income velocity of base, M1 and M2 monetary aggregates (Gillman and Kejak, 2004), the explanation of the effect of inflation on growth (Gillman and Nakov, 2004; Gillman and Kejak, 2005a, 2005b) and the specification of a role for financial development within the inflation–growth nexus (Gillman and Harris, 2004; Gillman et al., 2004). Using the credit production technology also has shown promise in explaining output movements during financial deregulatory periods at business cycle frequencies (Benk et al., 2005).

Here the chapter applies the credit production approach to the business cycle in order to compare this exchange technology extension to more standard approaches, the cash-in-advance and shopping time models. A simple money supply rule is maintained.[1] Velocity is endogenous and the results suggest that the credit production approach improves the ability of the inflation tax models to explain business cycle movements. In particular the paper demonstrates that the credit production model can explain procyclic movements in monetary aggregates, inflation and nominal interest rates while the standard models cannot.

Such potential improvements make sense intuitively in that they result from exploitation of an additional margin, relative to the standard cash-in-advance economy. A similar margin exists in the shopping time model but it is rarely exploited there; and shocking the shopping time is awkward in its rationale. The margin included by the credit approach is the ability of the agent to trade-off between using cash and using credit in exchange, depending on relative costs. Cash-only models do not have this freedom and shopping time approaches specify a general transactions cost that induces a margin between using money and using time for exchange. This money–time trade-off can be described as a broad-brush approach that the credit approach refines by specifying labor time that is used in a diminishing returns production function for credit services as an alternative to money in exchange. A distinct advantage of the credit approach relative to shopping time is that the credit production function can be shocked, and calibrated using time-series data from the bank sector. For example, the credit shock in a credit production approach has been identified robustly in Benk *et al.* (2005).

Exploitation of the additional margin allows for additional income and substitution effects that improve the monetary business cycle model's performance during certain periods. The income effect is important when for example there is a positive credit shock that also contributes significantly to GDP. Benk et al. (2005) demonstrate that several of these appear to exist in the USA during the 1980s and 1990s, and for example that these contributed to even bigger increase in GDP during the upswings starting in 1982 and 1991. The income from the positive credit shock causes an additional upward increase in consumption and money demand not present in the other models. And this is the interpretation given for the model's ability to explain procyclic monetary aggregate (M1) movement.

The substitution effect is important in terms of the use of money versus credit in the purchase of the consumption basket. Consider that a positive shock to the productivity of the credit sector causes credit use to become less expensive, and induces more credit to be used relative to cash in exchange. This acts to decrease money demand in the face of an unchanged money supply growth rate. The level effect on money demand causes the price level to jump and the inflation rate to pulse upwards. Continuing with the example of the financial deregulation of the 1980s in the USA, the inflation rate would have been pulsed upwards from the deregulatory acts even while the money supply growth rate began to fall; the result would be an inflation rate that did not fall as quickly as expected (by the money supply growth rates) and a tendency for a procyclic inflation rate when the credit shock contributes significantly to output changes. This significant effect on output would only occur with relatively large, occasional, credit shocks such as major deregulations. This type of substitution likewise carries over to explain how the credit model better explains observed procyclic nominal interest rate movements not explained with the shopping time or standard cash-in-advance models. And so the credit model improves upon the ability to explain an observed procyclic nature of monetary aggregates, the inflation rate and the nominal interest rates, but does this most plausibly during subperiods containing strong credit shocks.

18.2 Exchange-based business cycle models

Three representative agent models are examined: the standard cash-in-advance, a shopping time economy and the credit production economy. Here a nested model of the three economies is presented. With utility over consumption c_t and leisure x_t given by

$$U = E_0 \sum_{t=0}^{\infty} \beta^t (\log c_t + \Psi \log x_t) \quad 0 < \beta < 1 \tag{1}$$

the consumer faces a minimum of two shocks in all three models: an aggregate output productivity shock and a money supply growth rate shock. The third shock introduced in the credit economy is to the productivity of credit production.

Current investment i_t plus the depreciated capital from the last period comprise the current capital stock k_t:

$$k_t = (1 - \delta) k_{t-1} + i_t \tag{2}$$

Output y_t is produced by the agent with the previous period capital stock k_{t-1} and current labor n_t via a Cobb-Douglas constant-returns-to-scale production function with the productivity shock z_t:

$$y_t = e^{z_t} k_{t-1}^{a} n_t^{1-a} \tag{3}$$

$$z_t = \varphi_z z_{t-1} + \varepsilon_{zt} \qquad \varepsilon_{zt} \sim N(0, \sigma_{\varepsilon z}^2) \qquad 0 < \varphi_z < 1 \tag{4}$$

Firms maximize their profits $y_t - r_t k_{t-1} - w_t n_t + (1-\delta) k_{t-1}$, implying the equilibrium real wage rate w_t and the real gross capital rate of return net of depreciation δ, or r_t:

$$w_t = (1-a) e^{z_t} k_{t-1}^{a} n_t^{-a} \tag{5}$$

$$r_t = a e^{z_t} k_{t-1}^{a-1} n_t^{1-a} + 1 - \delta \tag{6}$$

Current income from labor, capital and lump-sum transfers of new money T_t are spent on consumption c_t and capital, yielding the change in money stock $M_t - M_{t-1}$. With P_t the nominal price of the consumption good, this gives the period t budget constraint as

$$w_t P_t (1 - x_t - l_{Ft}) + P_t r_t k_{t-1} + T_1 - P_t c_t - P_t k_t \geq M_t - M_{t-1} \tag{7}$$

The money supply is subject to a sequence of random nominal transfers that satisfy

$$T_t = \Theta_t M_{t-1} = (\Theta^* + e^{u_t} - 1) M_{t-1} \tag{8}$$

where Θ_t is the random growth rate of money, Θ^* is the stationary growth rate of money and u_t is a random autoregressive process given by

$$u_t = \varphi_u u_{t-1} + \varepsilon_{ut} \qquad \varepsilon_{ut} \sim N(0, \sigma_{\varepsilon u}^2) \qquad 0 < \varphi_u < 1 \tag{9}$$

The other resource constraint allocates the total time endowment among leisure, labor hours in producing the aggregate output and time spent in exchange activity, denoted by l_{Ft}:

$$n_t + x_t + l_{Ft} = 1 \tag{10}$$

18.2.1 Exchange

An extended cash-in-advance constraint is specified so that it encompasses three alternative exchange technologies. The general form is

$$M_{t-1} + T_t \geq P_t c_t (B_1 - B_2 c_t^{b_1} \tilde{A}_{Ft} l_{Ft}^{b_2}) \tag{11}$$

where B_1, B_2, b_1 and b_2 are parameters, and $\tilde{A}_{Ft}$ is a variable, specified in the following special cases.

18.2.1.1 Cash-only

For the standard cash-in-advance economy that uses only cash, let $B_1 = 1$ and $B_2 = 0$.

18.2.1.2 Shopping time

The shopping time case assumes that $\tilde{A}_{Ft}$ is a positive parameter A_F, $B_1 = 0$, $B_2 = -1$, $b_1 = 0$ and $b_2 = -1$; or

$$M_{t-1} + T_t \geq P_t c_t A_F / l_{Ft} \tag{12}$$

This implies a proportionality of the time spent in 'shopping' to the consumption velocity of money; or that $l_{Ft} = A_F[c_t/(M_t/P_t)]$. While the more general form of the shopping time function is $l_{Ft} = f(c_t, M_t/P_t), f_c > 0, f_{M/P} < 0$, the particular specification with proportionality to velocity is found in Gavin and Kydland (1999) and Lucas (2000), justified because it yields a constant interest elasticity of money demand equal to –0.5 as in Baumol (1952).

Given that time in exchange activity is proportional to velocity, this implies a unitary elasticity of exchange time with respect to velocity; $(\partial l_{Ft}/\partial V_t)(V_t/l_{Ft}) = 1$ where $V_t \equiv c_t/(M_t/P_t)$. Or if the elasticity is defined in terms of the ratio of exchange time to consumption, where $\eta \equiv [\partial(l_{Ft}/c_t)/\partial V_t][V_t/(l_{Ft}/c_t)]$, then again $\eta = 1$.

18.2.1.3 Credit production

Here $\tilde{A}_{Ft} = A_F e^{v_t}$, $B_1 = 1$, $B_2 = 1$, $b_1 = -\gamma$ and $b_2 = \gamma$, or

$$M_{t-1} + T_t \geq P_t c_t (1 - c_t^{-\gamma} A_F e^{v_t} l_{Ft}^{\gamma}) \tag{13}$$

It is assumed that $\gamma \in (0,1)$, $A_F > 0$ and that the shock v_t follows an autoregressive process:

$$\upsilon_t = \varphi_v V_{t-1} + \varepsilon_{vt} \qquad \varepsilon_{vt} \sim N(0, \sigma_{\varepsilon v}^2) \qquad 0 < \varphi_v < 1 \tag{14}$$

Note that the credit sector specification, supplying only a means of exchange and not intertemporal credit, is parallel to the aggregate output sector specification in several ways. First the credit shock is similar to the productivity shock above, except that the credit shock is a sectoral productivity shock rather than an aggregate shock across all sectors. But it is still a shock to the shift parameter of the production function both in the credit sector case and in the aggregate production case. To see this, consider letting $a_t \in (0, 1]$ denote the fraction of consumption goods that are purchased with money. Then $c_t a_t$ is the total amount purchased with money and $c_t(1 - a_t)$ is the remainder: the total amount of goods purchased with credit. Now consider producing this quantity of credit used for exchange with the following production function involving labor time: $c_t(1 - a_t) = A_F e^{v_t}(l_{Ft}/c_t)^{\gamma} c_t$, where l_{Ft} is the labor time. This can be rewritten as $1 - a_t = A_F e^{v_t}(l_{Ft}/c_t)^{\gamma}$ which says that the share of credit production is produced with the labor per unit of consumption, with a diminishing marginal product of normalized labor. Solving for $a_t = 1 - A_F e^{v_t}(l_{Ft}/c_t)^{\gamma}$, writing the exchange constraint as $M_t = a_t P_t c_t$ and substituting for a_t gives the exchange constraint (13). This clarifies that the assumption behind the exchange constraint is simply that the credit share is produced in a diminishing returns fashion. And it shows that the shock affects the productivity factor of this production function.

The credit production function is also similar to the Cobb–Douglas form of the aggregate production function. Writing it as $c_t(1 - a_t) = A_F e^{v_t} l_{Ft}^{\gamma} c_t^{1-\gamma}$, it is of the Cobb–Douglas form in l_{Ft} and c_t. However, just as American Express offers credit for exchange (no intertemporal loans) with its standard card, and just as American Express takes the total economic activity as a given in its production of the exchange credit for the economy, so also does our credit production take the total output as a given in its production of the exchange credit.

The degree of diminishing returns depends on the parameter γ. Gillman and Kejak (2005b) illustrate that a value of γ between 0 and 0.5 results in a marginal cost of credit production that is upward sloping and convex, as in the right-hand side of a standard U-shaped marginal cost curve, while values between 0.5 and 1 give an upward sloping but concave marginal cost curve. The values used in the robustness (Section 5 below) range between 0 and 1 but values above 0.5 are suspect in that they yield a marginal cost that rises at a diminishing rate, unusual if found in the industrial organization literature. The baseline value in the simulations is $\gamma = 0.21$, as estimated in Gillman and Otto (2003) from the time-series estimation of US money demand that is derived from a similar credit technology.

18.2.1.4 Comparison

In comparison to the shopping time case, one key difference is the ability to shock the productivity of the credit production in a standard way, in that it is similar to the shock to any sector or to the aggregate output. The other key difference concerns the elasticities of these models to nominal type changes. Consider that the exchange time in the credit model is not proportional to the consumption velocity of money as it is in the common shopping time specification. Rather the exchange time to velocity ratio rises with the inflation rate. This implies a significant difference in the underlying money demand function. And a similar difference exists between the cash-only and the credit production economies.

Consider the elasticity of exchange time relative to velocity ($1/a_t$). While zero in the cash-only case, and one in the shopping time case, the elasticity of exchange time with respect to velocity is larger than one in the credit production case. For the credit case, let $V \equiv c/(M/P)$ and $\eta \equiv [\partial(l_{Ft}/c_t)/\partial V_t][V_t/(l_{Ft}/c_t)]$; then $\eta = (1/\gamma)[1/(V-1)]$. If, for example, $a_t = 0.5$ and $\gamma = 0.21$, then $V = 2$ and $\eta \approx 5$. This means that the exchange time rises much more than proportionally with increases in the velocity. And this is just a standard feature of a production function with a diminishing marginal product in each of its factors. To see this, consider a standard Cobb–Douglas production function of output, say Y, that depends on a labor quantity L and capital K, as in $Y = L^{\gamma}K^{1-\gamma}$. Then the elasticity of the ratio of labor to capital with respect to the ratio of capital to output, denoted by $\tilde{\eta}$, compares directly to η, the labor elasticity of velocity as defined above; this Cobb–Douglas elasticity can be found to be equal to $\tilde{\eta} = -1/\gamma$. With $\gamma = 0.21$, $\tilde{\eta} \approx -5$, similar to $\eta \approx 5$ when $V = 2$ (the difference in signs results because the credit output is $1 - a_t$ and not a_t). These elasticity results in the production functions reflect the same thing: that the marginal cost curve is positively sloped and rising at an increasing rate. Increasingly more labor time is used because of increasing marginal costs of production. So the elasticity result in the credit production function is a natural consequence of using a standard microeconomic relation and is not found in the standard shopping time and cash-only models.

The consequence of the credit specification can be put in terms of income and substitution effects. There can be significant income effects from using an increasing amount of time in banking, as the inflation rate increases. Cash-only has no such real resource use in avoiding inflation and shopping time has what might be called a unitary elastic cost. During the business cycle, a significant positive credit productivity shock can free up a measurable amount of time and have a significant income effect on the credit model.

The substitution effect can be stated in terms of the interest elasticity of money demand. The cash-only model has a very sluggish interest elasticity of money that rises slightly in magnitude as the inflation rate goes up; it does not allow for exchange time to be used as an alternative to money; and therefore the consumer has no alternative by which to buy goods and only slightly substitutes away from money as inflation rises. The shopping time model has a constant interest elasticity similar to the Baumol (1952) model that results from its assumption of a unitary time elasticity with respect to velocity. And the credit, or banking time, model produces an interest elasticity that rises in magnitude with the inflation rate in a way very similar to the Cagan (1956) model;[2] this is a result of using a more standard production function. These differing substitution effects can influence business cycle results if there is a large shock that significantly affects the use of money versus its credit alternative in the credit model. The only exchange alternative in the cash-only model is leisure, not typically subject to shocks; in the shopping time model, the exchange alternatives are leisure or shopping time, also not typically shocked. And note that, at high rates of inflation, the elasticity tends to be higher in the credit model than in both the cash-only and shopping time (depending on calibrations) and the substitution effect would then be significantly greater and the effect of a shock larger, such as one that possibly may have occurred during the moderately high US inflation of the early 1980s when deregulation began.

18.2.2 Equilibrium

The consumer's exchange constraint can alternatively be written in the nested model as

$$M_{t-1} + T_t \geq a_t P_t c_t \tag{15}$$

where

$$\begin{aligned} a_t &= 1 \text{ cash-only} \\ &= A_F / l_{Ft} \text{ shopping time} \\ &= 1 - A_F e^{v_t} \left(\frac{l_{Ft}}{c_t}\right)^{\gamma} \text{ credit production} \end{aligned} \tag{16}$$

or, expressed in terms of l_{Ft}, in each of these cases, gives that

$$\begin{aligned} l_{Ft} &= 0 \text{ cash-only} \\ &= A_F / a_t \text{ shopping time} \\ &= [(1 - a_t)/(A_{Ft} e^{v_t})]^{1/\gamma}\, c_t \quad \text{credit proudction} \end{aligned} \tag{17}$$

This formulation summarizes the nested model developed above and is convenient for defining the equilibrium and for calibration.

The consumer chooses consumption, leisure, capital stock, the fraction of goods bought with money, time spent in exchange activity and the money balances over time, $\{c_t, x_t, k_t, a_t, l_{Ft}, M_t\}_{t=0}^{\infty}$, to maximize lifetime utility (1) subject to the budget constraint (7), the cash-in-advance constraint (15) and the exchange technology given in equation (17) for the three cases:

$$\begin{aligned} L = E \sum_{t=0}^{\infty} \beta^t \Big\{ & (\log c_t + \Psi \log x_t) + \lambda_t \left(\frac{M_{t-1} + T_t}{P_t} - a_t c_t \right) \\ & + \mu_t \left[w_t (1 - x_t - l_{Ft}) + r_t k_{t-1} + \frac{M_{t-1} + T_t}{P_t} - c_t - k_t - \frac{M_t}{P_t} \right] \Big\} \end{aligned} \tag{18}$$

A competitive equilibrium for this economy consists of a set of allocations $\{c_t, x_t, l_t, n_t, l_{Ft}, k_t, a_t, M_t\}_{t=0}^{\infty}$, a set of prices $\{w_t, r_t\}_{t=0}^{\infty}$, exogenous shock processes $\{z_t, v_t, u_t\}_{t=0}^{\infty}$, a money supply process and initial conditions k_{-1} and M_{-1} such that, given the prices, shocks and government transfers, the allocations solve the consumer's utility maximization problem, solve the firm's profit maximization problem and make the goods, labor and money markets clear.

In a stationary deterministic steady state we use the transformation $p_t = P_t/M_t$ (and also denote real money balances by $m_t = M_t/P_t$). There is no uncertainty and time indices can be dropped, denoting by an asterisk the steady-state values and by $R^* = r^*(\Theta^* + 1)$ the steady-state interest rate factor.

18.2.3 Log-linearization and calibration

The first-order conditions and log-linearization of the model, following Uhlig (1995), are presented in Appendix 18.A1. This uses the first-order Taylor approximation of the log variables around the steady state and replaces all equations by approximations which are linear functions in the log-deviations of the variables. For example, the variable x_t is replaced with $x_t = x^*(1 + \hat{x}_t)$, where $\hat{x}_t$ is the percentage deviation (log-deviation) from the steady state, or $\tilde{x}_t \approx \mathrm{d} \log x_t$, and x^* is the steady-state value of the variable x_t.

The baseline calibration uses standard values that are found in the literature. For the more novel credit sector parameter A_F, its value is set to 1.422 which follows from setting $\gamma = 0.21$ (as estimated in Gillman and Otto (2003)). The table in Appendix 18.A2 presents the values used in all three models.

18.3 Impulse responses

Figures 18.1–18.3 show the impulse responses for the credit model to goods productivity shocks, money shocks and the additional credit productivity shock. The impulse responses of the cash-only and shopping time models to goods productivity and money shocks are similar to those of the credit model, with the exceptions mentioned below.

18.3.1 Goods productivity shock

Across the three models, a positive goods productivity shock (Figure 18.1) causes more output, consumption, capital, labor, real wages, real interest rate and real money, and lower leisure and prices. Shopping time falls slightly while banking time falls a lot, as labor time is more valuable.

18.3.2 Money shock

Across the three models, a positive shock to the nominal money supply growth rate (Figure 18.2) causes an increase in capital, real wages and prices, and a decrease in output, consumption, labor, the real interest rate and real money. Leisure falls in the shopping time model but increases in the cash-only and credit models. At the same time, the exchange time in the credit model rises by some 10-fold more than the shopping time. Also consumption falls

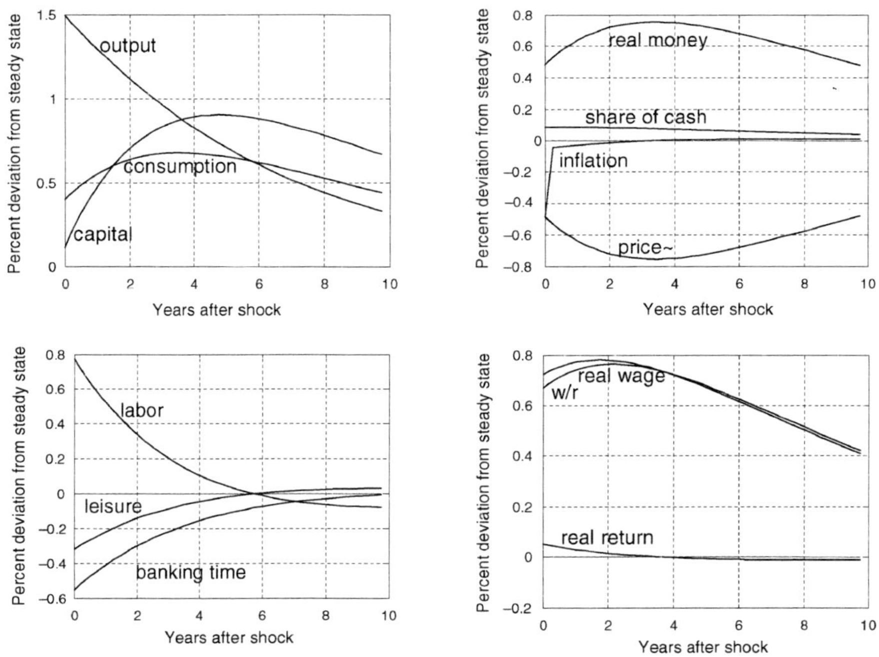

Figure 18.1 Impulse responses to 1 per cent productivity shock: credit model.

strongly in the cash-only model, less so in the credit model, and hardly at all in the shopping time model. The cash-only and credit models show the typical goods to leisure substitution, but the shopping time model does not. This can be interpreted as the shopping time model having 'too much' substitution towards exchange time at low inflation rates, because of the constant –0.5 interest elasticity of money; the credit model in contrast has a near-zero interest elasticity of money at very low inflation rates. The credit model's inelastic money demand at low inflation rates causes more substitution from goods to leisure.[3]

18.3.3 Credit productivity shock

The third shock (Figure 18.3) appears only in the credit model, giving it potentially more explanatory power through this additional dimension. Here the key difference, with a positive credit productivity shock, is that while consumption and output rise, so do prices. In comparison, for a money shock, consumption and output fall as prices rise, in all three models. This is the reason why the additional shock allows for a better explanation of procyclic inflation. And this feature makes sense: an increase in credit productivity during say financial deregulation causes more banking and less money use, with the same money supply growth rate; thus more inflation. If the credit

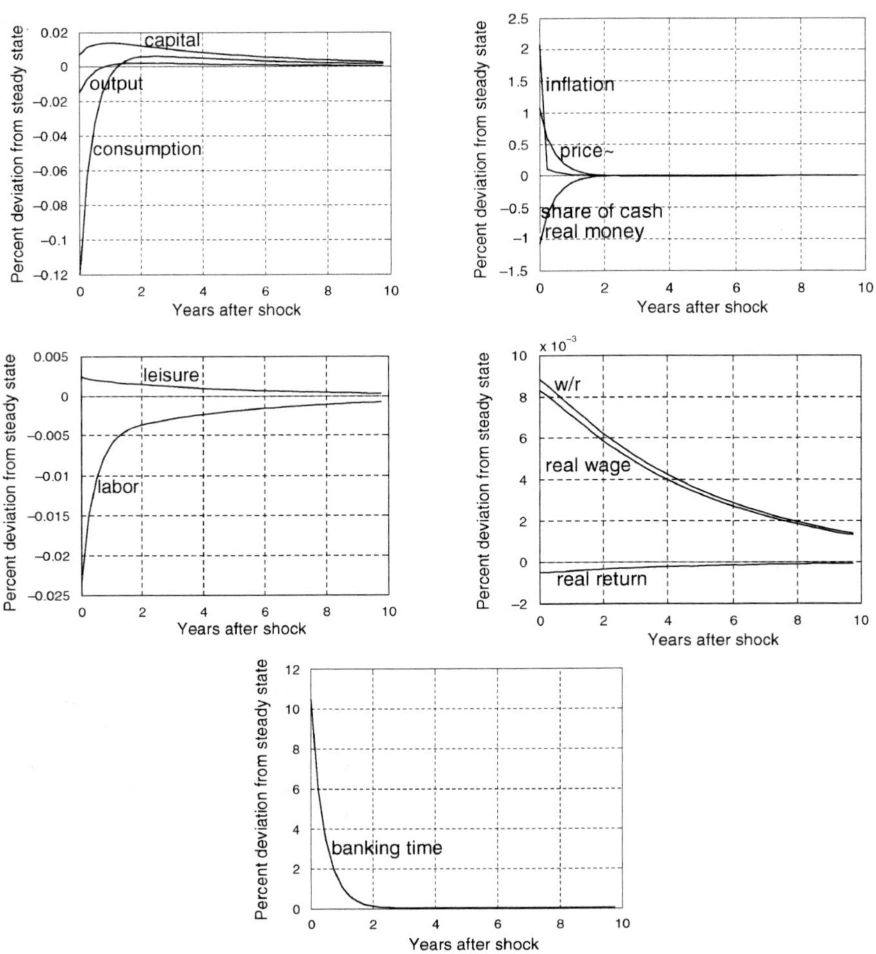

Figure 18.2 Impulse responses to 1 per cent money supply shock: credit model.

shock also leads to a positive GDP impulse, then inflation moves up at the same time as GDP. This is a feature found in US post-war data, and as elaborated upon next, the impulse responses show that neither the goods productivity or the money shock yields such procyclic inflation.

18.4 Puzzles

Table 18.1 first sets out the actual cyclical behavior of the post-war US economy over the 1959:I–2000:IV period. This updates the facts presented in Cooley and Hansen (1995). It shows the standard deviations and the cross-correlations with real GDP and with M1 growth for real and nominal variables.

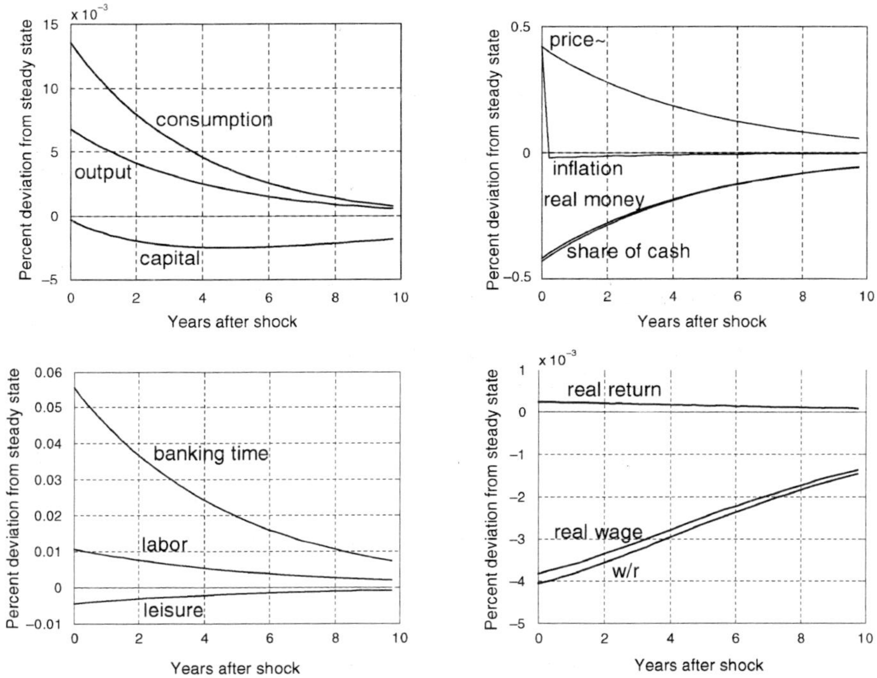

Figure 18.3 Impulse responses to 1 per cent credit productivity shock: credit model.

18.4.1 Simulations

Simulations were conducted for all three models, in order to see how they perform compared with the puzzles in the literature; only the credit model simulations are presented in Table 18.2. This table presents the results of simulating the credit model economy 50 times, each simulation being 168 periods long, to match the number of observations underlying the US statistics reported in Table 18.1. Each simulated time series is filtered with the Hodrick–Prescott filter; the standard deviations of the key variables are reported as well as their cross-correlation with output.

A comparison with the actual cross-correlations in Table 18.1 shows noteworthy features. While the credit model does not capture the actual output correlation with banking hours, it does do rather well with the inflation rate and the nominal interest rate. The actual data show a positive correlation of future output with inflation and nominal interest rates, and a negative correlation with lagged output with inflation and nominal interest rates. The credit model simulation shows a similar pattern although it is not exactly in phase with actual data. For example, the actual data show a positive current output correlation, and in the simulation the correlation turns positive only with the one-period-ahead output.

Table 18.1 Cyclical behavior of the US economy: 1959:I–2000:IV

			Cross-correlation of output with										
Variable	*SD %*	*Corr. with M growth*	$x(-5)$	$x(-4)$	$x(-3)$	$x(-2)$	$x(-1)$	x	$x(+1)$	$x(+2)$	$x(+3)$	$x(+4)$	$x(+5)$
Output	1.43	–0.13	0.06	0.26	0.46	0.67	0.86	1.00	0.86	0.67	0.46	0.26	0.06
Consumption	1.47	0.01	0.42	0.57	0.69	0.80	0.84	0.79	0.62	0.43	0.23	0.04	–0.13
Investment	4.77	–0.11	0.20	0.37	0.52	0.70	0.83	0.89	0.80	0.63	0.43	0.20	–0.01
Banking hours	1.23	–0.01	–0.53	–0.50	–0.42	–0.32	–0.15	0.04	0.21	0.34	0.45	0.47	0.50
Real wage	1.16	0.18	0.43	0.53	0.57	0.60	0.58	0.45	0.29	0.14	–0.02	–0.18	–0.30
Prices (CPI)	1.22	–0.15	–0.61	–0.68	–0.71	–0.70	–0.64	–0.51	–0.37	–0.22	–0.09	0.04	0.16
Inflation	0.42	–0.32	–0.33	–0.25	–0.10	0.02	0.20	0.38	0.47	0.47	0.49	0.49	0.41
Money (M1)	3.98	0.11	0.14	0.15	0.15	0.14	0.11	0.07	0.00	–0.06	–0.09	–0.12	–0.15
Money growth	1.00	1.00	0.08	0.09	0.05	0.03	–0.09	–0.13	–0.25	–0.19	–0.14	–0.08	–0.07
Real money	3.32	0.20	0.35	0.40	0.43	0.44	0.39	0.30	0.17	0.06	–0.04	–0.13	–0.21
Interest rate (TBill)	1.15	–0.51	–0.61	–0.50	–0.33	–0.14	0.13	0.36	0.48	0.51	0.50	0.47	0.43
Cons. velocity	2.68	–0.25	–0.24	–0.21	–0.17	–0.11	–0.02	0.07	0.14	0.18	0.18	0.18	0.17
Income velocity	3.27	–0.28	–0.38	–0.34	–0.26	–0.16	–0.01	0.15	0.23	0.27	0.27	0.26	0.23

Table 18.2 Standard deviations in per cent and correlations with output of the simulated economy (Hodrick–Prescott filtered series)

			Cross-correlation of output with										
Variable	*SD %*	*Corr. with M growth*	*x(−5)*	*x(−4)*	*x(−3)*	*x(−2)*	*x(−1)*	*x*	*x(+1)*	*x(+2)*	*x(+3)*	*x(+4)*	*x(+5)*
Output	1.44	−0.01	−0.03	0.09	0.25	0.45	0.70	1.00	0.70	0.45	0.25	0.09	−0.03
Consumption	0.47	−0.25	−0.23	−0.12	0.03	0.24	0.51	0.86	0.73	0.60	0.48	0.37	0.26
Investment	4.51	0.09	0.04	0.15	0.30	0.49	0.71	0.99	0.65	0.38	0.17	0.00	−0.11
Capital	0.40	0.02	−0.45	−0.39	−0.29	−0.14	0.07	0.36	0.54	0.63	0.66	0.64	0.59
Banking hours	11.02	1.00	0.02	0.01	0.00	−0.01	−0.04	−0.06	−0.05	−0.03	−0.03	−0.02	−0.01
Share of cash	1.09	−0.92	−0.02	0.00	0.00	0.02	0.05	0.08	0.06	0.04	0.04	0.03	0.02
Real wage	0.72	−0.01	−0.12	0.00	0.16	0.38	0.65	0.98	0.74	0.54	0.37	0.22	0.10
Leisure	0.31	0.04	−0.06	−0.18	−0.32	−0.50	−0.72	−0.98	−0.62	−0.34	−0.13	0.04	0.15
Labor	0.75	−0.06	0.06	0.18	0.32	0.50	0.72	0.98	0.62	0.34	0.13	−0.04	−0.15
Prices	2.79	0.59	0.05	0.03	0.01	−0.03	−0.08	−0.16	−0.13	−0.11	−0.09	−0.08	−0.07
Inflation	2.00	0.84	0.00	−0.03	−0.03	−0.05	−0.08	−0.09	0.03	0.03	0.02	0.02	0.02
Real return	0.05	−0.04	0.10	0.21	0.35	0.52	0.72	0.96	0.59	0.29	0.07	−0.09	−0.20
Money	2.33	0.23	0.01	0.01	0.02	0.02	0.02	0.01	0.01	0.01	0.00	−0.01	−0.02
Money growth	1.06	1.00	0.02	0.01	0.02	0.01	0.00	−0.01	−0.02	−0.01	−0.02	−0.02	−0.02
Real money	1.31	−0.87	−0.10	−0.04	0.01	0.10	0.22	0.37	0.31	0.25	0.21	0.16	0.11
Interest rate	2.00	0.84	0.00	−0.02	−0.02	−0.03	−0.06	−0.07	0.05	0.04	0.02	0.02	0.02
Wage rate	0.68	−0.01	−0.14	−0.02	0.15	0.36	0.63	0.97	0.75	0.55	0.39	0.24	0.12
Cons. velocity	1.09	0.92	0.02	0.00	0.00	−0.02	−0.05	−0.08	−0.06	−0.04	−0.04	−0.03	−0.02
Income velocity	1.54	0.73	0.06	0.13	0.22	0.34	0.46	0.60	0.38	0.21	0.06	−0.05	−0.12

18.4.2 Explanation of puzzles with simulations across models

The various puzzles from Cooley and Hansen (1989, 1995, 1998) and Gavin and Kydland (1999) are enumerated in Table 18.3 and organized into credit effects and inflation tax effects categories (Table 18.3). Columns 2–4 summarize the extent to which the three models, credit, cash-only and shopping time respectively, are able to explain puzzles when faced with joint productivity and money shocks. Columns 5–8 show when the credit shock is also active, applying only to the credit model.

First note that, when subject to joint productivity and money shocks, the credit model generates the procyclic monetary aggregates and the money–output phase shift, as found in the actual data. These facts are not replicated by the two alternative models with the joint shocks. This shows an advantage of the credit model using standard shocks.

Credit shocks alone (column 5) generate procyclic monetary aggregates and income velocity as well as the phase shift between money and output, as seen in the data. This simulation also replicates the procyclic inflation and nominal interest rate, with values very close to the data. The other models cannot match the data here. Column 8 presents results of the credit model with all three shocks, as in the simulations presented in Table 18.2. Here the inflation procyclic movement with current output is lost, but as noted above the simulation still matches the correlation of inflation with one-period-ahead output.

What emerges primarily from this comparison with the puzzles is that the credit shock can be important in explaining inflation movements. Put differently, when the economy is in a period during which the credit shock is important, such as banking deregulation, the procyclic inflation movement can be explained in this way.

18.5 Sensitivity and robustness

It is important that the simulations prove robust to variations in key parameters, in particular the degree of diminishing returns in credit production, γ, the productivity shift parameter in credit production, A_F, and the inflation rate level.

For the γ values of 0.21 (the baseline calibration), 0.3, 0.5, 0.6 and 0.8, two of the most important cases are examined: the credit-shock-only case and the case when the economy is faced with all three shocks. When faced with credit shocks only, the procyclicality of monetary aggregates remains unchanged under all γ values except for the largest value 0.8. The procyclic natures of income velocity, inflation and nominal interest rate are extremely robust; the correlation coefficients remain approximately constant under all values of γ. The same robustness is found in the phase shift between output and money. When subject to all three shocks, the economy demonstrates the same robustness. Moreover, when γ increases, the correlation coefficients

Table 18.3 The extent to which productivity, money or credit shocks can explain the monetary puzzles

(1)	*(2)* *Credit model*	*(3)* *CIA model*	*(4)* *SHT model*	*(5)* *Credit model with credit shocks*	*(6)*	*(7)*	*(8)*
Facts and puzzles	*PR + M shocks*	*PR + M shocks*	*PR + M shocks*	*CR shocks*	*PR + CR shocks*	*CR + M shocks*	*CR + PR + M shocks*
A. Credit							
1. Monetary aggregates are procyclical (+0.07; +0.33 in CH, 1995)	Yes 0.03	No –0.04	No 0	**YES** 0.26	**YES** 0.05	No –0.05	Yes 0.01
2. Phase shift in the correlation between output and money = lagged money is correlated with present output	Yes	No	No	**YES**	No	Yes	Yes
3. Positive correlation between output and inflation (+0.38)	No –0.11	No –0.12	No –0.08	**YES** 0.39	No 0.39	No –0.79	No –0.09
4. Positive correlation between output and nominal interest rate (+0.35)	No –0.08	No –0.09	No –0.05	**YES** 0.39	No –0.30	No –0.79	No –0.07
B. Inflation tax							
1. Income velocity is procyclical (+0.15)	Yes 0.63	Yes 0.88	Yes 0.61	Yes 1	Yes 0.90	No –0.73	**YES** 0.60
2. Negative correlation between money growth and output (–0.13)	**YES** –0.03	**YES** –0.05	Yes –0.02	N/A	N/A	Yes –0.91	Yes –0.04
3. Negative correlation between money growth and hours (–0.15 in CH, 1995)	**YES** –0.05	**YES** –0.10	Yes –0.03	N/A	N/A	Yes –0.91	Yes –0.06
4. Negative correlation between money growth and consumption (–0.1 in CH (1998) but 0.02 in Ch (1995); 0.01 here)	Yes –0.30	Yes –0.79	**YES** –0.08	N/A	N/A	Yes –0.99	**YES** –0.25
5. Negative correlation between output and prices (–0.51)	Yes –0.15	Yes –0.20	Yes –0.15	No 1	Yes 0.72	Yes –0.35	Yes –0.16

CH, Cooley and Hansen; CIA, cash-in-advance; SHT, shopping time; PR, productivity; M, money; CR, credit; N/A, not available; 'Yes' indicates that the shock explains the puzzle; '**YES**' indicates the best explanatory power of the different models for a given puzzle.

of the money growth with output and hours worked move closer towards their observed values. The only exception is the correlation of output with monetary aggregates, which, at higher γ values, becomes acyclical or slightly countercyclical.

For the productivity parameters (A_F) of 0.6, 1.0, 1.4, 1.7 and 2.0, when only credit shocks operate in the economy, the model remains robust under various productivity parameters with one exception: at low productivity the nominal money supply becomes slightly countercyclical. Under joint productivity, money and credit shocks the system proves to be robust; however, just as with varying γ values, monetary aggregates display a rather acyclical pattern, although the shift in the correlation coefficient is almost negligible.

Under various inflation rates (–4, –2, 0, 2, 5, 10, 20, 100 per cent), the results are robust with all of the shock processes. The exception is the behavior of nominal money supply under credit shocks, which turns out to be procyclic only at moderate inflation rates but countercyclical at deflationary or hyperinflation rates.

18.6 Discussion

The impulse responses show that the shopping time model has differences such as its leisure decrease when the money supply growth rate is shocked upwards. This feature is not found in the other two models and it appears to be related to the assumption of its exchange time moving proportionally with velocity. This may create a lesser performance of the shopping time model to explain the inflation tax puzzles. For example, the credit model with goods productivity and money shocks seems better at explaining procyclic monetary aggregates.

However, the performance differences among the three models are somewhat marginal in comparison with the advantage of having the additional credit shock in the credit model. This gives the procyclic aggregate movements found in the data and can generate procyclic inflation rate movements. A related type of shopping time shock can be added to the shopping time framework, as Dittmar et al. (2005) show, but this has less intuition in that the specification of the shopping time function is not linked to any microfoundations other than a fixed interest elasticity of money demand. The advantage of the credit model is that the additional credit productivity shock helps to capture substitution away from money use during important financial sector innovation periods, and to generate income effects in terms of saved time in banking.

The inflation movements are not persistent in the credit model, however, when using the simple money supply growth rule, and this makes the overall model's performance with all three shocks still inconsistent with observed inflation–output contemporaneous correlation. But since the credit-shock-only model gives the right magnitude and positive sign for the inflation correlation, an increase in inflation persistence such as from a Taylor feedback rule as in Dittmar et al. (2005) may lead to overall improvement. Another area for improvement in the model is liquidity effects. Cooley and Hansen (1995, 1998) modify cash-in-advance economies with nominal rigidities and the non-neutralities so introduced cause larger velocity and interest rate volatility that are closer to the facts. However, the inflation tax models of Section 18.2 better fit for example the negative correlation between current output and the price level. And the nominal rigidity models poorly explain real variable movements, and do not capture money growth, inflation and interest rate correlations. A credit approach may still be useful for the liquidity problem if cash transfers can be injected first into the credit sector with a subsequent increase in the supply of credit before the inflation rate increases.

18.7 Conclusion

The chapter analyzes three different models of exchange technology within a business cycle framework. The first two are the standard cash-only and shopping time models and the third is a credit model that is a stochastic version of the Gillman and Kejak (2005b) economy. The credit model allows for an additional shock to the usual goods productivity and money shocks. It is found that this addition allows the co-movement of monetary aggregates, inflation and the nominal interest rate with output at different points in the phase of the business cycle to be captured better than other models. Impulse responses confirm this feature in the credit model that is not available in the cash-only and standard shopping time models. The chapter thus is able to argue that the credit production approach is an extension that, based in a microfoundations-linked calibration, improves the performance of the monetary business cycle model. The contribution represents a step that allows the general equilibrium business cycle to account for important changes in banking and for the more standard inflation tax effects.

Appendix 18.A

18.A1 First-order conditions and log-linearization

The first-order conditions with respect to c_t, x_t, k_t, a_t, M_t are

$$\frac{1}{c_t} - \lambda_t a_t - \mu_t w_t \left(\frac{1-a_t}{A_F e^{v_t}}\right)^{1/\gamma} - \mu_t = 0 \qquad \text{(A1)}$$

$$\frac{\Psi}{x_t} - \mu_t w_t = 0 \qquad \text{(A2)}$$

$$-\mu_t + \beta E_t(\mu_{t+1} r_{t+1}) = 0 \qquad \text{(A3)}$$

$$-\lambda_t c_t + \mu_t w_t c_t \frac{1}{\gamma\, A_{\mathrm{F}} \mathrm{e}^{v_t}} \left(\frac{1-a_t}{A_{\mathrm{F}} \mathrm{e}^{v_t}}\right)^{(1/\gamma)-1} = 0 \tag{A4}$$

$$\frac{-\mu_t}{P_t} + \beta E_t\left(\frac{\lambda_{t+1} + \mu_{t+1}}{P_{t+1}}\right) = 0 \tag{A5}$$

These can be simplified to

$$R^* - 1 = \frac{w^*}{\gamma A_{\mathrm{F}}}\left(\frac{1-a^*}{A_{\mathrm{F}}}\right)^{(1/\gamma)-1} \tag{A6}$$

$$\frac{x_t}{\Psi c_t} = \frac{1 + a^*(R^*-1) + w^*(1-a^*/A_{\mathrm{F}})^{1/\gamma}}{w^*} \tag{A7}$$

$$r^* = \frac{1}{\beta} \tag{A8}$$

The log-linearized system of equilibrium conditions includes the consumer's first-order conditions

$$(\lambda^*\, a^*\, c^* + \mu^*\, c^*)\hat{c}_t + \lambda^*\, a^*\, c^*\, \hat{a}_t + \mu^*\, w^*\, l_{\mathrm{F}}^* \hat{w}_t + \mu^*\, w^*\, l_{\mathrm{F}}^* \hat{l}_{\mathrm{F}t} + \lambda^*\, a^*\, c^*\, \hat{\lambda}_t + (\mu^*\, w^*\, l_{\mathrm{F}}^* + \mu^*\, c^*)\hat{\mu}_t = 0 \tag{A9}$$

$$\hat{x}_t + \hat{\mu}_t + \hat{w}_t = 0 \tag{A10}$$

$$-\hat{\mu}_t + E_t\hat{\mu}_{t+1} + E_t\hat{r}_{t+1} = 0 \tag{A11}$$

$$-\hat{\lambda}_t + \hat{\mu}_t + \hat{w}_t + (1-\gamma)\hat{l}_{\mathrm{F}t} - (1-\gamma)\hat{c}_t - v_t = 0 \tag{A12}$$

$$-\hat{\mu}_t + \hat{p}_t + E_t\left(\frac{\lambda^*}{\lambda^* + \mu^*}\hat{\lambda}_{t+1} + \frac{\mu^*}{\lambda^* + \mu^*}\hat{\mu}_{t+1} - \hat{p}_{t+1} - u_{t+1}\right) = 0 \tag{A13}$$

the firm's equilibrium conditions

$$-\hat{w}_t + z_t + \alpha\hat{k}_{t-1} - \alpha\hat{n}_t = 0 \tag{A14}$$

$$-\hat{r}_t + [1-\beta(1-\delta)]z_t + (\alpha-1)[1-\beta(1-\delta)]\hat{k}_{t-1} + (1-\alpha)[1-\beta(1-\delta)]\hat{n}_t = 0 \tag{A15}$$

$$-\hat{y}_t + z_t + \alpha\hat{k}_{t-1} + (1-\alpha)\hat{n}_t = 0 \tag{A16}$$

and the resource and money market constraints

$$-\hat{l}_{\mathrm{F}t} + \frac{a^*}{\gamma(a^*-1)}\hat{a}_t + \hat{c}_t - \frac{1}{\gamma}v_t = 0 \tag{A17}$$

$$l_{\mathrm{F}}^*\hat{l}_{\mathrm{F}t} + x^*\hat{x}_t + n^*\hat{n}_t = 0 \tag{A18}$$

$$\hat{p}_t + \hat{a}_t + \hat{c}_t = 0 \quad \text{(A19)}$$

$$-w^* n^* \hat{w}_t - w^* n^* \hat{n}_t - r^* k^* \hat{r}_t - r^* k^* \hat{k}_{t-1} + c^* \hat{c}_t + k^* \hat{k}_t = 0 \quad \text{(A20)}$$

$$\hat{p}_t - \hat{p}_{t-1} - \hat{\pi}_t + u_t = 0 \quad \text{(A21)}$$

Equations (A9)–(A21), together with the three shock processes for goods productivity, money supply and credit productivity, form the complete recursive system of linear stochastic difference equations in the endogenous state variable $\hat{k}_t$, exogenous state variables z_t, v_t, u_t, endogenous control variables $\hat{c}_t$, $\hat{x}_t$, $\hat{n}_t$, $\hat{l}_{Ft}$, $\hat{a}_t$, $\hat{w}_t$, $\hat{r}_t$, $\hat{y}_t$, $\hat{p}_t$, π_t, and shadow prices $\hat{\lambda}_t$,$\hat{\mu}_t$.

18.A2 Calibration

	Credit	*Cash only*	*Shopping time*
α	0.36	0.36	0.36
δ	0.05	0.05	0.05
β	0.99	0.99	0.99
A_F	1.422	N/A	0.0034
Ψ	2.03	2.03	1.876
Θ	0.0125	0.0125	0.0125
γ	0.21	N/A	N/A
φ_z	0.95	0.95	0.95
σ_z	0.0075	0.0075	0.0075
φ_v	0.95	N/A	N/A
σ_v	0.0075	N/A	N/A
φ_u	0.57	0.57	0.57
σ_u	0.01	0.01	0.01
c	0.8098	0.8072	0.8463
x	0.7055	0.7069	0.6847
n	0.2940	0.2930	0.3072
l_F	0.00049	0	0.0080
a	0.7002	1	0.425
w	2.3706	2.3706	2.3706
r	1.0101	1.0101	1.0101
π	1.0125	1.0125	1.0125
y	1.0891	1.0855	1.1381
k	11.1695	11.1333	11.6725
m	0.5670	0.8072	0.3598

N/A, not available.

Notes

* Benk, Szilárd, Max Gillman and Michal Kejak (2005). 'A Comparison of Exchange Economies within a Monetary Business Cycle', *Manchester School*, 73(4), 542–562.

† The authors are grateful to Central European University and to the World Bank Global Development Network for grant support, the third author to the Czech Republic grant 402/02/0393. We are also grateful to participants at the North

American Econometric Society 2005 Meetings, the Society for Economic Dynamics 2004 Meetings, the CGBCR 2004 conference, the GDN 2004 workshop in Prague and the RES 2005 meeting.

1 Both Alvarez et al. (2001) and Schabert (2003) show conditions under which Taylor interest rate rules can be equivalent to simple money supply growth rules.
2 See Gillman and Kejak (2002).
3 See also how Lucas (2000) contrasts the constant interest elasticity function versus the constant semi-interest elasticity function at low inflation rates.

19 Money velocity in an endogenous growth business cycle with credit shocks*

Szilárd Benk, Max Gillman and Michal Kejak

Summary

The chapter sets the neoclassical monetary business cycle model within endogenous growth, adds exchange credit shocks, and finds that money and credit shocks explain much of the velocity variation. The role of the shocks varies across sub-periods in an intuitive fashion. Endogenous growth is key to the construction of the money and credit shocks since these have similar effects on velocity, but opposite effects upon growth. The model matches the data's average velocity and simulates well velocity volatility. Its Cagan-like money demand means that money and credit shocks cause greater velocity variation the higher is the nominal interest rate.

19.1 Introduction

Explaining velocity at business cycle frequencies involves a rich literature. Freeman and Kydland (2000), Hodrick, Kocherlakota and Lucas (1991) and Cooley and Hansen (1995) endogenize money velocity in models with shocks to the goods sector productivity and the money supply. Cooley and Hansen call the procyclic behavior of US velocity "one of the most compelling features of aggregate data" (Cooley and Hansen, 1995, p.179). Their model reproduces this but its correlation of velocity with output is high compared to data. Here the goods sector productivity shock drives velocity changes, in a way similar to Friedman and Schwartz's (1963) velocity theory as based on the application of the permanent income hypothesis to money demand (p.44). A positive temporary output shock (productivity) causes income to rise temporarily while money demand depends on consumption demand and is not much affected by the temporary income increase; a procyclic velocity results. However the most common explanation of velocity, that it depends on monetary-induced inflation effects on the nominal interest rate, as in McGrattan (1998), has no role in explaining velocity at business cycle frequencies, as Wang and Shi (2006) note in their alternative search-theoretic approach to velocity. Also missing is a role for financial sector shocks (King and Plosser 1984), financial innovation (Ireland 1991), technological progress (Berger 2003), or deregulation (Stiroh and Strahan 2003).

The chapter explains 75% of the variability of velocity seen in 1972–2003 US quarterly data, by confronting the problems of velocity movements that are too procyclic, that are little affected by money shocks, and that have no role for financial sector shocks. In particular, it adds shocks to the productivity of providing exchange credit, which is introduced instead of the trips-to-the-bank approach of Freeman and Kydland (2000) or the cash-good, credit-good framework in Hodrick et al. (1991) and Cooley and Hansen (1995), and uses an endogenous growth framework instead of an exogenous growth one (Section 19.2). Money and credit shocks both positively affect velocity but affect growth in opposite ways (Section 19.3). This allows both shocks to get picked up by the shock construction process (Appendix), thereby inducing a large role for the shocks in the velocity variation and a subsequently less procyclic velocity as the goods productivity shock is relatively less important. The velocity variance decomposition for post-1972 data show all three shocks playing large roles that vary by subperiod. Money shocks have the largest effect during the high inflation period of 1972–1982, as might be expected; credit shocks are relatively more important during the financial deregulatory period of 1983–1995, also as expected (Section 19.4). The results are discussed relative to other velocity studies (Section 19.5), with conclusion (Section 6).

19.2 Endogenous growth with credit

The representative agent economy is an endogenous growth extension of Benk, Gillman & Kejak (2005), with a Lucas (1988b) human capital investment technology causing growth. The agent allocates resources amongst three sectors: goods production, human capital investment, and exchange credit production as a means to avoid the inflation tax. There are three random shocks at the beginning of the period, observed by the consumer before the decision process, which follow a vector first-order autoregressive process for goods sector productivity, z_t the money supply growth rate, u_t, and credit sector productivity, v_t:

$$Z_t = \Phi_Z Z_{t-1} + \varepsilon_{Zt} \tag{1}$$

where the shocks are $Z_t = [z_t\ u_t\ v_t]'$, the autocorrelation matrix is $\Phi_Z = diag\{\varphi_z, \varphi_u, \varphi_v\}$ and $\varphi_z, \varphi_u, \varphi_v \in (0, 1)$ are autocorrelation parameters, and the shock innovations are $\varepsilon_{Zt} = [\varepsilon_{zt}\ \varepsilon_{ut}\ \varepsilon_{vt}]' \sim N(\mathbf{0}, \Sigma)$. The general structure of the second-order moments is assumed to be given by the variance-covariance matrix Σ. These shocks affect the economy as described below.

The representative agent's period t utility over consumption c_t and leisure x_t is $\frac{(c_t x_t^{\Psi})^{1-\theta}}{1-\theta}$, with $\theta \geq 0$ and $\Psi > 0$. Output of goods (y_t) is produced with physical capital (k_t) that depreciates at the rate $\delta_k \in [0,1)$ and with effective labor, through Cobb-Douglas production functions. Investment (i_t) is given by the accumulation equation $k_{t+1} = (1 - \delta_k)k_t + i_t$. A unit of time is divided amongst leisure (x_t) and work in goods production (l_t), human capital investment (n_t), and exchange credit production (f_t):

$$1 = x_t + l_t + n_t + f_t. \tag{2}$$

With h_t denoting human capital, the effective labor employed across sectors is $l_t h_t$, $n_t h_t$, and $f_t h_t$ respectively. Given $A_H > 0$, $\delta_h \in [0,1)$, human capital accumulates with a labor-only technology (Lucas 1988):

$$h_t + 1 = (1 - \delta_h) h_t + A_H n_t h_t. \tag{3}$$

Let $a_t \in (0, 1]$ denote the fraction of consumption goods that are purchased with money (M_t); then the exchange constraint can be expressed as

$$M_t + T_t \geq a_t P_t c_t, \tag{4}$$

where M_t is the money stock carried from the previous period and T_t is the nominal lump-sum money transfer received from the government at the beginning of the current period. Exchange credit (q_t) is produced by the consumer acting in part as a bank to provide a means to pay for the rest of the purchases, without having to hold cash in advance of trading, and instead paying off the debt at the end of the period; this gives that

$$q_t = c_t (1 - a_t). \tag{5}$$

The consumer deposits all income that is not invested, of $y_t - i_t = c_t$, in its bank, makes purchases of goods c_t with the cash and credit taken out of deposits d_t, where $d_t = [(M_t + T_t)/P_t] + q_t = a_t c_t + (1 - a_t) c_t = c_t$. As a bank, the consumer uses a case of the now-standard Clark (1984) financial services technology to produce the exchange credit q_t. Clark assumes a constant returns to scale function in labor, physical capital, and financial capital that equals deposited funds.[1] Here for simplicity no physical capital enters; with $A_F > 0$ and $\gamma \in (0,1)$, the CRS production technology is $q_t = A_F e^{\upsilon_t} (f_t h_t)^{\gamma} d_t^{1-\gamma}$, where v_t is the shock to factor productivity; since deposits equal consumption, this can be written as

$$q_t = A_F e^{\upsilon_t} (f_t h_t)^{\gamma} c_t^{1-\gamma}. \tag{6}$$

Solving for q_t/c_t from equation (6), substituting this into the relation $a_t = 1 - (q_t/c_t)$ from equation (5), and substituting this relation for a_t back into the exchange constraint (4), yields an exchange constraint analogous to a shopping time constraint as extended to endogenous growth:[2]

$$M_t + T_t \geq [1 - A_F e^{\upsilon_t} (f_t h_t/c_t)^{\gamma}] P_t c_t. \tag{7}$$

Let w_t and r_t denote competitive wage and rental rates. Nominal wages ($P_t w_t l_t h_t$) and rents ($P_t r_t k_t$) plus any unspent cash ($M_t + T_t - a_t P_t c_t$), make up the consumer's income, while set-aside cash (M_{t+1}) plus end-of-period credit debt payments [$c_t(1 - a_t)$], and investment (i_t) are expenditures:

$$P_t w_t l_t h_t + P_t r_t k_t + T_t + M_t - M_{t+1} - P_t c_t - P_t k_{t+1} + P_t(1 - \delta_k)k_t \geq 0. \tag{8}$$

The government transfers a random amount T_t given by

$$\frac{T_t}{M_t} = \Theta_t = \Theta^* + e^{u_t} - 1 = \frac{M_{t+1}}{M_t} - 1, \tag{9}$$

so that Θ^* is the stationary gross growth rate of money.

The competitive firm maximizes profit given by $y_t - w_t l_t h_t - r_t k_t$, with production technology $y_t = A_G e^{z_t} k_t^{1-a} (l_t h_t)^a$. Then

$$w_t = a A_G e^{z_t} \left(\frac{k_t}{l_t h_t}\right)^{1-a}; \tag{10}$$

$$r_t = (1 - a) A_G e^{z_t} \left(\frac{k_t}{l_t h_t}\right)^{-a}. \tag{11}$$

Definition of equilibrium Denoting the state of the economy by $s = (k, h, M, z, u, v)$, and with $\beta \in (0, 1)$, the representative agent's optimization problem can be written in a recursive form as:

$$V(s) = \max_{c,x,l,n,f,k',h',M'} \left\{ \frac{(cx^{\Psi})^{1-\theta}}{1-\theta} + \beta EV(s') \right\} \tag{12}$$

subject to the conditions (2), (3), (7) and (8). Define the competitive equilibrium as a set of policy functions $c(s)$, $x(s)$, $l(s)$, $n(s)$, $f(s)$, $k'(s)$, $h'(s)$, $M'(s)$, pricing functions $P(s)$, $w(s)$, $r(s)$ and the value function $V(s)$, such that (i) households maximize lifetime welfare given the pricing functions and that the value function $V(s)$ solves the functional equation (12); (ii) firms maximize profits, with the functions w and r given by (10) and (11); (iii) the goods and money markets clear, in equations (8) and (9).

Description of equilibrium Here the focus is on the effects of shocks on velocity, the output growth rate, and the capital to effective labor ratio across sectors. Equilibrium money demand, and its velocity, is solved primarily from the first-order condition with respect to the choice of hours employed in credit production, this being the additional condition compared to a cash-only economy. Combined with equations (4) to (7), and other conditions to determine the constraint multipliers, the consumption-normalized money demand is given by

$$\frac{M_{t+1}}{P_t c_t} = a_t = 1 - (A_F e^{\upsilon_t})^{1/(1-\gamma)} \left(\frac{\gamma R_t}{w_t}\right)^{\gamma/(1-\gamma)}. \qquad (13)$$

A positive money supply growth rate shock increases R_t through its inflation rate component and lowers normalized money demand (raises consumption velocity). A positive credit productivity shock v_t reduces money demand directly (raises consumption velocity). A positive goods productivity shock increases w_t and R_t through equations (10) and (11), and the Fisher equation of interest rates, by which the real interest rate r_t affects the nominal interest rate R_t; the net effect on R_t/w_t is small since there is no effect of this shock on r_t/w_t.

The magnitude of the interest elasticity of money demand (denoted η_t, where w_t is held constant) is $\eta_t = [\gamma/(1-\gamma)]\,(1-a_t)/a_t$; this rises with R_t as in the Cagan (1956) model; $\partial\eta_t/\partial R_t = \frac{\eta_t \gamma}{a_t R_t (1-\gamma)} > 0$. With the baseline calibration values of $a_t = 0.224$, and $\gamma = 0.13$, then at $R_t = 0.10$, the interest elasticity is –0.52. The importance of the elasticity can be seen by considering that there is a bigger increase in velocity from an interest rate increase, the higher is the interest rate (and elasticity); $\partial^2(1/a_t)/\partial R_t^2 = \frac{\eta_t}{(a_t R_t)^2}\frac{2\gamma - a_t}{1-\gamma} > 0$ for $a_t < 2\gamma = 0.26$, and w_t constant. And also a credit shock causes a bigger change in velocity the higher is the interest rate (and elasticity); with w_t and R_t constant, $\partial(1/a_t)/\partial\upsilon_t = \frac{\eta_t}{\gamma_{at}} > 0$ for $R_t > 0$; and with w_t constant, $\partial^2(1/a_t)/(\partial R_t \partial\upsilon_t) > 0$ for $R_t > 0$. This can explain, for example, why there would be a large response to the model's velocity from deregulation in the early 1980s when interest rates were higher: nominal interest rates fell rapidly after 1981 but velocity stayed high as deregulation began.

Note that in Cooley and Hansen (1995), the comparable normalized money demand is equal to $\phi/[1 + R_t\,(1-\phi)]$, where ϕ is a preference parameter for cash goods. A positive money supply shock and goods productivity shock both increase R_t and reduce the money demand; but with their calibrated value of $\phi = 0.84$, and say $R_t = 0.10$, the interest elasticity of the normalized money demand is –0.016, compared to –0.52 in our model.

The total effect on income velocity depends not only on $\frac{P_t c_t}{M_{t+1}}$ but also on the income-consumption ratio: $V_t \equiv \frac{yt}{M_{t+1}/P_t} = \left(\frac{P_t c_t}{M_{t+1}}\right)\frac{y_t}{c_t}$. To the extent that income rises temporarily from a goods productivity shock, y_t/c_t will increase, increasing velocity as in Cooley and Hansen (1995) and Friedman and

Schwartz (1963).[3] With the impact of credit and money shocks on $\frac{P_t c_t}{M_{t+1}}$, the temporary income channel can be of relatively less importance.

Shocks to velocity affect the growth rate (g_t) through the effect on the percent of labor employed ($1 - x_t$); this can be seen intuitively by deriving the balanced-path growth rate as $1 + g_t = (\beta\,[1 + A_H(1 - x_t) - \delta_h])^{1/\theta}$ and the marginal rate of substitution between normalized goods and leisure as $\frac{x_t h_t}{\Psi c_t} = \frac{1 + a_t\, R_t + (1(- a_t)\gamma R_t}{w_t}$. A positive money shock increases R_t and the goods shadow price $[1 + a_t R_t + (1 - a_t)\,\gamma\, R_t$ relative to the leisure shadow price w_t, induces substitution from goods (c_t / h_t) towards leisure (x_t), and decreases the growth rate; a positive credit shock in reverse decreases the cost of exchange, induces substitution from x_t towards c_t / h_t, increases the employment rate ($1 - x_t$) and g_t.

Shocks to velocity also involve a Tobin effect on input price and quantity ratios (Gillman and Kejak 2005b). A positive money shock causes more leisure, an increase in w_t / r_t, and an increase in the capital to effective labor ratio $\frac{k_t}{l_t h_t}$; since it is also true that $1 + g_t = [\beta\,(1 + r_t - \delta_k)]^{1/\theta}$, the fall in r_t goes in tandem with the fall in the marginal product of human capital, $A_H(1 - x_t)$. A positive credit shock conversely decreases w_t / r_t and $\frac{k_t}{l_t h_t}$, and increases g_t. A goods productivity shock directly increases r_t and g_t.

19.3 Impulse responses and simulations

Standard solution techniques can be applied once growing real variables are normalized by the stock of human capital so that all variables in the deterministic version of the model converge to a constant steady state. We define $\tilde{c} \equiv c/h$, $\tilde{\imath} \equiv i/h$, $\tilde{k} \equiv k/h$, $\tilde{m} \equiv M/Ph$ and $\tilde{s} \equiv (\tilde{k}, 1, 1, z, u, v)$, log-linearize the equilibrium conditions of the transformed model around its deterministic steady state, and use standard numerical solution methods.

The calibration uses standard parameters for the goods production labor share of $a = 0.6$, a factor productivity normalized at $A_G = 1$, capital depreciation of $\delta_k = 0.012$ and $\delta_h = 0.012$, leisure preference of $\Psi = 3.2$, consumption elasticity of $\theta = 2$, and time preference of $\beta = 0.99$. The human capital sector is labor only, with factor productivity of $A_H = 0.12$. Time division at baseline is that leisure's share is 0.70, goods production time 0.16, and human capital investment time 0.14; labor in credit production is 0.0008, or 0.0008/0.3= 0.27% of total productive time.

For nominal factors, the consumption velocity of money is set to the 1972–2003 average of the consumption velocity of M1, at 4.5 ($a = 0.224$). Shock characteristics are set to estimated values from the constructed shocks: persistences of $\varphi_z = 0.86$, $\varphi_u = 0.93$, $\varphi_\upsilon = 0.93$, standard deviations of

$\sigma_{\varepsilon_z} = 2.39$, $\sigma_{\varepsilon_u} = 0.85$, $\sigma_{\varepsilon_\upsilon} = 1.9$, and correlations of $corr(\varepsilon_z, \varepsilon_u) = -0.03$, $corr(\varepsilon_z, \varepsilon_\upsilon) = -0.24$, $corr(\varepsilon_u, \varepsilon_\upsilon) = 0.85$. The credit sector productivity parameter is set at $A_F = 1.86$, and its Cobb-Douglas parameter γ is calibrated using financial industry data at $\gamma = 0.13$. The γ is calibrated by first noting that the Cobb-Douglas function implies a decentralized bank sector profit of $Rq(1-\gamma)$: since R is the unit credit equilibrium price (equal to the real wage divided by the marginal product of labor in credit production, or the marginal cost), profit equals $Rq - wfh$ subject to $q = A_F(fh)^\gamma d^{1-\gamma}$; by the CRS technology property, $\gamma Rq = wfh$; so $Rq(1-\gamma)$ is profit returned to the consumer (interest dividend on deposits); and γRq is the resource cost of the credit. Per unit of credit this is γR, so γ is the per unit cost of credit divided by R. Now, since credit is given by $q = c - m$, and $m = ac$, then $q = c(1-a)$ (equation 5). With the calibration of $a = 0.224$ then $q = c(1 - 0.224) = c(0.776)$. Then $\gamma = (\text{total credit cost})/Rc(0.776)$. The estimate of 100 is used as the average annual cost over the data period at 2006 prices of an exchange credit card (American Express) and it is assumed to reflect the total interest costs of using the annual exchange credit (not roll-over intertemporal credit) for a single person (other ad-on charges such as penalties are not included). Then $\gamma = 100/Rc(0.776)$. Using US annual average data for 1972–2003, with $c = 15780$ at 2006 prices, being per capita consumption expenditure, and $R = 0.0627$ the 3-month Treasury Bill interest rate (annual basis), then $\gamma = 100/[(0.0627)15780(0.776) \simeq 0.13$.

Sensitivity to alternative values of γ affect mainly the relative effect of money versus credit shocks on velocity. A larger γ makes the interest elasticity of money demand higher, causes money shocks to affect velocity more, credit shocks to affect velocity less, and thereby increases the importance of the money shock relative to the credit shock. Our low calibrated value of γ thus could be viewed as on the conservative side of the importance of money shocks. And note that a value of γ greater than 0.5 is less plausible as this gives a concave marginal cost curve per unit of credit produced, rather than a convex marginal cost that applies for $\gamma < 0.5$ (Gillman and Kejak, 2005b).

The impulse responses in Figure 19.1 show the effects of the shocks over time, and illustrate the discussion of the effects of shocks on the equilibrium in Section 19.2. A positive money shock (M) increases velocity (vel), causes an output growth rate (gY) decrease that persists for more than 50 periods, and an increase in the investment to output ratio, as in a positive Tobin effect. Opposite effects occur for a positive credit shock (CR) on the growth rate and investment ratio, with a positive effect on velocity. The productivity shock (PR) increases velocity, the output growth rate, and the investment ratio over time before the effect turns slightly negative and dies out.

Simulations show that the relative volatility of the output velocity of money, of 1.40, is 75% of the actual 1972–2003 average for the output velocity of M1, of 1.88; this 75% substantially improves on previous work, such as less than 50% in Benk et al. (2005), and 57% for the comparable case (of

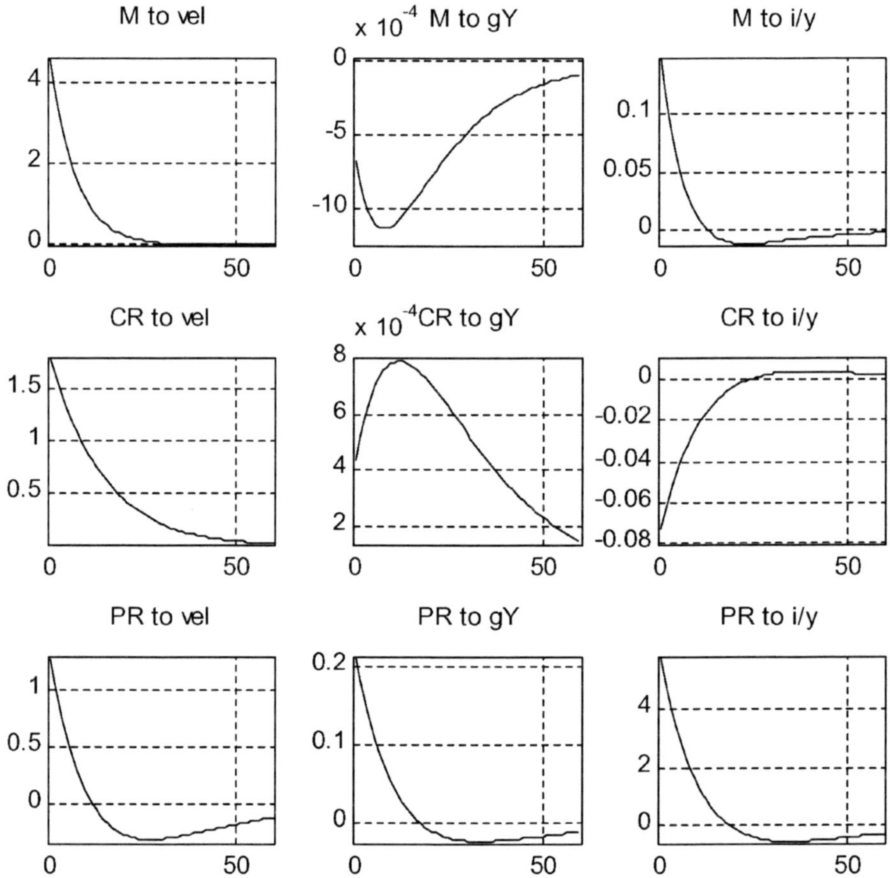

Figure 19.1 Impulse responses: velocity, output growth, investment ratio.

a relative risk aversion coefficient of 2 in table 3) in Wang and Shi (2006). The model's contemporaneous correlation of velocity with the output ratio y/h is 0.07, lower than the comparable 0.24 found in the data (where data for h is described in the Appendix), rather than too high as in Cooley and Hansen (0.95 compared to 0.37 in their data sample). Also, Freeman and Kydland's (2000) simulation shows a real M1 correlation with real output of 0.98 compared to 0.26 in their 1979–1995 subsample. We have a 0.53 output correlation of m/h compared to the data's $(M1/P)/h$ output correlation of 0.31 for the 1972–2003 sample; plus, a 1.67 relative volatility of m/h versus 2.14 in data; a 0.85 correlation of c/h with output versus 0.79 in data; and a 0.59 relative volatility of c/h versus 1.03 in data. With only the goods productivity shock active, the c/h relative volatility is the same, but the velocity relative volatility drops by more than half to 0.56 and m/h volatility drops in half to 0.83. The model's ability to come close to the data for velocity and *m/h* depends on the money and credit shocks being operative.

19.4 Variance decomposition of velocity

From the shock construction (please see Appendix), a standard variance decomposition of velocity is conducted, similar to the variance decomposition for output described in Benk et al (2005) for an exogenous growth case. The endogenous and exogenous growth results are compared in Table 19.1, for the baseline (five-variable) case of the shock construction, with six possible orderings of the shocks, and for US quarterly data from 1972–2003; here the exogenous growth case used for comparison is the economy set out in Benk et al (2005). For the whole period, the table shows an average effect of 4% for the money shock in exogenous growth but 45% for the endogenous growth model. The credit shock effect on velocity drops from 86% for the exogenous growth results to 46% in endogenous growth. The productivity shock explains an average of 9% of the variance in endogenous growth.

Table 19.1 also breaks the period into subperiods of 1972–1982, 1983–1996, and 1997–2003. The first subperiod is when the high accelerating inflation rate took place, and credit was restrained by financial sector regulations. The money shock shows a 50% average share, more than twice that of the 20% for credit, while the productivity share is at 30%. In the next subperiod, when financial deregulation was taking place and the inflation rate was much lower but still variable, credit shocks had their highest effect at 48%; money shocks also had a 48% share. In the last subperiod, with a lower, more stable, inflation rate and a significantly deregulated financial market, the money and credit shocks had lower effects, and the goods shock a high of 32%.

The variance decompositions vary with the definition of the subperiod.

Table 19.1 Velocity variance decomposition, with different shock orderings

Shock ordering			*Endogenous model*			*Exogenous model*		
CR	PR	M	79%	18%	3%	84%	16%	0%
CR	M	PR	84%	8%	8%	88%	5%	7%
PR	CR	M	5%	92%	3%	5%	95%	0%
M	CR	PR	84%	8%	8%	2%	88%	10%
M	PR	CR	84%	11%	5%	2%	16%	82%
PR	M	CR	5%	89%	6%	5%	14%	81%
Average			*PR*	*M*	*CR*	*PR*	*M*	*CR*
1972–2003			*9%*	*45%*	*46%*	*10%*	*4%*	*86%*
1972–1982			30%	50%	20%	29%	11%	60%
1983–1996			4%	48%	48%	7%	10%	83%
1997–2003			32%	31%	37%	33%	8%	59%

For example, if the period of 1983–2003 is considered without further subperiods, the goods productivity share is 6% while money and credit shares are 47% and 47% respectively. This masks the fact that the goods productivity played a much bigger role in the latter part of the subperiod, with a share of 32% from 1997–2003, compared to 4% during 1983–1996.

What emerges is that the productivity shock, and the permanent income theory of velocity, takes on more importance during the latter subperiod when there are less episodes of large credit and money shocks. Money shocks are relatively important during the inflation acceleration and deceleration of the 1970s and 1980s; credit is relatively important during financial deregulation.

19.5 Discussion

Prescott (1987) presents a goods continuum with an exogenous division between cash and credit that Freeman and Kydland (2000) and Gillman (1993) make endogenous, resulting in an endogenous velocity. These models involve general transaction costs and a goods continuum that can be cumbersome relative to a more standard single-good model. Alternatively, the Section 19.2 model has a single good with a credit industry production function from banking microfoundations, allowing plausible credit shocks to sectoral productivity to be identified. This uses the producer side of banking rather than the consumer-side shopping time or trips-to-the bank: consider that with internet banking, shifting funds from savings to current accounts is nearly costless to consumers, getting hold of cash is simple with ubiquitous cash machines or with debit cards at point of purchase, and trips to the bank are optional. However, costs on the production side are real and measurable.

Hodrick et al. (1991) use the cash-good, credit good, economy and find that velocity variability, coming from substitution between cash and credit goods, and from the precautionary demand for money when the exchange constraint is not binding, is not fit well relative to evidence for reasonable parameter values. In our model, the exchange constraint always binds, the shocks drive velocity variability, the velocity volatility is within 75% of actual, while the average velocity is matched exactly and parameter specifications are standard except for the credit sector. However a fitness-of-model comparison using the Hodrick et al. approach is not conducted and would be useful.[4]

Ireland (1996) specifies exogenous velocity shocks and productivity shocks, and shows how to maintain the Friedman optimum in the face of such shocks using various money supply regimes. In our model, with an endogenous velocity that is affected by various shocks, it would be interesting to derive how the effects on velocity could be offset through money supply rules in order to establish the optimum or, more topically, an inflation target.

19.6 Conclusion

The chapter extends a standard monetary real business cycle by setting it within endogenous growth and adding credit sector shocks. A large portion of the variability of velocity found in the data is simulated in the model, an advance for the neoclassical exchange model. While the standard explanation focuses on the goods productivity shock only in explaining velocity in an exchange economy, here two other factors combine together to play an important role. Shocks to the money supply growth rate have a significant impact on velocity, especially during the high inflation period; credit shocks, found to have an important impact on GDP during the deregulatory era, for example in Benk et al. (2005), also effect velocity strongly during this period. Thus while temporary income deviations can be dominant, as in Friedman and Schwartz's (1963) permanent income hypothesis explanation of velocity, during times when money supply growth rates and credit markets are significantly shocked, these other factors can dominate swings in velocity.

The results suggest for example that episodes in monetary regimes could cause different degrees of money supply shocks. This can help explain why there might be higher inflation persistence in the 1970s and 1980s, and less such persistence during the inflation targeting period, a possible topic for future work. It might also be a useful extension of this methodology to examine jointly the effects of the shocks on GDP as well as on velocity with a view towards explaining whether having the credit outlet to increase velocity can take pressure off GDP volatility. If so this could be viewed as part of the Jermann & Quadrini (2006) thesis that financial deregulation and increases in finance activity contributed to the post 1983 moderation in GDP, or even to moderations in GDP experienced in the 1930s and 1950s. Another extension could be to examine money and credit shocks in countries outside of the US. Transition countries, with large inflations post-1989 and subsequent banking deregulations, might also reveal significant roles for money and credit influences. Extension of the model to include intertemporal credit that is intermediated through a costly process similar to that of exchange credit would allow for financial shocks that are more of the banking crisis genre.

Appendix 19.A: construction of shocks

Based on the solution of the model from Section 19.2, the log-deviations of the model variables be written as linear functions of the state $\hat{s}_t = (\hat{\tilde{k}}_t, z_t, u_t, v_t)$. By stacking the equations, the solution can be written in matrix form as $X_t = A[\hat{\tilde{k}}_t] + B[z_t\ u_t v_t]'$, where $X_t = [\hat{\tilde{c}}_t\ \hat{x}_t\ \hat{l}_t \hat{f}_t\ \hat{a}_t\ \hat{m}_t\ \hat{\tilde{k}}_t]'$. Given the solution for matrices A and B, the series of shocks $[z_t u_t\ v_t]$ are constructed using data on at least three variables in X_t plus data for $\hat{\tilde{k}}_t$, and then backing-out the solution for the shocks in each period. Identification of the three series of shocks requires at least three variables from X_t. More variables can be used, with the aim of finding robust solutions for the shocks; in this over-indentified case a least-square procedure is used. To do this, we use data for the state variable $\hat{\tilde{k}}_t$, plus the normalized variables of $\widehat{c_t/y_t}$, $\widehat{i_t/y_t}$, $\widehat{m_t/y_t}$, $\hat{f}_t$ and $\widehat{mplb}_t$, where $mplb_t$ represents the marginal product of labor in banking from equation (6). Then we let $XX_t = AA[\hat{\tilde{k}}_t] + BB[z_t\ u_t\ v_t]'$, where $XX_t = [\widehat{c_t/y_t}, \widehat{i_t/y_t}, \widehat{m_t/y_t}, \hat{f}_t \widehat{mplb}_t]'$ and the rows of the matrices AA and BB result from the linear combinations of the corresponding rows of matrices A and B. Then the baseline estimated three shocks (est) are given by least squares as $est\ [z_t\ \ u_t\ \ v_t]'_t = (BB'BB)^{-1}BB'(XX_t - AA[\hat{\tilde{k}}_t])$.

Here the data series on $\tilde{k}_t$, where $\tilde{k}_t = k_t/h_t$, and $\hat{\tilde{k}}_t$ is its log deviation, is constructed with the capital accumulation equation and data on investment, giving $\hat{i}_t$ (with $\hat{\tilde{k}}_{t-1} = 0$), and with the human capital series of Jorgenson & Stiroh (2000), extrapolated forward until 2003. We also use data on labor hours f_t from the Finance, Insurance and Real Estate sector (FIR), and the wage rate in FIR for the marginal product ($mplb_t$); please see the not-for-publication Appendix for further data description and other details.

A crosscheck of the model calibration is to estimate the shock persistence parameters φ_z, φ_u and φ_v from the constructed shock series. For this reason we estimate a system from equation (1) by the method of seemingly unrelated regressions (SUR). The resulting estimates of the autocorrelation parameters are 0.86 (0.04), 0.93 (0.03) and 0.93 (0.03) respectively (with standard errors in parentheses), which equal the assumed values and thereby show internal consistency of the calibration. From this estimation, the cross-correlations and variances of the error terms are used in the model simulation in Section 19.3. The corresponding variance-covariance matrix Σ_t for equation (1) contains the following elements: $var(\varepsilon_{zt}) = 5.698$, $var(\varepsilon_{ut}) = 0.720$, $var(\varepsilon_{vt}) = 3.617$; and $cov(\varepsilon_{zt}, \varepsilon_{ut}) = -0.056$, $cov(\varepsilon_{zt}, \varepsilon_{vt}) = -1.106$, $cov(\varepsilon_{ut}, \varepsilon_{vt}) = 1.376$.

Notes

* We thank Toni Braun, Bye Jeong, Patrick Minford, Charles Nolan, editor Masao Ogaki, anonymous referees, participants at Cardiff University, CERGE-EI, and Durham University seminars, at the 3rd CDMA Conference, St Andrews, and we gratefully acknowledge support from a World Bank Global Development Network RRC IV grant and from the third author's grant No. 402/02/0393 of the Grant Agency of the Czech Republic.

1 Many studies have empirically verified this CRS specification including deposits as the third factor, and this specification has become dominant in current work, for example Wheelock and Wilson (2006).

2 Solve $f_t h_t = g(c_t, M_{t+1}/P_t)$. Then the main shopping time restrictions follow: that $g_1 \geq 0$ and $g_2 \leq 0$, as shown in Gillman and Yerokhin (2005); the specification of $f_t h_t$ results from the credit technology rather than a pre-determined interest elasticity of money demand as in shopping time models.

3 Such an effect from y_t/c_t on velocity is included econometrically for US data in Gillman, Siklos and Silver (1997).

4 See Basu and Dua (1996) and Hamilton (1989) for other empirical considerations in testing velocity in related cash-good/credit-good models.

20 Epilogue

The perspective going forward

The contributions of this collection can be put in the perspective of the ups and downs of integrating inflation theory in general equilibrium over its long history. Wicksell's (1898) *Interest and Prices* focused on the determination of the real interest rate in capital markets. Patinkin (1989) determined in his *Money, Interest and Prices* to show how the monetary side enters into the general equilibrium setting. And Woodford (2003) tries to return the theory of monetary policy to one without money at all, calling his book *Interest and Prices*.[1]

Patinkin's *Money, Interest and Prices* argues that the neoclassical quantity theory of Irving Fisher (1911) vintage should not have money neutrality in the sense that when the money supply increases, the price level increases proportionately. He says the income level may change when money increases because of a "real balance" effect. Here he says that the interest rate is not included in the quantity theory analysis but that real money can act as capital that affects the real interest rate and the real output level.

The Patinkin analysis is fine for a one-time change in the money supply. But policy is generally about changes in the rate of growth of the money supply. Here the effect of money supply growth is to imply a certain level of inflation tax seigniorage finance, one of several tools for the government to raise funds. As all of these tools are distortionary, the government must balance these distortions.

The effect of the inflation tax distortion has been the subject of this book. In contrast, Woodford's (2003) Prices and Interest Rates is a deliberate attempt to set out a macroeconomic framework without the money of Patinkin's text, and without any inflation tax distortions of the collection here that are at the heart of modern neoclassical monetary theory. In Woodford, instead that text is only about policy in the sense of setting the nominal interest rate. The idea is that then money demand is set equal to money supply implicitly in a way so as to bring about the desired interest rate that is chosen by the policy maker; in this way it is argued that money does not matter.

Using the cash-in-advance models also allows for the money supply growth rate to be implicitly set through the use of an interest rate policy rule. But then there is no artificial assumption that there is no inflation tax distortion. If it is desired to assume away issues of fiscal tax distortions, such as from the inflation tax, then it is fine to somehow assume away the inflation tax distortion. And the recent international adoption of low inflation rate targets, with a subsequently small inflation tax, is sometimes used to justify such an assumption.

Would it be that worldwide inflation was no longer an issue. But wars still arise that result in large deficits, and that coincide with (if not cause) large run-ups of the inflation rate. During fiat money regimes, this has happened in the US not only with the 2003–2008 Iraq war, but also with the Vietnam War, the Korean War and WWII. And inflation tax distortions that arise during wars tend to last subsequently for many years. This on-going inflation tax remains an endemic part of fiat monetary regimes, dating back at least as far as the Bank of England's suspension of the gold standard, and adoption of fiat money supply, during the 1797–1821 period involving the Napoleonic Wars; during this period the inflation rate rose steadily until the war ended and then reversed to an deceleration.

The distortion of the inflation tax remains a part of the macroeconomic world in which we live. This is true no matter how much price rigidity we may believe exists, and no matter whether the central bank uses an interest rate rule or money supply rule to set monetary policy.

The collection here shows how the inflation tax distortion can cause substitution that reduces money demand, increases credit production, reduces the output growth rate, and causes business cycle volatility effects. These are significant non-neutralities that go way beyond that discussed in the original quantity theory literature. And these non-neutralities are important to policy.

Going forward from here are many policy issues that open up with a banking approach to the derivation of the endogenous money demand function. First, our work on the inflation tax can be generalized to all taxes. Preliminary work shows that the effect of the inflation in causing the growth rate to decrease, at a decreasing rate, is mirrored in the effect of capital, labor and value-added goods taxes (VAT) on the growth rate, when evasion of the taxes is allowed through the banking sector. This reflects the result that credit supplied through the banking system is a way to avoid the inflation tax and that money demand becomes increasingly price elastic as the tax rate rises (because of its Cagan, 1956, form). With evasion of taxes through banking, using the financial intermediation approach of the collection, the same rising price elasticity results with respect to each tax, giving the increasingly smaller negative effect of the tax increase on growth, be it capital, labor, VAT, or inflation. This gives an extension of public finance and growth theory.

Other preliminary new empirical work also finds econometrically with panel data that the negative and marginally decreasing effect of inflation on growth is robust across developed country and transition country samples. This work has added "splines" to estimate the different effect of each range of inflation on growth. This gives promise also for investigating empirically whether there is such a negative and marginally decreasing effect of other taxes on growth, an area yet unexplored.

Another area needing more attention is the implication of these models in the collection that the employment rate falls as the inflation rate rises. This is the mechanism at work throughout and, with leisure interpreted as unemployment, it implies the cointegration of inflation and unemployment which has been found in published work such as Ireland (1999) and Shadman-Mehta (2001). This long run effect of inflation is consistent with the stagnation part of the stagflation period during the high-inflation times of the 1970s and 1980s, and with the fall in the unemployment rate during the low inflation, high growth times of the 1990s and into the twenty-first century. Now again inflation and unemployment are rising and growth falling, also consistent with these models. But an active unemployment feature could easily be built into these models to give unemployment explicitly instead of only using leisure, and conversely the employment rate.

Stochastically, the monetary business cycle model of Chapter 19 is also well-positioned to study the volatility of GDP and inflation over long historical periods, another topic of preliminary research. Here it appears that money and credit shocks play a significant role. And "policy" seems to come out ahead of "luck" in explaining the moderation of volatility post 1983; in particular, along with the deceleration of inflation, the financial deregulation in the early 1980s that freed up credit seems to be important in explaining the recent moderation of volatility.

And another important policy area is the Taylor rule itself. Our preliminary research has found that the basic perfect foresight endogenous growth model of this book, with money supply growth exogenously determined by the government, implies an endogenous equilibrium condition exactly analogous to the original Taylor rule. And a full "central bank policy model" also results endogenously. In the stochastic endogenous growth monetary economy, an interest smoothing version of the Taylor condition emerges endogenously whereby the weights of the smoothing depend precisely on the endogenous velocity of money demand. It suggest that Taylor rules are found in estimation because they are part of the equilibrium of the economy, rather than because the central bank has exogenously imposed them on the economy. These exciting results follow directly from the models of the collection and suggest a wide area of policy-related research that remains to be seen.

Note

1 See also Laidler (2006).

Bibliography

Ahmed, S. and J. H. Rogers (2000), 'Inflation and the great ratios: long term evidence from the US,' *Journal of Monetary Economics*, 45(1), 3–36.

Aiyagari, S., R. Braun and Z. Eckstein (1998), 'Transaction services, inflation, and welfare,' *Journal of Political Economy*, 106(6), 1274–1301.

Alvarez, A., R. E. Lucas and W. E. Weber (2001), 'Interest rates and inflation,' *American Economic Review*, 91(2), 219–225.

Alvarez, F., P. Kehoe and P. Neumeyer (2004), 'The time consistency of monetary and fiscal policies,' *Econometrica*, 72(2), 541–567.

Andrews, D. W. K. (1993), 'Tests for parameter instability and structural change with unknown change point,' *Econometrica*, 61, 821–856.

Andrews, D. W. K. and W. Ploberger (1994), 'Optimal tests when a nuisance parameter is present only under the alternative,' *Econometrica*, 62, 1383–1414.

Arrau, P., J. De Gregorio, C. M. Reinhart and P. Wickham (1996), 'The demand for money in developing countries: assessing the role of financial innovation,' *Journal of Development Economics*, 46, 317–340.

Azariadis, C., J. Bullard and B. Smith (2000), 'Private and public circulating liabilities,' Manuscript.

Baba, Y., D. F. Hendry and .–. R. o. E. S. .–. R. M. Starr (1992), 'The Demand for M1 in the U.S.A.' (1992), 'The demand for M1 in the U.S.A., 1960–1988,' *Review of Economic Studies*, 59(1), 25–61.

Bai, J. (1997), 'Estimating multiple breaks one at a time,' *Econometric Theory*, 13(3), 315–352.

Bai, J. and P. Perron (1998), 'Estimating and testing linear models with multiple structural changes,' *Econometrica*, 66, 47–78.

—— (2003), 'Computation and analysis of multiple structural change models,' *Journal of Applied Econometrics*, 18, 1–22.

Bailey, M. J. (1956), 'The welfare costs of inflationary finance,' *Journal of Political Economy*, 64(2) 93–110.

—— (1992), *Introduction, Studies in Positive and Normative Economics*, Aldershot, England: Edward Elgar Publishing.

Balfoussia, C. and M. Wickens (2005), 'Inflation prediction from the term structure: the Fisher equation in a multivariate SDF framework,' *Money Macro and Finance Research Group 37th Annual Conference*.

Baltensperger, E. (1980), 'Alternative approaches to the theory of the banking firm,' *Journal of Monetary Economics*, 6, 1–37.

Balvers, R. and J. Ran (1997), 'Price stickiness under menu and convex adjustment costs,' *Journal of Economic Research*, 2(2), 269–278.

Bansal, R. and W. J. Coleman (1996), 'A monetary explanation of the equity premium, term premium, and risk-free rate puzzles,' *Journal of Political Economy*, 104(6), 1135–1171.

Barnett, W. A. (1980), 'Economic monetary aggregates: an application of index number and aggregation theory,' *Journal of Econometrics*, 14(Summer), 11–48.

—— (1997), 'Which road leads to stable money demand?' *Economic Journal*, 107, 1171–1185.

Barro, R. J. (1972), 'A theory of monopolistic price adjustment,' *Review of Economic Studies*, 39, 17–26.

—— (1995), Inflation and economic growth, NBER Working Paper 5326.

—— (1997), *Determinants of economic growth: a cross country empirical study*, Cambridge, MA: MIT Press.

—— (2001), 'Human capital and growth,' *American Economic Review* 91(2), 12–17.

Barro, R. J. and X. Sala-I-Martin (1995), *Economic Growth*, New York: McGraw-Hill, Inc.

Basu, P. and P. Dua (1996), 'The behaviour of velocity and nominal interest rates in a cash-in-advance model,' *Journal of Macroeconomics*, 18(3), 463–478.

Baumol, W. (1952), 'The transactions demand for cash: an inventory-theoretic approach,' *Quarterly Journal of Economics*, 66, 545–566.

Beaulieu, J. J. and J. A. Miron (1993), 'Seasonal unit roots in aggregate US data,' *Journal of Econometrics*, 55(1–2), 305–328.

Beaurepaire, R. A., P. J. Higgins and P. C. Mercovich (1974), 'A study into the impact of continuing inflation – with particular reference to Shell (Australia) Ltd., 1974–1985,' Research Report, Master of Business Administration, University of Melbourne.

Becker, G. S. (1965), 'A theory of the allocation of time,' *Economic Journal*, 75(299), 493–517.

—— (1975), *Human Capital*, 2nd edn. Chicago: University of Chicago Press.

Benati, L. and G. Kapetanios (2003), 'Structural breaks in inflation dynamics,' *Computing in Economics and Finance* 169, Society for Computational Economics.

Benk, S., M. Gillman and M. Kejak (2004), 'Credit shocks in a monetary business cycle,' Working Paper 7/2004, Budapest: Central European University.

—— (2005), 'Credit shocks in the financial deregulatory era: not the usual suspects,' *Review of Economic Dynamics*, 8(3), 668–687.

—— (2008), 'Money velocity in an endogenous growth business cycle with credit shocks,' *Journal of Money, Credit and Banking*.

Berger, A. N. (2003), 'The economic effects of technological progress: evidence from the banking industry,' *Journal of Money, Credit, and Banking*, 35, 141–176.

Bewley, T. (1983), 'A difficulty with the optimum quantity of money,' *Econometrica*, 51(5), 1485–1504.

Billmeier, A. and L. Bonato (2004), 'Exchange rate pass-through and monetary policy in Croatia,' *Journal of Comparative Economics*, 32(3), 426–444.

Bishop, R. L. (1948), 'Alternative expansionist fiscal policies: a diagrammatic analysis,' in L. A. Metzler (ed.), *Income, Employment, and Public Policy*, 317–340. New York: W. W. Norton & Company.

Black, R. T. M.and S. Poloz (1993), 'Non-superneutralities and some benefits of disinflation: a quantitative general equilibrium analysis,' Manuscript, Bank of Canada, October.

Bohn, H. (1991), 'On cash-in-advance models of money demand and asset pricing,' *Journal of Money, Credit, and Banking* 23, 224–242.

Bordo, M. D. and L. Jonung (1987), *The Long-Run Behavior of the Velocity of Circulation*. Cambridge: Cambridge University Press.

Bordo, M. D., L. Jonung and P. L. Siklos (1997), 'Institutional change and the velocity of money: a century of evidence,' *Economic Inquiry* 35(4), 710–724, October.

Boskin, M. J., M. Gertlet and C. Taylor (1980), 'The impact of inflation on US productivity and international competitiveness,' Washington, DC: National Planning Association.

Brand, C. and N. Cassola (2004), 'A money demand system for Euro area M3,' *Applied Economics*, 36(8), 817–838.

Brand, C., D. Gerdesmeier and B. Roffia (2002), 'Estimating the trend of M3 income velocity underlying the reference value for monetary growth,' Discussion Paper ECB Occasional Paper 3, European Central Bank.

Braun, R. A. (1994a), 'Another attempt to quantify the benefits of reducing inflation,' *Federal Reserve Bank of Minneapolis Quarterly Review*, 18(4), 17–25.

—— (1994b), 'How large is the optimal inflation tax?,' *Journal of Monetary Economics*, 34(2), 201–214.

Bruno, M. and W. Easterly (1998), 'Inflation crises and long-run growth,' *Journal of Monetary Economics*, 41(1), 3–26.

Bry, G. and C. Boschan (1971), 'Cyclical analysis of time series: selected procedures and computer programs,' Technical Paper 20, National Bureau of Economic Research, Columbia University.

Bullard, J. and B. Smith (2001), 'The Value of Inside and Outside Money,' Working Paper 2000–027C, The Federal Reserve Bank of St. Louis.

Butkiewicz, J. L. and M. M. McConnell (1995), 'The stability of the demand for money and M1 velocity: evidence from the sectoral data,' *Quarterly Review of Economics and Finance*, 35 (Fall), 233–243.

Cagan, P. (1956), 'The monetary dynamics of hyperinflation,' in *Studies in the Quantity Theory of Money*, ed. by M. Friedman, 25–120. Chicago: University of Chicago Press.

Calvo, G. A. and C. M. Reinhart (2002), 'Fear of floating,' *Quarterly Journal of Economics*, 117(2), 379–408.

Campbell, J. (1994), 'Inspecting the mechanism: an analytical approach to the stochastic growth model,' *Journal of Monetary Economics*, 33, 463–506.

Canova, F. and B. E. Hansen (1995), 'Are seasonal patterns constant over time?: a test of seasonal stability,' *Journal of Business and Economic Statistics*, 13(3), 237–252.

Canzoneri, M. and B. Diba (2005), 'Interest rate rules and price determinacy: the role of transactions services of bonds,' *Journal of Monetary Economics*, 52(2), 329–344.

Carlstrom, C. T. and W. T. Gavin (1993), 'Zero inflation: transition costs and shoe leather benefits,' *Contemporary Policy Issues*, 11(1), 9–17.

Cetorelli, N. (2004), 'Real effects of bank competition,' *Journal of Money, Credit and Banking*, 36(3, Part 2), 543–558.

Chari, V., L. E. Jones and R. E. Manuelli (1996), Inflation, growth, and financial intermediation. *Federal Reserve Bank of St. Louis Review*, 78(3), 41–58.

Chari, V., P. Kehoe and E. McGrattan (2007), 'Business cycle accounting,' *Econometrica*, 75(3), 781–836.

Chow, G. (1960), 'Tests of equality between sets of coefficients in two linear regressions,' *Econometrica*, 28, 591–605.

Christiano, L. J., M. Eichenbaum and C. L. Evans (1997), 'Sticky price and limited participation models of money: a comparison,' *European Economic Review*, 41(6), 1201–1449.

Christoffersen, P. and P. Doyle (2000), 'From inflation to growth: eight years of transition,' *Economics of Transition*, 8(2), 421–451.

Clark, J. A. (1984), 'Estimation of economies of scale in banking using a generalized functional form,' *Journal of Money, Credit, and Banking*, 16(1), 53–68.

Clower, R. (1967), 'A reconsideration of the microfoundations of monetary theory,' *Western Economics Journal*, 6(1), 1–9.

Cochrane, J. H. (1994), 'Permanent and transitory components of GNP and stock prices,' *Quarterly Journal of Economics*, 109, 241–266.

Colander, D. (1995), 'The stories we tell: a reconsideration of AS/AD analysis, *Journal of Economic Perspectives*, 9(3), 169–188.

Cole, H. and L. Ohanian (2002), 'The US and UK great depressions through the lens of neoclassical growth theory,' *American Economic Review*, 92(2), 28–32.

Coleman, W. J., II, (1989), Asset prices in a cash-in-advance economy, Manuscript. December.

Collins, S. and R. Anderson (1998), 'Modeling U.S. households' demands for liquid wealth in an era of financial change,' *Journal of Money, Credit and Banking*, 30(1), 83–101.

Cooley, T. and G. Hansen (1989), 'The inflation tax in a real business cycle model,' *American Economic Review*, 79(4), 733–748.

—— (1995), 'Money and the business cycle,' in T. Cooley (ed.), *Frontiers of Business Cycle Research*, 175–216. Princeton, NJ: Princeton University Press.

—— (1998), 'The role of monetary shocks in equilibrium business cycle theory: three examples,' *European Economic Review*, 42, 605–617.

Cooley, T. F. and G.D. Hansen (1991), 'The welfare cost of moderate inflations,' *Journal of Money, Credit, and Banking* 23, 482–503.

—— (1992), 'Tax distortions in a neoclassical monetary economy,' *Journal of Economic Theory*, February, 290–316.

Correia, I. H. and P. Teles (1999), 'The optimal inflation tax,' *Review of Economic Dynamics*, 2(2), 325–346.

Council of Economic Advisors, Economic report of the President, 1991, 286, 356, 363, Washington, DC.: Government Printing Office.

Crowder, W. J. (1997), 'The long-run Fisher relation in Canada,' *Canadian Journal of Economics*, 30(4), 1124–1142.

—— (1998), 'The long-run link between money growth and inflation,' *Economic Inquiry*, 36(2), 229–343.

—— (2003), 'Panel estimates of the Fisher effect,' Manuscript, University of Texas at Arlington.

Crowder, W. J. and D. L. Hoffman (1996), 'The long-run relationship between nominal interest rates and inflation: the Fisher equation revisited,' *Journal of Money, Credit and Banking*, 28(1), 102–118.

Culver, S. and D. Papell (1997), 'Is there a unit root in inflation rate? evidence from sequential break and panel data analysis,' *Journal of Applied Econometrics*, 12(4), 435–444.

Cziráky, D. (2002), 'Cointegration analysis of the monthly time-series relationship between retail sales and average wages in Croatia,' *Croatian International Relations Review*, 8(28–29), 139–156.

Cziraky, D. and M. Gillman (2006), 'Money Demand in an European Union accession country: a vector-error correction study of Croatia,' *Bulletin of Economic Research*, 58(2), 105–127.

Darity, W., Jr. and W. Young (1995), 'IS-LM: an inquest.' *History of Political Economy*, 27 (1), 1–41.

Davidson, J. E. H., D. F. Hendry, F. Srba and S. Yeo (1978), 'Econometric modelling of the aggregate time series relationship between consumers' expenditure and income in the United Kingdom,' *Economic Journal*, 88(352), 661–692.

Den Haan, W. J. (1990), 'The optimal inflation path in a Sidrauski-type model with uncertainty,' *Journal of Monetary Economics* 25, 389–410.

—— (2000), 'The comovement between output and prices.' *Journal of Monetary Economics*, 46(1), 3–30.

Diamond, P. and J. Mirrlees (1971), 'Optimal taxation and public production I: production efficiency,' *American Economic Review*, 61, 8–27.

Dickey, D. A. and W. A. Fuller (1979), 'Distribution of the estimators for autoregressive time series with a unit root,' *Journal of the American Statistical Association*, 74, 427–431.

Dickey, D. A., D. P. Hasza and W. A. Fuller (1984), 'Testing for unit roots in seasonal time series,' *Journal of the American Statistical Association*, 79(386), 355–367.

Dimand, R. W. (1988), *The Origins of the Keynesian Revolution*. Aldershot, England: Edward Elgar.

—— (1999), 'Irving Fisher and the Fisher relation: setting the record straight,' *Canadian Journal of Economics*, 32(3), 744–750.

Dittmar, R., W. Gavin and F. Kydland (2005), 'Inflation persistence and flexible prices,' *International Economic Review*, 46(1), 245–261.

Dixon, H. (1997), 'Controversy: microfoundations and the demand for money,' *Economic Journal*, 107, 1169–1170.

Dotsey, M. (1991), 'Monetary policy and operating procedures in New Zealand,' *Economic Review*, Federal Reserve Bank of Richmond, September/October 1991, 13–19.

Dotsey, M. and P. N. Ireland (1994), 'The welfare cost of inflation in general equilibrium,' Manuscript, Federal Reserve Bank of Richmond, March.

—— (1996), 'Inflation in general equilibrium,' *Journal of Monetary Economics*, 37(1), 29–47.

Dotsey, M. and P. D. Sarte (2000), 'Inflation uncertainty and growth in a cash-in-advance economy.' *Journal of Monetary Economics*, 45(3), 631–655.

Dowd, K. (1990), 'The value of time and the transactions demand for money,' *Journal of Money, Credit and Banking*, 22(1), 51–64.

—— (1992), 'The costs of inflation,' Manuscript, University of Nottingham, November.

—— (1994), 'A proposal to end inflation,' *Economic Journal*, 104(425), 828–841.

Duca, J. and W. C. Whitesell (1995), 'Credit cards and money demand: a cross-sectional study,' *Journal of Money, Credit and Banking*, 27 (May), 604–623.

Easterly, W. and R. Levine (2002), 'It's not factor accumulation: stylized facts and growth models,' Working Paper 164, Central Bank of Chile.

Eckstein, Z. and L. Leiderman (1992), 'Seigniorage and the welfare cost of inflation: Evidence from an intertemporal model of money and consumption,' *Journal of Monetary Economics*, 29(3), 389–410.

Eichenbaum, M. and K. J. Singleton (1986), 'Do equilibrium real business cycle theories explain postwar US business cycles?' *NBER Macroeconomics Annual*, 1986, Cambridge, MA: MIT Press, 91–135.

Eichenbaum, M. and L. J. Christiano (1992), 'Liquidity effects and the monetary transmission mechanism,' *American Economic Review* 82, 346–354.

Eichenbaum, M. and N. Wallace (1985), 'A shred of evidence on public acceptance of privately issued currency,' *Federal Reserve Bank of Minneapolis Quarterly Review*, Winter, 2–4.

Einarsson, T. and M. H. Marquis (1999), 'Transitional and steady-state costs of disinflation when growth is endogenous,' *Economica*, 66, 489–508.

—— (2001), 'Bank intermediation over the business cycle,' *Journal of Money, Credit and Banking*, 33(4), 876–899.

Engle, R. F. and C. W. J. Granger (1987), 'Cointegration and error correction: representation, estimation, and testing,' *Econometrica*, 55, 251–276.

Englund, P. and L. E. O. Svensson (1988), 'Money and banking in a cash-in-advance economy,' *International Economic Review*, 29, 681–705.

Erosa, A. and G. Ventura (2002), 'On inflation as a regressive consumption tax,' *Journal of Monetary Economics*, 49(4), 761–795.

Espino, E. and T. Hintermaier (2004), 'Occasionally binding collateral constraints in RBC models,' Society for Economic Dynamics, Meeting Papers 449.

Estrella, A. and J. C. Fuhrer (2003), 'Monetary policy shifts and the stability of monetary policy models,' *The Review of Economics and Statistics*, 85(1), 94–104.

Fama, E. and K. R. French (1988), 'Permanent and temporary components of stock prices,' *Journal of Political Economy*, 96, 246–273.

Feldstein, M. (1982), 'Inflation, tax rules and investment,' *Econometrica*, 50, 825–862.

Fender, J. (1990), *Inflation: Welfare Costs, Positive Theory, and Policy Options*, Ann Arbor: University of Michigan Press.

Fischer, S. (1981), 'Towards an understanding of the costs of inflation: II,' *Carnegie–Rochester Conference Series on Public Policy*, 15, 5–41.

—— (1993), 'The role of macroeconomic factors in growth,' *Journal of Monetary Economics*, 32, 485–512.

Fisher, I. (1907), *The Rate of Interest*, New York: Macmillan.

—— (1911), *The Purchasing Power of Money*, New York: Macmillan.

—— (1920), *Stabilizing the Dollar*, New York: Macmillan.

—— (1930), *The Theory of Interest*, New York: Macmillan.

Fluet, C. and L. Phaneuf (1997), 'Price adjustment costs and the effect of endogenous technique on price stickiness,' *European Economic Review*, 41(2), 245–258.

Franses, P. H. (1990), 'Testing for seasonal unit roots in monthly data,' Discussion Paper, Econometric Institute Report 9032/A, Rotterdam: Erasmus University.

Freeman, S. and F. E. Kydland (2000), 'Monetary aggregates and output,' *American Economic Review*, 90(5), 1125–1135.

Frenkel, Jacob A. (1976), 'Some dynamic aspects of the welfare costs of inflationary finance,' in *Money and Finance in Economic Growth and Development: Essays in*

Honor of E.S. Shaw, Ronald I. McKinnon, ed., 177–195, New York: Marcel Dekker, Inc.

Friedman, B. M. and K. N. Kuttner (1992), 'Money, income, prices, and interest rates,' *American Economic Review*, 82(3), 472–492.

Friedman, M. (1953), 'Discussion of the inflationary gap,' in *Essays in Positive Economics*, The University of Chicago Press, Chicago, Ill., 251–262.

—— (1956), 'The quantity theory of money: a restatement,' in M. Friedman ed., *Studies in the Quantity Theory of Money*, Chicago: University of Chicago Press.

—— (1957), *A Theory of the Consumption Function*, Princeton: Princeton University Press for the National Bureau of Economic Research.

—— (1959), 'The demand for money – some theoretical and empirical results,' *Journal of Political Economy*, 67, 327–51.

—— (1960), *A program for monetary stability*. New York: Fordham University Press.

—— (1969), *The optimum quantity of money and other essays*, 1–50, Chicago: Aldine.

—— (1988), 'Money and the stock market,' *Journal of Political Economy*, 96, 221–245.

Friedman, M. and A. J. Schwartz (1963a), *A Monetary History of the United States, 1867–1960*, Princeton: Princeton University Press.

—— (1963b), 'Money and business cycles,' *Review of Economics and Statistics*, 45, 32–64.

—— (1982), *Monetary trends in the United States and the United Kingdom*, Chicago: University of Chicago Press.

Fuhrer, J. and G. Moore (1992), 'Monetary policy rules and the indicator properties of asset prices,' *Journal of Monetary Economics*, April, 303–336.

Fusfeld, D. R. (1985), 'Keynes and the Keynesian cross: a note,' *History of Political Economy*, 17, 385–389.

Gaspar, V., F. Smets and D. Vestin (2007), 'Is time ripe for price level path stability?,' Working paper series 818, European Central Bank.

Gavin, W. and F. Kydland (1999), 'Endogenous money supply and the business cycle,' *Review of Economic Dynamics*, 2, 347–369.

Ghosh, A. and S. Phillips (1998), 'Inflation, disinflation and growth,' IMF Working Paper WP/98/68.

Gillman, M.(1987), 'The time value of money,' Doctoral dissertation, University of Chicago, December.

—— (1993), 'Welfare cost of inflation in a cash-in-advance economy with costly credit,' *Journal of Monetary Economics*, 31(1), 22–42.

—— (1994a), 'Second-best credit policy: the optimality of exchange credit restrictions,' working paper, University of Otago, December.

—— (1994b), 'Foundations in macroeconomics,' Manuscript, University of Otago, June.

—— (1995), 'A comparison of partial and general equilibrium estimates of the welfare cost of inflation,' *Contemporary Economic Policy*, 13(4), 60–71.

—— (1996a), 'Optimality of exchange credit restrictions,' Research Paper no. 519, Department of Economics, University of Melbourne.

—— (1996b), 'Price stability as optimal policy: costly nominal adjustment in general equilibrium,' Research Paper no. 515, Department of Economics, University of Melbourne.

—— (1998), 'Macroeconomic analysis of the transition economies,' in *Handbook on the Globalisation of the World Economy*, A. Levy-Livermore, ed. Cheltenham, England: Edward Elgar.
—— (2000), 'On the optimality of restricting credit: inflation-avoidance and productivity,' *Japanese Economic Review* 51(3), 375–390.
—— (2002), 'Keynes's treatise: aggregate price theory for modern analysis.' *European Journal of the History of Economic Thought*, 9(3), 430–451.
Gillman, M. and M. Harris (2004), 'Inflation, financial development and endogenous growth,' Working Paper 24–04, Monash University.
Gillman M., M. Harris and L. Mátyás (2001), 'Inflation and growth: some theory and evidence.' Central European University Department of Economics Working Paper WP1/2001.
—— (2004), 'Inflation and growth: explaining a negative effect', *Empirical Economics*, 29(1), 149–67.
Gillman, M. and M. Kejak (2002), 'Modeling the effect of inflation: growth, levels, and Tobin,' in D. Levine (ed.), *Proceedings of the 2002 North American Summer Meetings of the Econometric Society: Money*. http://www.dklevine.com/proceedings/money.htm
—— (2003), 'A revised Tobin effect from inflation: relative input price and capital ratio realignments, US and UK, 1959–1999,' *Economica*, 70(279), 439–450.
—— (2004), 'Causality of the inflation–growth mirror in accession countries,' *Economics of Transition*, 12(4), 653–682.
—— (2004), 'The demand for bank reserves and other monetary aggregates,' *Economic Inquiry*, 42(3), 518–533.
—— (2005a), 'Contrasting models of the effect of inflation on growth,' *Journal of Economic Surveys*, 19(1), 113–136.
—— (2005b), 'Inflation and balanced-path growth with alternative payment mechanisms,' *Economic Journal*, 115(500), 247–270.
Gillman, M., M. Kejak and A. Valentinyi (1999), 'Inflation and growth: Nonlinearities and financial development,' *Transition Economics Series 13*, Vienna: Institute of Advanced Studies.
Gillman, M. and Nakov, A. (2001), 'A monetary explanation of oil and gold prices.' Central European University Department of Economics Working Paper, WP5/2000, Revised.
Gillman, M. and G. Otto (1997), 'The velocity of non-interest bearing means of payment during a period of financial innovation: Australia, 1975–96,' Mimeo, University of New South Wales, & Economics Institute, Academy of the Sciences of the Czech Republic.
—— (2002), 'Money demand: cash-in-advance meets shopping time,' Department of Economics Working Paper WP03/02, Budapest: Central European University.
—— (2003), 'Money demand in a banking time economy,' Discussion Paper 254, Hamburg: Hamburg Institute of International Economics.
—— (2007), 'Money demand in general equilibrium endogenous growth: estimating the role of a variable interest elasticity,' *Quantitative and Qualitative Analysis in Social Sciences*, 1(1), 1–25.
Gillman, M., P. Siklos and J. L. Silver (1997), 'Money velocity with costly credit.' *Journal of Economic Research*, 2, 179–207.
Gillman, M. and M. Wallace (2003), 'Growth and inflation in a Baltic Sea transition economy: the case of Latvia,' Manuscript.

Gillman, M. and O. Yerokhin (2005), 'Ramsey-Friedman optimality in a banking time economy,' *Berkeley Electronic Journals in Macroeconomics: Topics in Macroeconomics*, 5(1), article 16.

Godfrey, L. G. (1988), *Specification Tests in Econometrics*, Cambridge: Cambridge University Press.

Gomme, P. (1993), 'Money and growth: revisited,' *Journal of Monetary Economics*, 32, 51–77.

Goodfriend, M. (1997), 'A framework for the analysis of moderate inflations,' *Journal of Monetary Economics*, 39, 45–65.

Gordon, D., E. Leeper, and T. Zha (1998), 'Trends in velocity and policy expectations,' *Carnegie-Rochester Conference Series on Public Policy*, 49, 265–304.

Granger, C. (1969), 'Investigating causal relations by econometric models and cross-spectral methods,' *Econometrica*, 37, 424–438.

Granger, C.W.J. and N. Swanson (1996), 'Further developments in the study of cointegrated variables,' *Oxford Bulletin of Economics and Statistics*, 58(3), 537–553.

Gray, C. W. and A. Holle (1996), 'Bank-led restructuring in Poland,' *World Bank Policy Research Working Paper, 1650*, Washington, DC: The World Bank.

Guzman, M. (2003), 'Slow but steady progress toward financial deregulation.' Southwest Economy 1, Federal Reserve Bank of Dallas.

Gylfason, T. and T. Herbertsson (2001), 'Does inflation matter for growth?' *Japan and the World Economy* 13(4), 405–428.

Hafer, R. W. and D. W. Jansen (1991), 'The demand for money in the United States: evidence from cointegration tests,' *Journal of Money, Credit and Banking*, 23 May, 155–168.

Hamilton, J. D. (1989), 'The long run behavior of the velocity of circulation: a review essay,' *Journal of Monetary Economics*, 23(2), 335–344.

—— (1994), *Time Series Analysis*. Princeton, N.J.: Princeton University Press.

Hanc, G. (1998), 'The banking crises of the 1980s and early 1990s: summary and implications,' *FDIC Banking Review*, 11(1).

Hancock, D. (1985), 'The financial firm: production with monetary and nonmonetary goods,' *Journal of Political Economy*, 93(5), 859–880.

Hansen, B. (1997), 'Approximate asymptotic P values for structural change tests,' *Journal of Business and Economic Statistics*, (1), 60–67.

Harberger, A. C. (1974), 'Three basic postulates for applied welfare economics: an interpretive essay,' in *Taxation and Welfare*, Chicago, Ill.: The University of Chicago.

—— (1998), 'A vision of the growth process,' *American Economic Review*, March 88(1), 1–32.

Harding, D. and A. Pagan (2002), 'Dissecting the cycle: a methodological investigation,' *Journal of Monetary Economics*, 49, 365–381.

Haslag, J. H. (1998), 'Monetary policy, banking, and growth,' *Economic Inquiry*, 36(3), 489–500.

Hernandez-Cata, E. (1999), 'Price liberalization, money growth, and inflation during the transition to a market economy,' *International Monetary Fund Working Paper 99/76*, Washington, DC: IMF.

Hicks, J. R. (1935), 'A suggestion for simplifying the theory of money,' *Economica*, 2(5), 1–19.

—— (1937), 'Mr. Keynes and the Classics: a suggested interpretation.' *Econometrica*, p. 147–159.
—— (1950), *A Contribution to the Theory of the Trade Cycle*. London: Oxford University Press.
Hodrick, R. J., N. R. Kocherlakota and D. Lucas (1991), 'The variability of velocity in cash-in-advance models', *Journal of Political Economy*, 99(2), 358–384.
Hoenig, T. (2000), 'Discussion of "The Australian financial system in the 1990s,"' in *The Australian Economy in the 1990s: Conference Proceedings*, Reserve Bank of Australia.
Hoffman, D. L. and R. H. Rasche (1991), 'Long-run income and interest elasticities of money demand in the United States,' *Review of Economics and Statistics*, 73(4), 665–674.
Hoffman, D. L., R. H. Rasche and M. A. Tieslau (1995), 'The stability of long-run money demand in five industrial countries,' *Journal of Monetary Economics*, 35(2), 317–339.
Hopenhayn, H. and P. Neumeyer (2002), 'The Argentine Great Depression 1975–1990,' Department of Economics Working Paper 26, Universidad Torcuato Di Tella, University of Rochester.
Hotelling, H. (1938), 'The general welfare in relation to problems of taxation and of railway and utility rates,' *Econometrica*, July, 242–269.
Howitt, P. (1987), 'The optimum quantity of money,' in *The New Palgrave: Money*, eds. J. Eatwell, M. Milgate and P. Newman, New York: Macmillan.
Hylleberg, S., R. F. Engle, C. W. J. Granger and B. S. Yoo (1990), 'Seasonal integration and cointegration,' *Journal of Econometrics*, 44(1–2), 215–238.
Ingram, B., N. Kocherlakota and N. Savin (1994), 'Explaining business cycles: a multiple-shock approach,' *Journal of Monetary Economics*, 34, 415–428.
—— (1997), 'Using theory for measurement: an analysis of the cyclical behavior of home production,' *Journal of Monetary Economics*, 40, 435–456.
International Financial Statistics (2002), Database. Washington, DC: International Monetary Fund.
Ireland, P. N. (1991), 'Long-run behavior of velocity: new evidence from US regional data,' *Federal Reserve Bank of Richmond Economic Review*, 16–25.
—— (1993), 'Price stability under long-run monetary targeting,' *Federal Reserve Bank of Richmond Economic Review*, 79(1), 25–45.
—— (1994a), 'Economic growth, financial evolution, and the long-run behavior of velocity,' *Journal of Economic Dynamics and Control*, 18(3/4), 815–848.
—— (1994b), 'Money and growth: an alternative approach,' *American Economic Review*, 84(1), 47–65.
—— (1995), 'Endogenous financial innovation and the demand for money,' *Journal of Money, Credit and Banking*, 27(1), 107–123.
—— (1996), 'The role of countercyclical monetary policy,' *Journal of Political Economy*, 104(4), 704–723.
—— (1999), 'Does the time-consistency problem explain the behavior of inflation in the United States?,' *Journal of Monetary Economics*, 44(2), 279–291.
—— (2004), 'Money's role in the monetary business cycle,' *Journal of Money, Credit and Banking*, 36(6), 969–985.
—— (2005), 'The liquidity trap, the real balance effect, and the Friedman rule,' *International Economic Review*, 46(2), 1271–1301.

Jayaratne, J. and P. Strahan (1996), 'The finance-growth nexus: evidence from bank branch deregulation,' *Quarterly Journal of Economics*, 111, 639–670.

Jermann, U. J. and V. Quadrini (2006), 'Financial innovations and macroeconomic volatility,' NBER Working Papers 12308, NBER.

Johansen, S. (1991), 'Estimation and hypothesis testing of cointegration vectors in gaussian vector autoregressive models.' *Econometrica*, 59, 1551–1580.

—— (1995), *Likelihood-based Inference in Cointegrated Vector Autoregressive Models*, Oxford: Oxford University Press.

Johansen, S. and K. Juselius (1990), 'Maximum likelihood estimation and inferences on cointergration-with applications to the demand for money,' *Oxford Bulletin of Economics and Statistics*, 52, 169–210.

Johnson, H. G. (1969), 'Inside money, outside money, income, wealth, and welfare in monetary theory,' *Journal of Money, Credit and Banking*, 1(1), 30–45.

Jones, L. and R. Manuelli (1995), 'Growth and the Effects of Inflation,' *Journal of Economic Dynamics and Control*, 19, 1405–1428.

Jones, L. E., R. E. Manuelli and P. E. Rossi (1997), 'On the optimal taxation of capital income,' *Journal of Economic Theory*, 73, 93–117.

Jones, L., M. Rodolfo and R. Rossi (1993), 'Optimal taxation in models of endogenous growth,' *Journal of Political Economy*, 101, 485–517.

Jorgenson, D. W. and K. J. Stiroh (2000), 'Raising the speed limit: U.S. economic growth in the information age,' OECD Economics Department Working Papers 261, OECD.

Judson, R. and A. Orphanides (1999), Inflation, volatility and growth. *International Finance* 2(1), 117–138.

Karni, E. (1974), 'The value of time and demand for money,' *Journal of Money, Credit, and Banking*, 6, 45–64.

Kehoe, T. J. and E. C. Prescott (2002), 'Great Depressions of the twentieth century,' *Review of Economic Dynamics*, 5(1), 1–18.

Keynes, J. M. (1923), *A Tract on Monetary Reform*; Collected Works, Vol. IV, 1971 ed., London: Macmillan.

—— (1930), *A Treatise on Money*, 2 Volumes. New York: Harcourt, Brace and Company.

—— (1936), *The General Theory of Employment, Interest, and Money*. London: Macmillan.

—— (Lord) (1971–1983), *Collected Writings*, London: Royal Economic Society.

Khan, A., R. G. King and A. L. Wolman (2003), 'Optimal monetary policy,' *Review of Economic Studies*, 70(4), 825–860.

Khan, M. S. and A. S. Senhadji (2000), 'Financial development and economic growth: an overview,' Working Paper WP/00/209, International Monetary Fund.

—— (2001), Threshold effects in the relationship between inflation and growth, *IMF Staff Papers* 48(1), 1–21.

King, J. E. (1995), 'Aggregate supply and demand analysis since Keynes: a partial history,' *Journal of Post Keynesian Economics*, 3–31.

King, R. G. (1988), 'Money demand in the United States': a quantitative review – a comment, Carnegie–Rochester Conference Series on Public Policy 29, 169–172.

King, R. G. and C. I. Plosser (1984), 'Money, credit and prices in a real business cycle,' *American Economic Review*, 74(3), 363–380.

—— (1986), Money as the mechanism of exchange, *Journal of Monetary Economics* 17, 93–115.

King, R. G., C. I. Plosser and S. Rebelo (1987), 'Production, growth and business cycles: technical appendix,' Manuscript, Rochester: University of Rochester.

King, R. G. and S. Rebelo (1990), 'Public policy and economic growth: deriving neoclassical implications,' *Journal of Political Economy*, 98(2), S126–S150, Part 2.

Kiyotaki, N. (1998), 'Credit and business cycles,' *Japanese Economic Review*, 49, 19–35.

Kiyotaki, N. and J. Moore (1997), 'Credit cycles,' *Journal of Political Economy*, 105, 211–248.

Knight, F. (1922), *Risk, Uncertainty and Profit*. Boston: Houghton-Mifflin.

Kocherlakota, N. (2000), 'Creating business cycles through credit constraints,' *Federal Reserve Bank of Minneapolis Quarterly Review*, 24(2), 2–10.

Kontolemis, Z. G. (2002), 'Money demand in the Euro area: where do we stand (today)?,' Discussion Paper WP/02/185, International Monetary Fund.

Kormendi, R. C. and P. G. Meguire (1985), 'Macroeconomic determinants of growth: cross-country evidence,' *Journal of Monetary Economics*, 16, 141–163.

Kraft, E. (2003), 'Monetary policy under dollarisation: the case of Croatia,' *Comparative Economic Studies*, 45(3), 256–277.

Kuznets, S. (1941), *National Income and Its Composition*, Cambridge: National Bureau of Economic Research.

Kwiatkowski, D., P. C. B. Phillips, P. Schmidt and Y. Shin (1992), 'Testing the null hypothesis of stationarity against the alternative of a unit root,' *Journal of Econometrics*, 54, 159–178.

Kydland, F. and E. C. Prescott (1977), 'Rules rather than discretion: the inconsistency of optimal plans,' *Journal of Political Economy*, 85(3), 473–491.

Lacker, J. M. and S. L. Schreft (1996), 'Money and credit as means of payment,' *Journal of Monetary Economics*, 38(1), 3–24.

Laidler, D. (2006), 'Woodford and Wicksell on interest and prices: the place of the pure credit economy in the theory of monetary policy,' *Journal of the History of Economic Thought*, 28(2), 151–159.

Leigh-Pemberton, R. (1992), 'The case for price stability,' *Bank of England Quarterly Bulletin*, 32(4), 441–448.

Leijonhufvud, A. (1977), 'Costs and consequences of inflation,' in: H. Harcout (ed.), *Microeconomic Foundations of Macroeconomics*, Boulder, CO.: Westview Press.

Levy, D., M. Bergen, S. Dutta and R. Venable (1997), 'The magnitude of menu costs: direct evidence from large U.S. supermarket chains,' *Quarterly Journal of Economics*, (107)3, 791–825.

Li, V. (2000), 'Household credit and the monetary transmission mechanism,' *Journal of Money, Credit and Banking*, 32(3), 335–356.

Lipsey, R. G. and K. Lancaster (1956), 'The general theory of second best,' *Review of Economic Studies*, 23, 11–23.

Ljungqvist, L. and T. Sargent (2000), *Recursive Macroeconomic Theory*. Cambridge, MA: MIT Press.

Lougani, P. and N. Sheets (1995), 'Central Bank independence, inflation and growth in transition economies,' *Board of Governors of the Federal Reserve System, International Finance Discussion Papers*, 519.

Lourenco, R. D. and D. Gruen (1995), 'Price stickiness and inflation,' *Research Discussion Paper 9502*, Sydney: Reserve Bank of Australia.

Love, D. and J. Wen (1999), 'Inflation, welfare, and the time-costs of transacting,' *Canadian Journal of Economics*, 32(1), 171–194.

Lowe, P. (1995), 'Labour-productivity growth and relative wages: 1978–1994.' DP 9505, Sydney: Reserve Bank of Australia.

Lucas, R. E., Jr., (1967), 'Adjustment costs and the theory of supply,' *Journal of Political Economy*, 75(4), 321–334.

—— (1972), 'Expectations and the neutrality of money,' *Journal of Economic Theory*, 4, 103–124.

—— (1976), 'Econometric policy evaluation: a critique,' *Carnegie-Rochester Conference Series on Public Policy*, 1(2), 19–46.

—— (1980), 'Equilibrium in a pure currency economy,' *Economic Inquiry*, 43, 203–220.

—— (1981), 'Discussion of Stanley Fischer, "Towards an understanding of the costs of inflation: II",' in *The Cost and Consequences of Inflation*, K. Brunner and A. Meltzer, eds., North Holland Publishing Co., 1981, 43–52.

—— (1984), 'Money in a theory of finance,' *Carnegie–Rochester Conference Series on Public Policy* 21, 9–46.

—— (1988a), 'Money demand in the United States: a quantitative review.' *Carnegie-Rochester Conference Series on Public Policy*, 29, 169–172.

—— (1988b), 'On the mechanics of economic development,' *Journal of Monetary Economics*, 22, 3–42.

—— (1993b), 'Making a miracle,' *Econometrica*, 61, 251–272.

—— (1996), Nobel lecture: monetary neutrality. *Journal of Political Economy*, 104, 661–682.

—— (2000), 'Inflation and welfare,' *Econometrica*, 68(2), 247–275.

Lucas, R. E., Jr. and N. L. Stokey, Jr. (1983), 'Optimal fiscal and monetary policy in an economy without capital,' *Journal of Monetary Economics* 12, 55–93.

—— (1987), "Money and interest in a cash-in-advance economy," *Econometrica* 55, 491–514.

—— (1993a), 'On the welfare costs of inflation,' paper prepared for the Hitotsubashi International Symposium on Financial Markets in the Changing World.

MacKinnon, J. (1991), *Critical Values for Cointegration Tests*, Chapter 13. Oxford: Oxford University Press.

Mankiw, N. G. (1985), 'Small menu costs and large business cycles: A macroeconomic model of monopoly,' *Quarterly Journal of Economics*, 100(2), 529–537.

—— (1989), 'Real business cycles: a new Keynesian perspective,' *Journal of Economic Perspectives*, Summer 3(3), 79–90.

Mankiw, N. G. and L. H. Summers (1987), 'Money demand and the effects of fiscal policies,' *Journal of Money Credit and Banking*, 18, 415–429.

Manuelli, R. and T. J. Sargent (1988), Models of business cycles: a review essay, *Journal of Monetary Economics* 22, 523–542.

Marcet, A. and J. Nicolini (2003), 'Recurrent hyperinflation and learning,' *American Economic Review*, 93(5), 1476–1498.

Mark, N. C. and D. Sul (2003), 'Cointegration vector estimation by panel DOLS and long run money demand,' *Oxford Bulletin of Economics and Statistics*, 65(5), 655–680.

Marquis, M. H. and K. L. Reffett (1994), 'New technology spillovers into the payments system,' *Economic Journal*, 104, 1123–1138.

—— (1995), 'Equilibrium growth in a monetary economy with transactions costs,' *Bulletin of Economic Research*, 47, 233–251.

Marshall, A. (1920), *Principles of Economics*, 8th edn., London: Macmillan.

Marty, A. (1969), 'Inside money, outside money, and the wealth effect,' *Journal of Money, Credit and Banking*, 1(1), 101–111.

Mátyás, L. and P. Sevestre, eds. (1996), *The econometrics of panel data*, The Netherlands: Kluwer Academic Publishers.

McCallum, B. T. (1983), The role of overlapping-generations models in monetary economics, *Carnegie–Rochester Conference Series on Public Policy* 18, 9–44.

—— (1989), *Monetary Economics*, New York: Macmillan.

—— (1990), 'Could a monetary base rule have prevented the Great Depression?' *Journal of Monetary Economics*, 26, 3–26.

—— (1999), 'Recent developments in the analysis of monetary policy rules,' *Federal Reserve Bank of St. Louis Review*, 81(6), 3–11.

McCallum, B. T. and M. S. Goodfriend (1987), 'Demand for money: theoretical studies,' in *New Palgrave Money*, M. J. Eatwell and P. Newman (ed.). New York: Macmillan.

McCandless, G. (2008), *The ABCs of RBCs*. Cambridge, MA: Harvard University Press.

McGrattan, E. R. (1998), 'Trends in velocity and policy expectations: a comment,' *Carnegie-Rochester Conference Series on Public Policy*, 49, 305–316.

Mehra, R. and E. C. Prescott (1985), The equity premium: a puzzle, *Journal of Monetary Economics* 15, 145–161.

Melnick, R. (1995), 'Financial services, cointegration, and the demand for money in Israel,' *Journal of Money, Credit, and Banking*, 27, 140–153.

Meltzer, A. (1963), 'The demand for money: the evidence from the time series,' *Journal of Political Economy*, 71, 219–246.

—— (1987), 'Limits of short-run stabilization policy,' *Economic Inquiry*, 25, 1–14.

—— (1988), *Keynes's Monetary Theory: A Different Interpretation*, Cambridge: Cambridge University Press.

Mishkin, F. (1997), *The Economics of Money, Banking and Financial Markets*, 5th edn., New York: Addison-Wesley.

Mondschean, T. S. and T. P. Opiela (1997), 'Banking reform in a transition economy: the case of Poland,' *Federal Reserve Bank of Chicago Economic Perspectives*, 16–32.

Monnet, C. and W. E. Weber (2001), 'Money and interest rates,' *Federal Reserve Bank of Minneapolis Quarterly Review*, 25(4), 2–13.

Mosconi, R. and C. Giannini (1992), Non-causality in cointegrated system: representation, estimation and testing. *Oxford Bulletin of Economics and Statistics*, 54, 399–414.

Mulligan, C. B. and X. Sala-I-Martin (1997), 'The optimum quantity of money: theory and evidence,' Working Paper 5954, National Bureau of Economic Research.

Mussa, M. (1977), 'The welfare cost of inflation and the role of money as a unit of account,' *Journal of Money, Credit, and Banking*, 9(2), 276–286.

Neville, J. W. and B. Bhaskara Rao (1996), 'The use and abuse of aggregate demand and supply functions,' *The Manchester School*, 64, 189–207.

Newey, W. K. and K. D. West (1987), 'A simple positive semi definite heteroskedasticity and autocorrelation consistent covariance matrix,' *Econometrica*, 55, 703–708.

Niehans, J. (1969), 'Efficient monetary and fiscal policies in balanced growth,' *Journal of Money, Credit, and Banking*, 1(2), 228–251.

Nikolic, M. (2000), 'Money growth-inflation relationship in postcommunist Russia,' *Journal of Comparative Economics*, 28(1), 108–133.

Obstfeld, M. and K. Rogoff (1996), *Foundations in International Macroeconomics*, Cambridge, MA: MIT Press.

Orden, D. and L. A. Fisher (1993), 'Financial deregulation and the dynamics of money, prices, and output in New Zealand and Australia,' *Journal of Money, Credit and Banking*, 25, 273–292.

Otto, G. and M. Crosby (2000), 'Inflation and the capital stock,' *Journal of Money, Credit, and Banking*, 32(2), 236–253.

Paal, B. and B. Smith (2000), 'The sub-optimality of the Friedman rule and the optimum quantity of money,' Manuscript, Stanford University.

Parkin, M. (1986), 'The output–inflation trade-off when prices are costly to change,' *Journal of Political Economy*, 94(1), 200–224.

—— (1988), 'A method for determining whether parameters in aggregative models are structural,' *Carnegie-Rochester Conference Series on Public Policy*, 29, 215–252.

Parry, R. (2000), 'Monetary policy in a new environment: the US experience,' in *Recent Developments in Financial Systems and Their Challenges for Economic Policy: A European Perspective*, Federal Reserve Bank of San Francisco, The Bank for International Settlements and the Deutsche Bundesbank.

Patinkin, D. (1989), *Money, Interest, and Prices An Integration of Monetary and Value Theory*. 2nd edition, abridged. Cambridge, MA: MIT Press.

—— (1976), *Keynes' Monetary Thought*. Durham: Duke University Press.

Perron, P. (1989), 'The great crash, the oil price shock, and the unit root hypothesis,' *Econometrica*, 57, 1361–1401.

Persky, J. (1998), 'Price indexes and general exchange values,' *Journal of Economic Perspectives*, (12)1, 197–205.

Petrovic, P. and Z. Mladenovic (2000), 'Money demand and exchange rate determination under hyperinflation: conceptual issues and evidence from Yugoslavia,' *Journal of Money, Credit, and Banking*, 32(4), 785–806.

Phillips, P. and P. Perron (1988), 'Testing for a unit root in time series regression,' *Biometrika*, 75, 335–346.

Plosser, Charles I. (1984), 'Money in a theory of finance. Some observations on the Lucas paper,' *Carnegie–Rochester Conference Series on Public Policy* 21, 47–56.

Prescott, E. C. (1987), 'A multiple means of payment model,' in *New Approaches to Monetary Economics*, ed. by W. A. Barnett, and K. J. Singleton, chap. 2, 42–51. Cambridge: Cambridge University Press.

Quah, D. (1992), 'The relative importance of permanent and transitory components: identification and some theoretical bounds,' *Econometrica*, 60, 107–118.

Quandt, R. (1960), 'Tests of the hypothesis that a linear regression system obeys two separate regimes,' *Journal of the American Statistical Association*, 55, 324–330.

Ramsey, F. (1927), 'A contribution to the theory of taxation,' *Economic Journal*, 37, 47–61.

Ramsey, J. B. (1969), 'Tests for specification errors in classical linear least squares regression analysis,' *Journal of the Royal Statistical Society*, 31, 350–371.

Rapach, D. (2003), 'International evidence on the long-run impact of inflation,' *Journal of Money, Credit, and Banking*, 35(1), 23–48.

Romer, D. (1986), 'A simple general equilibrium version of the Baumol–Tobin model,' *Quarterly Journal of Economics* 101, 663–685.

—— (1987), 'The monetary transmission mechanism in a general equilibrium version of the Baumol–Tobin model,' *Journal of Monetary Economics* 20, 105–122.
Romer, P. (1986), 'Increasing returns and long-run growth,' *Journal of Political Economy*, 94(5), 1002–1038.
Ross, K. (2000), 'Post-stabilization inflation dynamics in Slovenia,' *Applied Economics*, 32(2), 135–149.
Roubini, N. and X. Sala-i-Martin (1995), 'A growth model of inflation, tax evasion, and financial repression,' *Journal of Monetary Economics*, 35, 275–303.
Sahay, R. and C. A. Vegh (1995), 'Inflation and stabilization in transition economies: a comparison with market economies,' *International Monetary Fund Working Paper No. 95/8*, Washington, DC: IMF.
Samuelson, P. A. (1951), *Economics*, 2nd edn. London: McGraw-Hill.
Sargent, T. J. (1972), 'Anticipated inflation and the nominal rate of interest,' *Quarterly Journal of Economics*, 86(2), 212–225.
—— (1973), 'Interest rates and prices in the long run: a study of the Gibson paradox,' *Journal of Money, Credit, and Banking*, 5(1), 385–449.
Schabert, A. (2003), 'On the equivalence of money growth and interest rate policy,' Working Paper 2003/6, Department of Economics, University of Glasgow.
—— (2005), 'Identifying monetary policy shocks with changes in open market operations,' *European Economic Review*, 49(3), 561–577.
Schreft, S. (1992), 'Welfare-improving credit controls,' *Journal of Monetary Economics*, 30, 57–73.
Schultz, T. W. (1964), *Transforming Traditional Agriculture*, New Haven: Yale University Press.
Schumpeter, J. A. (1952), *Ten Great Economists from Marx to Keynes*, London: Allen & Unwin.
Sephton, P. S. (1995), 'Response surfaces estimates of the KPSS stationarity test,' *Economics Letters*, 47, 255–261.
Shadman-Mehta, F. (2001), 'A re-evaluation between wages and unemployment in the United Kingdom,' *Economica*, 68(272), 567–606.
Sidrauski, M. (1967a), 'Inflation and economic growth,' *Journal of Political Economy*, 75, 796–810.
—— (1967b), 'Rational choice and patterns of growth in a monetary economy,' *American Economic Review*, 57(2), 534–544.
Siklos, P. L. (1993), 'Income velocity and institutional change: some new time series evidence, 1870–1986,' *Journal of Money, Credit, and Banking*, 25 August, 377–392.
Siklos, P. L. and C. W. J. Granger (1996), 'Temporary cointegration with an application to interest rate parity,' Discussion Paper 96–11, San Diego: University of California.
Sims, C. A. (1972), 'Money, income and causality,' *American Economic Review*, 62(4), 540–542.
Sims, C., J. H. Stock and M. W. Watson (1990), 'Inference in linear time series models with some unit roots,' *Econometrica*, 58(1), 113–144.
Stemp, P. J. (1996), 'The role of monetary policy in Australia: a minimalist approach,' *Australian Economic Review*, 1st quarter, 10–28.
Stiroh, K. J. and P. E. Strahan (2003), 'Competitive dynamics of deregulation: evidence from U.S. banking,' *Journal of Money, Credit, and Banking*, 35(5), 801–828.

Stock, J. H. and M. W. Watson (1989), 'Interpreting the evidence on money-income causality,' *Journal of Econometrics*, 40(1), 161–181.
Stockman, A. (1981), 'Anticipated inflation and the capital stock in a cash-in-advance economy,' *Journal of Monetary Economics*, 8(3), 387–393.
Stokey, N. and R. E. Lucas, Jr. (1989), *Recursive Methods in Economic Dynamics*. Cambridge, MA: Harvard University Press.
Strahan, P. (2003), 'The real effects of U.S. banking deregulation,' *Federal Reserve Bank of Saint Louis Review*, 85, 111–128.
Svensson, L. E. O. (1985), Money and asset prices in a cash-in-advance economy, *Journal of Political Economy* 93, 919–944.
—— (1997), 'Inflation forecast targeting: implementing and monitoring inflation targets,' *European Economic Review*, 41(6), 1111–1147.
—— (1999), 'Inflation targeting as a monetary policy rule,' *Journal of Monetary Economics*, 43(3), 607–654.
Szapary, G. (2001), 'Banking sector reform in ungary: lessons learned, current trends and prospects,' *National Bank of Hungary Working Paper 2001/5*.
Taub, B. (1989), 'The optimum quantity of money in a stochastic economy,' *International Economic Review*, 30(2), 255–273.
Taylor, J. B. (1993), 'Discretion versus policy rules in practice,' *Carnegie-Rochester Conference Series on Public Policy*, 39 (December), 195–214.
—— (1999), 'The robustness and efficiency of monetary policy rules as guidelines for interest rate setting by the European Central Bank,' *Journal of Monetary Economics*, 43(3), 655–679.
—— (2001), 'The role of the exchange rate in monetary policy rules,' *American Economic Review*, 91(2), 263–267.
Tobin, J. (1956), 'The interest elasticity of transactions demand for cash,' *Review of Economics and Statistics*, 38, 241–247.
—— (1965), 'Money and economic growth,' *Econometrica*, 33(4, part 2), 671–684.
Topel, R. and R. Sherwin (1988), 'Housing investment in the United States.' *Journal of Political Economy*, 96(4), 718–740.
Tower, E. (1971), 'More on the welfare cost of inflationary finance,' *Journal of Money, Credit, and Banking*, November, 850–860.
Townsend, R. M. (1978), 'Intermediation with costly bilateral exchange,' *Review of Economic Studies*, 45(3), 417–425.
—— (1989), 'Currency and credit in a private information economy,' *Journal of Political Economy* 97, 1323–1345.
Turnovsky, S. (1997), *International Macroeconomic Dynamics*. Cambridge, MA: MIT Press.
U.S. Council of Economic Advisors, *Economic Report of the President*, 1991, Washington, D.C: Government Printing Office.
U.S. Department of Commerce, Bureau of Economic Analysis, *The National Income and Product Accounts, 1929–1982*, Washington, DC: Government Printing Office.
—— *Survey of Current Business*, July 1985, 1986, 1987, 1988, 1989, 1990, Washington, DC: Government Printing Office.
Uhlig, H. (1995), 'A toolkit for analyzing nonlinear dynamic stochastic models easily,' *Discussion Paper 101*, Institute for Empirical Macroeconomics, Federal Reserve Bank of Minneapolis.
—— (2004), 'What moves real GNP,' Econometric Society 2004 North American Winter Meetings, 636.

Vilasuso, J. (2000), 'Trend breaks in money growth and the money-output relation in the U.S.,' *Oxford Bulletin of Economics and Statistics*, 62(1), 53–60.
Wallace, N. (1980), 'The overlapping generations model of fiat money,' in J. Kareken, and N. Wallace, eds., *Models of Monetary Economics*, Federal Reserve Bank of Minnesota, Minneapolis, 49–82.
Walsh, C. E. (1998), *Monetary Theory and Policy*. Cambridge, MA: MIT Press.
—— (2003), *Monetary Theory and Policy*, 2nd edn., Cambridge, MA: MIT Press.
Wang, W. and S. Shi (2006), 'The variability of velocity of money in a search model,' *Journal of Monetary Economics*, 53(3), 537–572.
Wheelock, D. C. and P. W. Wilson (2006), 'Robust non-parametric quantile estimation of efficiency and productivity change in US commercial banking, 1985–2004,' *Working Paper Series 2006–041A*, Federal Reserve Bank of St Louis.
White, H. (1980), 'A heteroskedasticity-consistent covariance matrix and a direct test for heteroskedasticity,' *Econometrica*, 48, 817–838.
Wicksell, K. (1898), *Interest and Prices*, English Translation by R. F. Kahn of *1936*. London: Royal Economic Society 1936.
Woodford, M. (2003), *Interest and Prices*. Princeton: Princeton University Press.
Wright, R. (1991), 'Comment on the welfare cost of moderate inflations,' *Journal of Money, Credit, and Banking* 23, 514–518.
Wyplosz, C. (2000), 'Ten years of transformation: macroeconomic lessons,' *Center for Economic Policy Research Discussion Paper*, 2254.
Zivot, E. and D. Andrews (1992), 'Further evidence on the great crash, the oil-price shock, and the unit-root hypothesis,' *Journal of Business and Economic Statistics*, 10, 251–270.

Index